FLORIDA STATE
UNIVERSITY LIBRARIES

FEB 11 2000

TALLAHASSEE, FLORIDA

The Lion and the Eagle

THE LION AND THE EAGLE

Interdisciplinary Essays on German-Spanish
Relations over the Centuries

Edited by
Conrad Kent, Thomas K. Wolber,
and Cameron M. K. Hewitt

Published in 2000 by

Berghahn Books

Editorial offices:
604 West 115th St., New York, NY 10025 USA
3, NewTec Place, Magdalen Road, Oxford, OX4 1RE, UK

© 2000 Conrad Kent, Thomas K. Wolber, and Cameron M. K. Hewitt

All rights reserved.
No part of this publication may be reproduced
in any form or by any means
without the written permission of Berghahn Books.

Library of Congress Cataloging-in-Publication Data

The lion and the eagle : interdisciplinary essays on German-Spanish relations over the centuries / edited by Conrad Kent, Thomas Wolber, and Cameron M. K. Hewitt
 p.   cm.
 Includes bibliographical references.
 ISBN 1-57181-131-1 (alk. paper)
  1. Germany–Relations–Spain. 2. Spain–Relations–Germany.
 3. German literature–Appreciation–Spain. 4. Spanish literature–Appreciation–Germany. I. Kent, Conrad, 1942– . II. Wolber, Thomas, 1953– . III. Hewitt, Cameron M. K.
 DD120.S7L56 1999   99–18156
 303.48'243046—dc21   CIP

British Library Cataloguing in Publication Data

A catalogue record for this book is available from the British Library.

Printed in the United States on acid-free paper.

Contents

List of Illustrations — viii
Preface — x
Introduction *by Conrad Kent and Thomas K. Wolber* — 1

I. From the Middle Ages to the End of the Spanish Habsburg Dynasty

1. Spain and Germany in the Middle Ages: An Unexplored Literary-Historical Area of Exchange, Reception, and Exploration
   Albrecht Classen — 47

2. The Archduchess Elizabeth: Where Spain and Austria Met
   Joseph F. Patrouch — 77

3. A Woman's Influence: Archduchess Maria of Bavaria and the Spanish Habsburgs
   Magdalena S. Sánchez — 91

4. Germany's Indies? The Spanish Monarchy and Germany in the Reign of the Last Spanish Habsburg, Charles II, 1665–1700
   Christopher D. Storrs — 108

II. From the Enlightenment to the Modern Imagination

5. The Motifs of Incest and Fratricide in Friedrich Schiller's *The Bride of Messina* and Their Possible Calderonian Sources
   Henry W. Sullivan — 133

6. Francisco López de Úbeda and Johann Wolfgang von Goethe as Participants in the Shared German-Spanish Tradition of Kabbalistic Rhetoric
   Patricia D. Zecevic — 152

7. The Influence of Neogrammarian Scholarship on Ramón 177
Menéndez Pidal's Historical Grammars of Spanish
Donald E. Lenfest

8. Reassessing Friedrich Schlegel's Reading of *Don Quixote* 188
in Light of His Early Writings
Rachel Schmidt

9. Spain in Heine—Heine in Spain: Notes on a Bilateral 214
Reception
Berit Balzer

10. *La Abeja* of Barcelona and German Literature in Spain, 235
1862–1870
John W. Kronik

11. Clarín's Krausism 255
Nelson R. Orringer

12. Configurations of German and Spanish Intellectual 273
History and Aesthetics: Goethe, Novalis, Ortega y Gasset,
and Unamuno
Francisco LaRubia-Prado

13. The Fame of Miguel de Unamuno in Germany: Its Growth 290
and Decline, 1924–1930
Shirley King

III. From the Spanish Civil War to the Present

14. Hitler and the Spanish Civil War: A Shifting Balance 313
of Power
Robert H. Whealey

15. What the Condor Saw: Nazi Propaganda Images of the 325
Spanish Civil War
Conrad Kent

16. Writing War: German Women and the Spanish Civil War 360
Friederike B. Emonds

17. The Reluctant Belligerent: Franco's Spain and Hitler's War 383
Norman J. W. Goda

18. The Last Defenders of the New Order: Spaniards and 397
Nazi Germany, August 1944–May 1945
Wayne Bowen

19. Pablo Neruda and the German Literary Exile Community 423
Vera Stegmann

20. *La insurrección/Der Aufstand*: Cultural Synergy, Film, 442
and Revolution
Rachel J. Halverson and Ana María Rodríguez-Vivaldi

21. The Reception of Spanish-American Fiction in Germany: 457
    The Tide of Bestsellers, 1980–1995—Rising and Ebbing?
    Meg H. Brown

Notes on Contributors 467

Bibliography 473

Index of Names 511

Index of Subjects 525

List of Illustrations

Figures

1. Franco's Moroccan troops in February 1937. — 328
2. A Spanish photograph appropriated for an anticommunist Nazi propaganda exhibition at the Reichstag: "Bolschewismus ohne Maske" (Bolshevism unmasked). — 332
3. Refugees in Madrid. — 332
4. Communist on her way to the front to fight with the volunteers. — 334
5. The "Margaritas" who aided the Falange by sewing woolens for the battle of San Sebastián. — 335
6. The Renaissance tower, the "Torre del Clavero," as part of the architectural and military heritage of Salamanca. — 336
7. Francoist forces examining the destruction of buildings in Madrid. — 337
8. Guernica after the bombing of 26 April 1937. — 338
9. Guernica several days after the bombing. — 339
10. German instructors in the Ávila training grounds. — 341
11. Moving artillery with beasts of burden at the Ávila training grounds. — 341
12. Chemical warfare exercises at the Salamanca "Gasschule." — 342
13. A photomontage of Ju 52 planes over Burgos. — 342
14. Moroccan soldiers leaving the city of Leganés. — 343
15. Captured Republican soldiers guarded by the Moroccan soldiers. — 343
16. Moroccan soldiers rendered as leisurely cosmopolites in Barcelona, March 1939. — 344
17. Italian propaganda photograph of Franco's Moroccan color guard, 22 February 1939. — 344
18. A Moroccan guardsman preparing for a ceremonial march in Barcelona, March 1939. — 345

19.	Republican refugees moving toward the French border at Perthus, January 1939.	346
20.	Republican refugees on entering France at Perthus, January 1939.	347
21.	Spanish Nationalist officers at leisure in a captured Barcelona.	349
22.	Spanish Nationalist soldiers in a café.	349
23.	A Gypsy offering to tell the fortune of a soldier in Barcelona after the fall of the city.	350
24.	A market in Barcelona during the last weeks of the war.	351
25.	Franco's victory parade in Madrid, 19 May 1939.	352
26.	Maidens adorning the legionnaires with flowers in Hamburg.	353
27.	Hitler and his staff honoring the Condor Legion, 6 June 1939.	354
28.	Generals Wilhelm Keitel, Wolfram von Richthofen, Walther von Brauchitsch, and Erhard Milch, Admiral Erich Raeder, Field Marshall Hermann Göring, and Adolf Hitler celebrate the returning German legionnaires.	354
29.	Condor legionnaires at the Brandenburg gate, 6 June 1939.	355
30.	The División Azul arriving by train in France in June 1941.	357
31.	Members of the Spanish División Azul in Paris before transfer to the Russian front.	357

Preface

German-speaking and Spanish-speaking lands have long influenced each other. Relationships and reciprocities between the two spheres have been profound and enduring. The Visigoths who arrived in Spain after the fall of Rome shared their culture, their institutions, and their own version of an imperial legacy with the Iberian Peninsula. The medieval pilgrimage to Santiago de Compostela brought Germanic peoples and their northern culture to Iberia. Through two centuries of the Habsburg dynasty, Germanic and Hispanic ruling houses were united in yet another imperial era. Golden Age writers in Spain inspired the German romantics, and, throughout the nineteenth century, German art, music, literature, and philosophy shaped significant areas of Spanish urban culture. By the early twentieth century, Germany and Spain shared seminal roles in the creation of the avant-garde in art and literature, and yet by the 1930s they were united through totalitarian collaboration. Since World War II, Latin American poetry and, more recently, the "magic realism" of Gabriel García Márquez and his contemporaries have inspired German-speaking peoples in their search for new forms of expression.

Paradoxically, the connections between the Germanic and Hispanic lands have received only isolated critical attention. Although individual monographs on German-Spanish relations in literature, philosophy, and history have been written, notably the pioneering work of Gerhart Hoffmeister, the enduring influences between the two spheres have never enjoyed sustained or comprehensive scholarly interest. No interdisciplinary study or compendium of essays devoted to the comparative study of German and Spanish culture exists, and, as a consequence, many facets of an immense realm of shared culture and history have been neglected.

In *The Lion and the Eagle: Interdisciplinary Essays on German-Spanish Relations over the Centuries*, the editors have attempted to provide a foundation for this area of inquiry. Bringing together contributions by scholars from diverse fields using different methodologies, we have sought a framework for the exploration of relations between two major spheres of language and culture from the Middle Ages to recent years. When brought together in a single volume, these scholarly inquiries into German-Spanish relations reveal an intensity and continuity of association that provide astonishing insights. Equally important, such scrutiny gives access to subtleties of each culture that have eluded scholars who have not engaged in comparative and interdisciplinary studies.

This book continues traditions at both Ohio Wesleyan University and Berghahn Books of a dedication to interdisciplinary and comparative studies. At Ohio Wesleyan, numerous conferences sponsored by grants from the Andrew Mellon Foundation and the Lilly Endowment have supported cultural studies and cultural history. For Berghahn Books, this volume is an addition to crosscultural and interdisciplinary titles whose primary emphasis has been on German studies. Indeed, Berghahn Books has made it possible for this kind of publication to see the light of day.

While organizing interdisciplinary conferences for Ohio Wesleyan University's National Colloquium, Conrad Kent and Thomas Wolber were struck by connections between our respective fields of Spanish and German studies. Intrigued as much by the variety of shared topics as by the depth of connections that link the two cultures to which we have devoted our careers, we began to focus on the relationships we had observed between German and Spanish cultures. Conversations regarding the avant-garde in Germany, Austria, Spain, and Latin America drew attention to remarkable figures from both language areas who not only became leading innovators in world art and architecture in the 1920s and 1930s but also projected their creations across language and cultural boundaries. Subsequent conversations on the similarities between Vienna and Barcelona at the turn of the century and between the novels of Thomas Mann and Miguel de Unamuno led us back to the intricate web of connections linking Germany and Spain during their shared Habsburg history. It was this search that eventually inspired the conference "The Lion and the Eagle," held at Ohio Wesleyan University from 25 through 27 April 1996, and that has resulted in this Berghahn volume.

Two scholars, Henry W. Sullivan and Nelson R. Orringer, were crucial contributors to the conference and to this volume. Henry W. Sullivan, Professor of Spanish and Portuguese in Golden Age Literature at Tulane University, is author of the seminal work

Calderón in the German Lands and the Low Countries: His Reception and Influence, 1654–1980 (Cambridge and New York, 1983). His work is a model for exploring the relationships between Spanish and German cultures. Through his long experience in the literature, philosophy, and music of the Germanic and the Hispanic worlds in general, and his investigations into the subtle literary and philosophical influences of the Spanish Golden Age on the German romantic imagination in particular, he has been instrumental in enhancing our venture.

Nelson R. Orringer, Professor of Comparative Literature at the University of Connecticut, is the author of several fundamental studies of the German influences on José Ortega y Gasset, Miguel de Unamuno, and Ángel Ganivet. Orringer has continued research on the influence of Krausism, the Germanic intellectual current that most influenced Spanish reformers during the last third of the nineteenth and the first third of the twentieth century. He has also provided insight, encouragement, and full cooperation during the development of the conference and the publication of its proceedings.

Through the planning stages of the conference, other scholars demonstrated interest in and commitment to a discussion of German-Spanish relations over the centuries. Maite Álvarez Oller, Wayne Bowen, Meg H. Brown, Kenneth Brown, Albrecht Classen, Friederike B. Emonds, Norman J. W. Goda, Shirley King, Helmut J. Kremling, Hera T. Leighton, Joseph F. Patrouch, Rachel Schmidt, Robert H. Whealey, and Istvan Varkonyi agreed to join Conrad Kent, Thomas K. Wolber, Henry W. Sullivan, and Nelson R. Orringer as participants in the symposium.

From 25 through 27 April 1996, conference participants shared in discussions that crossed time lines, languages, and disciplines. We discussed patterns reappearing in the relationships between the Germanic and Hispanic peoples, not only in Germany and Spain but also more generally in the intellectual exchange between Europe and the Americas. The conference demonstrated not only a commonality of ideas across a variety of fields but also an elevated level of academic discourse. Especially notable was the existence of a new generation of scholars willing and eager to embark on interdisciplinary and cross-cultural research. They were leaders in the roundtable discussion following the conference that saw the formulation of strategies and shared plans for continued programs and research activities in German-Spanish studies.

Conversations with Dr. Marion Berghahn during the summer of 1996 did much to shape the conference proceedings into a book.

She raised important questions regarding the areas and disciplines represented at the conference, and has helped us to delineate better the lacunae in the studies to be published. As a consequence, additional complementary essays have been included, resulting in a further enrichment of the contents of this book. In this effort, Nelson R. Orringer again offered wise counsel with recommendations for valuable additions to the publication.

Christopher D. Storrs and Magdalena S. Sánchez have pursued a historical inquiry into patterns of Habsburg culture and court patronage represented by Joseph F. Patrouch, and have enhanced our knowledge of the extraordinary connections between different branches of the Habsburg dynasty. Patricia D. Zecevic has introduced recent critical methods in her study of shared experience in the work of Johann Wolfgang Goethe and Francisco López de Úbeda.

Several scholars have offered important additions to our understanding of the nineteenth- and early twentieth-century German-Spanish relations. Berit Balzer has produced a study of the Spanish ballads and the poetry of Heinrich Heine; John W. Kronik demonstrates Spanish sensitivity and awareness of German literature through the Barcelona periodical *La Abeja*; and Francisco LaRubia-Prado has contributed a study of the role of German philosophy on Miguel de Unamuno and José Ortega y Gasset.

Although a half-century of intensifying relationships between Latin America and the German-speaking countries will undoubtedly receive heightened attention in future collections of studies on German-Spanish relations, two papers not delivered at the conference but added to the collection explore Germanic-Latin American reciprocities. Vera Stegmann considers the influence of the Chilean poet Pablo Neruda on the creative efforts of German exile writers of the Nazi era. Rachel J. Halverson and Ana María Rodríguez-Vivaldi discuss a close German-Spanish collaboration through film in the work of Peter Lilienthal and Antonio Skármeta.

Donald E. Lenfest, Professor of Modern Foreign Languages at Ohio Wesleyan University, has contributed an essay on the influence of German philology on the linguistic work of Ramón Menéndez Pidal. As Chairman of the Department of Modern Foreign Languages at Ohio Wesleyan University, he has also provided constancy, flexibility, and departmental support for both the conference and this publication.

Gerhart Hoffmeister, Professor of Comparative Literature at the University of California at Santa Barbara and a leading authority on the subject of German-Spanish relations in literature, has been the first outside scholar to evaluate the observations we have made in the introduction. Kindly scrutinizing our overview, he has made helpful suggestions to improve it, while vindicating our conviction that this collection of essays is a valuable contribution to several fields of scholarly inquiry in German, Spanish, and comparative studies.

Cameron M. K. Hewitt, a 1998 Ohio Wesleyan University graduate who attended the conference in 1996, became our editorial assistant during the spring of 1998, and finally, as a result of his diligence, joined us as coeditor. He has been responsible for regularizing the essays included in this collection, especially in unifying the different word-processing programs, but also in making a sustained effort to achieve consistency in stylistic matters. Cameron has also been helpful in proofreading essays at various stages of progress during the spring of 1998 and again during the spring of 1999.

Our copyeditor Shawn Kendrick has also been extremely effective in unifying the texts, in making each essay even more readable, and in helping to find ways to bring the diverse parts of this story together as a whole. Through her conscientious efforts, ostensibly remote connections become accessible to readers without technical training or specific background. Janine Treves, managing and production editor of Berghahn Books, has been consistently helpful in seeing this book through every stage of development.

We owe a special debt of gratitude to John C. Maxwell III, a 1980 Ohio Wesleyan graduate. Through his financial support and generosity of spirit, the 1996 conference was as successful as it was. And through his continued largesse, many cultural programs are made possible and sustained at our university.

We have been inspired by Karl-Ludwig Selig, born in Wiesbaden, Germany, and Professor Emeritus of Spanish and Portuguese at Columbia University and a *Honorarprofessor* at Greifswald University—an embodiment of German-Spanish relations. He has supported us morally and professionally.

William C. Louthan and Richard D. Fusch, Provost and Associate Dean of Academic Affairs of Ohio Wesleyan, ensured the success of the conference and the publication of this book. Both the Departments of Humanities/Classics and Modern Foreign Languages supported the conference, and the Department of Humanities/Classics has subsidized the volume through the department's Herbst fund. Dennis Prindle, as he has done for many Ohio Wesleyan University activities, provided the conference title, poster design, and many insights into the nature of the venture on which we embarked five years ago.

It is our hope that the culmination of our efforts, *The Lion and the Eagle: Interdisciplinary Essays on German-Spanish Relations over the Centuries*, will shed light on the subtle and evolving ways in which the German and Spanish intellectual lands have nourished and influenced each other for over a millennium. The bibliography assembled for this volume shows that the subject has intrigued many fine minds dedicated to German and Spanish themes in the humanities, social sciences, and natural sciences. The essays evoke the richness and complexity of the subject of German-Spanish relations and serve as a gateway for scholarly inquiry in the future.

INTRODUCTION

Conrad Kent and Thomas K. Wolber

Germany and Spain have influenced and at times transformed each other's literature, art, and culture. Since before the Habsburg dynasty of the Renaissance and baroque periods, the cross-fertilization and challenges have been both fruitful and complex. Novel inventions surfacing in one culture have often achieved their greatest prosperity in the other: Martin Luther's Protestant Reformation stimulated a response in Spain that was to define the European Counter Reformation. Spanish baroque writers were seminal in the development of German romanticism. Carl Christian Friedrich Krause and other nineteenth-century German liberals provided the foundation for Spanish reformist efforts on the one hand, while German conservatives like Novalis and Adam Müller inspired conservatives on the other. The music of Richard Wagner transformed Spanish music and the Spanish stage at the turn of the twentieth century, and yet Pablo Picasso and other artists of the Spanish avant-garde sparked the enthusiasm of the Germans before the Nazi era. Today, German and Spanish intellectuals and writers share a similar commitment to the creation of a European culture in the face of resistance from other members of the European Union. Yet rarely are the myriad connections between Germany and Spain addressed in a single program and joined in a single volume of essays.

In this anthology, we have gathered essays written by scholars from a variety of disciplines who have addressed many of the relationships between the Germanic world and the Hispanic world over the centuries. Thirteen of the essays were originally presented in a symposium held at Ohio Wesleyan University from 25 April through 27 April 1996. These papers represent a first dialogue among specialists from different fields who engaged in an exploration of the relentlessly consistent, albeit often forgotten, connections between the two linguistic and cultural groups. In addition to the contributions that evolved from the original symposium, other essays were solicited to expand further the range of inquiry into the subject. Chronologically organized, the twenty-one essays of this collection have become far more than an inventory of subjects. The papers of Albrecht Classen, Joseph F. Patrouch, Magdalena S. Sánchez, Christopher D. Storrs, Henry W. Sullivan, Patricia D. Zecevic, Donald E. Lenfest, Rachel Schmidt, Berit Balzer, John W. Kronik, Nelson R. Orringer, Francisco LaRubia-Prado, Shirley King, Robert H. Whealey, Conrad Kent, Friederike B. Emonds, Norman J. W. Goda, Wayne Bowen, Vera Stegmann, the team of Rachel J. Halverson and Ana María Rodríguez-Vivaldi, and Meg H. Brown provide a glimpse at the breadth and depth of the formative relationship between the Germanic and Hispanic worlds from the Middle Ages to the present.

We have not sought a rigorous definition of terms: German or Germanic and Spanish or Hispanic have been used, although we prefer the terms Germanic and Hispanic for the width of experience they connote. The language cultures that lie behind those terms are as mutable in history as they are vague for the purposes of definition. We have opted for an inclusive rather than an exclusive strategy for the rubrics of this collection. For example, we assume that scholars could be intrigued by the influence of the German-speaking, Bauhaus-affiliated Swiss artist Paul Klee on the Catalan-speaking Barcelona resident Antoni Tàpies, as well as other subjects that invite further study into significant areas of contact between the Germano-Hispanic worlds. With every twist and turn in dynastic, religious, social, economic, and cultural history, individuals and institutions have forged links between the two language groups with a persistence that defies easy generalization as much as it requires further investigation.

From the Middle Ages to the End of the Spanish Habsburg Dynasty

For German and Hispanic lands in both war and peace throughout the Middle Ages, the "imperial" legacy is the grid on which the course of historical change would be rendered coherent and meaningful. Indeed, for centuries German and Hispanic rulers, scholars, and clergy sought to bring their respective efforts under a Roman dispensation because Roman fortifications, road networks, political structures, and even Catholic liturgy were visibly evident in daily life. Bereft of the geographic and demographic forces that gradually led to the formation of nation-states elsewhere, the Iberian Peninsula and the lands of German-speaking people often appealed to Rome for claims of legitimacy. Through the language of empire, sovereigns in both Germanic and Hispanic lands sought authority in the face of adversaries on the outside and confusion from within. More than the parallel appropriation of imperial pretensions, the cultivation of an imperial mythology would resonate between the two cultural and language groups, making them receptive to habits of mind and sensibilities within each other's traditions.

The collapse of the Roman Empire resulted in a direct and seminal linkage between the German and Hispanic peoples, as the Germanic tribes of the Alans, Suevi, Vandals, and Visigoths were able to make their way across the Pyrenees into the Iberian Peninsula. In the year 411, the Suevi founded a kingdom in Galicia and northern Portugal—with Braga (Bracara Augusta) as its capital—that lasted until 585, when it was integrated into the empire of the Visigoths. While there is no consensus about the Suevi's origin, there is agreement that this Germanic tribe played a role in the later development of a distinct Galician and Portuguese identity.[1] The Visigoths made their first entry into Spain in 414, capturing Barcelona. Outnumbered by the Romanized residents of the peninsula, the Germanic peoples succeeded the Romans in material control, if not institutional order, and by the sixth century a Visigothic realm had replaced the Roman Empire in all of Spain. Enduring at least as a political and military force until the arrival of the Islamic peoples in 711, Visigothic Spain maintained a loose affiliation with the Byzantine heirs to Rome. With their capacity for contriving fortification and their leadership in warfare, the Germanic peoples bequeathed to Spain some semblance of the military strategies that had once allowed them to engage Rome so effectively in battle. The Visigoths' contributions in the realm of jurisprudence were particularly important: the code of laws promulgated by kings Chindaswinth and Recceswinth, called the *Lex Visigothorum* and later the *Fuero Juzgo*, served as a basis for later compilations.[2] In liturgical and ecclesiastical efforts maintained not by the Visigoths but by a priest class that kept alive the culture of an earlier era, the religious institutions of the Visigoths became by default residual expressions of Roman ritual. It was through the Visigoths in Romanized Spain that the art and culture of the eastern empire of Byzantium would find important expression.³ The last of the thirty-five Visigothic kings, Roderic (Rodrigo), a popular Spanish hero of perennial interest, is presumably identical with the prominent figure of Rüdiger in medieval German literature.⁴

Through the agency of Charlemagne, the Frankish armies and their religious associates brought Germanic culture to the Iberian Peninsula during the ninth century. The Carolingian intrusion into Hispanic lands established institutions, architectural innovations, and religious practices that were to link Spain to the rest of Europe, while distancing it from the Muslims to the south. By the end of Charlemagne's reign in 814, the Germanic lands and the northern tier of Hispanic lands were administered by a single system that owed much of its success to the tenacity with which bonds between the peoples of the kingdom were not only encouraged but enforced.

In the later Middle Ages, the association between Germanic and Hispanic cultures and traditions grew unequivocal as shared Germano-Spanish realities reached popular and material culture. Albrecht Classen introduces the essays of Part I, "From the Middle Ages to the End of the Spanish Habsburg Dynasty," with a study of Germano-Hispanic contacts, "Spain and Germany in the Middle Ages: An Unexplored Literary-Historical Area of Exchange, Reception, and Exploration," ranging from the time of Charlemagne to about 1500. According to the author, scholars have paid little attention to Germano-Hispanic relations in the Middle Ages. For Classen, the limited research in the field is cause for study of the cultural exchanges between Germany and Spain that has heretofore been based on speculation "harbored mainly by the romanticists." Classen has chosen to make his paper serve as a preliminary discussion to future in-depth investigations, outlining a basic framework for the study of the likely contacts between Spaniards and Germans. In looking at, among other names and works, Konrad's *Rolandslied*, Wolfram von Eschenbach's contacts with Spain, and Oswald von Wolkenstein's songs, Classen maintains that Spain and Portugal were not strange and exotic countries to medieval German audiences, but rather familiar territory, known by many and even visited by some adventurous travelers—mostly pilgrims, merchants, and poets. Pointing to "an almost uninterrupted flow of literary documents" that reflected Spain in Germany, Classen concludes that Hispanic-Germanic relations during the Middle Ages are indeed an important and most fruitful area of scholarly research.

Of all the medieval institutions that Germanic and Spanish peoples shared, the pilgrimages to Spain provided the most consistent contact between Germans and Spaniards. Both Santiago de Compostela, in Galicia, and Montserrat, in Catalonia, were important destinations for Central European peregrinators. Santiago de Compostela, in particular, became an attractive center of pilgrimages after the body of St. James the Apostle, Spain's patron saint, was discovered there during the reign of Alfonso II (791–842): "The spot became a center of pilgrimages ranking next to Jerusalem and Rome, and the road leading to it, the 'Way of St. James,' was trod by countless thousands of foreigners."[5]

As outlined by Classen, the Germanic impact on Spanish commerce and art in the late Middle Ages and early Renaissance was significant. Witness, for example, the construction of the great Gothic cathedral of Burgos, begun two centuries earlier in 1221. Queen Berengaria had sent Bishop Mauricio to Germany to ask for the hand of Philip II's daughter Beatrice of Swabia for her son Ferdinand III (married 1219). After six months of extensive traveling, the bishop returned, with the images of several French and German Gothic cathedrals fresh in his memory.[6] When the construction of the west side of the cathedral was started in 1442, not a French but a German master, Hans von Köln (John of Cologne or Juan de Colonia), was commissioned with the task. While the details were executed in the plateresque style of the time, the basic architectural blueprint remained Nordic. Thus, the two towers of the Burgos cathedral bear a striking resemblance to the Gothic domes of Germany (especially those in Cologne, Freiburg, and Ulm).[7] The result of this fusion of Hispanic and Germanic art forms was what might be called a German-Spanish cultural symbiosis.

Numerous craftsmen and artists from Flanders, the Netherlands, Burgundy, and Germany came to Spain in the fifteenth century, primarily for financial and artistic reasons. Throughout the century, contacts between Germanic countries and the Iberian Peninsula intensified, through trade as well as through political association. Under John II, the Flemish artist Jan van Eyck (c. 1390–1441) visited Spain, and his influence lasted for more than one hundred years; his impact on Luis de Morales (1509–1586) is well documented. Henry IV (1454–1474) made an effort to introduce modern state bureaucracy into the management of his crown's affairs, and hence drew upon resources from as far away as Hamburg.

One of the best sources of knowledge about the period is Hieronymus Münzer's *Itenarium sive peregrinatio per Hispanum et Alemanium*.[8] Not much is known about Münzer, an early scientist who died in 1508, but his travelogue of 1494/95 remains a treasure-trove from which modern researchers benefit. Münzer describes the Spain of Isabella the Catholic (1474–1504) and Ferdinand (1470–1504) at its moment of greatest splendor—the end of the Trastamaran dynasty. His descriptions suggest the vitality and economic prosperity that made it possible for the Spanish merchant class of both northern and southern Spain to cultivate the Flemish and Rhenish taste in domestic and institutional art, architecture, and craftsmanship that would come to be called the Isabeline style.

A visit to the Prado Museum reveals the extent to which Germanic high art reached Spain during the fifteenth century and the first half of the sixteenth century. Hieronymus Bosch (c. 1450–1516), "El Bosco," is represented with dozens of works, as are the Brueghels, Van Dyck, Rubens, and Rembrandt. The "German School" is made up of works by Hans Baldung Grien (1484/85–1545), Albrecht Dürer (1471–1528), Hans Holbein (1497/98–1543), and others. The Prado collection is living testimony to the intensity of Germano-Spanish commercial and cultural relations during this period.

By the time Charles I/V (1500–1558), the grandson of Isabella and Ferdinand, arrived in 1517 as the first Habsburg emperor of Spain, the Germanic presence was already pervasive. However, Charles raised the level of interaction even further by merging politically the German and Spanish components of the vast European realm of the Habsburgs: he was crowned King Carlos I of Spain in 1516, and Charles V, Holy Roman Emperor, in 1519. Raised in Burgundy and the Netherlands, and ruler of Germanic territories, he eventually made Spain the center of a vast Catholic empire. To bring efficiency to the organization of government, he transformed the now archaic medieval monarchy of Isabella and Ferdinand into a coherent, systematic state bureaucracy, sufficiently Hispanicized in tone and language to assure its function and survival.

In the 1996 symposium, Maite Álvarez Oller (not included in this collection), of the J. Paul Getty Museum, discussed the art collecting patterns of Charles, shedding insight into his political agenda as well. Unifying his Habsburg collection with that of Spain, and introducing Italian art into his royal galleries, Charles strove to create a truly "European" collection. Ever conscious of the concept of "empire," he used art to legitimize his claim as Europe's undisputed leader.

To the culture of Spain, Charles introduced an urbane religious sensibility associated with Erasmus of Rotterdam, whose *devotio moderna* led Charles to militate against the intellectual openness of the first years of his reign. On the one hand, he had surrounded himself with intellectuals who championed the Christian humanism associated with *Erasmismo*. On the other hand, he increasingly patronized the forces of conservative scholasticism that would in the end do battle with devotio moderna within Spain, and certainly with the Protestant Reformation that spread throughout much of Charles's realm during his lifetime. During the 1520s, deeper levels of spirituality would be cultivated in Spanish urban areas, and during the 1530s, the conservative forces of the church assigned themselves the responsibility of protecting the purity of the millennial kingdom and its institutions. Erasmian thought, which had entered the urban centers of Spain by 1520, was repudiated by orthodox members of the church by the end of the decade.[9] The Jesuit order was founded in 1534 as a further, institutional response to the developing power and spread of Protestantism. It was in Germany and Spain that in fundamental ways the "Wars of Truth" were to reach confrontational proportions; Charles I/V even traveled to Germany in 1532 in a futile attempt to resolve the emerging religious conflicts. As Protestantism expanded, and as the Council of Trent (1545–63) deliberated, the Reformation became a struggle for the minds and souls of Europeans everywhere. With the evolution of Charles away from the Germanic culture of his youth, and with ardor for the cause defined by the Jesuit order as a defense of the Catholic hegemony, the man who had once straddled the Germanic and Hispanic worlds was forced to make a choice. By the end of his career, Charles was an adamant defender of the conservative forces of the church and upheld their efforts in the Council of Trent.

Although Charles eventually drew away from his Germanic upbringing, during his reign Spanish institutions flourished, in part through the importation of Germanic culture and science. In the 1540s, the Belgian anatomist Andreas Vesal (1515–1564), also called Vesalius, who drew the human anatomy (*De humani corporis fabrica*) with astonishing exactness, became a figure in Charles's court. Within decades, anatomy would become a subject of study at the University of Salamanca, although it later ceased to be a permitted area of inquiry. The study of science could not be separated from that of theology within the kingdom, and questions pertaining to orthodoxy would eventually challenge the integrity of the scholarly enterprise of Spanish universities. Spanish literature was translated and read in German lands, and as several of our contributors demonstrate in their essays, texts in Spanish were part of German court life. During this period, the German banking house of the Fuggers was able to gain financial leverage in the Spanish realm by lending Charles over 500,000 guldens so that the king could bribe the German electors to vote for him after the death of Maximilian I in 1519.[10]

Philip II (1556–1598), Charles's son and, like him, a champion of Catholicism, intensified the opposition to the Protestant culture and religiosity that were spreading far beyond northern Germany. Suspecting his Central European relatives of secretly flirting with Protestantism, he saw to it that the sons of the Austrian-Habsburg dynasty would be educated in Madrid rather than Vienna. In 1559, he forbade Spanish students to travel abroad and instituted the *Index librorum prohibitorum*—five years before Pope Pius IV produced his own catalog of banned books. The Counter Reformation institutions of Spain penalized those who had once enjoyed access to European institutions. By 1580, there were fewer than fifty students of medicine at the University of Salamanca, once a virtual laboratory of the anatomical discoveries arriving from German lands during the first half of the century. By the end of the sixteenth century, the country was under the watchful eye of a severe inquisition, students were garbed in dark cloaks, and visitors from Germany were more apt to be vagabonds than scholars, merchants, or men of medicine.

In Germano-Hispanic literature, the shared roots of Italian humanism and dynastic authority have resulted in reciprocity in narrative and poetry. Although much inquiry remains to be done, Gerhart Hoffmeister, an essential authority on the presence of Spanish Renaissance literature and culture in the German imagination, has treated this topic in his paradigmatic study *Die spanische Diana in Deutschland* (1972). Since then, Hoffmeister has widened his Spanish interests by including the reception of several prose genres of the Spanish Golden Age in his research (the *novela pastoril*, the *novela sentimental*, and the *novela picaresca*), along with investigations of their adapters (Kuffstein, Ulenhart, and Augspurger), of the image of Spain (*La leyenda negra*), and of Spaniards in Germany (the Spanish *pícaro*). He has also published a comprehensive overview of Spanish-German literary relations (*Spanien und Deutschland*, 1976) and has recently turned his attention to Spanish-German contacts during the baroque and romantic periods.[11]

During the Renaissance, contacts between Spain and Germany are of special interest regarding art and court patronage. Several essays in this collection concern successive generations of patronage. Joseph F. Patrouch has written a study of the remarkable persistence of Spanish culture in the Viennese court of the Habsburg Archduchess Isabella (1554–1592); Magdalena S. Sánchez has produced a study of patronage in the court of Archduchess Maria of Bavaria (1551–1608); and Christopher D. Storrs has investigated the relationship between Germany and the court of the last Spanish Habsburg, Charles II (1661–1700).

Joseph F. Patrouch's essay, "The Archduchess Elizabeth: Where Spain and Austria Met," concentrates on the Habsburg Archduchess "Isabell," as she wrote her name, or Elizabeth, as she is often called in the literature. She was born and died in Vienna, but nevertheless spoke Spanish more than German since almost her entire family was born, educated, and/or betrothed in Spain. Her father Maximilian II and her mother Maria were married in Valladolid before moving to Austria; her older sister Anna later became queen of Spain, bride of Philip II, and mother of Philip III; and two of her brothers, the later Emperor Rudolf II and Ernst, were sent to Spain to be educated under the strict supervision of their uncle Philip II. In 1570, Elizabeth married the king of France, Charles IX, but her stay in war-torn France was brief. After her husband's death in 1574, she chose to devote her life to the sick and poor. She founded convents, supported the Jesuits, and in general "had the opportunity to implement Spanish-influenced ideas about religion and Counter Reformation Catholicism through pious foundations and courtly patronage." Elizabeth's life illustrates that the traditional separation between the Spanish and the Austrian branches of the Habsburg dynasty is misleading and only serves to obfuscate the close connections between the various Habsburg family members and their courts. In his essay, Patrouch makes a strong case that Spanish texts, court ceremonies, and religious rituals practiced in Vienna were significant in a time and place generally regarded as isolated from Spain and Spanish culture.

The authority that aristocratic women were able to wield in the area of politics has long been underestimated by historians. The Archduchess Maria of Bavaria (1551–1608), described by Magdalena S. Sánchez in her essay entitled "A Woman's Influence: Archduchess Maria of Bavaria and the Spanish Habsburgs," is an example of such a politically astute woman. Maria successfully used her considerable diplomatic skills to help bridge the gap between Spain and Central Europe. Of Wittelsbach descent, she married the Habsburg archduke of Styria, Karl II, in 1571. After his death in 1590, she served as regent until her eldest son Ferdinand assumed power in 1595. Her most pressing concern was to gain financial and military assistance for her son. She was able to achieve that objective through savvy diplomacy, familial ties, correpondence, the exchange of lavish gifts, and religious works. When one of her daughters, Margaret of Austria, became the wife of Philip III of Spain, Maria effectively used that connection as an entrée to the Spanish court. As a result of her tireless efforts, the Spanish monarchy assisted the Austrian branch of the Habsburgs throughout the reign of Philip III. In particular, Spain worked closely with Archduke Ferdinand and helped finance his numerous military campaigns—a relationship that continued long after Maria's death in 1608. The ties that the archduchess forged were instrumental in cementing the close relations between the Austrian and the Spanish Habsburgs.

In his essay, "Germany's Indies? The Spanish Monarchy and Germany in the Reign of the Last Spanish Habsburg, Charles II, 1665–1700," Christopher D. Storrs looks at Spanish-German relations during the second half of the seventeenth century. By then, Spanish military might was diminished, and Madrid now actively sought allies and support against the aggressive French king Louis XIV. Storrs notes that previously the Spanish Habsburgs had effectively evaded the obligations of membership in the Holy Roman Empire, but by the 1660s, this attitude began to change. Henceforth, Spain emphasized its membership in the Empire and presented itself as a defender of German freedom and liberty in order to secure German aid for the defense of its own territories in the Low Countries and Italy, and even in Spain itself. Storrs describes how Charles II attempted to rent troops from the German princes, many of whom were eager to comply—for a handsome profit, of course—even though payments were often maddeningly slow, if they arrived at all. At the same time, Spain offered considerable resources and opportunities for adventurous princes from Germany. Charles also forged familial ties with Germany, which enhanced prospects for a German throne succession. However, as more and more ambitious and greedy Germans arrived in Spain, anti-German resentment began to grow. Storrs argues that this contributed to the defeat of the Austrian Habsburgs in the War of the Spanish Succession. The House of Habsburg came to an ignominious end, and Bourbons were to occupy the Spanish throne until 1931.

Together, these essays on Renaissance patronage suggest that the continuing and intimate contact of the Habsburg courts in Germany and Spain entailed a shared religious conservatism and a propensity to cultivate art for the purpose of both religious edification and aesthetic refinement. This was not the sensibility or bias of the art of England and France, as those cultures moved toward the expression of secular grandeur. Separating gradually over the years, the Spanish and the German Habsburgs nevertheless maintained a rapport and similarities even in the baroque expansiveness of the Benedictine effulgence in Austria and Bavaria and the contemporaneous baroque of Spain.

During the 1630s, Francisco de Quevedo's (1580–1645) caricature of Germans in *La hora de todos* (Everybody's Hour) gave literary form to Spanish resentment against the Germans. Although Quevedo depicts the French as scavenger-merchants who gouge the Spanish out of their money, and the Dutch as such thieves that they have stolen their land from the sea, Germans from various principalities are viewed more critically as "heretics and Protestants," who are both drunk and disorderly.[12] Seventeenth-century German artists and writers were keenly aware of Spain and Spanish culture, especially the Spanish pícaro tradition, which they tried to emulate. A prime example of a German picaresque novel is Johann Michael Moscherosch's (1601–1669) remarkable work *Les Visiones de Don Francesco de Qvevedo Villegas oder Wunderbare satirische Gesichte, verteutscht durch Philander von Sittewald* (1640–42). Based on Quevedo's *Sueños* of 1608 (German translation 1635) and on autobiographical elements (Moscherosch's Jewish family had Aragonian roots), the novel represents the most comprehensive social criticism of the century and influenced Hans Jakob Christoffel von Grimmelshausen (c. 1622–1676), whose own German variation on the picaresque tradition in *Der Abenteuerliche Simplicissimus Teutsch* (1669) is also based on Spanish narratives. Modeled on the serial adventures of a cunning outcast, the figure of Simplicissimus moved through episodes following different masters and surviving only by his wits. Both the anonymous *Lazarillo de Tormes* (1554), translated into German in 1617, and Mateo Alemán's *Guzmán de Alfarache* (1599/1605), translated into German in 1615, are picaresque novels that were available to Grimmelshausen.[13] Miguel de Cervantes' *Don Quixote* (1605–15), a novel with some resemblance to the picaresque tradition, would endure as one of the most significant literary inspirations for German writers over the subsequent centuries.

Another component of the Germanic-Hispanic connections are the Sephardim—the Jews of the Iberian Peninsula and their descendants. Forced to leave Spain and Portugal because of the Inquisition, they settled all over Europe, including the Germanic regions along the Rhine. Their most prominent representative is probably the Dutch philosopher Baruch Spinoza (1632–1677). At the 1996 symposium, Kenneth Brown contributed a paper on Sephardic poetry from Germany, "Spanish and Portuguese Poetry Written by Seventeenth- and Eighteenth-Century Sephardim in Hamburg and Frankfurt" (not included in this collection), which gave focus to the fragments, tombstone inscriptions, Biblical translations, and rare editions that comprise the transitory legacy of the displaced Sephardim in Germany. In addition, Brown also assessed the poetic discourse for reasons of linguistic exclusion, autobiography, broad cultural aspects, and the connection with the Spanish Golden Age muse.

As a parenthetical remark, it might also be pointed out that the origins of the famous Spanish Riding School (Spanische Reitschule) in Vienna can be traced back to the sixteenth century. The Lipizzaners were brought to Austria from Spain by Archduke Charles II, who founded the riding academy in 1572. Originally, these Arabian stallions performed military functions; they were trained to kick and strike at opposing foot soldiers and to rear up and twist to avoid an avenger's sword. Today, however, the horses' unique training and skills merely serve to entertain audiences in Vienna and around the world.[14]

From the Enlightenment to the Modern Imagination

Compared to the rest of Europe, the eighteenth century in Spain was largely a period of "intellectual stagnation."[15] The Catholic Church continued to dominate the political, social, and cultural life, exercising an effective censorship on everything foreign, which it equated with heretical. In the words of Norman Hampson, "For the writers of the rest of Europe Spain was essentially the country of the Inquisition, a dreadful compound of poverty, ignorance and fanaticism."[16] Spain's image being tarnished by this *leyenda negra* (black legend), German intellectuals of this era received their stimuli instead from England (Locke, Hume, Pope, etc.) and especially from France (Descartes, Bayle, Voltaire, Montesquieu, Rousseau, Boileau, etc.)—countries in which the Enlightenment flourished in full force. It was not until the latter half of the eighteenth century that the forces and fashions of the capitals of Europe began to compete at the Bourbon court of Spain for the imagination of the Enlightenment monarchy. Although the influence was to be primarily French in architecture and public works as well as in taste and academic pretensions, the influence of German Enlightenment figures shaped neoclassicism, especially during the reign of

Charles III, who ruled from 1759 to 1788. Under Charles, the influence of Johann Joachim Winckelmann (1717–1768) gave Spaniards access to new perspectives on both Greece and Rome. Through his letters, essays, and history of ancient art, *Geschichte der Kunst des Altertums* (translated as *The History of Ancient Art* and *La historia del arte en la antigüedad*), Winckelmann popularized a taste for ancient art and architecture among his contemporaries. Francisco de Goya (1746–1828) himself was to come under Winckelmann's classicizing influence during his early years.

In Germany, on the other hand, Hispanic culture was rediscovered after about 1770. The circle of Johann Wilhelm Ludwig Gleim (1719–1803), Christoph Martin Wieland (1733–1813), and Johann Georg Jacobi (1740–1814) formed the nucleus of a renewed interest in things Spanish. Friedrich Justin Bertuch (1747–1822), who had studied Spanish with the help of a former Danish ambassador at Madrid, translated Cervantes' *Don Quixote* (1775–77) "aus der Urschrift" (from the original)—a rarity at that time. Gleim and others tried to emulate the Spanish ballads and romances.[17] In the literature of the Golden Age, but also in the ballads and folk traditions, German Sturm und Drang authors such as Johann Gottfried Herder (1744–1803) and Wilhelm Heinse (1746–1803) found a new, supposedly democratic vocabulary and language to be set in opposition to the rigorous, aristocratic French style. Gradually, Spanish motifs found their way into German dramas and prose. In 1776, for instance, Friedrich Maximilian Klinger (1752–1831), who gave the Sturm und Drang period its name, produced a play, *Simsone Grisaldo*, against the background of the Spanish battle with the Moors.

Strongly impacted by the Sturm und Drang, which they helped define, Johann Wolfgang Goethe (1749–1832) and Friedrich Schiller (1759–1805) shared a common interest in universal affairs, both in time and space. Schiller, a history professor at Jena University, was an expert on Spain and its relationship with the Low Countries. His *Geschichte des Abfalls der vereinigten Niederlande von der spanischen Regierung* (History of the Revolt of the United Netherlands against Spain) of 1788 provided the background for his influential drama *Don Carlos, Infant von Spanien* (1787), which served as the basis for Giuseppe Verdi's famous opera of the same name. As Schiller's Protestant view of Philip II and the Spanish Inquisition was sharply critical, it is not surprising that his drama was received coolly in Spain.[18] Goethe, on the other hand, enjoyed a warmer reception, beginning with the 1803 translation of his *Die Leiden des jungen Werthers* (The Sufferings of Young Werther).[19]

Schiller was well acquainted with Pedro Calderón de la Barca (1600–1681). But what exactly did he know about Calderón, and when did he know it? And to what extent was he influenced by the Spanish playwright? In his essay "The Motifs of Incest and Fratricide in Friedrich Schiller's *The Bride of Messina* and Their Possible Calderonian Sources," Henry W. Sullivan raises these questions and investigates the possible indebtedness of Schiller to Calderón. Schiller's *Bride of Messina* (written in 1802–03) bears what Sullivan calls "a striking resemblance" to Calderón's youthful saints-and-sinners drama entitled *La devoción de la cruz* (Devotion to the Cross, 1624–25). There is no doubt, Sullivan asserts, that Schiller knew of August Wilhelm Schlegel's translation of Calderón's play, completed in 1802 and published in 1803. Sullivan describes in detail not only the many similarities in plot, motifs, characters, and style, but also the aesthetic, philosophical, and theological implications of what the discovery of Calderón might have meant for the German dramatist. Though Calderón's aesthetics and ethics were in flagrant contravention of the neoclassical rules that Schiller had espoused earlier, and Goethe still practiced, Schiller nevertheless embraced them when he moved toward the romantic genre of *Schicksalsdrama* (drama of fate). The author suggests that only Schiller's untimely death in 1805 prevented him from coming to a tenable reconciliation of the dichotomy between freedom and destiny, based on Christian values. In his essay for this collection, Sullivan is redefining a field in which he is the acknowledged authority.[20]

Goethe, too, was initially influenced by the "black legend" cultivated by the eighteenth century in France and the Netherlands. His early Sturm und Drang drama *Clavigo* (1774) advocates freedom and opposition to tyranny and oppression; the Duke of Alba is portrayed as a diabolical figure devoid of humane thoughts and feelings. Gradually, however, Goethe's views became more differentiated, as did Schiller's. Under the influence of the romantics, especially Friedrich Schlegel, he discovered Calderón, and, as theater director at Weimar, he performed several of the Spaniard's plays. Calderón's impact on Goethe has not been studied systematically. For instance, it would be worthwhile to investigate the possible interconnection between Goethe's critique of Faust's hubristic transgressions and Calderón's subservience to Christian values.

Patricia D. Zecevic proposes another, unorthodox approach to the conceptualization of the relationship between Goethe and the Spanish tradition. In her essay "Francisco López de Úbeda and Johann Wolfgang von Goethe as Participants in the Shared

German-Spanish Tradition of Kabbalistic Rhetoric," she posits the notion that López de Úbeda's *La pícara Justina* (1605) and Goethe's *Wilhelm Meister* (1795ff.) share significant patterns of language and stylistic devices. In light of Luce Irigaray's theory of *parler-femme* (speaking-woman), López de Úbeda's Justina and Goethe's Makarie and Mignon are speechless and homeless in the male-dominated world and need to create their own *Haus der Sprache* (house of language)—a feminine, nonlinear voice that is fluid and asymmetrical. United through the picaresque tradition as well as probable roots in the Kabbala, accessible to both Spanish and German writers during and after the Renaissance, *La pícara Justina* and *Wilhelm Meister* share an expression of the "female voice" as shaped in the Kabbalistic mystical tradition. For Zecevic, the Kabbalistic tradition in both López de Úbeda and Goethe seems to function as a key intertext, providing a "literal bodiliness of language in order to express the (Divine) Feminine."

By the end of the eighteenth and the beginning of the nineteenth century, the synergy between Germanic and Hispanic voices was resulting in prodigious levels of creativity. Even in scientific explorations of the period, Hispano-Germanic connections blossomed and led to significant advances. Alexander von Humboldt (1769–1859), a friend of Goethe and Schiller, whose idealistic and humanistic outlook he shared, successfully negotiated with a Spanish ministry and received permission to explore Central and South America. Through the agency of the Marquis of Urquijo, a minister in the Bourbon Court of Madrid, the German explorer embarked in 1799 on a four-year expedition to the Spanish colonies. Humboldt applied himself to rigorous ethnological, zoological, botanical, geological, and meteorological studies. For example, he conducted inquiries into the course of the Orinoco and the Amazon rivers as well as the fertilizing properties of guano, all of which contributed to his laying the foundations of what would become physical geography. In the five volumes of his magnum opus, the *Kosmos*, translated into more than one hundred languages, and the thirty volumes of his *Ansichten der Natur* (Views of Nature), he laid down his observations about the Latin American countries in an encyclopedic fashion.[21]

Of even greater significance, Humboldt pursued yet another area of study that was to have a profound impact on Spanish culture for over a century. Together with his brother, Wilhelm von Humboldt (1767–1835), he initiated modern linguistic theory, which was to change the way northern Europeans saw Spanish linguistics and the way Spanish intellectuals were to conceive the study of philology in Spain. As Donald E. Lenfest points out in his essay, "The Influence of Neogrammarian Scholarship on Ramón Menéndez Pidal's Historical Grammars of Spanish," there is a clear line of development among German linguists, the *Junggrammatiker* (Young Grammarians), that led to the great accomplishments of Menéndez Pidal (1869–1968), Spain's premier linguist historian of the twentieth century. His linguistic, folkloristic, and literary studies are linked methodologically and thematically to German Romanist scholars such as Friedrich Diez (1794–1876), Gustav Gröber (1844–1911), and Wilhelm Meyer-Lübke (1861–1936), whose philosophical and philological origins, in turn, can be traced back to the brothers Grimm—Jacob Grimm (1785–1863) and Wilhelm Grimm (1786–1859)—and Johann Gottfried Herder (1744–1803). Collectively, these Germans formulated approaches that eventually led to a framing of studies of various areas of Hispanic life, literature, and culture.[22]

Conservatives developing integrist thoughts in Spain throughout the nineteenth century also owed much to Central European imagination. German romanticism, largely a counterreaction against the French Enlightenment, the French Revolution, and Napoleon, resorted back to an idealized medieval era or even prehistoric mythology. The 1799 work by Novalis (Friedrich von Hardenberg, 1772–1801), *Christenheit oder Europa* (Christianity or Europe), was among the early treatises on the fanciful eulogy of the Middle Ages as the splendid days when the European *imperium sacrum* was still united under the church. Adam Müller, in *Die Elemente der Staatskunst* (The Elements of State Government, 1809), also argued for the organic unity of medieval society. Other conservative and reactionary thinkers of the *politische Romantik* movement were Friedrich Schlegel (1772–1829), Joseph Görres (1776–1848), Achim von Arnim (1781–1831), and Franz Baader (1765–1841). As a result, the negative image of Spain—the "black legend" of the enlightened eighteenth century—began gradually to be replaced by a new, positive attitude toward the Iberian Peninsula. It is not a coincidence that the first Spanish-German dictionary appeared in the year 1795. Prior to that, Spanish works were typically translated into German from the French version.[23]

Among the literary pioneers in Spanish-German relations was Ludwig Tieck (1773–1853), who studied Spanish literature as early as 1793. His own translation of Cervantes' *Don Quixote* (1799–1801) provided the other romantics with a new poetic paradigm that was much discussed and helped define early romanticism. Tieck's next discovery was Calderón de la Barca, and he was instrumental in familiarizing the Schlegel brothers with the Spanish playwright, who was soon regarded by them as "der spanische Shakespeare."[24] In their wake, and prompted by none other than Goethe, Johann Dieterich Gries (1775–1842) undertook the tremendous task of translating all of Calderón's plays into German. The first volume appeared in 1815, the seventh and last in 1829, followed by a second edition in 1840–41.

Another influential romantic-Catholic writer and translator was Joseph von Eichendorff (1788–1857). He, too, began to study Spanish on his own and translated plays by Calderón. The Austrian playwright Franz Grillparzer (1791–1872) was likewise deeply influenced by Calderón and especially by Lope de Vega. Also a Hispanophile was the German philosopher Arthur Schopenhauer (1788–1860), whose idol was the Jesuit priest Baltasar Gracián (1601–1658). In 1864, Schopenhauer translated Gracián's *Oráculo manual y arte de prudencia* (Das Handorakel or The Art of Worldly Wisdom) into German, and only his failure to find a publisher prevented him from finishing the translation of Gracián's *El criticón* (The Critic) that he had begun. It would be an interesting research project to compare and contrast Schopenhauer's own pessimistic masterpiece, *Die Welt als Wille und Vorstellung* (The World as Will and Representation, 1819), with Gracián's philosophical novel *The Critic*.

The romantic period is represented in this collection by an essay on Friedrich Schlegel and his reaction to Ludwig Tieck's translation of *Don Quixote*. In her essay entitled "Reassessing Friedrich Schlegel's Reading of *Don Quixote* in Light of His Early Writings," Rachel Schmidt argues against scholarly claims that the German author perceived the Spanish work as a sentimental novel, devoid of satirical or parodistic intentions. Through a review of Schlegel's literary notebooks of 1797 to 1801, she documents the former's regard for *Don Quixote* as an all-inclusive work: "Cervantes' *Don Quixote* epitomizes the mixing of genres and the development of ironic tensions between objectivity and subjectivity that were to become intrinsic to the novel as a genre." According to Schmidt, Schlegel's reading of *Don Quixote* ignored neither the parody of chivalric romances nor the characters' absurdity, but rather incorporated these elements into a broader definition of the novel as the genre that encompasses the chaos and contradiction of sentiment and irony, folly and wisdom. Thus, Cervantes' novel was a cornerstone in the emerging self-definition of romantic literature, as propagated by Friedrich Schlegel.

In the 1830s and 1840s, a new intellectual group, the *Junges Deutschland* or Young Germany, developed in Germany. A politically charged movement that promoted democracy and freedom, it eventually led to the German Revolution of 1848–49. Prominent in that group, and in Germano-Hispanic contacts, was the German writer Heinrich Heine (1797–1856). In this collection, the ample inventory of existing studies of Heine's work are ably and comprehensively represented in Berit Balzer's "Spain in Heine—Heine in Spain: Notes on a Bilateral Reception." The author recapitulates facets of Heine's familiarity with early nineteenth-century German translations of *Don Quixote* and *El Cid*, and above all the *romancero*, which provided the poet with inspiration for his own lyrical works. In addition, Balzer also recounts the history and criticism of Spanish writers' familiarity with Heine's work, available in translations beginning in 1856 and known to be an influence on Mariano José de Larra (1809–1837), José de Espronceda (1808–1842), Gustavo Adolfo Bécquer (1836–1870), and Rosalía de Castro (1837–1885), as well as numerous *modernista* poets in Spain and Latin America. Between the age of Bécquer and the *modernismo*, there existed a veritable "Heine fever" in Spain. However, Balzer concludes that Heine enjoyed essentially not a "true" but a "'false' reception" in Spain, since only his early Byronian melancholic *Weltschmerz* was acknowledged, at the expense of his politically oriented later oeuvre.

The tradition of Georg Wilhelm Friedrich Hegel (1770–1831), Ludwig Feuerbach (1804–1872), and Karl Marx (1818–1883) must not be overlooked in even this cursory study of German-Spanish relations over the centuries. The German philosopher Hegel, claimed by rightists and leftists alike, left his mark in Spain,[25] as did his disciples Feuerbach[26] and Marx.[27] Marx, of course, was as central to nineteenth-century socialist thought in industrializing Spain as he was elsewhere in Europe and in America. In competition with the writings of Mikhail Bakunin (1814–1876) and other anarchists, especially in Barcelona, Marx's writings generated enthusiasm and provided the ideological basis, or at least the claims of legitimacy, for the left in its defense of the Spanish Republic in the twentieth century. After the fall of the Republic, Marx provided the intellectual framework on which opposition to the Franco regime coalesced, in both the writings and teachings of such figures as Enrique Tierno Galván, and as the subtext in the writings of Jaime Gil de Biedma, José María Castellet, Juan Goytisolo, and other poets, novelists, and critics of the 1950s.[28]

John W. Kronik's essay in this collection, "*La Abeja* of Barcelona and German Literature in Spain, 1862–1870," provides insight into the manner in which German literary culture was introduced into Barcelona even before the destruction of the city walls and the development of the *Ensanche/Eixample*, which led to further and more extensive contacts with European culture and commerce. *La Abeja* (The Bee) specialized in the publication of translations of German writings, both literary and scientific. Among the more prominent authors represented were numerous eighteenth- and nineteenth-century novelists, playwrights, and poets of Germany and Switzerland such as Lessing, Klopstock, Herder, Goethe, Schiller, Jean Paul, Novalis, Tieck, and Heine—not to mention dozens of lesser-known names. For the destinies of many German authors in Spain, Kronik writes, "*La Abeja* was a significant milepost if not a defining moment." On the other hand, it is equally indicative that many other great names of German literature were ignored by the editorial collective—both established writers (such as Eichendorff, Hebbel, Hölderlin, Kleist, Lenau, Mörike, and Wieland) and "problematic" authors (such as Büchner, Moritz, and Wezel) whose seminal significance was not recognized until decades later.

The most pronounced philosophical influence on late nineteenth-century Spanish progressives, however, was the German philosopher Karl Christian Friedrich Krause (1781–1832). Krause was eulogized as the formative influence on nineteenth- and early twentieth-century Spanish culture as a code for progressive thought, especially emanating from Madrid (Julián Sanz del Río). Although Krause was viewed with anathema by conservatives such as Marcelino Menéndez y Pelayo (1856–1912), his work informed the imagination and convictions of the Spanish reformers who identified themselves with the politics of Práxedes Mateo Sagasta and who formulated a culture aptly described by the late Juan López-Morillas (1913–1995).[29]

In this collection, Nelson R. Orringer, one of the leading experts on Krause, makes the case for the influence of Krause on Leopoldo Alas (1852–1901), known by his pseudonym Clarín. Orringer's essay, "Clarín's Krausism," effectively argues that Leopoldo Alas consistently grounded his work—including his major novel *La Regenta* (The Regent's Daughter, 1884–85), his shorter novel *Su único hijo* (His Only Son, 1891), and his short stories—on Krausist premises. Countering critics who have argued that Alas had moved away from Krausism toward "a vague idealism with Krausist underpinnings," Orringer convincingly demonstrates that Alas's Krausism, or "Krauso-positivism," continued throughout his life, reflecting and maintaining the Germanic influence he first internalized as a doctoral student in the 1880s when he wrote his dissertation on law and morality under the Krausist Francisco Giner de los Ríos (1839–1915).[30] This introduction would be remiss if it failed to mention Juan Eugenio Hartzenbusch (1806–1880) and Cecilia Böhl de Faber (1796–1877), who wrote under the pseudonym Fernán Caballero. Hartzenbusch, the son of a German cabinetmaker in Madrid, did much to cultivate German-Spanish relations. Besides writing sixty-nine plays of his own in the romantic style, he translated Lessing and Schiller into Spanish and edited critical editions of Lope, Calderón, and Tirso de Molina.[31] Böhl de Faber, the daughter of the consul to Cadiz from Hamburg, the ardent Hispanophile Johann Nikolas (or Juan Nicolás) Böhl von Faber, settled in Andalusia in 1821 and wrote several influential novels, the best and most important one being *La gaviota* (The Seagull, 1849). The plot involves a German doctor, Fritz Stein, and his tragic love and marriage to Marisalada, "the Seagull," who runs off with a bullfighter— a cross-cultural conflict that is reminiscent of Prosper Merimée's earlier novella *Carmen* (1845–46) and George Bizet's opera of the same name. While the motifs may be sentimental, Böhl de Faber certainly "deserves credit for founding the realistic regional novel in nineteenth century Spain,"[32] if not for establishing the modern Spanish novel as a genre.

By the end of the nineteenth century, German writers whose works influenced the Spanish included Friedrich Nietzsche (1844–1900), who became a significant catalyst for the renewal of Spanish culture through the Generations of 1898 and 1914. Ángel Ganivet (1865–1898), known to have been responsive to German writers in the formative stages of his career, is often associated as a figure parallel to the German Nietzsche.[33] Ramiro de Maeztu (1875–1936) has sometimes been called a "Spanish Nietzsche" in reference to his earlier works before he reverted to traditionalism, monarchism, and Catholicism. The Basque novelist Pío Baroja (1872–1956) freely admitted his admiration for Nietzsche and eventually got into trouble for his Germanophile tendencies. Another writer, Ángel Guimerà (1849–1924), wrote his rural plays (e.g., *Terra baixa*) under the influence of Gerhart Hauptmann (1862–1946) and Hermann Sudermann (1857–1928), prominent exponents of the new *Naturalismus* movement in Germany.

In photography, the French and English travelers who visited Spain in the nineteenth century are often seen as the principle seekers of romantic images and of travel souvenirs, especially for the traveler by rail. Charles Clifford from England and Jean Laurent from France were both photographers to the Spanish royal family. Yet the little-known work of Max Junghändel (born in 1861), *Die Baukunst Spaniens*, published in various printings from 1891 to 1898 with increasingly greater numbers of photographs of Spain, was an important source of illustrations for consumption in Germany and even in the United States. His images, primarily from the 1880s, are historical documentation that gave late nineteenth-century and early twentieth-century Germans a view of Spain that included facets of daily life seen in few other photographs of the period.[34]

By the early twentieth century, the Spanish embrace of German culture was at its peak. The works of Krause and Nietzsche were scrutinized through various texts, and German theater and opera riveted the attention of the urban bourgeoisie. The intellectuals of Madrid had by the 1870s begun an evaluation of the work of Krause as the cornerstone of a culture of progress that would manifest itself in such remarkable institutions as the Institución Libre de Enseñanza, while the less intellectually inclined bourgeoisie was embracing the language and song of Germany through the works of Richard Wagner (1813–1883) and Engelbert Humperdinck (1854–1921). The Belgian Maurice Maeterlinck (1862–1949) had an influence in both Germany and Spain, and in Spain was associated with the Germanic world of folk and fairy tales as well as romantic legends.

The 1901 premiere of Humperdinck's opera *Hänsel und Gretel* (1893), translated into Catalan by Antoni Gaudí's friend Joan Maragall (1860–1911), appears to have influenced Gaudí in the creation of the gatehouses in Barcelona's Park Güell. Maragall's translation of the work was first performed at the Teatro del Liceo in the winter of 1901, just months after Gaudí (1852–1926) had begun work on Park Güell and two years before he had created the park's gate lodges, which recall the "houses of sugar" in the light opera. The German's cautionary tale was ideally suited for the wit and charm of Barcelona's turn-of-the-century café society.[35]

While Humperdinck offered light entertainment for a culture that was amused by the Spanish *cuplé* (popular song), Wagner provided the operatic grandeur that had a profound impact on the expansive urban middle and elite classes of Barcelona. The Paris opera house of Charles Garnier was an important influence on the creation of ever more dramatic opera houses in Barcelona and Madrid. The Teatro del Liceo of Barcelona of the 1860s emerged at the end of the century as the flamboyant venue for the presentation of Wagnerian opera. In such works as *Parsifal* (1877–82), Wagner himself was inspired by themes and myths of Spain.

On the other hand, Spanish composers likewise enjoyed a growing audience in the German-speaking countries. Isaac Albéniz (1860–1909), a pupil of Franz Liszt (1811–1886), Enrique Granados (1867–1916), and Manuel de Falla (1876–1946) created a new national style of music, using regional tunes and rhythms, that resonated well with the German public. These three composers led Spanish music to European eminence.

Less conspicuous, but no less dramatic, was the influence on the Spanish church language by conservatives such as the German Jesuit Father Joseph Kleutgen (1811–1883), and on the health and personal lives of the Spanish populace by Sebastian Kneipp (1811–1883), adviser to Pope Leo XIII (1878–1903). For the body and soul of Gaudí and others in the Catalan elite at the turn of the century, Kneipp had contrived an austere health regimen and water treatments. The gymnast Müller provided the model for the physical exercise programs that were implemented in the workers' colonies in the Llobregat and Ter valleys.[36]

Seminal to Spanish thought of the twentieth century is the nineteenth-century German legacy in the work of Miguel de Unamuno (1864–1936) and José Ortega y Gasset (1883–1955). In his essay, "Configurations of German and Spanish Intellectual History and Aesthetics: Goethe, Novalis, Ortega y Gasset, and Umanuno," Francisco LaRubia-Prado argues that both Unamuno and Ortega developed their creative vision through a unique relationship with German culture. By reproducing in the Spanish context the issues and conflicts that were central intellectual causes in Germany, both Spanish figures helped to elevate Spain to a higher level of European discourse. In Unamuno, LaRubia-Prado examines uses of the Nietzschean concepts of *Übermensch* (superman) and the *ewige Wiederkehr* (eternal return), stemming from the romantic tradition; in Ortega, he explores facets of the classical tradition that contributed to *The Dehumanization of Art and Ideas on the Novel*. While German influences helped shape Unamuno's "organicism," they also contributed to Ortega's "classicist" understanding of the avant-garde.

Unamuno, in return, exercised a limited but decisive and lasting impact on German intellectuals of nonsocialist persuasion. Shirley King documents the German response to Unamuno during the Spanish writer's exile in France in her essay, "The Fame of Miguel de Unamuno in Germany: Its Growth and Decline, 1924–1930." She demonstrates that Unamuno, though sensationalized and trivialized in the press, had captured the imagination of the German elite of the period, including Hermann Bahr, Ernst Robert

Curtius, Hermann Hesse, Heinrich Mann, and Reinhold Schneider. King also suggests that it was Unamuno's exile during the 1920s that brought the pre–civil war situation in Spain into world-view.

Spain in the twentieth century had become far more than an exotic destination and a repository of ruins, folklore, and flamenco music; it was even to become an influence on the invention and refinement of the avant-garde. Having escaped many of the academic tendencies that dominated the culture of the Renaissance and the Enlightenment, the art and literature of Spain appeared to share the uninflected, basic, and essential qualities that the Germans were looking for in their own past or in exotic cultures uncontaminated by rationalism and industrialization. The revolutionary leader in twentieth-century art, the Spaniard Pablo Ruiz Picasso (1881–1973), was also among the most potent influences of the avant-garde in early twentieth-century German art. After moving to Paris from Barcelona at the turn of the century, he exercised an influence on German, Austrian, and Swiss artists as enduring as it was extensive in the international avant-garde milieu of the first decades of the century. In his aftermath, the way was paved for the reception of other Spanish artists such as Joan Miró (1893–1983) and Salvador Dalí (1904–1989)—household names in Germany even to the present day.

Concomitantly, the German vanguard contributed to the artistic revolution in Spain, especially in Barcelona. Otto Weber's 1915 exhibition at the Dalmau Galleries in Barcelona shocked the public. In 1931, the works of German avant-garde artists, including Hans Arp and Otto Freundlich, were exhibited. The symbolists and surrealists were indebted to the writings of Sigmund Freud (1856–1939), Carl Gustav Jung (1875–1961), and the culture of psychoanalysis.[37] Translations of Rainer Maria Rilke (1875–1926) and Stefan George (1868–1933) were part of the exercises in experimental art forms. The Mexican writer Jaime Torres Bodet (born in 1902) wrote his novel *Margarita de niebla* (Margarita of the Mist, 1927) with both direct and indirect allusions to Goethe's *Faust*. The German philosopher Paul Ludwig Landsberg lectured in Barcelona in 1935 after his escape from Nazi Germany.

In architecture, the German influence was likewise fundamental. By the time of the Barcelona Universal Exposition in 1929, the culture of the Bauhaus had become central to Spanish design and sensibility. Ludwig Mies van der Rohe's (1886–1969) German Pavilion on Monjuich (1929), as well as the aluminum and leather chair as part of the furniture within the pavilion, evoked the sensibility of functional modernism that would resonate with the austere design principles of José Luis Sert. Sert, along with Josep Torres Clavé, Francesc Fàbregas, and others, founded a neo-Bauhaus design group in 1928, the G.A.T.C.P.A.C. (Group of Catalan Artists and Technicians for the Progress of Contemporary Architecture), through which modern German design would enter and be propagated in Spain. Sert designed the culmination of the avantgarde in Catalonia with his 1937 Republican pavilion in the International Exposition of Paris, refining the purists' lessons of Mies van der Rohe, Walter Gropius (1883–1969), Swiss-born architect Le Corbusier (1887–1965), and others.[38] As director of the Harvard School of Design, once directed by Gropius himself, Sert would continue Bauhaus-inspired modernism. In the Gropius-designed Harvard graduate living environment at Harkness Commons, a significant Joan Miró painting was featured as a mural, in a parallelism recalling Miró's painting of a Catalan peasant and the revolution in Sert's 1937 Spanish pavilion in Paris. It could be argued that Sert's mid-1960s design of the Harvard University Holyoke Center is the culmination of Bauhaus construction in America.

The works of Thomas Mann (1875–1955) contemporaneously illustrate the complex response to Spain among many Germans of high culture. Although he writes conventionally in letters, essays, and novels of Spain as a land of austerity and inquisition, he also reveals more immediate and personal bonds with Spain and Spanish culture. For example, his protagonist Felix Krull has repeatedly been connected with the Spanish picaresque novel. The reactionary figure of Naphta, from *Der Zauberberg* (The Magic Mountain), shows affinities to the Spanish Jesuits and the Counter Reformation they propelled. And once again, as in the case of Goethe, it would be a rewarding endeavor indeed to locate and interpret further possible links by comparing, for instance, Mann's version of *Doktor Faustus* and the Spanish tradition of unquestioning obedience to God and the church.

On Thomas Mann's steamship departure from Germany to America during May 1934, Cervantes' *Don Quixote* had become Mann's deck chair reading. Published that summer in the *Neue Zürcher Zeitung*, Mann's "Meerfahrt mit Don Quixote" (Voyage with Don Quixote) narrates both the journey and the reading of the book, along with stunning commentary on Cervantes' literary style. In one of the most imaginative modern formulations of a Germano-Hispanic relationship, Mann concludes his overseas journey, Cervantes' book, and his own essay by recounting a dream that brings together, in conscious unity, Spain and Germany, Cervantes and Nietzsche:

I feel dreamy from the early rising and strange experience of this hour. And I dreamed in the night too, in the unfamiliar silence of the engines; now I try to recall the dream which assembled itself from my reading. I dreamed of Don Quixote, it was he himself, and I talked with him. How distinct is reality, when one encounters it, from one's fancy! He looked different from the pictures; he had a thick, bushy moustache, a high retreating forehead, and under the likewise bushy brows almost blind eyes. He called himself not the Knight of the Lions but Zarathustra.[39]

The concern for Spain by Romance languages scholars Karl Voßler (1872–1949), Ernst Robert Curtius (1886–1956), Leo Spitzer (1887–1960), Erich Auerbach (1892–1957), and their contemporary cultural historians and philologists was largely generated in the 1920s and matured in the following decades. If nineteenth-century history and linguistics were pursued by the romantic Germans, twentieth-century scholarship in similar areas was rigorously and often brilliantly pursued by German philologists and historians. Voßler's letter on Spain to Hugo von Hofmannsthal (1874–1929) in 1924 was to intensify the Austrian writer's Hispanic studies and made Voßler's commentaries on Spanish culture favorite books for Madrid publishers in the early 1940s, during the imperial era of the Franco regime. Curtius's work *European Literature in the Latin Middle Ages* (1948–53) outlined common Latinate features that linked the Germanic and Romance cultures. Spitzer wrote an essay on Catalan in 1915, as well as a vast number of studies on the language and literature of Spain and on other Romance languages. Auerbach's essay on Spanish and other Romance literature has been a milestone in scholarly erudition; especially notable are his hallmark observations on Don Quixote's encounter with Dulcinea in the second volume of Cervantes' *Don Quixote*. The research of Wolfgang Kayser (1906–1960) has extended aspects of that tradition in a brilliant interdisciplinary analysis of the grotesque in art and literature, including commentary on the Spanish sensibility from Cervantes through Goya to the surrealists.[40]

Two German writers in particular upon whom Spain and Spanish literature had a lasting impact must be singled out. In Austria, the conservative poet and playwright Hugo von Hofmannsthal (1874–1929) was heavily indebted to the Romance languages and literatures, in particular to Calderón, whose plays he translated and adapted for the Vienna Burgtheater.[41] A participant in the same "Conservative Revolution," the German writer Reinhold Schneider (1903–1958) also discovered Portuguese and Spanish history, as presented by Thomas K. Wolber in the 1996 symposium (not included in this collection). Initially pessimistic over Germany's state of military defeat and cultural bankruptcy in 1918, Schneider encountered a congenial mind in Unamuno's *The Tragic Sense of Life*, translated in 1925 by Robert Friesé as *Das tragische Lebensgefühl*. Schneider found positive inspiration in Spanish Catholicism and wrote numerous books with Spanish motifs, beginning with *Philip II*. (Philipp II, 1931).[42] Before Ludwig Pfandl and others, Schneider was the first German writer to rid Philip of the prevailing stigma as being "the epitome of an oppressor of spiritual freedom."[43] It has been argued that thinkers of the Conservative Revolution such as Hofmannsthal and Schneider, aided by the Spanish paradigm, may have contributed to the destruction of reason, liberty, and democracy in the Weimar Republic and thus facilitated the rise of the Nazis, much like the German romantics are often blamed for destroying the spirit of the Enlightenment. However, in fairness to these writers and philosophers it must be stated that few of them shared the ideology of the National Socialists; they preferred an "inner exile" (*Innere Emigration*). Hofmannsthal died before Hitler's *Anschluß* of Austria, but Schneider's fate was less fortuitous. He was harassed and censored by the Nazis, whom he tirelessly fought in the name of a higher authority, and was eventually accused of high treason. Schneider's best-known book is *Las Casas vor Karl V.: Szenen aus der Konquistadorenzeit* of 1938 (translated into English as *Imperial Mission*), which contains a courageous critique of Nazi antisemitism, concealed in Bartolomé de Las Casas's passionate plea for the native Americans.

From the Spanish Civil War to the Present

During the pivotal years of the Spanish Civil War (1936–39), the presence of the German Condor Legion was central to the military effort of the Franco assault on the Republic and to Germany's preparation for its imminent aggressions. Virtually from the beginning of the war, German "specialists" arrived in Spanish waters and in Spain itself for a collaboration as infamous to the world as it was perplexing to most of the parties involved. On the other hand, some twenty-seven German authors served in the Loyalist International Brigades, the largest contingency among international writers. A cluster of essays pertains to different aspects of the affiliation between the two countries and suggests the extent to which the collaboration conditioned the Civil War. Expanding on his seminal 1989 work *Hitler and Spain*,[44] Robert H. Whealey, in his essay "Hitler and the Spanish Civil War: A Shifting Balance of Power," provides an overview of the Civil War and suggests its importance in the imminent larger battle that was to be waged throughout the world. According to Whealey, the Spanish theater of war was a welcome stage on which the Germans could rehearse World War II: "Militarily, the Nazis used the Spanish Civil War for training and experimentation by their army, navy, and air force."

In "What the Condor Saw: Nazi Propaganda Images of the Spanish Civil War," Conrad Kent illustrates several of the anachronistic patterns by which the German soldiers and photographers in Spain, as well as the photographic curators in German archives, perceived their Spanish experience. An analysis of the contradiction between an atavistic vision and modern warfare reveals the archaism at the root of the German imagination of the 1930s. Irrespective of improvements in supply procedures, the concentration of armor in spearheads, and other modern military refinements, the German military continued to frame the war in monumentalist images founded on mythic assumptions little affected by the fluidity and complexity of their own experience in combat or their technical advances in photography. As Kent relates, "In photography more than in any other medium, the dual nature of the German experience in Spain reveals itself to be deeply rooted and shared by many different individuals."

In her essay, "Writing War: German Women and the Spanish Civil War," Friederike B. Emonds describes German women who observed the war, either on the Republican or the Francoist side. A significant number of women from German-speaking countries experienced the Civil War firsthand and produced fictional and nonfictional accounts of it, among them the antifascists Anna Seghers and Maria Osten, as well as Maria de Smeth, who was employed by the German propaganda ministry and supported the fascist forces in Spain. While German women were, by law, prevented from actual combat action at the front, their narratives nevertheless constitute authentic and credible testimony. In fact, precisely by focusing on matters other than trench warfare, maneuvers, and strategy, they were able to draw attention to the human dimension of the war.

With the end of the Spanish Civil War and the beginning of World War II in 1939, the relations between Franco and Hitler emerged as a silent rivalry between erstwhile partners. What had been in the middle of the 1930s a bond forged in anticommunist rhetoric and military convenience was by the beginning of the 1940s a series of diplomatic and social jousts by which Hitler,

Franco, and their advisers sought their respective advantage in the radically changing stages of the international conflict.

Norman J. W. Goda's essay, "The Reluctant Belligerent: Franco's Spain and Hitler's War," extends the discussion of the German-Spanish relationship under Hitler and Franco into the first years of World War II. Goda takes exception to the traditional argument that Franco steered a skillful and deliberate path of nonbelligerency in this war. According to the German, Spanish, and French documents Goda has consulted, Franco aggressively sought to enter the war on Germany's side from June to November 1940 with the goal of acquiring French Morocco for Spain. He and his ministers remained optimistic despite German vagueness about how much of Morocco Spain was to receive. However, the alliance with Germany ran aground, but not due to Madrid's unwillingness. Rather, Hitler's revelation in November 1940 that he wished to use the Gibraltar strait to station German troops in Morocco ended Madrid's interest in the war. Had Hitler and Göring had the circumspection to give Spain what it coveted, the alliance of forces, and thus the outcome of World War II, may have been different.

In the aftermath of the Spanish Civil War, both the fascist and antifascist sides produced large quantities of memoirs and fictional accounts of the events. The voluminous collection edited by Luis Costa and others, *German and International Perspectives on the Spanish Civil War: The Aesthetics of Partisanship* (Columbia, S.C., 1992), is an indication of the fecundity of the subject, much of which has yet to be fully explored. If there is one book that epitomizes the contemporary German view of the Spanish Civil War, it would have to be the Peter Weiss's (1916–1982) *Ästhetik des Widerstands* (Frankfurt, 1975–81)—written, ironically, by an author who spent his exile years in Prague and Stockholm, yet whose account of the years between 1936 and 1939 in the first volume of his seminal trilogy has shaped the German perception forever.

A half decade of World War II further altered the German-Spanish relationship. According to Wayne Bowen, "During the last nine months of World War II, the split between Francisco Franco's (1892–1975) Spain and Adolf Hitler's (1889–1945) Germany became a deep chasm." Bowen's contribution to the symposium and to this publication, "The Last Defenders of the New Order: Spaniards and Nazi Germany, August 1944–May 1945," argues that by the end of the war, political, economic, and diplomatic conflicts between the two governments echoed the physical separation between Germany and Spain caused by the Allied conquest of France. Bowen's contribution analyzes the *División Azul* (Blue

Division) and other Spanish "Naziphiles" who continued to collaborate with the Third Reich even in the final months of the war. Numbering just in the several thousands, these zealous adherents of a New Order led by Germany undermined Franco's efforts to distance himself from the Thousand Year Reich in late 1944 and the first five months of 1945.

Yet to be examined is the German presence in Spanish popular culture between the early official attempts to side with Hitler and the last official efforts to separate Spain from the Nazis' visionary extremes during both the Civil War years and most of World War II. Although American music, film, and automobiles had been central to the modernization of Spanish life during the first third of the twentieth century, and American influence was crucial during the "Roaring Twenties," German movies and popular culture were prevalent on the Nationalist side during the Civil War and throughout Spain for the first years of World War II. Especially during 1941 and 1942, the Spanish press gave prominence to the victories of the Axis powers and extolled the richness of culture in these countries. With the front pages of Spanish newspapers featuring news of German military exploits, the entertainment sections carried news about the films of Willy Fritsche, Hilde Krahl, Paul Hartmann, and Ilse Werner. Thus, German culture embedded itself subtly into the imagination of many Spaniards even as wartime news receded from the front pages, and after the Blue Division of Spanish soldiers became muffled in other drums of war. After 1945, the aesthetics of German culture were accepted by certain elitist Spaniards as an antidote to Walt Disney's empire and the "American Way of Life" in general, often ridiculed by an intelligentsia that was emerging in the middle of the 1940s.

The Spanish cultural landscape of these years was conducive to scholars who had received a German education and to those who became Germanophiles through the political tendency of the Franco government to favor German over Anglo-Saxon culture, even when the Wehrmacht was showing signs of fatigue. A group of Spanish and German writers produced works recalling an earlier era that would be accepted as academic dogma for decades. This shared Germano-Hispanic scholarly connection of the 1940s can be seen in the works of Gabriel Maura y Gamazo—the Duque de Maura (born in 1879)—and in the extensive publications of Karl Voßler. Both writers sought to find cultural links demonstrating an ancient closeness that would be the grounds for a contemporary conservative alliance—an affiliation emanating from medieval ballad times and shared imperial grandeur.

Germany played a role in the development of the progressive culture of Spain during the second half of the twentieth century. In the 1950s, Spanish poets coming of age after the Franco era traveled to Germany as well as to France. Germany was the country to which they first went because they were sponsored by church and official university organizations, which were reluctant to let the young leaders of Spain lose themselves in Paris. Given the favor in which Germany was held during the 1940s, it was inevitable that Germany would be a point of destination for the young who wished to see the world beyond the official culture of Franco's Spain. But it was not to Nazi Germany that these youths traveled. Heidelberg in the summer of 1950 was an environment in which Carlos Barral, Joan Reventós, Luis Martín Santos, and Manuel Sacristán worked on the foundations of what would become modern Spanish progressive culture while they studied German language and literature, sharing an opening to the world that would lead to France, Italy, England, and Ireland. More importantly, it was the study of German literature and philosophy—on which those writers developed their critical thinking skills—that would eventually lead to the Marxism and existentialism forged in Paris.[45] In his later years, Antoni Tàpies has often referred to this exploration of not only the artistic world of Paul Klee and Max Ernst but also the writings of the medieval mystic Meister Eckhart.

A younger member of this generation of Barcelona's prominent intellectuals, theater critic José María Carandell was destined to be the primary continuing intellectual link between Germany and Spain for the past half-century. After visiting the Federal Republic of Germany in 1950, he committed himself to the study of German writers and to being their spokesman in Spain. A 1969 book on Peter Weiss and a 1975 study of Hermann Hesse were seminal works in the development of modern culture before the transition away from Francoist culture.[46] Through prologues and studies on the works of Kleist, Büchner, Schnitzler, Brecht, and Thomas Mann, Carandell has given Spanish and Catalan readers an introduction to a wide range of German-language culture. His extensive essays in *El Observador* and *La Vanguardia* of Barcelona have allowed German literature and art to enter the popular culture of Catalonia, and his close personal friendships with Hans Magnus Enzensberger, Hans Mayer, José Agustín Goytisolo, Carlos Barral, Juan Marsé, and Ana María Matute have enhanced German-Spanish relations among the intelligentsia of both countries.

German travelers to Latin America have produced their own accounts of a wondrous world, peopled by strange beings and colored in a palette of rich vegetation and strong smells that betoken alluvial forests—mysterious paths to the center of exotic truths. By the middle of the twentieth century, those travels had taken the form of an appropriation of the Latin American boom. Continuing a long-standing tradition of seeking out primitivism and exoticism, German literary figures of the twentieth century have made the Latin American odyssey a sensuous version of the path once traveled by Germans to the depths of a "mysterious" landscape in Spain. Above all, Latin America has become for them a land of political exile and a literary landscape for the expression of alienation.

A German anarchist of mysterious origins, Ret Marut (who died in 1969) made his way to Tampico, Mexico, in 1924 as B. Traven, creating a personal mythology as compelling as that which he created for the screen in *The Treasure of the Sierra Madre*. Presented by Helmut J. Kremling in the 1996 symposium (not included in this collection), B. Traven's journeys and writings can be seen as both a search for utopian authenticity and a critique of capitalist corruption. Traven's major work is the *Caoba Cycle*, a series of six novels about the gruesome conditions that led to the Mexican revolution of 1910. As suggested by Kremling, Traven's legacy continues in the present-day Zapatista rebellion in Chiapas.[47] In a symmetry of curious proportions, sixty years later Werner Herzog created *Aguirre: Der Zorn Gottes* (Aguirre: The Wrath of God), a 1972 film that suggested the exotic, "outsider" experience of the Spaniard in Peru during the European conquest. The German's rendition of the conquistadors in Latin America suggests another curious parallel with the travels of B. Traven. Each artist represents humankind as obsessed in a world without coordinates and nature as an impersonal witness to human limitations. Obsession was also a theme in the writings of Juan José Arreola of Mexico beginning in the 1950s. Through an appropriation of the stylistic and thematic features of the work of Franz Kafka (1883–1924), Arreola prepared his readership for Kafka's works themselves.

For many German and other displaced writers in the twentieth century, Latin America was also a place of exile. After 1933, thousands of Germans fled abroad and became scattered all over the world—from Scandinavia and France to South Africa, and from the U.S. and Turkey to China. America, too, provided a welcome haven for Jews and/or intellectuals critical of the Nazi regime, among them many writers who had fought in the Spanish Civil War on the Loyalist side.[48] The most important Latin American country for the German refugees was Mexico, where even socialist and communist writers were welcome.[49] Other centers of exile were Buenos Aires, Santiago, and Rio de Janeiro.[50] Perhaps the best-known of these authors is Anna Seghers (1900–1983) who lived in Mexico from 1940 to 1947. Her exile novels *Das siebte Kreuz* (The Seventh Cross) and *Transit* belong to the very best of the genre. Several of her stories ("Die Hochzeit auf Haiti," "Wiedereinführung der Sklaverei auf Guadeloupe," and "Das Licht auf dem Galgen") deal with the Third World experience of her Mexican years.[51] Also among the writers who emigrated to Mexico were Alexander Abusch (1902–1982), who became the editor of the important exile monthly *Freies Deutschland/Alemania Libre*, published between 1941 and 1946,[52] and Gustav Regler (1898–1963), Egon Erwin Kisch (1885–1948), Ludwig Renn (1889–1979), and Bodo Uhse (1904–1963).[53] Like Seghers, several of these writers eventually produced stories and journalistic accounts of their stay in Mexico (e.g., Kisch's *Entdeckungen in Mexiko*, 1947, and Uhse's *Mexikanische Erzählungen*, 1957). Unfortunately, because of the liberal leanings of many of these authors, after 1945 the reception of exile writers was typically restricted to those from the German Democratic Republic (GDR). Even prolific writers such as Paul Zech (1881–1946), who died in Buenos Aires leaving a legacy of some fifty or so unpublished manuscripts written while in exile, remained largely forgotten and unpublished in the West.[54] Hence, the new-found knowledge of the émigré writers never found its way back to the Federal Republic of Germany (FRG)—one of the factors contributing to the myopic provinciality of the West German Adenauer years.

Another largely unexplored area of research pertains to the Jewish diaspora communities in Latin America.[55] While much has been written about the German-Jewish communities in Argentina and Brazil, other Latin American nations—namely Ecuador, Bolivia, and the Spanish Caribbean—also openly accepted fleeing refugees. At the 1996 symposium, Istvan Varkonyi presented a paper on this topic, "The Tropical Diaspora: German-Speaking Jewish Exiles in Cuba and the Dominican Republic" (not included in this collection). Varkonyi provided a general introduction to the life and culture of the exiles in Havana, Cuba, and Sosúa, Dominican Republic. He also included testimonies from autobiographies as well as personal interviews he conducted in the Dominican Republic.

Exiled European Jews found themselves in a culture very different from their own, yet, over time, a dialogue would emerge, sometimes even followed by complete assimilation. Max Aub

(1903–1972), a displaced writer who eventually played a crucial role as a mediator between the German, French, and Spanish avant-garde, is just such an example. Born in Paris of a German father and a French mother, the Jewish family moved to Spain at the outbreak of World War I, where Aub became passionately involved with his adopted country. At the end of the Spanish Civil War, he spent three years in various concentration camps and finally escaped to Mexico, where he continued to live until his death. While esteemed in the Romance countries, Aub was virtually forgotten in the German-speaking countries; it was only a few years ago that he was rediscovered and translated for the first time.[56]

"Pablo Neruda and the German Literary Exile Community" is the subject of a study by Vera Stegmann. She shows that in his memoirs Neruda (1904–1973) mentions his love for Hölderlin, Heine, Rilke, and Brecht, and that as early as 1926, he had translated Rilke's works for the journal *Claridad*. During the 1930s and 1940s, he opposed Nazi propaganda and defended exiles who had been persecuted under the Nazis. While in Mexico City during World War II, he took part in German exile community activities and supported its causes, and after the war wrote poetry in memory of the damages and suffering occasioned by Nazi Germany. Stegmann also demonstrates the inevitable influence that Neruda was to have on German poets, prose writers, and dramatists, including Bertolt Brecht. The poet Erich Arendt (1903–1984), a Spanish Civil War veteran and political refugee in Colombia, was Neruda's congenial and prolific translator into German.

Film is a relatively new medium, but in this field, too, numerous examples of Hispanic-Germanic cross-pollination can be found. One such case study is described by the German-Spanish team of Rachel J. Halverson and Ana María Rodríguez-Vivaldi, "*La insurrección/Der Aufstand*: Cultural Synergy, Film, and Revolution," itself an example of German-Spanish cultural synergy. In the 1970s and 1980s, the German film director Peter Lilienthal (born in 1929) and the Chilean film director Antonio Skármeta (born in 1940) joined forces to produce several movies together. Lilienthal, of Jewish descent, had grown up in exile in Uruguay and did not return to Germany until 1956; Skármeta, on the other hand, had to leave Chile in 1973 after the coup that deposed the government of Salvador Allende, and lived in Berlin until 1990. Among the several movies they collaborated on was *Der Aufstand* or *La insurrección* (The Uprising, 1980). The film, based on a true story from the 1979 Sandinista revolution in Nicaragua, describes the struggle for Leon, one of the last strongholds of Anastasio Somoza, Jr., the Nicaraguan dictator. After examining the respective careers of Lilienthal and Skármeta, the coauthors provide a detailed plot summary of *The Uprising* and explore the movie's structure and main themes. Their discussion offers interesting insights into the dynamics and challenges that arise when the Old and the New Worlds meet.

Meg H. Brown's essay, "The Reception of Spanish-American Fiction in Germany: The Tide of Bestsellers, 1980–1995—Rising and Ebbing?" provides a commentary on the changes in the fortunes of Latin American literature in Germany. Brown notes that before 1980, Spanish-American fiction went virtually unnoticed, but during the mid-1980s it became such a prominent literary phenomenon that Germans were among the most avid readers of Spanish-American novels. The German public found in the prose of Latin America certain literary characteristics that were not present in its own national literature—mainly the magic of the tropics and the vitality of exoticism. The success of Gabriel García Márquez and Isabel Allende paved the way for other Latin American writers. However, Brown has also ascertained that the literary tide has begun to ebb: "We must come to the conclusion that the trend of Spanish-American bestsellers in Germany has reached its peak and is on the decline."

In East Germany as well as West Germany, the Third World emerged as a major literary topic after 1971, the year Erich Honecker came to power and the GDR became an international player. Of course, the old Spanish Civil War fighters and the writers of the exile were still around, but now the younger generations started to include Latin American themes in their writings, kindled by the events in Chile. In 1975, Peter Hacks (born in 1928) wrote *Die Fische*, a play with Mexican motifs, and Volker Braun (born in 1939) devoted a play, *Guevara oder Der Sonnenstaat*, to the Cuban revolutionary Che Guevara. In 1979, Claus Hammel (1932–1990) published a play, *Humboldt und Bolívar oder Der Neue Continent*, based on a fictional encounter between Alexander von Humboldt and the revolutionary Simón Bolívar.[57]

At the 1996 symposium at Ohio Wesleyan University, Hera T. Leighton presented a paper entitled "The Influence of Latin American 'Magic Realism' on East German Fantastic Prose" (not included in this collection). Leighton's thesis was that authors such as Cortázar, Borges, and García Márquez inspired the so-called "middle generation" of East German writers to expand their "socialist realism" by trying their hands at the "surreal" or "fantastic."

Among these writers were Günter de Bruyn, Fritz Rudolf Fries, Sarah Kirsch, Helga Königsdorf, Günter Kunert, Irmtraud Morgner, Klaus Schlesinger, Rolf Schneider, Helga Schubert, and Christa Wolf. In her paper, Leighton emphasized the special position Fritz Rudolf Fries holds in German-Hispanic relations. Born in 1935 in Bilbao, Spain, he emerged as a particularly important mediator between Latin America and the GDR. Among his many translations of Spanish- and Latin American works and his own literary oeuvre is a 1977 biography of Lope de Vega.

The climate that existed in 1967 when Gabriel García Márquez's novel *One Hundred Years of Solitude* was rejected by major German publishing houses (Hanser, Rowohlt, S. Fischer, and Aufbau) is now long gone.[58] Latin American writers such as Isabel Allende, Jorge Luis Borges, Carlos Fuentes, Gabriel García Márquez, Juan Carlos Onetti, Octavio Paz, Ernesto Sábato, and Mario Vargas Llosa are well known, even popular, in the reunited Germany. However, the fascination that Latin America holds for Germans is not limited to the literary realm, but extends into the political arena as well. Since the student movement of the 1960s, many young Germans have openly sympathized with the various revolutionary movements in Central and South America, and some have even traveled there to join, for example, the Cuban revolution, the Nicaraguan Sandinistas, and the Mexican Zapatistas. It seems that very intriguing, yet little studied, "elective affinities" exist between Latin American revolutionaries and German philosophy. A case in point is Abimael Guzmán, the now imprisoned leader of the Peruvian *Sendero Luminoso* (Shining Path). When still teaching philosophy at the University of Ayacucho in the 1970s, he lectured on Kant, Hegel, and Marx and was said to be a great fan of Heidegger and Jaspers.

Coupled with the remnants of romantic sympathies for Latin American revolutions and an interest in "liberation theology," it is no wonder, then, that some of the younger German writers have begun to travel to Central and South America to find new inspiration for their own poems, plays, and novels. Hans Magnus Enzensberger, born in 1929, was among the first to travel to Cuba, but also one of the first to distance himself again from Fidel Castro's socialist regime. It is interesting to note that Enzensberger moved from his radical anarchist and pro-revolutionary beginnings of the 1960s and 1970s back to the influence of Calderón's *Tochter der Luft* (Daughter of the Air), a 1992 rewrite of the Spaniard's play that reveals the vanity of a human life devoid of transcendental values. Hubert Fichte (1935–1986), a prolific but highly controversial traveler, ethnologist, and novelist, single-handedly created the "ethnopoetic" novel. Uwe Timm, born in 1940, has published novels that take place in Africa and South America. In *Der Schlangenbaum* (The Snake Tree, 1986), the German engineer Wagner is supposed to build a paper factory in the rain forest—a heroic but vain struggle that becomes a parable of the process of civilization itself. Writer Hans Christoph Buch, born in 1944, is another frequent traveler to the New World. In 1985, playwright Franz Xaver Kroetz, born in 1946, published his *Nicaragua Tagebuch*, followed in 1991 by *Brasilien-Peru-Aufzeichnungen*, the diary of a three-month trip taken through Brazil and Peru in 1989. Bodo Kirchhoff, born in 1948, published *Mexikanische Novelle* in 1984, followed by other "exotic" novels. They are part of a definite trend in contemporary German literature—a trend for which there is no end in sight. Today, Germany has successfully overcome the isolation and provinciality that existed between 1933 and 1966 and is once again an active part of the "global village." No peoples travel as much as the Germans do, and that new openness to foreign influences is clearly reflected in the national literature, music, and film.

In an interesting study, Michael Rössner has postulated that the "magic realism" and mythical exoticism for which Latin American literature is famous, is, in its origins, a Central European product.[59] Spanish-writing authors such as Mário de Andrade, Miguel Ángel Asturias, and Alejo Carpentier as well as Brazilian writers such as João Guimarães Rosa were very familiar with the European avant-garde and freely admitted their indebtedness to German expressionism and/or French surrealism. Jorge Luis Borges, for example, was intimately involved with German literature throughout his life. First conceived by German critics (e.g., Franz Roh) to address the novel artistic and literary experimentation in the first decades of the century, magic realism invites further study into the reciprocal literary influences of German and Latin American writers.

Both the end of a divided Germany and the rise of a European community have radically changed Germano-Hispanic relations in less than a decade. Spain and Germany are partners in a Eurocentric bloc that seeks to promote European unity over nationalistic impulses. Beginning in 1982, the Spanish government of Felipe Gónzalez and the German government of Helmut Kohl sought to find common ground on which to forge a new Europe. Given the traumatic past of both countries, the decade of the 1980s and 1990s has therefore been an era of assertive public relations efforts by both Germans and Spaniards to demonstrate to the world their shared commitment to democracy and a united Europe. With German support for Spanish attempts to become integrated into Europe in exchange for alliance with the Europeanist factions of European government, Spain has welcomed the presence of German culture as part of the redefinition of Spain as a center of world culture, especially in Barcelona, through which German culture has always been introduced into Spain. Just as French culture was the dominant influence on the nineteenth-century Spanish imagination, so Germany has become a significant means of access to cosmopolitan culture today. For example, in the 1992 Olympics-related bicentennial of Mozart's death in 1792, Barcelona focused on the life and art of the German-speaking composer as access to performances of international stature.[60]

More recently, German scholars in Catalonia celebrated an extensive conference in Sitges, near Barcelona. On 25–27 October 1997, the Associació de Germanistes de Catalunya (Association of Catalan Germanists) organized a seminal conference on twentieth-century German-language linguistic, literary, and cultural relations with other European nations: "Korrespondenzen: Literatur und Sprache der internationalen Moderne des 20. Jahrhunderts." Sponsored by the Goethe Institute, the Federación de Asociaciones de Germanistas en España (FAGE), the Generalitat de Catalunya, and other agencies and institutions, the conference was a watershed in intellectual cooperation, especially between German- and Spanish-language scholars. Especially notable in this symposium was the search for historical, literary, and pedagogical commonality. The participants were engaged in both theoretical inquiry and a search for practical solutions to conceptualizing and teaching culture in a united Europe. A glance in *Germanistik an Hochschulen in Spanien: Verzeichnis der Hochschullehrerinnen und Hochschullehrer* (Bonn, 1997)—the latest directory of German teachers at Spanish universities, issued by the Deutscher Akademischer Austauschdienst (DAAD)—confirms the strong interest in German-Spanish relations, exemplified perhaps by the recent volume *Deutsch-spanische Literatur- und Kulturbeziehungen: Rezeptionsgeschichte* (Madrid, 1995), coedited by Margit Raders and Luisa Schilling of the Universidad Complutense in Madrid.

In Germany, as the bibliography to *The Lion and the Eagle* clearly indicates, there is likewise a strong interest in German-Spanish relations, both in academic and nonacademic circles. Some publishing houses, for instance, Vervuert in Frankfurt, have produced numerous volumes devoted to Germano-Hispanic contacts. Given the fact that Europe is growing together and is now introducing a single new currency, the euro, the different nations are discovering the commonalities of their past as a step toward strengthening their existing ties and as an effort to develop a new, joint identity.

Still, there are vast unexplored areas of cross-cultural contacts. One literary example is Albert Vigoleis Thelen (1903–1989), who spent the years 1931 to 1936 on the Spanish island of Majorca where he worked as secretary for Graf Harry Kessler. In 1953, he published his picaresque novel, *Die Insel des zweiten Gesichts: Aus den angewandten Erinnerungen des Vigoleis*, in which he describes the German exile community of Majorca and the distant rumbling of the coming Civil War. Another example is the writer Hans-Joachim Sell (born in 1920), who worked as a radio reporter in Spain during the years between 1960 and 1968. He published numerous fictional and nonfictional books involving Spain and Latin America, his best-known work being *Der rote Priester: Eine spanische Erfahrung* (The Red Priest: A Spanish Experience, 1976). Unfortunately, his recent death remains unobserved, and to our knowledge, no scholarly study has been written on him.

A literary traveler from Germany to Spain, alert to the ironies of contemporary life, was among the first to narrate a new kind of Hispanic journey for the German people, and thus to reframe the dialogue between traveler and host. With remarkable timing, Peter Handke (born in 1942) foreshadowed a new conception of the world through his writings about Spain toward the fateful end of 1989, when he traveled to Soria, notable to him and others for its association with the poet Antonio Machado. Written in the third person, Handke's narrative situates this iconic Spanish city in contemporary culture, epitomized by the American jukebox. By the same token, the author uses references to modern, international realities in the daily life of Soria as a means to conjure up the cold austerity of Soria poignantly explored in poetry by Machado and not unlike the exotic spaces in search of which Germans have long traveled.[61]

The relationships between the Spanish- and German-language worlds explored in this overview and in the essays that follow suggest a profound linkage between the two spheres over many centuries. The multifaceted relationships also invite further inquiry into areas of shared sensibility, expectations, and self-perception. It may prove that geography itself should be considered in further studies, especially given the fact that both Germany and Spain have France as a neighbor, one whose influence is often too direct and too powerful to be easily accepted. Indeed, it may be in the German-Spanish response to France itself that many aspects of the Germano-Hispanic relationship can be better understood. Shared early historical, political, and religious patterns may, in fact, have been merely a pretext by which Germans and Spaniards from the seventeenth century on developed as kindred admirers-adversaries of the French. Whatever the nature of future explorations, however, it cannot be denied that for centuries Germans have gone to Spain in search of inspiration, and that Spaniards and Latin Americans have sought in German culture and technology the means to reframe the Hispanic world in modern terms.

Notes

1. See Erwin Koller and Hugo Laitenberger, eds., *Suevos—Schwaben: Das Königreich der Sueben auf der Iberischen Halbinsel, 411–585. Interdisziplinäres Kolloquium Braga 1996* (Tübingen, 1998).
2. See Nicholson B. Adams, *The Heritage of Spain: An Introduction to Spanish Civilization* (New York, 1959), p. 13.
3. Debates and discrepancies in recent scholarly thinking on the Visigoths in Spain can be found in catalogue essays for the exhibition of medieval Spanish art that was held at New York's Metropolitan Museum of Art: *The Art of Medieval Spain, A.D. 500–1200*, ed. John P. O'Neill (New York, 1993).
4. See Norbert Voorwinden, "Zur Herkunft der Rüdiger-Gestalt im Nibelungenlied," *Amsterdamer Beiträge zur älteren Germanistik*, vol. 29 (1989), pp. 259–270. Others—see, for example, B. Q. Morgan, "Rüedegêr," *Beiträge zur Geschichte der deutschen Sprache und Literatur*, vol. 37 (1911), pp. 325–336—have attempted to prove the identity of Rüdiger as the Spanish "Cid," who lived from c. 1040 to 1099.
5. Adams, *The Heritage of Spain*, p. 17. The many recent titles listed in our bibliography indicate that the interest in this *Jakobsweg* did not vanish with the Reformation of the sixteenth century, but has maintained its fascination until the present day.
6. See Adams, *The Heritage of Spain*, p. 83.
7. See Ernst Adam, *Baukunst des Mittelalters II* (Frankfurt and Berlin, 1963), p. 149.
8. Jerónimo Münzer, *Viaje por España y Portugal, 1494–1495* (Madrid, 1991).
9. The authority on Erasmus in Spain continues to be Marcel Bataillon. His book in French, *Érasme et l'Espagne: recherches sur l'histoire spirituelle du XVIe siècle* (Paris, 1937), has appeared in several editions after the first Spanish version: Marcel Bataillon, *Erasmo y España: estudios sobre la historia espiritual del siglo XVI*, trans. Antonio Alatorre (Mexico, 1950). We must also recall that scholars working in both German and Spanish were contemporaneous students of the Renaissance humanists in Italy. See *Renaissance Humanism*, 3 vols., ed. Albert Rabil, Jr. (Philadelphia, 1991). Of special note are Ottavio Di Camillo, "Humanism in Spain," and Noel L. Brann, "Humanismo in Germany."

10. Ramón Carande, *Carlos V y sus banqueros*, 3 vols. (Madrid, 1949), both describes the astonishing drain caused by debt payment to the Fuggers of Augsburg and makes claims of loyalty of the Fuggers to Charles when adversaries sought to disrupt the Fugger-Habsburg relationship.
11. Gerhart Hoffmeister's 1970 doctoral dissertation at the University of Maryland, *Die spanische Diana in Deutschland: Zur Rezeption des Schäferromans im XVII. Jahrhundert*, concerned the presence of the work of Jorge de Montemayor, Alonso Pérez, and Gaspar Gil Polo in German translation in the seventeenth century. The book appeared as *Die spanische Diana in Deutschland: Vergleichende Untersuchungen zu Stilwandel und Weltbild des Schäferromans im 17. Jahrhundert* (Berlin, 1972). See also Gerhart Hoffmeister, *Spanien und Deutschland: Geschichte und Dokumentation der literarischen Beziehungen* (Berlin, 1976); Spanish translation: *España y Alemania: Historia y documentación de sus relaciones literarias* (Madrid, 1980). Other pertinent books by Hoffmeister include *German Baroque Literature: The European Perspective* (New York, 1983); *Der deutsche Schelmenroman im europäischen Kontext: Rezeption, Interpretation, Bibliographie* (Amsterdam, 1987); *Deutsche und europäische Barockliteratur* (Amsterdam, 1987); *Der deutsche Schelmenroman in europäischer Barockliteratur* (Stuttgart, 1990); and *Deutsche und europäische Romantik* (Stuttgart, 1990).
12. Francisco de Quevedo y Villegas, *La fortuna con seso y la hora de todos*, in *Obras Completas*, 6th ed., vol. 1, ed. Felicidad Buendía (Madrid, 1966), pp. 256, 275.
13. See Volker Meid's "Einleitung" to his edition of Grimmelshausen's *Der abenteuerliche Simplicissimus* (Stuttgart, 1986), p. 16.
14. See Alois Podhajsky, *The White Stallions of Vienna*, trans. Frances Hogarth-Gaute (Munich, 1963), and Wolfgang Reuter, *The Lipizzaners and the Spanish Riding School* (Innsbruck, 1969).
15. See Norman Hampson, *The Enlightenment* (Harmondsworth, 1968), p. 58.
16. Ibid., p. 59.
17. See Beatriz Brinkmann Scheihing, *Spanische Romanzen in der Übersetzung von Diez, Geibel und von Schack: Analyse und Vergleich* (Marburg, 1975).
18. For the relationship between Schiller and Spain, see Herbert Koch, *Schiller y España* (Madrid, 1978).
19. For the relationship between Goethe and Spain, see Marie Mathilda Weinrich, *Goethe's Interest in Spanish Literature: Its Influence on His Works, and His General Relation to Spain* (Ph.D. diss. Washington University, 1937); Udo Rukser, *Goethe in der hispanischen Welt* (Stuttgart, 1958), translated into Spanish as *Goethe en el mundo hispánico* (Mexico, 1977); and Robert Pageard, *Goethe en España* (Madrid, 1958).
20. Students of Germano-Spanish relations owe a debt of gratitude to Henry W. Sullivan for his major work on the role of Calderón's influence on German culture. See Henry W. Sullivan, *Calderón in the German Lands and the Low Countries: His Reception and Influence, 1654–1980* (Cambridge and New York, 1983); a Spanish version appeared as Henry W. Sullivan, *El Calderón alemán: recepcion e influencia de un genio español, 1654–1980*, trans. Milena Grass (Frankfurt and Madrid, 1997).
21. The books about Alexander von Humboldt's life, travels, and work are too numerous to be listed here. However, for travels of German researchers to Latin America, see Herbert Scurla, ed., *Im Lande der Kariben: Reisen deutscher Forscher des 19. Jahrhunderts in Guayana. Alexander von Humboldt, Robert Schomburgk, Richard Schomburgk, Carl Ferdinand Appun*, 3rd ed. (Berlin, 1968); Herbert Scurla, ed., *Durch das Land der Azteken: Berichte deutscher Reisender des 19.*

Jahrhunderts aus Mexiko und Guatemala (Berlin, 1978); and Urs Bitterli, *Die Entdeckung Amerikas: Von Kolumbus bis Alexander von Humboldt* (Munich, 1991). See also Michael Zeuske and Bernd Schröter, eds., *Alexander von Humboldt und das neue Geschichtsbild von Lateinamerika* (Leipzig, 1992).
22. By the end of the nineteenth century, German scholarship of the Spanish language was remarkably sophisticated and thorough, as seen in the works of F. Diez, *Grammatik der romanischen Sprachen* (1836–43); W. Meyer-Lübke, *Grammatik der romanischen Sprachen* (1890–1902); G. Gröber, *Grundriß der romanischen Philologie* (1886–88); G. Körting, *Handbuch der romanischen Philologie* (1896); G. Baist, *Die spanische Sprache* (1904–06); E. Hübner, *Monumenta linguae ibericae* (1893); and many others.
23. See Reinhard Tgahrt, ed., *Weltliteratur: Die Lust am Übersetzen im Jahrhundert Goethes. Eine Ausstellung des Deutschen Literaturarchivs im Schiller-Nationalmuseum Marbach am Neckar* (Marbach, 1982), p. 575.
24. See Oskar F. Walzel, *Deutsche Romantik: Eine Skizze* (Leipzig, 1908), pp. 95–97. On Tieck's reception of Cervantes and Calderón, see Roger Paulin, *Ludwig Tieck: A Literary Biography* (Oxford, 1985), passim. On Calderón's influence on Germany, see Elisabeth Münnig, *Calderón und die ältere deutsche Romantik* (Berlin, 1912); Ernst Behler, "The Reception of Calderón among the German Romantics," *Studies in Romanticism*, vol. 20 (1981), pp. 437–460; and, of course, Henry W. Sullivan.
25. See Juan Francisco García Casanova, *Hegel y el republicanismo en la España del XIX* (Granada, 1982); and José Ignacio Lacasta Zabalza, *Hegel en España: un estudio sobre la mentalidad social del hegelismo hispánico* (Madrid, 1984).
26. Our bibliography includes a number of Spanish-language titles on Feuerbach, too numerous to list here. It is interesting to note, however, that while Feuerbach is known as "the first materialistic thinker" in the German-speaking countries, Spanish and Latin American books seem to emphasize his pre-Marxist theology.
27. See Pedro Ribas, ed., *Verbreitung und Rezeption der Werke von Marx und Engels in Spanien* (Trier, 1994); and Raúl Fornet-Betancourt, *Ein anderer Marxismus? Die philosophische Rezeption des Marxismus in Lateinamerika* (Mainz, 1994).
28. For a reprise of the Marxist influence in Spanish literature of the 1950s, see J. M. Castellet, *Literatura, ideología y política* (Barcelona, 1976).
29. Juan López-Morillas, *El Krausismo español: perfil de una aventura intelectual* (Mexico City, 1956); English translation as *The Krausist Movement and Ideological Change in Spain, 1854–1874*, trans. Frances M. López-Morillas, 2nd ed. (Cambridge, England, 1981). For a selection of original "Krausista" works, see Juan López-Morilla's *Krausismo: estética y literatura* (Barcelona, 1973). The *Urtext* of Spanish "Krausismo" was Julián Sanz del Río's version of Krause's *Urbild der Menschheit* as *Ideal de la humanidad para la vida* (Madrid, 1860). Partly in response to the influence of progressive German culture in Spain through the translations of Sanz del Río (1814–1869), Menéndez y Pelayo (1856–1912) dedicated a book on aesthetics to his conservative mentor, Manuel Milà y Fontanals (1818–1884): Marcelino Menéndez y Pelayo, *Historia de las ideas estéticas en España* (Madrid, 1883). Menéndez y Pelayo's review of German aesthetics is a vast compendium and ambivalent critique of German thought from Kant, Winckelmann, and Lessing through Goethe, Jean Paul, and Schlegel to Hegel, Krause, and Schopenhauer. In later editions, he even included comments on the influence of the aesthetics of Richard Wagner. But for the "theosophical fantasmagoria" of Krause's thought, Menéndez y Pelayo reserves

only scorn; see *Historia de las ideas estéticas en España*, 14 vols. (Buenos Aires, 1943), vol. 11, pp. 108: "Pero como en España, por una calamidad nacional, nunca bastante llorada, hemos sufrido durante más de veinte años de dominacion del tal Krause, ejercida con un rigor y una tiranía de que no pueden tener ideas los extraños, algo hay que decir de esa dirección funesta que de tanto contribuyó a incomunicarnos con Europa."

30. Nelson Orringer's contribution to Germano-Spanish studies is as extensive as it is profound. Notable is his study of the German roots of Ortega y Gasset's philosophy; see Nelson R. Orringer, *Ortega y sus fuentes germánicas* (Madrid, 1979). See also Nelson R. Orringer, *Unamuno y los protestantes liberales (1912): sobre las fuentes de "Del sentimiento trágico de la vida"* (Madrid, 1985).

31. An English summary of the author's life and work is provided by Carmen Iranzo, *Juan Eugenio Hartzenbusch* (Boston, 1978).

32. Adams, *The Heritage of Spain*, p. 244. For a critical study on *The Seagull*, see Maria Caterina Ruta, *Ideologia e strutture in "La gaviota" di Fernán Caballero* (Palermo, 1974). A summary of Böhl de Faber's life and work is provided by Lawrence Hadfield Klibbe, *Fernán Caballero* (New York, 1973).

33. Javier Herrero, *Angel Ganivet: un iluminado* (Madrid, 1966), pp. 198–203, traces specific relationships to the German romantics Novalis and Eichendorff. Miguel Olmedo Moreno, *El pensamiento de Ganivet* (Madrid, 1965), draws parallels between Ganivet and Nietzsche and other German writers he associates with an antitechnological stance.

34. Max Junghändel, *Die Baukunst Spaniens in ihren hervorragendsten Werken* (Dresden, 1891–98).

35. Conrad Kent and Dennis Prindle, *Park Güell* (New York, 1993), pp. 90 and 104. Among the students of Germanic influences in Spain is Lily Litvak; her work, *España 1900: modernismo, anarquismo y fin de siglo* (Barcelona, 1990), should be consulted for observations and for further bibliographic references, including her essay on Maurice Maeterlinck.

36. Joseph Kleutgen, *Ars dicendi* (Rome, 1847), provided the neo-Counter Reformation manual of rhetoric for Jesuits in Spain and elsewhere. Sebastian Kneipp, *Mi testamento*, 4th ed. (Barcelona, 1904), was the mentor in hydrotherapy and other health programs for antirationalists among the Catalan elites. The Colònia Güell in Santa Coloma de Cervelló adopted the Müller gymnastic techniques as part of the conservative religious and educational programs of the industrial colonies surrounding Barcelona.

37. The influence of Freud reached many progressive Spaniards' sensibilities through the work of Salvador Dalí and Luis Buñuel in Cadaques, Figueras, and Paris. For a recent study of the Freudian aspects of the 1929 film *Un chien andalou*, see Stuart Liebman, "'Un chien andalou': The Talking Cure," in *Dada and Surrealist Film*, ed. Rudolf E. Kuenzli (Cambridge, Mass., 1996), pp. 143–158.

38. See Oriol Bohigas, "El pavelló de la República espanyola a l'Éxposició de París del 37 va a ser el punt culminant de les avantguardes arquitectòniques a Catalunya," *Nexus*, no. 9 (December, 1992), pp. 50–59.

39. Thomas Mann, "Voyage with Don Quixote," in *Essays by Thomas Mann*, trans. H. T. Lowe-Porter (New York, 1958), p. 369. The English translation was first published in Thomas Mann, *Essays of Three Decades*, trans. H. T. Lowe-Porter (New York, 1947).

40. Karl Voßler's letter to Hofmannsthal can be found in Karl Voßler, *Spanischer Brief* (n.p., 1924). Throughout the early 1940s, his work concerning the reach and influence of Spanish culture in Europe was published widely, as in Karl

Voßler, *Algunos carácteres de la cultura española* (Madrid, 1941). Ernst Robert Curtius, *Europäische Literatur und lateinisches Mittelalter* (Berne, 1948); English translation: *European Literature in the Latin Middle Ages*, trans. Williard R. Trask (New York and London, 1953). Leo Spitzer, *Syntaktische Notizen zum Catalanischen* (Göthen, 1915). A representative selection of Spitzer's articles can be found in Leo Spitzer, *Romanische Literaturstudien, 1936–1956* (Tübingen, 1959). Erich Auerbach, *Mimesis: Dargestellte Wirklichkeit in der abendländischen Literatur* (Berne, 1946); English translation: *Mimesis: The Representation of Reality in Western Literature*, trans. Williard R. Trask (Princeton, 1953). Wolfgang Kayser, *Das Groteske: Seine Gestaltung in Malerei und Dichtung* (Oldenburg und Hamburg, 1957); English version: *The Grotesque in Art and Literature* (Bloomington, Ind., 1960).
41. See Vernon L. Anderson, *Hugo von Hofmannsthal and Pedro Calderón de la Barca: A Comparative Study* (Ph.D. diss. Stanford University, 1954); Helmuth de Haas, *Hofmannsthals Weg zu Calderón* (Ph.D. diss. Munich, 1955); and Egon Schwarz, *Hofmannsthal und Calderón* (Cambridge, Mass., 1962).
42. See Reinhold Schneider, *Gesammelte Werke*, ed. Edwin Maria Landau, 10 vols. (Frankfurt, 1977–81).
43. "Philipp wurde im Zeitalter der Demokratie zum Inbegriff eines Unterdrückers geistiger Freiheit." Elisabeth Frenzel, *Stoffe der Weltliteratur: Ein Lexikon dichtungsgeschichtlicher Längsschnitte* (Stuttgart, 1983), p. 619.
44. Robert H. Whealey, *Hitler and Spain: The Nazi Role in the Spanish Civil War* (Lexington, Ky., 1989).
45. See Carlos Barral, *Años de penitencia* (Barcelona, 1990), pp. 339–350.
46. José María Carandell, *Peter Weiss: Poesía y verdad* (Barcelona, 1969), and idem, *Hermann Hesse* (Barcelona, 1975).
47. The most comprehensive work on B. Traven remains Karl S. Guthke, *B. Traven: Biographie eines Rätsels* (Frankfurt, 1987).
48. See Wolfgang Kießling, *Exil in Lateinamerika* (Leipzig, 1980); Patrik von zur Mühlen, *Fluchtziel Lateinamerika: Die deutsche Emigration, 1933–1945. Politische Aktivitäten und soziokulturelle Integration* (Bonn, 1988); and Alisa Douer and Ursula Seeber, eds., *Wie weit ist Wien: Lateinamerika als Exil für österreichische Schriftsteller und Künstler* (Vienna, 1995).
49. Egon Schwarz, "Exilliteratur," in *Deutsche Literatur: Eine Sozialgeschichte*, ed. Horst Albert Glaser, vol. 9, p. 313. See also Fritz Pohle, *Das mexikanische Exil: Ein Beitrag zur Geschichte der kulturellen Emigration aus Deutschland, 1937–1946* (Stuttgart, 1986).
50. See Hans-Bernhard Moeller, ed., *Latin America and the Literature of Exile: A Comparative View of the 20th-Century European Refugee Writers in the New World* (Heidelberg, 1983).
51. See Werner Roggausch, *Das Exilwerk von Anna Seghers, 1933–1939: Volksfront und antifaschistische Literatur* (Munich, 1979); Kathleen J. LaBahn, *Anna Seghers' Exile Literature: The Mexican Years, 1941–1947* (New York, 1986); and Alexander Stephan, ed., *Anna Seghers im Exil: Essays, Texte, Dokumente* (Bonn, 1993).
52. See Volker Riedel, *Freies Deutschland: México, 1941–1946. Bibliographie einer Zeitschrift* (Berlin and Weimar, 1975).
53. See Renata von Hanffstengel, *Mexiko im Werk von Bodo Uhse: Das nie verlassene Exil* (New York, 1995).
54. See Ward B. Lewis, "Literature in Exile: Paul Zech," *German Quarterly*, vol. 32 (1970), pp. 535–538, for a brief description of Zech's exile years. See also Ward B. Lewis, *Poetry and Exile: An Annotated Bibliography of the Works and Criticisms*

of *Paul Zech* (Berne and Frankfurt, 1975); and Arnold Spitta, *Paul Zech im südamerikanischen Exil, 1933–1946: Ein Beitrag zur Geschichte der deutschen Emigration in Argentinien* (Berlin, 1978).
55. Gert Eisenbürger, ed., *Lebenswege: 15 Biographien zwischen Europa und Lateinamerika* (Hamburg, 1995); Achim Schrader and Karl Heinrich Rengstorf, eds., *Europäische Juden in Lateinamerika* (St. Ingbert, 1989).
56. Recently, Aub's novel *Las buenas intenciones* was translated by Eugen Helmlé as *Die besten Absichten* (Frankfurt, 1996). Reportedly, the Eichborn Verlag plans to publish more of Aub's books in the future. See Hannes Stein's review, "Im Meer der Tränen," *Der Spiegel*, 13 May 1996, pp. 228–229.
57. Arlene A. Teraoka, "Solidarity and Its Discontents: Latin American Revolutions in East German Drama," in *East, West, and Others: The Third World in Postwar German Literature* (Lincoln, Nebr., and London, 1996), pp. 79–104.
58. See Hans-Jürgen Schmitt, "Ein Kontinent der Literatur im Licht: Dieter Reichardts bahnbrechendes 'Autorenlexikon Lateinamerika,'" *Süddeutsche Zeitung*, 17–18 July 1993.
59. Michael Rössner, *Auf der Suche nach dem verlorenen Paradies: Zum mythischen Bewußtsein in der Literatur des 20. Jahrhundert* (Frankfurt, 1988), passim.
60. See *Nexus*, no. 7 (December, 1991), devoted to the Mozart Bicentennial. *Nexus* is a publication of La Fundació Caixa de Catalunya.
61. Peter Handke, *Versuch über die Jukebox* (Frankfurt, 1990). Spanish translation: Peter Handke, *Ensayos sobre el Jukebox*, trans. Eustaquio Barjau (Madrid, 1992).

Part I

FROM THE MIDDLE AGES TO THE END OF THE SPANISH HABSBURG DYNASTY

– 1 –

SPAIN AND GERMANY IN THE MIDDLE AGES

An Unexplored Literary-Historical Area
of Exchange, Reception, and Exploration

Albrecht Classen

Germany and Spain in the Middle Ages

The topic of Hispano-German relations promises to be a fertile ground if one dares to explore it in depth and take untrodden paths. In particular, the question of what these relations were like in the period prior to 1600 has hardly ever been raised, and even then only perfunctorily[1] or with the exclusive interest in the political and military relations since the early modern age.[2] Romanist scholars have certainly done their share to examine the history of Spanish literature and culture, reaching far back to late antiquity and the early Middle Ages.[3] Germanists have, however, hardly paid attention to the question of the degree to which medieval and early modern German literature might have been influenced by Spanish culture and language.[4] Admittedly, one intriguing theory has often been discussed, that is, the influence of the Mozarabic lyric poetry on troubadour and then also *Minnesang* poetry.[5] Arabic sources for Middle High German Minnesang might be a possibility, but it is more likely that such contacts occurred between the crusaders and their opponents in Palestine, rather than through cultural exchange on the Iberian Peninsula. Overall, no convincing evidence has so far been unearthed to support this theory, as fascinating as it might sound.[6]

Several approaches to the question of Hispano-German literary relations are possible, one of which I would like to pursue in this essay. First of all, one could examine the more or less direct influences of medieval Spanish literature on German poetry and prose. However, scarcity of concrete evidence produced so far, lack of historical circumstances in which German poets could have learned from their Spanish contemporaries, and remarkable differences in the cultural framework between Germany and Spain during that time period make it extremely difficult at this point to take this avenue. Second, the opposite flow of influence, that is, the impact of medieval German literature on Spain, might be possible and deserves our attention. Unfortunately, the same problem as in the case of the first option arises, as most of the groundwork still needs to be done, and we know far too little about the reverse flow of reception as to paint even a broadly conceived canvas with this question in mind.[7] Third, one could study translations of Spanish or German texts and their impact on the respective book markets in the late Middle Ages. But the first known translations were not produced until the sixteenth century, well beyond the time frame in question. Moreover, most of the previous assumptions about cultural exchanges and mutual influences have turned out to be speculations harbored mainly by the romanticists, whose ideas were not based on hard facts.[8]

For practical reasons, and particularly due to the lack of previous research into this topic, this chapter must discuss in more general terms the reflections in medieval German literature on the Iberian Peninsula as a geographical entity and on Spanish culture, literature, religion, and politics. Tracing direct connections in the respective literary texts seems to be premature at this point, yet we are in a good position to at least outline the cultural and historical horizon of potential contacts and of mutual familiarity—here limited to the German writers' knowledge about Spain. In this sense, the following essay will serve as a preliminary discussion to more in-depth investigations and will present the basic framework within which those presumed—indeed, likely—contacts took place.

Edmund Schramm emphasizes in his groundbreaking article that the influence of Spanish literature on Middle High German literature is "a very unevenly researched area."[9] In fact, in his own survey, he quickly passes over the Middle Ages and stresses instead that "in the area of literature, the first concrete contacts between the two countries were not established until the time of the Renaissance and the Reformation."[10] This is, however, not the case, as a number of poems, romances, and travelogues indicate. Even if direct forms of intertextual influences might be hard to demonstrate at this point, we can certainly claim that many medieval German poets introduced their audiences to Spanish scenarios, Spanish landscapes, and Spanish customs. Spain served as a backdrop to many religious crusade poems; Spain was the country of origin of many sophisticated ideas and arcane knowledge that was disseminated at the medieval European universities; and Spain is mentioned as the birthplace of many different protagonists in Middle High German romances and other narratives.[11]

Certainly, as soon as we turn to the Renaissance and Reformation in Germany, we observe more concrete contacts between both cultures, although current scholarly interest in those contacts has been, at best, meager.[12] Edmund Schramm points out that the first important work by a Spanish author to be translated into German was the *Tragicomedia de Calisto y Melibea*, or *Celestina*, from 1499, rendered into German in 1520 by Christoph Wirsung from Augsburg. He had discovered this text, an *acción en prosa* (action in prose), in Italy in an Italian translation, and he reached a wide audience with his German version. In 1534, he published a second edition in which the tragic love story was transformed into a moralistic tale.

The only Spanish writers who found their way to the German-speaking areas during the sixteenth century were, as far as is known, Garcilaso de la Vega and Cristóbal de Castillejo, the latter reflecting his experience at the Viennese court in his *Aula de Cortesanos* from 1547, which, in turn, might have been influenced by Ulrich Hutten's famous dialogues.[13]

Undoubtedly, Cervantes exerted a considerable influence on German-reading audiences with his famous *Don Quixote*,[14] during both the baroque and, especially, the romantic periods.[15] German baroque writers seem to have admired Spain and its literature more than ever before.[16] Later centuries also witnessed a strong exchange between both countries and their poets,[17] such as the reception of Lope de Vega's and Calderón's works in Germany and the adoption of the picaresque novel in early modern German literature.[18]

Irrespective of these literary-historical factors relevant for the sixteenth and seventeenth centuries, there is something basically wrong with the impression conveyed by Edmund Schramm's article and by the current state of scholarship as far as the earlier periods are concerned. The general assumption seems to be that people living in northern and central Europe during the Middle Ages knew nothing or very little about the world to the south and particularly the southwest, that is, Spain and Portugal. Marjatta Wis bluntly argues, "Spain and Germany lie far apart from each other, which makes the establishment of contacts difficult";[19] and, "Spain was, for the Germans, a far removed country."[20] This assumption is fed by the modern concept of nationhood, linguistic barriers, and cultural differences that prevent exchange, influence, and familiarity with the other, foreign world beyond one's own border,[21] although the concept of national border was anachronistic to the Middle Ages. Of course, individual languages were of importance even in the Middle Ages and marked separation, opposition, and alterity. But the notion of a nation in the modern sense of the word was alien to medieval people, as merchants, artisans, poets, and artists moved freely around Europe, learning from each other and communicating with a wide range of members of diverse communities.[22]

This is not to deny that, for example, Occitan troubadour poetry was different from Middle High German Minnesang, or Spanish mysticism from visions and revelations experienced by women and men in Germany. But such differences were of regional character, and had nothing to do with the modern concept of nationality. Feudalism and courtly society, as reflected in courtly love poetry and romances, were the dominant political and cultural features of the medieval European world, with the exception of the eastern, southeastern, and southern frontiers.[23] Hence it makes perfect sense to question what German medieval poets knew about Spain, what they wanted their audience to know about it, and what influences of Spanish literature they revealed in their own works.

Fundamentally, it is a question of cultural exchange, of interest in the foreign world, as well as an investigation of the intellectual horizon of the average aristocratic audience during the Middle Ages. We know of the astoundingly high level of mobility of medieval people, and we have learned to identify the degree to which numerous personal contacts took place between representatives of many different countries, regions, and provinces from all over Europe during major court festivals, church councils, and political meetings. In fact, courtly culture is best characterized by the concept of worldly, perhaps even cosmopolitan *urbanitas*, broadly defined as well-rounded and open-minded education and civil behavior, acquired both through communication with learned courtiers and teachers and through international travels and contacts.

Potentials and Limitations of Current Research: Literary, Economic, Religious, and Artistic Contacts

At the current state of research, it is not yet fully possible to examine specific intertextual relations and forms of collaborations between Spanish and German writers, since we are lacking most of the basic spadework in this field.[24] Instead, I will investigate some of the most important examples of Middle High German literature reflecting on Spain and will also consider additional global contexts between both cultures in order to demonstrate that Spanish culture and geography were well known in the north—that is, in the German-speaking countries—during the Middle Ages.[25] For the sake of convenience, I will refer to "Spain" and "Spanish culture" throughout my discussion, which is not to confuse the differences between Asturias, Galicia, Navarre, and Castile, among other independent territories and their varying languages. It was only after the wedding of Ferdinand and Isabella in 1469 that these territories merged to form the modern nation of Spain, with Castilian as the dominant language.

Although economic and religious criteria do not lend themselves easily to the discussion of Spanish-German literary contacts during the Middle Ages, they can, despite their different nature, open our eyes to the possible channels through which first cultural and literary contacts were made and then concrete relationships were developed.[26] Even as early as the eleventh and twelfth centuries, merchants and traders traversed large sections of Europe and the Near East.[27] In particular, the connections between merchants in Cologne and other cities along the Rhine and their counterparts in Catalonia and Navarre are noteworthy. Recently, many of these macroeconomical contacts have been unearthed, even though much still needs to be done to shed light on the microstructure when the relevant documents can be found and interpreted.[28]

In the twelfth century, Cologne established many business contacts with Portugal as a consequence of the various crusades that used Lisbon as the starting point for their campaigns. Simultaneously, large groups of pilgrims traveled from Germany to Santiago de Compostela to worship at the tomb of St. James (St. Jakob in German).²⁹ Nevertheless, far into the fourteenth century, most Spanish trade was carried out by the Spaniards themselves, who went to Flanders and the Champagne to sell their products. Beginning in the 1370s, German businessmen are mentioned in the official records of Barcelona, which soon turned into a major trading center for the Cologne companies. In 1396, the first written document was produced in which the existence of a Cologne colony in Barcelona is recorded. At the same time, German artists and printers, musicians and poets found their way to Spain because large profits could be made in this Mediterranean metropolis, which in turn provided the financial means for the merchants to subsidize the artists.³⁰

Once the printing press had been invented by Johann Gutenberg in 1455/56, many German artisans learned this trade and soon spread their business throughout Europe, including Spain.³¹ German book printers were especially drawn to Valencia, but many of their names are also found in Seville and Lisbon. If we pursued this investigative link further, we would be able to identify an entire network of German-Spanish contacts during the later Middle Ages. Gunther Hirschfelder now confirms, "In general, the Cologne merchants were present at all marketplaces on the Iberian Peninsula that were frequented by Germans. Here they were the only representatives of the Hanse region who were able to compete with the big southern German companies."³²

How are we to interpret these and similar observations? In particular, what do they mean for our literary-historical topic? Three conclusions are immediately relevant for us. First, the economic link between the Iberian Peninsula and the German territory was quite intensive and offered many opportunities for cultural exchanges during the late Middle Ages. Traveling took much time, and much time was also spent at the trading places and during the many evening hours along the way when the merchants had to rest. These were the moments during which the interaction of literature, music, paintings, and other forms of cultural expression took place.

Second, the religious fervor of many medieval people stimulated them to travel to the cathedral of Santiago de Compostela (built since 1078) to visit the grave of St. James, which forced them to traverse large sections of northern Spain.³³ In fact, throughout the Middle Ages, Santiago de Compostela was almost as important a pilgrim's goal as were Rome and Jerusalem. Since the eleventh century, we hear of the so-called *Jakobsbrüder*, although they have not left testimonies before the fifteenth century.³⁴ From that time on, many writers gave detailed accounts of their experiences and discussed at great length the route they took. Gotfrid von Pullen, for instance, informs us about his tour in a typical fashion: "Then from Bayonne to Pamplona, which is the capital of the kingdom of Navarre, the distance is 25 miles. From Pamplona to the area of Saragossa, the capital of the kingdom of Aragon, the distance is 30 miles. The distance between Burgos to Saint Jacob is 52 miles. The distance from Saint Jacob to Finisterre is 14 miles."[35]

Finally, many Christian knights sought renown and chivalric glory by fighting on the side of the Castilian, Aragonese, and other "Spanish" forces against the Arabs in the south of the peninsula.[36] In other words, many opportunities for contacts between Germans and Spaniards (Castilians, Catalans, and so on) existed, and the trade and travel routes were well known and open. The interest in the Spanish world was obvious, as the chronicles and literary documents inform us. Conversely, a number of Spanish writers left us accounts of their experiences in German-speaking areas, such as the travelogue by Pero Tafur, who visited the cities of Basel, Mainz, Cologne, and Brugge from 1438 to 1439.[37]

How did these many and very diverse contacts translate into literary reflections? Marjatta Wis points out that the history of Hispano-German relations does not really begin before the enthronement of Emperor Charles V in 1516, which opened multiple channels between Madrid and Vienna. The beginning of his rule, indeed, was the starting point for an unprecedented intensification of economic, military, artistic, and religious contacts. Thousands of Germans began to serve in the Spanish armies, many German artisans and artists were employed in Spain, and large numbers of Spanish Jesuits came to Germany after the Bavarian duke William V had invited them to his court.[38] Even Spanish cuisine exerted a considerable influence, as a cookbook by the Mainz cook Marx Rumpolt, *A New Cookbook: That Is, a Thorough Description of How to Properly Prepare All Kinds of Meals*, demonstrates.[39] Finally, scores of German book printers set up shops in various Spanish cities, and the German postal system, run by the house of Thurn and Taxis, was also established in Spain.[40]

Surprisingly, there are almost no studies available that examine the question of whether Middle High German poets had had any experience with Spain or were familiar with Spanish literature. By determining how much Spain figured as a political, geographical, and cultural entity in the mind of the German writers, we can proceed with further investigations of where and how they gained their knowledge. In the following pages, I will limit myself to an exploration of the first aspect to provide a solid framework for future studies on this subject.[41]

The Spanish Scene as Battlefield: Konrad's *Rolandslied*

One of the earliest and most important examples of crusade epics is the *Rolandslied* (Song of Roland) by the cleric known as Pfaffe Konrad. The historical basis for this epic poem was the military defeat of Emperor Charlemagne against the Saracens in northern Spain on 15 August 778, when, on his retreat through the Pyrenees, his rear guard was attacked and decimated by Basque troops. Konrad used as his model the French epic *Chanson de Roland*, in which a strongly nationalistic tone (*dulce France*) dominates. The German poet transformed this paradigmatic framework into a highly religious setting, attributing the character of a crusade to the battles between Christians and Muslims. Roland and his Christian compatriots fight for the divine truth and become martyrs in the wake of their desperate attempts to defend themselves against an overwhelmingly superior heathen enemy force. The idealization of the protagonist and his friends is matched with the radically negative view of the traitor Genelun, who had conceived of the plan to leave Roland in charge of the rear guard and thus to hand him over to the Saracens in return for monetary compensation.

We assume that Konrad was a Regensburg cleric and that he composed his work, commissioned by Duke Henry the Lion, around 1170 or shortly thereafter. Matilda, the English princess whom Henry had married in 1168, asked the monk to write the translation for her. The epic poem reflects a highly archaic style, which made scholars think for a long time that the text must have been written much earlier. Recently, however, we have come to understand that Konrad contributed to an entire ideological program espoused by Henry the Lion, who intended to claim the imperial throne in Germany for himself and therefore used both architecture and literature to demonstrate his close cultural association and family ties with Charlemagne.[42]

Judging from the relatively large number of extant fragments from the twelfth century onwards, we can be certain that the *Rolandslied* enjoyed considerable popularity. Later poets such as Wolfram von Eschenbach, the anonymous poet of the *Karlmeinet*, and the wandering poet called Der Stricker referred directly to this work or adapted it for their own purposes.[43] Although neither the historical events nor the geographical locations were really familiar to contemporary audiences, Konrad created with his epic a major literary work of profound ideological implications with which knighthood could identify. The *Rolandslied* provided the basis for the concept of *translatio imperii* and *renovatio imperii*, both placed within the Augustinian paradigm of *civitas dei* and *civitas mundi*. The battles between Saracens and Christians were no longer waged in order to achieve military superiority or to defeat a dangerous enemy. Instead, Konrad's *Rolandslied* emerged as a new crusade epic in which the Christian knights were given an opportunity to prove themselves as worthy warriors in the name of God.[44] Both Charlemagne and his army are presented in biblical imagery, as the battle between heathens and Christians is interpreted as a battle between good and evil. In this sense, the *Rolandslied* appears as an attempt to create an *imitatio Christi*, with the emperor gaining the rank of a *figura dei*, a new King Solomon. Nevertheless, the motivating factor for Duke Henry to commission Konrad to compose this epic was not to glorify the German emperor, but to claim the imperial rank for himself.[45]

The content and the literary-historical aspects of Konrad's *Rolandslied* do not easily lend themselves as support for our topic of German-Spanish relations during the Middle Ages. The poem did, however, play a major role in early Middle High German poetry and, as such, apprises us about the level of German familiarity with Spain as the battleground where the decisive conflict between Christian Europe and Muslim North Africa took place. The epic informs the reader about a different culture and about other forces in existence that could threaten both Christian and European dominance. In other words, Konrad presents a critical challenge to the prevalent ideology espoused by his audience, reconfirming it in the end, however, with the glorious victory of Charlemagne over the Saracens.[46] This challenge took place in northern Spain, and it is here that the narrator takes his listeners/readers to describe the actual battle scenes and the sites where the Muslims defended themselves.

In the prologue, we learn that Charlemagne was deeply dismayed to hear of the situation in "Yspania" because the population venerated false gods and had turned away from the Christian God (ll. 31–37). God then commissions the emperor to go to Spain himself and to convert the people (ll. 55–58); the obstinate ones who refuse to be converted would have to be killed and sent to hell. Soon the crusade is organized, and it is quickly carried out with a triumphant victory. Only the city of Saragossa, where the heathen king Marsilie holds out, cannot be conquered (l. 377). We hear that the mountains are high and the country well defended (ll. 382–383), but Charlemagne does not give up his siege. The Saracens then call for a council and meet on a hot day under an olive tree (ll. 395–398) to find a solution to their desperate situation. Without going into details, the narrator has provided sufficient signals to indicate how far the two hostile armies are apart from each other. Then he quickly turns to the gathering of the Saracens, no longer discussing the Castilian landscape until later in the course of events, when Charlemagne deliberates with his advisers and friends about the plan of action.[47]

Most of them simply discuss the deceptive offer to accept baptism, to pay large amounts of gold, and to leave the king's own son as a hostage in return for an end of the fighting and a retreat of the Christians to France. The Bishop St. John, on the other hand, argues for a vigorous pursuit of the Muslims across the river "Ualchart" or "Guadalquivier" and toward the city "Almarie" or Almeria in southern Spain (ll. 1061–1062) to crush the heathen. Next, Genelun refers to the cities of "Nables vn Morinde, / Ualterne vn Pine" (ll. 1211–1212) as locations where some Christian troops should stay behind, while the major part of Charlemagne's forces returns home. Eventually, Genelun is sent to the Saracens as the emperor's envoy, but the narrator does not specify anything about the location of the enemy's camp or Genelun's travels. When Marsilie begins to carry out his deceptive plan, he announces to his allies that Córdoba is in flames and the Islamic troops are defeated (l. 2588ff.) to convince them finally to rally to his support. Otherwise, we do not hear much more about the geography of the events, except that the heathen armies march toward the north where Roland and Olivier are defending Charlemagne's rear (l. 3813ff.). The ensuing battle takes up the entire following part without providing us any details of the location. Nevertheless, we know that the heathens and Christians battle in distant Spain, specifically in the valley of Ronceval (l. 6952), which would have been well known to all pilgrims from their journey to Santiago de Compostela.[48]

The battle assumes enormous dimensions because incredible numbers of Muslims attack Roland and his tiny group of friends. The Bishop Turpin exclaims, for instance, that "so many people have never been assembled on earth" (ll. 5742–5743),[49] indicating that the battle is of a biblical nature because it will determine the destiny of all of Europe. But the Christian audience is only confronted with the horrible news of the assault, and so can only hope for a victory with God's help. Nevertheless, the important point is that the distance to Spain builds a safeguard and allows the listeners/readers not to worry about the direct impact of that historical conflict on their own lives. At the same time, there are enough references to known localities on the Spanish peninsula to indicate to the audience that the military events actually occurred in that distant country.

Since the text explicitly characterizes the heroes as martyrs (l. 5763), the identification of their last battlefield as Ronceval supports the ultimate purpose of this epos. During the Middle Ages, stories of martyrdom usually took place in the past of Roman antiquity and in very distant lands, inspiring awe, belief, and humility in the face of God.[50] To transpose the ultimate battle between Christianity and Islam into the known and yet unknown Spain therefore served a twofold purpose, that is, to indicate how relevant those heroic acts by Roland and Turpin, among others, were for the contemporary audience, and to show that they reflected historical events that had a direct bearing on the readers/listeners. In fact, Spain is given the role of a new Israel, where events of global significance unfold.[51] After Roland's death, the earth begins to shake, thunderstorms rage, and trees fall down both in "Karlingen unt ze Yspania" (l. 6930) as God signals his rage and his grief over this victim in the fight for Christianity.[52] Immediately following, the narrator reconnects these heavenly messages with the concrete geographical site in the Pyrenees: "The emperor and his heroes came rushing down from the mountains into the valley of Ronceval" (ll. 6950–6952).[53]

After the corpses have been recovered, Charlemagne pursues the enemies down to the Ebro River, which had become impassable for the Christians because of inundations and because their ships had been lost (l. 7045ff.). Then a new enemy arrives from the Middle Eastern region, but only to give the emperor a chance to avenge his dead men and to prove the absolute superiority of Christianity. Charlemagne kills the new king Paligan, whereas Marsilie dies of grief over his total defeat. Now the Christians cross the Ebro and gain control over all the Muslim lands: "The emperor and his heroes crossed the Ebro" (ll. 8607–8608).[54] The last fortress, Saragossa, opens its gates, and the population is baptized (l. 8631). The victory is complete; only Genelun has to be put to trial, but this event takes place back in France.

Konrad's *Rolandslied* can be interpreted from many different angles, either as a deeply Christian epos or as a historical account of the battles between Saracens and Carolingians. We might take it as testimony of medieval attitudes toward Islam and toward foreigners in general.[55] But we can also, as I have done here, take the text as an important source material to demonstrate how much or how little a German writer, and hence also his audience, knew about the Iberian Peninsula. At that early stage, Spain served as the backdrop of the historical struggle for supremacy between Islam and Christianity, and it was exactly at that frontier where the latter's superiority was demonstrated through Charlemagne's victory. The literary canvas of medieval Spain is here only a very rough one, with few geographical markers, taking us from the Pyrenees to the Ebro River, from Saragossa even down to Córdoba. But the focus point remains the battlefield and the struggle between warriors representing their individual religions.

Wolfram von Eschenbach's Contacts with Spain

Wolfram von Eschenbach and his *Parzival* serve as our principal witness in the investigation of how well medieval Spain and its culture were known by German audiences. Again, Spain plays a major role as the basic stage where the narrative takes place; above all, it is Spain where the kingdom of the Holy Grail is located. In addition, Spanish literature and history seem to have been a significant source of inspiration for the poet, as we will see in our subsequent discussion.[56]

The romance is too complex for us to explain in great detail here; exploring the function and purposes of the geographical scenery as far as Spain is concerned will suffice.[57] Gahmuret, Parzival's father, marries twice in his life: first to the black queen Belacane, and later, after he has departed from her and arrived in southern Spain near Seville, to Herzeloyde, a member of the Grail family. His travels have led him there because he knew the king: "[I]t was his cousin Kaylet, and he traveled on to Toledo to see him" (section 58, ll. 27–58). Obviously, Gahmuret enjoys immediate respect and is freshly equipped with lances to prepare him for the next tournament in Waleis near Kanvoleis. Herzeloyde needs a husband and wants to use the chivalric game to select one. The reward is a very rich one—both herself and two countries—which makes many a knight a miserable victim in the tournament, as the narrator comments (sec. 60, ll. 18–19). The subsequent events center on the jousts and other challenges but do not provide additional information about Spain and its countryside. Nevertheless, two aspects deserve our attention, one being the lack of specific references to the geographical environment, and the other being the international character of the tournament. Gahmuret has come to a major event whose promised rewards have attracted knights from all over Europe: "There is the worthy King of Ascalun, and the proud King of Aragon, Cidegast of Logrois, and the King of Punturtois;... and there is the bold Lehelin; and there is Morholt of Ireland ... Out on the plain are encamped the proud Alemans: the Duke of Brabant has come to this country" (sec. 67, ll. 13–24).

The contrast to Konrad's picture of Spain is striking. Whereas in the *Rolandslied*, the valley of Ronceval and the area north of Barcelona had been the decisive battlegrounds between Christians and Saracens, here Spain has turned into the kingdom where the elite of European chivalry is meeting and testing its ability. Wolfram does not indicate that the people there might speak Castilian; instead, he has some of his protagonists express themselves in sophisticated French (sec. 76, l. 10), already then the language of courtly refinement. More important, Gahmuret is engaged in important dialogues with an esteemed Spanish knight whom he trusts and in whom he confides his love relationships with Queen Belacane and the French queen Amphlise, and with whom he even shares his grief over the news of his brother's death: "The report was so sad that the worthy Spaniard's eyes were filled with tears" (sec. 91, ll. 14–15).

The following events soon demonstrate that the entire narrative is supposed to take place on Spanish soil, whether in Castile, in Granada, or near Toledo. Wolfram locates the Grail somewhere in the Iberian Peninsula and indicates to his audience that only there can the ultimate key to wisdom be found. Parzival's later drama—his failing at castle Munsalvœsche, his many attempts to regain the Grail's grace, the recovery of chivalry, even the interactions between King Arthur and the Grail community—all seem to be located in that area. To a large extent, of course, Wolfram is not really interested in a detailed geographical description and instead sets his narrative in a kind of dream world, one that is far away from familiar territory. Especially Munsalvœsche is surrounded by a mysticism of a deeply religious nature, wherefore the search for its actual identity on medieval maps would have been a futile endeavor.

Of course, Wolfram copied large sections of his *Parzival* from Chrétien de Troyes's *Perceval* or *Le Conte du Graal* and thus seems to be oriented toward French literature, not toward its Spanish counterpart. Wolfram reveals, however, that his work is not simply a translation from the French model, but rather a retelling of stories he has heard from a learned man, Kyot, who studied in Toledo, where he had come across an account of the Grail recorded by the Arabic scholar Flegetanis.[58] The latter was a descendant of King Solomon and studied the stars, in which he eventually discovered the message about the Grail. The Grail thus turns out to be a "hidden message" (sec. 454, l. 20) from God, and is revealed only to the most learned of men. Kyot heard about it and searched for the true story in archives all over the world until he found it in an Anjou chronicle (sec. 455, l. 12).

Although Kyot has never been identified by modern scholarship, Wolfram seems to insist on his historical existence because he refers to him repeatedly as an authentic source.[59] According to Wolfram's account, Kyot was a Provençal who possessed many skills and intellectual abilities (sec. 416, ll. 20–25). The original story was hidden in a Toledo library and written in a secret language and in an unknown script (sec. 453, ll. 11–16). Wolfram claims in his epilogue that he learned of this tale in an Occitan language version and translated it into German (sec. 827, ll. 1–11). Even if all of these strange references are to be identified as fictionalized author references, and even though traditional scholarship has disregarded any attempt to take the narrator's allusions seriously,[60] the *Parzival* romance nevertheless allows us to pursue our topic one step further.

Wolfram refers to Spain, Toledo, Seville, and other Iberian cities often enough to demonstrate that he was both very familiar with that part of the world and also wanted to leave traces in his text indicating some kind of connections with the culture and literature from that region. Toledo or "Dolet" is mentioned four times (sec. 48, l. 8; sec. 58, l. 30; sec. 261, l. 2; sec. 453, l. 12); Spain or "Spâne" is mentioned four times (sec. 48, l. 9; sec. 58, l. 27; sec. 64, l. 13; sec. 400, l. 4); several times we read of Spaniards (sec. 39, l. 15; sec. 91, l. 15); and, of course, Munsalvœsche plays a major role (sec. 251, l. 2; sec. 251, l. 19; sec. 255, l. 26; sec. 286, l. 11; sec. 316, l. 29; sec. 318, l. 29; etc.). Other Spanish names to which the narrator refers, and which are still recognizable, are Galicia (sec. 416, l. 10; sec. 419, l. 19) and Catalonia or "Katelangen" (sec. 186, l. 21; sec. 477, l. 5; sec. 799, l. 28); the many references to "Waleis," Herzeloyde's kingdom somewhere in southern Spain, should also count toward the total of Spanish geographical terms (sec. 59, l. 23; sec. 60, l. 9, sec. 64, l. 12; etc.).[61]

This handful of names does not actually prove that Wolfram had been to Spain and knew the country well. We can only say with certainty that the Iberian Peninsula was of significance for Wolfram, and that he clearly signaled to his audience that the events surrounding Parzival and the Holy Grail indeed took place there. However, André de Mandach has recently provided startling new evidence that the alleged fiction of Kyot and the Spanish connection was more than pure imagination. Relying on a plethora of new findings concerning the Spanish royal houses and their family histories during the eleventh and twelfth centuries, he argues that most of the personal names found in *Parzival* are directly borrowed from the local chronicles. Moreover, both Munsalvœsche and the Grail as a sacred object are identifiable, the first as the cave monastery San Juan de la Peña, founded in 920 and located near the mountain Mont San Salvador, and the second as the famous chalice today housed in the cathedral of Valencia, formerly part of the monastery's treasure from 1076 until 1399.

Whether or not we accept de Mandach's theses regarding the identifications of Wolfram's localities with those in Spain, the discovery of many name identities between the "fictional" characters and historical persons documented in the Spanish chronicles provides solid evidence. Anfortas, the ailing king of the Grail, bears the nickname applied to Alfonso I, king of Aragon and Navarre; Parzival himself bears the name of Rotrou II de Perche; Kyot would be the same as Ramón Berenguer IV, count of Barcelona, who was also known as Kyot; Kailet of Spain bears the name of King Alfonso VII of Spain; and so on. In addition, a surprisingly large number of geographical names in Wolfram's *Parzival* that are not easy to decode can be equated with specific rivers, cities, mountains, and other features in modern Spain, such as the town of Vedrun, today Pontevedra, at the Vedra River (ll. 12–15, 22–29, 60–61, 62–67). De Mandach does not totally disregard the literary-political connections to Wales and the Cymric origins of the Grail and Arthurian tales, but he claims, with surprisingly forceful arguments, that the actual narrative material derives from the chronicles of the Catalonian, Castilian, and Aragonese royal houses.[62] If this thesis holds against philological criticism, it would substantially support this essay's argument that the literary connections between medieval Spain and Germany were not negligible despite the extensive physical distance. In that case, the intellectual map of medieval Europe would have to be redrawn, especially because many more literary, philosophical, and scholarly links seem to have existed between both worlds than heretofore assumed.

Considering the wealth of references to astronomy, astrology, and other scientific fields in Wolfram's *Parzival*, we might even assume that the author spent time in Toledo or was familiar with a scholar who had taught at that city's famous Hebrew and Muslim university. Arthur Gross, after a meticulous source study, concludes, "Whatever we wish to make of Kyot and Flegetanis, Wolfram was clearly familiar with the massive influx of Arabic science into twelfth-century Latin culture; indeed, his narrative constitutes one of the primary documents of its reception."[63] Insofar as Toledo was well known throughout Europe for the accomplishment by its local scholars, under the guidance of Archbishop Raymond, of translating Arabic treatises and other texts into Latin, thus making them available to all European intellectuals, Wolfram's narrative gains even more significance as a testimony of this cross-cultural process.[64]

Other Personal Contacts

In this context we also have to consider that many German scholars, such as Hermannus Teutonicus and Johannes von Jandun, lived in Spain during the High Middle Ages, and many German philosophers, such as Albertus Magnus, closely studied the works of their Spanish colleagues Averroës and Maimonides.[65] Allegedly, the German woman writer Hrotsvita von Gandersheim composed her saint's legend *Pelagius* (before 959) on the basis of an oral account from Spain, where the martyr had been killed in 925. This point would be difficult to prove, because Hrotsvita mostly relied on the available literature in the monastic library, which was not arranged by country, but according to topics and areas of research.[66] H. J. Hüffer emphasizes, however, that many direct contacts existed between the imperial court in Germany and the royal houses in Córdoba and Granada during the tenth century. The chronicler Liutprand, for instance, is said to have received the idea for writing his *Antapodosis* from the Spanish bishop Recesmund in 956. At about the same time, Emperor Otto the Great's ambassador to Córdoba, Johann von Gorze, composed a detailed report about his experiences in Spain.[67]

References to Spain in the High and Late Middle Ages

When we turn to other Middle High German writers, we do not find the same weight of evidence for Hispano-German connections. Nevertheless, even when the plots have nothing to do with the peninsula as such, we can still discover an interesting smattering of references to Spain and Spanish culture. Gottfried von Straßburg includes, for instance, a line about the origin of Tristan's horse, which proves to be an even more classy animal than the horses raised in Spain: "His horse was held by a squire. There was not a more beautiful horse raised in Spain or elsewhere."[68] Of course, the Arabic horses bred in Spain were famous, but the narrator here wants to highlight that Tristan's animal is an even better breed.

In the *Nibelungenlied*, we hear of "Spânje" as the home of Walther, who had escaped from Attila's court together with Hiltegund: "He and Walther of Spain grew up here. I sent Hagen home, whereas Walther escaped together with Hiltegunde."[69] No specific explanations are given as to why this Spaniard later served King Attila in the final battle against the Burgundians (sec. 2344, l. 3), but it clearly heightens the sense of a struggle involving the entire known world to have warriors from many different countries join the Hunnish court only to be killed at the Burgundians' hands.[70] The anonymous author may also have relied on some early oral Spanish sources for the portrait of Rüdiger (Roderic)—an intriguing thesis by Norbert Voorwinden, who perceives significant parallels between this fictional character and Don Rodrigo, the last king of the Visigoths in Spain. This Don Rodrigo—a popular hero in late medieval Spanish ballads—expresses deep grief over the loss of a battle and searches for an alternative destiny for himself in the war against his enemy; moreover, there are intriguing parallels between Witege, the murderer of Rüdiger's son, and Witiza, the murderer of Rodrigo's father. Voorwinden concludes, "The fact that the positive image of Rodrigo served as a model for Rüdiger allows us to assume that this figure became known in the north of Spain, in Asturias."[71]

In several religious tales from the first half of the thirteenth century that focus on the lives of St. Francis and St. George, we also hear of Spain, if only in fleeting passages. Lamprecht von Regensburg, who translated the *Vita of St. Francis*, written by Thomas of Celano, incorporates the following lines: "Germans and French, Spaniards and Englishmen thronged in the street."[72] In a similar vein, Reinbot von Durne uses a reference to Spaniards to indicate the international backdrop to the events surrounding St. George.[73] The original tale came from Spain (l. 523); the battles with the heathens take place in Spain (ll. 365, 379); and great warriors come from Spain (l. 614). And as in the case of Gottfried von Straßburg's *Tristan*, some of the best horses are bred in Spain (l. 2273). In Johann von Würzburg's late medieval romance *Wilhelm von*

Österreich, written in 1314, the protagonist encounters a secondary figure lifted from Wolfram von Eschenbach's *Parzival*, Gahmuret's cousin Kaylet of Spain, who now plays a major role in Wilhelm's endeavors to win the hand of his beloved, the princess Aglye.[74] In addition, the narrator also refers to Portugal (ll. 13751, 14280, 14485, 14493, 14883), Catalonia (l. 16964), Navarre (ll. 13748, 14285, 14449, 14465, 14861, 14868), and Aragon (ll. 14477, 14885, 16963, 18369, 18063) as the origins of some of the mighty kings participating in court festivities and, specifically, at tournaments.

Tournaments were events at which the entire chivalry of a region, a country, and even all of Europe convened: many nationalities and languages met as knights from the Spanish kingdoms came into contact with their colleagues from France, Germany, and England, among other countries, and vice versa.[75] Johann von Würzburg reflects on this political and cultural framework as an element relevant both for his fictional account and for the actual conditions at his time. In other words, the casual mention of the kings of Aragon, Navarre, Catalonia, and so on reveals to us the degree to which a German audience would have been able to identify those countries. Of course, the use of those names is in itself not enough to demonstrate an intimate knowledge of Spanish culture and politics; instead, Johann primarily refers to these names as markers of foreignness, the internationality of the tournament, and the high social rank of its participants. The presence of Spanish royalties, then, was considered with awe and respect. In utilizing both the literary tradition (Wolfram von Eschenbach) and general knowledge of Spanish kingdoms, Johann's romance confirms, once again, that German readers and listeners were well aware of the southwestern parts of Europe and thus might have known more about Spain's culture than simply the names of individual kingdoms.

The Late Middle Ages: Oswald von Wolkenstein

Not until the late fourteenth and early fifteenth centuries, however, are more direct contacts and influences documented in German literature. Whereas Wolfram von Eschenbach's texts are the most important sources for the High Middle Ages, the works of Oswald von Wolkenstein (1376/77–1445) function as the principal source for the late Middle Ages.[76] This South Tyrolean poet is famous for his many autobiographical songs, in which he describes the extensive travels that took him all over Europe and the

Near East.⁷⁷ Although the intriguing mixture of fiction and fact in his songs is not easy to disentangle, and although we have learned to see in his work both a reflection of his own life and an allegorical interpretation of it, much information about fifteenth-century culture can be culled from these texts.⁷⁸ Most importantly for our topic, Oswald also toured Spain and Portugal and, in some of his songs, paints a picture of the culture and the countryside he encountered.

Oswald served Emperor Sigismund as translator, ambassador, negotiator, and perhaps also as entertainer, and accompanied him on several important diplomatic missions. Sigismund tried to resolve the difficult problem of the schism within the Catholic Church and went to Perpignan in July 1415 to meet King Ferdinand I of Aragon, the dauphin Alfonso of Aragon, and the prince of Navarre, among other dignitaries. In the meantime, Oswald had traveled through England, Scotland, and Ireland to rally support for the emperor's plan to find a new candidate for the Holy See, and arrived on the Iberian Peninsula in August 1415. On 21 August, Oswald joined the Portuguese and Spanish forces in the conquest of the Arabic town Ceuta (Septa), and from there he traveled north to meet Sigismund. We can assume that Oswald carried the official news of the victory over the Muslims with him and was therefore well received by the royal courts. In one of his extensive autobiographical poems, he reports that the queen of Aragon graced him with a valuable ring that she attached to his long beard ("willingly I let her have the beard"⁷⁹) and then warned him never to take it out again. The curious linguistic strategy employed by Oswald here is to fall back to the original statement "non maiplus dis ligaides" (sec. 19, l. 36), demonstrating to his audience that he was indeed capable of understanding and repeating the Catalan language.⁸⁰ In addition, he presents snippets of concrete sceneries of his adventures at the Aragonese court in Perpignan—at that time still considered to be part of Spanish/Aragonese territory—where the queen attached rings to his beard (sec. 18, ll. 33–48), but he deliberately refrains from painting a more specific picture of his Spanish experiences. Instead, Oswald primarily focuses on his own personality and jokingly pretends to have been the most important figure in the entire imperial mission: "[W]omen and men looked at me and laughed; nine royal personalities were present."⁸¹ Although the poet specifically locates himself in the foreign context where international political decisions are made, in the final analysis, Spain simply serves as the backdrop for his self-presentation:

> Noch ist es als ein klainer tadel,
> seid mir die schöne Margarith
> stach durch die oren mit der nadel
> nach ihres landes sitte.
> Dieselbe edle künigin,
> zwen guldin ring sloss si mir drin
> und ain in bart verhangen,
> also hiess si mich prangen.
> (Sec. 19, ll. 153–160)
>
> There is no blame involved
> when the beautiful Margarith poked,
> according to her country's customs,
> a hole through my ear lobes.
> This noble queen
> attached two golden rings into them
> and one into my beard;
> in this way she decorated me.

Oswald seems to have spent a considerable period of time in Spain, whose culture might have imbued him more than he openly admits in his songs. In section 23, for instance, we only hear of his travels through Portugal, Granada, and Castile by simple name reference to these countries (sec. 23, ll. 101–102); in section 26, he mentions that he had traveled from Scotland and Ireland to Portugal (ll. 5–6), where he participated in the battle for Ceuta (l. 12). He also visited Granada to see the "rotte küng" (l. 16), that is, the Almoravidian King Yusuf III,[82] and later also refers to his stops in Aragon and Navarre, among other countries on the Iberian Peninsula (sec. 44, ll. 13–15). Cape Finisterre also plays an important role, because having reached that point meant that Oswald had indeed covered all significant geographical areas in the southwest of Europe.[83] Based on many curious references in his work to military events, political leaders, and special bodily appearances (such as Oswald's beard), and based on the intriguing game the poet plays with his own involvement in the battle for Ceuta, it has been argued that the Tyrolean imitated the national "Spanish" hero El Cid and gained his royal audience's respect with his successful reenactment of the Campeador's achievements in a playful presentation.[84] Since the early fifteenth century was a time of major political and military transitions for all of the Spanish kingdoms, the revival of the heroic image of El Cid served the royal houses well. Consequently, a linguistically versed poet and entertainer such as Oswald von Wolkenstein could easily pick up on these tendencies and gain great personal renown in this respect.

When Oswald had returned to Germany and worked on his song, he arbitrarily changed the reference to El Cid into that of a Turkish leader, "wisskunte von Türkei" (sec. 19, l. 162)—"many thought I was a heathen noble."[85] At that time, the Turks already presented a much larger danger than the Arabs, so the poet acted out a more up-to-date role. Nevertheless, the heroic epic *El Cid*, with which Oswald might have been familiarized through ballads popular in Spain at the time, still stands in the background.

Oswald's works helped to build links between the cultures of Germany and Spain, although his songs are so individualistic and creative that it would be difficult, if not impossible, to unearth all of the various sources influencing him and his poetic creativity. Through his texts he established personal connections and also introduced novel images of Spanish court life, such as his discussions of culinary specialties (sec. 19, l. 8) and women's fashion (sec. 19, ll. 49–56). We can detect subtle references to the literary tradition in Spain, but Oswald proves to be too idiosyncratic to reveal more than some curious aspects and his personal activities there, which is not atypical for his entire œuvre.[86]

The Knightly Adventure in Spain and Other Personal Contacts: Georg von Ehingen and Empress Leonora

Finally, one of the many noteworthy voices in medieval German literature that reflects Spain is Georg von Ehingen (1428–1508), who, having visited Rhodes, Palestine, and France, also traveled throughout the entire Iberian Peninsula and eventually participated in battles against the Saracens.[87] Georg von Ehingen's travelogue is famous for its detailed accounts and lively descriptions of countries and peoples. Georg presents himself as a good Christian knight who wins honor through fighting heathens wherever he encounters them. After he and his friends have arrived in "Pampillion" (Pamplona), they decide to spend more time in Spain before moving on to Portugal. The court of Navarre promises the best opportunities, as they are warmly welcomed and invited to join in various court activities, such as hunting, dancing, and celebrations (pp. 44–45). As soon as Georg learns that the king of Portugal is planning a military campaign against the Arabs in northern Africa, he and his companions bid farewell and travel on, making a detour over Santiago de Compostela and Finisterre and then taking a ship down to Lisbon. Once the Portuguese king is informed that they have arrived as representatives from the Austrian court, he greets them with great respect, provides them with housing and, after a rest of three days, invites them to a reception. Here, Georg mentions their linguistic difficulties because, lacking any knowledge of Portuguese, they have to resort to body language and gestures (p. 47) until a translator for Dutch and Flemish helps them out. Next follows an extensive report about the ensuing war campaign in which Georg gains a glorious victory in a single battle against a heathen leader (pp. 58–60), which determines the outcome of the war. The next event is the Castilian king's war against Granada, in which Georg also participates. Several accounts about sieges and attacks follow, in which he receives a deep wound at his shin (p. 67). Eventually, after another trip to Portugal, this traveling knight returns to France, from where he moves on to England and then to Ireland.

Like Oswald von Wolkenstein, Georg von Ehingen documents through his accounts that knighthood was an international institution that provided a familiar framework for all of its members, wherever they went in Europe. In Spain and Portugal, for instance, although they faced some linguistic difficulties, they enjoyed the same privileges as other aristocrats and participated in official cultural activities. In this sense, they were both ambassadors and learners, bringing with them in their cultural package the knowledge of German courtly literature and also acquiring new knowledge of Spanish poetry, romances, and songs. Georg does not mention this specifically, but indicates that he and his compatriots enjoyed the various aspects of courtly entertainment and spent much time in ladies' chambers (p. 48).

We do not know whether Georg von Ehingen or Oswald von Wolkenstein came into contact with Spanish poets, or whether they became familiar with the contemporary literature circulating at the Spanish courts.[88] Nevertheless, for both writers, and thus also for many other aristocratic travelers, Spain was by no means an exotic and remote country; instead, it shared most of the characteristics of any other courtly society. This familiarity would then become the basis for poetic and artistic exchanges that we can infer but not yet prove.

Moreover, we also know that intermarriage among European ruling families connected the various courtly centers in Germany, Spain, and Portugal. Famous among the German empresses was Leonora (1434–1467), a princess of Portugal, and the wife of Frederick III, who exchanged many letters with her family and friends back home. It would seem very likely that Leonora brought to

Germany literature written in her homeland, and that her influence facilitated many subtle but important exchanges. What these exchanges were remains to be seen, but Leonora would certainly be another important contact point for Germano-Hispanic literary exchanges.[89] Heinrich Finke has pointed out the wealth of correspondence between German and Spanish rulers in the late Middle Ages, which also serves as powerful evidence for close cultural ties between both intellectual worlds.[90]

Conclusion

To summarize, Spain and Portugal were not so strange and unknown to medieval German audiences as the literary histories generally assume. Admittedly, we are not yet in a position to demonstrate fully that the personal meetings and exchanges that are documented actually led to literary and artistic influences, since too little material has been made available from which more definitive conclusions could be drawn. But on the basis of our Middle High German sources, we have discovered an almost uninterrupted flow of literary documents that either reflect Spain as a backdrop to a narrative's plot (*Rolandslied*) or refer to Spain as the country of origin of the most arcane knowledge (Wolfram von Eschenbach). Johann von Würzburg simply indicates his knowledge of geographical names from the Iberian Peninsula, whereas Oswald von Wolkenstein and Georg von Ehingen specifically discuss their travels and experiences in Spain and Portugal. *Fortunatus* (1509), an early modern *Volksbuch*, pursues the same agenda as these travel authors, but the protagonist simply tours from city to city in Spain, listing the distances from each other and mentioning their political rank, without giving us any concrete data concerning Spanish culture and the geographical conditions.[91] Nevertheless, even at that early date, the Iberian Peninsula was already a highlight on the agenda of more ambitious travelers and tourists, as the many famous convents and cathedrals made the visit a worthwhile object for both religious and cultural purposes. In Thüring von Ringoltingen's *Melusine* (1456), the protagonist Reymund retires into the monastery of "Our dear Virgin Mother of Monserat in Aragon," without ever returning home.[92]

Irrespective of how we interpret these various literary sources, they all demonstrate that a Germano-Hispanic connection existed even in the Middle Ages, as the many references to the Iberian Peninsula and its inhabitants in Middle High German literature indicate. This cross-association provided a historical and cultural framework for writers from both cultures. As we have seen, some German authors utilized the given possibilities of the foreign world for a discussion of their own world. Others simply assumed that foreignness was not an issue because Castile, Aragon, and other Spanish realms belonged to the wider circle of European feudal kingdoms. Finally, Spain was an important partner in trade and politics, as some of the fleeting references also reveal. In other words, the question of Spanish-German relations during the Middle Ages emerges as a highly fruitful one, for it clearly reflects fundamental issues of cross-culturation and inspiration that existed in many different forms. This is not to deny the overwhelming influence of French literature on German poets and writers, but we can now at least argue that other sources, such as texts from Spain—and so also from other frequently traveled countries such as Italy and the Netherlands—have to be included in comparative studies.[93] Medieval Europe was an open world, where ideas flowed freely and travelers did not encounter national borders. To be sure, French court life, an elite cultural development, had a crucial impact on German writers. Nevertheless, other sources of influence, such as medieval Spanish texts, also need to be considered to gain a full understanding of the overall course of development of Middle High German literature.[94]

Notes

1. Gerhart Hoffmeister, *Spanien und Deutschland: Geschichte und Dokumentation der literarischen Beziehungen* (Berlin, 1976), pp. 20–25; Angela Mendoza, "Einleitung," in *Spanisch-deutscher Kulturdialog: Ein Handbuch deutscher Aktivitäten* (Gütersloh, 1990), pp. 10–21; Benedikt Rüchardt, *Deutsch-spanische Beziehungen*, Ph.D. diss. (Munich, 1988).
2. Dietrich Briesemeister, "'Allerhand iniurien schmehkarten pasquill vnd andere schandlose ehrenrurige Schriften vnd Model': Die antispanischen Flugschriften in Deutschland zwischen 1580 und 1635," *Wolfenbütteler Beiträge: Aus den Schätzen der Herzog-August-Bibliothek*, vol. 4, no. 1 (1981), pp. 147–190.
3. Francisco López Estrada, *Introducción a la literatura medieval española*, 3rd ed. (Madrid, 1966); Alan D. Deyermond, *The Middle Ages* (London, 1971); Joseph F. O'Callaghan, *A History of Medieval Spain* (Ithaca, N.Y., 1975); Hans Flasche, *Geschichte der spanischen Literatur*, vol. 1 (Berne, 1977); Juan Ignacio Ferreras, ed., *Historia crítica de la literatura hispánica* (Madrid, 1987–91).
4. Kurt Voßler, *Spanien und Europa* (Munich, 1952); Barbara Becker-Cantarino, "The Rediscovery of Spain in Enlightened and Romantic Germany," *Monatshefte*,

vol. 72 (1980), pp. 121–134; Volker Roloff and Hans Wentzlaff-Eggebert, eds., *Der spanische Roman: Vom Mittelalter bis zur Gegenwart* (Düsseldorf, 1986).
5. Theodor Frings, "Altspanische Mädchenlieder aus des 'Minnesangs Frühling,'" *Beiträge zur Geschichte der deutschen Sprache und Literatur*, vol. 73 (1951), pp. 176–196; Günther Schweikle, *Minnesang* (Stuttgart, 1989), pp. 71–77.
6. Aleya Khattab, *Das Bild der Franken in der arabischen Literatur des Mittelalters: Ein Beitrag zum Dialog über die Kreuzzüge* (Göppingen, 1989).
7. P. Groult, "Las fuentes germanicas de la mística española," *Arbor*, vol. 46, no. 14 (1961), pp. 23–39.
8. The best example for this theory is the German "chapbook" *Fortunatus* (1509), which was believed to have been a translation from the Spanish. This pet idea by the romanticists was deftly destroyed by Julius Zacher, "Fortunatus," in *Allgemeine Encyklopädie der Wissenschaft und Künste*, ed. J. S. Ersch and J. G. Gruber, vol. 46 (Leipzig, 1847); see also my study "Die Weltwirkung des *Fortunatus*: Eine komparatistische Studie," *Fabula*, vol. 35, nos. 3/4 (1994), pp. 209–225; an overview can be found in Hoffmeister, *Spanien und Deutschland*, p. 26ff. and passim; for the understanding of Spain on the part of the romantics, see Elisabeth Münnig, *Calderón und die ältere deutsche Romantik* (Berlin, 1912), and Wilhelm Schwartz, *August Wilhelm Schlegels Verhältnis zur spanischen und portugiesischen Literatur* (Halle, 1913).
9. "ein sehr ungleichmäßig erforschtes Gebiet." Edmund Schramm, "Die Einwirkung der spanischen Literatur auf die deutsche," in *Deutsche Philologie im Aufriß*, 2nd ed., ed. Wolfgang Stammler, vol. 3 (Berlin, 1962), pp. 147–199, here p. 147.
10. Ibid., p. 147. See also Michael Aichmayr, "Eulenspiegel-Picaro: Eine motivvergleichende Untersuchung," *Eulenspiegel-Jahrbuch*, vol. 28 (1988), pp. 53–67; Christoph Rodiek, *Sujet—Kontext—Gattung: Die internationale Cid-Rezeption* (Berlin and New York, 1990); and G. L. Pinette, "Die Spanier und Spanien im Urteil des deutschen Volkes zur Zeit der Reformation," *Archiv für Reformationsgeschichte*, vol. 98 (1957), pp. 182–191.
11. Traditionally, the literary relations between France and Germany have been the object of close analysis (see, for instance, Joachim Bumke, *Die romanisch-deutschen Literaturbeziehungen im Mittelalter: Ein Überblick* [Heidelberg, 1967]), but not those between Spain and Germany, as far as the Middle Ages are concerned; see, however, the few sketches drawn by Hoffmeister, *Spanien und Deutschland*, pp. 17–25.
12. See, for instance, *Beiträge zur Aufnahme der italienischen und spanischen Literatur in Deutschland im 16. und 17. Jahrhundert*, ed. Alberto Martino (Amsterdam and Atlanta, 1990); the editor admits, however, that the contributions offer only preliminary approaches and individual investigations, whereas the extent and quality of these exchanges and mutual influences remain uncertain (pp. 1–2); see also Marjatta Wis, "Über den ältesten Einfluß des Spanischen auf die deutsche Sprache," *Neuphilologische Mitteilungen*, vol. 66 (1965), pp. 619–634.
13. Schramm, "Die Einwirkung der spanischen Literatur," p. 149.
14. J.-J. A. Bertrand, *Cervantes en el país de Fausto*, trans. José Perdono García (Madrid, 1950).
15. W. Brüggemann, *Cervantes und die Figur des Don Quijote in Kunstanschauung und Dichtung der deutschen Romantik* (Münster, 1958).
16. Adam Schneider, *Spaniens Anteil an der deutschen Literatur des 16. und 17. Jahrhunderts* (Strasbourg, 1898).
17. Hermann Tiemann, *Das spanische Schrifttum in Deutschland von der Renaissance bis zur Romantik: Eine Vortragsreihe* (Hamburg, 1936).

18. Hoffmeister, *Spanien und Deutschland*, pp. 53–85; see also Christoph E. Schweitzer, *Spanien in der deutschen Literatur des 17. Jahrhunderts*, Ph.D. diss. (New Haven, Conn., 1954).
19. "Spanien und Deutschland liegen ja weit entfernt voneinander, und somit wird die Berührung der beiden Völker erschwert." Wis, "Über den ältesten Einfluß des Spanischen," p. 619.
20. "Spanien war für die Deutschen ein entferntes Land." Ibid., p. 622.
21. Burkhardt Krause, "Interkulturelles Erbe Europäisches Mittelalter und Ethnologie," in *Gegenwart als kulturelles Erbe: Ein Beitrag der Germanistik zur Kulturwissenschaft deutschsprachiger Länder*, ed. Bernd Thum (Munich, 1985), pp. 55–83.
22. Arno Borst, *Lebensformen im Mittelalter* (Frankfurt, 1973), pp. 296–297. The emergence of political territory and the concept of nationhood did not begin until the fourteenth century; see Rolf Sprandel, *Verfassung und Gesellschaft im Mittelalter* (Paderborn, 1975), pp. 247–272, especially pp. 268–272; and Rüdiger Schnell, "Deutsche Literatur und deutsches Nationsbewußtsein in Spätmittelalter und Früher Neuzeit," in *Ansätze und Diskontinuität deutscher Nationsbildung im Mittelalter*, ed. Joachim Ehlers (Sigmaringen, 1989), pp. 247–319.
23. Willi Erzgräber, ed., *Europäisches Spätmittelalter* (Wiesbaden, 1978); Anna Eörsi, *International Gothic Style in Painting*, trans. Lili Halápy, rev. trans. Margaret Davies (Budapest, 1984).
24. Ulrike Draeser, *Wege durch erzählte Welten: Intertextuelle Verweise als Mittel der Bedeutungskonstitution in Wolframs "Parzival"* (Frankfurt and New York, 1993).
25. Despite the common concept of the Middle Ages as a highly stationary and narrow-minded culture, many indicators inform us of a surprisingly high level of mobility, even in the twelfth and thirteenth centuries; see O. Borst, *Alltagsleben im Mittelalter* (Frankfurt, 1983), pp. 542–549; see also my study "Die Mystikerin als Peregrina: Margery Kempe, Reisende in corpore—Reisende in spiritu," *Studies in Spirituality*, vol. 5 (1995), pp. 127–145.
26. C.-E. Deforcel, "L'Espagne de la Conquête arabe au siècle d'or (travaux parus de 1969 à 1979)," *Revue historique*, vol. 263 (1980), pp. 425–461.
27. C.-E. Deforcel and Jean Dautier-Dalché, *Histoire économique et sociale de l'Espagne chrétienne au Moyen Age* (Paris, 1976).
28. Gunther Hirschfelder, *Die Kölner Handelsbeziehungen im Spätmittelalter* (Cologne, 1994), p. 8ff.
29. *Deutsche Jakobspilger und ihre Berichte*, ed. Klaus Herbers (Tübingen, 1988); Ursula Ganz-Blättler, *Andacht und Abenteuer: Berichte europäischer Jerusalem- und Santiago-Pilger, 1320–1520* (Tübingen, 1990). Regarding travel literature and traveling in the Middle Ages, see *Reisen und Reiseliteratur im Mittelalter und in der Frühen Neuzeit*, ed. Xenja von Ertzdorff, Dieter Neukirch, and Rudolf Schulz (Amsterdam and Atlanta, 1992); unfortunately, the authors have not taken into account Spain as a travel destination.
30. Hirschfelder, *Die Kölner Handelsbeziehungen im Spätmittelalter*, p. 1; Johannes Vincke, "Zu den Anfängen der deutsch-spanischen Kultur- und Wirtschaftsbeziehungen," *Gesammelte Aufsätze zur Kulturgeschichte Spaniens*, vol. 14 (1959), pp. 111–136.
31. Aloys Schulte, "Die Deutschen und die Anfänge des Buchdrucks in Spanien," in *Festgabe Friedrich von Betzold* (Bonn and Leipzig, 1921), pp. 165–180, here p. 168; Konrad Haebler, *Die deutschen Buchdrucker des 15. Jahrhunderts im Auslande* (Munich, 1924), p. 248ff.; Hermann J. Hüffer, "Deutsch-spanische Beziehungen unter Kaiser Karl V.," *Gesammelte Aufsätze zur Kulturgeschichte Spaniens*, vol. 14 (1959), pp. 183–193; Rudolf Juchhoff, *Kölnische*

und niederrheinische Drucker am Beginn der Neuzeit in aller Welt (Cologne, 1960), pp. 44–45.
32. "Ingesamt gesehen waren Kölner im Spätmittelalter an allen von Deutschen besuchten Handelsplätzen auf der Iberischen Halbinsel präsent. Hier waren sie die einzigen Vertreter des Hanseraumes, die in Konkurrenz zu den großen oberdeutschen Unternehmen treten konnten." Hirschfelder, *Die Kölner Handelsbeziehungen im Spätmittelalter*, p. 24.
33. Karl Bertau, *Deutsche Literatur im europäischen Mittelalter*, vol. 1 (Munich, 1972), pp. 131–137.
34. Arturo Farinelli, "Spanien und die spanische Literatur im Lichte der deutschen Kritik und Poesie," *Zeitschrift für vergleichende Literaturgeschichte*, new ser., vol. 5 (1892), pp. 135–206, 267–332.
35. "Item von Biania gen Pamplion, ist die haubtstat des königreychs Nafaren, ist bey. XXV. meylen. Item von Pamplion auff die seyten Saragosa, die haubtstat des Königreychs Arrogan. XXX. meyl. Item von Burges gen dem heyligen sant Jacob. LII. meyl. Item von dem heyligen sant Jacob gen Finisterre. XIIII. meyl." *Ein hubscher tractat wie durch Hertzog Gotfrid von Pullen ...* (Nuremberg, 1479), quoted in Wis, "Über den ältesten Einfluß des Spanischen," p. 623.
36. Farinelli, "Spanien und die spanische Literatur," p. 140.
37. Ibid., pp. 138–139.
38. Wis, "Über den ältesten Einfluß des Spanischen," pp. 625–626.
39. *Ein new Kochbuch / Das ist Ein gründtliche beschreibung wie man recht vnd wol ... allerley Speisz ... kochen vnd zubereiten solle* (Frankfurt, 1581), quoted in Wis, "Über den ältesten Einfluß des Spanischen," p. 633.
40. Cf. Hüffer, "Deutsch-spanische Beziehungen."
41. Curiously, even contemporary literary connections between modern Spanish and German literature do not seem to attract sufficient attention; see Christoph Rodiek, "Die hispanisch-deutschen Literaturbeziehungen: Ein Bericht zur komparatistischen Forschung der 80er Jahre," *Arcadia*, vol. 24 (1989), pp. 225–238.
42. Bertau, *Deutsche Literatur im europäischen Mittelalter*, vol. 1, pp. 462–470.
43. Marianne Ott-Meimberg, "Karl, Roland, Guillaume," in *Epische Stoffe des Mittelalters*, ed. Volker Mertens and Ulrich Müller (Stuttgart, 1984), pp. 81–110.
44. Friedrich-Wilhelm Wentzlaff-Eggebert, *Kreuzzugsdichtung des Mittelalters: Studien zu ihrer geschichtlichen und dichterischen Wirklichkeit* (Berlin and New York, 1960), p. 77ff.
45. Horst Richter, *Kommentar zum Rolandslied*, vol. 1 (Berne and Frankfurt, 1972); Horst Richter, "Das Hoflager Kaiser Karls: Zur Karlsdarstellung im deutschen Rolandslied," *Zeitschrift für deutsches Altertum und deutsche Sprache*, vol. 102 (1973), pp. 81–101.
46. The relationship between the two peoples is not informed by the idea of tolerance; rather, Konrad painted a highly negative image of the Saracens bound for hell as lost souls and sinners. See Hans Naumann, "Der wilde und der edle Heide (Versuch über die höfische Toleranz)," in *Vom Werden des deutschen Geistes: Festgabe Gustav Ehrismann* (Berlin and Leipzig, 1925), pp. 80–101.
47. For further comments, see Richter, *Kommentar zum Rolandslied*, vol. 1.
48. Robert Plötz, "Santiago-peregrinatio und Jacobus-Kult mit besonderer Berücksichtigung des deutschen Frankenlandes," *Gesammelte Aufsätze zur Kulturgeschichte Spaniens*, vol. 31 (1984), pp. 24–135.
49. "... so getan magen / gesamt sich nie uf di erde."
50. E. Sauer, *Bekenner seiner Herrlichkeit: Das Zeugnis frühchristlicher Märtyrer* (Innsbruck, 1964).

74 | Albrecht Classen

51. Ibid.
52. *Das Rolandslied*, ed. D. Kartschoke, p. 728; see Matthew 27:45, 51ff.; Mark 15:33. 38; Luke 23:44–45.
53. "Der kaiser unt sine helde / uon perge zeuelde / chomen si ze Runzeual."
54. "Der kaiser un di sine helde / schiften uber die Seibere."
55. See, for instance, *Medieval Christian Perceptions of Islam: A Book of Essays*, ed. John Victor Tolan (New York and London, 1996).
56. *Wolfram von Eschenbach*, ed. Karl Lachmann, 7th ed., ed. Eduard Hartl, vol. 1: *Lieder, Parzival und Titurel* (Berlin, 1952); for the English translation, I used Wolfram von Eschenbach, *Parzival*, trans. Helen M. Mustard and Charles E. Passage (New York, 1961).
57. For the most recent critical positions in Wolfram research, see Arthur Groos, *Romancing the Grail: Genre, Science, and Quest in Wolfram's 'Parzival'* (Ithaca, N.Y., and London, 1995).
58. Rolf Bräuer, "Wolfram von Eschenbach," *Geschichte der deutschen Literatur: Mitte des 12. bis Mitte des 13. Jahrhunderts*, ed. R. Bräuer (Berlin, 1990), pp. 259–326, closely analyzes the so-called Kyot problem, but claims that the reference to Kyot is nothing but a "Germanistenfiktion," p. 269; see also J. Bumke, *Die romanisch-deutschen Literaturbeziehungen*, p. 32; idem, *Geschichte der deutschen Literatur im hohen Mittelalter* (Munich, 1990), p. 166.
59. *Parzival*, sec. 416, l. 20ff; sec. 431, l. 2; sec. 453, l. 5ff.; sec. 776, l. 10; sec. 805, l. 10; and sec. 827, l. 1ff.
60. Bräuer, "Wolfram von Eschenbach," p. 269.
61. Clifton D. Hall, *A Complete Concordance to Wolfram von Eschenbach's 'Parzival'* (New York and London, 1990).
62. André de Mandach, *Auf den Spuren des heiligen Gral: Die gemeinsame Vorlage im pyrenäischen Geheimcode von Chrétien de Troyes und Wolfram von Eschenbach* (Göppingen, 1995), especially p. 27ff. passim.
63. Groos, *Romancing the Grail*, p. 204.
64. O'Callaghan, *A History of Medieval Spain*; Myriam Salama-Carr et al., "Translators and the Dissemination of Knowledge," in *Translators through History*, ed. Jean Delisle and Judith Woodsworth (Amsterdam and Philadelphia, 1995), pp. 101–127, here pp. 115–119.
65. Hoffmeister, *Spanien und Deutschland*, pp. 18–19; Sir Hamilton Gibb, "The Influence of Islamic Culture on Medieval Europe," *Bull of the John Rylands Library*, vol. 38 (1955), pp. 82–98.
66. Wiebke Freytag, "Geistliches Leben und christliche Bildung: Hrotsvit und andere Autorinnen des frühen Mittelalters," in *Deutsche Literatur von Frauen*, vol. 1: *Vom Mittelalter bis zum Ende des 18. Jahrhunderts*, ed. Gisela Brinker-Gabler (Munich 1988), pp. 65–87.
67. Hüffer, "Aus 1200 Jahren," *Gesammelte Aufsätze zur Kulturgeschichte Spaniens*, p. 88. Johann von Gorze's report is printed in *Monumenta Germaniae Historica, Scriptores*, vol. 4 (Hanover, 1841).
68. Gottfried von Straßburg, *Tristan*, ed. Friedrich Ranke, trans. Rüdiger Krohn (Stuttgart, 1980), ll. 6659–6661: "sîn ors daz habete ein knappe dâ. / in Spanjenlant noch anderswâ / wart nie kein schoenerez erzogen"; see also l. 9211; for horses in the Middle Ages, see Beate Ackermann-Arlt, *Das Pferd und seine epische Funktion im mittelhochdeutschen 'Prosa-Lancelot'* (Berlin and New York, 1990).
69. "… er und von Spânje Walther, die wuohsen hie ze man. / Hagenen sande ich wider heim: Walther mit Hiltegunde entran." *Das Nibelungenlied*, 13th ed., ed. Helmut de Boor (Wiesbaden, 1956), stanza 1756, verses 3–4.

70. This element is given additional weight in the follow-up epic poem, *Diu Klage*, quoted here from *The Lament of the Nibelungen*, trans. Winder McConnell (Columbia, S.C., 1994). Etzel laments the death of the many men "di ich von manegem lande. / zv miner hohzit her gevvan" (ll. 844–845).
71. "Die Tatsache, daß das positive Rodrigo-Bild für Rüdiger Pate gestanden hat, läßt vermuten, daß man diese Figur im Norden Spaniens, in Asturien, kennengelernt hat." Norbert Voorwinden, "Zur Herkunft der Rüdiger-Gestalt im Nibelungenlied," *Amsterdamer Beiträge zur älteren Germanistik*, vol. 29 (1989), pp. 259–270, here p. 269. He assumes that the familiarity with Spanish ballads at the bishop of Passau's court was established through migrating goliards who had accompanied German pilgrims on their way to Santiago de Compostela (p. 156); see also Norbert Voorwinden, "Pilgrim und das Bistum Passau im Nibelungenlied: Grenzen und Möglichkeiten der Datierung und Lokalisierung aufgrund geographischer und historischer Bezüge," in *Pöchlarner Heldenliedgespräch: Das Nibelungenlied und der mittlere Donauraum*, ed. Klaus Zatloukal (Vienna, 1990), pp. 139–156.
72. "Tiutsche und Franzoise / Spanjole und Engeloise / sich ûf der strâzen drungen." Quoted from Jacob Grimm and Wilhelm Grimm, *Deutsches Wörterbuch* vol. 10, no. 2 (Leipzig, 1905), col. 1883. See also J. Heinzle "Lamprecht von Regensburg," *Die deutsche Literatur des Mittelalters: Verfasserlexikon*, 2nd ed., ed. Kurt Ruh et al., vol. 5, nos. 1–2 (Berlin and New York, 1984), cols. 520–524.
73. Reinbot von Durne, *Der Heilige Georg Reinbots von Durne*, ed. Carl von Kraus (Heidelberg, 1907); see Werner Williams-Krapp, "Reinbot von Durne," *Die deutsche Literatur des Mittelalters: Verfasserlexikon*, vol. 7, nos. 3–4 (1989), col. 1156ff.
74. Johann von Würzburg, *Wilhelm von Österreich*, ed. Ernst Regel (Dublin and Zurich, 1906/1970). For a critical examination of this text, see Albrecht Juergens, *"Wilhelm von Österreich": Johanns von Würzburg "Historia Poetica" von 1314 und Aufgabenstellungen einer narrativen Fürstenlehre* (Frankfurt, Berne, New York, and Paris, 1990).
75. Helmut Nickel, "The Tournament: A Historical Sketch," in *The Study of Chivalry: Resources and Approaches*, ed. Howell Chickering and Thomas H. Seiler (Kalamazoo, Mich., 1988), pp. 213–262.
76. *Die Lieder Oswalds von Wolkenstein*, 3rd ed., ed. Karl Kurt Klein (Tübingen, 1987).
77. The contacts between Tyrol and Spain were, at least during the late Middle Ages, quite significant; see N. Grass, "Tiroler in Spanien," *Gesammelte Aufsätze zur Kulturgeschichte Spaniens*, vol. 20 (1962), pp. 236–263.
78. Alan Robert Shaw, "Oswald von Wolkenstein: Pilgrim and Travelling Salesman," *Jahrbuch der Oswald von Wolkenstein Gesellschaft*, vol. 8 (1994/95), pp. 321–339; Anton Schwob, *Oswald von Wolkenstein: Eine Biographie*, 3rd ed. (Bozen, 1979).
79. "… zu willen raicht ich ir den bart." *Die Lieder Oswalds von Wolkenstein*, ed. Klein, sec. 19, l. 34.
80. In ibid., sec. 19, ll. 21–23, for instance, Oswald lists ten languages that he commanded. He most probably exaggerated with this claim, but we can still assume that his linguistic abilities were astounding; see Burghart Wachinger, "Sprachmischung bei Oswald von Wolkenstein," *Zeitschrift für deutsches Altertum und deutsche Literatur*, vol. 106 (1977), pp. 277–296; see also Jens Lüdtke, "Oswald von Wolkenstein und die romanischen Sprachen," in *Logos Semantikos: Studia Linguistika in Honorem Eugenio Coseriu, 1921–1981*, ed. H. Geckelen et al., vol. 1 (Berlin and New York, 1981), pp. 303–312.
81. "Weib und ouch man mich schauten an mit lachen so; / neun personier kungklicher zier, die waren da." *Die Lieder Oswalds von Wolkenstein*, ed. Klein, sec. 18, ll. 45–46.

82. Norbert Mayr, *Die Reiselieder und Reisen Oswalds von Wolkenstein* (Innsbruck, 1961), p. 74.
83. Sieglinde Hartmann, "Oswald von Wolkenstein et la Méditerranée: Espace de vie, espace de poésie," *Jahrbuch der Oswald von Wolkenstein Gesellschaft*, vol. 8 (1994/95), pp. 289–320, here p. 314.
84. Albrecht Classen, "*El Poema de Mío Cid* and Oswald von Wolkenstein: A Playful Form of Masquerading and Literary Reception: The Spanish-German Connection," *Jahrbuch der Oswald von Wolkenstein Gesellschaft*, vol. 8 (1994/95), pp. 341–361.
85. "Vil manger wont, ich sei gewesen / ain haidnischer frei." *Die Lieder Oswalds von Wolkenstein*, ed. Klein, sec. 19, ll. 163–164.
86. Ulrich Müller, "*Dichtung*" *und* "*Wahrheit*" *in den Liedern Oswalds von Wolkenstein: Die autobiographischen Lieder von den Reisen* (Göppingen, 1968).
87. Gabriele Ehrmann, *Georg von Ehingen: Reisen nach der Ritterschaft. Edition, Untersuchung, Kommentar* (Göppingen, 1979). In addition, see the travelogue by Leo von Rožmital who, on his European travels from 1465–1467, also visited Aragon, Castile, and Portugal: Leo von Rožmital, *Des böhmischen Herrn Leo's von Rožmital Ritter-, Hof- und Pilger-Reise durch die Abendlande, 1465–1467: Beschrieben von zweien seiner Begleiter*, ed. J. A. Schmeller (Stuttgart, 1844).
88. Such a possibility, however, has recently been suggested by Sieglinde Hartmann in her talk "German and Spanish Seranillas: Oswald von Wolkenstein and the Marquéz de Santillana," presented at the 33rd International Congress on Medieval Studies, 7–10 May 1998. Her paper will appear in an upcoming *Jahrbuch der Oswald von Wolkenstein Gesellschaft*.
89. Katherine Walsh, "Verkaufte Töchter? Überlegungen zu Aufgabenstellung und Selbstwertgefühl von in die Ferne verheirateten Frauen anhand ihrer Korrespondenz," *Jahrbuch des Vorarlberger Landesmuseumsvereins* (1991), pp. 129–144; idem, "Deutschsprachige Korrespondenz der Kaiserin Leonora von Portugal: Bausteine zu einem geistigen Profil der Gemahlin Kaiser Friedrichs III. und zur Erziehung des jungen Maximilian," in *Kaiser Friedrich III. (1440–1493) in seiner Zeit: Studien anläßlich des 500. Todestags am 19. August 1493/1993*, ed. Paul-Joachim Heinig (Cologne, Weimar, and Vienna, 1993), pp. 399–445. There were many similar cases in which marriage facilitated cultural exchanges even on a larger scale; see Susan Groag Bell, "Medieval Women Book Owners: Arbiters of Lay Piety and Ambassadors of Culture," in *Women and Power in the Middle Ages*, eds. Mary Erler and Maryanne Kowaleski (Athens, Georgia, and London, 1988), pp. 149–187.
90. Heinrich Finke, "Zur Korrespondenz der deutschen Könige und Fürsten mit den Herrschern Aragons im 14. und 15. Jahrhundert," *Gesammelte Aufsätze zur Kulturgeschichte Spaniens*, vol. 5 (1935), pp. 458–505.
91. Quoted from *Romane des 15. und 16. Jahrhunderts: Nach den Erstdrucken mit sämtlichen Holzschnitten*, ed. Jan-Dirk Müller (Frankfurt, 1990).
92. "Z vnser lieben frawen z Monserat in Arraguny̆," here quoted from *Romane des 15. und 16. Jahrhunderts*, pp. 153 and 155.
93. Bumke, *Die romanisch-deutschen Literaturbeziehungen*; Albrecht Classen, *Zur Rezeption norditalienischer Kultur des Trecento im Werk Oswalds von Wolkenstein (1376/77–1445)* (Göppingen, 1987).
94. For a continuation of the observations in this article, see my study "Spain in Medieval German Travel Accounts," forthcoming, *Jahrbuch der Oswald von Wolkenstein Gesellschaft*, vol. 10 or 11.

– 2 –

THE ARCHDUCHESS ELIZABETH

Where Spain and Austria Met

Joseph F. Patrouch

Historians' oft-repeated division of the early modern Habsburg dynasty into two separate branches, one based in Iberia and one in Central Europe, serves to obscure the close connections between the various family members and their courts in the sixteenth and seventeenth centuries.[1] It distracts attention from the cultural consequences of these ties, particularly those consequences attributable to the various undertakings of the Habsburg archduchesses who traveled between Iberia and Central Europe. While perhaps the division is of use in a political discussion of wide dynastic aspirations tied to the males of the house, it has less utility in a discussion of the day-to-day undertakings of the women and men of the Habsburg lines.

It is precisely through such a discussion, however, that significant aspects of the Habsburgs' activities come more into focus. By examining the Habsburgs of this period as men and women living "on the ground" in Iberia or Central Europe, participating in court lives that connected closely to wider social worlds, one can see how this dynasty facilitated cultural communication between the Iberian lands of the post-Reconquest period and the Danubian lands of the years of the Reformation and the Turkish wars. The women who traveled and corresponded along the route that led between Valladolid and Barcelona, by sea to Genoa, and then over the Alps and Innsbruck along the Inn and Danube rivers to the castles of Vienna and Bratislava, implemented religious reforms, founded convents, bankrolled propagandists and artists, and brought their geographically separated worlds together.[2]

This essay will concentrate on the undertakings of one Habsburg archduchess, "Isabell," as she wrote her name, or Elizabeth, as she is often called in the literature.[3] I will briefly sketch the outline of her life in the later decades of the sixteenth century, which will serve to highlight some of the general features of the Iberian-Central European exchanges so characteristic of the Habsburg dynasty. I will then examine a number of the sources now in Vienna's Haus-, Hof- und Staatsarchiv concerning this archduchess. These include her final testament and an inventory of her library, recorded after her death in 1592. The documents show a woman who was born and died in Vienna, but who apparently spoke Spanish more than German, collected a respectable library of Spanish books, was surrounded with Spanish clerics and courtiers, and had the opportunity to implement Spanish-influenced ideas about religion and Counter Reformation Catholicism through pious foundations and courtly patronage.

Elizabeth was born in the Danubian trading city of Vienna in 1554. She was of double imperial blood: both her mother and her father were children of emperors and empresses.[4] Her mother Maria (1528–1603) was the daughter of the king of Spain and Holy Roman Emperor Charles I/V and Holy Roman Empress Isabella of Portugal. Elizabeth's father Maximilian II (1527–1576), the son of the emperor Ferdinand I and the empress Anna of Bohemia and Hungary, would become Holy Roman Emperor ten years after Elizabeth's birth.[5] She was born not long after her parents, who had been married in Valladolid, moved to Austria. Her older sister, Anna, who would later become the queen of Spain, bride of Philip II and mother of Philip III, had been born in Spain. Educated partially under the tutelage of the Salamanca professor and theologian—and eventual cardinal-archbishop of Toledo—Juan Martínez Siliceo,[6] Maximilian had also served as Spanish regent with his wife for a few years before traveling to Central Europe to take over rule of the contested border territories of the Habsburg lands: the Austrian archduchies, the kingdom of Bohemia, and the disputed kingdom of Hungary.[7] There, Ottoman troops posed a threat that made the castles of Vienna and the nearby Hungarian city of Bratislava almost border fortresses.

Two of Elizabeth's brothers, the later Emperor Rudolf II and Ernst, were sent to Spain to be educated under the supervision of the Spanish king, their uncle Philip II.[8] Elizabeth remained in Vienna, growing up in the newly erected Stallburg (the present home of the horses of the famous Spanish Riding School). There, it is reported, she was taught at some level German, French, Italian, Czech, Hungarian, and Latin.[9] The education was supervised by her grandfather Ferdinand, who, like her mother, had grown up in Spain.[10] While she was still a young child, her relatives began discussing marriage plans for her, which culminated in 1570 with her marriage to the king of France, Charles IX, one of the last of the Valois dynasty.

Her stay in France as queen of that country, torn by religious war, was brief. The historian Arthur Léon Imbert de Saint-Amand described Elizabeth as "[a]n angel astray in hell."[11] She experienced the threats of the great massacres of St. Bartholemew's Day, gave birth to a girl, christened Marie Isabelle, and lost her husband to a strange illness—all in the span of four or five years. Leaving her baby daughter behind and in the care of her mother-in-law, Catherina de Medici, Elizabeth returned to the Habsburg courts in Prague and Vienna. Reports of her stay in France describe Elizabeth as pious, a devout supporter of saints' cults and icons. She is said to have helped found a new Jesuit college in Bourges,[12] and seems in France to have generally represented the reformed Catholic cause (known as the Counter Reformation) that was slowly gaining ground in the years following the Council of Trent, the great reform council which set the rules for Roman Catholicism that stayed in effect until the late nineteenth and twentieth centuries.[13]

After her husband's death and her return to Central Europe, Elizabeth chose not to remarry, following instead the example of a number of her Habsburg predecessors, such as the regent of the Netherlands, her great-aunt Mary of Hungary, who had never remarried after losing her husband to the Ottomans on the battlefield of Mohacs in 1526.[14] Instead, like her thirteenth-century namesake Elizabeth of Thuringia, Elizabeth dedicated her life to helping the poor and sick and to sponsoring various pious undertakings.[15]

In her widowhood, Elizabeth seems to have participated in the Prague court of her mother, the empress Maria (who was widowed not long after Elizabeth, in 1576). In 1581, Maria returned to Spain with her daughter (Elizabeth's sister) Margaret of the Cross to retire in the Madrid convent Nuestra Señora de la Consolación de las Descalzas.[16] Maria was accompanied by two Bohemian noblewomen of the Pernstein family. Their father, the Bohemian high chancellor, Vratislav von Pernstein, had married a Spanish noblewoman, María Manríquez de Lara, in 1555. Another daughter, Polyxena, would later marry Bohemian High Chancellor Zdenek Adalbert Popel von Lobkowitz, and strongly supported the Counter Reformation in Bohemia.[17] The Madrid convent where Empress Maria died in 1603 had been founded by her sister, the widowed Queen Juana of Portugal. One of the Pernstein daughters would become prioress of the convent,[18] which was also entered by Anna Dorothea, known as the Marquesa de Austria, one of the illegitimate children of Elizabeth's brother Rudolf.[19]

In her Central European widowhood, Elizabeth actively sponsored efforts of reformed Catholic clergy. In Prague, she was responsible for the reconstruction of the All Saints Chapel in the Hradschin castle hill complex. This castle had been—like much of Prague's "small side"—heavily damaged in a fire in 1541.[20] Now Elizabeth and her brother Rudolf were engaged in rebuilding and expanding the castle district, perhaps influenced by Rudolf's having watched the construction of El Escorial (1563–84), Philip II's palace near Madrid. Part of the reconstructed wing of the Prague castle, the "Spanish Salle," was the home of some of Rudolf's idiosyncratic art collection.[21] At Elizabeth's request, the relics of the eleventh-century Slavic saint Procop were transferred to Prague as well.

In Vienna, as her aunt Juana of Portugal had done in Madrid, Elizabeth founded a new convent, buying property for it near the house in which she lived, around the corner from the Hofburg and the Stallburg where she had grown up. She received from her brother Ernst, the administrator of the Austrian archduchy of Lower Austria, various incomes associated with an abandoned religious house in the countryside and some properties about the city,[22] which she used to support the new foundation of Poor Clares, a house dedicated to Our Lady of Angels and known colloquially as the "Königinkloster." The church was consecrated in 1583, and Elizabeth was buried there after her death, at age 38, on 22 January 1592. Later, when the Enlightenment emperor Joseph II sold the church to the Vienna Protestant community, Elizabeth's remains were transferred to one of the crypts under St. Stephen's cathedral. There she remains.[23]

Elizabeth's life is representative of the lives of many of the Habsburg archduchesses of the sixteenth and seventeenth centuries whose worlds were a mixture of Spanish and Central European influences. Ever since the fateful double marriage of Juan and his sister Juana of Spain to Margaret and Philip of Austria in 1496 and 1497, the political leadership of important parts of Iberia, Central

Europe, and the Low Countries had been united by the idea of dynasty. The Habsburg family, which had started as petty nobility, protecting ecclesiastical properties from their base in a small Alpine castle dedicated to the hawk, in the sixteenth and seventeenth centuries claimed sovereignty over a large portion of Europe and the New World.

Elizabeth's grandfather, Emperor Ferdinand I, had been particularly responsible for the large influx of Spanish speakers and Iberian culture into the Central European Habsburg lands. Born in Alcalá de Henares near Madrid, he lived at the Spanish courts for years before going with his courtiers over the Alps to Vienna. There, he spoke Spanish, took notes in Spanish, and left much of the daily business of his regime in the hands of Spanish noblemen like Martín de Guzmán, Martín de Parades, the treasurer Gabriel de Salamanca, and others. Spanish troops helped defend Vienna when it was besieged by the Ottoman armies in 1529.[24] While the poet Garcilaso de la Vega was only briefly in Vienna in this period, another writer, Ferdinand's secretary Cristóbal de Castillejo, remained in Central Europe until his death in Vienna in 1550.[25]

Ferdinand, who took a personal interest in the upbringing of Elizabeth and his other grandchildren, set up a court structure that was to have a particular role in the political and cultural patronage strategies of the Habsburg archduchesses, and that also served as an important point of linkage between the Iberian and the Central European worlds. In 1529, Ferdinand organized the structure of the *Hofstaat*, the court, for his children and grandchildren, and particularly emphasized the role of the chaplains in it. These men were to watch over the religious training of the children, in addition to their duties supervising the court chapel choirs and the organization of the masses.[26] The court choirs and musical groups, monitored by the court preachers and chaplains, represented a particularly influential avenue for cultural interchange.

The courts also provided opportunities for wealthy noblemen and women who were looking to "get ahead" by serving as sources of credit for the cash-strapped Habsburg archduchesses and archdukes. The Carinthian and Styrian nobleman Adam, Freiherr von Dietrichstein, for example, who worked at the courts of the Archdukes Rudolf and Ernst and the empress Maria, loaned money to his lords; married one of Maria's ladies-in-waiting, Margarita de Cardona (the daughter of the Spanish viceroy of Sardinia, Antonio de Cardona); became established as one of the permanent ambassadors between the Iberian and Central European

Habsburg courts; and married his daughters into a number of Spanish noble families.[27]

The courts, of course, had not only up-and-coming nobles, but a wide variety of musicians, dancers, singers, jesters, doctors, secretaries, and scholars. Maximilian II, for example, is recorded as having recommended to Elizabeth in 1572, while she was queen of France, the services of the famous composer-musician Maddelena Casulana da Mazari.[28] Elizabeth's court records for 1581 reveal payments for the dwarves Madalena Leopartius (who received wax, candles, wine, and dumplings daily, in addition to her regular salary) and Hanns Leophart (who received a horse along with his salary).[29]

The Habsburg archduchesses like Elizabeth who supervised these courts had in their hands important tools for influence, patronage, and propaganda. Conversely, the clerics who occupied positions in the courts were ideally situated to influence the decisions of those in power, especially if they provided links between the worlds of Iberia and those of Central Europe. The court of the empress Maria, Elizabeth's mother, illustrates this facet of the Hofstaat well, particularly as it relates to the various clerics who were employed there. The well-known Spanish composer Matteo Flecha the Younger (1530–1604) worked as a tutor to Maria when she was a child in Spain. After a brief stay in a Spanish Carmelite house following his release from service, Flecha returned to Maria's court, now in Vienna, in the 1560s. In addition to serving Maria, he also appears in the records of the court of her daughter Anna when Anna went to Spain to marry Philip II in 1571.[30] Reports find him with the court of Archduchess Elizabeth at times, as well.[31]

The courts—and particularly the clerics employed at them as musicians, confessors, and chaplains—were popular with the Habsburgs partly because ecclesiastical benefices could provide them with support when regular court operating funds were insufficient. As Robert Lindell points out in his study of musicians at the court of Elizabeth's father Maximilian II, before Maximilian took the imperial throne, he had limited access to patronage, and "an important aspect of Maximilian's patronage was his willingness to intervene for members of his court chapel in their efforts to gain ecclesiastical benefices."[32] The same holds true, perhaps even in a more pronounced way, for the Habsburg archduchesses like Elizabeth, whose dowry properties in France were chronically behind in paying any incomes. Her modest courts in Prague and Vienna therefore had to rely on ecclesiastics who could draw incomes from elsewhere. Her mother's chaplain,

Matteo Flecha, received the position of head of the Benedictine house of Tihanny in Hungary.[33] One of Elizabeth's court priests, the Italian bassist Hieronymus Spinola, became provost of the religious house of Erlakloster in Lower Austria.[34] It was by appointments such as these through the mechanism of patronage, supervised by courtiers like the archduchess Elizabeth, that the cultures of Iberia (and Italy) reached out into the countryside of Hungary and Austria.

The structure of the court served not only as a mechanism for cultural diffusion but also as an avenue for personal expression. In addition to providing opportunities through which her court chaplains found positions and accumulated incomes, Elizabeth also was influenced by these men and their ideas—and these men and their ideas were influenced by her. An analysis of sources for Elizabeth's world-view reveals some of the ideas she and her court spread, connecting in Elizabeth's case Iberia to Central Europe, with a little of France and the rest of the world thrown in for good measure.

Some of Elizabeth's actions speak of her interests. We have already seen how, as resident queen in France, she supported the recently founded Jesuit order. Her grandfather Ferdinand had called the Jesuits to Vienna in 1551, three years before Elizabeth's birth. Three of the original eleven members of the Vienna house who made the journey north from Rome were Spanish.[35] Years later, in her will, drawn up shortly before her death in January 1592, Elizabeth remembered the Viennese Jesuits with 700 guilders and some of the tapestries that hung in her apartments, to be used to support ten students.[36] In addition, Elizabeth upheld a type of piety tied to objects such as the relics of Saint Procop, which she had transferred to the newly rebuilt chapel in the Prague castle. Her will mentions a variety of relics, which she donated to the nuns in the Vienna convent of Poor Clares. These relics included a piece of the True Cross that her mother had given her.

The devotional activities outlined in Elizabeth's will place her firmly within the camp of the reformed Catholic Church. Elizabeth's father had been suspected of deviating from the orthodox line, and Vienna and Prague were cities with large numbers of people not always in total agreement with this line. In Bohemia, generations of religious heterogeneity stretched back to the Hussites of the previous century, and in the Austrian duchies and in Hungary, with the tremendous popularity in some circles of the teachings and ideas connected with Luther, the promotion of reformed Catholic ideas and practices could have been seen as a provocation.³⁷ Elizabeth, tied socially to Iberia through her mother and her court, represented a source of consistent support for reformed Catholicism that was in some ways insulated from the general populace's leanings. In this way, the supporters of the reformed Catholic cause could establish institutional backing as a basis for future successes that the next century would bring. In the seventeenth century, large portions of the populations of Central Europe accepted the practices outlined by the Trent decrees, resulting in a flowering of baroque Catholicism.

Elizabeth's will stipulated the saying of large numbers of masses for her soul. She donated money to the poor and established a fund for the daily celebration of a sung mass in the church of the Our Lady of the Angels convent, where she was to be buried beneath a simple slab. Touchingly, Elizabeth donated money for masses for the soul of her deceased husband, King Charles IX, for her own soul, and for the souls of all the departed.³⁸ Churches throughout the city were to receive money to pay for vigils and masses. The will emphasizes music and singing and recalls the importance of the court chapel for this archduchess. Prisoners and poor soldiers on the Hungarian front were to receive gifts, as were poor girls, so that they could establish dowries and marry. Various personal objects were bequeathed to Elizabeth's brothers, including a necklace for Emperor Rudolf and her wedding ring for Archduke Ernst.

A marginal note on the German copy of the will implies that the original had been written in Spanish. It remarks that one passage is unclear concerning the number of boys or girls to receive gifts, because the reading of a passage was either "muchachos" or "muchachas."³⁹ This point also indicates the ties to Iberia that Elizabeth evidenced. Although she grew up in Vienna and spent most of her life in a Central Europe convulsed with religious controversies and violence, she seems to have consistently advocated reformed Catholic religious practices, which can no doubt be at least partially explained by her close cultural ties to Spain through her language, her mother, and her court. The variety of languages at her Viennese and Prague courts allowed her to advocate a religious program; in this case, reformed Catholicism "spoke" Spanish.⁴⁰

A survey of the books in Elizabeth's modest library, inventoried after her death, helps to make a similar point.⁴¹ The list begins with the comment that the books were to be found in a leather-covered trunk. Fifty-seven titles are given, mostly without authors or other information. From the list, the following general information can be gleaned. The largest single number of books—twenty-two—were in Spanish. Of the remaining thirty-five, German works (fourteen) slightly outweighed French and Latin ones (ten each), while one title was listed in Italian. Perhaps not surprisingly for one who would found a convent, and given what has already been said about the activities of this archduchess, the majority of the titles deal with religious subjects, particularly religious orders. Elizabeth owned a copy of the story of Saint Dominic, a chronicle of the Franciscans, and the rules of the order of Saint Benedict. She had a number of handwritten books of hours, written on vellum and bound in elaborate velvet, leather, or satin. One of them was decorated with pearls, as well. Elizabeth owned a copy of the famous *Légende dorée* of Jacques de Voragine. A Latin vita of Saint Leopold, a saint the Habsburgs were promoting as their own, was among the devotional works that the clerks found in the chest.

Many of the French works obviously dated from Elizabeth's brief stay in France. These included David Chambers's *Histoire abrégée de tous les roys de France, Angleterre et Escosse* and a funeral oration for Charles IX.[42] Two of the French works deal with astrological subjects: *Prophéties par l'astrologue du très chretien roy France et de madame la duchesse de Savoye* and *Prognostication avec ses présages pour l'an 1571 Nostradami*. Another work that dates from Elizabeth's French years is a Latin marriage song dedicated to her.[43] She also owned a copy of Sophocles' *Antigone*.

The German volumes include several works of the Tyrolean Jesuit preacher Georg Scherer (1539/40–1605). Scherer was active at the court of Elizabeth's brother Ernst, and claimed in one publication owned by Elizabeth to have delivered a poor girl in a Vienna hospital of 12,652 demons.[44] His polemical publications make up a good number of the German books in Elizabeth's possession.[45] A manual for widows and an illustrated life of Jesus were also among the German texts Elizabeth owned.[46]

Not content to survey only the world of her court and the courts of her brothers, sisters, and mother, Elizabeth owned a number of works in various languages that reveal a lively interest in the world outside of Europe as it was being described by various contemporary authors. A work on the religious position of the Indians of the New World and various editions of the 1580s reports of the Jesuits in the Far East are reminders that the missionizing that was taking place in the world, and the religious patronage undertaken by people such as Archduchess Elizabeth, must be placed—as it no doubt was by them—in a larger context.[47] There was more to their world than Spain and Austria.

The Spanish works, which made up the largest single group of books in Elizabeth's library, reveal the types of Iberian cultural influences that Elizabeth could pass on through her court into Austria. Most of the works were devotional or theological in nature. A favorite author of Elizabeth's appears to have been the Dominican Luis de Granada; her library contained several of his works, including his *Guia de peccatore*, his *Libro de la oracion y meditacion*, and his *Memorial de la Vida Christiana*. Luis Ponce de León was another contemporary author represented in Elizabeth's holdings, with his *De los nombres de Christo*.

Saint Teresa of Ávila, perhaps not surprisingly, plays a large role in the library. Elizabeth owned a copy of her autobiography, as well as *Los libros de la madre Teresa de Jesus, fundatore de los monasterios de Marias y frayles Carmelitas descalcas de lo primero regle*. Surprisingly, given the role of Georg Scherer's works, the reports from the Americas and Asia, and the supportive undertakings of Elizabeth in relation to the Jesuits in France and Vienna, there is little evidence of other Jesuits' works. Elizabeth appeared to be well informed about the female religious reform that was taking place in Iberia. Through the reading of the ideas of Saint Theresa, Elizabeth could have conveyed such Iberian influences into the churches of Vienna and elsewhere in Central Europe in the 1580s.

Elizabeth's library catalog allows us a glimpse into some of the types of cultural productions originating in Iberia that could have been transmitted into the messy Central European context of the 1580s by Habsburg archduchesses such as this one-time French queen. The Habsburg women who corresponded and traveled back and forth between Iberia and Central Europe tied a dynasty together and provided institutional contexts, their courts, for the advocacy of reformed Catholic ideas and general social and cultural trends originating in Iberia. In the decades between the Council of Trent (which ended in 1563), and the outbreak of the Thirty Years' War (1618), mechanisms such as this patronage by archduchesses were the means by which reformed Catholic ideas were transmitted into the courts and the countryside of Central Europe. The life story of Archduchess Elizabeth reminds us that in the sixteenth and seventeenth centuries, Spain and Austria met not only on the maps of politicians negotiating alliances, but in the hearts and minds of women who participated in the social worlds of Habsburg history.

Notes

1. This point has been made in a general fashion in Andrew Wheatcroft's new work, *The Habsburgs: Embodying Empire* (New York, 1995). See pp. 175–176: "I have deliberately not differentiated between the branches of the Habsburg lineage, but it is more normal practice to treat the 'Spanish' and 'Austrian' Habsburgs as separate entities." The standard work on the Habsburgs in the period of interest to this essay is R. J. W. Evans, *The Making of the Habsburg Monarchy, 1550–1700* (New York, 1979).
2. Recently, more attention has been given to the ties between Central Europe and Iberia under the Habsburgs. This could at least partially be the result of efforts at European integration by these two relatively recent EU members. It could also be the result of the commemorations surrounding the magic year of 1492: five hundred years of European connections to the Americas. See Wolfram Krömer, ed., *Spanien und Österreich in der Renaissance: Akten des fünften Spanisch-Österreichischen Symposions, 21.-25. September 1987 in Wien* (Innsbruck, 1989); Ferdinand Opll and Karl Rudolf, *Spanien und Österreich* (Vienna, 1991); *Hispania-Austria: Die katholischen Könige, Maximilian I. und die Anfänge der Casa de Austria in Spanien, Kunst um 1492* (Milan, 1992). For a review of this exhibition, which was also held in Toledo under the title "Reyes y Mecenas," see Andrea Scheichl, "Hispania-Austria: Die katholischen Könige. Maximilian I. und die Anfänge der Casa de Austria. Österreichische und spanische Kunst um 1492," in *Frühneuzeit-Info*, vol. 3, no. 2 (1992), p. 116. The classic discussion of political relations between the Habsburgs in Iberia and those in Central Europe remains Bohdan Chudoba, *Spain and the Empire, 1519–1643* (New York, 1977).
3. Marianne Strakosch, *Materialien zu einer Biographie Elisabeths von Österreich Königin von Frankreich*, unpublished Ph.D. diss. (University of Vienna, 1965). Here (p. 86), the point is made about Elizabeth's signature in reference to the "Hofstaat der KöniginWitwe Elisabeth v. France," dated 1 July 1581, no. 58 in the Haus-, Hof- und Staatsarchiv, Vienna (HHStA), Oberhofmeisteramt (OMeA), Sonderreihe, Schachtel 183.
4. Very little has been written concerning this Habsburg archduchess. I am presently collecting materials for a biography of her. For general background, see *Die Habsburger: Ein biographisches Lexikon*, ed. Brigitte Hamann (Munich, 1988), pp. 87–88. The literature cited concerning Elizabeth consists of a mid-nineteenth-century French historical novel and Strakosch's University of Vienna dissertation of 1965.
5. Maximilian has received increased attention recently. An excellent collection of essays on his court, placing him into the broader European context instead of dealing with him simply as a German prince, has recently been published: *Kaiser Maximilian II: Kultur und Politik im 16. Jahrhundert*, ed. Friedrich Edelmayer and Alfred Kohler (Vienna, 1992).
6. Alfonso E. Pérez Sánchez, "The Madrid-Prague Axis," in *The Arcimboldo Effect: Transformations of the Face from the Sixteenth to the Twentieth Century*, ed. Ponus Hulten (New York, 1987), pp. 55–65, here p. 56. On Juan Martínez Siliceo, see J. H. Elliott, *Imperial Spain, 1469–1716* (New York, 1964), pp. 213–215, 221–222.
7. Ana Díaz Medina, "El Gobierno en España de Maximiliano II (1548–1551)," in *Kaiser Maximilian II*, ed. Edelmayer and Kohler, pp. 38–54.
8. On Elizabeth's brother Rudolf, see R. J. W. Evans, *Rudolf II and His World* (New York, 1973). On the two boys' stay in Spain, see Erwin Mayer-Löwenschwerdt,

Der Aufenthalt der Erzherzöge Rudolf und Ernst in Spanien, 1564–1571 (Vienna, 1927), pp. 1–64.
9. Strakosch, *Materialien*, p. 4.
10. Paula Sutter Fichtner, *Ferdinand I of Austria: The Politics of Dynasticism in the Age of the Reformation* (New York, 1982).
11. Arthur León Imbert de Saint-Amand, *Women of the Valois Court* (New York, 1894), p. 247. Original title: *Les femmes à la cour des derniers Valois*.
12. Strakosch, *Materialien*, p. 64. The main source regarding Elizabeth's stay in France is the Seigneur de Brantôme, a courtier at the royal court; see his *Illustrious Dames of the Court of the Valois Kings* (New York, 1912). On Brantôme, see Henri Hauser, *Les sources de l'histoire de France: XVI siècle (1494–1610)*, vol. 3: *Les guerres de religion (1559–1589)* (Paris, 1912), pp. 33–34.
13. Two good, brief introductions to the Counter Reformation, which include references and background on the Council of Trent, are A. G. Dickens, *The Counter Reformation* (New York, 1969), and Martin D. W. Jones, *The Counter Reformation: Religion and Society in Early Modern Europe* (New York, 1995).
14. Ghislaine de Boom, *Marie de Hongrie* (Brussels, 1956); David P. Daniel, "Piety, Politics and Perversion: Noblewomen in Reformation Hungary," in *Women in Reformation and Counter-Reformation Europe: Public and Private Worlds*, ed. Sherrin Marshall (Bloomington, Ind., 1989), pp. 68–88; Jane de Iongh, *Mary of Hungary, Second Regent of the Netherlands* (New York, 1958); and *Maria von Hongarije, 1505–1558*, ed. Jacqueline Kerkhoff and Bob van den Boogert (Utrecht, 1993).
15. David Hugh Farmer, *The Oxford Dictionary of Saints*, 2nd ed. (New York, 1987), p. 139 (with bibliography). See also Johann Stadler, ed., *Vollständiges Heiligen-Lexikon*, vol. 2 (Augsburg, 1861), pp. 41–45, and Hiltgart L. Keller, *Reklam Lexikon der Heiligen und der biblischen Gestalten*, 5th ed. (Stuttgart, 1984), pp. 196–199.
16. Pérez Sánchez, "The Madrid-Prague Axis," p. 63; Opll and Rudolf, *Spanien und Österreich*, pp. 70, 81.
17. Joachim Bahlcke, *Regionalismus und Staatsintegration im Widerstreit: Die Länder der böhmischen Krone im ersten Jahrhundert der Habsburgerherrschaft, 1526–1619* (Munich, 1994), pp. 172–73, 185.
18. Pérez Sánchez, "The Madrid-Prague Axis," p. 63.
19. Opll and Rudolf, *Spanien und Österreich*, p. 89.
20. Strakosch, *Materialien*, pp. 81–82.
21. For a general discussion of Rudolf's world-view, see Evans, *Rudolf II*. On his art collecting, which is receiving ever more attention, see Thomas DaCosta Kaufmann, *The School of Prague: Painting at the Court of Rudolf II* (Chicago, 1988).
22. Documents concerning these incomes, dating from 1583, 1588, and 1594, can be found in the Niederösterreichisches Landesarchiv, Klosterrat Akten 3, "Erlakloster."
23. Strakosch, *Materialien*, pp. 85–119. On the convent generally, see Felix Czeike, *Historisches Lexikon Wien*, vol. 3 (Vienna, 1994), p. 567; Felix Czeike, *Das große Groner-Wien-Lexikon* (Vienna, 1974), p. 590; and Gustav Gugitz, *Österreichs Gnadenstätten*, vol. 1 (Vienna, 1955), pp. 19–20. On the closing of the convent, see Gerhard Winner, *Die Klosteraufhebungen in Niederösterreich und Wien* (Vienna, 1967), pp. 96–97, 102–104.
24. Opll and Rudolf, *Spanien und Österreich*, pp. 31–32, 43–44, 51.
25. Ibid., p. 101.
26. Walter Pass, *Musik und Musiker am Hof Maximilians II* (Tutzing, 1980), pp. 5, 53.

27. Friedrich Edelmayer, "Ehre, Geld, Karriere: Adam von Dietrichstein im Dienst Kaiser Maximilians II," pp. 109–142, and Susanne Herrnleben, "Zur Korrespondenz Kaiser Maximilians II. mit seinen Gesandten in Spanien (1564–1576)," both in in *Kaiser Maximilian II*, ed. Edelmayer and Kohler, pp. 95–108.
28. Robert Lindell, "New Findings on Music at the Court of Maximilian II," in *Kaiser Maximilian II*, ed. Edelmayer and Kohler, pp. 231–245, here p. 236.
29. HHStA, OMeA/SR 183, no. 58: "Hofstaat der KöniginWitwe Elisabeth v. Fr.," dated 1 July 1581: ff. 4, 5.
30. Pass, *Musik und Musiker*, pp. 55–56. On the general importance of lesser royal courts, and especially female entourages, see R. J. W. Evans, "The Court: A Protean Institution and an Elusive Subject," in *Princes, Patronage, and the Nobility: The Court at the Beginning of the Modern Age, c.1450–1650*, ed. Ronald G. Asch and Adolf M. Birke (London, 1991), pp. 481–491, here, p. 482. On the Habsburgs' courts generally, see Volker Press, "The Imperial Court of the Habsburgs, from Maximilian I to Ferdinand III," pp. 289–312 in the same volume. See also R. J. W. Evans, "The Austrian Habsburgs: The Dynasty as a Political Institution," in *The Courts of Europe: Politics, Patronage, and Royalty, 1400–1800*, ed. A. G. Dickens (New York, 1977), pp. 121–146.
31. Evans, *The Making of the Habsburg Monarchy*, p. 191. See esp. note 3.
32. Lindell, "New Findings on Music," p. 235.
33. Pass, *Musik und Musiker*, p. 55, note 302.
34. Ibid., pp. 60–61. Erlakloster was an abandoned house of Benedictine nuns in Lower Austria which was given to Elizabeth to support her convent in Vienna.
35. Opll and Rudolf, *Spanien und Österreich*, p. 93.
36. HHStA, Familien Akten 74. Testament Abschrift dated Vienna, 16 September 1591.
37. For an introduction to the general context of religious developments in Central Europe in the period, see Winfried Eberhard, "Bohemia, Moravia and Austria," pp. 23–48, and David P. Daniel, "Hungary," pp. 49–69, both in *The Early Reformation in Europe*, ed. Andrew Pettegree (Cambridge, 1992). As Eberhard points out, "It is commonly assumed that eastern Central Europe was always a stronghold of Catholicism. This assumption ... ignores the fact that Protestantism was so widespread in the area throughout the sixteenth century that it largely reduced the Catholic church to a minority" (p. 23).
38. Her will stated, "für den künig (d. in d. glori sei)."
39. See folio 3r, "Nota."
40. Randolph C. Head has recently discussed the issue of multiple languages and their possibilities using a case study drawn from a Graubünden-based family living in an area where a dialect of Romansch was spoken in his "A Plurilingual Family in the Sixteenth Century: Language Use and Linguistic Consciousness in the Salis Family Correspondence, 1580–1610," *Sixteenth Century Journal*, vol. 16 (1995), pp. 577–593. See p. 593: "The authors of these letters lived in a world in which multiple languages represented distinct possibilities for organizing different kinds of communication and helped define their identities in both local and European terms." See also Paul J. Smith, "Mehrsprachigkeit und Sprachbetrachtung bei Rabelais," *Frühneuzeit-Info*, vol. 3 (1992), pp. 40–47.
41. The list of books is transcribed in Strakosch, *Materialien*, pp. viii-ix. The original is in HHStA, Familienakten, Karton 75. As a point of comparison, it is useful to look at Christian Gries's discussion of the (much more extensive) library of Elizabeth's uncle Ferdinand of Tyrol, "Erzherzog Ferdinand II. von

Tirol und die Sammlungen auf Schloß Ambras," *Frühneuzeit-Info,* vol. 5 (1994), pp. 7–37. The inventory used by Gries dates from 1596, only four years after Elizabeth's death. In this library of over three thousand titles, religious writings take a subordinate place in relationship to other areas of interest such as geography, architecture, art theory, geometry, history, law, and medicine. Ferdinand's collections were originally in Vienna's Hofburg castle, and it seems certain that if Elizabeth did not see them in Innsbruck, she at least saw them while growing up across the street in Vienna.
42. *Oraison funèbre du très hault etc. Charles IX.*
43. *Epithalamion serenissimae Elisabethae, reginae Franciae.*
44. *Histori ainer erledigten besessnen junkfrauen patris Georgii Scherer.* On this work, see Evans, *The Making of the Habsburg Monarchy,* p. 391.
45. At least four of the fourteen German works are attributed to Georg Scherer.
46. *Der wittfrauen spiegel* and *Zierliche und schöne gebett illuminirten Bildern etc. von dem leben und sterben Jesu Christi.*
47. *Indianischer religionsstand durch fratrem Valentinum Friccium* and *Avoisi del Giapone degli anni 1582, 1583, 1584, etc.*

– 3 –

A Woman's Influence

Archduchess Maria of Bavaria and the
Spanish Habsburgs

Magdalena S. Sánchez

Archduchess Maria of Bavaria (1551–1608), a princess from the Wittelsbach family, is an excellent example of a politically powerful woman who helped bridge the distance between Spain and Central Europe.[1] Known in her day as a model wife, mother, and woman, Maria also freely displayed her political influence. She worked to further the interests of her children as well as to spread Tridentine Catholicism in Central Europe. Both of these goals brought her into direct contact with the Spanish Habsburgs, and in 1599 her daughter Margaret of Austria became the wife of Philip III of Spain. The relations of Archduchess Maria to the Spanish Habsburgs give us an opportunity to examine the familial, personal, and diplomatic connections between Spain and Central Europe in the late sixteenth and early seventeenth centuries. They also allow us to consider the powerful role played by women in these contacts.

Archduchess Maria was the daughter of Duke Albert V of the Bavarian Wittelsbach family. In 1571, she married Habsburg Archduke Karl of Styria (who had previously courted Queen Elizabeth I of England).[2] Karl was also Maria's uncle, as he was the brother of Anna, Maria's mother. Maria was therefore herself both a Wittelsbach and a Habsburg. Karl and Maria had fifteen children, twelve of whom survived into adulthood.³ Unlike many politically influential women of her day, Maria was able to exercise power directly. When her husband died in 1590, their eldest son Ferdinand, who was still completing his studies at the Jesuit college in Ingolstadt, was not old enough to govern Styria. For that reason, Archduchess Maria served as regent of Styria from 1590 until 1595, when Ferdinand assumed political authority. Maria continued to counsel her son, who remained very much under her influence until her death in 1608. From his mother, Ferdinand learned to promote orthodox Catholicism, which caused him to push for the implementation of Tridentine decrees in his lands.⁴

Archduchess Maria was consistently praised as a pious and virtuous woman. In fact, observers noted her piety more than her obvious political activities. Pedro Salazar de Mendoza, the Castilian chronicler who wrote a biography of the archduchess after she died, detailed her pious deeds,⁵ describing her life as that of a "true and perfect religious."⁶ Fray Alonso de Herrera, a Benedictine monk, also wrote an account of her pious actions.⁷ The archduchess's life included a daily ritual of strenuous devotional exercises: she woke up as early as four or five in the morning to pray in bed until her servants awoke; she attended two masses every morning in her private oratory; and on Sundays and holy days, she would attend one or two masses in one of the parish churches in Graz. She also visited convents regularly and founded a convent for cloistered nuns. Salazar de Mendoza recounted that the archduchess went at least once a week to a church or hermitage, where she would hear three masses. Every Saturday she would go to confession, and every Sunday she received communion.⁸ She prayed each evening, fasted dutifully throughout Lent, and performed other penitential deeds. As a young girl, when she felt the desire to dance, she would put pins in her shoes so as to make it impossible, or at least too painful, to do so.⁹ In this manner, Archduchess Maria followed the example of so many Catholic women who mortified their bodies to avoid, at least in part, the temptations of the flesh.¹⁰

Salazar de Mendoza and Fray Alonso de Herrera both emphasized that Archduchess Maria set a good example for her people in many ways. She regularly took communion publicly and would accompany public religious processions on foot.¹¹ These devotional practices supposedly gained her much popular support. Salazar de Mendoza claimed that even heretics, by whom he meant Protestants, respected her and held her dear, and they saw her as a means to reach her husband.¹² Salazar de Mendoza's comments, however, do not fully ring true. Maria was certainly less tolerant in her religious attitudes than was her husband. Although Karl attended daily mass and followed other typically Catholic practices,[13] he initially seems to have tolerated Protestants and was not so determined to insist on religious orthodoxy in his lands. His marriage to Maria and the influence of his confessors had the effect of making him much less tolerant in the last two decades of his life.[14] Indeed, Maria was determined to make her own family and her servants conform to Catholic orthodoxy. Fray Alonso de Herrera reported that she insisted that everyone in her family and her household receive communion every month.[15] Herrera also noted that by performing pious deeds in a public fashion, Maria openly fought the Calvinist rejection of good works.[16] In this case, Herrera drew attention to the powerful religious and political use of devotional practices. Thus, Salazar de Mendoza's claim that Maria served as an intercessor for Catholics and Protestants with Archduke Karl is questionable. Salazar de Mendoza was no doubt following a conventional practice in eulogies and biographies of royal women: to praise them as peace-loving individuals who brought tranquility to their husband's lands and who acted as mediators for all people with kings and with God.[17] Salazar de Mendoza even credited Archduchess Maria with preserving peaceful relations with the nobility.[18] While we cannot say for sure that Protestants did praise her and that she did act as an intermediary for them—and for nobles in general—with her husband, we can see what was expected of royal women and what characteristics they were supposed to embody.[19]

An essential part of Archduchess Maria's piety was charity. She regularly gave alms to the poor, inviting them into the palace, where she and her children waited upon them. Fray Alonso de Herrera reported that every Monday, the archduchess would personally wait upon twelve poor individuals,[20] using the occasion to instruct them in the Catholic faith: while they ate, the archduchess's confessor would preach to them.[21] When her son Ferdinand was defending the fortress of Canisia from the Turks, Archduchess Maria had a poor person dine with her and her family every night.[22] On Holy Thursday, she and her children washed the feet of and clothed twelve poor women.[23] Every Friday, Maria would abstain from food until the evening. While her children ate the evening meal, she would tend to the needs of her house and the family finances.[24] Archduchess Maria also visited hospitals to give alms to the sick.[25] When they went to hospitals, she and her children supposedly were in disguise, and they also performed the Holy Thursday ceremony in private.[26] These charitable deeds were therefore all the more notable because Maria did not want to draw attention to herself while carrying them out.

Maria was also held up as the model of a virtuous woman. Both Salazar de Mendoza and Fray Alonso de Herrera commented that she maintained her household in perfect order. She served as an example to the ladies at her court because she did not allow herself or her servants to be frivolous or idle; she always kept her hands busy and insisted that all her ladies-in-waiting do likewise. According to Salazar de Mendoza, Archduchess Maria also loved books and reading. In fact, the chronicler claimed that the archduchess learned to read earlier than most women.[27] She had someone read to her and her children at all hours, though the books had to be religious in nature and were only for personal and familial edification.[28] She did not allow her children to play cards or other frivolous games, and she supposedly said that she would rather see her children dead than see them offending God in such a manner.[29] She was also praised for never lying and for not allowing others to dissimulate.[30] Once again, Salazar de Mendoza, like other biographers of royal women, emphasized that women acted as counterbalances to the Machiavellian practices common to an early modern court.[31]

In all of these ways, Archduchess Maria greatly influenced her daughter Margaret of Austria, who married Philip III of Spain. As a young girl in Graz, Margaret of Austria visited the sick in hospitals and dispensed alms to the poor. Legend has it that when she received word that she was to be the bride of Philip III, Margaret of Austria was making beds in a hospital.[32] On the trip from Graz to Spain, Margaret of Austria visited numerous convents with her mother. As queen of Spain, Margaret followed practices almost identical to those of her mother: early mass in her private oratory, one or two masses publicly, visits to cloistered convents. Margaret even requested and received papal dispensation to enter the cloistered sections of convents so as to converse and spend time with nuns.[33] Like her mother, Margaret of Austria founded a convent for cloistered nuns.[34] She gave alms to hospitals and patronized Jesuit institutions. The inventory of her library also shows that the great majority of the volumes were devotional in nature.[35] Perhaps the one area in which Margaret differed from her mother was in the former's love of theater, particularly of drama.[36]

Pious deeds clearly linked mother to daughter. We would probably find that other daughters of Archduchess Maria followed these same practices. Moreover, these deeds were not limited to women; Archduchess Maria encouraged her sons to follow similar devotional routines. In the letters she wrote to her son Ferdinand, Archduchess Maria urged him to attend mass, go on pilgrimages (in particular to Mariazell), and pray in hospitals.[37] Ferdinand's daily religious rituals were much like those of his mother and his sister.[38] Moreover, Habsburgs in general had ties to convents and monasteries. Many Habsburgs, such as Charles V, his daughters Juana and María, María's daughter Margaret of the Cross, and Rudolf II's illegitimate daughter Anna Dorothea, retired to monasteries. Archduchess Maria's daughters Maria Christina and Eleanora retreated to and died in a convent in Innsbruck.[39] Both the Spanish and the Austrian Habsburgs attended several masses a day; had regular devotion to confessors, to the Eucharist, and to the Trinity;[40] and founded and patronized convents and monasteries.[41] Pious deeds were therefore not specific to a particular branch of the family or group of individuals. Nonetheless, devotional practices connected the Austrian and Spanish Habsburgs in concrete political ways in the early modern period. Religious devotion, especially when performed in a public fashion, assumed political significance in a world in which Catholics and Protestants vied for religious and political control. Catholic religiosity served as a bridge between Central Europe and Spain, one which Archduchess Maria did her utmost to encourage and promote.

A salient feature of the religious practices of Habsburg women in Central Europe was their devotion to the Jesuits. Most Austrian Habsburg women had Jesuit confessors and ensured that their children would also have Jesuits for confessors and as educators. Archduchess Maria, for example, sent her sons to the Jesuit college at Ingolstadt, and she and all her children had Jesuit confessors; the archduchess even founded three Jesuit schools.[42] Empress María, the widow of Maximilian II, patronized Jesuit schools and bequeathed part of her wealth to the Jesuit school in Madrid. Archduchess Maria's daughter Margaret of Austria had great devotion to her Jesuit confessor, Richard Haller, and showed considerable favor toward the Jesuits, bequeathing a sizable portion of her wealth to the Jesuit college in Salamanca.[43] The Habsburg women's support for the Jesuits was part of their efforts to support Tridentine Catholicism in Central Europe. Women such as Empress María and Margaret of Austria brought this support of the Jesuits with them to Spain and thus created yet another link between Central Europe and the Iberian Peninsula.

Pious deeds clearly connected Archduchess Maria not only to her daughter but also to two other women of the Habsburg dynasty, who resided in the Descalzas monastery in Madrid: Empress

María and Margaret of the Cross.[44] The former was a daughter of Charles V (and a sister of Philip II) who had been married to Holy Roman Emperor Maximilian II. In 1581, five years after Maximilian's death, María returned to Spain and retired to the convent of the Descalzas. Her youngest daughter, Margaret of the Cross, accompanied her to Madrid and entered the Descalzas as a cloistered Franciscan nun. Empress María and Archduchess Maria had been in contact while the former was still in Central Europe. Like Archduchess Maria, Empress María had worked to protect and further the Catholic faith in Central Europe. She had attempted, somewhat unsuccessfully, to instill orthodoxy in her husband and her sons.[45] Empress María and Margaret of the Cross no doubt thought that Archduchess Maria's daughters were religiously orthodox, as they found them to be good candidates to marry Philip III, and Empress María considered them possible matches for her son Rudolf II.[46]

The personal and political links among these women were clearly evident when Archduchess Maria accompanied her daughter, Margaret of Austria, to Spain. Even before leaving Graz, Archduchess Maria requested permission to visit the empress and her daughter; she planned to accompany Margaret of Austria all the way to Madrid and visit the two women in the Descalzas.[47] This meeting was crucial: the archduchess wanted to discuss several issues that were of importance to her son Archduke Ferdinand, and she also wanted to speak with the imperial ambassador, Hans Khevenhüller.[48] The meeting paved the way for Empress María and Margaret of the Cross to look after the young queen, Margaret of Austria. The archduchess recognized that her daughter would share common interests with the two Habsburg women, that all three would represent the needs of the Austrian Habsburgs, and that they would work together. Royal women welcomed the company of relatives, particularly other women. Empress María, Margaret of Austria, and Margaret of the Cross were joined by shared interests, pious deeds, and common experiences.

Archduchess Maria had not been originally scheduled to accompany her daughter from Graz to Madrid. However, Margaret of Austria asked Philip II to allow her mother to go with her, and the king approved this request. When Philip II died in September of 1598, Margaret of Austria and her mother were already en route to Spain. Archduchess Maria and Margaret of Austria realized that the new king might not feel bound to uphold his father's decision. Almost immediately upon hearing of Philip II's death, the two women petitioned Philip III to allow the archduchess to continue her journey to Spain.[49] As they had suspected, Philip III and his royal favorite, Francisco Gómez de Sandoval y Royas, First Duke of Lerma, decided not to honor Philip II's promise. Most probably at Lerma's insistence, Philip III instructed the Spanish ambassador to the imperial court, Guillén de San Clemente, who accompanied the women, to send the archduchess home to Graz.

In denying the archduchess's request, Philip III was perhaps following the common practice of trying to sever a foreign bride's ties to her native country.[50] Perhaps the Spanish king was trying to lessen the burden of paying for Archduchess Maria's and Margaret's entourage, which supposedly numbered more than six hundred individuals.[51] More likely, the denial of her request formed part of a larger effort to limit the archduchess's activities in Spain. Hans Khevenhüller claimed that the Duke of Lerma sought to preclude any contact between the archduchess and the Habsburg women at the Descalzas because he feared that the women would use their familial connections to influence Philip III in ways that Lerma did not desire and thus would challenge Lerma's power. Khevenhüller argued that with these goals in mind, Lerma had made sure that Philip III's and Margaret of Austria's wedding ceremonies were transferred from Madrid to Barcelona and then to Valencia so as to prevent Archduchess Maria from meeting with Empress María.[52] Lerma's efforts were ultimately unsuccessful, and, as previously discussed, Archduchess Maria did meet with the women in the Descalzas.

Archduchess Maria reacted strongly against Spanish attempts to control her activities. In her letters to Ferdinand, the archduchess regularly noted her frustration with the Spanish, particularly with Guillén de San Clemente. She called the Spanish *falsch* (false) and complained that she was plagued by San Clemente, who in her opinion did everything in his power to silence her and govern her actions.[53] Archduchess Maria also expressed her frustration with Albert, the Habsburg archduke. She blamed Albert and San Clemente for the attempts to prevent her from proceeding to Spain. She wrote Ferdinand that the two men wanted her to return to Graz after reaching Ferrara, Italy.[54] When it became clear that she would nonetheless go to Spain, Archduchess Maria claimed that the two men warned her not to speak to Philip III and his ministers about any political matters. She implied that they feared that she was pressing some sort of agenda. Indeed, rumor had it that the archduchess wanted Philip III to invest her son, Archduke Leopold, with the recently vacant archbishopric of Toledo, which the Duke of Lerma sought for his uncle.[55] Archduke Albert and

Guillén de San Clemente were no doubt following orders when they tried to prevent Archduchess Maria from going to Spain. Nevertheless, San Clemente, who was saddled with financing and finding provisions for the huge entourage, must have also welcomed the chance to limit expenses. These expenses mounted as the trip was delayed by the outbreak of plague in Central Europe and then by the numerous stops along the way, which were lengthened by the daily visits that the women paid to convents and churches.[56] Moreover, Margaret of Austria insisted on sending expensive gifts to her siblings, gifts which San Clemente had to finance.[57] San Clemente was in the unenviable position of having to inform the women of Philip III's new orders and of implementing them.[58] Thus, while Archduchess Maria complained about his "false" or treacherous nature, the ambassador was in fact dealing with a thorny diplomatic issue. Caught in the power struggle between the royal favorite Lerma and the new queen, San Clemente needed to tread lightly so as not to offend either one.

The stubbornness of the archduchess and Margaret of Austria's strength of character ultimately prevailed. Archduchess Maria explained to Ferdinand that Margaret of Austria used her authority as queen to gain permission for her mother to accompany her all the way to Spain. In this way, the women were able to circumvent the efforts of Lerma, Albert, and San Clemente. Certainly Maria saw the trip to Spain as an opportunity to win support for Archduke Ferdinand and to negotiate issues that were beneficial to her children. This was precisely what the Duke of Lerma sought to avoid. Through San Clemente and Archduke Albert, Lerma was attempting to silence a strong, politically powerful woman. These efforts were very similar to those Lerma would later use to try to limit Margaret of Austria's influence with Philip III. In combating Archduke Albert and Guillén de San Clemente, Archduchess Maria appealed to her daughter's power as queen, to the authority that she wielded over all others—including powerful men— precisely because she was the queen. Margaret of Austria would, in fact, use this authority later to fight the Duke of Lerma at the Spanish court.[59]

Archduchess Maria and Margaret of Austria clashed with the Duke of Lerma on yet another issue. Lerma, arguing that Spanish queens always had Franciscan confessors, tried to replace the Jesuit Richard Haller with Fray Mateo de Burgos, who was head of the Franciscan order in Spain. Lerma's actual motive, however, was to sever the queen's ties with Central Europe, surround her with individuals loyal to him, and remove Haller, who had the potential to and eventually did become a strong political opponent.[60] The queen went directly to Philip III and emphasized that her poor grasp of Castilian made it imperative for her to keep her German confessor. Philip III acquiesced, and Margaret of Austria, with Archduchess Maria's help, was able to retain Haller as confessor for the rest of her brief life. Lerma was correct to see Haller as a potential opponent: Margaret of Austria and Richard Haller together challenged Lerma's power at the Spanish court. Archduchess Maria no doubt encouraged her daughter to see that Haller remained as her confessor since, after all, the archduchess had been instrumental in choosing Haller.[61] Moreover, as a native of Nuremberg, Haller would almost instinctively defend the interests of Archduchess Maria's family, the Bavarian Wittelsbachs, along with those of the Austrian Habsburgs. Haller ultimately did negotiate many issues for Archduchess Maria and carried messages for the archduchess to influential members at the Spanish court.[62] Thus, when Archduchess Maria wrote to Lerma that she was "very pleased that Father Haller stays" as Margaret's confessor and that she knew that she had only Lerma to thank, she was honestly assessing the advantages she stood to gain from having Haller at Philip's court.[63]

Archduchess Maria's letters to her son Ferdinand during her trip to Spain show that she was anxious to return to Central Europe in order to help her son with governmental matters. She frequently asked Ferdinand about the progress of the Landtag (Styrian Diet), about his brother Leopold's appointment to the bishopric of Passau, and about many other issues that concerned her.[64] Her departure from Spain by no means signaled the end of her ties with her daughter or with Philip III. At her departure, Philip III gave her numerous presents, including a jewel worth twenty thousand ducats; a diamond necklace worth twenty-seven thousand ducats; several objects from the West Indies, such as thread, sugar, and coconuts; and twelve black slaves.[65]

Gifts such as those from Philip III to Archduchess Maria cemented the connection between Central Europe and Spain. The Spanish Habsburgs regularly sent costly presents to their relatives in Central Europe, and, as mentioned above, Margaret of Austria sent gifts to her siblings as she traveled to Spain. Once Archduchess Maria returned to Graz, the queen sent her presents, including Portuguese porcelain and silver objects.[66] When Archduchess Maria visited the Descalzas, Empress María and Margaret of the Cross gave many presents to her and to her children.[67] Empress María sent gifts to the Duke of Bavaria and sent numerous gifts to her children.[68] In most cases, Philip III requested that no duties be exacted from the goods and that the deputies see that the merchandise be transported swiftly and safely. The Habsburgs in Spain sent objects from the New World, religious items, furniture, gems and precious stones, silver objects, and porcelains, among other things. The Austrian Habsburgs saw Spain as the source of desirable goods. Certainly, the imperial ambassador Hans Khevenhüller regularly procured objects for Rudolf II. These pieces included small objects, such as gold buttons and unusual stones, as well as more substantial things, such as paintings and prized stallions for the imperial stables.[69] Thus, there was always a material connection between the two Habsburg branches, one from which the Austrian Habsburgs benefited.

Upon leaving Spain, the archduchess quickly began long correspondences with her daughter, Richard Haller, Philip III, and the Duke of Lerma. She thus made use of one of the common features of an early modern woman's influence—a network of correspondence—to press for individual concerns, particularly for those of her family.[70] Her most immediate goal was to gain financial and military assistance for her son Archduke Ferdinand, and she enlisted the assistance of Margaret of Austria and Richard Haller in this task. She also took it upon herself to put pressure on Philip III and on Lerma by writing them regularly and reminding them of Ferdinand's needs. As a politically savvy woman, Maria knew how to win Philip's and Lerma's attention. When in December 1600 she wrote to Lerma requesting assistance for Ferdinand, she added that she would try to negotiate with Emperor Rudolf II and encourage him not to make peace with the Turks.[71] The archduchess recognized that Philip might be more likely to help Ferdinand if, in turn, Ferdinand and Archduchess Maria would use their influence with the emperor in a matter that was very important to Philip III. While this influence might not have been very significant, Rudolf II's behavior was sufficiently eccentric and his relations with the Spanish ambassador were strained enough to ensure that Philip would welcome any assistance he could get in negotiating with the emperor. Archduchess Maria's letter also shows that she was conscious of the need to bring a certain degree of reciprocity to the relations between the Austrian and the Spanish Habsburgs. The Spanish government during the reign of Philip III believed that the Austrian Habsburgs demanded and took financial assistance from Spain but never reciprocated in kind. The archduchess was offering to repay Spanish assistance in one of the few ways available to her, namely, intercession with politically powerful men.

Archduchess Maria also knew the ways of the Spanish court. Though she must have realized that Lerma monitored her daughter Queen Margaret of Austria's activities and that he could not have welcomed the archduchess's frequent requests for Spanish assistance, Archduchess Maria still knew that she had to win his support for her petitions: in order to reach Philip III, she would have to deal with Lerma. At least one historian has argued that the Duke of Lerma succeeded in winning the archduchess over with lavish gifts, large sums of money, and financial assistance to her son Ferdinand.[72] María Jesús Pérez Martín cites the letters that the archduchess wrote to Lerma, which were filled with references of respect, regard, and even affection. According to this interpretation, Lerma used gifts to silence Archduchess Maria, a woman who could have been a powerful opponent.

Yet there is another, more plausible reading of this situation. Archduchess Maria was a knowledgeable political player. She had, after all, been in charge of the Styrian lands for five years on her own, and her son Ferdinand still sought and received political assistance and advice from her. Maria knew that to win Spanish financial and military aid for Ferdinand, she had to court the Duke of Lerma. When she first met Lerma, she wrote to Ferdinand that she hoped that Lerma would be of great value to them. She remarked that Lerma was "like a German" and that she was pleased that her daughter would have such a faithful servant close by. She and Lerma had spoken about the Venetians and undoubtedly about Ferdinand's problems with them.[73] From the beginning, therefore, Archduchess Maria recognized that Lerma was someone whom she should court and from whom she and her children could benefit. When, in 1605, she referred to Lerma as "father" to her and her children, she was appealing to a father's duty to provide and was thus trying to encourage him to see to her children's concerns.[74]

Through Lerma she found one avenue to Philip III, who was not easily accessible to her at first. To Ferdinand, she described Philip as a child to whom she could barely speak. He spent little time with her and negotiated almost everything through the Duke of Lerma.[75] The archduchess quickly realized that Lerma was her means of access to the monarch. She also knew that Lerma, who was melancholic, welcomed the attention and esteem of others and often had to be reassured of people's loyalty and friendship.[76] Thus, her affectionate words were designed to win the *privado*'s (royal favorite's) favor and to gain his assistance. Archduchess Maria also was aware that one of Lerma's closest associates, Magdalena de Guzmán, Marquesa del Valle, wielded much influence at the Spanish court.⁷⁷ Individuals requested audiences with the marquesa so that she would then carry their requests to Lerma and to Philip III. In her letters to Lerma, Archduchess Maria sent her greetings to the Marquesa del Valle.⁷⁸ In this case, as in so many others, the archduchess demonstrated her political acumen.

The archduchess was correct in her reading of Lerma and the Spanish court. She sought Lerma's favor because she feared that her connection to the king and queen were becoming tenuous, in particular, that her correspondence network was weakening. In several letters to Philip III, she complained that she failed to receive letters from the king and queen. She also feared that her letters were not reaching them, either.⁷⁹ She tried sending letters through several routes—through the Spanish ambassador in Prague, through Venice, through Flanders. She wrote to Philip III that she regretted that he did not understand German, because then her letters would not need to be translated for him, and she could speak more freely. She expressed her fear that others were reading her letters to the queen,⁸⁰ though Philip III assured her that her letters were being translated by a very trustworthy individual (*mano muy segura*).⁸¹ The archduchess's comments, however, point to correspondence as the key to maintaining the ties between Central Europe and Spain. Maria's remarks also indicate the inherent problems of long-distance relations and of the language barriers between the Habsburg branches.

Through the continued efforts of Archduchess Maria, and because of her strong influence over Queen Margaret of Austria, the Spanish monarchy assisted the Austrian Habsburgs throughout the reign of Philip III. In particular, Philip worked closely with Archduke Ferdinand and helped finance his numerous military campaigns. This cooperation between the Spanish king and the Austrian archduke continued long after Archduchess Maria's death in 1608. When Ferdinand was forced to suppress the Bohemian revolt of 1618, the Spanish king provided him with financial and military assistance. In this way, the Spanish monarchy became involved in what proved to be a thirty-year war, a war that was ultimately disastrous for Spain. Philip's assistance to Ferdinand was predicated upon the familial ties that had been strengthened by the marriage of Philip to Margaret of Austria, a marriage which Archduchess Maria had helped to arrange. The archduchess thus bound the future of her children to that of the Spanish Habsburgs. In turn, however, the archduchess's actions also ensured that Spain's fortunes depended on the outcome of events in Central Europe.

Archduchess Maria thus provides us with a compelling example of how an aristocratic woman helped shape political events. Through marriage strategies designed to benefit her children, and by maintaining close, affectionate ties with those children, the archduchess exercised an important role in international politics. In this way, maternal responsibilities could and did translate into political influence. Archduchess Maria successfully navigated the murky diplomatic waters between the Spanish and the Austrian Habsburgs. As such, she emerges as a savvy woman who worked to focus Spanish attention on Central Europe for the benefit of her sons. The present essay only begins to scratch the surface of Archduchess Maria's story. This fascinating, powerful woman deserves a full-length biography that considers how she exercised political authority and how that authority affected cultural and political events in Central Europe and in Europe as a whole. Her ability to win favor at the Spanish court is but one example of how she wielded authority.

Notes

1. Research for this article was made possible through a Research and Professional Development Grant from Gettysburg College. I would like to thank the college and the Grants Advisory Committee for their generous support.
2. See Carole Levin, *The Heart and Stomach of a King: Elizabeth I and the Politics of Sex and Power* (Philadelphia, 1994), pp. 48–54.
3. For a list of their children, see Friedrich von Hurter, *Bild einer christlichen Fürstin: Maria, Erzherzogin zu Österreich, Herzogin von Bayern* (Schaffhausen, 1860), pp. 72–73.
4. Johann Franzl, *Ferdinand II.: Kaiser im Zwiespalt der Zeit* (Graz, 1978), pp. 73–75.
5. Pedro Salazar de Mendoza, *Succession de la inclyta casa de Baviera con la vida de la serenissima Señora Archiduquesa María* (Toledo, 1608). Salazar de Mendoza dedicated this biography to Queen Margaret of Austria. The inventory of Margaret's books lists a genealogy of the house of Bavaria, which was also contained in Salazar de Mendoza's book. I therefore conclude that Margaret owned a copy of Salazar de Mendoza's book.
6. Salazar de Mendoza, *Succession de la inclyta casa de Baviera*, fol. 61r.
7. Fray Alonso de Herrera, *Sermon que predico el Padre Fray Alonso de Herrera monge de la orden de S. Benito a las honras que hizieron sus Magestades á la Serenissima Archiduquesa de Austria Maria en San Benito el Real de Valladolid, a 13 de Agosto de 1608* (Valladolid, 1608).
8. Ibid., fols. 8v-9r; Salazar de Mendoza, *Succession de la inclyta casa de Baviera*, fols. 64v-65r.
9. Salazar de Mendoza, *Succession de la inclyta casa de Baviera*, fol. 61v.

10. Caroline Walker Bynum details the self-mortification and suffering of many medieval women, even as she argues that these women welcomed pain as a way to share in Christ's suffering. See Caroline Walker Bynum, *Holy Feast and Holy Fast: The Religious Significance of Food to Medieval Women* (Berkeley, Calif., 1987), passim. See also Donald Weinstein and Rudolph M. Bell, *Saints and Society* (Chicago, 1982), pp. 31–45.
11. Salazar de Mendoza, *Succession de la inclyta casa de Baviera*, fol. 65r-65v.
12. Ibid., fol. 63v.
13. When he visited Elizabeth I in England, he attended daily mass. See Levin, *The Heart and Stomach of a King*, p. 51.
14. Johann Andritsch argues that up until the 1570s, Karl's religiosity was much like that of Maximilian II. See Johann Andritsch, "Landesfürstliche Berater am Grazer Hof (1564–1619)," in *Innerösterreich, 1564–1619* (Graz, 1968), pp. 88–89.
15. Herrera, *Sermon que predico el Padre Fray Alonso de Herrera*, fol. 9r.
16. Ibid., fols. 8v-9v.
17. See, for example, Juan de la Cerda, *Vida política de todos los estados de mujeres* (Alcalá de Henares, 1599), fols. 306v-307r; Jeronimo de Florencia, *Sermon que predicó a la Magestad del Rey Don Felipe III en las honras que Su Magestad hizo a la serenissima Reyna D. Margarita su muger, que es en gloria, en San Gerónimo el Real de Madrid a 18 de noviembre de 1611* (Madrid, 1611), fol. 17–17v; idem, *Sermon segundo que predicó el Padre Gerónimo de Florencia de la Compañia de Jesus, y predicador del Rey N.S. en las honras que hizo á la Magestad de la serenissima Reyna Doña Margarita N.S. (que Dios tiene) la nobilíssima villa de Madrid en Santa Maria, á los 19. de Diziembre de 1611* (Madrid, 1612), fol. 11v; Juan de la Palma, *Vida de la serenissima Infanta Sor Margarita de la Cruz, religiosa Descalza de Santa Clara* (Seville, 1653), fol. 120.
18. Salazar de Mendoza, *Succession de la inclyta casa de Baviera*, fol. 63v.
19. One can also detect the religious prejudices of Fray Alonso de Herrera and Pedro Salazar de Mendoza, as well as those of their audience.
20. Herrera, *Sermon que predico el Padre Fray Alonso de Herrera*, fol. 9v.
21. Ibid.
22. Salazar de Mendoza, *Succession de la inclyta casa de Baviera*, fol. 64r.
23. The English kings followed similar practices. For those of Queen Elizabeth, see Levin, *The Heart and Stomach of a King*, pp. 22–25, 33–35.
24. Salazar de Mendoza, *Succession de la inclyta casa de Baviera*, fol. 66r.
25. Herrera claimed that Maria and her daughters went three times a month. See Herrera, *Sermon que predico el Padre Fray Alonso de Herrera*, fol. 10r.
26. Salazar de Mendoza, *Succession de la inclyta casa de Baviera*, fol. 61v.
27. Ibid.
28. Ibid.
29. Ibid., fol. 63r; Herrera, *Sermon que predico el Padre Fray Alonso de Herrera*, fol. 7v.
30. Salazar de Mendoza, *Succession de la inclyta casa de Baviera*, fol. 63r.
31. For similar descriptions of Margaret of Austria, see Diego de Guzmán, *Reyna Católica: Vida y muerte de Doña Margarita de Austria, Reyna de España* (Madrid, 1617), fol. 116v; Jeronimo de Florencia, *Sermon que predicó a la Magestad del Rey Don Felipe III*, fol. 11v.
32. Guzmán, *Reyna Católica*, fol. 46r; María Jesús Pérez Martín, *Margarita de Austria, Reina de España* (Madrid, 1961), p. 22.
33. Archivo Segreto Vaticano, Correspondence of the Patriarch of Alexandria, nuncio in Spain, Fondo Borghese, ser. 1, 649, fol. 21r-21v; letter from the nuncio to Cardinal Aldobrandino, Madrid, 10 January 1599; fol. 199r-199v; letter

from the nuncio to Cardinal Aldobrandino, 6 June 1599; fols. 391r-393v; letter from the nuncio to Cardinal Aldobrandino, Saragossa, 28 September 1599.
34. This convent was the royal convent of the Encarnación in Madrid. Margaret was also instrumental in renovating the royal convent of Santa Isabel in Madrid. On the Encarnación, see María Leticia Sánchez Hernández, *El Monasterio de la Encarnación de Madrid: Un modelo de vida religiosa en el siglo XVII* (Salamanca, 1986). On Santa Isabel, see José Luis Saenz Ruiz-Olalde, O.A.R., *Las Agustinas Recoletas de Santa Isabel la Real de Madrid* (Madrid, 1990). Archduchess Maria founded at least one convent; see Franzl, *Ferdinand II.*, p. 75.
35. See Archivo del Patrimonio Real, Registro 239, Inventario de los Bienes de Margarita de Austria, fols. 209r-218r.
36. Melveena McKendrick, *Theatre in Spain, 1490-1700* (New York, 1992), pp. 209-210.
37. Ferdinand Khull, *Sechsundvierzig Briefe der Erzherzogin Maria an ihren Sohn Ferdinand aus den Jahren 1598-99* (Graz, 1898), p. 235, letter from 25 January 1599. Archduchess Maria wrote these letters to her son when she accompanied Margaret of Austria to Spain.
38. For a brief description of these rituals, see R. J. W. Evans, *The Making of the Habsburg Monarchy, 1550-1700* (New York, 1984), pp. 72-73.
39. Hurter, *Bild einer christlichen Fürstin*, pp. 72-73.
40. See Anna Coreth, *Pietas Austriaca: Österreichische Frömmigkeit im Barock* (Vienna, 1982), especially pp. 15-37.
41. So, for example, Philip II founded the Jeronimite monastery of San Lorenzo el Real at the Escorial. His sister Juana founded the royal convent of the Descalzas in Madrid. For other examples, see Geoffrey Parker, *Philip II*, 3rd ed. (Chicago, 1995), p. 171.
42. Salazar de Mendoza, *Succession de la inclyta casa de Baviera*, fol. 67r.
43. Testamento de Margarita de Austria, Real Academia de la Historia, Madrid, Colección Salazar y Castro, M63, fols. 313v-314r.
44. On these women, see Magdalena S. Sánchez, *The Empress, the Queen, and the Nun: Women and Power at the Court of Philip III of Spain* (Baltimore, 1998), passim.
45. Empress María's concern about the religious beliefs of her husband and sons is clearly evident in the diplomatic correspondence of Francisco Hurtado de Mendoza, Count of Monteagudo, Spanish ambassador at the imperial court from 1570 to 1577. See, for example, "Carta descifrada del Conde de Monteagudo a S.M., fechada en Viena á 14 de mayo de 1573," *Colección de documentos inéditos para la historia de España* (hereafter *CODOIN*), vol. 111, p. 233; "Carta Original del Conde de Monteagudo á Su Magestad, Fechada en Espira á 15 de Agosto de 1570," *CODOIN*, vol. 110, p. 51.
46. In fact, portraits of the four Styrian archduchesses were sent to Empress María, and they now form part of the art collection of the Descalzas convent. On these portraits, see María Teresa Ruiz Alcón, *Monasterio de las Descalzas Reales* (Madrid, 1987), pp. 80, 82.
47. See Archivo General de Simancas (hereafter cited as AGS), Estado Alemania, Legajo 705, Guillén de San Clemente to Philip II, Graz, 20 September 1598.
48. See Khull, *Sechsundvierzig Briefe der Erzherzogin Maria*, p. 103, letter from 9 April 1599; p. 381, letter from 7 November 1598.
49. AGS, Estado Alemania, Legajo 705, Guillén de San Clemente to Philip II, Graz, 20 September 1598.
50. Ruth Kleinman, *Anne of Austria: Queen of France* (Columbus, Ohio, 1985), pp. 38-42; Caroline M. Hibbard, "The Role of a Queen Consort: The Household

and Court of Henrietta Maria, 1625–1642," in *Princes, Patronage, and the Nobility: The Court at the Beginning of the Modern Age, c. 1450–1650*, ed. Ronald G. Asch and Adolf M. Birke (Oxford, 1991), pp. 404–407; Kevin Sharpe, "The Image of Virtue: The Court and Household of Charles I, 1625–1642," in *The English Court: From the Wars of the Roses to the Civil War*, ed. David Starkey et al. (London, 1987), pp. 247–248, 256–257.
51. Guzmán, *Reyna Católica*, fol. 54r; Khull, *Sechsundvierzig Briefe der Erzherzogin Maria*, p. 4.
52. Biblioteca Nacional, Madrid (hereafter BNM), Ms. 2751, "Historia de Joan Kevenhuller de Aichelberg," p. 1139.
53. Khull, *Sechsundvierzig Briefe der Erzherzogin Maria*, p. 34, letter from 2 November 1598.
54. Ibid.
55. Pérez Martín, *Margarita de Austria*, p. 36.
56. Ibid., pp. 26–27.
57. Ibid., pp. 48–49.
58. Ibid., pp. 27, 36.
59. See ibid., pp. 99–102, 113–115, 117–119; and Sánchez, *The Empress, the Queen, and the Nun*, pp. 42–44, 95–105.
60. See Sánchez, *The Empress, the Queen, and the Nun*, pp. 21–22, 50–51, 102–103.
61. For the selection of Haller as Margaret's confessor, see Andritsch, "Landesfürstliche Berater am Grazer Hof," pp. 105–106.
62. See, for example, BNM, Ms. 915, fols. 70v–71r, Archduchess Maria to Philip III, 16 December 1602.
63. BNM, Ms. 915, fols. 58v–59r, Archduchess Maria to the Duke of Lerma, 10 December 1600.
64. Hurter, *Bild einer christlichen Fürstin*, pp. 16, 257–258, 275.
65. For the list of presents, see Haus-, Hof- und Staatsarchiv, Vienna (hereafter cited as HHStA), Spanien Varia 3, fol. 316r and 316v, 2 June 1599.
66. Archivo Histórico Nacional, Madrid (hereafter cited as AHN), Consejos, Curia Catalonia (Registros de Cancilleria), book 2302, fols. 70v–71r, Philip III to Diputados de Aragon.
67. Hurter, *Bild einer christlichen Fürstin*, p. 264, letter from 10 May 1599.
68. AHN, Consejos, Curia Catalonia (Registros de Cancilleria), Libro 2302, fols. 58v–59r, fol. 67r–67v, fols. 71v–72r, fols. 73v–74v, fol. 77r–77v, fols. 145v–146v, Philip III to Diputados de Aragon.
69. For examples, see HHStA, Spanien Diplomatische Korrespondenz, Karton 12, fol. 72r (4 March 1591); fol. 144r (29 September 1593); fol. 178r–178v (24 April 1594); fol. 281r–281v (18 February 1596); fol. 438r (20 October 1599). These references are to the typescript volume compiled by Georg Graf Khevenhüller, entitled *Die geheime Korrespondenz des kaiserlichen Botschafters am Königlich spanischen Hof in Madrid, Hans Khevenhüller, Graf von Frankenburg*. The volume is located within the *Kartons* of the Spanien Diplomatische Korrespondenz in the Haus-, Hof- und Staatsarchiv in Vienna. The references in this note are taken from volume 5, parts 1 and 2, of the typescript version.
70. For an example of another woman who skillfully developed a correspondence network to benefit her children, see Robert J. Kalas, "The Noble Woman's Place in the Patriarchal Household: The Life and Career of Jeanne de Gontault," *Sixteenth Century Journal*, vol. 24, no. 3 (1993), pp. 531–534.
71. BNM, Ms. 915, fols. 58v–59r, Archduchess Maria to the Duke of Lerma, 10 December 1600.

72. See Pérez Martín, *Margarita de Austria*, pp. 102–105. Ciriaco Pérez Bustamante also argues that through large monetary gifts, Lerma was able to get Archduchess Maria to return to Graz. Pérez Bustamante implies that once she left Spain, the archduchess lost any influence with Philip III and Lerma. See Ciriaco Pérez Bustamante, *La España de Felipe III*, 3rd ed. (Madrid, 1983), p. 119.
73. Khull, *Sechsundvierzig Briefe der Erzherzogin Maria*, p. 104, lettter from 9 April 1599.
74. BNM, Ms. 915, fol. 67, Archduchess Maria to the Duke of Lerma, 29 August 1605.
75. Khull, *Sechsundvierzig Briefe der Erzherzogin Maria*, p. 128, 7 July 1599.
76. See Sánchez, *The Empress, the Queen, and the Nun*, pp. 169–171.
77. On the Marquesa del Valle, see Luis Fernández Martín, "La Marquesa del Valle: Una vida dramática en la corte de los Austrias," *Hispania*, vol. 39, no. 143 (1979), pp. 559–638.
78. BNM, Ms. 915, fols. 58v-59r, Archduchess Maria to the Duke of Lerma, 10 December 1600.
79. Ibid., fol. 80, Archduchess Maria to Philip III, 2 November 1600; fol. 58, Archduchess Maria to the Duke of Lerma, 10 December 1600.
80. Ibid., fol. 80, Archduchess Maria to Philip III, 2 November 1600.
81. Ibid., fol. 123, Philip III to Archduchess Maria, June 1601.

– 4 –

Germany's Indies?

The Spanish Monarchy and Germany in the
Reign of the Last Spanish Habsburg,
Charles II, 1665–1700

Christopher D. Storrs

Spanish foreign policy and Spain's international role during the reign of the last Spanish Habsburg Charles II (1665–1700) are among the least-studied aspects of an age in which the Spanish succession is generally regarded as one of the key issues in European politics.[1] One simple explanation for this is the widespread view that Spain, once so powerful, was by the late seventeenth century a second-, even third-rank power, unable to defend itself alone against Louis XIV's France and only fit to be the object of international rivalry. Spain was certainly not as dominant a power in the reign of the physically and mentally weak Charles II, the so-called *hechizado* (bewitched), as it had been in that of the more robust first Spanish Habsburg Charles I, that is, the Holy Roman Emperor Charles V, and his son and successor in Spain, Philip II. Spanish naval power had been smashed in 1588, with the defeat of the Armada against England, and again in 1639 at the Downs. Spanish military might, the foundation of Spain's power in the sixteenth century, which was deployed very effectively in Germany in the first decade or so of the Thirty Years' War (1618–48), had also suffered disastrously, above all at Rocroi (1643). Thereafter, Spain was obliged to recognize the independence of the

Dutch Republic (1648) and Portugal (1668), while Louis XIV seized parts of the Spanish Low Countries (1667/68), Franche-Comté (1674), and Luxembourg (1683/84). Not surprisingly, Madrid now sought allies and support against the French king, and attempted to make the most of its claim to be one of the German states and a member of the Holy Roman Empire.[2]

Spain's seventeenth-century decline, however, has been greatly overstated. Despite its losses, the Spanish monarchy (as it was known) remained enormous, stretching from Flanders and the Mediterranean across the Atlantic to the Pacific. That empire, and particularly the Americas or West Indies, continued to provide substantial funds in the form of precious metals, which helped finance a foreign policy aimed at the preservation of both empire and status. There was some success: at the conclusion of the Nine Years' War or War of the League of Augsburg (1688–97), Louis XIV returned Luxembourg to secure peace with Spain and its partners in the Grand Alliance. Spain clearly remained a member of that small elite of great powers (the others were Austria, the Dutch Republic, England, and France), distinguished from the great mass of small states by its extensive interests and resources and its determination and ability to play a leading role in Europe. As one of Europe's diplomatic centers, Madrid also remained an important battleground for the struggle for status and precedence between numerous lesser princes and states, including those of Germany.[3] More importantly, however, Spain's determination to use its still vast resources to maintain the monarchy provided a cornucopia of opportunities for lesser nobles and states and inevitably drew those seeking their own interest. In the last decade of Habsburg Spain, the way some German princes and their followers seemed to be thriving at the expense of the monarchy fueled the faction-fighting that characterized politics in Madrid. It also stimulated an anti-German feeling that contributed to the victory of the French Bourbon Philip V (1700–1746) over his Austrian Habsburg rival in the War of the Spanish Succession.[4]

Spain remained a reservoir of opportunities for German states, princes, and individuals between 1665 and 1700 because of Spanish determination to hang on to southern Flanders, which had been salvaged from the Dutch revolt in the later sixteenth century (and which was only finally lost by Spain during the War of the Spanish Succession). This needs emphasizing because some historians believe that Spain was increasingly tired of the cost of empire and, in particular, of the burden represented by the Low

Countries.[5] The Dutch and English certainly suspected—and resented—that Madrid sought to transfer the burden of the defense of Spanish Flanders to them, and there is some contemporary evidence to support their suspicions. According to King William III's envoy to the Spanish court, following Spain's traumatic loss to Louis XIV's forces of the town of Mons in 1691, Spanish ministers considered handing over the Low Countries to the Dutch, but were restrained by (among other things) the opposition of a *junta de teólogos* to the transfer of its Catholic population to the Protestant Dutch.[6]

Spain's Army of Flanders certainly dwindled in size significantly after 1659, to 20,000 men and less, and made but a meager contribution to the allied armies facing Louis XIV in Flanders during the Nine Years' War.[7] Nevertheless, throughout Charles II's reign, Spain continued to pour men and money into the Spanish Low Countries, which remained both strategically important and a source of prestige. In 1667, while Spain was still fighting to restore its sovereignty over Portugal, 5,000 men were raised in Spain for Flanders, and in 1683/84, at least 2,500 men were ferried there from Spain.[8] Similar efforts were made during the Nine Years' War. In August 1689, eight ships arrived at Ostend carrying 3,000 Spanish troops from Galicia.[9] As for money, in the winter of 1691/92, of two million ducats remitted abroad from the so-called *indulto* (levy) on the *galeones* fleet recently arrived in Cadiz from America, nearly 900,000 went to the Low Countries (and 600,000 and 400,000, respectively, to those other theaters of war, Lombardy and Catalonia).[10] Spain's independent efforts alone may not have sufficed—necessitating some reliance on Spain's allies[11] and on Flanders' German neighbors—but they demonstrate Madrid's determination to preserve both its dominion and reputation.[12] Spain's Army of Flanders could still also represent a threat to some of those lesser German princes neighboring the Spanish Low Countries.[13]

Spain Exploits Its Status as a German Power

Spain was itself, of course, a German power, by virtue of its possession of Franche-Comté, Luxembourg, and the Low Countries (acquired by the Habsburgs following the collapse of the Burgundian "state" during and after 1477). Together these had comprised since 1548 one of the ten Circles of the Holy Roman Empire: the Burgundian.[14] Hitherto, however—and despite a new concern of

Spanish propagandists in the 1630s to appeal to the German "nation" against French propaganda that urged the defense of German "liberty" against the Habsburgs during the Thirty Years' War[15]—Spain had made little of its identity as a German power. Indeed, the Spanish Habsburgs had preferred to evade the obligations of membership in the Empire, and to effectively regard these territories as independent of the Empire.[16] This attitude changed with the transformation of the international scene, beginning in the 1660s, to Spain's disadvantage. Henceforth, Spain would seek to affirm its status as a "German" power in order to secure the support of the Empire in the defense of Spain's imperial territories against Louis XIV.

This new interest in asserting Spain's full membership in the Empire, and its German identity, became clear following the invasion of Flanders by Louis XIV's forces in May 1667 and the invasion of Franche-Comté in January 1668. In the immediately preceding period, Spain had been content to have its interests looked after in the Imperial Diet (in perpetual session at Regensburg/Ratisbon since 1663) by the representative of the emperor. However, in 1667, the governor of Spanish Flanders and of Franche-Comté, the Marquis of Castel Rodrigo, who claimed to have only 20,000 troops to face Louis XIV's 50,000, decided to restore the permanent delegation of the Burgundian Circle (i.e., of Spain) at the Diet, sending there two representatives, both natives of Franche-Comté. Their mission was to have the Burgundian Circle included in the so-called Guarantee of the Empire, implying a promise of military support against France, and to contribute to measures to put the Empire in a state to resist. Fortunately for Spain, Louis XIV's more aggressive policy in the Rhineland undermined Cardinal Mazarin's League of the Rhine, in which a number of Rhenish princes had allied with France against Spain. These included the elector of Trier who, in August 1668, concluded a treaty of alliance with the governor of Spanish Flanders, abandoning the French alliance.[17] Some other German princes—notably the archbishop of Salzburg and, to a lesser degree, the great elector of Brandenburg—and their delegates sympathized with Spain. Others, however, including the electors of Bavaria and Cologne and the influential archbishop of Mainz, favored Louis XIV. In September 1667, one of the Spanish representatives urged in the College of the Princes that the Burgundian Circle must be defended as an outpost of the Empire, and thus of German freedom, of which Spanish power was now a guarantee against an aggressive France. This represented another strand in the evolution of the meaning of "German freedom" in the sixteenth and seventeenth centuries. Spain was now clearly trying to present itself in Germany as a German power and defender of German liberty in order to secure German aid for the defense of territories it had until recently effectively sought to withdraw from the Empire. Unfortunately, although the College of the Princes accepted that the Burgundian Circle was part of the Empire, it would not extend to it the Guarantee, while the College of the Electors merely proposed mediating between France and Spain.[18]

Although its diplomacy had clearly suffered a defeat, Spain remained determined to make the most of its German credentials. This was one reason why Charles II (or rather the regency headed by his mother during his minority, which lasted until 1675) rejected Louis XIV's offer to return his conquests in the Low Countries in exchange for being allowed to retain Franche-Comté. Of course, Franche-Comté was part of Charles II's Burgundian inheritance in an age in which proprietary dynasticism, rather than natural frontiers, inspired princely policy. But his possession of Franche-Comté also strengthened Spain's case for help from Germany and the Empire. Unfortunately for Madrid, however, not until September 1674 would the Empire (following its declaration of war against France) extend the Guarantee to the Burgundian Circle. By then it was too late, Louis XIV's forces having already conquered Franche-Comté. Nevertheless, by virtue of its retention of Flanders, Spain remained a member of the German body. That Spain continued to want to make a reality of its German status is evident from its positive response to proposals to reform the military contributions of the circles, agreeing to a contribution from the Burgundian Circle of 3,000 men (to a total imperial force of 30,000), a reform which was effected in 1681. The loss of Luxembourg (1683–84) further undermined Spain's German status and exposed the fragility of the German Guarantee, but Luxembourg was recovered in 1697, and that status was never wholly lost.[19] As head of the Burgundian Circle, Charles II was able to join in 1686 that defensive association of German princes, the League of Augsburg, which was formed to shield the Empire more effectively against Louis XIV,[20] and during the Nine Years' War, the representative of the Circle of Burgundy (i.e., of Charles II) at Regensburg usefully supplemented Spanish diplomacy.[21] In the spring of 1697, the deputies of the Imperial Circle in the Rhine area, fearful of French attack, sought the help of Charles II as head of the Burgundian Circle, according to the quotas agreed at Regensburg in 1681.[22]

Spain's Use of German Subsidy Troops

If Spain could not secure a guarantee or an imperial army, it might obtain German help in other ways, including the purchase of troops from one or more German princes in return for subsidies. After 1665, the so-called Army of Flanders was normally only sufficient to provide garrisons for the many fortresses that dotted the Low Countries. Spain could no longer send troops from Italy along the now dismantled "Spanish Road," and sending troops from Spain by sea could be both time-consuming and risky. It was therefore often simpler to reinforce the Army of Flanders in wartime by purchasing troops in neighboring Germany,[23] exploiting the well-established trade in troops, or *Soldatenhandel*, which was increasingly the preserve of the German princes, rather than of the independent military entrepreneurs of an earlier period. The system was advantageous to the princes since it allowed them to maintain troops they might not otherwise have been able to afford and which might serve their own military ambitions and even to make a profit. In 1668, for example, Sweden, which was desperate for funds to support the army that underpinned its own imperial position, offered to supply 16,000 troops in Flanders in case of emergency, in return for an annual subsidy of 480,000 escudos.[24] During the Dutch War, Spain paid subsidies for troops to various German princes, including the electors of Brandenburg and Trier; the dukes of Celle, Hanover, and Wolfenbüttel; and the bishop of Osnabrück.[25]

However, these Spanish subsidies were generally paid only very slowly. In 1675, Great Elector Frederick William (1640–1688) of Brandenburg sent a minister, Melchior Ruck, to Madrid, ostensibly to congratulate Charles II on the end of his minority. His main purpose, however, was to press for payment of growing subsidy arrears owed by Spain for the support of both the elector's troops and (during the revolt of Messina, on the island of Sicily, in 1674) his ships. Unfortunately, Spain's extensive military commitments and the relative lack of clout of the elector of Brandenburg (which was still very much a second-rank power)[26] meant that these demands went unsatisfied. Early in 1680, Ruck demanded immediate payment from Charles II's recently appointed chief minister, the duke of Medinaceli, who offered 30,000 escudos in cash and the rest of the debt (800,000 escudos) in assignations on the next West Indies fleet to reach Cadiz. Given the many other assignations on this same source, Ruck returned in disgust to Berlin. In September 1680, six vessels flying the elector's standard seized in Ostend harbor a newly built Spanish ship, the *Carlos Segundo*, which was about to leave with a cargo worth 300,000 escudos. With Spain refusing to negotiate the settlement of the debt until the ship was released, the elector sold the seized vessel, pocketing the proceeds in settlement of his debt—a humiliation by a lesser prince about which Spanish ministers felt deeply, not least because of its likely impact elsewhere in Europe. The duke of Hanover also had to wait until after the Dutch War for the subsidies due for troops he had provided during that conflict, while the duke of Neuburg attempted (unsuccessfully) to trade his arrears in Madrid for territorial concessions on the Lower Rhine.[27]

There were clearly drawbacks to providing Spain with troops for cash, although the Spaniards also complained—of German princes who took subsidies and failed to deliver men.[28] Yet Spain continued to seek, and the German princes to supply, subsidy troops. The duke of Hanover, for example, negotiated another deal of this sort, as war seemed imminent between Louis XIV and Spain in 1683/84.[29] As for the elector of Brandenburg, during the Nine Years' War, his troops again served Spain in Flanders and on the Rhine, while the promised subsidies were again paid slowly. By the spring of 1692, the elector was said to be owed 400,000 escudos for 5,000 infantry and 2,000 cavalry that had been in Spanish service since the autumn of 1690.[30] Substantial numbers of the elector's troops also served in the pay of Duke Victor Amadeus II of Savoy in Piedmont, which stood between the Milanese and Louis XIV's armies. When the duke of Savoy abandoned the Grand Alliance in the summer of 1696, concluding a separate peace with Louis XIV, the elector's troops were soon defending Milan itself from a Franco-Savoyard invasion before the war in Italy was ended by the treaty of Vigevano (October 1696). The elector's troops then left Italy altogether.[31]

The elector of Brandenburg was not alone in supplying Spain with subsidy troops in these years. In 1690, Spain hoped to obtain imperial troops for Milan, from which in 1689 a regiment of Germans had been sent to Catalonia,[32] and whose governor offered 500 Germans and Burgundians for a projected invasion of France from Piedmont in 1690.[33] Since the imperial troops did not materialize, it was suggested that men might be supplied instead from Württemberg and Hesse-Kassel. The governor of the Milanese, Count Fuensalida, was unenthusiastic, claiming that the negotiation and the march of the troops would take too long.[34] However, the duke of Württemberg did supply Spain with three regiments (totaling 2,364 men) for service in the Milanese between 1690 and

1696, but these, too, were rather slowly paid.[35] As for Spanish Flanders, troops from a number of other German states served there in 1690, although the 12,000 men supplied by the duke of Hanover were dismissed at the end of the campaign by the governor, the Marquis of Gastañaga, on the grounds that he had no funds to pay them.[36] Towards the end of 1694, it was widely known that Charles II was hoping to obtain German troops to serve in Catalonia in 1695 from the bishop of Münster and the elector of Bavaria,[37] who did send some of his troops to Spain from Flanders.[38] As for the elector of Trier, in 1699, he was still seeking subsidy arrears owed for troops provided in the last war.[39]

Elector Max Emanuel and the Prospects of the Bavarian Wittelsbachs

If supplying subsidy troops to Spain for Flanders and Italy was the means whereby some German princes found their own advantage in Spain's imperial commitments and difficulties during the reign of Charles II, one princely dynasty, the Bavarian Wittelsbachs, enjoyed prospects of aggrandizement that completely dwarfed the fortunes of other princes. As one of the royal families with a claim on the Spanish monarchy, should Charles die without heirs, they would have to be compensated if they were not to pose a permanent threat to peace in Europe. Most of them emerged from the wars provoked by the Spanish succession to 1713 with substantial gains. Max Emanuel, who even aspired to replace the Austrian Habsburgs as the dominant power in Germany, did not do so well and was lucky to recover the territories he had lost in the War of the Spanish Succession (including Bavaria itself) at the end of that conflict. Nevertheless, his failure to achieve more must not be allowed to obscure the glittering prospects opening up to the Bavarian Wittelsbachs in the final decades of Habsburg Spain— prospects that could have transformed their position in Germany and altered the future course of German history.[40]

The Wittelsbach claim on the Spanish succession derived from Elector Max Emanuel's marriage to Archduchess Maria Antonia, whose maternal grandfather was Philip IV of Spain.[41] In 1684, after the loss of Luxembourg and on the occasion of Max Emanuel's marriage, an anonymous Spanish *arbitrista* suggested that in order to withstand Louis XIV in the future, Spain should create a territorial bloc dedicated to the defense of Spanish Flanders, with the Wittelsbachs at its center. It was proposed that Charles II should give Flanders to Max Emanuel and his wife, who would contribute 10,000 infantry and 1,500 to 2,000 cavalry toward a permanent force there of 40,000 (34,000 infantry and 6,000 cavalry). The arbitrista also hoped that Max Emanuel's uncle would agree to appoint the elector's brother coadjutor of the sees of Cologne and Liège, and that the Neuburg duke of Jülich-Berg, whose territories bordered the Spanish Low Countries and Cologne, might be drawn into the scheme, if the bishop of Cologne would appoint the duke's brother as his own coadjutor in the bishoprics of Münster and Hildesheim. This plan was never completely realized, then or later, but was symptomatic of the way some Spaniards looked on the German princes as the solution to the preservation of Flanders and of the extent to which Max Emanuel (both because of his marriage and the proximity of his armed forces) stood out in schemes of this sort.[42] In fact, within a decade, during the Nine Years' War, Max Emanuel was appointed governor of Spanish Flanders. This occurred at the end of 1691, after another disappointing campaign in the Low Countries and amid growing fears of revolution there if the Spanish governor were not replaced.[43] The appointment, which was backed by William III as a means to invigorate Spain's war effort in Flanders, was the first step toward the partition of the Spanish monarchy while Charles II was still alive.[44]

Max Emanuel, in fact, proved something of a disappointment in Flanders, not least because he failed to provide there the numbers of troops he had promised—although this was due in part to the fact that he was not adequately supplied with funds from Madrid.[45] However, he remained a key figure to the Spanish succession, despite the death of his wife in childbirth (1692), because their son Joseph Ferdinand was seen by many Spaniards as the solution to avoid the partition of the monarchy among the rivals for the Spanish crown. These included the powerful primate of Castile, Cardinal Portocarrero, archbishop of Toledo, and his followers in Charles II's faction-ridden court. In 1695/96, there were suggestions that the Castilian Cortes (which had not met since 1664) might assemble to declare Charles II incapable of ruling and install Joseph Ferdinand as king, under the regency of Charles's mother, and in November 1698, Charles did designate Joseph Ferdinand his heir, to wide acclaim in Spain. In the meantime, Max Emanuel tightened his hold on Flanders. He secured Charles's permission, against the opposition of both the emperor and Charles's own German queen, to introduce there another 10,000 of his own troops, and he got rid of many of the Spanish troops already in situ. Clearly, largely on the basis of the Wittelsbach role in the Spanish succession, Spanish Flanders was being incorporated into an expanding Bavarian state, making the latter a potentially formidable power in northwest Germany and the Low Countries. There was even a plan for Max Emanuel himself to come to Spain (following a suggestion that the emperor's son, Archduke Charles, go to Spain) in order to strengthen the Wittelsbach position in the developing struggle over the Spanish succession, under the guise of bringing troops for Catalonia—a project that was effectively squelched by William III (who had to supply the ships to carry the troops from Flanders). William would not agree to cooperate before the Cortes had ratified the designation of Joseph Ferdinand as Charles II's heir.[46]

Max Emanuel sought to further strengthen his hold on the Spanish Low Countries, although it was increasingly clear that the governorship of Flanders was proving a great strain for his hereditary realm, the Bavarian states, both because of his absence from the latter and because of the drain on his finances. He concluded a secret agreement with the Dutch in 1698 promising to cede the fort Santa Maria, which dominated the port of Antwerp, and to stymie the import trade of Spanish Flanders in return for Dutch recognition of his position there. Unfortunately, all these plans for Wittelsbach aggrandizement collapsed with Joseph Ferdinand's premature death in February 1699, leaving the field to the two main contenders for the Spanish succession, the French Bourbons and the Austrian Habsburgs. Max Emanuel still hoped to salvage something from the wreckage of his aspirations in the form of the Low Countries. However, the revelation of his agreement with the Dutch, the suspicion that his administration of Flanders was corrupt, and the growing anti-German sentiment in Madrid further undermined his position in Spain. Max Emanuel remained governor of Flanders, not least because Madrid was unable to pay the sums it owed him, but the favorable outlook of the recent past, which at one point seemed to include a Bavarian Wittelsbach world empire, had largely evaporated.[47]

Mariana of Neuburg and the Prospects of the Pfalz-Neuburgs

Max Emanuel's glittering prospects had been founded largely on the expectation of receiving at least something by way of satisfaction of family claims on the Spanish succession, and to a lesser degree on the troops he could contribute to the defense of Spanish

Flanders. But for another German prince, Philip William of Neuburg, duke of Jülich-Berg, and Elector Palatine (since 1685, following the death without direct male heirs of the previous elector),[48] the opportunities promised by Spain derived from a more immediate connection, the marriage of his daughter to Charles II. For princely and noble families throughout Europe, the marriages of daughters could be a crucial steppingstone to further honors, offices, territory, and wealth. The importance of women in achieving valuable alliances of this sort is evident in the marriages of Philip William's daughters: Leonora to Holy Roman Emperor Leopold, Maria Sofia to King Peter II of Portugal, and Mariana to Charles II. These marriages promised gains that not only would enable the Elector Palatine to provide for his eight sons and six daughters by Elizabeth Amalia of Hesse in ways which otherwise he could not, but also would bolster his status and that of his family and his state within both Germany and Europe.[49]

The extent to which this was the common view is evident from the general interest in whom Charles II would take as his second wife following the death of his first, Marie Louise of Orleans, in 1689, and from the divisions the issue provoked in Madrid.[50] The majority of Charles's Council of State reportedly favored the daughter of the Medici grand duke of Tuscany because of the promised dowry and the inevitable reinforcement a Tuscan alliance would mean for Spain's position in Italy. However, both Charles's mother, Mariana of Austria, and Emperor Leopold urged marriage with Mariana of Neuburg (who came with no dowry), not least because the Neuburg princesses seemed fertile, suggesting that the marriage would produce the heir that the Spanish monarchy desperately needed.[51] Charles opted for Mariana of Neuburg, who was accompanied on her journey from Germany to Madrid via Flanders and Galicia by her brother, the grand master of the Teutonic Knights. He was en route for Lisbon to negotiate the marriage of his and Mariana's recently widowed brother, and Elector Palatine since 1690, John William, to the Portuguese infanta, heiress to the crown of Portugal, and thus to secure for the Neuburgs access to the extensive Portuguese overseas trading empire.[52]

The prospects for Mariana (and her relations) as mother of the heir who would remove the problem of the Spanish succession, and perhaps even as regent, should any son succeed as a minor, are obvious enough. They help explain her many false pregnancies throughout the 1690s, the marriage in fact proving childless. As early as 1689, there were rumors that her brother, the future elector John William, would be appointed governor of the Spanish Milanese, another key appointment within the monarchy (and traditionally the preserve of the Castilian grandees).[53] The Elector Palatine clearly saw Mariana as his agent in Madrid, his letters to her requesting grants of territory, appointments (for example, of another brother, Charles Philip, as viceroy of Naples or governor of Milan), and even pictures. In fact, Mariana did not secure everything she sought for her family. Her abortive efforts to secure the governorship of the Low Countries for her brother provoked her first clash with her mother-in-law, the champion at Charles II's court of Max Emanuel of Bavaria. In 1693–94, following the death of a previous Neuburg nominee, Mariana pressed unsuccessfully for the election of her brother, the grand master of the Teutonic Knights, and following his death, of another brother, the bishop of Breslau, as bishop of Liège—against the opposition of the Wittelsbachs. Nor was Mariana able to obtain for the Elector Palatine permission to trade in the Spanish Americas, which he had sought since 1695.[54] However, these very setbacks reveal the many possibilities Spain seemed to offer, while Mariana's brothers were by no means completely disappointed. Charles Philip, for example, received the prestigious Order of the Golden Fleece in 1696. More importantly, in 1697, John William was allowed by Charles II to appoint the governor of, and to garrison, the recently recovered fortress of Luxembourg, which Max Emanuel of Bavaria had wanted for himself. Clearly, although not all of her family's many expectations were satisfied, Mariana did exploit her position to their benefit—and to the disadvantage of some Spaniards (particularly those outside of the faction she promptly built up) who would normally have expected to enjoy the royal patronage that she diverted to her relations and court favorites.[55]

Prince George of Hesse-Darmstadt

The long-term prospects of the Neuburgs depended upon Mariana's ability to influence (as queen and prospective queen dowager, and perhaps even regent) the distribution of the extensive patronage still at the disposal of the Spanish king. For yet another German prince who found his fortune in Spain in the 1690s, the foundation of success was different again. Prince George of Hesse-Darmstadt, younger brother of Ernst Ludwig, landgrave of Hesse-Darmstadt, and a cousin of Mariana of Neuburg, was typical of generations of younger sons of lesser princes throughout Europe who sought their fortune in the military service of one of the greater princes, including both the emperor and the king of Spain. In 1695, George led the German troops sent by the emperor from Italy to Catalonia.[56] There he distinguished himself in the defense of Barcelona—which was later successfully besieged by the French in 1697, at the end of the Nine Years' War—and revealed an awareness of Catalan political sensitivities by approaching the *Generalitat* or *Diputació* (the standing committee of the Catalan Cortes), and not Madrid, with a request to levy another 5,000 men for Barcelona's defense. Following the conclusion of the peace of Rijswijk in 1697, which ended the war, George was rewarded by Charles II for his service in Catalonia with promotion to grandee first class (the most senior rank in the Spanish nobility), the Order of the Golden Fleece, and a Guards regiment.[57]

Last, but by no means least, and with the support of Mariana, George was appointed viceroy of Catalonia, the Catalans having vetoed Charles II's initial appointment of the Conde de Corzana (who was unpopular with the Catalans for his part in the siege of 1697).[58] As in Flanders, a German prince had effectively inserted himself into one of imperial Spain's most important viceroyalties and, as a supporter of the Habsburgs' claim to the Spanish succession, could be expected to use his influence on their behalf. George was soon using his military patronage in Catalonia to appoint Germans, often to replace Spaniards. This caused some difficulties with both the Diputació, which preferred to see Catalans appointed, and the Council of State in Madrid, which suspected George of corruption and deliberately kept him short of funds. These difficulties with Madrid were also related to the larger factional struggles at Charles II's court. Indeed, in the spring of 1698, George considered using his troops in a military coup to "liberate" Mariana and Charles from Portocarrero's faction and to exile the cardinal himself to Spain's African outpost at Oran.[59]

George's difficulties with the politically sensitive Catalans continued in the interval between the death of Charles II and the arrival of the first Bourbon king of Spain, Philip V, in 1700—the Catalans questioning the viceroy's right to function as representative of the monarch during an interregnum. Despite being promptly dismissed as an Austrian Habsburg sympathizer by Philip V, the prince was able to exploit his position and contacts in Catalonia to further Habsburg interests. Before leaving Barcelona, he issued a manifesto appealing to Catalan separatism on behalf of the Habsburg emperor in the succession struggle. Subsequently, as imperial envoy at Lisbon and an acknowledged expert on Spanish affairs,

George shared in the planning and execution of the abortive allied expedition against Cadiz (1702) and the more successful attempt on Gibraltar (1704). He also continued to exploit his Spanish contacts in the hope of igniting an anti-Bourbon revolt, particularly in eastern Spain. Among his correspondents was the Catalan economist, historian, and publicist Narciso Feliu de la Penya. Prince George's death—he died of his wounds at the allied conquest of Barcelona in 1705—was a blow to the Austrian cause because he was widely felt to be the only one of the Habsburgs who was at all liked in Spain.[60]

Anti-German Sentiment in Spain

Although Prince George of Hesse-Darmstadt established a rapport with at least some Catalans, exploiting their sensitivity to suspected infringements of their constitutional freedoms by Madrid, most of the Germans who flocked to Spain in the 1690s achieved the opposite, alienating Spaniards by their greed and their diversion of pensions, honors, and other prizes of the patronage system away from its traditional Spanish recipients. The main offenders were Mariana's secretary, Henry Wiser, younger son of the chancellor of the Palatinate, who had originally accompanied Mariana's sister to Lisbon, and who was known in Spain as *el Cojo* (the lame), and Mariana's *camarera mayor*, Gertrudis Maria Josefa Bohl von Gutenberg, dowager Countess of Berlepsch (the widow of a member of the lesser nobility of Hesse), who was popularly known by a Hispanicized version of her name as *la Perdíz* (the partridge). Their acquisitiveness on behalf of themselves, their friends, and their relations seemed to know no bounds. On one typical occasion, Wiser sought from the Councils of Finance and Castile a ruling against the farmer of the tobacco revenues who had promised Wiser 6,000 doubloons if the farm was continued, but had not paid up; while in 1696 (after the extent of mourning for Charles II's recently deceased mother was reduced on the grounds of the need for economy), Mariana secured for Berlepsch a fief in the kingdom of Naples valued at 12,000 escudos and additional sums.[61]

Inevitably, there was growing hostility in Madrid toward Mariana's German entourage. Such anti-German sentiment was not entirely new. During Charles II's minority, his illegitimate half-brother Don Juan had mobilized similar feeling to oust his own political rival, the Austrian Jesuit confessor Nithard, upon whom Charles's mother, the regent, largely depended—and whom she had promoted to inquisitor general.[62] But Nithard was an isolated individual, whereas in the 1690s, the Germans, although still relatively few in number, were more numerous and visible. The extent of anti-German feeling is suggested by Berlepsch in a letter to the Elector Palatine in July 1697. Reporting on Prince George of Hesse-Darmstadt's request to the Diputació for troops for the defense of Catalonia, which had offended royal ministers in Madrid, she noted, "But he's a German, and the Spaniards would not tolerate even Jesus Christ if he were one."[63] That this anti-German sentiment comprised many different strands is evident from the insulting declaration in 1698 to Mariana of one of her ladies in waiting, the Countess of Benavente. According to the latter, she respected Mariana only as the consort of her king, Charles II, not as Princess Palatine, since Mariana's lineage was inferior to her own. Spanish grandees, she declared, were far superior to German electoral princes. Berlepsch's attempt to mediate between the two women only provoked the countess to abuse her as well.[64]

Whatever its sources, this anti-German sentiment had important political consequences in Madrid. A session of the Council of State in December 1694, called to discuss the funding of Spain's war effort, culminated in a call for the expulsion of the Germans around Mariana. The Count of Monterrey thought this as necessary as had been the expulsion of the *moriscos* (christianized Moors) in 1609.[65] In January 1695, Cardinal Portocarrero echoed this demand, claiming that Mariana's Germans were corrupting the administration of justice and undermining relations between the king and his subjects. Indeed, satirical verses, posters, "prophecies," and other expressions of hostility toward Mariana and her German entourage were rife, suggesting that, even if the (Castilian) Cortes did not assemble, public opinion found channels for the expression of political resentments.[66] In February 1695, partly to placate that opinion before the introduction of new tax-raising measures to finance Spain's effort in the Nine Years' War, the grandees achieved the expulsion of Wiser, who was sent (with many parting gifts) as Charles II's envoy to one of Mariana's brothers-in-law, the Duke of Parma.[67] The Countess of Berlepsch was expelled in 1700, following the triumph of Portocarrero's faction. But she, too, left with money and honors, including the promise of the prestigious Order of the Golden Fleece for the future husband of her niece.[68] With the departure of the most visibly grasping Germans, the resentment they had provoked diminished. Nevertheless, anti-German sentiment and Mariana's support of the Austrian Habsburgs in the struggle for the succession,[69] helped ensure that, during the War of the Spanish Succession, Spain—and above all Castile—would prefer the French Bourbons to the Austrian Habsburgs, who were also handicapped by their reliance on Protestant German, English, and Dutch troops in that struggle.[70]

Conclusion

It has been impossible to address every aspect of relations between Spain and Germany in the later seventeenth century. Little has been said, for example, about economic links, although in 1667 Spain sent an unprecedentedly high volume of wool (still a major Spanish export) to Hamburg, more than to any other destination.[71] More could also be said about the way Madrid continued to subsidize the Austrian Habsburgs,[72] about Madrid's exploitation of the revival of the emperor's authority within the empire (above all in Italy) in the 1690s,[73] and about the degree to which that revival also made Charles II (like any German or Italian prince of the empire) and his ministers anxious (again, particularly about Spanish power and influence in Italy).[74] But enough has been said to show that Spain's determination to remain a great power during the reign of the last Habsburg had important implications for Germany. A weaker Spain now sought to represent itself as a German power in order to secure the support of the German states against Louis XIV, and had some success with many princes (including the electors of Bavaria, Brandenburg, and Trier) who had once looked to France as a protector against an overmighty Spain.

At the same time, Spain's difficulties and still considerable resources also offered enormous opportunities. For the Bavarian Wittelsbachs, helping Spain provided the chance of realizing, in part at least, their new family claims on the Spanish monarchy in a way that would have transformed their state beyond anything conceivable within the scope of its existing resources. For the Elector Palatine's family, the marriage of a daughter and sister to the king of Spain held out prospects of a different kind—access to the still extensive and invaluable (for a German prince) patronage dispensed by the Spanish monarch—that might also in the longer term have transformed their fortunes both in Germany and in Europe as a whole. In some respects, indeed, Madrid witnessed in the 1690s a struggle between these two German princely houses for what Spain had to offer. For other Germans, too, including that archetypal younger son, Prince George of Hesse-Darmstadt, and those who followed Mariana of Neuburg to Madrid, Spain in the

1690s offered prestigious prizes. But, although Spanish resentment of foreigners having access to the wealth of the monarchy was by no means new, this unusual German influx provoked an anti-German feeling, which initially, at least, distinguished between Max Emanuel, or rather his son, of Habsburg descent and the Germans from the Palatinate. This sentiment ultimately contributed to the defeat of the Austrian Habsburgs in the War of the Spanish Succession, limiting the role of Germans in Spanish affairs. When Spain subsequently lost its European territories after that war and Philip V demonstrated a preference for recovering Spain's former Italian dominions rather than those in the Low Countries and the Rhineland, a period of intense German involvement in Spanish politics and culture was brought to a close.[75]

Notes

1. I wish to thank Dr. Derek McKay of the London School of Economics for his comments on an earlier draft of this paper. Among the most important studies of the reign, particularly for its account of court politics, is the one by Duque de Maura (i.e., Don Gabriel Maura y Gamazo, created first duke of Maura in 1930 in honor of his father, the Conservative politician Antonio Maura), *Vida y reinado de Carlos II* (Madrid, 1942), recently reissued in one volume, ed. P. Gimferrer (Madrid, 1990), which is the edition used in the present study. This work contains no references (Maura's notes were burnt, by "Reds," during the Civil War) but was well founded: the Duque de Maura also wrote *Carlos II y su corte* (Madrid, 1911–15), dealing with the period 1661–79, and, with Adalbert of Bavaria, coedited the important five-volume collection of state and other papers from Charles II's reign, *Documentos inéditos referentes a las postrimerías de la Casa de Austria* (Madrid, 1927–35), including the correspondence of some of the German princes with their agents in Madrid. Maura, whose research dated from much earlier, clearly found Franco's Spain, which encouraged the study of Spain's imperial past, very sympathetic. His collaboration with Adalbert of Bavaria suggests that the German presence in Charles II's Spain had already attracted the interest of some German historians. In 1940, the Hispanophile Ludwig Pfandl's *Karl II.* was published in Berlin. It was later published in Spain as *Carlos II* (Madrid, 1947). Pfandl was criticized by Maura for not having exhausted the published or manuscript sources for Charles II's reign, and (along with all German and French historians) for not fully understanding the Spanish succession or, indeed, Spain itself, but without specifying exactly why; see *Vida y reinado de Carlos II*, p. 22. However, Pfandl's work remains valuable, not least as a check on that of Maura. It would be tempting, but stretching things, to see this German-Spanish interaction as symptomatic of the political affinities between Franco's Spain and Hitler's Germany. The best recent study of Carlos II's Spain, H. Kamen's *Spain*

in the Later Seventeenth Century, 1665–1700 (London, 1980), relies greatly on Maura's account of the politics of the reign.
2. The best general account of international relations in this era is to be found in D. McKay and H. M. Scott, *The Rise of the Great Powers, 1648–1815* (London, 1983). For Spain's role, cf. R. Stradling, *Europe and the Decline of Spain, 1580–1720* (London, 1981).
3. In 1693, following the grant of the so-called "royal treatment" to the ambassadors in Madrid of Charles II's ally, Duke Victor Amadeus II of Savoy, the latter's Italian rival, the grand duke of Tuscany, sought to mobilize against it the ministers of the German electors, those other great competitors of the Dukes of Savoy in the struggle for status; Wiser to Elector Palatine, 24 December 1693, in *Documentos inéditos*, vol. 2, p. 154.
4. H. Kamen, *The War of Succession in Spain, 1700–1715* (London, 1969), p. 4.
5. The works of Henry Kamen are informed by a view of this sort; cf. his *Spain, 1469–1714: A Society of Conflict*, 2nd ed. (London, 1991), p. 255ff., for one aspect of this, the nostalgic view of the pre-imperial and pre-Habsburg era of the Catholic monarchs, Ferdinand and Isabella.
6. Alexander Stanhope to Earl of Nottingham, 9 May 1691, Madrid, Public Record Office/State Papers (henceforth SP) 84 (Spain)/73, f. 31.
7. J. I. Israel, *The Dutch Republic: Its Rise, Greatness and Fall, 1477–1806* (Oxford, 1995), p. 739ff.
8. Stradling, *Europe and the Decline of Spain*, pp. 156–157, 181.
9. *London Gazette*, no. 2383, news dated The Hague, 2 September 1689.
10. Stanhope to Nottingham, 9 January 1692, Madrid, SP 94/73 f. 51.
11. Cf. Israel, *The Dutch Republic*, p. 739ff., for the contribution of the Army of Flanders to the allied forces in Flanders in the 1690s. Israel's focus on "effectives" may exaggerate the decline and the disparity, while all army figures in this period must be treated with caution.
12. Many of these issues are discussed in C. Storrs, "The Army of Lombardy and the Resilience of Spanish Power in Italy in the Reign of Carlos II, 1665–1700 (Part One)," *War in History*, vol. 4, no. 4 (1997), p. 371ff.
13. In December 1683, the elector of Trier asked the governor of the Low Countries to order his subordinates not to levy contributions in the Elector's territories in the current conflict between Charles II and Louis XIV; see A. Sprunck, "Die Trierer Kurfürsten Karl Kaspar von der Leyen und Johann Hugo von Oberseck und die Statthalter der Spanischen Niederlande von 1675 bis 1700," *Rheinische Vierteljahrsblätter*, vol. 32 (1968), p. 318ff. This article is, in effect, a detailed calendar of the correspondence between successive electors of Trier and successive governors of the Spanish Low Countries in this period, contained in the Archives Générales du Royaume, in Brussels. The author wishes to thank Dr. Peter Wilson of the University of Newcastle upon Tyne for drawing this to his attention and supplying a copy.
14. G. Parker, *The Army of Flanders and the Spanish Road, 1567–1659* (Cambridge, Mass., 1972), p. 251. For the investiture of successive Spanish monarchs with the Low Countries by the emperor in the sixteenth and seventeenth centuries, see that of Charles II in 1670, in H. Lonchay et al., eds., *Correspondance de la Cour d'Espagne* (Brussels, 1935), vol. 5, pp. 91–92.
15. R. G. Asch, *The Thirty Years' War: The Holy Roman Empire and Europe, 1618–1648* (London, 1997), pp. 110–111.
16. The Burgundian Circle was largely exempt, for example, from the subsidy known as the Roman Months, but Spain had contributed troops to the

imperial army fighting the Turks in 1664 (and made much of this fact in the 1667/68 negotiations).
17. Cf. R. Pillorget, "Louis XIV and the Electorate of Trier, 1652–1676," in *Louis XIV and Europe*, ed. R. M. Hatton (London, 1976), p. 115ff.
18. These paragraphs draw heavily upon J. Schillinger, "La Franche-Comté et les enjeux diplomatiques Européens au XVIIIe [sic] siècle: Les Deputés du Cercle de Bourgogne à la Diète de Ratisbonne, 1667–1674," *Revue d'histoire moderne et contemporaine*, vol. 39, no. 4 (October–December 1992), p. 531ff., although the interpretive emphasis is largely my own.
19. R. Wines, "The Imperial Circles, Princely Diplomacy and Imperial Reform, 1681–1714," *Journal of Modern History*, vol 39 (1967), p. 1ff. (and p. 5, note 20 for the king of Spain as prince of the Burgundian Circle until 1713).
20. S. Baxter, *William III* (London, 1966), pp. 213–214.
21. Charles's minister at Regensburg was a useful source of intelligence regarding discussions of peacemaking at the Diet; Neuveforge to Borgomanero, 21 August 1693, Regensburg, copy, SP 80/17 f. 328.
22. Charles II to Max Emanuel, 5 July 1697; see Lonchay, *Correspondance de la Cour d'Espagne*, vol. 5, p. 657.
23. P. H. Wilson, *War, State and Society in Württemberg, 1677–1793* (Cambridge, Mass., 1994), p. 85.
24. Maura, *Vida y reinado de Carlos II*, p. 134.
25. Cf. Baxter, *William III*, pp. 123, 140; M. Garzón Pareja, *La hacienda de Carlos II* (Madrid, 1981), pp. 196–197; and, for Trier, Sprunck, "Die Trierer Kurfürsten," p. 318ff.
26. Cf. D. McKay, "Small Power Diplomacy in the Age of Louis XIV: The Foreign Policy of the Great Elector during the 1660s and 1670s," in *Royal and Republican Sovereignty in Early Modern Europe: Essays in Memory of Ragnhild Hatton*, ed. R. Oresko, G. C. Gibbs, and H. M. Scott (Cambridge, Mass., 1997), p. 188ff.
27. Maura, *Vida y reinado de Carlos II*, p. 272; Pfandl, *Carlos II*, p. 229ff.; E. Opgenoorth, *Friedrich Wilhelm, der Große Kurfürst von Brandenburg* (Göttingen, 1971–78), vol. 2; Garzón Pareja, *La hacienda de Carlos II*, pp. 191, 196, and 209. Cf. SP 84/21 f. 21 for Spanish anxiety about the impact of the Ostend episode on the prince of Parma.
28. Cf. the consulta of the Council of State, February 1684; Stradling, *Europe and the Decline of Spain*, pp. 181–182.
29. Baxter, *William III*, p. 188.
30. Cf. de la Tour to Victor Amadeus, 25 April 1692, The Hague, Archivio di Stato, Torino (henceforth AST)/Letter Ministri (LM)/Olanda m. 2.
31. Cf. C. Storrs, *Diplomatic Relations between Victor Amadeus II of Savoy and William III, 1690–96*, Ph.D. diss. (University of London, 1990), passim.
32. British Library, Egerton collection, 328 f. 25.
33. Cf. the protest of Albert van der Meer (Dutch commissary in Piedmont), 1690, AST/Negoziazioni/Olanda m. 1/8.
34. Consulta of Council of State, 9 May 1690, Archivo General de Simancas [henceforth AGS], Estado, 3411/87. Not surprisingly, Fuensalida preferred the widely admired Spanish troops.
35. Wilson, *War, State and Society in Württemberg*, pp. 114–115. According to the Savoyard minister in Madrid in late 1691, Charles II intended to send 300,000 escudos to Milan to pay the Württemberg troops there, following representations from his allies; Operti to Victor Amadeus, 6 December 1691, Madrid, AST/LM/Spagna m. 35. A review of the army of Lombardy in November

1695 revealed three regiments of Germans, totaling 2,447 men, in a total force of 12,198 men; *Relación*, AGS/Estado/3423.
36. Terriesi to Grand Duke of Tuscany, 22 August 1690, London, Add. Mss. f. 277 (on Spain's desperate efforts to pay its subsidy troops in Flanders); Bishop of Paderborn to his minister at The Hague, 17 November 1690, Neuhaus, SP 84/222 (on departure from Spanish Flanders of Swedish, Hanoverian, Wolfenbüttel and Celle troops); de la Tour to Victor Amadeus, 1 December 1690, London, AST/LM/ Inghilterra m. 8. Following a French incursion, levying substantial sums in contributions, de la Tour observed that these might have paid the Hanoverians; idem, 19 January 1691, The Hague, AST/LM/Olanda m. 1.
37. Cf. van der Meer to Fagel, 10 September 1694, Turin, Algemeen Rijks Archief, The Hague/Staten Generaal/8644/144; and Stanhope to the Earl of Galway, 2 December 1694, Madrid, Kent Record Office [henceforth Kent RO], U1590 015/4.
38. Maura, *Vida y reinado de Carlos II*, p. 445ff. A Bavarian regiment was still stationed in Catalonia in 1700; cf. *Historia de España Menéndez Pidal*, vol. 28: *La transición del siglo XVII al XVIII: Entre la Decadencia y la Reconstrucción*, ed. P. Molas Ribalta (Madrid, 1994), p. 361.
39. Sprunck, "Die Trierer Kurfürsten," p. 329.
40. Generally, cf. L. Hüttl, *Max Emanuel, der Blaue Kurfürst (1679–1726): Eine politische Biographie* (Munich, 1976).
41. Cf. family tree of claimants to the Spanish succession in H. Kamen, *Spain in the Later Seventeenth Century*, p. 385.
42. The abortive scheme is outlined in Maura, *Vida y reinado de Carlos II*, pp. 311–312.
43. Cf. de la Tour to Saint Thomas, 4 May 1691, The Hague, AST/LM/Olanda, m. 1.
44. Maura, *Vida y reinado de Carlos II*, p. 399. The Low Countries had, from 1598, been briefly held as an independent sovereignty by Philip II's daughter, the Infanta Isabella and her husband.
45. In the winter of 1695/96, Max Emanuel was offering some of his regiments to other princes since his Spanish subsidy was unpaid and he could not now afford all the troops in his pay; Saint Thomas to de la Tour, 3 December 1695, Turin, AST/LM/Olanda m. 4.
46. Maura, *Vida y reinado de Carlos II*, pp. 412, 437, 500–501, 541–542, 547; Pfandl, *Carlos II*, pp. 349–350.
47. Maura, *Vida y reinado de Carlos II*, pp. 552–553, 557, 575–577; Pfandl, *Carlos II*, pp. 350–351.
48. Maura, *Vida y reinado de Carlos II*, p. 319.
49. For the family of the Elector Palatine, cf. Pfandl, *Carlos II*, p. 253ff; and for Mariana, Adalbert of Bavaria, *Mariana de Neoburgo, Reina de España* (Madrid, 1938).
50. Maura, *Vida y reinado de Carlos II*, p. 349.
51. Hopes of the new queen's fertility were expressed in a contemporary rhyme, "Razones para esperar que la reina nuestra senora sea fecunda," in *Satíras políticas de la España moderna*, vol. 1, ed. T. Egido (Madrid, 1973), p. 198, no. 47.
52. Terriesi to Grand Duke of Tuscany, 11 April 1689, London, Add. Mss. 25,378 f. 199; same to Bassetti, 15 July 1689, London, Add. 25,378 f. 217. Cf. consulta of Council of State, 16 May 1689 regarding orders for Borgomanero, on the journey of the new queen from Vienna; in *Documentos inéditos*, vol. 1, p. 101ff.
53. Consul Kirk to Duke of Shrewsbury, 5 November 1689, Genoa, SP 79/3 f. 83. 54 Pfandl, *Carlos II*, p. 291; Maura, *Vida y reinado de Carlos II*, pp. 420ff., 448–449, 452, 506–507, 563. Since the king of Portugal was rewarded (for supplying troops for

the defense of Spain's outposts in North Africa in 1695) with privileged access at Buenos Aires, the Elector Palatine fixed his attention on Darien (Panama). Unfortunately, this was the site of an intrusive Scots colonization scheme between 1698 and 1700. By the time Spain had recovered Darien, the throne had passed to Philip V, extinguishing Mariana's influence. See C. Storrs, "Disaster at Darien (1698–1700)?" *European History Quarterly*, vol. 29 (1999), p. 5ff.
55. Maura, *Vida y reinado de Carlos II*, pp. 448, 494–495, 507.
56. During the 1695 campaign, George sought satisfaction from the Spanish court as commander of the imperial troops, in a precedence quarrel with Neapolitan troops who were also serving in Catalonia; Stanhope to Galway, 11 August 1695, Madrid, Kent RO, U1590/015/4.
57. Maura, *Vida y reinado de Carlos II*, pp. 475–476, 490. De Soto de Clonard, *Historia Organica de las Armas de Infantería y Caballería Española desde la Creación del Ejercito Permanente hasta el Dia* (Madrid, 1851–62), vol. 15, p. 5ff. (This invaluable history of the Spanish army, based on archival sources, contains many extremely useful regimental histories.) There is no good modern study of Prince George, but cf. H. Kunzel, *Das Leben und der Briefwechsel des Landgrafen Georg von Hessen-Darmstadt* (London and Friedberg, 1859) and D. Francis, "Prince George of Hesse-Darmstadt and the Plans for the Expedition to Spain of 1702," *Bulletin of the Institute of Historical Research*, vol. 42 (1969), p. 58ff.
58. A. Rodriguez Villa, *Don Diego Hurtado de Mendoza y Sandoval, Conde de la Corzana* (Madrid, 1907), p. 201; *Historia de España Menéndez Pidal*, vol. 28, p. 357. The emperor was pressing Prince George's promotion to viceroy in the summer of 1695; Stanhope to Galway, 11 August 1695, Madrid, Kent RO, U1590/015/4.
59. Maura, *Vida y reinado de Carlos II*, p. 508ff.
60. *Historia de España Menéndez Pidal*, vol. 28, pp. 311, 321, 334 ff., 359ff.; Francis, "Prince George," passim. According to D. Francis, *The Methuens and Portugal, 1691–1708* (Cambridge, Mass., 1966), p. 142, George argued against a bombardment of Cadiz in 1702 on the grounds that it would alienate potential Spanish supporters. Cf. ibid., p. 300, for the implications of the prince's death. For Feliu de la Penya, author of *Fénix de Cataluña* (1683), cf. Kamen, *Spain in the Later Seventeenth Century*, p. 81ff.
61. Maura, *Vida y reinado de Carlos II*, pp. 435–436, 470; Pfandl, *Carlos II*, p. 322ff.; Garzón Pareja, *La hacienda de Carlos II*, pp. 155–156, 165. The farmer of the tobacco tax had had to pay much more (after competitive bidding) than in previous years to retain his farm and believed Wiser did not deserve his commission. Berlepsch's son secured a Spanish noble heiress and was admitted to the prestigious Order of Santiago. He also received a valuable *encomienda* of the order.
62. For verses calling for Nithard's return to Germany, 1669, cf. *Satíras políticas de la España moderna*, p. 35.
63. Maura, *Vida y reinado de Carlos II*, p. 475.
64. Ibid., pp. 522–523.
65. Between 1609 and 1614, three hundred thousand (of a total of 320,000) moriscos were expelled from mainland Spain; see Kamen, *Spain 1469–1714*, p. 221. See also Maura, *Vida y reinado de Carlos II*, pp. 436–437; Kamen, *Spain in the Later Seventeenth Century*, p. 388; *Historia de España Menéndez Pidal*, vol. 28, p. 239; Pfandl, *Carlos II*, p. 322ff. The duke of Montalto cited earlier consultas calling for the expulsion of not only Nithard but also—linking the present agitation to the earlier Comunero revolt (1520–22) with its xenophobic anti-Flemish (and

anti-German) undertones—of Charles V's minister, Guillaume de Croy, lord of Chièvres. Some additional details are contained in the report of the French adventuress and agent, the marchioness of Gudannes, 23 December 1694, Madrid. This (and her other reports from Madrid between 1693 and 1695) was published by A. Marin in *Revue Hispanique*, vol. 47 (1919), here p. 492.

66. Maura, *Vida y reinado de Carlos II*, p. 437; and Pfandl, *Carlos II*, p. 326. In May 1693, the Elector Palatine's minister in Madrid, informing his master of these satires, observed that the freedom with which the monarchs themselves were discussed was unheard of, and that no German prince would tolerate half of what was allowed in Madrid; *Documentos inéditos*, vol. 3, p. 118. This suggests, of course, yet another fruitful sphere for research into Spanish-German relations (notably mutual perceptions) in this era.
67. Pfandl, *Carlos II*, p. 327ff.; Garzón Pareja, *La hacienda de Carlos II*, p. 165. There was talk of his representing Charles II at the Imperial Diet at Regensburg; Maura, *Vida y reinado de Carlos II*, pp. 442–443.
68. Pfandl, *Carlos II*, p. 364ff.; Maura, *Vida y reinado de Carlos II*, p. 618; Garzón Pareja, *La hacienda de Carlos II*, p. 157.
69. Maura, *Vida y reinado de Carlos II*, pp. 645–646.
70. Cf. María Teresa Pérez Picazo, *La Publicistica española en la Guerra de Sucesión* (Madrid, 1966), passim. Unfortunately, I have been unable, due to the prolonged temporary inaccessibility of some of the holdings of the National Library of Scotland, Edinburgh, to consult the Spanish pamphlets from the War of the Spanish Succession in its rich Astorga Collection.
71. Cf. C. R. and W. Phillips, *Spain's Golden Fleece: Wool Production and the Wool Trade from the Middle Ages to the Nineteenth Century* (Baltimore, Md., 1997), p. 263.
72. Spain subsidized the emperor's war against the Turks, although a memorialist of 1687 urged that this could be done equally well, and without remitting money to Germany, by a strong Spanish Mediterranean fleet. The memorial is in Garzón Pareja, *La hacienda de Carlos II*, p. 443ff.
73. Inevitably, the emperor bombarded Madrid with requests for subsidies to support his troops in Italy, which the Italian states could not (or would not) do; cf. consulta of Council of State, 25 April 1693, AGS/Estado/3083, on a recent report from Borgomanero.
74. Cf. consulta of 2 August 1694 on reports from Vienna of Borgomanero regarding imperial ambitions in North Italy, about which he had been ordered to find more earlier that year, AGS/Estado/3937.
75. Cf. P. Molas Ribalta, *Manual de Historia de España*, vol. 3: *Edad Moderna, 1474–1808* (Madrid, 1989); and W. Coxe, *Memoirs of the Kings of Spain of the House of Bourbon*, 2nd ed. (London, 1815), vol. 2. The abortive attempt of Philip V and his first queen, Marie Louise of Savoy, during the Utrecht peace negotiations (1712–13), outlined in ibid., vol. 2, p. 155ff., to secure an independent sovereignty (that of the Duchy of Limburg) in the former Spanish Low Countries for their favorite, the Princess des Ursins, represents the last real effort to retain a Spanish presence of sorts in the vicinity of the Lower Rhine. However, the Bourbon kings of Spain continued to maintain distinct Walloon regiments and to attract members of the Flemish elite into their (military) service; see G. Desdevises du Dezert, *L'Espagne de l'Ancien Régime*, 3 vols. (Paris, 1897–1904), recently issued in one volume in Spanish translation (the edition used here) as *La España del Antiguo Régimen* (Madrid, 1989), p. 496.

Part II

FROM THE ENLIGHTENMENT TO THE MODERN IMAGINATION

The Motifs of Incest and Fratricide in Friedrich Schiller's *The Bride of Messina* and Their Possible Calderonian Sources

Henry W. Sullivan

It is a topos of comparative literature to remark that the German romantics—either in the revolutionary or the reactionary aspects of their literary program for the future—lionized the last of the great Golden Age Spanish playwrights, Pedro Calderón de la Barca (1600–1681). As a major eighteenth-century German writer who kept the early romantics at a safe but cordial distance, Friedrich Schiller (1759–1805) was well aware of the Jena school's manifesto of 1798, as well as of their new ideas and preferences for a Catholicizing and medievalizing art. Schiller's premature death in 1805 put an end to any franker involvement with the romantic program on his part, either for it or against it; however, as studies by Petersen, Tiemann, Rehm, Bertrand, von Wiese, Sullivan, Paulin, and Lamport have shown, Schiller had definitely become acquainted with Calderón toward the end of his life.[1] He only wished that Goethe and Schiller himself had come to know the Spanish dramatist much earlier, thus, in Schiller's own phrase, "having spared ourselves many a blunder [*Fehlgriff*]."[2]

The question that interests me for the purposes of this investigation, however, is not whether Schiller was actually acquainted with Calderón. He was. The question is, rather, what did he know of Calderón and when did he know it? In particular, I wish to inquire into Schiller's possible indebtedness to the inspiration of Calderón in one of his last plays, *The Bride of Messina*, a classicizing verse tragedy composed between 1802 and 1803. For reasons that I hope will become clear, this tragedy from the Weimar period bears a striking resemblance to Calderón's own youthful saints-and-sinners drama entitled *La devoción de la cruz* (Devotion to the Cross). Calderón's Spanish play of 1624–25 was a kind of German Sturm und Drang tragedy before its time, and was taken up mightily by Ludwig Tieck, the two Schlegels, the philosopher Schelling, and many others at the turn of the eighteenth century. This possible direct use of Calderón as a model for one of Schiller's own plays is a connection that no critic, to my knowledge, has ever previously suggested.

The triangular sibling relationship at the heart of each drama is, with minor variations, the same: Calderón's incestuous and fratricidal tragedy contains two brothers (Lisardo and Eusebio) at odds, not aware that they are brothers, and a sister (Julia) who loves, and is loved by, her brother Eusebio, unaware that she and he are fraternal twins. Eusebio kills his elder brother Lisardo in a duel. In the dénouement, the younger son Eusebio dies by his father's hand. Schiller's incestuous and fratricidal tragedy also contains two brothers (Don Manuel and Don Cesar) at odds, who *are* aware that they are brothers, and a sister (Beatrice), who is loved by both brothers, each unaware that they love the same girl and also unaware that she is their sister. Cesar kills his elder brother Manuel in an impulsive stabbing. In this tragedy's dénouement, the younger son Cesar dies by his own hand.

Before coming to consider any further parallels and resemblances between the two works, or any speculation as to the whys and wherefores of Schiller's interest in the Spanish model—or, indeed, before assuming any definite connection between the two works at all—it is necessary to look at the historical context of the introduction of Calderón's *Devotion to the Cross* into early romantic Germany. Is there sufficient circumstantial evidence to suggest that Schiller could have known the Spanish work in question, possibly or probably in a German translation, during the *Entstehungsgeschichte*, or creation, of his own tragedy? More specifically, since *The Bride of Messina* was written in the latter part of 1802 and early part of 1803—its first performance at Weimar falling on 19 March 1803—was the text of *Devotion to the Cross* available to Schiller in one form or another within that framework of time?

The answer here must be a resounding "yes." Ludwig Tieck, the two Schlegels, the von Humboldt brothers, and the Grimm brothers had all come to know Spanish literature firsthand during their undergraduate days at the University of Göttingen in the late 1780s and early 1790s. Tieck was so forcibly struck by *Devotion to the Cross* in 1798, especially in its use of the incest motif, that he brought the play to the attention of August Wilhelm Schlegel. At first lukewarm toward Tieck's discovery, Schlegel suddenly turned from his translations of Shakespeare to the translation of Calderón in 1801, and his first German samples were available by the summer and autumn of 1802. Completed by September 1802, *Devotion to the Cross* was eventually printed in Berlin, along with *El mayor encanto amor* (Love, the Greatest Enchantment) and *La banda y la flor* (The Scarf and the Flower), in time for the Easter fair of 1803 as volume one of Schlegel's *Spanisches Theater*.[3]

The question now arises: did Schiller have prior knowledge of, or access to, Schlegel's translation of *Devotion to the Cross*, shortly after the manuscript was completed in September 1802, and at the period when *The Bride of Messina* had begun to take shape in his imagination from July of that same year? Or had he, via Weimar correspondence or conversations with Goethe and his circle, come to know the plot or gist of *Devotion to the Cross* even before July 1802, the moment of the play's initial conception, such that the basic idea of Calderón's precocious "destiny drama" (*Schicksalstragödie*) actually became the starting point for *The Bride of Messina*?

A first important sidelight on this question is provided by the philosopher Friedrich Wilhelm Joseph von Schelling (1775–1854). He had himself received a copy of the Schlegelian manuscript as early as October 1802, a mere month after its completion. In an enthusiastic letter of 21 October 1802, he wrote to A. W. Schlegel, "the play by Calderón has thrown me into a high delight and a profound wonderment. It is a completely new viewpoint and opens up, more than I can find the words to say, perspectives into the greatness of which romantic poetry is capable."[4] If he had ever known a play, Schelling went on, which is all matter and form, then it is this one. Calderón's work converts both into absolute transparency. The playwright's intention is completely fused in the object, so that if such involuntary revelation of inner intentions may be called naiveté, then Calderón's poem is—according to Schelling—one of the most "naive" that one may read. One sees into the depths of the playwright's soul; Calderón himself speaks his mind and views repeatedly.[5]

Schelling's reference here to "naive" poetry obviously draws on Schiller's own typological distinction in his theoretical essay of 1795–96, "Über naive und sentimentalische Dichtung" (Concerning Naive and Reflective Poetry).[6] According to Schiller, naive poets were at one with nature, neither separated from it nor longing to return to it. Typically, the Greeks were naive and tended to realism, while the naive sense of an indivisibility of nature was also characteristic of Goethe's poetry. Schiller, by contrast, saw himself in the reflective "sentimental" and idealistic category. This Schillerian distinction explains the thrust of Schelling's remark about the naive poet's fusion of matter and form into absolute transparency, and his fusion of dramatic intention in the object: they are both features of an intact and ingenuous (or "naive") perception concerning the indivisibility of poetry and nature that the philosopher delightedly descried in Calderón's Christian destiny drama. This would also rank Calderón, according to the Schelling-Schiller typology, with the ancient Greeks, rather than with modern dramatic poets such as Shakespeare, for example. This alignment of Calderón with the ancient Greek dramatists is extremely pertinent, as we shall see.

A second important sidelight on the same question is provided by Goethe. On 28 January 1804, just over ten months after the Weimar premiere of *The Bride of Messina*, Goethe sent Schiller a manuscript of A. W. Schlegel's new translation of Calderón's specifically Christian martyr-tragedy *El príncipe constante* (The Steadfast Prince). The text itself did not find its way into print until 1809 (in Schlegel's second volume of the *Spanisches Theater*), but the Goethe-Schiller correspondence here demonstrates that the elder dramatist felt compelled to keep the interested Schiller abreast of the most recent Calderoniana in Germany. The terms of the accompanying letter are hardly lukewarm. Goethe writes:

> As in the previous dramas, one is perturbed in the enjoyment of the detail for very different reasons, above all on a first reading; nevertheless, when one reaches the end [of *The Steadfast Prince*] and the idea, like a phoenix, rises from the flames before the eyes of the spirit, then one thinks one has never read anything more splendid. It certainly deserves to be ranked alongside *Devotion to the Cross*; in truth I place it higher, perhaps because one has read it most recently and because both the subject and the plot are in the highest sense delightful. I would even venture to say, if poetry vanished entirely from this world, it would be possible to reconstitute it on the basis of this play.[7]

The above exchanges between Schelling and Schlegel on the one hand, and between Goethe and Schiller on the other, suggest that the German intelligentsia of the period were eager to learn more of the dramaturgy of Calderón, either for all the wonderful things it might bring them through reading or performance satisfaction, or as a sui generis model for the rapidly evolving German classical drama. It is really this latter consideration, it seems to me, that furnishes the high circumstantial likelihood that Schiller had already been acquainted with *Devotion to the Cross* at the moment of conceiving *The Bride of Messina*.

What seems virtually undeniable, given the two plays' uncanny similarities, is that in the months of September and/or October of 1802, Schiller had received some manuscript copy of *Devotion to the Cross* prior to its 1803 publication, either from Schlegel himself or via Schelling, or perhaps through the customary good offices of Goethe. Another possibility is the mediation of Tieck, who in 1797 wrote his novella *Der blonde Eckbert* (Blond Eckbert), containing elements of the supernatural, guilt, and brother-sister incest, the year before his first enraptured reading of *Devotion to the Cross*. Regrettably, to my knowledge, no letter or covering note to (or from) Schiller confirming his receipt of some version of the play in 1802 has come to light in any of the extant sets of correspondence, or *Briefwechsel*, from the time.

But we do know for sure that Schiller finally read the first volume of Schlegel's *Spanisches Theater* in 1803—containing *Devotion to the Cross*—on the basis of a letter written by Johann Diederich Gries. Having paid a visit to Schiller in that year, Gries reported that the author of *Wilhelm Tell* dropped his customary reserve about the romantic school's innovations and exclaimed to Gries, "Have you read Calderón yet? With him, a whole new world has opened up before me."[8] Further valuable testimony from the same period illustrates Schiller's indisputable familiarity with and admiration for Calderón, as though he had come to know him through some exercise of practical application. In a letter to Christian Georg Körner dated 16 October 1803, seven months after the Weimar premiere of *The Bride of Messina*, Schiller reproved Körner for his negative comments about the Spanish playwright, while admitting that he was ready to recognize the weaknesses of Calderón. Sensuality and passion mark the southern spirit, he said, more than the moral depth of soul that befits the northern spirit. But he found himself unable to deny Calderón's theatrical skills; indeed, in his words, "a high art and the whole circumspection of the master are peculiar to him, even in that which may appear to be irregular."[9]

I would submit that the peculiar mastery Schiller detected in Calderón, as well as that "high art" and the Spanish playwright's "circumspection" that transcended the confines of so-called regular composition, were concretely that "whole new [Calderonian] world" that had opened up before him and which he described to Gries in the same year, 1803. I would further submit that the example of Calderón, and particularly the idea of *Devotion to the Cross*, available through hearsay or in a German manuscript at the time Schiller conceived and elaborated *The Bride of Messina*, provided him with not only a model of irregular drama that succeeded despite flagrant contravention of neoclassical rules, but one that was steeped in a sense of fateful tragedy, inseparable from the spirit of ancient Greece. At the same time—and this must have proved irresistible to Schiller—Calderón's works raised the issue of a specifically Christian tragedy, a concept that had in theory been disallowed completely by the respected German playwright Lessing. For Calderón appeared, far more than Shakespeare, to present plays of clearly tragic quality that no less clearly expressed Christian themes.

Indeed, the relationship between ancient tragedy and the modern character play had become a burning theoretical issue in Germany by the end of the eighteenth century. The more the German dramatists followed ancient tragedy, as Schiller did in his *Bride of Messina*, the more the idea of a blind and compelling fate that drove men to guilty acts and their own destruction (an idea also present in the native Sturm und Drang tradition) gained prominence. As a fact of life or a literary motif, the idea of blind destiny inspired throughout Germany a multitude of so-called "destiny dramas," and the question of how the ancient concept of fate might be united with modern consciousness gave a fresh interest to Spanish drama, for it was widely felt that Spanish drama lay closer in character to antiquity than it did to any modern European drama. Calderón de la Barca himself was viewed as having more of the ancient ethos than Shakespeare (in the Spaniard's systematic use of oracles, premonitions, and doom-laden properties such as daggers, pictures, and mirrors, for example). More importantly still, Calderón was seen as an example of how ancient drama might be—indeed, *had* been—united with the modern.

Though Calderón's *Devotion to the Cross* is thoroughly Spanish in character, mood, and theme, Calderón chose the Tuscan city of Siena in Italy and its surrounding areas as the setting for his play, though without specifying a particular century. Schiller likewise chose Italy as the setting for *The Bride of Messina*, but in a beautifully evoked medieval Messina on the island of Sicily. Moreover, Schiller painted his Messina under Spanish domination, as is indicated first and foremost by the character names. The recently widowed princess of Messina is called Isabella—an Italian variant of Isabel—but her two warring sons are named Don Manuel and Don Cesar (not the Italian-style Emanuele or Cesare), and the faithful old servant is called Diego, not Iago.

Some authorities place the play's action in the Sicily of the Norman conquest during the eleventh century. But the clear Hispanicization of the dramatis personae reveals Schiller's wish to evoke the period after 1268, when the rights of the former Swabian house in Sicily were held to have passed to Pedro, king of Aragon. The connection with Spain, which so deeply affected the whole later history of Sicily, actually began, then, in the last third of the thirteenth century.[10] Since Calderón was widely regarded in Germany as a guardian of medieval values, particularly of honor, chivalry, and a reaffirmed Catholicism, Schiller's Sicilian setting provided him scope to evoke a late medieval world, decidedly Christian, with clear Islamic elements evidenced, as well as the repeatedly invoked presence of the ancient Greco-Latin deities and their fateful intervention in the action.

In Calderón's original drama of 1624–25, Eusebio is in love with Julia, unaware that she is his sister, and she, likewise unaware, passionately returns his love. At the beginning of the play, her elder brother Lisardo, who is zealous of the family honor and his sister's purity, discovers Eusebio's love letters to Julia in a desk drawer and summons Eusebio to a deserted spot in order to confront him regarding their authorship and to challenge the nameless and unworthy suitor to a duel. As a consequence of the duel, Lisardo is the one mortally wounded, and he begs only that Eusebio bring him to a priest for confession, saying that he will return the favor, once in heaven, should Eusebio ever find himself in the same extremity. Neither antagonist is aware at this stage that they are brothers. The cruel, wastrel old father, Curcio, has meanwhile decided that a convent is the only place where Julia can atone for her affront to family honor by engaging in the exchange of love letters, ignoring her own vehement protests against becoming a novice nun.

Critical opinion on the matter seems united in saying that, apart from Schiller's borrowing of the dream oracle motif from Sophocles' *Oedipus Tyrannos*, the rest of the plot of his *Bride of Messina* was the German dramatist's own invention.[11] I would suggest, on the contrary, that Schiller's play is a remarkable remake *more suo* of the fundamental theme and plot of Calderón's *Devotion to the Cross* (though without any wish on my part to diminish in any way the remarkable lyric and dramatic intensity of Schiller's own invention). In the opening of Schiller's tragedy, the bereaved princess of Messina explains that she has forsaken her widow's weeds in order to resolve the terrible civil war that has broken out in the city since the old ruling prince's death three months previously, waged by her sons, the two perennially jealous and hostile brothers Don Manuel and Don Cesar. She succeeds in reconciling them through her pleadings, but this reconciliation is a volatile one at best. Manuel, in a subsequent scene, privately informs his retinue, or chorus, how he discovered his bride-to-be while out hunting and pursuing a white hind.

At this point, the similarities between Schiller's and Calderón's treatments become so uncanny that is hard to believe that they could actually be coincidental. Calderón's Julia, against her wishes, has been enclaustrated in a convent, though still retaining her secular status as novice. In Act II, Eusebio scales the convent walls with a ladder and abducts Julia from her convent cell by night, still unaware that she is his sister. In Schiller's play, Don Manuel—separated from his hunting companions—pursues the white hind into a convent, where it crouches, protected by a beautiful nun with whom Don Manuel falls in love and embraces at first sight, unaware that this nun is Beatrice, his younger sister. Like her counterpart Julia, Beatrice is also a novice and has not taken her vows. Thus the heinousness of wooing a nun in holy orders is both dwelt upon and technically avoided in both plays, and by the same device. And subsequently, just as in Calderón, Don Manuel abducts Beatrice by night at the end of Act I.

Both Calderón and Schiller insist on the desecration and monstrousness of abducting a novice bride from her convent by stealth. In both plays, furthermore, the motif of the ladder for scaling convent walls remains the same. In Schiller's Act III, old Diego enters to report to Isabella that her daughter has been abducted by Barbary pirates, a sincere and genuinely mistaken interpretation on his part. But when asked how this could happen, he replies, "The cloister garden's walls were easily / Scaled and swarmed o'er on lofty ladder rungs."[12]

As regards other palpable Calderonian influence, we can point to Schiller's rich polymetry throughout the play: unrhymed iambic pentameter for the most part, but much lyric meter in shorter lines, as well as complex rhyme schemes, especially in the speeches given to the two choruses. The most obvious use of Calderonian metrical practice is an eighteen-line soliloquy delivered by Beatrice in Act II, scene iii, cast in so-called Spanish trochees, or trochaic tetrameters. The easiest way to convey this ponderous rhythm is to quote the German:

> Schaudernd hört ich oft und wieder
> Von dem Schlangenhaß der Brüder,
> Und jetzt reißt mein Schreckenschicksal
> Mich die arme, rettungslose
> In den Strudel dieses Hasses
> Dieses Unglücks mich hinein.[13]
>
> Shúdd'ring / díd I / óften / héar of /
> Thís the / bróthers' / snáke-like / hátred; /
> Nów my / hórrid / Fáte doth / cást me, /
> Mé the / póor one, / sáns de- / lív'rance /
> Dówn the / vórtex / óf this / hátred, /
> Dównward / ín this / fóul mis- / fórtune. /
> (Accented translation mine)

The interest here lies in the fact that, when A. W. Schlegel first faced the difficulty of rendering Calderón's numerous octosyllabic verse forms into German (the ballad meter or *romance*, for example), he hit on just this solution: trochaic tetrameters. This German metrical solution, first found in *Devotion to the Cross*, was widely adopted in Germany by Zacharias Werner, Adolf Müllner, Franz Grillparzer, and others. Other metrical fingerprints that point to Calderón are Schiller's long passages of stichomythia, that is, dialogue in alternate lines of verse (used for disputation in Greek drama) characterized by brief antitheses and repetitions. The device was much cultivated by the disputatious, neo-Scholastic Calderón.

There are even more notable similarities between the two plays. Schiller had treated the theme of fratricidal enmity in his first drama *Die Räuber* (The Brigands) of 1781, which portrayed outlaws and their Robin Hood-like leader, Karl Moor, whose antagonist, his evil brother Franz Moor, commits suicide in the course of the play. Similarly, Schiller had treated the incest motif in *Don Carlos, Infant von Spanien* of 1787, in which the youthful Don Carlos is betrothed to Elizabeth of Valois, but his father, King Philip of Spain, appropriates Elizabeth as his own bride. Despite her marriage to his father, Carlos passionately continues to love the woman who is now his stepmother, a dangerous liaison, however much their incestuousness might be construed as purely "legal." His friend Posa eventually pays with his life for his loyal advocacy, and Don Carlos is mercilessly handed over to the Inquisition by the king.

In *Devotion to the Cross*, Schiller rediscovered the motif of the brigand chieftain in Eusebio, as well as the themes of fratricide and incest, inseparably combined. The Calderonian father Curcio is every bit as suspicious, jealous, and heartless as Schiller's King Philip of Spain, and just as ruthlessly sends his son Eusebio to his doom. But, more importantly, *Devotion to the Cross* raised the issue of human liberty and free will in conflict with the mysterious forces of doom and divinely ordained miracles. For his part, this Kantian theme of human liberty runs like an unbroken river through Schiller's dramatic productions and is present in *The Brigands, Don Carlos, The Bride of Messina, William Tell,* and many more. It is easy to imagine, then, bearing all of the above in mind, the electric and instantaneous impact Calderón's play must have exerted on Schiller. In view of Schiller's prior interests in liberty, fratricide, and incest, it was thematically tailor-made to captivate him. Moreover, Calderón also provided that link to a doom-laden antiquity blended with medieval Christianity that Schiller sought to revive in a classical verse tragedy for the Weimar stage.

Having laid his dramatic bets, however, Schiller did not learn all he might have done from a Calderonian portrayal of the workings of fate. In the Spanish original, the theological background of the play's action cannot be divorced from the Counter Reformation furor in Spain over grace and free will, known as the *De auxiliis* controversy. The Council of Trent had denied Luther's heretical propositions advocating "faith alone" as the true way to salvation, as well as his discarding the efficacy of good works. But the council never adequately clarified how divine power, omnipotence, and prescience could function if they were not to annul man's free will, nor, conversely, how man could choose freely in his actions, for bad or for good, if this were not to impugn the might and majesty of God.

The Thomistic distinction between "sufficient grace" and "efficacious grace," by which the council sought to paper over the difficulty, led to a passionate division within Spain, a doctrine of "physical predetermination" being adopted by the more conservative and Thomistically inclined Dominicans, and the doctrines of Luis de Molina that favored the human liberty to choose being adopted by the more humanistically inclined Jesuits.[14] There could not be two varieties of grace, argued the Jesuits, a sufficient one providing the potential to perform good acts and then a second, efficacious one that permitted the active execution of the act. All men possessed sufficient grace as a birthright of the soul. When man, of his own free will, chose to perform a good act, then the grace that had hitherto been sufficient was rendered efficacious. He could also avail himself of an "active indifference," declining to perform the good act, such that the grace in question remained "merely sufficient." Molina also developed a theory of God's "middle knowledge" (*scientia media*) to reconcile his system with the problem of divine foreknowledge.

Calderón was trained in his boyhood by the Jesuits at their Colegio Imperial in Madrid from 1609 to 1614. He clearly adopted the Jesuit line on this burning question in his dramas, *Devotion to the Cross* being only a single example of his adherence to Jesuit views. In the play, Eusebio's life has been miraculously shielded by the cross, and his devotion to the holy object provides the title of the play. It was at the foot of a cross in the wilderness that his mother Rosmira, unjustly accused by Curcio of having become pregnant by another man, gave birth to Eusebio, as well as to Julia, although the twins were separated at birth. Both siblings, however, bear the sign of the cross on their breast as a birthmark of talismanic powers. Subsequently, a miraculous series of crosses saves Eusebio from drowning in a well, dying in a burning house, drowning at sea, and so on. Finally, he dies at the foot of the selfsame cross where he was born, is miraculously revived and confessed by the old priest Alberto (thus making good on his act of mercy toward the moribund Lisardo), and goes to heaven, despite his desperado's career of highway robbery, murder, and incorrigible defiance of civil authority.

The theme of personal liberty is introduced by Julia in Act I, as she argues with her father about her choice of a future career. She tells him that impious fate cannot bend a free will. The theme is ingeniously developed in the love affair of Julia and Eusebio. When he attempts to abduct her from the convent, his pleadings have finally overcome her resistance to the point that he is about to possess her. But then Eusebio notices the mark of the cross on her naked breast and recoils in horror. We might argue that this moment has been divinely predetermined to prevent the act of incest, that no free will is in play here.

But Calderón's text is very precise. Eusebio says, "The Cross which I have seen on your breast / has been a sign, a prodigy; / And let not the Heavens permit / That, although I so sorely offend them, / I should sacrifice respect for the Cross."[15] The sight of the birthmark was an influx of sufficient grace, with which Eusebio cooperated. He makes this even more explicit in a soliloquy at the beginning of Act III, where he says,

> Julia, I found myself in your arms
> When I was so touched by good fortune

> That Love could have made new bonds
> Of those selfsame arms.
> But, at last, I left without enjoying
> The glory which I possessed not;
> But the cause was not mine,
> It was a more secret cause;
> Because, since my free will commands
> A superior efficaciousness,
> It ensured I respected on your breast
> The Cross which I do bear on mine.
> And since both of us were born,
> Ah Julia!, with that same mark,
> This has been a secret mystery
> Which God alone can understand.[16]

In Calderón's conception, then, man has free will within the purview of a divine providence that moves in mysterious ways. He is not alone in the universe and abandoned to a nameless fate or fickle fortune. God provides sufficient grace to all men; it is up to the individual to choose freely to cooperate with that grace, thus producing the salvific acts that will bring closer the attainment of salvation. In what has been called "the sublime of antinomianism," the homicidal brigand Eusebio, devoted to the symbol of Christ's ultimate sacrifice, and Julia, a victim of purely human wrongs, both achieve salvation.

The source of evil is not in God, nor in any dualist or diabolic machinations. The guilt for his family's tragic destruction lies squarely with Curcio, brutal to his innocent wife, tyrannical toward his daughter, and indifferent to the fate of the second twin, born in the wilds at the foot of the cross, who transpires to be his own son. Evil lies in the savage character of Curcio, not in any blind destiny or unmotivated caprice of the gods. Thus, Christian tragedy is shown by Calderón to lie in a web of human evildoing and errors of judgment, the whole presided over by a providential God who provides the means for salvation (*auxilia*) but does not force them on his creatures against their free will. The harder we scrutinize Calderón's tragic causality, the more we are drawn into the cause, the cause of the cause, the cause of the cause of the cause, and so on.

Schiller, by contrast, groping toward a similar sense of transcendence in the fateful mix of divine ordinance and human wrongdoing, lacks Calderón's theological precision and rigor. This would, in and of itself, not matter. But, obviously, if a tragedy speculates keenly on the human condition and its disasters, deserved or not, then the theological or tendentious underpinnings that frame the drama should bear up satisfactorily under scrutiny. Schiller seems to have had his own misgivings about the way he handled this issue in *The Bride of Messina*. Schiller's dramatic text is preceded by an essay, "On the Use of the Chorus in Tragedy," defending his revival of this ancient Greek convention in the Weimar theater.

It is of no real literary interest here to pursue the controversies concerning Schiller's innovation or its dramatic effectiveness. More pertinent to our purposes are the author's misgivings expressed at the very end of the prefatory essay concerning his own theological license. He writes:

> Another licence it may be more difficult to excuse. I have blended together the Christian Religion and the Pagan Mythology, and introduced recollections of the Moorish superstition. But the scene of the drama is Messina, where these three religions either exercised a living influence, or appealed to the senses in monumental remains. Besides, I consider it a privilege of Poetry to deal with different religions as a collective Whole, in which everything that bears an individual character, and expresses a peculiar mode of feeling, has its place. Religion itself, the idea of a Divine Power, lies under the veil of all religions; and it must be permitted to the poet to represent it in the form which appears the most appropriate to his subject.[17]

The difficulty here lies in the fact that we never know for sure wherein the causes behind the House of Messina's tragic disasters really lie. In the catastrophes of the play, the old ruling prince is already dead; the two rival brothers have unleashed a civil war in Messina; both have nearly committed incest with their own sister; one brother has been stabbed to death by his junior; and the surviving brother commits suicide before his brother's catafalque in the last scene, resisting pleadings and tears from both mother and sister, in order to atone for his fratricidal crime.

The nearest Schiller comes to providing a dramatic "cause of the cause" is in a speech by Manuel's retinue, doubling as chorus, at the end of Act I. This speech suggests some unnatural carnal union prior to the play's beginnings. The nineteenth-century English translator, Adam Lodge, did the best he could to render this delicately allusive and truly obscure passage in 1841:

> And thus to sad unhallowed rites
> Of an ill-omened nuptial tie,
> Too well ye know their father bore
> A bride of mournful destiny,
> Torn from his sire, whose awful curse has spread

> Heaven's vengeance on the impious bed.
> This fierce unnatural rage atones
> A parent's crime—decreed by Fate
> Their mother's offspring, Strife and Hate![18]

But a closer, hermeneutic look at the Schillerian text yields just a little more in the way of meaning. But this "little more" is highly significant. In my own retranslation, it would read as follows:

> It was a rape as well, as we all know,
> Which tore the ruling prince's wifely consort
> Into a marriage bed with outrage stained,
> Because she was the chosen of her father.
> At which the wrathful ancestor rained down
> Ghastly curses and a hideous seed
> Upon the marriage bed of sin.
> This house conceals atrocities without
> A name and darkest acts of crime.[19]

The best we can make of this is to infer that Isabella, the old prince's legitimate wife, was raped by her own father and gave birth to the two brothers in question, though they were not twins. Hence, we must suppose the father/daughter incest occurred at least twice. But this is intelligent guesswork. If we seek the cause of the cause in Schiller's tragedy, we can at most presume that the maternal grandfather of Don Manuel and Don Cesar was the unnatural progenitor who initiated the cycle of doom. In this sense, the violated incest taboo hangs over the play as the cause of dynastic disaster, and the love of Manuel and Cesar for their sister Beatrice would simply be a doom-laden repetition of family history.

If this be the kernel of Schiller's play, then it must be admitted that ancient Greek motifs, inspired by the Oedipus story of incest and parricide, gave him his main idea. And yet Schiller, attempting to wrestle with issues of freedom and destiny relevant to his modern day, could not dispense with Christianity and the notion of free choice. This is where Calderón's *Devotion to the Cross* must have seemed to him most provocative and advanced in tragic thought. The Spaniard's play is not a cycle of inscrutable doom and retribution wreaked by capricious deities from Olympus. While it brings the same themes of incest and fratricide (alias parricide) to the fore, it also clearly allows Eusebio free will within the dispensations of Christian grace and salvation through the meaning of Christ's passion on the cross. So Schiller, by his strategic decision to blend Greek mythology with both Christianity and Moorish superstition, was faced in his *Bride of Messina* with the problem of how his tragic hero was, in any meaningful way, to combine personal freedom with a destiny fatefully imposed from above.

There is much stress on this problem in Schiller's play. The widowed Isabella will make paradoxical observations such as the following: "I see it clearly; Destiny wills to tread / Its own free pathway with my children."[20] In the same speech, she refers to "the ungovernably stronger hand divine / That darkly spins the Fortune of my house."[21] But this raises the question of how destiny can tread freely, or what agent it is, precisely, that is free to command fortune. Schiller equivocates between attributing the divinity that shapes our ends to pagan deities on the one hand, and to the Christian God on the other. The problem comes most strongly to the fore in the play's climax, when Don Cesar declares that only his own suicide can atone for his slain brother's death.

Cesar tells the pleading chorus, in Lodge's translation, "The curse of old / Shall die with me! Death self-imposed alone / Can break the chain of Fate."[22] But Schiller actually wrote: "Der freie Tod nur bricht die Kette des Geschicks,"[23] and it is this "free death," or "freier Tod," which goes to the heart of the romantic understanding of Calderón and his *Devotion to the Cross*. Schiller's message is repeated by the chorus in the lines, "Behold! with willing steps and free, / Thy son prepares to tread / The paths of dark eternity,—/ The silent mansions of the dead."[24] The line in Schiller, however, "Hinabzugehen mit freiem Schritte" ("Freely to go down the abyss step by step"), is taken virtually verbatim from Friedrich Schlegel's *History of European Literature* of 1803 and 1804.[25] The phrase actually occurs in F. Schlegel's discussion of Calderón, of Christian tragedy, and of *Devotion to the Cross* in particular.

So far as the tragic catastrophe is concerned, argued the younger Schlegel, the ancient tragedians showed a marked preference for the hero's total destruction, which outcome corresponded to their view of preordained destiny. But such a tragedy would be more excellent, he says, insofar as the hero were not the victim of a fate from above, but *went step by step down an inner abyss* to his ruin, being destroyed through his own guilt while retaining some degree of freedom.[26] Schlegel distinguished a "third kind" of dramatic resolution, for him the highest kind of tragedy, which allows the portrayal of spiritual transfiguration to emerge from the utmost suffering.

This last is preeminently appropriate for a Christian poet, he says, and in this, Calderón is the first and the greatest exemplar. The Christian elements in *Devotion to the Cross* and *The Steadfast*

Prince lie not in the subject matter, but in the individual manner of feeling and treatment, which is predominant in Calderón as a whole. Even in cases where the story offers no scope for new life to develop completely out of death and suffering, everything, nevertheless, is conceived in the spirit of this Christian love and transfiguration; everything is seen in their light and painted in their colors. According to Schlegel, Calderón is under all conditions, and among all other dramatic poets, the most Christian, and for that reason the most romantic.[27]

This Schlegelian theory of tragedy in Calderón sounds like a blueprint for Schiller's *Bride of Messina*. And if we wonder how Christian love and transfiguration come into the picture in Schiller, it is important to remember the pleas of Cesar's mother, urging him to turn from suicide to penance. She entreats:

> All Christendom is rich
> In shrines of mercy, where the troubled heart
> May find repose: Oh! many a heavy burden
> Have sinners in Loretto's mansion laid;
> And Heaven's peculiar blessing breathes around
> The grave that has redeemed the world. The prayers
> Of the devout are precious—fraught with store
> Of grace, they win forgiveness from the skies;
> And on the soil by gory Murder stained,
> Shall rise the purifying fane [temple].[28]

At the same time that Friedrich Schlegel composed his essay on Calderonian tragedy and—as we suggest—Schiller composed his own classical neo-Calderonian tragedy entitled *The Bride of Messina*, the philosopher Schelling also gave a series of lectures in 1803 at Jena, the home of romanticism, entitled *A Treatise on Tragedy*. The lectures argued, like Schlegel, from the unique example of *Devotion to the Cross*. Schelling's desire, again, was to show how freedom and necessity in tragedy must both be given the scope to triumph. In other words, tragic necessity must somehow be accepted by the hero as an act of free will. This difficult and ingeniously argued treatise effectively worked out, on the basis of Calderón's *Devotion to the Cross* alone, a complete theory of Christian tragedy.[29]

In closing, I should like to offer a judgment by Goethe on the relationship between Schiller and Calderón—more intimate (it would seem) than previously admitted—taken from a conversation with Eckermann on 12 May 1825. Did Goethe, looking back over the years, have Schiller's mixed success with *The Bride of Messina* in mind in the following remark? He told Eckermann,

It is always, and only, a question of whether that person from whom we wish to learn is compatible with our nature. Thus, for example, Calderón, however great he may be and however much I may esteem him, has not exerted the least influence on me, either for good or for bad [sic]. But to Schiller he would have been dangerous; [Schiller] would not have known what to make of him, and it is a piece of good fortune, therefore, that Calderón came into general fashion only after [Schiller's] death [in 1805]. Calderón is infinitely great in the technical and the theatrical; Schiller, on the other hand, is far more capable, more serious, and greater in intention. And hence it would perhaps have been a shame to suffer some loss in virtues of this kind, while not attaining to Calderón's greatness in other respects.[30]

Did Schiller, in fact, "not [attain] to Calderón's greatness" in his own experiment with *The Bride of Messina*? Did Goethe know that Schiller had taken the much-studied and discussed *Devotion to the Cross* as his model for their classical Weimar theater? Was he happier that Schiller had never become more "Calderonized"? We shall probably never know the answer to these questions for sure. But one historical detail cannot be passed over in the context. Some six years after Schiller's death, on the night of 30 January 1811, Goethe mounted a production of Calderón's *The Steadfast Prince* at Weimar, using A. W. Schlegel's translation, slightly adapted by himself.[31] The premiere brought Goethe a ringing triumph, and the faithfully translated Calderón was born at last on the German stage. The telling detail I refer to is the identity of the person Goethe placed at his side for the first performance. It was Charlotte von Schiller, the widow of his great friend. Was this perhaps to say to her, if only your dear husband, my bitterly missed collaborator, were present now to witness this long-awaited moment? If only Schiller had been sitting here between us on this Calderonian night of nights!

Acknowledgment

For Dennis Melvin Mueller, in gratitude.

Notes

1. Of the Schiller-Calderón connection, see Julius Petersen, *Schillers Gespräche: Berichte von seinen Zeitgenossen* (Leipzig, 1911); Hermann Tiemann, *Das spanische Schrifttum in Deutschland von der Renaissance bis zur Romantik* (Hamburg, 1936); Walther Rehm, *Götterstille und Göttertrauer: Aufsätze zur deutsch-antiken Begegnung* (Berne, 1951); J. J. A. Bertrand, "Encuentros de F. Schiller con España," *Clavileño*, vol. 6, no. 35 (1955), pp. 38–42; Benno von Wiese, *Friedrich Schiller*, 4th ed. (Stuttgart, 1959), and his *Die deutsche Tragödie von Lessing bis Hebbel* [1948], 5th ed. (Hamburg, 1961); Henry W. Sullivan, *Calderón in the German Lands and the Low Countries: His Reception and Influence, 1654–1980* (Cambridge and New York, 1983), and the recent Spanish translation by Milena Grass, *El Calderón alemán: Recepción e influencia de un genio hispano, 1654–1980* (Frankfurt and Madrid, 1998); Roger Paulin, *Ludwig Tieck: A Literary Biography* (Oxford, 1986); and F. J. Lamport, *German Classical Drama* (Cambridge and New York, 1990).
2. Cf. Petersen, *Schillers Gespräche*, p. 358, and von Wiese, *Friedrich Schiller*, p. 760.
3. Cf. August Wilhelm Schlegel, *Schauspiele von Don Pedro Calderón de la Barca*, 2 vols. (Berlin, 1803–09).
4. Cf. Gustav Leopold Plitt, ed., *Aus Schellings Leben in Briefen*, 3 vols. (Leipzig, 1869), vol. 1, p. 430.
5. Ibid.
6. Cf. Johann Christoph Friedrich von Schiller, *Über naive und sentimentalische Dichtung* (Oxford, 1951).
7. See Stuart Atkins, "Goethe, Calderón and Faust: *Der Tragödie zweiter Teil*," *Germanic Review*, vol. 28 (1953), pp. 83–98. Quoted by Atkins, pp. 85–86. All translations are mine unless otherwise noted.
8. See Elisabeth Campe, *Aus dem Leben von Johann Diederich Gries* (Leipzig, 1855), p. 112.
9. See Fritz Jonas, ed., *Schillers Briefe* (Stuttgart, 1892–96), vol. 7, p. 88.
10. Cf. the article "Sicily" in *Encyclopaedia Britannica*, 11th ed. (Cambridge, 1910–11), vol. 25, pp. 20b–35b, here p. 35a.
11. See Henry and Mary Garland, *The Oxford Companion to German Literature*, 2nd ed. (Oxford and New York, 1986), p. 109a, and Lamport, *German Classical Drama*, p. 120.
12. "Des Klostergartens Mauren waren leicht / Auf hoher Leiter Sprossen überstiegen." Friedrich Schiller, *Die Braut von Messina*, in *Schillers Werke: Dramen II*, ed. Herbert Kraft (Frankfurt, 1966), p. 295.
13. Ibid., p. 285.
14. See Henry W. Sullivan, *Tirso de Molina and the Drama of the Counter Reformation* (Amsterdam, 1976), pp. 28–40.
15. "… la Cruz que he visto en tu pecho, / Señal prodigiosa ha sido, / Y no permitan los cielos / Que, aunque los ofenda, / Pierda a la Cruz el respeto." Quoted from Juan Eugenio Hartzenbusch, *Comedias de D. Pedro Calderón de la Barca* (Madrid, 1944), vol. 1, p. 63b.
16. "Julia, yo me vi en tus brazos / Cuando tan dichoso era, / Que de tus brazos pudiera / Hacer amor nuevos lazos. / Sin gozar al fin dejé / La gloria que no tenía; / Mas no fue la causa mía, / Causa más secreta fue; / Pues teniendo mi albedrío / Superior efecto, ha hecho / Que yo respete en tu pecho / La Cruz que tengo en el mío. / Y pues con ella los dos, / Ay Julia!, habemos nacido, / Secreto misterio ha sido / Que lo entiende sólo Dios." Ibid., p. 64a-64b.

17. Quoted from Friedrich Schiller, *The Bride of Messina: A Tragedy with Choruses*, trans. Adam Lodge, 3rd ed. (London, 1863), pp. 13–14.
18. Friedrich Schiller, *The Bride of Messina: A Tragedy with Choruses*, trans. Adam Lodge (London, 1841), p. 36.
19. "Auch ein Raub wars, wie wir alle wissen, / Der des alten Fürsten ehliches Gemahl / In ein frevelnd Ehebett gerissen, / Denn sie war des Vaters Wahl. / Und der Ahnherr schüttete im Zorne / Grauenvoller Flüche schrecklichen Samen / Auf das sündige Ehebett aus. / Greueltaten ohne Namen / Schwarze Verbrechen verbirgt dies Haus." *Schillers Werke: Dramen II*, p. 277.
20. "Den eignen freien Weg, ich seh es wohl, / Will das Verhängnis gehn mit meinen Kindern." Ibid., p. 293.
21. "Der unregiersam stärkern Götterhand, / Die meines Hauses Schicksal dunkel spinnt." Ibid., p. 293.
22. Cf. Schiller, *Bride of Messina* (1863), p. 125.
23. "Den alten Fluch des Hauses lös ich sterbend auf, / Der freie Tod nur bricht die Kette des Geschicks." *Schillers Werke: Dramen II*, p. 325.
24. Cf. Schiller, *Bride of Messina* (1863), p. 127. Schiller actually wrote, "Entschlossen siehst du ihn, festen Muts, / Hinab zu gehen mit freiem Schritte / Zu des Todes traurigen Toren." *Schillers Werke: Dramen II*, p. 326.
25. See Friedrich Schlegel, *Geschichte der europäischen Literatur*, in *Kritische Friedrich-Schlegel-Ausgabe*, ed. Ernst Behler (Paderborn and Munich, 1958), vol. 9, p. 165.
26. On F. Schlegel's triple distinction of tragedy, see Sullivan, *Calderón in the German Lands*, pp. 214–215. Emphasis mine.
27. Ibid.
28. Cf. Schiller, *Bride of Messina* (1863), p. 124. "Reich ist die Christenheit an Gnadenbildern, / Zu denen wallend ein gequältes Herz / Kann Ruhe finden. Manche schwere Bürde / Ward abgeworfen in Lorettos Haus, / Und segensvolle Himmelskraft umweht / Das heilige Grab, das alle Welt entsündigt. / Vielkräftig auch ist das Gebet der Frommen, / Sie haben reichen Vorrat an Verdienst, / Und auf der Stelle, wo ein Mord geschah, / Kann sich ein Tempel reinigend erheben." *Schillers Werke: Dramen II*, p. 327.
29. See F. W. J. von Schelling, *Abhandlung über die Tragödie*, in *Sämmtliche Werke*, sec. I, vol. 5 (Stuttgart and Augsburg, 1859), p. 353ff. Also summarized in Sullivan, *Calderón in the German Lands*, pp. 216–220.
30. See Johann Peter Eckermann, *Gespräche mit Goethe in den letzten Jahren seines Lebens*, in *Goethe Gedenk-Ausgabe* (Zurich, 1948), vol. 24, p. 158. Quoted in Sullivan, *Calderón in the German Lands*, p. 185.
31. See my previous articles on this subject, "Un manuscrito desconocido de la refundición por Goethe del *Standhafter Prinz* (Calderón/A. G. Schlegel)," in *Hacia Calderón: V Coloquio Anglogermano* (Oxford 1978), ed. Hans Flasche (Wiesbaden, 1981), pp. 74–82; and the enlarged version, "Ein unbekanntes Manuskript von Goethes Bearbeitung des 'Standhaften Prinzen' (Calderón/August Wilhelm Schlegel)," in *Pedro Calderón de la Barca: Vorträge anläßlich der Jahrestagung der Görres-Gesellschaft 1978*, ed. Theodor Berchem and Siegfried Sudhof (Berlin, 1983), pp. 58–68.

– 6 –

Francisco López de Úbeda and Johann Wolfgang von Goethe as Participants in the Shared German-Spanish Tradition of Kabbalistic Rhetoric

Patricia D. Zecevic

My point of departure is a striking and, I argue, mutually illuminating similarity between the style of two works that may appear rather disparate at first sight: the Spanish picaresque novel *Libro de entretenimiento de la pícara Justina* (1605) by Francisco López de Úbeda (fl. 1590?) and the German Bildungsroman par excellence *Wilhelm Meister* (Apprenticeship, 1795, and Journeyman Years, 1821–29) by Johann Wolfgang Goethe (1749–1832). There is, in my view, not simply a thematic coincidence in that both novels deal with the problem of female self-presentation; there is also a remarkable similarity in the stylistic devices that each author deploys in order to give expression to the discourse of women. Guided by contemporary discussion of the cultural representation of the woman and by feminist stylistics (in particular, by the speculative-cum-theological variety associated with the work of the French philosopher Luce Irigaray), I suggest that both writers, for all the evident differences of period and temper in mind, are drawing on the common tradition of the Kabbalah, both for its elaborated account of the (divine) feminine and for its doctrine and practice of the Speaking (divine) Woman.

In an extraordinarily powerful passage in *La Pícara Justina*, Francisco López de Úbeda lends to his fictional narrator-character one of those "linguistic pirouettes,"[1] as they have been called, by means of which the (already highly ambiguous) meaning of the text is given yet one more turn:

> Sólo un pelo de mi pluma ha parlado que soy pobre, pícara, tundida de cejas y de vergüenza, y que de puro pobre he de dar en comer tierra, para tener mejor merecido que la tierra me coma a mí, que si me rasco la cabeza no me come el pelo, y según mi pluma lleva la corriente atrevida y disoluta, a poca más licencia, la tomará para ponerme de lodo, porque quien me ha dado seis nombres de P, conviene a saber: pícara, pobre, poca vergüenza, pelona y pelada, ¿qué he de esperar, sino que como la pluma tiene la P dentro de su casa y el alquiler pagado, me ponga algún otro nombre de P que me eche a puertas? Mas antes que nos pope, quiero soplarle, aunque me llamen soplona.

> A mere hair of my quill has spoken out that I am poor, *pícara*, stripped of eyebrows and of shame, and that because I am pure poor, I have to take to live on nothing [literally, eat earth/dirt], so that I can better deserve to die [literally, to be eaten by the earth]; that if I scratch my head, the hair will not bother me [literally, not eat me], and since my pen is holding forth in a bold and dissolute manner; with a little more license it will take the liberty of discrediting me [literally, covering me in mud], because whoever has given me six names of P, and it is important to know them: pícara, poor, very-little shame, bald [socio-economically inferior/lacking], and bald [deprived/oppressed], what can I expect but that, since the pen has the P inside its house, and has paid the rent [that is, it is free to speak], it will cast another name of P at my door to exclude me? But before it belittles/patronizes us, I wish to blow it away/whisper its secrets, even if they call me telltale.[2]

Here the frequent (29) occurrences of the "p" sound create an alliterative pattern that reaches its climax in the self-defining phrase, "pícara, pobre, poca vergüenza, pelona y pelada." Besides suggesting a whispering tone of confidentiality, semantic items are linked by this figure in a wholly alogical way, suggesting an identity of some sort between the pícara and poverty and between belittlement and baldness (with its connotations of low social status and gender blurring). In the words, both the physical and the moral predicament of the feminine pícaro are intimately associated with socioeconomic factors in an acausal, one might say "poetic," nexus—and all of this is linked, by the same alliteration, to writing (the pen).

A very similar thickening of the linguistic texture—until it begins to approach the density of poetry—is evident, too, in the language of the women in Johann Wolfgang Goethe's *Wilhelm Meister*. The Beautiful Soul, for example, in writing that "my convictions were a mystery to no one," builds in an anaphoric link that condenses "convictions" and "mystery" in a way that runs counter to the surface sense: "Meine Gesinnungen waren niemand ein Geheimnis."[3] And in the final paragraph of her "Confessions," the same technique is used to suggest that "commandment" and "law" are essentially mere "formalities": "Ich erinnere mich kaum eines Gebotes; nichts erscheint mir in Gestalt eines Gesetzes; es ist ein Trieb, der mich leitet und mich immer recht führet; ich folge mit Freiheit meinen Gesinnungen" (H.A. 7, p. 42; "I recall hardly any commandment; nothing appears to me in the form of a law: a drive of some sort always leads and guides me aright; I follow freely my own convictions," *Apprenticeship*, p. 256). Moreover, alliteration likewise links *Trieb* ("drive"), *leitet* ("lead"), and *führet* ("guide"), as well as *führet, folge* ("follow") and *Freiheit* ("freedom"), in an alogical cluster of meaning that binds together "being led (by impulse)" and "freedom."

The similarity of style employed in these two passages (by no means an isolated phenomenon in either novel, as I will show) is underlined by the fact that both López de Úbeda's and Goethe's exploitation, in prose, of the sound-look relations of language,[4] to insinuate a further refinement of meaning, can be conveniently and illuminatingly categorized, bringing to bear some of the key concepts of the French feminist philosopher Luce Irigaray, especially her "speaking-woman."[5] Her *parler-femme* refers to the possibility of female subjectivity being expressed in language, in contrast to (male) discursive, theoretical, or meta-language. Parler-femme is likened to the dynamic immediacy of the "enunciation" in the psychoanalytic process, in which not only the unconscious, but gender, too, can be articulated. But parler-femme is not only a psycholinguistic description; it also articulates women's real dilemma in the current situation, the fact that a woman's position as object is already given, and that the real challenge for her is to enter language as a subject in her own right (as an epistemological subject); in Irigaray's terms: "Her economy is that of the *between-subjects*, and not that of the subject-object relation."[6] Referring to language as a home, in imaginary and symbolic terms, Irigaray contends that women are homeless in the male-dominated symbolic order, that they need their own house of language.

In Irigaray's writing, the strategy for creating a female symbolic in broad terms seems to be twofold: first, intervention, so as to infiltrate and free up the discursive system by opening it and revealing its hidden foundations, its unconscious; and second, recoding, so that, having opened up a site for women in the dominant discourse, a house of language—*langage* (language as used) as opposed to *langue* (language as formally prescribed)—might be built to secure women's own place in the symbolic order. With this in mind, Irigaray elaborates a series of linguistic devices that women might exploit in order to construct a house of language which, to some degree at least, gives expression to their identity. Central to this attempt to construct a house of language is the trope of *mimesis,* or mimicry—a deliberate strategy involving a parasitic adoption of the male ego-identity and its ideological point of view by more or less parodying it, and in so doing, by a diversion from the male model, to point to a female identity. Markers of female specificity in Irigaray's work include a fluid, nonlinear identity characterized by processes being set in motion, and passages (thresholds) between spaces, all suggestive of dynamic movement and process. Added to that, she recommends both a refusal to entertain the either-or of male specificity and the strategy of revealing the (underlying) sexual bias of Western culture's patriarchal mythology by inserting and inscribing the material feminine and preventing, however temporarily, the dominant (male) discourse from occupying that space. The essential strategy for Irigaray, then, is to overcome the "either-or" logic of the male imaginary by means of the "both ... and" intuition of the female imaginary—in which she has been famously anticipated by Goethe's Werther, who likewise deplored "either-or" thinking as inadequate to the realities of human experience.[7]

Moreover, in terms that are distinctly evocative of kabbalistic rhetoric, Irigaray expressly links the feminine principle with our (human) relationship to God, the elemental world, and "our lost sense of touch."[8] This double relationship, fruit of the sensuous-emotional aspects of our psychological life—traces of which survive, according to Irigaray, in the dark and mysterious aspects of myths and folktales, and are expressed in poetry—is, in her view, otherwise left out of everyday (male) language and discourse that "forgets the [particular] matter it names and by means of which it speaks."[9] The status here of the feminine-divine-elemental, the Great Goddess by another name, is as a forgotten and neglected sensuous medium through which the fundamental relationship with the mother and with nature-God can be expressed. Woman, in her "becoming," as Irigaray calls it, lacks a sense of herself as more than finite flesh, more than bodily self. In other words, she lacks a sense of herself as simultaneously transcendental, as divine: "In order to become, it is essential to have a gender or an essence (consequently a sexuate essence) as *horizon*. Otherwise becoming remains partial and subject to the subject."[10]

Of greater interest from a historical point of view is the fact that the similar stylistic devices employed by López de Úbeda and Goethe (and recommended anew by Irigaray) to give expression to the female voice are also very close indeed to the kabbalistic tradition of expressing the Divine Feminine (the *Shekhinah*) through the manipulation of the outward forms of language.

In mythology, the Kabbalah begins with the oral tradition given to Moses in Sinai. But, historically, the earliest form (the *Merkova*) flourished in Palestine in the first century A.D., and centered on mystical contemplation of the divine throne or "chariot" (*merkova*) seen by the prophet Ezekiel. The *Sefer yetzira* (Book of Creation, appearing between the third and sixth centuries A.D.) envisioned creation as a process of ten divine emanations, or *sefirot*, embodied in the twenty-two letters of the Hebrew alphabet. The influential *Sefer ha-bahir* (Book of Brightness, twelfth century) introduced to the ongoing oral tradition the notion of the transmigration of souls and an elaborate mystical symbolism. The anonymous *Sefer ha-temuna* (Book of the Image, thirteenth century) appeared in Spain and contributed to the idea that the sefirot provide a mystical interpretation of the Torah. The *Sefer ha-zohar* (Book of Splendor, probably thirteenth century), known as *The Zohar*, was likewise produced by Spanish Kabbalists. *The Zohar*, in which every word and every letter of the Torah was given a mystical explanation and in which Shekhinah is central, became (and has remained) the major text of kabbalism. After the Jews' expulsion from Spain in 1492, the Kabbalah became ever more popular and a "practical Kabbalah" evolved, absorbing and enhancing traditional folk magic and superstition. By the sixteenth century, the center of Jewish kabbalistic scholarship had shifted to Galilee and Palestine, where the influence of Isaac ben Solomon Luria (1534–1572) rivaled that of even *The Zohar*. Partly through the doctrines of (eighteenth-century) Hasidism and partly through a continuous tradition of its cultivation in Jewish communities, Kabbalah as a mystical exercise in piety and approximation to God continues to flourish to the present day, and not only among Jewish followers. For instance, at the time of the Renaissance, many notable scholars—such as Pico della Mirandola (1463–1494) and Jakob Böhme (1575–1624)—began to assimilate kabbalistic thought as a way of identifying Christian doctrine with ancient pagan traditions.

The female voice of God (of the Shekhinah)—the oral Torah—can be heard only by means of the kabbalistic reading of the written Torah; that is, by means of a reading that plays, much in the manner of both López de Úbeda and Goethe, with the sound and look of the texts (even to the extent, by some, of giving letters of the alphabet numerological value). This exploitation of the literal medium of language to reveal the Divine Feminine fosters a high degree of sensitivity to the physicality of the language: "combining and separating the letters ... composing whole motifs of separate groups, combining several of them with one another and enjoying their combinations in every direction."[11] The Kabbalah provided the most fully articulated version available of the Eternal Feminine, offering to writers a rich—and accessible—store of imagery and ideas with which to articulate the female voice. The Kabbalah's conception of the key archetype of the Shekhinah represents a radical departure from the old rabbinical conception of it: in Talmudic literature and nonkabbalistic rabbinical Judaism, the Shekhinah is simply God Himself in His omnipresence in the world, equivalent to His "face" in the Bible, with no distinction made between the two. In the Kabbalah, however, the feminine potencies in God achieve their most succinct expression in a quasi-independent aspect of God. She is Binah, the third *sefirah*, or upper mother or Shekhinah, who, as demiurgic potency, gives birth to the seven lower sefirah.[12] Henricus Agrippa's feminism in his *De nobilitate* (1529)—"which sees in woman an immediate manifestation of the divine"[13]—is an early example of the formative influence of the Shekhinah on Western writers' attempts to give expression to the female divine identity, one in which traces of the ancient Great Goddess are unmistakably present.[14]

Indeed, Shekhinah's style—her mode of thought embodied in language—is necessarily based on her own sexuate woman's body. Eros is the origin of her bodily style, and erotic love the "enabling symbol to express union with God."[15] Like Luce Irigaray's self-made woman, the Shekhinah's articulation of the (Divine) Feminine is fundamentally an exploitation of her body.[16] The language of the Kabbalah, of *The Zohar* in particular, like the style recommended by Irigaray, is characterized by explicit sexual symbolism, which to many may well seem offensive, in particular in relation to its most developed attribute, the female Shekhinah, and her relations with her male counterpart in the mystical marriage. Just as Irigaray is not advocating the invention of a new language, but rather a skillful manipulation of the only available (male) rhetoric in order to create a new (female) style, so in kabbalistic terms would this parler-femme be a Shekhinah-space, a "house of language," however restricted, enabling a female identity to express itself. In other words, a distinctly female "I" or ego, envisaged—however tentatively, and however inadequately—as articulating an authentic, distinctly female imaginary, points toward a potentially female semiotic system that is very close indeed to the kabbalistic system of signification, for Shekhinah's voice speaks her position in the scheme of things. She speaks her own *langage*, her own style, but always, too, the *langue* of God.[17] Above all, she articulates her relationship with the masculine principle in the Godhead—her father, her brother, and her beloved—*and* that with her mother and sisters. She is on the border, between transcendence and immanence, between the earthly realm and the divine, belonging to both and not wholly visible in either.

My argument in what follows is that a reading of the female voice in *La Pícara Justina* and *Wilhelm Meister* in the light of Irigaray's theory of parler-femme reveals striking stylistic similarities in the two novels, similarities that internal and external evidence suggests may well be the result of both López de Úbeda's and Goethe's participation in the kabbalistic tradition of exploiting the literal bodiliness of language in order to express the (Divine) Feminine. In essence, my suggestion is that the Kabbalah may well be functioning here as the key intertext.

In the *Apprenticeship*, Wilhelm, the young son of well-to-do middle-class parents, sets out—after mistakenly supposing his first love, Mariane, to have been unfaithful to him—on what begins as a business trip but turns very quickly into a picaresque wandering. His encounters with a series of fascinating women give his free and easy lifestyle a degree of structure: the carefree Philine, the mysterious androgyne Mignon, the hysterical Aurelie, the practical Thérèse, and the "beautiful Amazon" (as he calls Natalie, to whom he is eventually betrothed but whom he consistently confuses with her sister, a married countess)—they all make a marked impression on him. Early on, Wilhelm forms his own troupe of actors, which is disbanded after an ambush by robbers; he then joins another troupe, with which he plays the lead role in *Hamlet*, a character with whom he clearly identifies at this stage. After this performance, and during a dire set by a mysterious harper, Wilhelm learns that he has a son, Felix (by Mariane, now dead). Wilhelm eventually comes under the influence of the exclusively male Society of the Tower—a secret organization devoted to educating its members for life—to which he is admitted at the end of the *Apprenticeship*. The Society insists that Wilhelm complete some years of travel to prepare himself for his vocation in life. Goethe's last novel, *The Journeyman Years* (published in 1821 and, in an extended form, in 1829, but written between 1807 and 1828), is the sequel to the *Apprenticeship*, tracing Wilhelm's further development. Every three days Wilhelm must move on, to a point at least three leagues from his last port of call. In company with his son, he comes across a series of groups of men and women who have gathered together to work out a distinctive lifestyle on the basis of differing values and attitudes, though each group has connections with the others. In the practical sphere of the Oheim, Wilhelm is confronted with the tenets of liberal political economy, while in the circle around the mysterious wise woman, Makarie, he must come to terms with mystical cosmic consciousness. Wilhelm learns of the experience of others indirectly, too, through a series of interpolated novellas, only tenuously related to the main plot (like the "Confessions of a Beautiful Soul," inserted into book VI of the *Apprenticeship*), and through two collections of aphorisms, both of which are associated with Makarie. At the end of the novel, Wilhelm, having found his vocation as a surgeon, is able to save the life of his injured son, thus underlining what Goethe insisted was the thoroughgoing "symbolic" nature of his novel.

In *La Pícara Justina*, the protagonist Justina (one of five children, and the most astute and talented of three daughters), whose parents are innkeepers in the village of Mansilla, begins her story with a detailed, highly symbolic account of her narrative point of view as being distinctly female. (Justina's sustained use of the adjective *real*, meaning both "real" and "royal," is one way in which she uses language to express her full identity both as a real, flesh-and-blood woman and as a divine (royal) goddess, in the tradition of the Great Goddesses of antiquity.) On the death of her parents, whose genealogy she traces with burlesque humor, Justina sets out for the first time from her native village with, like Wilhelm Meister, a desire for freedom and experience of life—a journey that she refers to throughout as a "pilgrimage." In her wanderings through Spain, during which time she takes part in various rustic festivals and burlesque fetes, Justina encounters a number of male adversaries, all of whom attempt to take advantage of her in various ways. Beginning with her abduction from the festival by a gang of youths who attempt to rape her, she undergoes a series of painful learning experiences in which her innate intelligence and wit, expressed in her consummate skill with language, come to her rescue and bring about a process of increasing self-confidence and self-awareness. Returning home, her humiliated abductors in tow, she is hailed as a heroine in her village. On her second departure from home, ostensibly to gain firsthand knowledge of the city (León) with all the sophistication that this promises, Justina takes the reader on a highly personal and deeply symbolic tour of the city with its artistic and cultural wealth. She continues to engage in battles with the male *pícaros* she meets on her travels, assuming various identities in order to do so, and at the same time comes to terms with several highly significant relationships with female (mother) figures who play a key role in her emerging self-identity. On her second victorious return to her village, Justina discovers that she is the victim of the cruel envy of her selfish and envious siblings, who deprive her of her legal inheritance. In order to finance her court action against her brothers, she assumes various identities, plays tricks on various male pícaros, and ingeniously manages to convince the authorities, once again using her formidable linguistic prowess, that she is the rightful heir to the inheritance of an old Moorish witch. Having won her lawsuit, she returns to her village for the third and final time, where, after being courted by a series of very "unsuitable suitors," she eventually falls in love and marries the soldier-gambler Lozano.

Makarie is "the most taciturn of women" ("die schweigsamste aller Frauen"; H.A. 8, p. 223) in Goethe's *Wilhelm Meister*. When she does talk, she speaks in the measured tones and the heightened aesthetic discourse of the written aphorisms in her archive.[18] While it is left open to whom the writing of the aphorisms in her archive is to be ascribed, the presumption must be that one or all of the women who use and take care of it (Makarie herself, Hersilie, Juliette, or Angela) write them out. Whoever the particular author may be, the aphorisms seem to be the precipitate of a woman's writing. And just as these aphorisms evince a highly stylized linguistic organization—"an unrepeatable concordance of sense, rhythm, and sound"[19]—so, too, is Makarie's talk marked by an unusual formal intensity. In her opening conversation with Wilhelm, she picks up her cue from the terms used by the astronomer (in discussing the misuse of *means*, which are, in themselves, potentially useful) and then plays with them in a curiously fractured chiasmus: "'Ich geb' es zu,' versetzte Makarie, 'denn man kommt in doppelte Verlegenheit. Spricht man von Mißbrauch, so scheint man die Würde des Mittels selbst anzutasten, denn es liegt ja immer noch in dem Mißbrauch verborgen; spricht man von Mittel, so kann man kaum zugeben, daß seine Gründlichkeit und Würde irgendeinen Mißbrauch zulasse'" (H.A. 8, p. 116; "'I agree,' Makarie answered, 'because you face a dilemma. If you talk about misuse, then you seem to impugn the dignity of the means themselves since the means are still implicit in their misuse; if you talk about means, then you scarcely concede the possibility that their thoroughness and dignity might allow any misuse,'" *Journeyman Years*, pp. 175–176).

In ways reminiscent of what is, according to Irigaray, characteristic of a specifically feminine discourse—asymmetry, in particular[20]—Makarie's language at once associates in German "means" (*Mittel*) and "misuse" (*Mißbrauch*) by the play on their near-identical first syllable, thrown into relief by the chiasmus, *Mißbrauch, Mittel, Mittel, Mißbrauch*, which is disrupted by an "extra" appearance of *Mißbrauch* in the middle of the four terms. It is as if the dilemma—the tangled inextricability of the two concepts—were being enacted in the particular use of language. Here, the meaning is embodied in the language rather than simply designated by it. Probably the most striking case in *Wilhelm Meister* of a woman employing language in a nonlinear, apparently illogical, and disruptive way is that of Mignon. Far from being a source of mere involuntary comedy,[21] Mignon's mangled German is curiously expressive: "Manche Tage war sie ganz stumm, zuzeiten antwortete sie mehr auf verschiedene Fragen, immer sonderbar, doch so, daß man nicht unterscheiden konnte, ob es Witz oder Unkenntnis der Sprache war, indem sie ein gebrochenes, mit Französisch und Italienisch durchflochtenes Deutsch sprach" (H.A. 7, p. 110; "Some days [Mignon] would be completely silent; on others she would answer certain questions, but always strangely, so that it was difficult to decide whether her German mixed with French and Italian was intentionally witty or simply the result of an imperfect knowledge of German," *Apprenticeship*, p. 61).

The undecidability of Mignon's use of language has the advantage, for her, that her unique style of German protects her from being fully understood, and thus renders her—like Justina—difficult to manipulate. Moreover, her German, however broken, is accompanied by an impressive tone ("einer sonderbar feierlichen Art," H.A. 7, p. 8; "a curiously solemn air"), reinforced (again like Justina) by a peculiarly affecting body language: her egg dance—for all its mechanical, clockwork nature—is nonetheless powerfully expressive of her character (H.A. 7, pp. 115–116). That such a communicative nature should try so hard to master writing, then, is hardly surprising (H.A. 7, p. 135). Despite her failure at acquiring this particular technique, Mignon is shown to be, along with the harpist, the most articulate of all the characters in the novel. She is, after all, the author—within the fiction of the novel—of some of Goethe's most admired poems ("Kennst du das Land, wo die Zitronen blühn," H.A. 7, p. 145; "So laßt mich scheinen, bis ich werde," H.A. 7, p. 515). The narrator emphasizes that the power of the first song disappears completely once Mignon's interpretation is lost in its being set down on paper: "Melodie und Ausdruck gefielen unserm Freunde besonders, ob er gleich die Worte nicht alle verstehen konnte. Er ließ sich die Strophen wiederholen und erklären, schrieb sie auf und übersetzte sie ins Deutsche. Aber die Originalität der Wendungen konnte er nur von ferne nachahmen. Die kindliche Unschuld des Ausdrucks verschwand, indem die gebrochene Sprache übereinstimmend und das Unzusammenhängende verbunden ward. Auch konnte der Reiz der Melodie mit nichts verglichen werden" (H.A. 7, pp. 145–146; "The melody and the expression pleased our friend [Wilhelm] greatly, though he could not make out all the words. So he asked her to repeat the stanzas, and explain them; then he wrote them down and translated them into German. He found, however, that he could only approximate the originality of her phrases, and the childlike innocence of her expression was lost when the broken language was smoothed over and the disconnectedness removed. The charm of the melody was also quite unique," *Apprenticeship*, p. 83). It is, then, precisely the brokenness, the nonlinear connectedness of Mignon's expression that moves her listeners—and gives expression to her own psyche.

Much later in the novel, this point is made again with some emphasis by the narrator: "Sie sprach noch immer sehr gebrochen deutsch, und nur wenn sie den Mund zum Singen auftat, wenn sie die Zither rührte, schien sie sich des einzigen Organs zu bedienen, wodurch sie ihr Innerstes aufschließen und mitteilen konnte" (H.A. 7, p. 262; "She still spoke a very broken German; and only when she opened her mouth to sing, or played the zither, did she seem to use the one organ with which she could open up and express her innermost self," *Apprenticeship*, p. 156). Mignon's ability to express herself aesthetically, but not discursively, is manifest in her manner of articulating general principles, in much the same way as the infinitely more sophisticated Makarie. For example, in response to Wilhelm's decision that she get a formal education, she famously answers, "Ich bin gebildet genug, um zu lieben und zu trauern" (H.A. 7, p. 488: "I am educated enough to love and to mourn"). Parallelism and near-rhyme on the endings of the two infinitives coalesce "love" and "mourning" in her powerfully effective German in a way that is quite untranslatable. Similarly, her formulation of the age-old "reason-emotion" antithesis is charged and heightened: "Die Vernunft ist grausam ... das Herz ist besser" (H.A. 7, p. 489; "Reason is cruel ... the heart is better"). The sibilant-alliteration in German, in combination with the assonance-repetition, links "heart" with "better" in a dense knot of quasi-identity between the terms. Mignon puts great store by physical appearance; indeed, the opening line of her song ("So let me seem till I become") makes this as clear as her keenness to keep wearing the (female) clothes she has grown to love. The rhyme of *Weib* ("woman") on *Leib* ("body") in the third stanza of her song fully articulates the theme of "embodied meaning," which the female speakers and writers in the novel also exemplify: "Und jene himmlischen Gestalten, / Sie fragen nicht nach Mann und Weib, / Und keine Kleider, keine Falten / Umgeben den verklärten Leib" (H.A. 7, p. 516; "For all those glorious heavenly forms, / They do not ask about man or woman, / No garments long or draperies fine / Surround the body now transformed," *Apprenticeship*, p. 316). What at first sight appears to be inarticulateness is, in fact, the most profound articulation of felt life.

In López de Úbeda's *La Pícara Justina*, Justina makes frequent reference to the nature of her style as being "de espacio" (e.g., pp. 412, 525, 642), an opening up of the word "despacio" ("slow") to suggest also "of space." Her style takes its time and sees in the round.[22] Her repeated plea to the reader to wait for her suggests that she does not want the reader to jump, at first glance, to any rash judgments about her and the intentions or meanings of her words: "Y noten que cuando les parezca que murmuro, me aguarden, no me maldigan luego. Espérenme, que cuando no piensen, volveré con la lechuga" (p. 525; "and note that when it seems to you that I criticize, wait for me, don't condemn me right away. Wait for me, for when you least expect it, I shall return with the lettuce" [a reference to the interpolated story in book II, part II, cap. I, no. 3, p. 379]). Rather, she urges her readers to savor what she writes, that they might appreciate that she returns "más honra que la que debo" (p. 525; "more honor than I owe"). Justina, once again, articulates the notion of balancing, which in her case involves her in giving a little more honor than she owes—more, that is, than has been given to her. Later, in the chapter dedicated to Sancha Gómez, she underlines her style as cat-like, slowly stalking and ever waiting to pounce—a style that she claims has an advantage over that of other women, who usually make sudden moves.

One illustration in particular sums up the dilemma that Justina faces in her role as woman-as-writer and her need to write herself subtly and indirectly into discourse. In the interpolated tale of the Catholic monarchs (Isabel and Ferdinand), Isabel, who, as a woman, is unable to speak directly to the king to tell him that he is making a mistake, wonders aloud what the marshmallow plants on the side of the road would say if *they* were the only ones who could speak, a rhetorical question to which she herself provides the playfully serious punning answer: "En esta ocasión [no supieran ... decirnos] otra cosa, sino mal vas" (p. 89; "on this occasion [they would not know how ... to tell us] anything, except 'you are going wrong'"). The term for marshmallows ("malvas") has been literally opened up to yield "mal vas" ("you are going wrong"). Unable to assume directly the "I" of discourse in her own right, Isabel, like Justina, is forced to speak indirectly sub rosa. By disrupting the very morphology of the Spanish word, Justina-as-writer creates the space in which a woman's truly intended meaning can find expression.

One of the most remarkable passages in which the eponymous heroine of *La Pícara Justina* gives tongue to her frustration at her inability to articulate her self—to speak her "identity as a woman"[23]—comes in chapter 4, book 4, on the occasion of the bans of her marriage to Lozano: "¡Mirábanse unos a otros, y luego todos me miraban a mí!" (p. 727; "they looked at each other, and then they all looked at me!"). Unable to tolerate her brothers' hostile stares, she secures her grip on the coffer containing her hard-won inheritance, and, composing herself, affirms, "¡Yo soy! ¿No me conocéis? ¿Qué me miráis?" (p. 728; "I am! Don't you know me? Why do you look at me?"). Justina's words not only reveal her real (royal-divine) identity; they also betray her real (human) frustration and disbelief at her brothers' failure to recognize her true self, and so pay due respect to her autonomy, her integrity, and her status: "comencé a cobrar bríos de hidalga, mas no por eso mis hermanos me tenían más respeto" (p. 728; "I began to acquire a noblewoman's spirit, but that did not mean that my brothers showed me more respect"). The rhetorical emphasis in this episode on "looking at" (and implicitly not really seeing) is clearly linked to a notion of respect (or recognition of the object as an other, different, and equally valid subject), for her brothers, retaining their position of authority as subjects of the verb, reaffirm their male solidarity by looking at (and really seeing) one another, a solidarity, or "seeing-one-another," which is exploited and underscored in the verbal form "mirábanse" ("they looked at each other"), common enough in Golden Age Spanish usage. But their male solidarity sees itself in opposition to her, for they then turn, all-men-together ("todos"), to look at her, an action that, in its linguistic formulation ("todos me miraban a mí"), speaks not of solidarity with the object of the looking, that is, Justina, but of a divisive and fragmenting gaze.

This is really a not-seeing, which, experienced as it is from Justina's standpoint, is a powerful expression of the root cause of her isolation and exclusion—indeed, alienation—from the dominant (male) group, and hence, in the public sphere at least, from her inner self. Compare this to Justina's earlier references to her unsuitable suitors, her "novios" ("grooms") as "no vios" ("did-not-see's"); in other words, those who did not truly see and (implicitly) respect her (cf. p. 455). Her sense of herself as thus split between subjective and objective identities is underlined in the two distinct (one objective, the other disjunctive) pronouns for "me," which are, significantly, separated by the male subjects' divisive and reductive gaze. And it is in courageous response to their concerted attempt to suppress her hard-won (ego-) identity, her transcendent integrity as a subject in her own right, that Justina, grown in stature and self-awareness by this point in her narrative (hi)story (on the threshold of her union with Lozano), is emboldened to utter those all-important and all-powerful words, "I am." But it is at the beginning of her summary prologue (cf. pp. 81–84) to her life story that Justina makes a linguistic gesture that—unlike the defiant public declaration of self-affirmation ("I am") at her wedding, made to an unreceptive and, therefore, unworthy brotherhood—tenderly articulates (in the form of a letter addressed to Lozano prior to their wedding) a very private amorous exchange between her and her significant other. She does this by literally including the male "other" in her statement of self-affirmation—"Yo, mi señor don Pícaro, soy" (p. 82; "I, my señor Don Pícaro, am")—in an oddness of expression similar to that employed by Goethe's Makarie or Mignon. Moreover, in keeping with her self-determined holistic (inclusive) style of "telling all" (p. 170), she hereby opens up the linguistic space between the "I" and the "am," and, encompassing the male beloved in her womb-like, liminal interiority, inscribes her self, in indirect fashion, as archetypal woman.

One of Justina's most remarkable stylistic features is the sheer pleasure she takes in expressing herself, which is conveyed to the reader in two fundamental ways: first, through her constantly alluding to her body as playing a vital role in her self-expression; and second, by the playful way with which she handles the physicality of her linguistic medium, appearing to set words free from their rigid semantic import by exploiting their sound-look properties to the full. Many of the expressions she uses to refer to her words (such as "aires bola," "air ball")[24] suggest the playfulness, airy lightness, seductiveness, and extreme subtlety so characteristic of López de Úbeda's contemporaries, to whom such playfulness is second nature. Justina's playfulness can, however, also convey deeply felt emotion and profound truths—all expressive of her woman's touch. She is, of course, equally skilled at reproducing its opposite, for example, the heavy, clumsy, ugly, and repellent style of the unsuitable suitors, whose belching overtures she finds so "inappropriate." She cannot speak to her unsophisticated apprentice Bertol in her usual witty "coded" ("en cifra") style because, she says, she may as well be speaking in Arabic, so she has to say it "pan por pan" (p. 567; "to spell it out") before he grasps her meaning. In keeping with her womanly reflection of the "morphological marks of the female body,"[25] Justina's pen— the symbol of her empowerment and the instrument of her style, her parler-femme—like her readers-interlocutors, takes on a multiplicity of different identities, an expression of her dynamic sense of empowerment and delight in her fluid self-identity: "porque para de lejos, me servía de lanza; para de cerca, de trompa de elefante; para en pie, de azote, y para asentado, de sceptro" (p. 329; "from afar [the pen] served me as a lance; from near, an elephant's trunk; on foot, a whip; and seated, a scepter")—a series of identities (the first three of which are linked by homeoteleuton, words with similar endings) that, she claims, give her pleasure by confusing her abductors (cf. p. 329). Justina, who "jugaba de rebenque floridamente" (p. 329; "played with her whip-pen with rhetorical flowers"), rejoices in her chameleon-like qualities, her floriferous style, her skill, we might say, at that parler-femme that she shares with Goethe's Mignon and Makarie.

Justina is not only adept at winning verbal battles; she uses— literally—her body in her battles with her male opponents, a tactic she reproduces in the textual detail of her style. One example of the way she uses her face, for example, occurs in an encounter with Pavón in the chapter "Del desenojo astuto" ("Of the astute appeasement"), when she turns the tables on him by mimicking the Gorgon-Medusa-like vision of the demonized feminine. Confident of frightening her opponent, who has struck a blow at her with his two fingers hidden in his fist, she reminds herself (and the reader) that "no era yo la primer mesonera[26] que triunfó de hominicacos" (p. 605; "I was not the first landlady who triumphed over insignificant little men"). Justina gestures like a wild cat, thereby stopping her opponent in his tracks; in a typically playful use of the body of language, his "enojo" ("anger") is "deformed" into "desenojo" ("dis-anger" or appeasement, cf. pp. 602–605). She literally re-creates her own body language in the bodily detail of the language, as she does when she describes the way in which she retracts her bodily parts (here, her eyes and arms) as if they were a formidable and very effective weapon: "Retraje el brazo, eché a mis espantadores ojos las cortinas de mis párpados y plegué el pendón de mis extendidas cejas" (p. 605; "I retracted my arm, closed the curtains of my eyelids on my frightening eyes, and folded the banner of my extended eyebrows"). The striking alliterative play on "párpados," "plegué," and "pendón" associates (in the same nonlogical way as Goethe identifies "being led (by impulse)" with "freedom" in the writing of the "Beautiful Soul") the human body ("párpados") with the instrumentality of heroic action ("pendón"). The result of their encounter and her strategy is success, for she loses her fear and he, his anger (cf. p. 605). She sums up this particular episode by making a general statement about the seemingly arbitrary way in which life's fortunes can change and cause a setback, and, significantly, she uses the weaving leitmotif, pervasive in her text, to illustrate this: "Un buen decidor o decidora es de casta de lanzadera, la cual aunque muchas veces y mucho tiempo ande aguda y sutilmente sobre los hilos de la tela, pero si por desdicha encuentra en uno solo, aquél la ase y detiene. Así yo, aunque había gran rato dicho con agudeza, topé en este hilo y perdí el hilo" (p. 277; "A good speaker (masculine) or speaker (feminine) is like a shuttle that runs shrewdly and subtly over the threads of the cloth many times and for a long time; but if, by misfortune, it chances upon one (thread) only, that one catches it and stops it. So I, although I had for a long time spoken with wit, came across this particular thread, and I lost the thread"). She compares herself to the dynamic movement of the weaving shuttle, a constant interactive rhythm that is crucial to the creation of the whole tapestry-cloth and to her growth narrative; but, like the clock mechanism that misses a beat and is forced to stop in its tracks, the Justina-shuttle, when caught in one thread, is similarly balked, and she is forced to contemplate (albeit only momentarily, for melancholy is anathema to the pícara) the other of her pleasure-seeking enjoyment of life: death as the silent (ineffable) other of her delight in linguistic self-expression.

This analogy of speaking and weaving not only reveals Justina's sophisticated awareness of the etymological basis of the concept of "text"; it also focuses attention on her adroitness in drawing threads of sound and look over the surface of her writing, in the process creating a dense "texture" of apparently playfully arbitrary relations which yet are expressive of what would otherwise remain repressed: namely the "both ... and" structure of the felt life in which, for example, apparent (either-or) logical opposites like "anger" ("enojo") and "appeasement" ("desenojo") are, in a polyptoton (play on different forms of the same root or stem), made to sound and look quasi-identical in a way that is faithful to the (feminine) ambivalence of human feeling (cf. pp. 602–605). The fact that, in general usage,[27] the agent of "desenojo" (appeasement) is the same person who provoked the "enojo" ("anger") in the first place underlines the power of this subtle subtext.

Similarly, when her relatives confiscate her inheritance before the courts, she claims, using a palpable figure of *distinctio* (which is, of course, also a play on her own name), to emphasize the injustice of the law in application: "Para mí fue la *justicia justicia*, para mis hermanas misericordia" (p. 631, my italics; "for me, justice was justice; for my sisters, [it was] mercy"). And, in one of her most startling exploitations of the bodiliness of the Spanish language to express the way in which her brothers repress her, take away her pleasures, and summon the whole of the "hermandad" ("brotherhood") and their weapons against a woman if she makes just one small move to assert herself, Justina literally opens up the word "brother" ("hermano") and then inserts her own interpretation of the word: "her[ir con la] mano" (to wound by hand), based on her own experience of brothers: "there are no worse nor more crude executioners for a woman than brothers ... A bad brother is enemy like the flesh, for we cannot cast it from us. Whoever said brother, said to injure with the hand" (p. 628; "no hay peores ni más crudos verdugos para una mujer que hermanos ... Un mal hermano es enemigo como la carne, que no la podemos echar de nosotras. Quien dijo hermano, dijo herir con la mano"). In her differentiating—"finicky" ("melindrosa")—female voice, she makes it clear that it is not all brothers (indirectly, not all men), but only those "whose love is as corrupt as their name" (p. 629, "que tienen tan corrompido el amor como el nombre"). With this statement, she pinpoints stylistically the distorting, pathologizing influence of a one-sided psychology that corrupts the inherently positive meaning enshrined in the part-homonym—"hermano" meaning "loving affinity," "correspondence," and "harmony"—and endows it with negative and destructive significance.

Wilhelm Meister shares the episodic structure of the picaresque novel, and, as in *La Pícara Justina*, the hero's point of view is that of an outsider. More specifically relevant here is that the two works share a similar ironic viewpoint, arising from the same structural contrast (between realism and mythology), which is articulated in very similar stylistic terms, certainly in respect to the expression given to the female/feminine voice. In his 1823 review of a collection of Spanish romances,[28] it was precisely the "higher, benevolent irony" that Goethe singled out for particular praise, favorably comparing it with what he admired in Goldsmith's and Sterne's novels—a humor that "liberated the soul."[29] And, as Eric Blackall notes, there is some evidence to suggest that the picaresque novel played a significant role in shaping Goethe's own practice as a novelist.[30] What is certainly clear is that in both *La Pícara Justina* and *Wilhelm Meister*, the perplexing discrepancy between the "real" world of contingency and error and the mythological world produces an interruptive narrative framework,[31] which in turn furnishes opportunity for an indirect, nonlinear, allusive style that challenges the reader to find coherences in the textual detail that are, apparently, lacking in the narration. The power of this ironic play of language to disturb and to stimulate new insights is manifested in both novels in the organization of the language used by women, whether ostensibly spoken or written. Marie Cardinal's tenet—that words are a valuable means of a woman's self-determination[32]—is corroborated by the way in which in *La Pícara Justina* and *Wilhelm Meister* what women have to say takes on "embodied meaning" rather than simply "designative meaning."[33]

While Goethe's intense interest in Spanish literature is well documented,[34] there is only oblique evidence that he may have been familiar with *La Pícara Justina* (via Hans Jakob Christoffel von Grimmelshausen's *Simplicissimus* [1669–72], which seems to have drawn on the Spanish novel, though probably on the German translation [of 1626] of an earlier Italian translation).[35] But what Goethe almost certainly shared with López de Úbeda is that most cogent articulation of the female voice that appeared in the kabbalistic mystical tradition. Classical Kabbalah, coming to full fruition in Spain in the thirteenth century, culminated in the appearance there, toward the end of the century, of what was to become its central text, a kind of kabbalistic bible, the pseudo-epigraphic *Zohar*, literally "Book of Splendor," usually attributed to Rabbi Moses de León. In thirteenth-century Spain—the cradle of the European Kabbalah—the anonymous *Sefer ha-temuna* ("Book of the Image") continued the doctrine of the ten "emanations" (sefirot, or "numbers") of the *Sefer yetzira*, the extensive mystical symbolism of the *Sefer ha-bahir*, and advanced the notion of cosmic cycles or eons, each of which had a different *Torah*.[36] The kabbalistic tradition (and in particular, *The Zohar*),³⁷ in granting to Shekhinah, the female element of God, the central position that Sophia occupied in gnostic speculation marked "a relapse into, or ... revival of, the mythical consciousness," in which all metaphors, figures of speech, and above all, symbols were inherited from gnosticism.³⁸ Moreover, the sometimes fantastic and frequently indelicate anthropomorphisms employed in *The Zohar* to express Shekhinah's relations with God as with the human individual are reminiscent of the Great Goddess's sexual prowess—an explicitness that persuaded, as late as 1926, the English translator of Christian Knorr von Rosenroth's influential Latin translation of *The Zohar*, the *Kabbala Denudata* (vol. 1, Sulzbach, 1677/78; vol. 2, Frankfurt, 1684), to leave certain passages in Latin.³⁹

Even before the keen interest taken in *The Zohar* by such influential Renaissance figures as Pico della Mirandola and Johann Reuchlin (1455–1522), its influence in Christian Spain was being felt.⁴⁰ Long before *The Zohar* appeared in print, it was exerting a widespread influence across southern Renaissance Europe;⁴¹ in Latin translations and polemic pamphlets, it caught the interest of such thinkers as Paracelsus, Agrippa, Luther, and Newton. Between 1480 and 1650, not many Christian thinkers and writers were left untouched by the influence of what one writer has called a "fad" of the Renaissance.⁴² The interest of the Christian interpreters was primarily to corroborate Christological doctrine: "The primary intention of the Christian interpretations of cabala, as first shown in the earliest of the Christian interpreters, was to seek for new means of confirming the truths of the Christian religion."⁴³ But other aspects also had their appeal and made their way into writings of Renaissance figures only twenty-five years after the introduction of *The Zohar* into Europe. Indeed, one of the earliest references to the Kabbalah in a history of philosophy calls attention to "the similarity between the Kabbalah and the late Greek mystery cults."⁴⁴

The earliest critical discussions of the Kabbalah seem to have taken place in Provençal literature during the thirteenth century, though Castile, as early as the last two decades of the thirteenth century, was a meeting point in Spain for those interested in the Kabbalah and a fertile breeding ground for the elaborate flourishing of its symbolism.⁴⁵ But it is undoubtedly the publication of Pico della Mirandola's *Conclusiones Philosophicae Cabalisticae et Theologicae* of 1486 (in which he saw the Kabbalah as the best way of bridging the gap between Christianity and ancient Greek philosophy) that marks the true beginning of the widespread interest in the Renaissance for kabbalistic thought.⁴⁶ Kabbalistic ideas became part of the Platonic-Pythagorean-hermetic Renaissance synthesis, which itself was widely disseminated in Latin, Italian, Spanish, German, French, and English.[47] Reuchlin, in his *De Verbo Mirifico* of 1494, took up Pico's idea that all religions, each in its own way, express the same divine, cosmic truth[48]—an idea that was to play a central role in the Enlightenment of the eighteenth century.

The cross-fertilization during the early Christian era that had apparently given rise to the eclectic cosmological speculations and formulations of the Kabbalah, along with its systematic compression, seems to have recommended *The Zohar* in particular to Renaissance thinkers, keen to codify the complex symbology of the general hermetic tradition to which they were grateful heirs. And in this melting pot of Christian, pagan, and esoteric traditions, the Kabbalah provided a *lingua franca* of seductively exact macrocosmic correspondence, as well as a mythological framework. The personification of wisdom as a heavenly virgin who, like the philosophers' stone (the ancient alchemical symbol of the *coniunctio oppositorum*), is represented as hermaphroditic in her reconciliation of opposites, is an idea that Goethe could just as easily have taken directly from the writings of the Christian kabbalists (like Johann Reuchlin or Friedrich Christoph Oetinger) or, more likely, indirectly from his secondary sources. Similarly, Jakob Böhme's kabbalistic symbolization of the final attainment of wisdom as the loving embrace of bridegroom and bride—a commonplace of mystical writing since the Song of Songs—was available to Goethe in Arnold, whose sympathetic passages on the Spanish "heretics" Saint Teresa, Saint John of the Cross, and Saint Ignatius Loyola Goethe found particularly congenial because of their emphasis on an in-dwelling God.[49] And, as Goethe tells us in *Dichtung und Wahrheit*, such notions in any case were mother's milk to him, raised as he was under the influence of the German Pietist movement, itself inspired by Böhme, an influence dramatically reinforced by his Pietistic mother's friend Fräulein von Klettenberg and her enthusiastic endorsement of the strongly occultist sect of Pietism founded by Nikolaus Ludwig von Zinzendorf. Moreover, long before he read in 1772, at the insistence of his great teacher Johann Gottfried Herder (1744–1803), Shaftesbury's Neoplatonic writings, Goethe had at the age of fifteen read Plotinus himself, and had gone on absorbing Neoplatonism, along with the tenets of alchemy and the Kabbalah, during the period 1768–70 (when he had even conducted alchemical experiments). Although, as he tells us in *Dichtung und Wahrheit*, he hid this "mystical-cabbalistic chemistry and all that pertained to it" from Herder (H.A. 9, p.

414), he continued to read in hermeticism, "in order to develop it more consistently" than the confused form in which he—and the late eighteenth-century fashion for quasi-mysticism—received it. Indeed, his interest in the hermetic tradition, including its kabbalistic expression, continued until the very end of his life, as the closing scenes of *Faust*'s second part make clear.

In the case of López de Úbeda, the influence that the Kabbalah may have had on his writings is suggested strongly by the reception of *The Zohar* in Renaissance Spain, but also by very compelling internal evidence. Justina's symbolic "return to her mother's womb" marks the beginning of the process of her becoming herself by retracing her own family tree, in particular by returning to her maternal origins. Reference to the name of her mother's hometown, Cea, associates her lineage with that of the goddess Ceres (p. 173), just as her roles as mediator (encapsulated in her name)—she has to "mantener la justa de la picardía" (p. 173; "umpire the joust—the just balance—of the picaresque life")—and as the "fundadora de la picardía" ("founder of the picaresque life") associate her with the Shekhinah as *Malkuth* (or foundation). And to ensure that the Justina-Shekhinah identification is not missed by the reader ("whether Christian or Moor"), the novel (and in particular the chapter dealing with her mother) is shot through with Shekhinah symbols such as the "reverendísima cuba" ("most reverent vat for collecting wine or cereal"), which is also described as a "beautiful whale" (p. 172), the moon, the bridge(s), the saddlebags (maintaining balance), and the date palm (cf. p. 173). Her surname, Diez ("Ten"), and her statement in relation to her ancestors, "porque soy la décima esencia de todos ellos, cuanto y más la quinta" (173; "because I am the tenth essence, as well as the fifth [quintessence] of all of them"), reveal most blatantly her self-identification with the tenth sefirah, Shekhinah. The close parallel of Justina with the all-powerful, gentle, but penetrating voice of the goddess, represented as the balmy "céfiro" breeze (*ruh*: holy spirit) that is the Shekhinah's ("sefirot") poetic veil (already alluded to in the abduction scene with Perro Grullo [cf. p. 304]) is given full expression in the chapter entitled "De la mirona fisgante" ("Of the looker spy"; pp. 523–539). Here, in a poem constructed in the strict form of a series of rhetorical parallelisms (reflected in the repeated rhyme scheme between the first two and the second two stanzas), each of the attributes of the Holy Spirit is extended in the second half of the poem to Justina.

In the first two stanzas of the poem, we have an eloquent recitation of the Shekhinah's essential attributes and functions, which in stanzas three and four are associated with Justina, indeed, identified with her. The animating Spirit of the World is characterized by constant movement (lines 2 and 7), mediating between the upper and the lower realms (ll. 5 and 6) and between the poles of earthly existence (ll. 7 and 8). The animating Spirit shares all of her attributes with Justina: for example, they both penetrate into the innermost (ll. 3 and 19), they are both antidotes to evil (ll. 12 and 29), and they both bring delight and health (ll. 14 and 16, 17 and 32). So close indeed is the parallel between the two figures that Justina takes on qualities that are not explicitly ascribed to the animating Spirit, but which are implicitly divine. It is she, Justina, who is said to have the divine power of naming things (l. 19)—a power that underlines her identification with Adam. And it is she who is able to divine that eminently female sphere, the waters (l. 20). The female voice is here the voice of divine wisdom (l. 11) and compassion (ll. 15–16, 30–32). Both the disembodied Spirit and its earthly embodiment in Justina move in a fluid, circular, dynamic mode that embraces extremes.

When Justina ironically repeats the age-old defamation of Eve—"Woman was the first to falsify the good and nature" (p. 563)—she is alluding to her office as writer-poet, in revaluing semblance as positive; for she gives expression, by means of the aesthetic manipulation of her medium, to the inner, feminine, life—the voice of the soul, as she puts it—which she "simulates" or "falsifies"—in other words, re-creates "artificially"—in her poetic style. She has already told us in her introduction (cf. p. 90) that she paints "with art." And artifice—an allusion to her rich arsenal of linguistic strategies, her "jokes," "tricks," "deceptions," and so on, as well as to her distinct writing style, for she is, after all, the "melindrosa escribana," the affected, finicky (i.e., not natural) scribe—is paradoxically what she must avail herself of, in order to achieve what can only ever be an approximation to "truth" and "nature." The use of the lies and tricks of her parler-femme are justified, moreover, in that they are valid self-expressive tools within a cultural discourse that is weighted against her. Whether it is "lo de veras" ("to do with truths") or "lo de burlas" ("to do with deception"), she assures the reader that it is all truth: "es verdad todo esto y otro tanto que callo" (p. 530; "all this, and more that I keep to myself, is truth"). She tells the reader, addressing him/her affectionately with the diminutive as "letorcillo" ("little reader"), that woman is the first inventor of strategies and "fictiones," for, she continues, it is women's legacy to be "fingidoras, disimuladas, recetistas, bizmadoras, saludadoras, y todo sobre falso, y más que yo me callo" (p. 564; "pretenders, deceivers, prescribers of cures, appliers of poultices, health-bringers, and all based [above all] on falseness, and more that I keep to myself"). In other words, her female voice, by means of poetic expression, forges the healing, redeeming link between the inner ("divine") and the outer ("human") spheres, overcoming superficial (and often unjust) distinctions of gender. Or, as Goethe's Mignon expresses the same thought, "Und jene himmlischen Gestalten / Sie fragen nicht nach Mann und Weib" (H.A. 7, p. 516; "for all those glorious heavenly forms, / They do not ask about man or woman," *Apprenticeship*, p. 316).

Such close congruence of both theme and style suggests "a shared cultural background ... in which the texts compared in some measure participate."[50] That shared background, I propose, is the kabbalistic tradition of exploiting the literal medium of language in order to express the female voice.

Notes

1. See Immaculada Delgado Cobos, "Algunos cultismos en la Picaresca del Siglo de Oro: cultismos en la 'Pícara Justina,'" in *Estudios filológicos en homenaje a Eugenio de Bustos Tovar*, ed. José Antonio Bartol Hernández et al. (Salamanca, 1992), vol. 1, pp. 219–234; here, p. 221: "[Nuestra preocupación se centra en] las voces que los autores considerados, en especial la sin par Justina, emplean para construir su inigualable forma de expresión. Quien ve chocarrería y vulgaridad en el pícaro, no se ha detenido a desmenuzar las voces recreadas que, para expresar las piruetas lingüísticas, son necesarias: las voces cultas, y no sólo plebeyas y vulgares, que daban el tono vital a la geografía léxica resultante."
2. Francisco López de Úbeda, *La Pícara Justina*, ed. Antonio Rey Hazas (Madrid, 1977). This passage comes at the end of the introductory number entitled "From the Sweetmeat/witticism to the hair of the pen" (pp. 103–104), in which Justina refers to her pen with the hair stuck to it as emblematic of her position as the writing woman, as the "summary" or "essence" ("in a nutshell") of her narratorial stance. For the elucidation of difficult Spanish terms, I have drawn on the *Diccionario de uso del español*, ed. María Moliner (Madrid, 1970).
3. *Goethes Werke in 14 Bänden: Hamburger Ausgabe*, ed. Erich Trunz (Hamburg, 1949ff.), vols. 7 and 8, p. 383, hereafter abbreviated in the text and endnotes as "H.A. 7" (*Wilhelm Meisters Lehrjahre*) and "H.A. 8" (*Wilhelm Meisters Wanderjahre*). The English translations of *Wilhelm Meister* are taken from *Goethe: The Collected Works in 12 Volumes*, vols. 9 and 10, ed. Victor Lange, Eric Blackall, and Cyrus Hamlin (Princeton, 1994–95), abbreviated in the text and endnotes as *Apprenticeship* and *Journeyman Years*, respectively. I have changed the English where necessary.
4. The phrase is Elizabeth Sewell's; see her *The Structure of Poetry* (London, 1951).
5. See, for example, Luce Irigaray, *Speculum of the Other Woman*, trans. Gillian C. Gill (Ithaca, N.Y., 1985), p. 79: "[women's writing] resists and explodes every firmly established form, figure, idea or concept."

6. Luce Irigaray, *Sexes and Genealogies,* trans. Gillian C. Gill (New York, 1993), p. 196.
7. Luce Irigaray, *Parler n'est jamais neutre* (Paris, 1985), p. 313. Cf. Margaret Whitford, *Luce Irigaray: Philosophy in the Feminine* (London and New York, 1991), p. 59; H.A. 6, p. 43.
8. Irigaray, "Divine Women," in *Sexes and Genealogies,* pp. 55–72, here pp. 59–60.
9. Ibid., p. 58.
10. Ibid., p. 61.
11. G. G. Scholem, *Major Trends in Jewish Mysticism* (New York, 1954), p. 134, discusses Abraham Abulafia's kabbalistic manuals, including "The Words of Beauty" and "The Book of Combinations."
12. G. G. Scholem, *On the Kabbalah and Its Symbolism,* trans. Ralph Manheim (New York, 1965), p. 105.
13. Barbara Newman, *From Virile Woman to Woman Christ: Studies in Medieval Religion and Literature* (Philadelphia, 1995), p. 227.
14. Scholem compares Shekhinah with the Shakti of the latent God of Indian religion which is "entirely active energy, in which what is concealed within God is externalized"; in *Mystical Shape of the Godhead: Basic Concepts in the Kabbalah,* trans. Joachim Neugroschel (New York, 1991), p. 174.
15. B. McGinn, "The Language of Love in Christian and Jewish Mysticism," in *Mysticism and Language,* ed. Steven T. Katz (New York, 1992), p. 227. See also Karen Guberman, "The Language of Love in Spanish Kabbalah: An Examination of the 'Iggeret ha-Kodesh,'" in *Approaches to Judaism in Medieval Times,* ed. David R. Blumenthal (Chico, Calif., 1984), vol. 1, pp. 53–105; her examination of the kabbalistic marriage manual provides a detailed analysis of the organizing principle of resemblance in the relationship between human and divine language and behavior.
16. Irigaray herself points to the Kabbalah as furnishing an example of such symbolism of the body: "Hebrew culture, or at least the Kabbalah, shows the lips in the form of a double inverted yod, a double inverted tongue"; "The Female Gender," in *Sexes and Genealogies,* pp. 105–123, here p. 115.
17. *Zohar: The Book of Enlightenment,* trans. and ed. D. C. Matt (New York, 1983), p. 230: "Shekhinah expresses divine language."
18. See R. H. Stephenson, *Goethe's Wisdom Literature: A Study in Aesthetic Transmutation* (Berne, 1983), pp. 157–163, for an aesthetic analysis of Goethe's aphoristic style.
19. Michael Hamburger, "A Perilous Multiplicity," in *Goethe Revisited: A Collection of Essays,* ed. Elizabeth M. Wilkinson (London, 1983), pp. 11–30, here p. 19.
20. Cf. Patricia Elliot, *From Mastery to Analysis: Theories of Gender in Psychoanalytic Feminism* (Ithaca, N.Y., 1991), pp. 162–165.
21. Stefan Blessin, *Goethes Romane: Aufbruch in die Moderne* (Paderborn, 1996), p. 167.
22. Cf. M. Whitford, *Luce Irigaray* (London, 1991), p. 5; the phrase "time of understanding" is used by Whitford to describe Irigaray's style, which needs the reader and requires of the reader that he/she take time for the process of making the connections, and thus be a vital part in "thinking the unthought" and effecting the change in the symbolic order that is her aim.
23. Irigaray, *Sexes and Genealogies,* p. 196.
24. Rey Hazas alludes to this playfully cryptic phrase, commenting that it evokes the speaker's pleasure (*La Pícara Justina,* p. 747).
25. Irigaray, *Sexes and Genealogies,* pp. 179–180.
26. A ubiquitous epithet in the text, used to express her female genealogy.
27. See *Diccionario del uso del español,* p. 935.

28. *Gedenkausgabe Goethes Werke*, ed. E. Beutler (Zurich, 1948–59), vol. 14, p. 508.
29. Ibid., vol. 8, p. 513.
30. Eric A. Blackall, *Goethe and the Novel* (Ithaca, N.Y., 1976), pp. 142–144.
31. S. Blessin, *Goethes Romane*, p. 39, argues that this structuring polarity holds true for all of Goethe's novels: "Seit dem *Werther* erzählt Goethe in seinen Romanfiguren zwei Geschichten: eine historische und eine musterhafte" ("Since *Werther*, Goethe narrates two stories in terms of the characters of his novels, one historical, the other exemplary").
32. See Elliot, *From Mastery to Analysis*, pp. 52–67.
33. The distinction is taken from James L. Guetti, *Word-Music: The Aesthetic Aspect of Narrative Fiction* (New Brunswick, N.J., 1980), p. 172.
34. See Marie Mathilda Weinrich, *Goethe's Interest in Spanish Literature, Its Influence on His Own Works, and His General Relation to Spain*, Ph.D. diss. (Washington University, 1937).
35. Ulrich Stadler, "Parodistisches in der *Justina Dietzin Picara*: Über die Entstehungsbedingungen und zur Wirkungsgeschichte von Úbedas Schelmenroman in Deutschland," *Arcadia*, vol. 7 (1972), pp. 158–170.
36. For a useful history of the Kabbalah in the pre-Zoharic period (i.e., before 1300), see Joseph Leon Blau, *The Christian Interpretation of the Cabala in the Renaissance* (New York, 1965), pp. 7–10.
37. Cf. Alice Raphael, *Goethe and the Philosophers' Stone: Symbolical Patterns in "The Parable" and the Second Part of "Faust"* (London, 1965), p. 31: "The book *Zohar* ... concerns the relations of God to his consort—the Matrona, who at the same time, meant Divine Wisdom."
38. Scholem, *Major Trends in Jewish Mysticism*, pp. 28 and 35.
39. *The Kabbalah Unveiled*, trans. S. L. M. Mathers (London, 1926), p. 231.
40. See G. G. Scholem, "Considérations sur l'histoire des débuts de la Kabbale chrétienne," in *Kabbalistes Chrétiens* (Paris, 1979), pp. 17–48 (especially pp. 31 and 36); Catherine Swietlicki, *Spanish Christian Cabala: The Works of Luis de Léon, Santa Teresa de Jesús, and San Juan de la Cruz* (Columbia, Miss., 1986), pp. 28–43.
41. See *Zohar: The Book of Enlightenment*, pp. 198–201 and 209–210.
42. Blau, *The Christian Interpretation of the Cabala*, pp. vii and 13.
43. Ibid., p. 20. "Knowledge [of the Kabbalah] has been found in every type of scholar, everywhere in Europe. From Italy to Scandinavia knowledge of cabala spread," p. 112.
44. Ibid., pp. 101–102.
45. See Moshe Idel, *Kabbalah: New Perspectives* (New Haven, Conn., 1988), pp. 9ff, 210–213, and 250ff.
46. Ibid., pp. 257–263.
47. The resultant theosophy was of interest to "English Platonists and scientists such as Newton, and German idealistic thinkers, such as Schelling"; ibid., p. 264.
48. Cf. Charles Zika, "Reuchlin's *De Verbo Mirifico* and the Magic Debate of the Late Fifteenth Century," *Journal of the Warburg and Courtauld Institutes*, vol. 39 (1976), pp. 104–138.
49. See Ronald D. Gray, *Goethe the Alchemist: A Study of Alchemical Symbolism in Goethe's Literary and Scientific Works* (London, 1952), p. 49.
50. S. S. Prawer, *Comparative Literary Studies: An Introduction* (London, 1973), p. 57. Prawer sees a shared tradition as a necessary implication of comparative work; cf. pp. 53–55.

THE INFLUENCE OF NEOGRAMMARIAN SCHOLARSHIP ON RAMÓN MENÉNDEZ PIDAL'S HISTORICAL GRAMMARS OF SPANISH

Donald E. Lenfest

Throughout his academic career, Ramón Menéndez Pidal (1869–1968), Spain's outstanding cultural historian, dedicated considerable time to the diachronic study of the Spanish language, combining the principles of classical philology, his chosen field of university study, with the more modern precepts of comparative philology, a discipline largely dominated by German scholars. Under the inspiration of romanticism, these comparativists had turned their attention from the literature of Greek and Latin antiquity to folk literature and to the evolution of the Indo-European family of languages. By the second half of the nineteenth century, the *Junggrammatiker* (Neogrammarians), a circle of young scholars who followed the Indo-Europeanist Karl Brugmann (1849–1919), had taken up the pioneering work of Rasmus Rask (1787–1832), Franz Bopp (1791–1867), and Jakob Grimm (1785–1863). The main concerns of this essay are Menéndez Pidal's own romantically inspired interest in the popular literature of Spain, his discovery of Neogrammarian linguistic scholarship, and his application of Neogrammarian principles to the study of the Spanish language.

As a youth, Menéndez Pidal was introduced to the iconoclastic enthusiasm of the romantics by his older brother Juan (1861–1915), whose interest in authors such as Johann Wolfgang von Goethe, Heinrich Heine, Sir Walter Scott, and Gustavo Adolfo Bécquer inspired Ramón not only to investigate the folk literature of his native Asturias, but also to read Manuel Milà y Fontanals's (1818–1884) monumental *De la poesía heroico-popular castellana* (1874). Later in life, Ramón Menéndez Pidal would continue to pursue this interest with his wife María Goyri, with whom he took many trips into the countryside to collect variants of the traditional ballads from unschooled country people. This, of course, is similar to what the brothers Grimm had done in their compilation of German fairy tales, an activity which eventually led Jakob Grimm to publish his *Deutsche Grammatik* (1819–34), in which he formulated his well-known "law" concerning the evolution of Germanic obstruents from corresponding Indo-European stops and fricatives, preparing the way for the Neogrammarian dictum that sound change laws have no exception ("die Lautgesetze kennen keine Ausnahmen").[1]

Despite the romantic effervescence within his own family, Menéndez Pidal's schooling imbued him with a respect for traditional culture. The *bachillerato* that he completed at the Instituto Cardenal Cisneros (1886) emphasized history, literature, and languages—disciplines that attracted the young scholar and held his interest throughout his professional career.[2] In history classes, he learned about the Greco-Roman past and about the European Middle Ages. In literature, he read not only the classics of Greek and Roman literatures, but also the masterpieces of European vernacular literatures, particularly those of Spain. In languages, he followed the traditional curriculum, initiating his study of Greek, Latin, and French. The classical languages eventually provided him with an entrée into the professorial ranks, while French furnished him with an invaluable tool for research in medieval literature, allowing him, for example, to read the works of the great French philologist Gaston Paris (1839–1903). French was also an important tool for historical linguistics because it permitted Menéndez Pidal to consult, in translation, philological works written in German.

When contemplating university studies, Menéndez Pidal was inclined toward the humanities rather than toward the more utilitarian curriculum of engineering urged upon him by his mother. In 1886, he entered the University of Madrid, following his own interests by enrolling in *Filosofía y Letras* but yielding in part to family pressure by agreeing also to study law. By the spring of 1887, he had completed introductory courses in Greek and Latin literatures and was about to begin studies with Marcelino Menéndez y Pelayo (1856–1912), a scholar who would play a decisive role in his literary orientation.³ During the 1887–88 academic year, Menéndez Pidal continued studying Greek literature and began to learn Arabic, a language important to Spanish philology and to the history of the Spanish language because of the Muslim occupation of much of Spain from the eighth to the fifteenth centuries. Later, Menéndez Pidal would turn his attention to documents from the ninth to the eleventh centuries in order to produce *Orígenes del español* (1923), by far the most authoritative study of medieval Spanish, one in which he not only cites Friedrich Diez (1794–1876) and Wilhelm Meyer-Lübke (1861–1936) but also confidently takes issue with them on controversial points, such as the distinctive loss of the initial *f-* in Castilian. As in the case of his introduction to the work of Milà y Fontanals, his discovery of historical grammar in the Neogrammarian mold occurred by chance when out of curiosity he started reading the French translation of Diez's *Grammatik der romanischen Sprachen* (1836–43). Legend has it that Menéndez Pidal continued to show his independence by dedicating himself to this landmark of comparative scholarship against the recommendation of Sánchez Moguel, a professor of Spanish literature who had warned him that the work would "muddle his head unnecessarily."⁴ Nevertheless, Menéndez Pidal persisted in reading the multivolume *Grammaire des langues romanes* (1874), as the work was called when it was translated into French by Gaston Paris, a disciple of Friedrich Diez and, therefore, an exponent and practitioner of Germanic philological principles as well as an authority on French medieval literature.

Despite Menéndez Pidal's admiration for Diez's *Grammaire des langues romanes*, he quickly recognized the advance in Romance linguistics represented by Wilhelm Meyer-Lübke's *Grammatik der romanischen Sprachen* (1890–1902), which gradually became available in French as it was being translated by the Doutrepont brothers, professors who worked on the project at the University of Fribourg (Switzerland) between 1890 and 1906. The importance of Meyer-Lübke's commitment to the Neogrammarian goal of systematically discovering the regular sound changes that underlie linguistic evolution is implicit in Gustav Körting's observation that "the strict linguistic method, in use since 1876 by the so-called Neogrammarians, has brought essential progress to Romance philology as well."⁵ In the decade before the publication of Menéndez Pidal's first version of his Spanish historical grammar, Körting not only praised the contributions of the Neogrammarians, but lamented, "as yet Spain has contributed comparatively little to Romance scholarship."⁶ The profound effect of these historical grammars upon Menéndez Pidal's intellectual development can be seen in the publication of his *Manual elemental de gramática histórica española* (1904), the first historical grammar of Spanish and the logical extension of the principles derived from Indo-European scholarship to specific languages of the Iberian Peninsula. The second edition, expanded and improved, was published the following year with "elemental" removed from the title. In his introduction to the second edition, Menéndez Pidal recognized useful suggestions in letters from his former rival Miguel de Unamuno, from foreign Hispanists Charles Carroll Marden and Carlo Salvioni, and, most significantly, from Meyer-Lübke himself. Among the reviewers were Ernest Mérimée, who had been Menéndez Pidal's professor at the University of Toulouse in 1898, and the outstanding Portuguese philologist José Leite de Vasconcelos, who had been first introduced to him by the aforementioned Sánchez Moguel.[7] There were also reviews by Axel Gabriel Wallensköld in *Neuphilologische Mitteilungen* and by Heinrich Morf in *Archiv für das Studium der neueren Sprachen*, all of which proves that the young scholar had attracted the attention of numerous philologists trained in comparative and Neogrammarian principles.

Not only did Menéndez Pidal recommend in the introductory pages of the *Manual de gramática histórica española* (1905) that his readers keep Meyer-Lübke's grammar "at hand," but he also cited Diez and Meyer-Lübke throughout the text, as he would again in the grammar that he prepared as part of his three-volume work dedicated to the *Cantar de Mío Cid* (1908) and also in the aforementioned *Orígenes del español* (1923), a detailed study of the earliest documents of Hispano Romance.

In addition to suggesting that readers of his grammar familiarize themselves with the grammars of Diez and Meyer-Lübke, Menéndez Pidal recommended that they study Meyer-Lübke's *Einführung in das Studium der romanischen Sprachwissenschaft* (1901), translated into Spanish by Menéndez Pidal's disciple, Américo Castro, as *Introducción al estudio de la lingüística romance* (1926). Other important works consulted were separate etymological dictionaries by Diez and Meyer-Lübke, both entitled *Romanisches Etymologisches Wörterbuch*. Also listed in the preliminary pages of the *Manual de gramática histórica española* are the encyclopedic *Grundriß der romanischen Philologie* (1886–88, 2nd ed. 1904–06), edited by Gustav Gröber (1844–1911), and the *Zeitschrift für romanische Philologie* (1876ff.), from which Menéndez Pidal cited many articles in his three grammars. Gröber was an "idealist" who had Neogrammarian training but challenged strict interpretation of the doctrine of the regularity of the sound change. Referring to the "Vulgar Latin substratum of Romance words" ("vulgärlateinische Substrate romanischer Wörter"), he envisioned a reconstructed stage between Latin and Romance, now called proto-Romance.[8] Of particular interest to Menéndez Pidal was the first volume of the *Grundriß der romanischen Philologie*, in which appeared Gottfried Baist's *Die spanische Sprache* (1904–06), a sequel to *Die spanische Literatur*, which was a history of Spanish letters from *Poema del Cid* to Cervantes and Lope de Vega, prepared by Baist for the first edition. After mentioning the indispensable works by German scholars, Menéndez Pidal listed Édouard Bourciez's *Eléments de linguistique romane* (1910) and Georges Millardet's *Linguistique et dialectologie romanes* (1923), both works being indebted not only to the grammars of Diez and Meyer-Lübke, but also to Adolf Tobler's *Vermischte Beiträge zur französischen Grammatik* (series 1–4, Leipzig, 1886–1908).

Finally, Menéndez Pidal recommended the works of three Latin American philologists: Andrés Bello's *Gramática de la lengua castellana* (1898), Rufino José Cuervo's *Apuntaciones críticas sobre el lenguaje bogotano* (1914), and Federico Hanssen's *Gramática histórica de la lengua castellana* (1913). Of these, Andrés Bello's grammar represents the classical tradition, first applied to a modern spoken language by Antonio de Nebrija in his *Gramática de la lengua castellana* (1492), continued after 1771 in periodically revised grammars of the same title published by the Real Academia Española. Bello's grammar is prescriptive in nature but respects Castilian tradition, making allowances for regional divergence from the established norm. Amado Alonso, in his introduction to a 1951 edition of Bello's grammar, saw the Venezuelan as a follower not only of Karl Voßler (1872–1949), but also of Wilhelm von Humboldt (1767–1835), who corresponded regularly with Friedrich Schiller and Johann Wolfgang Goethe and theorized about the inner and outer forms of language. Humboldt's view that the inner form, the grammatical pattern or structure, was more significant than the outer form, or sounds of language, prefigured twentieth-century structuralism.[9] Federico Hanssen and fellow Chilean Rodolfo Lenz combined the neoclassicism of Andrés Bello with the positivism of the Neogrammarians. Hanssen first published his *Spanische Grammatik auf historischer Grundlage* (1910) in Halle, citing not only Bello's grammar and Menéndez Pidal's *Manual elemental de gramática histórica española*, but also works by Friedrich Diez, E. Geßner, Gustav Körting, Wilhelm Meyer-Lübke, Erik Staff, Adolf Tobler, and Adolf Zauner—the same scholars of comparativist or Neogrammarian orientation frequently cited by

Menéndez Pidal and generally agreed to be among the pioneers in Romance linguistics. From the titles of the books recommended in the *Manual de gramática histórica española*, it is obvious that Menéndez Pidal was indebted to the work of comparativists and Neogrammarians, but also that, in the beginning at least, their works were more accessible to him in French—a language which he had begun to study at the Instituto Cardenal Cisneros, and which he greatly perfected while studying with Ernest Mérimée and Alfred Jeanroy at the University of Toulouse in 1898.[10]

Although Menéndez Pidal had long been interested in German because of his youthful enthusiasm for Goethe, Schiller, and Heine, by the time he began his thesis research on sources of *El Conde Lucanor* in 1891–92, he realized that he needed access to standard works in their original language and that many useful books and articles by German scholars were unavailable in translation into any of the Romance languages. Claiming that Menéndez Pidal's first interest in learning German came from his fascination with German romantic poetry, his biographer Joaquín Pérez Villanueva observed that "the young Pidal composed verses that he translated from German as a pedagogical exercise."[11] In order to pursue research on the sources of *El Conde Lucanor* for his doctoral dissertation (1892), Menéndez Pidal studied German and read on his own initiative articles on the Charlemagne cycle by Gaston Paris and on the transmission of Oriental tales by Friedrich (Max) Müller.[12] That Menéndez Pidal's determined independent study of German was successful is apparent in his recommendation that students of the *Manual de gramática histórica española* read Gröber's *Grundriß der romanischen Philologie* and Baist's *Die spanische Sprache*. Moreover, in his notes, Menéndez Pidal cited numerous books written in German and a great many articles from journals such as R. Herrig's *Archiv für das Studium der neueren Sprachen und Literaturen* (1846ff.), the *Zeitschrift für romanische Philologie* (1876ff.), and the *Romanische Forschungen* (1883ff.)—all journals well respected for their high standards of scholarship. It is interesting to note here that 1876 was the date cited by Körting for the original application of Neogrammarian principles to Romance philology. As one might expect, these same studies—and others—are also cited in the grammar that Menéndez Pidal prepared for his edition of the *Cantar de Mío Cid* and in *Orígenes del español*.

Menéndez Pidal's study of Greek and Latin led him to a knowledge of the Greco-Roman grammatical tradition going back to Plato and Aristotle; back to the debates between naturalists, who thought that language corresponded to its referents, and conventionalists, who believed that different societies established an arbitrary link between language and reality;[13] back to the Stoics, who prefigured the structuralist advances of Ferdinand de Saussure on the relationship between *signifiant* and *signifiée*;[14] and back to the Alexandrians, who understood and described most of the parts of speech, as well as the concepts of case, gender, number, tense, and voice.[15] Through classical philology, Menéndez Pidal knew Marcus Terentius Varro's *De lengua latina*, Aelius Donatus's *Ars Minor*, and Priscian's *Institutiones grammaticae*, which led him to Nebrija's application of Latin grammar to Spanish in his bold *Gramática de la lengua castellana* and eventually to the aforementioned Andrés Bello's *Gramática histórica de la lengua castellana*. Through his knowledge of classical philology, Menéndez Pidal won competitions for professorships against the likes of Ángel Ganivet and Miguel de Unamuno on his way to becoming professor in Greek at the University of Granada in 1891.[16]

Nevertheless, it was not Menéndez Pidal's expertise in classical philology that led him to diachronic linguistics, but rather the intersection of romanticism and positivism, movements that were characteristic of the age in which he lived and underlay his immediate interest in Milà y Fontanals's work on folk literature and in the compendious grammars and etymological dictionaries of the Romance languages by Diez and Meyer-Lübke—reference works consulted by Latin American investigators Federico Hanssen and Rufino José Cuervo, who also recognized the preeminence of Diez and Meyer-Lübke in Romance linguistics. For instance, Federico Hanssen (1857–1919) wrote in 1910, "The historical study of the Spanish language was founded by Diez, *Grammatik der romanischen Sprachen* (5th ed., 1882). While it is still an important work, especially in the area of syntax, it has been replaced by Meyer-Lübke's *Grammatik der romanischen Sprachen* (1890, 1894, 1899), currently the standard reference work."[17] Like Menéndez Pidal, Hanssen was familiar with Baist's *Die spanische Sprache*, Adolf Zauner's *Altspanisches Elementarbuch* (1908), and Paul Förster's *Spanische Sprachlehre* (1880), as well as with articles by E. Geßner, C. Michaëlis, G. Baist, and Axel M. Munthe.[18]

In the introduction to Cuervo's *Apuntaciones críticas sobre el lenguaje bogotano* (4th ed., 1885), there is evidence of an even more profound interest in the work of the comparativists and Neogrammarians whose work preceded Gustav Körting's *Lateinisch-romanisches Wörterbuch*—Diez's and Meyer-Lübke's *Grammatik der romanischen Sprachen*. For example, Cuervo cited Friedrich (Max)

Müller, who had summarized the findings of comparativists in a series of lectures at Oxford entitled *Lessons in the Science of Language* and thereby made Neogrammarian doctrine known to a wider audience.[19] Cuervo went on to credit Franz Bopp with establishing the etymological criteria that underlay Diez's work, but he also came to the soon disproved conclusion that Diez's "skill and ambition had left little work for his successors."[20]

Friedrich (Max) Müller (1823–1900), whose work on Oriental storytelling interested Menéndez Pidal during his investigation of the sources of *El Conde Lucanor*, had been a student of Franz Bopp, who inaugurated comparative philology with his *Vergleichende Grammatik des Sanskrit, Zend, Griechischen, Lateinischen, Gothischen und Deutschen* (1833). From 1876 to 1888, Müller worked on his *Grundriß der Sprachwissenschaft*, a work that, even more than Grimm's *Deutsche Grammatik*, emphasized the regularity of sound change, which was to become the basis for the Junggrammatiker's claim that sound change laws have no exception aside from contextual restraints like those admirably illustrated by Karl Verner's corollary to Grimm's law. Although Menéndez Pidal made little or no reference to these groundbreaking works, in all of his grammars he assiduously applied the principle of gradual, regular sound change, claiming, for example, that the diphthongization of stressed *Ŏ* to *ue* [we] involved four separate sound changes.[21]

Conscious of linguistics as a science, Cuervo also concluded that—as of 1885—only Reinhart Dozy and W. H. Engelmann had done any work on Spanish "with the precision of modern criticism,"[22] undoubtedly referring to their *Glossaire des mots espagnols et portugais dérivés de l'arabe* (1869). Cuervo also mentioned Franz Bopp and Jakob Grimm, along with the Dane Rasmus Rask, all three universally considered to be the nineteenth-century founders of modern linguistics.[23]

Menéndez Pidal, Meyer-Lübke, Gaston Paris, and other scholars admired by Menéndez Pidal—such as Federico Hanssen, Rufino Cuervo, and Georges Millardet, author of *Linguistique et dialectologie romanes*—considered Diez to be the founder of historical Romance linguistics. Even though Menéndez Pidal relied less upon Diez's scholarship after the appearance of Meyer-Lübke's grammar and dictionary, we have seen that there are, throughout his three grammars, references to the works that Diez had written after being appointed to the chair of Romance Philology at the University of Bonn in 1830. His three-volume *Grammatik der romanischen Sprachen* was published from 1836 to 1843, shortly after the completion of Grimm's *Deutsche Grammatik* in 1834.[24] It is interesting to note that, like Menéndez Pidal, Diez had studied classics and had come to an early appreciation of Spanish medieval ballads, publishing many in an anthology in 1818.[25]

Like Cuervo's *Apuntaciones críticas sobre el lenguaje bogotano*, Meyer-Lübke's *Einführung in das Studium der romanischen Sprachwissenschaft* reveals much about linguistic study at the beginning of the twentieth century. Meyer-Lübke lists among other works under general linguistics Berthold Delbrück's *Grundfragen der Sprachgeschichte* (1901), Wilhelm Wundt's *Völkerpsychologie* (1904), and Hermann Paul's *Prinzipien der Sprachgeschichte* (4th ed., 1909). For works treating Romance, he includes Friedrich Diez's *Grammatik der romanischen Sprachen* (1870–79), Gustav Gröber's *Vulgärlateinische Substrate romanischer Wörter* (1883–92), Adolf Zauner's *Romanische Sprachwissenschaft*, and Gustav Körting's *Handbuch der romanischen Philologie* (1886) and his *Lateinisch-romanisches Wörterbuch* (1907), as well as Gröber's aforementioned *Grundriß der romanischen Philologie*.

Of great interest, because of Meyer-Lübke's association with the Junggrammatiker, is the inclusion of Karl Brugmann's *Grundriß der vergleichenden Grammatik der indogermanischen Sprachen* (1900) and his *Kurze vergleichende Grammatik der indogermanischen Sprachen* (1906). Breaking with the older comparativists, Brugmann had moved to Leipzig to found the Neogrammarian school of linguistics, based on the principle that phonetic laws admit no exceptions.

Despite the interest of scholars cited by Menéndez Pidal in the work of Indo-Europeanists and Neogrammarians, the father of the Spanish school of historical linguistics preferred to familiarize himself with a wide variety of works that referred specifically to the evolution of Latin on the Iberian Peninsula. By having his academic training in classical philology, and by discovering Neogrammarian scholarship through French translation at the stage of its application to the Romance languages, Menéndez Pidal may have had only indirect exposure to the pioneering work done on Indo-European linguistics in the half-century before his birth. He seems to have been less interested in the philosophical works of Humboldt and Voßler and in the theoretical works of Delbrück, Wundt, Paul, and Brugmann than in the practical and concrete work of studying medieval documents and of fieldwork done by European scholars. He dedicated himself to the empirical goal of describing the evolution of Spanish from Latin and to amassing a quantity of primary and secondary evidence that his conclusions were correct, that they could resist the scrutiny of German-trained philologists or linguists. He was less interested in the schools of linguistics, in the Neogrammarians led by August Leskien (1840–1916) and Brugmann, in the structuralists guided by de Saussure, and in the functionalists gathered around Vilém Mathesius (1882–1945) and Count Nikolai Sergeevich Trubetzkoi (1890–1938) in Prague than he was in following the lead of those European scholars who were beginning to turn their attention to Spanish. As Manuel Peñalver concluded, "until the advent of Menéndez Pidal, the Spanish language had been investigated by Germans and Swedes. There was no philological tradition."[26]

Certainly, Manuel Peñalver is correct to assert that Menéndez Pidal created the Madrid school of linguistics. We have seen how Menéndez Pidal discovered Neogrammarian advances in Romance linguistics and applied those principles to Spanish, reading and evaluating everything that the German and Scandinavian philologists and linguists had written about his language in order to find additional evidence, to correct misconceptions, and to expand greatly what was known about its history. He adapted the methods of the Neogrammarians, accepting the challenge to meet their level of objectivity and thoroughness in order to make obsolete Gustav Körting's dour observation in 1896 that there had been little contribution to Romance linguistics from Spain. With the 1904 publication of the *Manual elemental de gramática histórica española*, Menéndez Pidal attracted the attention of the great Wilhelm Meyer-Lübke and that of other recognized scholars of Neogrammarian orientation. With the publication of *Orígenes del español*, he established himself as the world's outstanding expert on the history and development of the Spanish language, a scholar whose articles appeared not only in his own journal *Revista de Filología Española* but also in prestigious foreign journals; for example, his article "Sobre el sustrato Mediterráneo occidental" was published in the *Zeitschrift für romanische Philologie*.[27] To this day, the *Manual de gramática histórica española*, the first volume (text, grammar, and vocabulary) of his three-volume *Cantar de Mío Cid* (1908), and *Orígenes del español* (1926)—all made possible by Menéndez Pidal's early recognition of the advances in linguistic science accomplished by scholars of Neogrammarian orientation—are indispensable for the study of the evolution of Spanish from Latin.

Notes

1. Robert A. Hall, Jr., *External History of the Romance Languages* (New York, 1974), p. 237.
2. Steven Hess, *Ramón Menéndez Pidal* (Boston, 1982), pp. 2–3.
3. Joaquín Pérez Villanueva, *Ramón Menéndez Pidal: su vida y su tiempo* (Madrid, 1991), pp. 51–53.
4. Ibid., p. 53.
5. "Die seit 1876 von den sog[enannten] Junggrammatikern zur Anwendung gebrachte strenge sprachwissenschaftliche Methode … hat auch der romanischen Philologie wesentliche Förderung gebracht." Gustav Körting, *Handbuch der romanischen Philologie* (Leipzig, 1896), p. 79.
6. "… verhältnismäßig wenig hat bis jetzt Spanien zur romanischen Wissenschaft beigetragen." Ibid., p. 79.
7. Hess, *Ramón Menéndez Pidal*, p. 3.
8. R. E. Asher et al., eds., *Encyclopedia of Language and Linguistics*, vol. 3 (Oxford, 1994), p. 1506.
9. J. Lyons, "Linguistics," *The New Encyclopedia Britannica*, vol. 10 (Chicago, 1977), pp. 992–1013.
10. Hess, *Ramón Menéndez Pidal*, p. 5.
11. "… el joven Pidal metrificaba versos que traducía del alemán, como ejercicio de aprendizaje." Villanueva, *Ramón Menéndez Pidal*, p. 133.
12. Ibid., p. 56.
13. Sebastià Serrano, *La lingüística* (Barcelona, 1983), p. 26.
14. Ibid., p. 23.
15. Ibid., p. 25.
16. Villanueva, *Ramón Menéndez Pidal*, p. 111.
17. "Das historische Studium der spanischen Sprache ist durch Diez, *Grammatik der romanischen Sprachen* (5. Aufl., Bonn 1882) begründet worden. An die Stelle dieses namentlich in der Syntax noch immer wichtigen Werkes ist als übliches Handbuch gegenwärtig die *Grammatik der romanischen Sprachen* von Wilhelm Meyer-Lübke getreten (Leipzig 1890, 1894, 1899)." Federico Hanssen, *Spanische Grammatik auf historischer Grundlage* (Halle, 1910), p. 1.
18. Ibid., p. 2.
19. Fred West, *The Way of Language: An Introduction* (New York, 1975), p. 31.
20. Rufino J. Cuervo, *Apuntaciones críticas sobre el lenguaje bogotano con frecuente referencia al de los países de Hispano-América*, 4th ed. (Chartres, 1885), p. xiv.
21. Ramón Menéndez Pidal, *Orígines del español*, 5th ed. (Madrid, 1964), p. 126.
22. "… con la escrupulosidad de la crítica moderna." Cuervo, *Apuntaciones críticas sobre el lenguaje bogotano*, p. xiv.
23. West, *The Way of Language*, p. 29.
24. See Asher et al., *Encyclopedia of Language and Linguistics*, vol. 2, p. 926.
25. See Yakov Malkiel, "Friedrich Diez and the Birth Pangs of Romance Linguistics," *Romance Philology*, vol. 30, supplement pp. 1–15.
26. "… hasta que vino él (Menéndéz Pidal) la lengua de España había sido investigado por alemanes y suecos. No existía tradición filológica." Manuel Peñalver Castillo, *La escuela de Menéndez Pidal y la historiografía lingüística hispánica, aproximación a su estudio* (Almería, 1995), p. 29.
27. Ramón Menéndez Pidal, "Sobre el sustrato Mediterráneo occidental," *Zeitschrift für romanische Philologie*, vol. 59 (1938), pp. 189–206.

– 8 –

REASSESSING FRIEDRICH SCHLEGEL'S READING OF *DON QUIXOTE* IN LIGHT OF HIS EARLY WRITINGS

Rachel Schmidt

In October 1797, Friedrich Schlegel (1772–1829) received a request to translate anew *Don Quixote* (1605–15) into German. Although he assigned the task to his friend Ludwig Tieck (1773–1853), the moment sparked in Schlegel a profound interest in the novel, as well as the other works of Miguel de Cervantes (1547–1616), which gave rise to Schlegel's theoretical consideration of the Spanish author's place in his emerging definition of romantic literature.[1] In the following two years, he undertook a voracious reading of Cervantes' oeuvre, at times in the original Spanish, as well as the works of other major Spanish authors of the sixteenth and seventeenth centuries, such as Pedro Calderón de la Barca (1600–1681) and Lope de Vega (1562–1635). As Schlegel's notebooks and published works of the following three years reveal, Cervantes would take a favored place within the pantheon of Renaissance authors prized by the young critic as the modern masters of the four genres of literature who rivaled those of antiquity. This grouping is shown most succinctly in a diamond configuration appearing in Schlegel's *Literary Notebooks* (1797–1801): Petrarch, at the top, represents the lyric; Shakespeare, to the middle left, represents drama; Dante, to his right, represents the epic; and finally, Cervantes, at the bottom, represents the specifically romantic genre of the novel (IX 683; KA 16, p. 311).[2]

The question that arises, then, for the Cervantes scholar interested in the reception of *Don Quixote*, concerns the meaning of the term "romantic" for Friedrich Schlegel. This essay will serve as a response to the Hispanists who view the reading of *Don Quixote* by the early German romantics as a sentimentalization of the novel that stripped from it Cervantes' intention to parody the literature of knight errantry and attributed to it unwarranted serious philosophical meaning. Not only does this misreading simplify Schlegel's complex understanding of the novel, it also misses his central point: that *Don Quixote* is an exemplary romantic novel, a model to be followed by his contemporaries. Of particular importance to my interpretation of the young Schlegel's reading of Cervantes' major work is an examination of the terms *das Romantische* (the romantic), *Witz* (wit), *Narrheit* (foolishness), *Dummheit* (stupidity), and *Duplizität* (duplicity) as used in relation to *Don Quixote* and, more broadly, the theory of the novel. The full range of meaning of these terms is to be found not only in Friedrich Schlegel's review of Tieck's translation of the novel and the *Dialogue on Poetry* (1800), but also in his literary notebooks and fragments. Through this analysis of seemingly marginal references, I will argue that Friedrich Schlegel's reading of *Don Quixote* in the early romantic period did not discard the parodic or satiric elements of the work, but rather incorporated them into a theoretical framework in which *Scherz* (joking) was essential to the existence of *Ernst* (seriousness).

Der romantische Roman / The Romantic Novel

The one term that Schlegel most consistently and insistently applies to Cervantes' work in general and *Don Quixote* in particular is "romantic." For example, Schlegel writes, "Don Quixote [is] still the only completely romantic novel."[3] In his influential *Dialogue on Poetry*, *Don Quixote* serves as a principal representative of romantic literature in the various discourses on its history, content, and form. Perhaps due to its popularization during the nineteenth century, and perhaps also due to Schlegel's own complex and never clearly articulated usage, the word "romantic" has led to an oversimplification of his reading of the novel. Most typical of this critical tendency is Anthony Close's definition of the characteristics of what he calls "the Romantic approach to *Don Quixote*," which he sees originating in Friedrich Schlegel's thought. Basic to this interpretation, as analyzed by the Hispanist, is "the idealisation of the hero and the denial of the novel's satiric purpose."[4] In this essay, I will show that the statement denying the author's "satiric purpose" overlooks the essential role that humor, parody, and irony play in Schlegel's reading of *Don Quixote* as a romantic novel. Only through an exploration of the complex semantic play of the term "romantic" in Schlegel's early critical writings can his interpretation's complexity and influence be ascertained.

Concerning the mixed nature of romantic literature, its "fusion and transferral" of play and seriousness, Schlegel leaves no doubt. He even writes of "romantic thrashing and witty mud" ("romantische Prügel und witziger Dreck") as well as "romantic roguery" ("romantische Spitzbüberei," VII 163; KA 16, p. 216). Both the work of Cervantes and Shakespeare, the two giants of romantic, that is to say, modern literature as defined by Schlegel, exemplify the melding of the seemingly contradictory attitudes of play and seriousness (V 1032, IX 302; KA 16, pp. 170, 278). This understanding of the romantic as a mixture of humor and sobriety leads to an acknowledgment of the intermingling of genres within its masterpieces, seen to be in contrast to the closed purity of classical works. Schlegel's concept of the *Roman* (novel) as a mixed genre indicates part of his debt to the philosopher Johann Gottfried Herder (1744–1803), as well as his belief that it "is the dominant form both of the earliest and the most recent postclassical poetry."[5] By referring to the early modern romances and literature in Romance languages that he finds so unclassical in their eroticism and fantasy, and also the novel of his own period, the word "romantic" encompasses for Schlegel both the tradition of Shakespeare, Dante, and Cervantes, as well as the aesthetic ideal toward which he and his contemporaries should strive.[6] To sum up, the expression "romantic" was used both as a historical term and as a normative term, referring simultaneously to a segment of the past and to setting up a goal for the future.[7]

A diamond-like configuration clarifies the manner in which Schlegel visualizes the genres and the "poetic elements" that the exemplary romantic writers of the early modern period represent (IX 683; KA 16, p. 311):

$$\begin{array}{ccc} & \text{Petr[arca]} & \\ & 0/1 & \\ \text{<Shaksp[eare] [\textit{sic}]} & & \text{Dante>} \\ - & & + \\ & \text{Cerv[antes]} & \\ & 1/0 & \end{array}$$

The figure itself requires comparison with other notes in order to be comprehended. First, it represents the historical development of romantic literature, headed by Petrarch and Dante and culminated by Shakespeare and Cervantes, with Boccaccio, Ariosto, Tasso, and Guarini chronologically and in terms of literary importance enveloped between them (IX 728; KA 16, p. 315). Within the cycle, Dante is characterized by the transcendental and epic quality of the *Divine Comedy*, whereas Petrarch is characterized by the sentimental and lyrical quality of his poetry. The mimetic and dramatic qualities of his plays distinguish Shakespeare as a more progressive figure. This movement from epic to drama represents a movement from the one epic to the many dramas through lyric (IX 209; KA 16, p. 271). It also represents a transition from the objective nature of epic through the subjective nature of lyric to the objective-subjective nature of drama (IX 215; KA 16, pp. 271–272), or from the objective-subjective nature of epic through the subjective nature of lyric to the objective nature of drama (IX 749; KA 16, p. 317).[8] In Schlegel's terms, this tendency away from objectivity toward a mimetic mixture of objectivity and subjectivity, whether it be from epic to drama or vice versa, represents the movement from the classical to the romantic.[9]

The mixing of genres is clearly most important in the case of the novel, given both its emergence in the modern era and its obvious connection to the term "romantic." In fact, Schlegel views the novel as arising historically from the other three genres. He describes it thus: "Steps of the romantic: 1) among the ancients: epic and drama. The beginning of the mixed poem in prose and mystical sentimental love, erotica; 2) the absolutely mystical marvelous, the peculiarly romantic; 3) *Don Quixote*."[10] This simple fragment reveals both the generic and expressive qualities of the romantic. A. O. Lovejoy, Hans Eichner, and Ernst Behler have debated whether Friedrich Schlegel's definition of the romantic is specifically generic—that is to say, a definition of the novel.[11] Certainly, the term encompasses the Roman in Schlegel's reading of *Don Quixote* as a romantic work. As Antonio asserts in *Dialogue on Poetry*, "Indeed, I can scarcely visualize a novel but as a mixture of storytelling, song, and other forms. Cervantes always composed in this manner, and even the otherwise so prosaic Boccaccio adorns his collections of stories by framing them with songs."[12]

Several of Schlegel's literary notes concerning the Roman express his thoughts on the genre in an algebraic manner that, in turn, throws light upon the previously cited diamond of romantic masters. For example, he writes of the novel as an absolute form that embraces all literary genres.¹³ Therefore, the space of the Roman is a mediating space, one so defined by polarities and dualities that it encompasses and transcends them all. Significantly, absoluteness in Schlegel's notebooks is often indicated mathematically by $1/0$, the notation Schlegel attributes to Cervantes in the romantic diamond.¹⁴ Lovejoy suggests that this concept of the absolute, or infinity (*Unendlichkeit*), is borrowed from Kant via Fichte, and implies that "art should be characterized by a constant enlargement of its boundaries and an endless progression toward an unattainably remote ideal."¹⁵ The Roman, as a space circumscribing polarities, is therefore the most suitable medium for an all-embracing art. Thus, the novel as a genre blends into Schlegel's understanding of the romantic as the aesthetic of the modern: "Romantic poetry is a progressive, universal poetry."¹⁶

Paradoxically, the symbol appearing under Cervantes in the above-mentioned diamond, $1/0$, also mathematically represents meaninglessness, and thus highlights the significance of chaos, understood as multiplicity and plurality, as the ground of the Roman.¹⁷ At the apex of the diamond appears, of course, the $0/1$ of Petrarch, Cervantes' antithesis. This figure signifies zero, a very curious reduction of the unity of the subject's lyrical vision and identity to absence.¹⁸ Schlegel, in this instance, insists on the poet's subject, Laura, who walks "heavenly" before us (KA 2, p. 337). His purity of vision reduces poetry to the contemplation of a divine absence. Unlike the multiplicity of Dante's poetic world, which represents the true origin of modern poetry, Petrarch's poetic unity and abstraction lead him to laugh at his own sentimentality (V 565; KA 16, pp. 131–132), and perhaps even to parody himself (V 839; KA 16, p. 156). At the opposite pole from Cervantes, Petrarch's work thus links up to the classical (V 354, VII 262; KA 16, pp. 114, 223). The mathematical symbols of plus (+) and minus (-), referring to the positive, constructive powers of Dante's epic and to the negative, ironic unravelings of Shakespeare's drama, are now seen to relate to the antithesis of chaos and system that forms the romantic. Schlegel writes, "Positivity and negativity alternate in chaos; in system they are both fused together."¹⁹ In another literary diamond referring to the chaotic in Shakespeare, Schlegel places "chaotisch" in the same position at the bottom. He then continues to describe the term as based in mathematics, springing from the irrational (!), the potentialized, the combinatory, and the progressive.²⁰ Thus, the author takes the all-inclusive field of chaos and melds its contradictions, without subsuming them, into the chaotic system that is the Roman.²¹ Like the epic, it contains the idealized, transcendent quality of positivity (+); like the drama, it embraces the mimetic stuff of theater negating transcendence (-). The subjectivity of sentimental love nullifying the objectivity of either drama or epos (0/1) counterbalances the chaos (1/0) from which the novel takes form.

Nonetheless, the movement of the Roman toward infinity is also a movement toward the chaos of the world in its mimetic attempt to embrace and transform it. For Schlegel, totality does not arise from the striving after similarity or uniformity, but from difference, and thus differs from unity (V 46; KA 16, p. 89). Likewise, "system" cannot be understood independently from its antithesis, irrationality. Schlegel notes that from the confusion of chaos a world can spring forth (*Athenäum Idee* 71, KA 2, p. 263). Versatility, more precisely, many-sidedness, does not only arise from a far-reaching system, but also from a sense of chaos, pointing toward a world beyond (*Athenäum Idee* 55, KA 2, p. 262). Schlegel repeats on various occasions that the romantic is chaotic (IX 226, IX 774; KA 16, pp. 272, 318) and that the Roman gives form to an artfully developed chaos (VII 37, IX 274; KA 16, pp. 207, 276).[22] The plurality of genres and their respective elements defining the mediating space of the Roman in Schlegel's romantic diamond is revealed, then, as the confusion from which the created worlds and their inherent systems of romantic art emerge. The chaos of the world is the stuff of the novel, and, inversely, the novel's chaotic aspects are mimetic.

In the "Letter about the Novel" from Schlegel's *Dialogue on Poetry*, the character Antonio imagines a theory of the novel, which would itself be a novel, surging forth from the chaos of the chivalric world.[23] Within this novel would coexist the "quadrumvirate" of early modern authors who serve as the founding figures for his consideration of romantic literature: "The things of the past would live in it in new forms; Dante's sacred shadow would arise from the lower world, Laura would walk heavenly before us, Shakespeare would converse intimately with Cervantes, and there Sancho would jest with Don Quixote again."[24] Despite this homage to the other modern giants, this theory as formulated by Antonio resembles Cervantes' creative vision expressed in *Don Quixote* through the juxtaposition of the protagonist's imagination fevered by chivalric fantasy with his chaotic encounters with the world itself. The similarity is noted in the phrase highlighting the joking interchange between Don Quixote and Sancho Panza. Thus, "the chaos of the world of knight errantry," to which Schlegel refers in Antonio's concept of a theory of the novel, signifies the disorganized, contradictory, and even meaningless elements from which Cervantes created the novel *Don Quixote*. The novel as a genre, the Roman, results from this attempt to wrest meaning from meaninglessness, while simultaneously preserving the multiplicity of chaos. Significantly, Cervantes' masterpiece is for Schlegel the culmination of the Roman and the romantic, and the blueprint for future writers to follow.

Der Witz / Wit

The term *Witz* is, for Friedrich Schlegel, the joking, playful element that differentiates the antique, classical era from the modern one by causing romantic literature to be perhaps even more artful than its predecessor (V 1032, IX 302; KA 16, pp. 170, 278).[25] Interestingly, the consideration of Witz dominates the young man's literary notebooks during the years 1797 and 1798, the same years in which he read *Don Quixote* in Spanish. This mixture of genres, defined by form and by historical moment (classical versus modern), points to the dual nature of romantic Witz, which in Schlegel's thought is both that of the modern era beginning with the Italian Renaissance and that of the genre of the novel, the Roman. What, then, is Witz? Schlegel comes closest to a definition when he writes, "Wit's form is the appearance of absolute antithesis. That is to say, in false humor merely absolute antitheses are synthesized without positing anything."[26] True wit synthesizes absolutes without consuming them, whereas false wit fails to arrive at such a thesis. In this note one sees how Schlegel can argue that Witz is the principle and organ of universal philosophy, since it presents what the thinker calls logical chemistry, the mixing of antithetical concepts (*Athenäum Fragment* 220, KA 2, p. 200). Witz itself is the outer lightning expressing *Fantasie*, understood as the creative imagination (*Athenäum Idee* 26, KA 2, p. 258). Of course, as seen earlier, Schlegel considers the "absolutely mystical wonderful" to be the "uniquely romantic" (V 69; KA 16, p. 91).

The artistic image to which Schlegel consistently turns in order to express the coexistence and interdependence of opposites, without pointing toward their mutual subsumption and consumption, is the *Arabeske*. As used in early modern printing, the arabesque is unique in its folding of meaning into ornament, or vice versa. The graphic essence of writing springs forth in its juxtaposition to, melding with, and even transformation into more "purely" decorative line. For Schlegel, all the components of language—sound, meaning, tropes, cited text, and textual fragments—present potential combinations and constructions, just as various images compose the arabesque. Concerning the arabesque opposition and juxtaposition of signifying elements and signified meaning in Schlegel's work, Gerhart von Gravenitz argues that it potentially produces a semiotic "Chaos" in which both rise to a "Sinnüberfluß," an overflow of meaning.[27] In fact, Schlegel writes that chaos, in the forms of the arabesque and the fairy tale, is the essential element of the romantic (IX 274; KA 16, p. 276). For Gravenitz, then, the doubling of poetry and mimesis in Schlegel's art follows from the very image of the arabesque.[28] As Schlegel neatly sums up, the principle of romantic prose and verse is the coexistence of symmetry and chaos—the very image of the arabesque (IX 539; KA 16, p. 298).

The consideration of Witz in relation to *Don Quixote* is particularly relevant given the consistent coupling of the term and its formal manifestation, the arabesque, with Cervantes' novel. In fact, the multiplicity of Schlegel's references to the term indicates that Witz functions within the novel on various levels. For example, his assertion that parody represents epic Witz certainly calls to mind Cervantes' parodic rendering of the conventions of chivalric literature (V 783; KA 16, p. 152). In general, Witz in *Don Quixote* is innocent, thus indicating that it rises above a negative joking based solely on grotesque parody toward its romantic manifestation (V 538, V 409; KA 16, pp. 129, 119).[29] Schlegel also writes that fantastic humor, that is to say, the arabesque balance of imagination and joking, prevails in the first book of *Don Quixote* (*Dialogue on Poetry*, KA 2, p. 299). In fact, Polheim has found the outline for a literary work centered on Sancho Panza, provisionally entitled *Zu den Arabesken*, that itself embraces fantastic adventures and parodic joking.[30] As will be shown, the coexistence of fantasy and ironic parody made possible by the arabesque forms the crux of Schlegel's assertion that *Don Quixote* is a novel par excellence. It is impossible, therefore, to argue that Friedrich Schlegel's early reading of *Don Quixote* ignored the work's humorous and parodic elements. Without them, there would have been no Witz, and Cervantes himself would have been no model for the young German romantic.

Romantic Witz, then, marks both content and its arabesque form in Cervantes' *Don Quixote*, as well as in Shakespeare's dramatic works. As Schlegel asserts, "Indeed, this artfully ordered confusion, this charming symmetry of contradictions, this wonderfully perennial alternation of enthusiasm and irony which lives even in the smallest parts of the whole, seem to me to be an indirect mythology themselves. The organization is the same, and certainly the arabesque is the oldest and an original form of human imagination."[31] This description of the function of Witz in the two great masters of postclassical drama and novel provides us with Schlegel's most succinct definition of the term. The symmetry of opposites takes form in the arabesque, which arises out of fantasy understood as the imaginative, creative faculty. The opposing elements that comprise the romantic arabesque are enthusiasm and irony. Enthusiasm, of course, refers to the unself-conscious absorption of the individual in an idea or cause, a trait frequently attributed by eighteenth-century readers to *Don Quixote*, often using the pejorative term *Schwärmerei*. For Schlegel, however, enthusiasm is elevated to a more dignified station, representing the "light chaos" of divine thoughts and feelings of moral and religious persons (*Athenäum Idee* 18, KA 2, p. 258). Irony, it then follows, stands as the contrasting, negative side of the arabesque, which gives form to Schlegel's understanding of the humor in *Don Quixote*.

Romantic irony has been a concept of much interest to critics of the period, although this precise term was never actually used by the early romantics.[32] Nonetheless, Schlegel offers an indisputably new "reformulation" of irony, which had previously referred to the rhetorical expression of a statement meant to signify its opposite.[33] Albert has most succinctly defined Schlegel's definition of irony as the "simultaneous presence of *two* meanings between which it is not possible to decide."[34] Various notes and fragments underline the basis of irony in paradox, most notably the oft-quoted reference to irony as the form of paradox (*Lyceum Fragment* 48, KA 2, p. 153). But Schlegel's understanding of irony goes beyond form to refer to the perspective of the romantic writer on the chaotic and contradictory matter of his world and work. "Irony is a clear consciousness of the eternal agility, of the infinitely abundant chaos," writes Schlegel.[35] The ironic stance of the romantic author depends upon a hovering and agile transcendence of these contradictory circumstances, which allows him to indulge in paradox as play.[36] Or, as Ernst Behler points out, "The function of irony does not reside so much in the destruction of creative production, but rather in a mediating position between enthusiasm and scepticism."[37] This hovering stance of the author is described as essential to romantic poetry: "And yet it can also—more than any other form—hover at the midpoint between the portrayed and the portrayer, free of all real and ideal self-interest, on the wings of poetic reflection, and can raise that reflection again and again to a higher power and multiply it in an endless succession of mirrors."[38] An endlessly self-duplicating row of images resembles, of course, an arabesque. Thus, Polheim astutely notes that the arabesque is the formal, compositional equivalent of irony, because it represents the potential to be found in the romantic poetic as a mediation between the finite and the infinite.[39] The link, then, between the arabesque as the form constructed from opposing parts, Witz as the joking expression of antithesis, and irony as a high-minded, playful acceptance of the coexistence of opposite meanings, clearly indicates that Schlegel did conceive of irony as an essential part of romantic art.

More important for our purposes is Schlegel's indication that Witz, arabesque, and irony are mimetic. For example, he writes, "Romantic life's form is that of wit—wit exists between art and virtue, love and fantasy. [It is] the purest indifference, hence it is extremely philosophical."[40] Indifference turns out to be a key term for the understanding of Schlegel's concept of the mimetic novel, which Schlegel defines algebraically as a combination of indifferent fantasy and indifferent sentimentality, using the sign ± to indicate indifference (V 843; KA 16, p. 157).[41] As one sees from the notation, indifference implies the coexistence of positive and negative values. Parody, the literary form of indifference, simultaneously brings into existence imaginative and sentimental literature and denies its value through its *witzige* attitude. Schlegel states elsewhere that humor is involved in both presence and absence, and can arise only from reflection, that is to say, the distanced stance of irony (*Athenäum Fragment* 305, KA 2, p. 217).[42] As Schlegel clearly indicates, parody is most complete in *Don Quixote* because its object of fun is a strong romantic form seen in a rear-view mirror, so to speak (V 843; KA 16, p. 157). The lens of parody, its backward reflection of a literary genre normally taken seriously, creates the arabesque between chaos and totality upon which the novel relies. Cervantes' parody of chivalric literature, a highly sentimentalized and fantastic genre based on the degradation of epic, clearly underlies Schlegel's espousal of the text's novelistic perfection.

Schlegel compares and contrasts irony and parody in various literary notes in a manner that allows us to trace further the coexistence of the two terms in relationship to his conception of the novel.[43] At one point, Friedrich Schlegel places irony and parody on equal footing as components of Witz, while simultaneously differentiating between them: "Irony and parody are the two absolute types of wit—the first the ideal, the second the real. Systematic wit = irony and parody."[44] Irony, as ideal wit, refers to the hovering self-positioning of the romantic author above his circumstances, whereas parody, understood as real wit, deals with the substantive, given material of his work. By applying this observation to *Don Quixote*, one glimpses how irony and parody coexist in Schlegel's reading of the novel. Cervantes ironically hovers above his creation by creating all the various and conflicting layers of narration, whereas he uses the real stuff of the chivalric romance in parody. Thus, a conventional understanding of parody as the burlesquing of a well-known genre accompanies Schlegel's insistence upon the removed and playful perspective of the literary creator. Nonetheless, another fragment deepens the contrast between irony and parody through clarifying Witz vis-à-vis genre: "Irony = self-parody? Parody is epic wit."[45] Whereas this note reinforces the understanding of parody as a joking stance toward the exterior, extant substance of epic, it suggests the centrality of a playful consciousness of self in irony. If one allows that the romantic, understood as the basis of irony and self-parody, is the missing term in these two equations, then parody, as epic Witz, stands in arabesque contrast to irony as romantic Witz. If one also allows, in the following logical step, that romantic Witz is itself combinatory as an element of the romantic, then it contains within itself the opposing force of parody. Consequently, Schlegel could not have conceived of Cervantes' incorporation of Witz in *Don Quixote* without taking into consideration its parodic element.

In one literary note, Schlegel, writing of romantic Witz, states that Socratic irony belongs to it (V 53; KA 16, p. 90). According to a rather lengthy fragment, Schlegel introduces the problem of the reader's or listener's stance before Socratic irony—can the reader distinguish the *Scherz* (the joking) from the *Ernst* (the serious)? (*Lyceum Fragment* 106, KA 2, p. 160). The fragment concludes with the observation that it is a good sign if "die harmonisch Platten" ("the harmonious bores") misunderstand the irony, presumably because they "insist on equating irony with deception, and on preferring one interpretation—either one—to the other."[46] Significantly, the Roman represents for Schlegel the modern form of Socratic irony: "Novels are the Socratic dialogues of our time. And this free form has become the refuge of common sense in its flight from pedantry."[47] Thus, the meaning of a novel would not be self-evident, but rather self-contradictory, requiring that the reader take an ironic stance toward the material, jokingly allowing for the coexistence of paradox.[48]

In his review of Ludwig Tieck's translation of *Don Quixote*, Friedrich Schlegel challenges the readers to just such a dualistic approach to the text. He poses the rhetorical question as to whether the reader will take up the text not only at the time of digestion, presumably for light, entertaining reading, but also at other hours. Thus, the reader might appreciate the serious poetry of the novel in addition to its comic elements.[49] As Lowry Nelson, Jr. observes, "Just as Shakespeare should no longer be considered a raving 'Sturm-und-Drangdichter' but a highly conscious artist, so Cervantes must no longer be taken as a jester but rather seen, in his hidden intentionality, as likewise canny and crafty ('schlau und arglistig')."[50] Referring again to the possible failure of the reader to appreciate the complexities of the novel, Schlegel also writes in the review that whoever does not find it divine does not understand *Don Quixote* (KA 2, p. 282). Nonetheless, what Schlegel finds divine in the novel may be surprising—it is the representation of *Narrheit*, foolishness (V 429; KA 16, p. 121). According to this fragment, the novel's philosophical polemics, character development, and insistent presence of the narrative voice are not divine for Schlegel—it is the foolishness that enchants him.

Dummheit and *Narrheit* / Stupidity and Foolishness

Another arabesque intertwining opposing elements that Schlegel sees in *Don Quixote* remains to be studied: foolishness and stupidity. Without a consideration of these terms, it is impossible to appreciate fully why and how the joking elements of the novel must intermingle with the serious. Both *Dummheit* (stupidity) and *Narrheit* (foolishness), however, are distinguished from *Tollheit* (craziness) by their arbitrary nature.[51] That is to say, stupidity and foolishness are connected to issues of personal will. In his fictional work *Lucinde*, Schlegel defines both Narrheit and Dummheit: "A stupid person is he who does not believe what he sees. A fool is he who is willfully stupid and does not believe that he is; he is stupid out of cunning."[52] Dummheit, then, is a simpler form of Narrheit, since the person is not aware of the condition. Narrheit, on the other hand, is a willful, arbitrary condition that the individual chooses, yet fails to acknowledge. The *Narr* suffers from the same incapacity to believe one's own eyes as the *Dummkopf*, yet does so out of cleverness. The deceptive power of the fool is such that he fools even himself. Schlegel further differentiates the fool from the stupid one by stating that the former is a man of book learning (*Scholastiker*), whereas the latter is a man of the world (*Weltmensch*; V 616; KA 16, pp. 136–137). The fool's capacity to deceive himself and others arises out of a willful insistence upon systematic knowledge that denies experiential truth; the stupid person's blindness arises out of his own adherence to common sense, that which is generally accepted as worldly knowledge.

These definitions of the Narr and the Dummkopf beg to be applied to Cervantes' pair of deluded protagonists, Don Quixote and Sancho Panza. It is possible, in fact, that the interpretation of the pair as polar opposites common to later romantic readings, in which Don Quixote represents ideals and Sancho Panza represents reality, could spring from Schlegel's observations. Nonetheless, Friedrich Schlegel never attributes either label to a specific character. Rather, he argues that the intertwining of the general attitudes are central to certain types of novels. Both a Narr and a Dummkopf ground the philosophical novel, because the wise man must himself be the fool and the blockhead, the enthusiast and the ironist, as well as the holy and the evil man, in order to embrace everything.[53] Thus, the characters of the fool and the stupid man become elements of an arabesque that intertwine with wisdom in the philosophical novel. Reason cannot exist without irrationality in Schlegel's conception of the novel. Subsequently, Schlegel does refer specifically to the arabesque of wisdom and foolishness in *Don Quixote* in several places. Writing of synthetic genres, Schlegel clarifies how Cervantes' novel can be considered philosophical. *Don Quixote* achieves philosophical indifference through the juxtaposition of negative imagination and positive criticism, parodic sentimentality and constructive philosophy, yet even this critical canceling out of the negative and the positive is grounded in the opposition of the Narr and the Dummkopf.[54] Nonetheless, the critical and philosophical elements are themselves rendered negative, given their grounding in Narrheit and Dummheit. Reason springs forth only from the representation of the characters' irrationality. In this interpretation of the interplay between wisdom and foolishness, Friedrich Schlegel actually approaches the insistence of various eighteenth-century critics upon Cervantes' satirical use of his protagonist's foolishness in order to educate the reader. Schlegel's reading of *Don Quixote* does not, therefore, stand alone as a definitive break from earlier traditions of interpreting the novel as a satire. Unlike the earlier eighteenth-century readers, however, Schlegel does perceive that the critical elements of the novel turn in upon themselves, as the foolishness and stupidity of the characters upon which it depends invert the positive values of the lesson once again. Schlegel, thus, sets the work, complete with its parodic and critical facets, within a new conception of the Roman as a mixed genre and the romantic as an all-encompassing art form representative of the modern world that values irony in itself. Significantly, Schlegel refers to the arabesque of reason and irrationality in his discussion of the romantic Witz of Cervantes' and Shakespeare's work as related to a romantic mythology:

> Neither this wit nor a mythology can exist without something original and inimitable that is absolutely irreducible, and in which after all the transformations its original character and creative energy are still dimly visible, where the naive profundity permits the appearance of the absurd and of madness, or of simplicity and foolishness, to shimmer through. For this is the beginning of all poetry, to cancel the progression and laws of rationally thinking reason, and to transplant us once again into the beautiful confusion of imagination, into the original chaos of human nature, for which I know as yet no more beautiful symbol than the motley throng of the ancient gods.[55]

According to Schlegel, neither romantic Witz nor mythology can exist without a basis in the original and inimitable. It is ironic, of course, that this primal ground is to be approached through the contemplation of the negative qualities of inversion and madness, silliness and stupidity. Implicit in the concept of inversion is Narrheit, as *Athenäum Fragment* 276 clarifies that Narrheit is the absolute inversion of the trend toward historicity (KA 2, p. 212). Thus, the appearance of willful foolishness and stupidity informs the old way in which one seeks the stuff of literature. Only then can the other side of the arabesque, reason, emerge and produce the beautiful confusion of imagination. Several paradoxes underlie the arabesque of Schlegel's description: the inimitable chaos of human nature will be transferred into imaginative confusion, in itself an attempt at imitation; the intermingling of irrationality and reason will give rise to this confusion; and the romantic mythology will finally resemble the classical mythology of the many, varied, and discordant gods of antiquity. Thus, Narrheit can be divine, for it, along with all the other negative manifestations of human irrationality, forms the ground for romantic Witz and mythology.

Dualismus and *Duplizität* / Dualism and Duplicity

As mentioned earlier, Friedrich Schlegel never attributes Narrheit or Dummheit to any specific characters in *Don Quixote*, although he does insist that the attributes' presence is essential to the novelistic character of the work. How, then, can one speak of foolishness or stupidity in the novel? Once again, the dual and paradoxical nature of the arabesque informs Schlegel's thought concerning characterization. For Schlegel, the individual contains within him/herself the paradox of chaos, the arabesque of finitude and infinity (*Athenäum Idee* 98, KA 2, p. 266). To create a novel in the form of cultivated, artistic chaos, Schlegel recommends the use of duality in characterization (VII 37; KA 16, p. 297). In this case, then, life and art—or, by extension, chaos and system—form the basis of both characterization and the novel. Thus, the algebraic artistry of dualism of character introduces into the novel the indifferent juxtaposition of opposing qualities constitutive of an arabesque. It also introduces into the novel a polemical or, as Schlegel wrote elsewhere, philosophical dimension (*Lyceum Fragment* 81, KA 2, p. 157). Literary characters, therefore, begin to serve as signs for abstractions in a manner that may, indeed, resemble the algebraic formulations of the relationships between Schlegel's ubiquitous categories—the sentimental, the fantastic, etc. Nonetheless, the basis for these idealizations of character are the negative qualities of foolishness and stupidity. The abstraction of literary figures into polemical ideals does not lose its grounding in what Schlegel views as the irrational chaos of human nature.

In his treatment of the specific characters of *Don Quixote*, however, Schlegel does not abstract the pair of protagonists into polemical signs. Rather, he writes approvingly of Cervantes' handling of Don Quixote and Sancho Panza, and signals the play of arbitrary willfulness present in both: "Cervantes also treats the characteristics of Don Quixote and Sancho in a thoroughly musical and playful manner, without any psychology, development, or even conventional consistency. The arbitrariness and the sudden rage are the purest elements of their character. The dualism between them is original and necessary."[56] Significantly, the dualism does not exist as a dialectic between the characters, in which one statically represents Narrheit and the other Dummheit, but rather springs from the witty dialogue between them. Thus, Cervantes' *Don Quixote* participates in the irony of Socratic dialogue, which Schlegel signals as the ground of the novel. Both "music" and "play," terms recurring throughout Schlegel's comments on *Don Quixote*, also imply the give-and-take between characters of dialogue. In the review of Tieck's translation, for example, Schlegel writes that in no other prose is the arrangement of words so symmetrical and musical (KA 2, p. 283). As Mennemeier notes, the notion of music is central to Schlegel's reading of *Don Quixote* for two reasons: music results from the apparent arbitrary claim of sublime ideas to unity, and it expresses the interchange of speech, in which enthusiasm constructs itself from the most ordinary and simplest words.[57] Music, then, would seem to offer another form of arabesque, in which counterpoint creates a transcendent form. In this note, Schlegel specifically praises the *donaires*, that is to say, the pithy and witty statements of both protagonists, characterizing the arbitrariness and even fury of their conversation.[58] In fact, in the ruminations over the theory of the novel quoted above from the *Dialogue on Poetry*, Schlegel ends his praise of the four romantic authors, Dante, Petrarch, Shakespeare, and Cervantes, by referring to the joking exchanges of Don Quixote and Sancho Panza (KA 2, p. 337). Thus, the pair's arabesquely witty conversation, based on the play of antithesis, dominates Schlegel's praise of their dualism.

In order to fully appreciate Schlegel's understanding of Don Quixote and Sancho Panza, however, it is necessary to focus upon the reference to their *Charakter* in one telling note (VII 91; KA 16, p. 211). Schlegel writes of their character (singular), not their characters (plural). We are given to understand that the pair incarnates a duality, creating another arabesque of foolishness and stupidity, willfulness and irascibility. The word *Dualismus* consistently appears in Schlegel's musings upon literature, a natural result of his interest in the juxtaposition of opposites. For example, he writes that individuality and universality are the agents of poetry, the original dualism (IX 103; KA 16, p. 262).[59] The duality of Don Quixote and Sancho Panza contains within itself an arabesque that expresses the potential of the novel to be both mimetic and polemical, to depict the individual and the abstract. Yet simple dualism is not the primary attribute of romantic literature. Schlegel later muses that objective poetry has more dualism, whereas romantic poetry has more *Potenzierung*, that is to say, the capacity to elevate the stuff of the world to a higher power.[60] Both depend on play, understood as an arabesque of contrasting elements (IX 458; KA 16, p. 291). Nonetheless, romantic literature moves beyond the balanced equation of its earlier counterpart toward a new form and substance, in short, a new form of art. Novalis clarifies how the Potenzierung of the world in art is linked to a romantic arabesquing of the lower self with the better self.[61] The arabesque of the characters of Don Quixote and Sancho Panza, rather than merely mirroring the worldly follies of each, actually elevates them in their juxtaposition to the higher realm of romantic art.

In his review of Tieck's translation of *Don Quixote*, Schlegel argues that Cervantes' prose is the only prose of the modern era that can be favorably set alongside that of the great ancients, Tacitus, Demosthenes, or Plato.[62] In his following description of Cervantes' work, the innovative arabesquing of form and content dominates Schlegel's praise: "In no other prose is the positioning of words so completely symmetrical and musical; no other so completely uses the differences of style, such as huge quantities of color and light; none is so fresh, so lively, and descriptive, in the general expression of social education (*Bildung*). Ever noble and ever delicate, it develops (*bildet*) on the one hand the sharpest acumen to its outermost point, and on the other hand wanders off in kindly, sweet flirtation."[63] Although a precursory reading of this text might focus on the abundance of seemingly frivolous and belletristic terms such as "light" and "sweetness," it is now clear that they can only be read in opposition to the other side of the arabesque—sharp-wittedness. It is this quality of sagacious Witz, if one will, that cuttingly raises the work to a new power, and yet wanders off again into sweet flirtation. The metaphor of music serves again to recall the symmetry, counterpoint, and transcendent effect that characterize romantic literature for Schlegel. Yet the centrality of Witz in counterbalance to feeling emerges in a note that repeats the comparison of Cervantes' prose to music: "In Cervantes there is often a concert of wit, rhyme, feeling, and love."[64] Thus, the dualism that informs *Don Quixote*, as well as the rest of Cervantes' prose, is sharp wit versus sentimentality.[65] Neither could exist in his arabesque work without the opposing tension of the other.

Another term related to Dualismus, *Duplizität*, suggests the manner in which opposition can transcend objective indifference and reach Potenzierung. Schlegel explores the term in the following note: "Duplicity in the novel—the algebraic foundations: nullity, identity, duplicity. So-called irony is an algebraic foundation."[66] Among the three possibilities listed for algebraic primary notions, Duplizität would, of course, be the one that corresponds to irony. Irony, as duplicity, depends on the simultaneous coexistence of opposite meanings. If one refers to the mathematical representation of these terms, nullity is $0/1$ and identity is $1/1$. Is duplicity, with its undermining of meaning, $1/0$? If so, then this note further illuminates the significance of the diamond of romantic literary giants referred to earlier (IX 683; KA 16, p. 311). On the vertical axis of the image, nullity and duplicity form the poles, whereas identity itself could only be found, but is not, somewhere in the center. Schlegel refuses to represent identity, and instead insists on the field of play between the two opposing terms of absence and duality. Petrarch represents the absence on which lyric depends, whereas Cervantes represents the use of the formless stuff of life in the novel. Absence, of course, marks the lyric, which arises from a yearning and longing for the beloved. Duplicity, then, characterizes the novel in its arabesque intertwinings of chaos and system, reason and irrationality, irony and sentiment. This dualism can be seen most evidently in *Don Quixote* in the interplay of its two protagonists, Don Quixote and Sancho Panza.

Several of Schlegel's literary notes indicate that, for him, *Don Quixote*'s duality goes much deeper to transform it into a self-reflexive work in the second part of the novel.[67] Published ten years later, the second book plays with the notoriety and popularity that the first part had achieved by representing episodes in which the main characters boast about and struggle with their fame, meet readers of the first part, and even encounter a man who claims to have met the apocryphal protagonist of Avellaneda's unauthorized continuation. For Schlegel, who personifies the two parts of Cervantes' masterpiece in the following fragment, the main protagonist of *Don Quixote II* is the first part of the novel. This results in a thorough reflection of the work upon itself (IX 185; KA 16, p. 269). The self-consciousness of the novel, expressed as a reflection of its earlier manifestation, embodies the self-consciousness of the romantic author, who hovers above his circumstances and thus achieves a transcendental awareness of the contradictions informing his world and his work. Schlegel sees this doubled, ironic vision as constitutive of self-parody in the second part of Cervantes' novel, in which education and understanding are both presented and parodied in the conversations and friendship of the two protagonists (IX 175; KA 16, p. 268). Notably, the self-parody transcends an ironic vision of the work's own generic play and polemic to embrace even the parody of noble society (*edle Gesellschaft*). This comment must refer, at the least, to the maltreatment of both protagonists at the hands of the duke and the duchess in the second part of the work, and thus indicates how the novel can rise above a mere canceling out of its own contradictions to deal with broader issues. In short, the work is elevated above mere parody and mere sentiment by the author's ironic vision of the arabesque contradictions composing it. The whole series of paradoxical juxtapositions—from sentiment to irony, reason to irrationality, humor to seriousness—gives body to *Don Quixote*. Clearly, Schlegel's reading of *Don Quixote* as the principal example of romantic prose, the novel, depends upon accepting and even reveling in these various contradictory elements.

Conclusion

Where, then, does Friedrich Schlegel's reading of *Don Quixote* fit within the history of the novel's reception? Given his recognition, even espousal, of the satirical and parodic elements of Cervantes' work, the argument that Schlegel's interpretation represented a definitive break from earlier readings cannot be sustained. The universalization of the work's humorous thrust already marked a broad spectrum of eighteenth-century reading. Peter Motteux stated in a 1706 English translation that Don Quixote poked fun at the foolish desires and delusions of every man.[68] Gregorio Mayans y Siscar asserted in a 1738 biography of Cervantes that his masterpiece parodied pernicious literature in general and the barbaric morality of the Middle Ages in particular.[69] Vicente de los Ríos wrote in a 1780 analysis of the novel that it satirized the gamut of social ills, from the lack of education in the nobility to the superstition of the lower classes, while simultaneously maintaining that Cervantes shared some of the chivalric and sentimental values of his deluded protagonist.[70] Friedrich J. Bertuch summarized the general German reception of the novel in 1775, when he wrote in the foreword to his translation that the novel represented in the figure of Don Quixote various types of foolish enthusiasts. In contrast, Sancho was seen as a faithful portrait of the lower class's vices, including innobility, superstition, avarice, talkativeness, and sloth.[71] Whereas translators and literary critics chose to read into the novel their own social agenda and literary ideals, visual artists began to use sentimental and even Christ-like models to elevate Don Quixote and Sancho Panza to more heroic stances.[72] There emerged, then, in the eighteenth century models of interpretation that represented the protagonists in a more sympathetic light and saw in Cervantes a congenial thinker interested in the same Enlightenment goals and neoclassical literary precepts. Schlegel's appropriation of Cervantes' work into his own theory as a masterpiece of romantic literature was, therefore, nothing new. What, perhaps, was new was his acceptance, even celebration, of the contradictions of a work that appeared to be both sentimental and parodic. From this fundamentally playful and serious reading, *Don Quixote* emerged as the model for the Roman, that is to say, the romantic novel.

Schlegel's interpretation of *Don Quixote* did, on the other hand, mark a turning point in Cervantine criticism, which has been dominated in the last two centuries by many of the German romantics' pet problems. The assertion that Cervantes' masterpiece initiated a new genre peculiar to the modern period has anchored various theories of the novel, ranging from Georg Lukács' early work based specifically on a romantic, ironic separation between the individual and society in *The Theory of the Novel*, to Mikhail Bakhtin's espousal of *Don Quixote* in his work on novelistics and carnivalesque culture as dialogic. Hispanists have chosen to view the generic innovations of *Don Quixote* within the fertilely inventive period of early modern Hispanic prose.[73] Other critics have focused on the dualities and doublings within the work, paying attention to the interaction of the protagonists, the importance of the interpolated stories and the various genres parodied, the contradictory attitudes of the various narrators, and the ubiquity of ironic and paradoxical play within the novel.[74] Nonetheless, many Hispanists have failed to appreciate the ironic complexity and necessarily contradictory elements of the young Friedrich Schlegel's reading of Cervantes' masterpiece. To assume that Schlegel's reading simplified the complexity of Cervantes' novel because he used seemingly ill-defined terms, or to state that the German romantic emasculated it by his emphasis on the arabesque, or to assert that Schlegel recommended its serious consumption above appreciation of its humor rather than in play with it is to grossly misinterpret the ironic complexity of the young Schlegel's thought.[75] The evidence to the contrary may be found in the elevation of *Don Quixote* to its status as the exemplary novel seen in the varied, even contradictory, yet critically challenging readings of Schlegel and his successors. As Schlegel mused, "The world is much too serious, but seriousness is nevertheless a rather rare phenomenon. Seriousness is the opposite of play."[76] *Don Quixote* continues to generate an arabesque of seriousness and play, as the young Schlegel would have heartily approved.

Notes

1. Jean-Jacques Achille Bertrand, *Cervantes et le romantisme allemand* (Paris, 1914), p. 88. Werner Brüggemann remarks that Cervantes was a constant topic of conversation among the early romantics, to the extent that Dorothea even reported a dream in which he appeared (*Cervantes und die Figur des Don Quijote in Kunstanschauung und Dichtung der deutschen Romantik* [Münster, 1958], note 162). Fervor for *Don Quixote* reached such a height that the Jena circle proposed staging part of the work, and Friedrich Schlegel took for himself the

name Cardenio, Don Quixote's counterpart in the Sierra Morena, who went mad from love (Bertrand, *Cervantes en el país de Fausto* [Madrid, 1950], p. 83).
2. All primary sources authored by Friedrich Schlegel from *Kritische Friedrich-Schlegel-Ausgabe*, ed. Hans Eichner (Paderborn), vol. 2, 1967 or vol. 16, 1981, will be indicated as either KA 2 with the title of the work and the page number, or as KA 16 with the numbers of the notebook and the fragment. English translations are mine, unless otherwise indicated.
3. "D[on] Q[uixote] noch immer d[er] einzige durchaus romantische Roman" (V 1110; KA16, p. 176).
4. Anthony Close, *The Romantic Approach to "Don Quixote": A Critical History of the Romantic Tradition in Quixote Criticism* (Cambridge, 1977), p. 1. The other two characteristics of this hermeneutic stance read as follows: "b) the belief that the novel is symbolical and that through this symbolism it expresses ideas about the human spirit's relation to reality or about the nature of Spain's history; c) the interpretation of its symbolism, and more generally, of its whole spirit and style, in a way which reflects the ideology, aesthetics, and sensibility of the modern era" (ibid.).
5. Hans Eichner, "Friedrich Schlegel's Theory of Romantic Poetry," *PMLA*, vol. 71 (1956), p. 1021.
6. Hans Eichner, "The Genesis of German Romanticism," *Queen's Quarterly*, vol. 72, no. 2 (1965), pp. 218–219.
7. Ibid., p. 229.
8. Peter Szondi, "Schlegel's Theory of Poetical Genres: A Reconstruction from the Posthumous Fragments," in *On Textual Understanding and Other Essays*, trans. Harvey Mendelsohn (Minneapolis, 1986), p. 85.
9. Arthur O. Lovejoy, "Schiller and the Genesis of German Romanticism," in *Essays in the History of Ideas* (Baltimore, 1948), p. 219.
10. "*Stufen des Rom[antischen]* 1) bei d[en] Alten: [Epos] und [Drama]. Anfang des Mischgedichts in *Prosa* und myst[ische] sentim[entale] Liebe, *erotika*. 2) Das absolute mystisch Wunderbare, d[as] eigentl[ich] Romantisch[e] 3) Don Quixote" (V 69; KA 16, p. 91).
11. Lovejoy most strongly represents the point of view that the definition of the *Roman* as novel is not the same as that of the romantic (see the article mentioned above in note 9, plus "The Meaning of 'Romantic' in Early German Romanticism," pp. 183–206, published in the same volume). The most salient rebuttal emerges in Eichner's article, "Friedrich Schlegel's Theory of Romantic Poetry," cited above in note 5, in which he argues that "*romantische Poesie, Romanpoesie* and *der Roman* were virtually synonymous in Schlegel's usage" (p. 1019). Ernst Behler argues the same point by distinguishing the use of the terms by the early Jena school from its appropriation by later authors in Germany and France ("The Origins of Romantic Literary Theory," *Colloquia Germanica*, vol. 1 [1968], pp. 110–113). In order to express what I perceive to be the inextricable intertwining of the novel as a genre and the romantic in Friedrich Schlegel's thought, I prefer to use the German word "Roman."
12. Friedrich Schlegel, *Dialogue on Poetry and Literary Aphorisms*, trans. Ernst Behler and Roman Struc (University Park, Pa., 1968), p. 102. "Ja ich kann mir einen Roman kaum anders denken, als gemischt aus Erzählung, Gesang und andern Formen. Anders hat Cervantes nie gedichtet, und selbst der sonst so prosaische Boccaccio schmückt seine Sammlung mit einer Einfassung von Liedern" (*Gespräch über die Poesie*, KA 2, p. 336).

13. In a typically algebraic formulation, he writes that the absolute Roman is composed of both positive and negative elements of psychological, philosophical, fantastic, and sentimental novels (V 420; KA 16).
14. Friedrich Schlegel, *Literary Notebooks, 1797–1801*, ed. Hans Eichner (Toronto, 1957), p. 12.
15. Lovejoy, "Schiller and the Genesis of German Romanticism," p. 216.
16. Friedrich Schlegel, *Philosophical Fragments*, trans. Peter Firchow (Minneapolis, 1991), p. 31. The original reads, "Die romantische Poesie ist eine progressive Universalpoesie" (*Athenäum Fragment* 116, KA 2, p. 182).
17. Robert James, *Mathematics Dictionary*, 5th ed. (New York, 1992), p. 133. Schlegel seems to understand meaninglessness as closely related to, if not synonymous with, chaos. Of course, this predates the current scientific fascination with chaos theory, which finds nonlinear repetition of forms in seemingly chaotic systems. It is hard not to speculate, however, that the young Schlegel would have been delighted by the arabesque patterns present in many chaotic systems, such as the edge of a leaf or a shoreline. Ironically, these patterns, as they are now understood, appear much more mimetic than those created by linear equations.
18. Schlegel recognizes this unifying of objectivity and subjectivity in Petrarch's lyrical stance into identity in his "Nachricht von den poetischen Werken des Johannes Boccaccio" (KA 2, p. 393).
19. "Im [Chaos] wechselt + und -[,] in [System] beides verschmolzen" (VII 249; KA 16, p. 222).
20. "Mathem[atik] ist Princ[ip] d[es] Chaotischen. Die [mathematische] Form entsteht durch d[as] Irrationale, Potenzirte/Combinatorische, Progress[ive]" (IX 973; KA 16, p. 336).
21. Behler believes that Schlegel's concept of the creative power of the author to form literature from chaos represents one of the few legitimate applications of Fichte's theory concerning the ego's power to create the non-ego (p. 124). Lowry Nelson, Jr. notes that the creative potential of chaos carries "cosmogonic pre-Socratic and Platonic overtones" ("Romantic Irony and Cervantes," in *Romantic Irony*, ed. Frederick Garber [Budapest, 1988], p. 18).
22. Franz Norbert Mennemeier notes that the change in the young Schlegel's thought about chaos, which he sees in 1795 as a negative value, occurs in the last few years of the century (*Friedrich Schlegels Poesiebegriff dargestellt anhand der literaturkritischen Schriften* [Munich, 1971], pp. 25–31).
23. "Eine solche Theorie des Romans würde selbst ein Roman sein müssen, der jeden ewigen Ton der Fantasie fantastisch wiedergäbe, und das Chaos der Ritterwelt noch einmal verwirrte" (KA 2, p. 337).
24. Schlegel, *Dialogue on Poetry and Literary Aphorisms*, p. 103. "Da würden die alten Wesen in neuen Gestalten leben; da würde der heilige Schatten des Dante sich aus seiner Unterwelt erheben, Laura himmlisch vor uns wandeln, und Shakespeare mit Cervantes trauliche Gespräche wechseln;—und da würde Sancho von neuem mit Don Quixote scherzen" (KA 2, p. 337).
25. Schlegel's earlier musings upon Witz proposed its existence in different forms, expressly the romantic, satiric, epic, lyric, dramatic, poetic, prophetic, classical, and progressive, of which the romantic is, of course, the highest manifestation (V 53, V 783; KA 16, pp. 90, 152). Steven E. Alford argues that romantic Witz, unlike simple Witz, is dialectical, because it combines sense and nonsense (*Irony and the Logic of the Romantic Imagination* [New York, 1984], p. 59).

26. "Die *Form* d[es] Witzes ist d[er] *Schein* absoluter Antithese. Oder so: im unächten Witz werden bloß absolute Antithesen synthesirt ohne daß ETWAS *thesirt* wird" (V 542; KA 16, p. 129).
27. Gerhart von Gravenitz, *Das Ornament des Blicks: Über die Grundlagen des neuzeitlichen Sehens, die Poetik, der Arabeske und Goethes "West-östlichen Divan"* (Stuttgart and Weimar, 1994), p. 23.
28. Ibid., p. 24.
29. In his book studying the complications of the concept of the arabesque in Friedrich Schlegel's work, Karl Konrad Polheim argues that the author sees the grotesque arising out of "sick" Witz, whereas the arabesque embodies romantic Witz (*Die Arabeske: Ansichten und Ideen aus Friedrich Schlegels Poetik* [Munich, 1966], p. 147); see also Mennemeier, *Friedrich Schlegels Poesiebegriff*, p. 344.
30. Polheim, *Die Arabeske*, pp. 313–360.
31. Schlegel, *Dialogue on Poetry and Literary Aphorisms*, p. 86. "Ja diese künstlich geordnete Verwirrung, diese reizende Symmetrie von Widersprüchen, dieser wunderbare ewige Wechsel von Enthusiasmus und Ironie, der selbst in den kleinsten Gliedern des Ganzen lebt, scheinen mir schon selbst eine indirekte Mythologie zu sein. Die Organisation ist dieselbe und gewiß ist die Arabeske die älteste und ursprüngliche Form der menschlichen Fantasie" (*Gespräch über die Poesie*, KA 2, pp. 318–319).
32. Lilian R. Furst, "Who Created 'romantische Ironie'?," *Pacific Coast Philology*, vol. 16, no. 1 (June 1981), pp. 30–32.
33. Ernst Behler, "The Theory of Irony in German Romanticism," in *Romantic Irony*, ed. Frederick Garber (Budapest, 1988), pp. 48–40.
34. Georgia Albert, "Understanding Irony: Three *essais* on Friedrich Schlegel," *MLN*, vol. 108, no. 5 (December 1993), p. 826.
35. Schlegel, *Dialogue on Poetry and Literary Aphorisms*, p. 155. "Ironie ist klares Bewußtsein der ewigen Agilität, des unendlich vollen Chaos" (*Athenäum Idee* 69, KA 2, p. 175).
36. Peter Szondi, "Friedrich Schlegel and Romantic Irony," in *On Textual Understanding, and Other Essays*, trans. Harvey Mendelsohn (Minneapolis, 1986), p. 23.
37. Behler, "The Origins of Romantic Literary Theory," p. 125. See also Eberhard Huge, *Poesie und Reflexion in der Ästhetik des frühen Friedrich Schlegel* (Stuttgart, 1971), p. 126.
38. Schlegel, *Philosophical Fragments*, p. 32. "Und doch kann auch sie am meisten zwischen dem Dargestellten und dem Darstellenden, frei von allem realen und idealen Interesse auf den Flügeln der poetischen Reflexion in der Mitte schweben, diese Reflexion immer wieder potenzieren und wie in einer endlosen Reihe von Spiegeln vervielfachen" (*Athenäum Fragment* 116, KA 2, pp. 182–183).
39. Polheim, *Die Arabeske*, p. 343.
40. "Die Form des romantischen Lebens ist die witzige.—Witz ist zwischen Kunst und Tugend —Liebe und Fantasie—die reinste Indifferenz, daher so äußerst [philosophisch]" (IX 908; KA 16, p. 330).
41. For an explanation of the sign for indifference, see Schlegel, *Literary Notebooks, 1797–1801*, p. 254.
42. "Humor hat es mit Sein und Nichtsein zu tun, und sein eigentliches Wesen ist Reflexion" (*Athenäum Fragment* 305, KA 2, p. 217).
43. For Schlegel, satire, like irony, participates in Witz and is the form most similar to romantic Witz (V 53; KA 16, p. 90). At another point he states that irony is a polemic with oneself and unending satire in the old sense (V 508; KA 16, p. 127).

44. "Ironie und Parodie s[in]d die absoluten Witzarten; der erste der ideale, d[er] zweite der reale.—'[Systematischer] Witz = Ironie + Parodie'" (V 1039; KA 16, p. 171).
45. "Ironie = Selbstparodie? Parodie ist der epische Witz" (V 783; KA 16, p. 152).
46. Albert, "Understanding Irony," p. 831.
47. Schlegel, *Philosophical Fragments*, p. 3. "Die Romane sind die sokratischen Dialoge unserer Zeit. In diese liberale Form hat sich die Lebensweisheit vor der Schulweisheit geflüchtet" (*Lyceum Fragment* 26, KA 2, p. 149).
48. As Lowry Nelson, Jr. writes, "A true feeling for irony allows one to avoid taking jest for earnest and vice versa. In general, we may conclude that irony is here presented as a transcendent and mature world view, far broader than mere seriousness and decorum would permit" ("Romantic Irony and Cervantes," p. 17).
49. "One also wonders if the reader will desire to share the translator's point of view, whether he can, in a nutshell, make up his mind to read *Don Quixote* at hours in addition to those of digestion, which, as one knows, becomes too easily disadvantageous to everything that does not make one laugh, chiefly serious or even tragic poetry." The German reads thus: "Es fragt sich also nur, ob der Leser wird in den Gesichtspunkt des Übersetzers eingehn wollen, ob er sich mit einem Worte entschließen kann, den DON QUIXOTE auch noch in andern Stunden als denen der Verdauung zu lesen, welcher bekanntlich alles, was nicht zu lachen macht, vorzüglich ernsthafte oder gar tragische Poesie, so leicht nachteilig wird" (Review of Ludwig Tieck's translation of *Don Quixote*, KA 2, p. 282).
50. Nelson, Jr., "Romantic Irony and Cervantes," p. 21.
51. "Die Narrheit ist bloß dadurch von der Tollheit verschieden, daß sie willkürlich ist wie die Dummheit" (*Athenäum Fragment* 79, KA 2, p. 176).
52. "Dumm ist, wer nicht glaubt, was er sieht. Ein Narr ist, wer willkürlich dumm ist und es nicht glaubt, daß er es ist; er ist aus List dumm," Schlegel, *Literary Notebooks*, p. 248. See also V 429 and 616 (KA 16, pp. 121, 136–137).
53. "Ein Dummkopf und ein Narr sind nothwendig im [philosophischen] R[oman]. —Die Männer haben mehr Anlage zur *Narrheit* und zur *Dummheit*; die *Weiber* aber zur *Bosheit*. (Der Weise muß zugl[eich] Narr und Dummkopf sein; Heiliger und Bösewicht; Schwärmer und Witz. Sonst umfaßt er nicht alles.—Der Narr ist ein Scholastiker, der Dummkopf ein Weltmensch. —)" (V 616, KA 16, pp. 136–137).
54. "D[on] Qu[ixote] ein [negativ Fantastisch-Sentimentaler Roman], [positiv kritisch-philosophischer Roman] (aber auch *dieser* in Rücksicht des [negativ philosophischen] Stoffs [Narr und Dummkopf] ein negativer)" (V 694; KA 16, p. 143).
55. Schlegel, *Discourse on Poetry and Literary Aphorisms*, p. 86. "Weder dieser Witz noch eine Mythologie können bestehn ohne ein erstes Ursprüngliches und Unnachahmliches, was schlechthin unauflöslich ist, was nach allen Umbildungen noch die alte Natur and Kraft durchschimmern läßt, wo der naive Tiefsinn den Schein des Verkehrten und Verrückten, oder des Einfältigen und Dummen durchschimmern läßt. Denn das ist der Anfang aller Poesie, den Gang und die Gesetze der vernünftig denkenden Vernunft aufzuheben und uns wieder in die schöne Verwirrung der Fantasie, in das ursprüngliche Chaos der menschlichen Natur zu versetzen, für das ich kein schöneres Symbol bis jetzt kenne, als das bunte Gewimmel der alten Götter" (*Gespräch über die Poesie*, KA 2, p. 319).

56. "Auch die Char[akteristik] des D[on] Q[uichote] und Sa[ncho] behandelt Cerv[antes] durchaus [musikalisch] und spielend, ohne alle [Psychologie], Entwicklung, ja gewöhnl[iche] Consequenz. Die Willkühr und *das plötzlich Auffahrende* im D[on] Q[uichote] und Sa[ncho]'s Donayres sind das feinste in ihrem Charakter. Der Dualismus zwisch[en] ihnen [ist] ursprünglich und nothwendig" (VII 91; KA 16, p. 211).
57. Mennemeier, *Friedrich Schlegels Poesiebegriff*, pp. 305–306.
58. Herder used the term "arabesque" in 1796 to refer to unrhymed, pleasant "Konversationspoesie" (Polheim, *Die Arabeske*, p. 21).
59. "Individualität und Universalität die Agenten d[er] [Poesie], d[er] ursprüngl[iche] Dualismus derselben" (IX 103; KA 16, p. 262).
60. "Der innre Grund d[er] Formverschiedenheit[en] der [Poesie] ist noch zu entdecken. Die objecktive hat mehr *Dualismus* in d[er] Form; die romantische mehr Potenzirung" (IX 458; KA 16, 291).
61. "Die Welt muß romantisirt werden. So findet man den urspr[ünglichen] Sinn wieder. Romantisiren ist nichts, als eine qual[itative] Potenzirung. Das niedre Selbst wird mit einem bessern Selbst in dieser Operation identificirt." Novalis, "Vorarbeiten zu verschiedenen Fragmentsammlungen 1798," *Werke*, ed. Hans-Joachim Mähl (Munich, 1978), vol. 2, p. 534. I would like to thank Dr. Paola Mayer for bringing this quote to my attention.
62. "Ich glaube, es ist die einzige *moderne*, welche wir der Prosa eines Tacitus, Demosthenes oder Plato entgegenstellen können" (Review of Ludwig Tieck's translation of *Don Quixote*, KA 2, p. 283).
63. "In keiner andern Prosa ist die Stellung der Worte so ganz Symmetrie und Music; keine andre braucht die Verschiedenheiten des Styls so ganz, wie Massen von Farbe und Licht; keine ist in den allgemeinen Ausdrücken der geselligen Bildung so frisch, so lebendig und darstellend. Immer edel und immer zierlich bildet sie bald den schärfsten Scharfsinn bis zur äußersten Spitze, und verirrt bald in kindlich süße Tändeleien" (KA 2, p. 283).
64. "Im Cerv[antes] oft ein *Concert* von Witz, von Reim, Gefühl und Liebe" (IX 24; KA 16, p. 257).
65. Schlegel writes in "Zur Poesie. 1802. II" (leaf 2) of two groups of Cervantes' works, the first including the *Galatea* and the *Numancia*, the second including *Don Quixote* and the *Novelas ejemplares* (Schlegel, *Literary Notebooks, 1797–1801*, p. 283). The dichotomy signaled here by Schlegel in Cervantes' collected works as typical of romantic poetry is the opposition between the idealized and heroic representation of love and valor in the first group and the parody of the same in the second.
66. "*Duplicität* zum Rom[an].—Die algebraischen Grundformen—Nullität, Identität, Duplicität. 'Die sogenannte *Ironie* ist algebraische Grundform'" (IX 756; KA 16, p. 317).
67. Lowry Nelson, Jr. notes that Schlegel praises a similar duplicity in *Wilhelm Meister*. Goethe begins the work as a *Künstlerroman* and then transforms it into the *Bildungslehre der Lebenskunst* (pp. 20–21). Cervantes, of course, did something similar in his transformation of a parody of chivalric literature into a novel. As the critic concludes, "At all events, the parallel in 'duplicity' between Goethe and Cervantes is of interest in suggesting the author's sovereign right to reveal his art by renewing or transforming it in process" ("Romantic Irony and Cervantes," p. 21).
68. "Every Man has something of *Don Quixote* in his Humour, some darling *Dulcinea* of his Thoughts, that sets him very often upon mad Adventures. What

Quixotes does not every Age produce in Politicks and Religion, who fancying themselves to be in the right of something, which all the world tells 'em is wrong, make very good sport to the Publick, and shew them that they themselves need the chiefest Amendment!" (Peter Anthony Motteux, "Translator's Preface," *The History of the Renoun'd Don Quixote de la Mancha* by Miguel de Cervantes Saavedra [London, 1706], n.p.).

69. Gregorio Mayans y Siscar, "Vida de Miguel de Cervantes Saavedra," in *Vida y hechos del Ingenioso Caballero Don Quixote de la Mancha* (London, 1738), p. 10.
70. Ríos's account of Cervantes' captivity by the Moors in Algiers is notable for its attribution of spiritual heroism to the author (Vicente de los Ríos, "Vida de Cervantes," in *El ingenioso hidalgo Don Quixote de la Mancha* [Madrid, 1780], pp. vii-x). For his description of Cervantes' objection to social ills, see p. cxxxiii. For Ríos, Cervantes was *not* a man of his age because, free of his time's preoccupations, he made them known and repudiated them in order to correct the vices of his contemporaries (p. cxxvi).
71. Brüggemann, *Cervantes und die Figur des Don Quijote*, p. 45.
72. Rachel Schmidt, "La ilustración gráfica y la interpretación del *Quijote* en el siglo XVIII," *Dieciocho*, vol. 19, no. 2 (Fall 1996), pp. 203–248, and idem, *Critical Images: The Canonization of Don Quixote through Illustrated Editions in the Eighteenth Century* (Montreal-Kingston, 1999).
73. See, for example, Edward C. Riley, *Cervantes's Theory of the Novel* (Oxford, 1962).
74. For a discussion of the interaction of the two protagonists, see Salvador de Madariaga, *Guía del lector del Quijote: ensayo psicológico* (Madrid, 1926); for a structuralist approach arguing for the unity of the novel, see Joaquín Casalduero, *Sentido y forma del Quijote, 1605–1615* (Madrid, 1970); for a discussion of the narrative levels in the work, see Ruth El Saffar, *Distance and Control in "Don Quixote": A Study in Narrative Technique* (Chapel Hill, N.C., 1975); and for a discussion of the ironic perspective in the novel, see Leo Spitzer, "Perspectivismo lingüístico en el Quijote," in *Lingüística e historia literaria* (Madrid, 1968).
75. Close, *The Romantic Approach to "Don Quixote,"* p. 35; Bertrand, *Cervantes en el país de Fausto*, p. 79; Lienhard Bergel, "Cervantes in Germany," in *Cervantes across the Centuries*, ed. Angel Flores and M. J. Benardete (New York, 1969), p. 334.
76. Schlegel, *Philosophical Fragments*, p. 84. "Die Welt ist viel zu ernsthaft, aber der Ernst ist doch selten genug. Ernst ist das Gegenteil von Spiel" (*Athenäum Fragment* 419, KA 2, p. 245).

SPAIN IN HEINE—HEINE IN SPAIN

Notes on a Bilateral Reception

Berit Balzer

The importance of Heinrich Heine (1797–1856) as a mediator between nations and cultures cannot be stressed enough. Few literary figures have brought about such an amount of varied and often contradictory material that deals with their artistic ideas, techniques, and aims. Although there are at present numerous studies on the reception of Heine in Germany and in other countries, few offer a coherent picture of how and why this reception took place. Heine's influence and scope have often been misinterpreted with a slant of partiality, according to individualistic interests among his critics. He has been acclaimed or rejected for particular aspects of his work, but rarely has the global meaning of his art—that is, the combination of a melodiously lyrical poetry with a poignant, irreverent sense of humor in pursuit of freedom from all restraints—been accepted for the uniquely modern outlook it offers. Also modern and relevant for our present time is his idea of a common ground where different cultures and creeds could live together in mutual tolerance and respect. Such utopia—or rather, paradise lost—is projected time and again in Heine's works and takes up a central part of his thought. On this general background, motifs from Spanish history play such a significant role in his entire work that they certainly deserve a closer look.

A Spanish point of view is present in Heine's early ballad "Die Romanze vom Rodrigo";[1] his drama *Almansor* (1822); his two ballads "Donna Clara" and "Almansor";[2] the ballads "Der Mohrenkönig," "Spanische Atriden," "Vitzliputzli," "Jahuda-ben-Halevy," and "Disputation," included in his *Romanzero* of 1851; and the long fragment of the unfinished "Bimini," edited posthumously in 1869. The Moorish-Christian conflict is present in three of these texts, the Jewish-Christian encounter in another three, and episodes from the Spanish Christian era yet again in three others. In the first group mentioned, Heine shows great sympathy for the Moors, drawing a "hymnic picture of the cultural conquests during the Moorish dominion in southern Spain."[3] Granada, Córdoba, and Toledo are the three Spanish cities he repeatedly refers to in a highly appreciative way for their brilliant cultural past. By trying to familiarize his German readers with the life and times of figures from Spanish history, with all that struck him as extraordinary and fascinating in it, Heine continued the work begun timidly by his predecessors Johann Wilhelm Ludwig Gleim (1719–1803), Johann Gottfried Herder (1744–1803), and the Schlegel brothers August Wilhelm (1767–1845) and Friedrich (1772–1829) by means of the popular ballad. In addition to adopting this already widely imitated form, Heine also greatly relied on and built upon Hispanic contents. At a time when little was known in Germany about the land beyond the Pyrenees, he drew information from all international sources available to convey a poetic picture of what he considered a real golden age in the sciences and humanities in medieval Moorish Spain, a mixture of cultural and economic flourishing, wisdom, and beauty. Such intermingling traditions, as well as religious and racial features, appealed to him for the cosmopolitan outlook they offered. Heine seems to have been especially intrigued by the fact that Muslims, Jews, and Christians had lived together symbiotically and fruitfully for several centuries, until the *Reconquista* was completed by the surrender of Granada in 1492, "destroying an admirable civilization with its poetry, astronomy, architecture, and refinement unique in this world."[4]

Excerpts from the Spanish *Romancero general*, a collection of historical, epic, or comical ballads of popular—and therefore anonymous—tradition, which had been partially translated by Herder, gave Heine the necessary sentimental and formal dimension to round up and make palatable to the public plain historical facts. He founded this knowledge on historiographic treatises like Ignaz Feßler's *Versuch einer Geschichte der spanischen Nation* (*Die alten und die neuen Spanier: Ein Völkerspiegel*). A more literary source for the *romance morisco* as an intertext was Ginés Pérez de Hita's *Historia de las guerras civiles de Granada* (1595), an epic poem interspersed with *romances*, which appeared in a German translation in 1805. Heine read it, certainly in French, in November 1820[5] before he started to work in Bonn on his drama *Almansor*, which he continued in Göttingen and finished in Berlin. It is highly probable that he also discussed Spanish subjects with the young scholar Wilhelm Havemann, his next-door neighbor in Göttingen (Don Henriques in one of his poems). Havemann was well read in Spanish history and later published his *Darstellungen aus der inneren Geschichte Spaniens während des 15., 16. und 17. Jahrhunderts*.[6]

Among the romances moriscos,[7] the recurrent dilemma faced by Muslims of either converting to Christianity or being expelled from "al-Andalus" (their own promised land) if they did not give up what the victorious Christians considered heresy was also a personal one for Heine, who converted from Judaism to Protestantism in 1825—a step from which he drew no personal profit and which he rather must have regretted in later times. Both his drama and his ballad "Almansor" pivot on such a religious conflict.

Hanne Gabriele Reck has studied in depth how Heine became familiar with the form and subject matter of the Spanish romance.[8] This notion had been introduced in Germany by Gleim as early as 1756.[9] Herder and the Schlegel brothers had translated some Spanish romances in 1778 and 1792.[10] It is noteworthy that Herder opens one of his first series in *Stimmen der Völker* (nos. 12–23) with the note that "Spanish romances are the simplest, oldest, and the most original of all *Romanzen*."[11]

The Schlegel brothers and Herder claimed that there was no way to make the typical assonant rhyme on even verses sound natural in a German translation because the ending on stressed "-ar," being inherent to the Spanish language, has practically no place in German. Herder also lamented that the "romance, a poetic form of noble and solemn origin, is used, or rather misused, in Germany only for vulgarly comical and adventurous subjects."[12] For his translation of romances into German, he chose rhymeless quartets in trochees, with four stresses in a verse. In the Spanish meter, the number of verses contained in a romance tends to be free, but it typically shows assonant rhyme on even verses. The uneven verses follow no determined rhyme pattern.[13] In his earlier works (especially the romances "Donna Clara" [1823] and "Almansor" [1825], and in *Lyrisches Intermezzo*), Heine occasionally tried to put into practice the assonant rhyme pattern typical for the traditional Spanish ballad, or he used assonant quartets alternatively,[14] but he abandoned this pattern completely in his later *Romanzero* (1851) for his own personal quartets with their characteristic metric pattern.

As we have already mentioned, Heine's readings of Spanish history go back to 1820 and 1821, when he studied in Bonn and Göttingen.[15] It is even conceivable that he borrowed books on the subject from the Düsseldorf public library before 1817, when he changed the title of his poem "Die Romanze vom Rodrigo" to "Don Ramiro."[16] This earliest of his Spanish ballads deals with rivalry in love. Although the names are Spanish, there is no description yet of a real geographic setting. The atmosphere is more spooky than heroic.

In German literature, the distinction between *Ballade* and *Romanze* is less a formal than a tonal one. The main difference lies in the mood: the Nordic Ballade is rather more melancholic and often contains supernatural elements; the Romanze is more lively and colorful, more sensuous and less subdued, as it contains more immediate action.[17] Herder at first made no distinction between the two denominations, not adopting the term "Ballade" until 1777, after he had closely studied English poetry. As a matter of fact, the name "Romanze" is not recovered until the romantic period. It is easy to see why Heine, its foremost heir, preferred to call his ballads "Romanzen," although many of them are in fact Nordic in mood and subject matter.

Heine's poetic grasp and inside view of the romantic spirit allowed him to introduce never-heard-of elements in his way of speaking. He turned romantic commonplaces into stunning hints at outdated concepts by conferring them an ironic twist. This technique also permitted him to elaborate on latent erotic motifs and make them popular, while scandalizing his reading public. This is especially true for certain elements contained in the Spanish ballad. Heine had a highly receptive as well as a sharply critical mind, which made him filter genuine from false feelings and perceptions. He was never lenient or indolent on any issue and sensed dormant intercultural relations and undercurrents long before his contemporaries were able to do so. His hedonistic treatment of topics, bound to be considered "exotic," "frivolous," or even "outrageous" by German nineteenth-century criticism, thus allowed him to give new impulses to a politically and socially stagnant literary world. Such choice of subject matter also documents Heine's self-elected role as a true ambassador of popular heritage.[18] In Spain, traditionally reluctant to embrace the French "enlightened" spirit, the contradictory or iconoclastic aspects of Heine's work were willfully omitted in most translations. The second half of this essay will show how and why this "false" reception occurred.

In Heine's tragedy *Almansor*, written between the summer of 1820 and the beginning of 1821, Jews are not mentioned at all, but only Moors, Christians, and *Moriscos*. Friedrich de la Motte Fouqué's insertion of the Christian-Muslim romance of Donna Clara and Don Gayferos in his novel *Der Zauberring* (1812),[19] as well as Clemens Brentano's *Romanzen vom Rosenkranz* (1804–12), undoubtedly inspired Heine's dramatic poem. The first volume of Friedrich Justin Bertuch's *Magazin der Spanischen und Portugiesischen Literatur*, which Heine read in 1821, included three popular Spanish romances, among them yet another version of "Don Gayferos." A third source for his *Almansor* is to be traced in the Persian epic love poem "Majnun and Layla" of Nezami of Ganjeh (who died in 1203). Heine read it in a German translation while in Bonn and mentions it in the drama as the favorite reading of the two lovers when they were children. Lord Byron's general Orientalism, as well as a more precise series of readings, like Franz von Dombay's *Geschichte der mauritanischen Könige* (Agram, 1794–97), Louis de Chénier's *Recherches historiques sur les Maures, et histoire de l'empire de Maroc* (Paris, 1787), and H. M. A. Cramer's *Briefe über Inquisitionsgericht und Ketzerverfolgung in der römischen Kirche* (Leipzig, 1784–85), must be taken into account as sources of information. In any case, Heine had at this time an exact perception of the Moorish dynasties (Abencerrages and Zegries) whose quarrels brought about the downfall of Granada. He also had a fair knowledge of political developments in contemporary Spain, proof of which is that he introduces in *Almansor* anachronisms like the reference to the Spanish revolutionaries Quiroga and Riego, thus establishing an analogy between the Reconquista onslaught and antiliberal repression of his own time. Heine contrasts the land of love and beauty with the dark barbarism of an African past, but also with King Fernando's intention to do away with "allem schönen Lichte," contrasting Catholic obscurantism with "enlightened" religious tolerance. Into this luminous and luscious southern setting[20] the author introduces two picaresque impostors, thus making it clear, by directly quoting passages from Francisco Quevedo y Villegas's (1580–1645) picaresque novel *El Buscón*, that the annihilation of a flourishing culture also brought about undesirable side effects like the newly rich converts and social opportunism.

Heine introduces reports of massacres and *autos de fe*, as well as the notion that the archbishop of Toledo ordered the burning of poetic and scientific Islamic literature of seven centuries. The following lines from *Almansor* have become famous: "When they burn books, they also burn people in the end" ("Wo man Bücher verbrennt, verbrennt man auch am Ende Menschen").[21] Although the reception of the play by its contemporary critics was mostly favorable, *Almansor* was, at its only performance on 23 August 1823 in Braunschweig, whistled and booed at. After this unexplainable fiasco, Heine turned away from the dramatic genre.

Heine's ballad "Donna Clara" also deals with Christian bigotry. A young foreign knight conquers Donna Clara's heart and favors. He makes her declare her hatred and repulsion of Jews, only to reveal himself in the end as the son of the rabbi of Saragossa. The final triumph of a Jew who has outwitted a Christian lady was an explosive subject to present to his German readers in times of smoldering or overt antisemitism. Heine thus transforms Fouqué's Christian-Muslim conflict of "Don Gayferos" into a Christian-Jewish one.[22]

Much attention has been paid to Heine's involvement with Judaism and the ample room this subject matter occupies in his work.[23] We can trace his growing interest from his early experience of visiting the Jewish ghetto in Frankfurt to his contact, later on in Berlin, with the Verein für Kultur und Wissenschaft der Juden and his subsequent friendship with Moses Moser. But his alleged final attachment to the religion of his ancestors has been refuted under the light of personal statements as well as the sacrilegious tone of his "Hebrew Melodies."[24] Not until recently has there been an effort to put this tendency to adopt a profane tone when speaking of religious issues in relation to the Islamic topic and Heine's evident esteem for the cultural contributions of Muslims in Spain.[25] His ballads "Der Asra" and "Der Mohrenkönig" and his ballad and drama *Almansor* strongly support this viewpoint that he values the contributions of Islam. A plainly Oriental background is present in "Der Asra," which is included in the "Historien" cycle of his *Romanzero*, although Spanish-Moorish architecture is again evoked by allusions to gardens and fountains. The poem belongs to a group which views the Orient "as a land of happy or unhappy, simple and sensitive or refined and sensual love."[26] Heine again undertook ample studies previous to the publication of these works, in which he consistently deals with religious repression of a non-Christian group by a Christian environment. In summary, this non-Christian group is sometimes Jewish (as in "Hebrew Melodies") and at other times Moorish.

Although Heine spoke no Spanish, he may have understood the original texts due to his knowledge of Latin and French. Among the books in his personal library, there was a Spanish grammar, practically unopened. But Heine felt so drawn to Cervantes' native country that he made plans twice for a trip to Spain from his Paris exile, first in November 1836 and then again in March 1844. As Susanne Zantop correctly points out, "In critical moments of his life, Spain was the land that Heine searched for with his soul."[27] The first time he had to give up his project because of ill health, the second because he decided to travel to Germany instead. But Heine obviously enjoyed hiding behind a Spanish mask. His interest in Spanish literature, history, and mythology dates back to the age of twelve, when he read his first novel, *Don Quixote*, which undoubtedly made a lasting impression on him. His famous foreword to the anonymous translation of *Don Quixote*[28] must be counted among the finest works of criticism produced worldwide on the fundamental role Cervantes played in the development of the modern novel. It shows a keen insight into the psychology of the author and his figures, as well as a complete identification with the ingenious knight of La Mancha, whose heroism consists for Heine in enduring ridicule as well as physical suffering. Instead of Dulcinea del Toboso, Heine "chooses freedom as his bride worth fighting for."[29] This idea stretches much further than the freedom of creed for a specific religious minority. In his writings Heine fights for the freedom of any individual from moral, social, and political restrictions and cultural conventions. This is also why he rejects all doctrines or ascetic sectarianism, shies away from any kind of chauvinistic nationalism, and is skeptical toward all maximalistic claims.

Heine took up the Spanish-Moorish subject again around 1850, while he was working on his *Romanzero*, a name once again more indebted to the meter that prevailed in the collection than to an ever present subject matter.[30] "Der Mohrenkönig," included in the first cycle ("Historien") of his *Romanzero*, deals with a well-known incident of 1492: the lamentations of Boabdil, the last Moorish king of Granada, at the moment he leaves for exile. This anonymous romance[31] is certainly one of the most famous of the Spanish *Romancero*. Heine takes a sympathetic stance toward Boabdil by not subscribing to his mother's view of his cowardice—a view which is also generally assumed by most writers who have occupied themselves with this figure—but rather by ensuring the unfortunate Boabdil's immortal fame through the songs of the poets. Critics have been surprised at the fact that Heine's grammatical gender of *Alhambra* is masculine. What they have overlooked is that in the entire *Romancero general* the citadel is referred to in the masculine form, whereas the city of Granada is often seen as a beautiful woman in Moorish captivity, waiting to be conquered by the Christian king.

The romance "Spanische Atriden" deals with the cruel fratricide of Don Pedro I, king of Castile. But, here again, Heine shows a certain sympathy for the tolerant attitude of the king toward Jews and Muslims. The cycle "Hebräische Melodien," the third and last part of the *Romanzero* after the "Book of Lazarus," stands for Heine's philosophical testament. It is highly probable that prior to setting himself to work, he read *Die religiöse Poesie der Juden in Spanien* by Michael Sachs, first published in 1845. The outstanding figure in this cycle is undoubtedly Jehuda-ben-Halevy, the most significant Jewish poet of medieval Spain, where Toledo was a melting pot of the three cultures. In the first half of the eleventh century, two other important members of the Toledo school of poetry were Moses ben Ezra and Salomo ben Gabirol. "Prinzessin Sabbath" contains no Spanish elements, but "Disputation" takes place in Toledo, at the court of the level-headed Don Pedro I, who "says many a good word to Jews and Moors" while he presides over the spiritual argument between the rabbi and the monk, who both appear in a dubious light at the end.

In these poems, none of Heine's emblematic figures is totally free of religious ambivalence, and it is easy to conceive why Heine's critics charged him with blasphemy, lack of respect, and impiousness. But it is also true that these poems do not represent a return to religiousness, as has often been maintained. Instead, they are a continuation in Heine's usual tone of irreverence, jocosity, and enlightened tolerance, which can be traced back to Gotthold Ephraim Lessing's *Nathan the Wise* (1779). Heine defends the feast of the flesh: erotic and sensual elements—food, drink, gaiety, and all bodily pleasures—have a firm place in his writings. In any case, "Hebrew Melodies" is not a simple glorification of Jews in medieval Spain.[32] "Disputation," the last poem of the *Romanzero*, ends discordantly on a rejection of both religions, that is, "dogmatic Judaism together with dogmatic Christianity."[33] The symbolic power and bitter truth, the "deeply stirring questions" of Heine's last poetry—questions that remain fundamentally unanswered—have long been underestimated. However, they offer a strikingly modern impact. "Vitzliputzli" is highly critical of the so-called feats of Spanish conquerers who, in yet another instance of religious intolerance, destroyed the advanced Aztec civilization in the name of Christianity. In this context, the unfinished poem "Bimini" implies a quixotic voyage, not to an Eldorado of eternal youth, but to the island of oblivion that cleans the individual of all past sorrows and pains.[34]

Why did Heine consider the Spanish historical subject exemplary, and why did he insist on it so conspicuously? Could German readers value this and follow Heine in his preference? Has the Spanish public ever duly appreciated Heine's exploration of their own popular heritage?[35] One should keep in mind that Heine definitely exported German romanticism to Spain, paving the way, so to speak, for Johann Wolfgang Goethe's work as a lyrical poet as late as 1864.[36] Heine's *Buch der Lieder* (1827) had the good fortune of being rather well translated by Eulogio Florentino Sanz and was immediately embraced by Spanish readers. Once Heine had opened this channel, the possibility was also given to convey to a receptive public his progressive ideas on political democracy, aristocracy of the spirit, and religious tolerance. But due to particular expectations in the Spanish readership around the middle of the nineteenth century, this facet of Heine was practically not assimilated at all, which explains in part why in Spain and the Hispanic world he was enthusiastically accepted and imitated as a composer of *Lieder*, whereas his liberal ideas, which could have served to introduce modern literature in Spain, remained widely unnoticed, if not ignored. Ernst Feise assures that, in general, nineteenth-century renderings of his poetry "did not have the audacity to present this rebel's poetry in the adequate ironic jargon."[37] Agnes Aregger has studied the model character of Heine's prose writings for the unfortunate Larra and the enterprising Fontcuberta.[38] Udo Rukser has given valuable information on Heine's repercussion on Spanish and Spanish-American writers. He also names some of the reasons why much of Heine's language could not be adequately translated into Spanish: "[Spanish writers] had a concept of poetry and tended, therefore, to rhetoric and pathos; the kind of cadence was different, the way of expression more pompous and far-fetched. Thus, a certain idea of poetry coincided with the fossilization of language."[39]

Hanna Geldrich traces Heine's enormous influence on *modernista* poets in Spain and Spanish America. Such important figures as Rubén Darío (1867–1916),[40] Manuel Gutiérrez Nájera (1859–1895), José Asunción Silva (1865–1896), Amado Nervo (1870–1919), and José Martí (1853–1895) received Heine by way either of French translations (Gérard de Nerval's prose version of *Poëmes et légendes* of 1855) or of Spanish translations (Jaime Clark [1872], José J. Herrero [1883], Teodoro Llorente [1885], but also Pérez Bonalde [1885] and Francisco Sellén [1875]), or by reading him in the original with the help of a German-speaking friend.[41] It is important to keep in mind that the Spanish public also had access to Spanish-American editions of Heine, and vice versa.

Modernismo had its roots in the romantic tradition and in the French symbolist movement (Charles Baudelaire, Paul Verlaine), as well as in the Parnassian writers. Other points of reference for modernista poets were Edgar Allan Poe, Arthur Schopenhauer, and Friedrich Nietzsche. Spanish modernistas such as Juan Ramón Jiménez (1881–1958) continued in the vein of the Bécquer tradition on one hand, and of the influential Nicaraguan Rubén Darío on the other. Bécquer was, so to speak, reexported by way of Rubén Darío, as was Heine, logically, in a second-degree reception, which means that his influence was extended indirectly even further on to Antonio Machado (1875–1939) and Miguel de Unamuno (1864–1936).[42] But it is also true that the main impact on the Spanish-speaking world was caused by Heine's earlier poetry, principally his *Intermezzo*, which was widely imitated in motifs, language, and rhythm.[43] However, much of his sarcastic and corrosive thought did not find its way to the Spanish public. This partial and biased reception seems to be due to the selection that Heine's first emulators had made of his work.

The Heine fever broke out in Spain between the age of Gustavo Adolfo Bécquer (1836–1870) and the modernismo wave. Eulogio Florentino Sanz first translated fifteen Lieder in 1857, in the magazine *El Museo Universal*, making Heine almost instantly popular. Bécquer could not read him in the original but was assisted by his friend Augusto Ferrán,[44] who had studied in Germany. Apart from Bécquer, Heine may also have been a source of inspiration for Rosalía de Castro (1837–1885)[45] and Ramón de Campoamor (1817–1901).[46] At a time when *Krausismo*—a philosophical amalgam between pantheism and Catholicism exported from Germany by Julián Sanz del Río—pervaded the Spanish literary world, readers there could not capture the ambiguity in Heine's poetic language, but only perceived the highly emotional timbre, the crisp shortness, and the unique flavor of his diction. Heine thus became the mediator between the popular folksong and Goethe's artistic *Kunstlied* at a time when little was known yet in Spain about contemporaneous German literature. In 1883, Marcelino Menéndez Pelayo explained the impact of Heine's poetry as a mental switch from plastic art to music.[47] The essayist Ramiro de Maeztu (1875–1936) tried to identify with Heine's skepticism for misunderstood confessional reasons.[48]

Heine's unrepentantly critical ideas and the unexpected ironic turning point at the end of many poems are usually lost or falsified in translation. So are, of course, most of his puns. The main difficulties seem to lie in the Spanish equivalent for the diminutives he abundantly uses, as well as in giving an adequate version of unpoetic, "coarse" expressions instead of omitting them completely, as has been consistently done. Heine's ludicrous paradoxes and frequent malicious statements have often been regarded as unworthy of the great poet he was. The use of foreignisms, rather common in Heine's poetry, seems to present a major problem to his translators, who opt to Hispanicize or paraphrase them. The principle of romantic disillusionment was not identified by the eager recipients of German romanticism. Even Bécquer, Heine's Spanish voice, was ideologically closer to Madame de Staël (1766–1817), the Schlegel brothers, and the Jena romantics.[49]

Heine's formal aesthetics of poetry remain undisputed on the whole, whereas politically he is highly polemical in Spain. While writing about Bécquer in 1875, in the preface of *Gritos de combate*, Gaspar Núñez de Arce (1834–1903) referred indirectly to Heine's poetry as "those minute lyrical sighs, of Germanic cut and flavor, exotic and full of mannerisms, with which our poetic youth expresses its disappointments in love, its luckless tenderness and premature loathing of life."[50] Several years later, in his "Discurso sobre la poesía" held on 3 December 1887 at the Madrid Ateneo, Núñez de Arce had to admit that "the overpowering influence due to productions by Goëthe [sic], Byron, Chateaubriand, Lamartine, Leopardi, Heine, and Victor Hugo on the intellectual movement of the world is so evident that I would offend your erudition should I linger on proving it."[51]

Emilia Pardo Bazán also praises Heine, but without perceiving—or purposely ignoring—the relevance of his satire:

> Heine seduced us not only with his intensity, fire, and tenderness, but also with his artistic shortness, with the sobriety of his procedures that contrasts with the verbal abundance that commonly diminishes the worth of our poets. The contradiction of Heine's poetry ... captured the Spanish public so deeply that it became fashionable to imitate Heine in the only way accessible to the rhyming rabble, that is, the size ... Here in Spain, until recent times, only the epigram and the popular *copla* were laconical: refined lyrical poetry which expresses the soul's emotions has always been of a diffuse rhetoric, forgetting that passion and sentiment, due to their very violence, tend to a quick expression, and their supreme form is an inarticulate stammering or shouting.[52]

Heine's most severe critics in Spain were the conservative Julián Sanz del Río and the traditionalistic Juan Valera (1824–1905), both of whom identified his ideas with impiousness and immorality and completely rejected his irony. Marcelino Menéndez Pelayo, in his 1883 introduction to Herrero's translation, stresses the affinity of Heine's cultural tradition to the Spanish essence. But Menéndez Pelayo, too, overlooks his hidden cynicism and sarcasm, thus furthering the erroneous impression of a kitsch German somnambulism and dreamy, starry-eyed romanticism. Peninsular Spanish poetry was, in fact, not prepared to give up its neoclassical isolation and *casticista* paralysis until the modernista movement. This is also why Spanish-American writers, in spite of a common language, paid practically no attention to "fashionable" peninsular writers like Bécquer, Campoamor, Núñez de Arce, or José Zorrilla (1817–1893), but rather turned to other European poets. They also assumed, long before the Spanish critics, the sensualistic and rebellious aspects of Heine's writings.

Another factor that greatly hampered Heine's reception in Spain was his anti-Catholic stance. In a country where the Catholic Church was still an all-pervasive force, there were two ways to deal with Heine: omit all that was conflictive or crush him for socalled aesthetic reasons. Spanish conservatives were Germanophiles when it came to brandishing philosophical idealism as a stronghold against the materialistic tendencies of French realism. When the Prussian state became strong while Spain was losing its last colonies, Spanish conservatives would admire Bismarck's policy as that of a man of action. The precursor of the Generation of 1898, Ángel Ganivet (1865–1898), used xenophobic arguments when viewing Heine's "otherness" in terms of envy of national heroes.[53] Pío Baroja (1872–1956) even revealed himself as a ferocious antisemite when it came to value Heine as a humorist.[54] Only several decades earlier, Heine had met with a more favorable, unprejudiced reception in Spain.

There had been a short period of liberalism after the death of Fernando VII in 1833. Mariano José Larra's (1809–1837) untimely suicide marks the end of this period. Larra, like Heine, saw literature as part of an emancipatory movement inherited from the Enlightenment; in congenial ideas, Larra in fact parallels Heine. Curiously enough, Baroja viewed them both as some kind of "underdogs" in their society: "As to Larra, his case is similar to Heine's, but without the expansiveness, poetry and cosmopolitanism of the German Jew. Larra has a strong, bitter, discontented talent that tends to ingenious satire rather than to humor. Larra, like Heine, feels crushed by a society that has ignored him, and he fights against it. Humorism cannot flow from someone who looks up at the world from below."[55] Baroja continues his hairsplitting appraisal of Heinean humor in the following way: "Heine does not give the impression of a humorist; he is a brilliant genius who bears a grudge; he is perfidious and poetic; there are many satirical, ingenious and incisive sentences, but no humorism."[56] Further on, Baroja deals with irony in Aristophanes, denying that it has anything to do with humorism. But toward the end of his essay, Baroja admits, not without a certain regret, that there is no purity of races as there is no pure sense of humor: "[T]here are no pure races among mankind, they are all intermingling. In such a way, a Jew of Spanish origin like Spinoza appears to us as the founder of German pantheism, later on developed by Hegel, Schelling, and Schopenhauer; and so, another Jew like Heine is one of the most significant representatives of German humorism."[57]

Agnes Aregger has compared selected passages of Heine's and Larra's works, concluding that they shared many viewpoints. Their congeniality consists in attitudes that rather differ from merely "looking at the world from below." Larra came across Heine's prose writings *De l'Allemagne* and *Reisebilder* during his stay in France. Heine's fervent attack on Madame de Staël's conservative views of German literature, as put forth in *De l'Allemagne,* is seen by Larra as totally justified. This shows what Heine could potentially have meant for the renewal of Spanish intellectual life. Some ideas about religion expressed in Heine's critique must have sounded offensive to Spanish ears at the time. Aregger makes the following comment: "Heine's bad reputation and his real anticlericalism make the reception of his critical writings in Spain very difficult. Their introduction happened partly in secret, even during the liberal years after the death of Fernando VII. To quote Heine was an act of civil courage and could mean getting into unnecessary trouble."[58]

Both Heine and Larra considered the word their main weapon and took a cosmopolitan and belligerent attitude, fighting for freedom from moral, religious, and political restrictions. Aregger claims that Fernando Corradi, having heard of *De l'Allemagne* through Larra, held a lecture on Heine in the Madrid Ateneo as early as 1836. José Andrés Fontcuberta, under the pseudonym of A. de Covert-Spring, quoted from *Die romantische Schule* in the Catalan press between 1835 and 1838, without even mentioning Heine's name. A few years later, in 1841, an anonymous review of Heine in the Barcelona *Museo de familias* does him justice for once by not separating the poet from the critic, as is normally the case: "The only truly original poet nowadays is ENRIQUE HEINE, that jester without piety whom the Germans, frightened by his sarcasm, have almost come to hate."[59]

There was at that point a radical division between reactionary and progressive forces in Spain. For instance, conservative writers considered even Hegel dangerous for Spanish orthodox religion and admitted more willingly Friedrich Schlegel's ideas.[60] And yet another anonymous Spanish review of Wolfgang Menzel's denouncement of the Young Germans, which resulted in their prohibition by the German government in 1835, takes the side of Schiller, thus dismissing Heine's defense of Goethe.[61] The latter are supposedly too epicurean and sensual for the Spanish character. Sanz del Río vehemently attacks the recently forbidden group of Young Germans—of which Heine was a member—even though he does not mention Heine's name in this context. It is a well-known fact today that the Heine-Bécquer issue, promoted among others by Pardo Bazán, distorted a true reception of Heine in Spain. Spanish romantic poetry tended to rhetorical pathos and avoided prosaic issues and expressions. It would admit romantic irony in the Schlegel style, but not the Heinean irony indebted to Karl Wilhelm Ferdinand Solger,[62] leaving the satirist widely underestimated. From approximately 1870 until the end of World War I (that is, during the second wave of Heine's reception in Spain), any anti-Prussian statement in print was ignored as unhealthy for the regeneration of Spain's own ailing national spirit. Thus, the preliminary biographical study of Heine's *Joyas Prusianas* ends with a rather colorful note: "By celebrating in his songs the ruin of old Germany, he revealed to his country many vices and many miseries in a pleasantly jocular style, but after abusing his talent, after profaning the sanctuaries of human conscience, history will have to judge him as a pygmy thinker and a giant poet."[63]

One of the first Spanish scholars to value Heine's importance for Spanish literature in its just dimensions was Max Aub (1903–1972).[64] He held that Heine's impact on Spanish literature should have been equal to that of Bécquer and Larra together and compared him to Quevedo in versatility.

What strikes us most is that, in spite of such a vast reception of Heine, there are hardly any significant studies, up to now, of the importance of the Spanish-Moorish topic in his works. Spanish criticism, as a whole, appears to have been too secluded for years, not only from Europe but also from Spain's natural partners, Spanish America and the Arab world. Often times its representatives have been too reactionary or too shortsighted to admit this citizen of the world, who paid such an important tribute to Spanish heritage. Müller calls this characteristic in nineteenth-century Spain a "strange tendency toward literary quietism" ("eigentümlicher Hang zum literarischen Quietismus").[65] As a matter of fact, the three strongest pillars—Church, military, and monarchy—were also the three evils for Heine. Spanish Catholicism seems to have been an important factor that prevented adequate reception of Heine in Spain.[66] It also kept certain intellectuals from coming to grips with their national history and admitting Moorish accomplishments. Ganivet, in his long essay "Granada la bella," is proud of what Christian faith made of the Arabic heritage: "Christianity, when it was Hispanicized and naturalized on our soil, was subjected to our historical sways, and from its battle with the Arab world, it came out even more cleansed and pure."[67]

It is rather striking that in an essay on the urban development of this emblematic city of Moorish Spain, Ganivet says nothing about Granada's past cultural splendor. One of the few comments the Moorish past deserves from him is a frivolous reference to polygamy: "We [Spaniards], who carry in our veins Arab—that is, polygamous—blood, have the illusion that a woman is a harem, and we live, if not happily, very close to happiness. Women should meditate on this."[68] What these thoughts reveal is that most Spanish intellectuals, when confronted with Heine's eulogistic picture of Moorish achievements in Spain, cannot or will not join him in his appraisal. This psychological barrier has long been a decisive impediment to Heine's full reception.

In recent years, Arturo Pérez-Reverte, a very successful young Spanish writer of adventure novels, consistently includes quotations from Heine's *Reisebilder* in his works. This means, if nothing more, that Heine's prose is just now being discovered in Spain.

Instead of an aggressive and heraldic "The Lion and the Eagle" topic, the masculine/feminine "fir and palm tree" ("Fichtenbaum und Palme") constellation (no. 33 of *Lyrisches Intermezzo*) would probably have been more to Heine's liking. If we spell out its underlying meaning, that is, the union of the isolated Orient with cold, solitary, and sleepy northern Europe, such a desirable union took place in Moorish Spain. Heine must have considered al-Andalus a bridge connecting Arabic culture to central Europe. Furthermore, he makes it clear in his work that the occidental Moorish dominion overtook the eastern in art, science, and lady courtship. He draws an intense picture of its positive influence in Spanish cultural history, a fact which has finally, if reluctantly, been accepted by official Spanish critics as part of their identity.

Notes

1. Written in 1817 and included in the first edition of his *Buch der Lieder* (1827).
2. The dramatic poem *Almansor* was first published in fragments in the Berlin magazine *Der Gesellschafter* in 1821. The two ballads were written in 1823 and 1825 and included in the first edition of his *Buch der Lieder*.
3. Heinrich Heine, *Sämtliche Werke* (Hamburg, 1973ff.), vol. 2, p. 388. Hereafter cited as Düsseldorfer Ausgabe (DHA).
4. Ibid., p. 388.
5. *Histoire chevaleresque des Maures de Grenade, précédée de quelques réflexions sur les Musulmans d'Espagne, avec des notes historiques et littéraires*, trans. A. M. Sané (Paris, 1809).
6. Two of Heine's poems, written in 1824 and included in the section "Die Heimkehr" of the *Buch der Lieder*, namely, "Auf den Wällen Salamankas" and "Neben mir wohnt Don Henriques," are transposed into a Spanish context, although the real references are Heine's relegation from Göttingen University, in the first case, and the character of his friend Havemann, in the second.
7. *Moriscos* is the name given to Muslims who submitted to Christian baptism; the Jewish counterpart would be the *marranos*. Jews under the Moorish rule were not only tolerated but, adopting Arabic as the literary and scientific language, made important contributions in all areas. Before the Reconquista was completed, many Christians lived in al-Andalus as *mozárabes*; those who converted to Islam were named *muladíes*. Max Aub, *Manual de la historia de la literatura española* (Madrid, 1974), p. 29, parallels the figures of Mosé ben Ezra (born in Granada in 1060) and Jehuda ben Halevi (Tudela 1071–1127), who both wrote in Hebrew and Arabic, with Provençal troubadours of their time. Aub also stresses the importance of *jarchyas* for the development of the popular *villancico*. The *Romancero general* is subdivided by subjects into morisco, chivalresque, historical, and common romances. For our purpose, we shall consider all those that Heine may have consulted in any then available translation.
8. Hanne Gabriele Reck, *Die spanische Romanze im Werke Heinrich Heines* (Frankfurt, 1987).
9. Johann Wilhelm Ludwig Gleim, *Romanzen* (Berlin and Leipzig, 1756). See p. 47 ("Nachricht"): "Die Spanier sind vermutlich die ersten Erfinder der Romancen, weil Eifersucht oder Ritterschaft (Chevalerie) bey ihnen mehr traurige Begebenheiten hervorbringen mag, als bey andern Voelkern, wo die Schoenen tugendhafter, oder die Männer versoehnlicher, und ritterliche Thaten keine Eigenschaften eines Liebhabers sind. In Erzählung vorstehender Geschichten, hat man versuchen wollen, ob die vorlängst bey den Spaniern, und neuerlich bey den Franzosen zu den romanzischen Liedern gebrauchte Schreibart, auch im Deutschen gefallen koenne. Je oefterer dieser Versuch, von den rühmlichen Virtuosen mit Stäben in der Hand, künftig gesungen wird, desto mehr wird der Verfasser glauben, dass er die rechte Sprache dieser Dicht-Art getroffen habe. Von der ersten Romanze findet sich in den Werken des Moncrif, eine so ähnliche Geschichte, dass man auf den Gedanken geraten möchte, sie sey übersetzt; allein, da ganz Berlin weiss, dass die darin erzählte Begebenheit, am eilften April des vorigen nicht aber dieses Jahres, wie auf dem Titul-Blatt durch einen Druckfehler stehet sich wircklich daselbst zugetragen hat, so kann die moncrifische Romanze, wohl nichts weiter, als eine ähnliche Geschichte seyn. Von der zwoten und dritten, werden die besten Kenner und fleissigsten Leser

anderwärts keine Spur finden. Geschrieben, Berlin den 1ten May 1756." The first of the three romances begins: "Die Ehe ist für uns arme Sünder / Ein Marterstand / Drum, Eltern zwingt doch keine Kinder / Ins Eheband."
10. Johann Gottfried Herder, *Sämtliche Werke*, vol. 7: *Zur schönen Literatur und Kunst* (Stuttgart and Tübingen, 1828). Herder includes "Die Herrlichkeit Granadas: Ein Gespräch König Juans und Abenamars," "Abenamars unglückliche Liebe," "Zaid und Zaida," "Gasul und Lindaraja," "Aljama," "Der blutige Strom," and "Zelindaja," most of these translated freely from Ginés Pérez de Hita's version, but at least one taken directly from the *Cancionero de romances* ("Río verde"). August Wilhelm Schlegel published in 1796 the first Moorish tale in German literature, "Morayzela, Sultanin von Granada: Eine mohrische Geschichte," for which he consulted Pérez de Hita, and later revealed this source to his pupil Heine.
11. Herder, *Sämtliche Werke*, vol. 7, p. 160. Friedrich Schlegel had sustained that the traditional Spanish romance had an Arabic origin (*Bonner Vorlesungen über die Geschichte der deutschen Sprache und Poesie*); see Max Trommer, *Herder und die Ballade*, typewritten manuscript (Göttingen, 1954). In fact, it seems impossible to trace the origin of this poetic form; cf. D. C. Clarke, "The Marqués de Santillana and the Spanish Ballad Problem," *Modern Philology* (1961), pp. 13–24.
12. Quoted by Trommer, *Herder und die Ballade*, p. 6.
13. See R. Baehr, *Spanische Verslehre auf historischer Grundlage* (Tübingen, 1962). The Spanish meter is counted in syllables (eight in the case of the romance), whereas German poetry versifies according to stressed and unstressed syllables. By not even attempting to reproduce syllable count, Herder and Schlegel made an important allowance to the German meter, even though they tried to maintain assonance.
14. It is rather futile to call Heine's metric form "redondillas de versos octosílabos," as his otherwise very capable translator Francisco Sellén has done (*Intermezzo lírico* [New York, 1875]; quoted in Hanna Geldrich, *Heine und der spanischamerikanische Modernismo* [Berne, 1971], p. 50).
15. See Fritz Mende, *Heine-Chronik* (Berlin, 1970), and W. Kanowsky, "Heine als Benutzer der Bibliotheken in Bonn and Göttingen," *Heine-Jahrbuch 1973*, pp. 129–153.
16. By this time, he had read Herder's translation of *El Cid* (Rodrigo Díaz del Vivar). Reck is convinced that Herder was a stronger point of reference than Friedrich de la Motte Fouqué for this ballad. Pierre Grappin even points out a possible influence by Clemens Brentano's comedy *Ponce de Leon* (1804), which in turn was inspired by Marie-Catherine d'Aulnoy's *Dom Gabriel Ponce de Léon*. Paul Beyer (*Der junge Heine* [Berlin, 1911]) hints at Ludwig Uhland's model for the ballad, but this must be discarded for the case of the Spanish romance.
17. See Trommer, *Herder und die Ballade*, p. 5.
18. Thus, in France he reported on German culture as he would have wanted it, whereas in the German press he commented on French conditions worth imitating. All of Heine's *Reisebilder* are highly subjective with elaborately literary views on German and foreign places and people. Ironically, his French critics, even when they praised him, thought his wit, his "esprit," totally un-German. In May 1833, when Heine was practically unknown in England—the first translation appeared there in 1858—Arnold J. Toynbee wrote, "It would be useless to deny the talent of this author, but it is perverted or unhealthy" (H. G. Fiedler, ed., *A.W. Schlegel's Lectures on German Literature from Gottsched to Goethe Followed by Toynbee's 'Continuation to Heine'* [Oxford, 1944], p. 71).

Toynbee considered Heine's praise for the French "unnatural from the lips of a German" (ibid.). Toynbee's diary or lecture notes are highly appreciative of Schlegel. His "Continuation to Heine" is, in fact, a refutation of Heine's *Die romantische Schule*, while Toynbee was under the influence of the negative critique by W. Menzel.

19. Friedrich de la Motte Fouqué, *Der Zauberring: Ein Ritterroman* (Nuremberg, 1812), p. 155. Many details of Fouqué's ballad are taken over by Heine in "Donna Clara" and "Almansor," as, for instance, the abduction by a Muslim of a lady converted to Christianity and the ensuing religious conflict. Fouqué's singer Hernandez points out in this respect, "In my country things are serious nowadays, because where Christians and heathens fight with each other for life and death, many times melancholy is at the rudder and not less often death."
20. He mentions jasmine and honeysuckle, fig trees, grapevines, melons, and pomegranate trees. The chorus reminds us, "Es ist ein schönes Land, das schöne Spanien, / Ein grosser Garten, wo da prangen Blumen, / Goldäpfel, Myrthen;—aber schöner noch/ Prangten mit stolzem Glanz die edlen Mauernstädte, / Das edle Maurenthum ... Und Schönes blühte, wo die Schönheit herrschte." See DHA, vol. 2, p. 47.
21. Ibid., p. 16.
22. In Herder's "Der blutige Strom," the Christian hero Don Alonso has a wife called Donna Clara.
23. L. Rosenthal, *H. Heine als Jude* (Frankfurt, 1973); Hartmut Kircher, *H. Heine und das Judentum* (Bonn, 1973); Jeffrey L. Sammons, *Heine, the Elusive Poet* (New Haven, Conn., 1969). Heine's *Rabbi von Bacherach*, which draws on reports of the persecution of Jews in this Rhenish city in 1287, was supposed to include a passage on Spanish Jews that was later omitted in the final version.
24. Siegbert Prawer, "Heine's Return," *German Life and Letters*, vol. 9 (1955–56), pp. 171–180.
25. Mounir Fendri, *Halbmond, Kreuz und Schibboleth: Heinrich Heine und der islamische Orient* (Hamburg, 1980).
26. DHA, vol. 2, p. 648.
27. Susanne Zantop, "Zwischen Aneignung und Enteignung. Heine in Südeuropa," in *Nationale Grenzen und internationaler Austausch: Studien zum Kultur- und Wissenschaftstransfer in Europa*, ed. L. Jordan and B. Kortländer (Tübingen, 1995), p. 95.
28. This edition was published in Stuttgart (1837–38) and included a biography by Viardot and illustrations by Joannot.
29. Sabine Bierwirth, *Heines Dichterbilder: Stationen seines ästhetischen Selbstverständnisses* (Stuttgart, 1995), p. 132.
30. Fendri, *Halbmond, Kreuz und Schibboleth*, p. 15, mentions the fact that Heine's brother Maximilian was an army physician in the Russian-Turkish war of 1830. He wrote to his brother about Turkish songs that dealt with the downfall of Granada and the Moorish dominions in Spain. According to Fendri, "the Spanish-Muslim history and culture stood at the center of Heine's spiritual interest from the beginning to the end of his poetic career." It could be added that Heine also felt a pronounced inclination toward the sense of justice of Muslim rulers in Andalusia.
31. No. 1064 of the *Romancero general*, "Paseábase el rey moro," was known through Pérez de Hita's *Historia de los bandos de Cegríes*. M. Staub maintains in her dissertation, *Die spanische Romanze in der Dichtung der deutschen Romantik, mit besonderer Berücksichtigung des Romanzenwerkes von Tieck, Brentano und*

Heine (Hamburg, 1970), that Heine's Boabdil was inspired by François René Chauteaubriand's novel *Les Aventures du dernier Abencérage* (1826), whereas P. Kabel ("Die Quellen für Heines 'Bimini' and 'Der Mohrenkönig,'" in *Das Archiv für das Studium der neueren Sprachen und Literaturen*, vol. 117 [1906], p. 256ff.) is convinced the sources are to be found in Washington Irving's *Conquest of Granada* (1829). Fendri suggests a possible inspiration from Théophile Gautier's poem "Le soupir du More," written between 1830 and 1845. Reck points to a similar ballad translated by Herder under the title "Aljama." The subject recently inspired Salman Rushdie for his novel *The Moor's Last Sigh* (New York, 1995).
32. As Prawer, "Heine's Return," pp. 175 and 177, points out, "Whenever Heine mentions modern Jews, he feels at once impelled to ridicule them"; and, "His return to the God of the Hebrews is therefore an opportunity for blasphemy. This attitude is diametrically opposed to that of the religious Jew."
33. Ibid., p. 172.
34. Apparently, Heine at first wanted to name the poem "Eldorado." Cf. DHA, vol. 3, p. 1566. See also Jürgen Jacobs, "Der späte Heine und die Utopie: Zu 'Bimini,'" *Etudes Germaniques*, vol. 4 (1967), pp. 511–516.
35. A. Hernández, *Bécquer y Heine* (Madrid, 1946), p. 41, tells of his first impression upon reading Heine's Hispanophile works: "Those of us Spaniards who read *Almanzor* and the first three stanzas of 'Don Ramiro' in German must exclaim enthusiastically, 'This is part of our own *Romancero*!'"
36. Johann Wolfgang Goethe had been read in Spain as the author of *Hermann und Dorothea* (1819). Emilia Pardo Bazán ("Fortuna española de Heine," in *Revista de España*, vol. 110 [1886], pp. 481–496) sustains that Goethe, in contrast to Heine, was "praised rather than loved." His *Werther* did not pass censorship and was read in French only by a few.
37. Ernst Feise, "Some Notes on Translating Heine," *German Life and Letters*, vol. 9 (1955–56), p. 189.
38. Agnes J. Aregger, *Heine und Larra: Wirkungsgeschichte eines deutschen Schriftstellers in Spanien* (Zurich, 1981).
39. Udo Rukser, "Heine in der hispanischen Welt," *Deutsche Vierteljahrsschrift*, vol. 30 (1956), p. 487.
40. See Rubén Darío's poem "Divagación" of his *Prosas profanas* (1896).
41. Geldrich, *Heine und der spanisch-amerikanische Modernismo*, p. 25.
42. About Heine's reception in Spain at the turn of the century, especially in Manuel Reina y Montilla, see Arno Gimber, "Perlen, Mond und Wasserfrauen: Die Heine-Rezeption in der spanischen Literatur der Jahrhundertwende," in *Aufklärung und Skepsis: Internationaler Heine-Kongreß zum 200. Geburtstag*, ed. Joseph A. Kruse, Bernd Witte, and Karin Füllner (Stuttgart, 1999), pp. 710–721.
43. William Rose's sentence about Heine's genius, "he could light up a situation with an epigram," is quoted by H. S. Reiss, "The Criticism of Heine since the War: An Assessment," *German Life and Letters*, vol. 9 (1955–56), p. 214.
44. Augusto Ferrán also translated Heine again in 1861 in *El Museo universal* and in *El Semanario popular*.
45. A. Machado da Rosa, "Heine in Spain (1856–1867): Relations with Rosalía de Castro," *Monatshefte*, vol. 99 (1957), pp. 65–82, has studied this issue in depth. See also Hernández, *Bécquer y Heine*, p. 63: "Rosalía de Castro gave Bécquer the French translation of Heine's works acquired by E. Florentino Sanz."

46. E. Díez-Canedo, "Heine en España" in *Enrique Heine, Páginas Escogidas* (Madrid, 1918), p. 493. See also J. M. Díez Taboada, "El germanismo y la renovación de la lírica española en el siglo XIX (1840–1870)," *Modern Philology*, vol. 2, no. 5 (1961), pp. 21–55.
47. See Marcelino Menéndez y Pelayo's foreword to José J. Herrero's translation of Heine, *Poemas y fantasías* (Madrid, 1909). About Heine's peculiarity, he writes, "A Hebrew by race, a German by birth, a Frenchman by long residence and some parts (not the best) of his genius, he looked to the South for heat, light, and liberty for his pensative Germanic poetry. All this bore a tart and pungent fruit, delicious and tender at the same time, which may never again arise in the world because the circumstances that produced it cannot be artificially created ... Heine without his irony is no more than half of Heine, and Heinean irony cannot be imitated nor parodied." Ibid., pp. xii-xiii.
48. Claude Owen, "Ramiro de Maeztu über Heine," *Heine-Jahrbuch 1967*, pp. 90–98.
49. Schlegel's ideas about the drama had been introduced in Spain in 1814 by Nicolás Böhl de Faber, a German Hispanist, trader, and consul who had established himself in Andalusia.
50. Gaspar Núñez de Arce, "Prefacio" to *Gritos de combate* (Madrid, 1930), p. xvi.
51. Ibid., p. 254.
52. Emilia Pardo Bazán, "Fortuna española de Heine," *Revista de España*, vol. 110 (1886), p. 484.
53. In his *Idearium español* of 1896 (*Obras completas*, vol. 1 [Madrid, 1961], p. 189), Ángel Ganivet feels obliged to defend the "leyenda negra" of Spanish conquerors against "foreign" judgments like Heine's "torpe leyenda": "Instead of becoming indignant about him, I think the most convenient [thing] is to say that they [those Germans?] do not understand our conquerors because they could not have any."
54. Pío Baroja, *La caverna del humorismo* (Madrid, 1986), pp. 77–78: "As far as Heine is concerned, he is a satirist, but I do not think he is a humorist. There is something in Heine which keeps him apart from humorism; for me the main reason for this is that Heine was a Jew ... We have witnessed the Jewish rabble [*canalla*] of Germany rise up jubilantly upon seeing the ruin of its fatherland and enthusiastically accusing it."
55. Ibid., p. 78.
56. Ibid., p. 77.
57. Ibid., p. 259.
58. Aregger, *Heine und Larra*, p. 71.
59. Ibid., p. 100.
60. See also Hans Juretschke, "Die Ursprünge der spanischen Romantik und ihre Darstellung in der Literaturgeschichte," *Gesammelte Aufsätze zur Kulturgeschichte Spaniens*, vol. 9 (Münster, 1954), pp. 224–242.
61. In 1837, the Spanish journal *Revista Europea* published an anonymous review of Menzel's revised edition of *Literatura Alemana*, which had first appeared in 1828 in Stuttgart.
62. See Oskar Walzel, *Romantisches* (Bonn, 1934), p. 74. Heine's *Reisebilder* were not translated in Spain until 1889 (vols. 1 and 2) and 1906 (vol. 3) by Lorenzo González Agejas (Madrid, Biblioteca Clásica).
63. M. M. Fernández, biographical note to Heine, *Joyas Prusianas* (Madrid, 1873), p. 39.

64. Aub, *Manual de la Historia de la Literatura española*, p. 439: "Bécquer ... es un Heine unilateral."
65. Bodo Müller, "Die Rezeption der deutschen Literatur in Spanien," *Arcadia*, vol. 2 (1967), p. 276.
66. See Fernández in Heine, *Joyas Prusianas*, p. 22, about the failure of Heine's early drama *Almansor*: "[I]t is not only an improper work for the stage, but it also attacks the Christian idea and even establishes the absurd belief that profane love is superior to all religions."
67. Ángel Ganivet, "Granada la Bella," *Obras completas*, vol. 1 (Madrid, 1961), p. 95.
68. Ibid., pp. 128–129.

– 10 –

LA *ABEJA* OF BARCELONA AND GERMAN LITERATURE IN SPAIN, 1862–1870

John W. Kronik

For some two centuries, the Iberian Peninsula has kindled a burning fascination in its Germanic neighbors to the north.[1] Long before modern means of transportation enabled Nordic travelers to bask in the Mediterranean sun en masse, German and Austrian literary figures with the stature of Johann Wolfgang von Goethe (1749–1832), Friedrich von Schiller (1759–1805), the brothers August Wilhelm and Friedrich Schlegel (1767–1845, 1772–1829), Ludwig Tieck (1773–1853), and Franz Grillparzer (1791– 1872), to name only the most notable, had succumbed to the seduction of those exotic lands that defined the extremes of southern Europe. With its legendary picturesqueness, the reach of its imperial power, and the brilliance of its classical playwrights, Spain was a source of inspiration for the literary imaginations of writers in the farther reaches of its former Habsburg dynasty. Thus developed between the Spanish- and German-speaking cultures an indelible bond that is a matter of record and that in the political arena (for example, Franco's anti-Republican alliances or Pío Baroja's wartime Germanophilia) incited periodic indignation and hostility among other national groups.

While for geographical, historical, and geopolitical reasons Germany could not compete with France in the ready diffusion of its culture beyond the Pyrenees, the manifestations of a Hispano-Germanic cultural interchange are substantial.[2] The curious devolution to Spain itself of the German notion of a "romantic Spain" spurred among Spaniards a foreign-inspired self-portrayal of lasting impact, if of questionable benefit. The late nineteenth-century appropriation and reassembly of the ideas of Karl Krause at the hands of Spanish thinkers and educators and the influence of German philosophy on José Ortega y Gasset are more recent examples. Even so, the reading public in Spain (numerically modest to begin with) had relatively little awareness of German culture until after the sway of romanticism.[3] At that time, direct contacts with German letters grew in consequence of a concerted propagandistic campaign of diffusion of Germanic culture over a period of several decades.

German philosophical and aesthetic theories were beginning to make themselves felt in Spain at the turn of the eighteenth century. By the middle of the nineteenth century—especially after 1860, at which time Julián Sanz del Río's proselytizing activities had gained significant followers and the struggles between neo-Catholics and pro-German Krausists had been engaged—German thought from Kant to Hegel had achieved canonical status, while German literature, though later and to a lesser extent, also enjoyed increasing recognition. These northern influences, as one would expect, reached to the heart of the peninsula, and Madrid did contribute to their dissemination; but, for reasons both historical and geographic, Catalonia, particularly in the years of the *Renaixença*, absorbed earlier and with greater intensity than the other regions of Spain the succession of new European artistic schools and the transformations that were occurring in England, France, and Germany. Barcelona has traditionally been the city most open to ultra-Pyrenean fashions and, more so than Madrid, has served as the peninsula's conduit for the import of fresh cultural trends from abroad, though Valencia, too, was a significant port of entry for European culture.[4] The activity and the example of individual writers and scholars were responsible in part for this diffusion process, which in yet larger measure was due to the collective labor of a series of journals. As often happens, these literary and scientific publications appeared and perished in rapid succession, some surviving longer than others, but all leaving their traces on the intellectual environment of the day.

Among the publications responsible for the dissemination of German culture in Spain during the nineteenth century, singular weight resides with one that bore the expressive title of *La Abeja*, which means "bee."[5] This crusading review, which specialized in the publication of translations of German writings, emerged precisely at the peak moment of the German intellectual and scientific invasion of Spain through Catalonia, so that it was at once a symptom of this phenomenon and its catalyst, abuzz with information Teutonic that it gathered in its seemingly random flits from text to text.

By way of contrast between Spain's two major cultural centers, one might cite the case of the Madrid journal *El Museo Universal*, predecessor to the well-known *Ilustración Española y Americana*. A weekly of eight, later twelve, pages per issue, *El Museo*, subtitled "Periódico de Ciencias, Literatura, Artes, Industria y Conocimientos Utiles, Ilustrado" (Periodical for Science, Literature, Art, Industry, and Other Useful Knowledge, Illustrated), ran for thirteen volumes between 1857 and 1869. At the start, its contents were exclusively Spanish. By its waning years, it had begun to print more foreign news, including some from Germany (notably a series of seven resonant articles by José Fernández Matheu,[6] also a contributor to *La Abeja*), but nothing on the scale of *La Abeja*: it published no translations, waged no campaign of international enlightenment, and remained national in its orientation. In fact, *El Museo* was statedly nationalistic in intent, hoping to show off Spain and its culture to Europeans and to legitimize Spain as a member of the European family of nations.[7] Also housed in Madrid, the long-lived semimonthly *La América* (1857–86), cast primarily as a purveyor of news to Spanish America, involved many of the foremost writers of the day and had a strong following on the peninsula. Goethe, Schiller, and Heine made appearances in its pages, and in an 1857 article, Pi y Margall held up the first two as exemplars of a great art that contemporary Spain lacked, that is, as writers who actively participated in the life of the century and did not dabble in art for its own sake.[8] Other contemporary journals that published translations from the German, though not as systematically as *La Abeja*, were *El Nene* (Madrid, 1859–60), *El Semanario Popular* (Madrid, 1862–65), and *El Eco de Euterpe* (Barcelona, 1862–64).

Students of the period's cultural interrelations know—or know of—*La Abeja*, and some have made at least passing reference to it. A close examination of its contents, and by extension of its aims and scope, is instructive on various counts: the review's ingredients reflect the weight that literature carried relative to the various fields represented in its pages; they signal the importance of German writings as compared to those of other nationalities; they make potentially telling statements about the authors selected for inclusion (or exclusion); and they provide insight into the possible effect that this importation of the German intellectual world may have had on writers and writings in Spain. Such a scrutiny presumes to be no more than a footnote to *Kulturgeschichte*, an exhumation of an archaeological bagatelle that in its time bridged two national frontiers. Even so, it is worth noting what José María de Cossío said of *La Abeja*: "The German influx has no better exponent than this publication, and it encompasses literature."[9] Commenting on Joan Maragall's translations of Goethe into Catalan, Egon Schwarz pays footnote obeisance to *La Abeja* as a curiosity, a "strange example," but concedes it its priority rights and its unique sweep, even though he was familiar with only three of its volumes.[10] Moreover, note should be taken of two significant details: first, the translations that appeared in this review were based directly on the original German texts rather than taken from French translations, as was the prevailing custom in Spain; and second, the journal, given its character and format, was directed not at specialists and scholars but at a more general reading public. In other words, *La Abeja* was an authentic and broadly grounded instrument of promulgation.

La Abeja was launched in January 1862 and appeared monthly until December 1866. With number 12 of volume 5, which corresponded to that month, its publication was interrupted. The journal was revived in 1870, with no change in format, but after another ten issues, it ceased publication definitively. The complete collection consists of seventy numbers in six volumes. That history testifies to the precarious economic existence of these noble leaps in the dark, but *La Abeja*'s life span is actually a respectable record. Each issue, not numbered as such but paginated sequentially throughout the volume, contained some thirty-two to forty-two pages, printed in packed double-column format in large-size folios measuring 21.5 cm by 30 cm.[11] The written texts were generously accompanied by illustrations of varied provenance in the style of the period. All the numbers of *La Abeja* displayed, in capitals and various typefaces, the subtitle "Revista Científica y Literaria Ilustrada, / Principalmente / Extractada de los Buenos Escritores Alemanes" (Illustrated Scientific and Literary Review, Mainly Extracted from Fine German Writers), though the word "Ilustrada" did not appear until the seventh number.

Those initially responsible for the selection and translation of the journal's contents represented a spectrum of disciplines. They were listed and identified on the masthead in the following order:

D. Antonio Bergnes de las Casas, catedrático de lengua griega, en la facultad de filosofía y letras, de la Universidad de Barcelona:
D. Miguel Guitart y Buch, doctor en Medicina:
D. Antonio Sánchez Comendador, catedrático de mineralogía y zoología, en la facultad de Ciencias, de la Universidad de Barcelona:
D. Antonio Rave, catedrático de física, en la facultad de Ciencias, de la Universidad de Barcelona:
D. Juan Font y Guitart.

The capitalization of "Ciencias" while "filosofía y letras" remained in lower case, like the punctuation, is copied from the original masthead but should not be taken to carry a hidden agenda. In fact, the humanist listed first was the driving force behind the venture. Antonio Bergnes de las Casas (1800–1879) was in his time what might be called a "Renaissance man" and a figure of great influence in Catalan intellectual circles during much of the nineteenth century. His publication record as a philologist, classicist, historian, and critic reflects his vast interests and capabilities. The author of a history of printing and of a four-volume history of Spain, he was also a true polyglot and a prolific translator. He held a chair at the University of Barcelona and was the university's rector between 1868 and 1875, and he spurred editorial activity in Barcelona with his own publishing business. *La Abeja* was the last of several periodicals that he initiated.[12]

Beginning with the seventh number (July 1862), the list of names disappeared from the editorial caption of the journal, replaced by the simple designation "una sociedad literaria" (a literary society). Apparently, the journal evolved out of the conversations of a group of colleagues, perhaps from one of those *tertulias* that enlivened nineteenth-century urban intellectual and café life, and, most likely, its management experienced some fluidity. The printing establishment responsible for the journal was the "Librería de D. Juan Oliveres, Editor," who in all volumes but the last designated himself as "Impresor de S. M." (His Majesty's printer) and who possibly was involved in the selection of unsigned translations.

In the inaugural issue, Antonio Bergnes presented his group's new enterprise to its readers in an ample introduction graced with an epigraph—in the original Greek side by side with its Spanish translation—taken from the Athenian orator Isocrates: "Just as we see the bee alight on all the flowers and extract what is useful from each of them, so too should the lovers of learning sample everything and gather what is good wherever it is to be found."[13] Bergnes made clear from the start that the underlying criteria for this project were of a pedagogical, ethical, aesthetic, and, to be sure, eclectic nature. He commended his review "to all lovers of rational progress" ("a todo amante del progreso racional"), and, following the example of the great German naturalist Alexander von Humboldt (1769–1859),[14] who had recently died and whom he called "the dean of European physicists and naturalists," he announced his intention to "convert to common good or property, by means of comprehensible and aesthetic exposition, the beautiful products of scientific investigation."[15] In other words—and it is interesting to note his insistence on the marriage of content and form—he would attempt to educate intelligent Spaniards in the realm of science, seducing his uninitiated readers "with the beauty of form and the liveliness of coloration" ("con la hermosura de la forma y la viveza del colorido") and making science both intelligible and savory by means of "the finery and the attractions of a pleasing and florid description" ("las galas y los atractivos de una descripción amena y florida").

Taking the high ground in the rhetoric of the times, Bergnes did not lose sight of the moral force that derives from a love for learning and from a closer approach to nature. To realize these objectives, *La Abeja*, he announced, would consist, for the most part, of "more or less amplified passages from German writers who, transported by their love of humanity, have taken upon their shoulders the by no means simple task of serving as interpreters and mediators between science and those who have barely hailed it."[16] He added, "We shall imitate the diligent bee who goes flying from flower to flower to sip its most precious nectar."[17] Given its utilitarian function of bringing scientific and philosophical discoveries into the public domain, *La Abeja* expected to pay service to teachers who might find between its covers materials that would enliven their lessons; but, favoring concise, attractive *apuntes* and *cuadros* (notes, sketches) over polished, methodical treatises, the journal aspired to include students in its public and even the common people ("el vulgo"), "so that all might find in these pages the choicest fodder for both spirit and heart."[18]

Further, the journal's founders wished to remedy the sparse contact that even educated Spaniards, for lack of initiative and curiosity, had experienced with their more removed neighbor's intellectual soil. Those who have struggled with the cases and constructions of the German language (or who have relished Mark Twain's parodies) will appreciate Bergnes's concession in this regard: "The language that is spoken there, doubtless the richest and most forceful while at the same time the most arduous one in the great European family, has been until now another Medusa's head for those who regard as badly applied the considerable time that its study requires."[19] But his astute sense of history and of *Völkerpsychologie* allowed Bergnes to locate the real causes for this neglect:

> Until now, Spain has been separated from Germany not only by geography but also, and singularly so, because of the French spirit, which is experiencing ever greater expansion in the two countries. It is true that Germans, so broadly indoctrinated in matters Roman, have not allowed this separation to prevent them from reaching the sources of Spanish literature. Spaniards, however, isolated by word and by manner from the Germanic world, which is completely strange to them, cannot help being at a great distance from that land; and if by chance they try to acquire some knowledge of German literature and art, they necessarily have to resort to French mediation. Perhaps there may fall to *La Abeja* the good fortune of initiating the desired union between the two countries.[20]

While scientists were in the majority on *La Abeja*'s staff and the thrust behind this review reflected the desire of a small group of Spanish academics to awaken their fellow citizens to the scientific advances being made abroad, belles-lettres was not neglected. The literary dimension was not at odds with the journal's stated aims, and Bergnes outlined the criteria for selection:

> In addition to scientific articles, other purely literary ones, no less instructive for being pleasurable, will occupy part of the columns of this review; and to this end we will select the most disinterested works of reflection and of poetry, those endowed with that moral appeal, with that genuine tranquility characteristic of a people who have contributed such finery to the intellectual scene. Consequently, there will be excluded from *La Abeja* all those deceitful and raving authors who, suppressing all that is beautiful, lead people along the paths of atheism toward a scorn of all authority and of tender family bonds.[21]

To some modern readers, this statement of editorial policy, shadowed by cautionary orthodoxy, might seem at odds with the cosmopolitanism of a gesture of openness to foreign ideas, but in this regard, too, *La Abeja* is a document of its times and reflects some of the tensions that the Spanish intelligentsia was to play out even more forcefully later, toward the end of the century. In an attempt at balance, Bergnes assured the desired purchasers of his periodical that he and his colleagues planned to favor neither the past for its conformity to established canons nor the modern simply because it was fashionable. Rather, the good and the beautiful were the blanket standards that would guide the editors' judgment. It is worthy of note that in the index at the end of each volume, where articles were grouped under subject headings, a single rubric joined "Literatura y Moral," a conjunction that surely influenced the selection of authors and texts. The project laid out in the introductory remarks reflects—and the contents of the journal (the specific passages as well as the chosen authors) confirm—its organizers' conservative and traditionalist bent; yet their vision was fixed on the future, and enlightenment was their goal.

At the conclusion of the second of two articles on Jean Paul Richter (vol. 1, no. 3, p. 117), Bergnes announced that *La Abeja* would avoid the system of free translation prevalent in Spain, France, and England and would adopt, instead, the German method of literal translation. Whether that distinction based on national lines can be sustained is open to debate, but the Germans' special knack for the art of translation can be readily documented, and Bergnes's admiration for their renditions of classical and modern authors was not misplaced. In any event, pains were taken to be as faithful as possible to the source so that the author's personal style and freshness of idea would be preserved. In this connection, Bergnes confessed that all his toil as a translator met with frustration in the face of the German language's "reduplicating compounds of two and more nouns and infinitives" ("redoblados compuestos de dos y mas nombres sustantivos e infinitivos"), and he bemoaned the inadequacy ("nulidad" is the word he chose) of the neo-Latin languages. Beginning with the issue that signaled an ostensible editorial revamping (no. 7), the translators' names were no longer appended systematically. Instead, covering this unexplained move toward anonymity, each issue carried at the end the note, "Responsible for what is unsigned and as editor, Juan Oliveres" ("Por lo no firmado y como Editor responsable.—Juan Oliveres").

La Abeja embraced a vast array of material in its columns, to which the subject headings in the indexes of each volume give ample testimony. The fields that appeared with greatest consistency were geography and travel, natural history, "literatura y moral," poetry, physics, physiology, and history; there also were articles on the arts, astronomy, biography, psychology, chemistry, archaeology, philosophy, geology, heraldics, medicine, botany, and zoology. Sometimes the classification of an article seems capricious ("artes," for example, comprised all sorts of matter). At the end of more than half of the numbers, a section entitled "Excerpta" offered maxims and snippets of wisdom from a great variety of authors, among whom there were also many Germans. The plan, announced in the introduction, to publish reviews of important books that were currently coming out of Germany remained an unfulfilled hope.

At the beginning, approximately one-fourth of each number was devoted to literary texts. Later, when the policy was introduced to print long works serially (much as the popular press of the day carried pulp novels "por entregas"), the literary section might occupy more than half the space in some issues. On other occasions, the literary content was materially reduced. The predominance of the German component is in evidence across the life of the journal if one surveys all the texts that it printed. In its early stages, *La Abeja* paraded a cavalcade of German literary figures before its readers, at least with selections from their writings. A new orientation became noticeable halfway into the second volume and more marked during the third year when the breathless pace adopted at the starting line ceded to a reduction in the number of authors selected for translation, partly as a consequence of the decision to serialize more extensive works.

Furthermore, while Germans still carried the majority, many non-German authors were now represented (for example, Dante, "Ossian," Milton), and the public taste for Oriental tales was reflected in the section of "Excerpta." The broader international perspective, which also included Eugène Sue, Walter Scott, and Washington Irving for the first time, prompted no change in the journal's subtitle, even though no morsels of German literature—only scientific and historical essays—graced *La Abeja* between August 1864 and February 1865. Subsequently, Germany again garnered more space and a wider representation of authors, though Goethe and Schiller were ever the dominant figures and *Faust, Werther,* and *Maria Stuart* now the favored texts. In fact, late 1865 and 1866 signaled a reinvigoration for *La Abeja*, a period of editorial revamping that led to peak performance just as it was about to interrupt publication. The reform involved an apparent diminution in the prevalence of moral criteria of selection relative to a text's artistic merits, the identification of translators by name, and the insertion of a considerable number of poems in verse translations.

A more specific scrutiny of *La Abeja*'s contents reveals that the literary section of the periodical's first number (pp. 28–40) brought a half-dozen writers to the attention of its readers, most in translation by Bergnes himself. Schiller led the assemblage with a story, "El criminal por la honra perdida" ("Der Verbrecher aus verlorener

Ehre"); there followed two brief parables, "Los dos ángeles" by Friedrich Krummacher (1767–1845) and "Los tres amigos" by Johann Gottfried von Herder (1744–1803), and a short story, "Encuentro inesperado," from the collection *Schatzkästlein des rheinländischen Hausfreunds* by the poet and popular writer Johann Peter Hebel (1760–1826). The star of this inaugural issue was Johann Paul Friedrich Richter (1763–1825), better known as Jean Paul, who was represented by two of his moral tales, "Sueño del entierro" and "El doble juramento de enmienda"; these were supplemented by the first installment of an extensive three-part article about him entitled "Juan Pablo Federico Richter: su biografía y juicio sobre sus obras," which included many quotations and excerpts from his writings and letters. *La Abeja*'s readers thus were provided with an opportunity to familiarize themselves thoroughly with an author who was to appear often in *La Abeja* and who later in the century did indeed become in Spain one of the more influential German writers. The issue closed with verses from Heinrich Heine (1797–1856), whose name, possibly because he was as Parisian in spirit as he was German by birth, was soon to be recognized by every cultured Spaniard.[22] Cossío makes reference to the sixteen Heine poems that *La Abeja* published in volume 1 and sees in the translations, by Font y Guitart, the influence of the style of Sanz del Río.

A collation of the Spanish versions in this first issue with the German originals brings to light two orientations in *La Abeja*'s transcriptions of literary texts. The translation of Goethe, true to the stated editorial policy, was faithful, generally accurate, and readable. In the Hebel selection, the translator took many liberties that did not alter the sense of the whole but that did at times destroy isolated touches and changed or interfered with the intended mood. This latter procedure typified a tendency to simplify structures and to neutralize nuances so as to make the text more accessible to the reader.

In the second number of *La Abeja*, Jean Paul and Heine were joined by Ludwig Uhland (1787–1862), represented by several of his poems in rather prosaic transcriptions, and in the March issue, Schiller made a renewed appearance, not with one of his creative works but with a lengthy speech, "El teatro considerado como una institución moral," that he had delivered in Mannheim in 1784. This choice of text, which today may appear curious to some, responded to the moral imperative that Bergnes had outlined as one of the touchstones of his new venture. Many of the journal's selections stood on that criterion, including, in number 4, under the heading of "Aforismos," the dozen moralizations of varying length and subject matter taken from the freethinking philosopher Ludwig Feuerbach (1804–1872), a student of Hegel. Font y Guitart and Bergnes each contributed a story by Jean Paul to the May 1862 issue, one a romantic evocation of nature, the other a philosophical text. These were framed by an ethical tract, "El mundo," from the *Monologen* [sic] by the theologian and thinker Friedrich Schleiermacher (1768–1834), and a long poem, "El amor de los amores," identified as a "Leyenda sacada de una balada alemana," whose translation was entrusted to a woman, María Mendoza de Vives. By the sixth issue, readers of *La Abeja* were encountering recognizable names—Jean Paul, Hebel, Herder—but in the following number, an important new player was introduced: the poet Friedrich Klopstock (1724–1803). The text of choice was the first part of his long epic poem *Messias*, rendered in a free and somewhat compressed prose adaptation that managed to retain the epic flavor of the original, although it greatly simplified the text syntactically and conceptually. Subsequent issues devoted plentiful space to a continuation of the epic until its completion with the "Zwanzigster Gesang" in July 1864. Klopstock shared these issues with E. T. A. Hoffmann in number 8, Krummacher and the Alsatian writer of fables Gottlieb Pfeffel (1736–1809) in number 9, Jean Paul in number 11, Herder and Ferdinand Freiligrath (1810–1876) in number 12, and only occasionally with a name that has not managed to survive as an entry in the *Knaurs Lexikon*.

The second volume of *La Abeja*'s existence (1863) opened with a burst of literary activity that covered pages 10 to 32 of the January issue's thirty-two pages and that was to continue through the first six months of the year. In addition to Klopstock's running *La Mesíada*, Goethe made his entry with an essay, "Última meditación: los naturalistas franceses," a personal evocation of his interest in the natural sciences. Schiller's famous ode "An die Freude" also appeared in this issue, as did selections from Hebel and from the writers of political verse, Christian Friedrich Schubart (1739–1791) and Ernst Moritz Arndt (1769–1860), from whom the readers of *La Abeja* received a taste of Germanic patriotism. Repeaters in the next five issues included Jean Paul (nos. 4 and 6), Schiller (with a prose version of "Das Lied von der Glocke" in no. 4), and Klopstock, a prose rendition of whose ode "Hermann und Thusnelda" interrupted the serialization of *La Mesíada* in number 6. But new entries dominated the scene, and, while an occasional interloper from an earlier period was admitted (for example, Johann Christian Günther [1695–1723], a transitional baroque poet, in no. 5), a predilection for poets of the romantic school is evident in the choices of Gottfried Bürger (1747–1794), Ludwig Tieck, Karl Immermann (1796–1840), Friedrich Rückert (1788–1866), Friedrich von Stolberg (1750–1819), and Novalis (1772–1801), among others. Goethe loomed larger with the publication (vol. 2, no. 6, pp. 222–225), under the title of "Recuerdos de Goethe," of extracts from the *Gespräche mit Goethe in den letzten Jahren seines Lebens* by Johann Eckermann (1792–1854), a student and friend of Goethe in Weimar and editor of his works. Fewer items accompanied the Klopstock serialization in the year's remaining issues, among them transcriptions of Heine's long poem "Don Ramiro" and, in the December issue, of Schiller's poem "Die Worte des Glaubens," a brief paean to freedom, virtue, and the existence of God. A novelty in that same number was "Langben el gigante y Vidrik hijo de Verland," an adaptation of one of the epic Danish legends collected by Wilhelm Grimm in his *Altdänische Heldenlieder*.

Volume 3 (1864) was sparser in its Germanic literary dimension; the few newcomers included Gotthold Ephraim Lessing (1729–1781) and the critic, literary historian, and minor poet of the romantic school Wolfgang Menzel (1798–1873). With the dedication and prologue to *Faust* in volume 4, number 3 (March 1865), *La Abeja* initiated its publication of Goethe's masterpiece: part 1 ran from number 4 through number 7, and part 2, one act per issue, filled the literary section of the remainder of that year's numbers. The only additions appeared in number 11: Goethe's "El amante multiforme" and Schiller's "Éxtasis" ("Die Entzückung an Laura"), rendered in verse by Teodoro Llorente, who maintained the rhythm and emotion of the originals more successfully than the translator of Heine. Goethe and Schiller again were the major players in the 1866 volume. The January issue contained isolated fragments from Goethe's projected third part of *Faust* alongside the first act of Schiller's tragedy *Maria Stuart*, offered in a literal prose translation faithful to the original in meaning and dramatic impact (though two minor characters suffered name changes). The remaining acts were strung out over the next four issues. In an impressive overlap, the February issue began the serialization of Goethe's *Die Leiden des jungen Werthers* (with the omission of some of the letters), which, skipping one issue, occupied readers until September (no. 9). Translations in prose and verse by José Fernández Matheu of Schiller's "Canto de victoria" and "El cazador de los Alpes" and of "Ditirambo" by Heinrich von Gerstenberg (1737–1823) accompanied the longer works, as did Schiller's "Las palabras de la ilusión," "El anillo de Polícrates," and "El guante," the last two in translations by Teodoro Llorente, arguably *La Abeja*'s most lyrical translator. The year's last two issues carried an array of shorter pieces: the Grimm brothers' "El Rey Barba aguda" ("König Drosselbart")[23] and free verse translations of three poems by Schiller and one by Goethe in number 11; and in number 12, a short dramatic presentation, "El homenaje á las artes," by Schiller, another brief fairy tale by the brothers Grimm, a religious composition by Krummacher, a selection from Jean Paul, and, under the rubric "Poesías alemanas," texts by the Swiss poet and painter Salomon Geßner (1730–1788), Klopstock, Goethe, Schiller, Heine, and Uhland. At this high point, *La Abeja* suspended uninterrupted publication.

Volume 6 of *La Abeja*, bound in 1870, comprises ten issues, of which the first four bear the printing date of 1867 (pp. 1–152), the next four 1868 (pp. 153–314), and the last two the current year (pp. 315–386).[24] This final volume witnessed a distinct diminution in the amount of German materials in all the disciplines covered despite the retention of the review's original subtitle that advertised its contents as "principally" extracted from German sources (though it is possible that some of the unsigned scientific and philosophical insertions were of German provenance). Germany had to sacrifice much of its space in the literary section to serializations of Dante's *Divine Comedy* and of writings from the Orient, then much in vogue as the epicenter of exoticism. This valedictory volume brought tales by the Grimm brothers in two issues; a poem by Gerstenberg and another by Ludwig Hölty (1748–1776); and a prose version of "Episodio del Diluvio Universal," the fifth *canto* of "La Noachida" by the Swiss writer Johann Jacob Bodmer (1698–1783). Goethe was represented by a rendition in assonance of "La leyenda del Pária" (no. 4) and Schiller by two more poems dedicated to "Laura" (no. 7).[25] The most significant contribution toward the dissemination of German culture in volume 6 was arguably Fernández Matheu's lengthy scholarly essay on "Las baladas de Schiller," followed by his verse translations of two of these poems (vol. 6., no. 4, pp. 117–121).

The gallery of names that appears in this register of *La Abeja*'s contents suggests that its editors inclined toward the canonical and did not seek out the forces of innovation. They did not provide its readers with an exhaustive picture of the very latest literary currents and activities in contemporary Germany, for that was not their aim; on the contrary, they shied away from adulation of the new for its newness. Nor did they aspire to full coverage of established writers from the period it favored, the late eighteenth and early nineteenth centuries.[26] The journal contented itself with a respectable cross section all the while that it was subject to the limitations of space, resources, and channels of information and to the tastes and values that governed its editorial board. Its practice of minimizing bibliographical source data and biographical introductions and its uneven provision of explanatory notes (quite a few do, for example, help the reader of *Faust*, part 2) indicate that it was bent on forming a retinue of readers of foreign, principally German, letters and only secondarily on providing an academic education. In any event, one must not lose sight of the fact that it was not purely, nor even primarily, a belletristic journal and that it contributed heavily to fields other than literature. It was the voice of a group of individuals more cosmopolitan, more internationally focused, and less Francophile than the average Spaniard, though not necessarily less tied to the reigning orthodoxies.

For the destinies of certain German writers in Spain—Heine, Goethe, Schiller, Klopstock—*La Abeja* was a significant milepost if not a defining moment. That is, the existence of prior translations did not necessarily assure their authors' popularity. Goethe's *Hermann und Dorothea*, for instance, appeared in Spanish during Goethe's lifetime a scant thirteen years after its composition, and translations of *Faust*, part 1, had preceded *La Abeja*'s, yet the wish of *La Abeja*'s editors clearly was to make available a readable dramatic version. The poetic qualities inherent in the language, structure, and imagery of the original were not abandoned but subordinated to the narrative demands of a prose transcription that made up for a certain loss of richness with the interest it held for readers.[27] Goethe in Spain, to usurp the title of Pageard's book, took a decisive step forward with this translation, while *La Abeja*'s presentation of part 2 of *Faust* and of the summary of Goethe's *Conversations* with Eckermann brought unfamiliar texts to its readers' attention. Emilio Lorenzo, tracking Spain's increasing awareness of Goethe, testifies to this development: "The allusions and references become more and more numerous, almost as much as the steady increase in versions of Goethe's works, in which task the scientific-literary review *La Abeja* is an important element."[28] This pro-Goethe campaign coincided chronologically with a series of lectures that Antonio Angulo y Heredia delivered at the Ateneo de Madrid and which, according to Lorenzo, was the first serious public attempt to bring Goethe and Schiller and their work to the notice of Spaniards.[29] It is difficult to name a Spanish thinker or cultural commentator since the demise of *La Abeja* who has not faced off with Goethe, from Alas and Valera to Joan Maragall, Eugenio d'Ors, and Ortega.

By the same token, critics have often remarked that the German factor was instrumental in the sorely needed renovation of Spanish poetry that took place after mid-century, and, apart from the obvious case of Bécquer's indebtedness to the *Lied*, most of the German poets credited with responsibility for these fresh inroads (alongside the continuing French influence) had appeared in *La Abeja*. Pageard and Ribbans have stressed the importance of literary magazines in the shaping of a new sensibility among a group of young poets that included Bécquer in the years between 1855 and 1870, the main sources of inspiration having been German lyric and folk poetry. They provide a long list of translations of Heine and of other writers published in Madrid in the *Semanario Popular* from 1862 to 1864, and they point out that some of the translations were lifted verbatim, or almost so, from *La Abeja*.[30] Díez Taboada, for his part, twice singles out the contents of *La Abeja* in a study of these international resonances in the lyric.[31] The insertion of Heine into the first issue is an immediate indication of the journal's conscious proselytizing mission.[32] A rare introductory note preceded Juan Font y Guitart's translations of seven poems from the *Buch der Lieder* (another fourteen followed in the second number). The translator apologized for the quality of his versions (in point of fact, some did lose much of the originals' rhythm and tenderness, the most successful being those least slavishly literal) and offered two reasons for his choice of Heine. One was a confession of a personal predilection. The other motive corresponded to his desire to facilitate access to the German poet:

> Eager to adorn the literary section of our review with some elegant blossoms from the enchanted garden of German poetry, we offer to our readers today, by way of first fruits, these light exercises that are free of any pretensions. For this number our choice has fallen on Heine ... Heine, more than Schiller, Goethe, and other German poets, is almost completely unknown in our country ... If not the best of the modern German lyric poets, Heine is undoubtedly the most original and the most popular; for from the Rhine to the Elbe, from the Danube to the North Sea, his songs ring out everywhere, in the most populous of cities no less than in the humblest of villages.[33]

In tracing the fate of Heine in Spain, Rukser gives full credit to *La Abeja* for the role it played during this period of Spain's self-evaluation of its cultural decadence and consequent reorientation toward northern Europe: "There was a desire to deal directly with Germany. One of the manifestations of these efforts was the founding in 1862 of the journal *La Abeja* by several professors from the University of Barcelona."[34]

Omissions notwithstanding, most of the luminaries of German letters were on exhibit in *La Abeja*, as were a series of lesser lights, some of whom have survived and some not. By any standard, the roster of presences is impressive. Many of the authors and texts translated here were making their first appearance in Spanish. More than anything else, the very existence of *La Abeja*, even as it stands as a barometer of the tastes of its times, records a step that Spain took in the mid-nineteenth century to open up toward its northern European neighbor. That course of action was salutary because it reflected a double effort to expand the national horizon and to transcend Spain's links to French culture. *La Abeja* coincided not with the beginnings of Spain's interest in German culture and science but with the flowering of that activity, and it contributed markedly to the expansion of Iberian tastes.

At the bottom of the last page of the final number of *La Abeja*, under the heading of "Advertencia de los editores" ("Editors' Notice") in blazing capitals, the review's most faithful followers may have been shocked and disappointed to find the following doleful reproach:

> Powerful and insurmountable reasons oblige us to suspend publication of this review indefinitely. We could recount them because they are no secret to those who are familiar with the intellectual and moral state of our country; but to relate them would be too, too sad and bitter, and we prefer to hold them back. We have struggled faithfully and with constancy for a long time; we have willingly sacrificed our leisure and our best interests in order to carry our idea forward; but, exhausted, we are forced to abandon it and to become mute; we do so with deepest personal regret and to the regret of a small number of people, admirers of knowledge, who have constantly encouraged us and who join us in the conviction, and deplore as we do, that it is impossible to acclimate Spain to publications in the style of our review.[35]

The editors' collective expressions of failure, frustration, and despair are chilling, and an assessment of their aptness belongs to a sociological examination of Spain's admittedly chaotic conditions at that moment in its history. The high hopes proclaimed in Bergnes's introduction eight years earlier seem to have crumbled and given way to disappointment and bitterness, undoubtedly prompted on one level by the economic stringencies that regularly doom worthy cultural enterprises, now as then. Perhaps the professors from Barcelona aimed too high or researched their market inadequately.

Yet in the long range, while these intellectuals' journal may have failed, their campaign did not. In historical perspective, *La Abeja* both reflected and spurred a cultural approximation between two countries. It deposited in Spain the "precious nectar" that it gathered from the blossoms that flowered in the distant fields of Germany. Its life span was limited, but its founders' laudable zeal and assiduous labor were not a vain investment.

Notes

1. A brief Spanish version of this essay was read at the 9th Congress of the Asociación Internacional de Hispanistas in Berlin in August 1986. I am grateful to Jean-François Botrel and José Escobar for useful comments on my paper. I also owe a debt to my colleague Joan Ramon Resina for spurring me on to completion of this project.
2. To these equations one must add the factor of censorship restrictions, both governmental and ecclesiastical, which delayed the entry of works like Goethe's *Werther*. For a thorough examination of the two-way literary flow between the two countries over the centuries, see Gerhart Hoffmeister, *Spanien und Deutschland: Geschichte und Dokumentation der literarischen Beziehungen* (Berlin, 1976), and *España y Alemania: historia y documentación de sus relaciones literarias*, trans. Isidro Gómez Romero (Madrid, 1980). An earlier systematic, chronological account of the German presence in Spain, not limited to literature, is Hugo Kehrer, *Deutschland in Spanien: Beziehung, Einfluß und Abhängigkeit* (Munich, 1953). A summary overview with useful bibliography is Egon Schwarz, "The Reception of German Culture in Spain," *Yearbook of Comparative and General Literature,* vol. 14 (1965), pp. 16–36.
3. For a succinct prehistory of German inroads into Spain in the nineteenth century, see Hans Juretschke, "La recepción de la cultura y ciencia alemana en España durante la época romántica," in *Estudios románticos* (Valladolid, 1975), pp. 63–120. The involvement of Nicolás Böhl de Faber, the German consul in Cádiz, in these early developments was decisive.
4. Goethe, for example, made his first appearance in Spain in Valencia in 1810 (Robert Pageard, *Goethe en España* [Madrid, 1958], p. 226), though an 1803 Spanish edition had appeared in Paris.
5. Santiago Olives Canals, *Bergnes de las Casas, helenista y editor* (Barcelona, 1947), p. 253, offers the following reasonable conjecture about the journal's title: "For the title, Bergnes could have found inspiration in O. Goldsmith's literary weekly *The Bee*, although other Spanish periodicals had adopted it." ("Para el título, Bergnes pudo haberse inspirado en el semanario literario de O. Goldsmith [1728–1774] *The Bee* [Edinburgh 1759], aun cuando otras publicaciones periódicas en España lo habían adoptado: Cádiz, 1812–1813, Madrid 1814, 1834–1836, 1845–1846 y 1864–1865.")
6. José Fernández Matheu, "Estudios de literatura alemana," *El Museo Universal*, vol. 11 (1867), pp. 19, 131, 162, 323, 330, 347, 354.

7. See John E. Englekirk, "*El museo universal* (1857–69): Mirror of Transition Years," *PMLA*, vol. 70 (1955), pp. 350–374.
8. Francisco Pi y Margall, "De la decadencia del arte," *La América*, vol. 1 (24 Sepember 1857), pp. 5–6.
9. "El influjo alemán no tiene mejor exponente que esta publicación, y alcanza la literatura." José María de Cossío, *Cincuenta años de poesía española, 1850–1950* (Madrid, 1960), vol. 1, p. 356.
10. Egon Schwarz, "Joan Maragall, Catalan Mediator of German Literature," *Modern Language Notes*, vol. 76 (1961), pp. 800–807.
11. The six volumes contained, respectively, the following number of pages: 484, 476, 471, 480, 476, 388.
12. His firm, Imprenta de A. Bergnes, had issued a translation of Goethe's *Las cuitas del joven Verther*, done by José Mor de Fuentes, as early as 1835. Prior to the birth of *La Abeja*, Bergnes had already opened the doors to German culture in a journal that he founded and directed between November 1838 and June 1841, *El Museo de Familias*, where he gave voice to the likes of Goethe, Schiller, Heine, and Bodmer, alongside English and Italian writers, and in 1850, he initiated a collection called "Germania" devoted to the same cause. Pageard remarks on the singularity of this pursuit (p. 32). Further information on Bergnes is available in Olives Canals.
13. "Bien así como vemos á la abeja posarse sobre todas las flores, y extraer lo útil de cada una de ellas, así mismo deben los amantes de la instruccion probarlo todo, y recoger lo bueno donde quiera que se encuentre." Antonio Bergnes de las Casas, "Introducción," *La Abeja*, vol. 1, no. 1 (January 1862), p. 1. In citations I respect the spelling, accentuation, and punctuation of the original. All translations are mine.
14. An early account of Humboldt's travels in and impression on Spain is Arturo Farinelli, *Guillaume de Humboldt et l'Espagne* (Paris, 1898), which also contains an appendix on "Goethe et l'Espagne" (pp. 219–250).
15. "… convertir en bien o propiedad común, por medio de una exposición comprensible y estética, los bellos productos de las investigaciones científicas." *La Abeja*, vol. 1, no. 1, p. 1.
16. "… pasages, más ó menos ampliados, de los escritores alemanes que, llevados de su amor á la humanidad, han echado sobre sus hombros la no fácil tarea de servir de intérpretes y mediadores entre la ciencia y los que apenas la han saludado." *La Abeja*, vol. 1, no. 1, p. 1.
17. "… á la abeja diligente, que va volando de flor en flor para libar el néctar mas precioso." *La Abeja*, vol. 1, no. 1, p. 2.
18. "… por cuanto unos y otros encontrarán en estas páginas el pasto mas selecto, así para el espíritu como para el corazón." *La Abeja*, vol. 1, no. 1, p. 2.
19. "La lengua que allí se habla, la mas rica y enérgica sin duda, á la par que la mas árdua, de la gran familia europea, ha sido hasta ahora otra cabeza de Medusa para los que creen mal empleado el tiempo, no escaso, que requiere su estudio." *La Abeja*, vol.1, no. 1, p. 2. Juretschke, "La recepción" (pp. 75–79), comments on the considerable linguistic barrier that separated Spaniards from Germans and on the steps that were taken to conquer it.
20. "Hasta ahora ha estado la España separada de la Alemania, no solo por su posicion, sino tambien, y de un modo muy señalado, por el espíritu francés, que se vá extendiendo mas y mas entre los dos paises. Verdad es que el Aleman, adoctrinado por tantos lados en el elemento romano, no ha consentido que esta separacion le imposibilitase llegar á las fuentes de la literatura

española. El Español, empero, apartado, así por la palabra como por el modo, del mundo germánico, completamente estraño para él, no puede menos de aparecer á grandísima distancia de aquel pais; y si por ventura trata de adquirir algun conocimiento de la literatura y del arte alemanes, tiene que acudir forzosamente á la mediacion francesa. Quizas le quepa á *La Abeja* la dicha de iniciar la union tan deseada entre los dos paises." *La Abeja*, vol. 1, no. 1, p. 2.

21. "Además de los artículos científicos, ocuparán parte de las columnas de esta *Revista* otros puramente literarios, no menos instructivos que agradables; y á este efecto elegiremos las obras mas desinteresadas del pensamiento y de la poesía, las dotadas de aquella gracia moral, de aquella tranquilidad genuina de un pueblo que ha dado tantas prendas á la cultura intelectual. Por consiguiente, quedan excluidos de *La Abeja* todos los autores de sistemas mentirosos y delirantes, que soterrando todo lo bello, conducen á los pueblos, por el ateismo, al menosprecio de toda autoridad y de los dulces lazos de familia." *La Abeja*, vol. 1, no. 1, p. 2.

22. Heine's role, along with Goethe, Schiller, and Uhland, in the formation of Bécquer as a poet has been amply documented. To cite but one such confirmation: José Pedro Díaz, *Gustavo Adolfo Bécquer: vida y poesía* (Madrid, 1958). For Heine, see especially pp. 325–336.

23. A translation of the Grimm brothers' "Hans im Glück" is to be found in *La Abeja Literaria, Científica e Industrial*, vol. 1, no. 14 (12 August 1864), pp. 5–6, an independent biweekly published in Madrid.

24. It is unclear if all of these issues saw the light of day in 1870 or had appeared sporadically and were simply bound as a volume in that year.

25. Emilio Lorenzo, in an informative article on the occasion of the bicentenary of Schiller's birth, contrasts Llorente's and Fernández Matheu's versions of "Die Entzückung an Laura" and tilts toward Llorente's (a version different from the one he did for *La Abeja*), explaining: "One must not forget, however, that T. Llorente is an excellent writer of poetry in Castilian, a translator of Goethe and Heine, although, as one can see, his translations are less faithful to the original." ("No hay que olvidar, sin embargo, que T. Llorente es un excelente poeta en lengua castellana, traductor de Goethe y Heine, aunque, como se ve, menos fiel en su traducción al original.") "Schiller y los españoles," *Arbor*, vol. 45 (1960), p. 355.

26. The lengthy list of absentees might include Winckelmann, Wieland, Hölderlin, Kleist, Brentano, Arnim, Eichendorff, Lenau, Mörike, Büchner, and Hebbel, among others.

27. Testimony to the success of this translation is that it appeared in book form in 1865 (Barcelona: Librería de D. Juan Oliveres) and in a second printing in 1876 as part of Bergnes's collection "Tesoro de Autores Ilustres." The translator is not identified; instead, a note advises, "Complete Castilian translation of this immortal work based on the best editions, done by a literary society." ("Traduccion completa en castellano hecha en presencia de las mejores ediciones de esta obra inmortal por una sociedad literaria.") Pageard's assumption that the translation was a collaboration between Fernández Matheu and Bergnes de las Casas cannot be verified (p. 226).

28. "Las alusiones y referencias son cada vez más numerosas, casi tanto como la versión paulatina de las obras de Goethe, en la que es un elemento importante la revista científico-literaria *La Abeja*, fundada en 1862." Emilio Lorenzo, "Goethe, visto por los españoles del siglo XIX," *Cuadernos Hispanoamericanos*,

no. 88 (1957), p. 61; for a brief, updated reprinting of this article, see the *Boletín Informativo* (Fundación Juan March), no. 122 (January 1983), pp. 38–40. For further data, consult Udo Rukser, *Goethe in der hispanischen Welt* (Stuttgart, 1958), and *Goethe en el mundo hispánico*, trans. Carlos Gerhard (Mexico, 1977).
29. The lectures were published in Antonio Angulo y Heredia's 420–page book, *Goethe y Schiller: su vida, sus obras y su influencia en Alemania* (Madrid, 1863).
30. Robert Pageard and G. W. Ribbans, "Heine and Byron in the *Semanario Popular* (1862–1865)," *Bulletin of Hispanic Studies*, vol. 33 (1956), pp. 78–86.
31. Juan María Díez Taboada, "El germanismo y la renovación de la lírica española en el siglo XIX, 1840–1870," *Filología Moderna*, vol. 2, no. 5 (1961), pp. 32–33, 52.
32. The same goal was explicitly stated at the conclusion of Bergnes' biographical articles about Jean Paul and his work. He explained that *La Abeja* offered its readers excerpts of Richter's work so that this German thinker might become known in Spain for the pleasure and instructiveness of his writings (*La Abeja*, vol. 1, no. 2, p. 117).
33. "Deseosos de adornar la parte literaria de nuestra *Revista* con algunas galanas flores del pensil de la poesía alemana, ofrecemos hoy, como primicias, á nuestros lectores estos ligeros ensayos, agenos de toda pretension. Para este número ha recaido nuestra eleccion en Heine ... Heine, mas que Schiller, Goethe y otros poetas alemanes, es casi enteramente desconocido en nuestro pais ... Si no el mejor de los líricos modernos alemanes, es Heine sin disputa el mas original y popular; pues desde el Rin hasta el Elba, desde el Danubio hasta el mar del Norte, resuenan sus canciones en todas partes, no menos en las ciudades mas populosas que en las mas humildes aldeas." *La Abeja*, vol. 1, no. 1, p. 39.
34. "Man wollte nun unmittelbar mit Deutschland verkehren. Diese Bestrebungen äußerten sich u.a. darin, daß einige Professoren der Universität Barcelona 1862 die Zeitschrift 'La Abeja' gründeten." Udo Rukser, "Heine in der hispanischen Welt," *Deutsche Vierteljahrsschrift für Literaturwissenschaft und Geistesgeschichte*, vol. 30 (1956), p. 481. By a statistical count, Heine led Schiller, Goethe, and Uhland, in that order, as Germany's most popular poet in Spain (Carey S. Crantford, "German Lyric Poetry in Spanish Translation through 1915," *Dissertation Abstracts*, vol. 22 [1962], pp. 3658–3659). Emilia Pardo Bazán paid him special attention some years later: "Fortuna española de Heine," *Revista de España*, no. 110 (1886), pp. 481–496.
35. "Motivos poderosos é invencibles, nos obligan á suspender indefinidamente la publicacion de esta Revista. Podríamos referirlos porque no son secretos para muchos que conocen el estado intelectual y moral de nuestra pátria; pero su relacion sería por demás triste y amarga, y preferimos callarla. Hemos luchado con fé y constancia por mucho tiempo; hemos sacrificado gustosos el reposo y los intereses para llevar adelante nuestra idea; pero rendidos, tenemos que abandonarla y enmudecer con hondo sentimiento propio y de un reducido número de personas amantes del saber que constantemente nos han alentado y que con nosotros deploran y estan convencidos de que es imposible aclimatar en España publicaciones de la índole de nuestra Revista." *La Abeja*, vol. 6, no. 10, p. 386.

– 11 –

CLARÍN'S KRAUSISM

Nelson R. Orringer

In memory of my teacher, Juan López-Morillas

Leopoldo Alas (1852–1901), the author of arguably the greatest nineteenth-century novel,[1] owes much of his achievement to the post-Kantian philosopher from Saxony, Carl Christian Friedrich Krause (1781–1832). Yet Alas's debt has received, at most, sporadic attention. In a typical treatment, Eduard Gramberg distinguishes three epochs in Alas's own fiction: a vaguely spiritualistic period dominated by Krausism (1873–80); a decade in which he heatedly defends and practices literary naturalism (1880–90); and a return to spiritualism, but of a deeper kind than in the first period (1890–1901).[2] Alas's most universal work, the long novel titled *La Regenta* (The Regent's Wife, 1884–85), would fall into the second period, affected as it is by Émile Zola's naturalism. But this tripartite division of Alas's writing into idealism, materialism, and a return to idealism is simplistic, involving monolithic appreciations of Krausist idealism and naturalistic materialism, as if they were mutually exclusive. Since 1985, historians of Krausism like Antonio Jiménez García have shown that in Spain that philosophy, after its importation by Julián Sanz del Río in 1860, evolved toward the various forms of positivism emerging from France and England in the 1870s. In the present essay, I wish to apply this new research on the history of Krausism to the aesthetics of Alas, popularly known as "Clarín." In doing so, this essay will be the first, I believe, to label Alas a Krauso-positivist. Initially, I shall examine his youthful espousal of Krausism at a time when it was merging with five types of positivism in Spain. Next, I shall summarize the most popular work of Spanish Krausism, *Ideal de la humanidad para la vida* (Ideal of Mankind for Life, 1860), a direct Spanish translation of Krause. Last, I shall show that Clarín fictionalizes Krausist premises, which he buttresses with positivistic techniques transposed to literature in his own most acclaimed works.

When he was twenty, Alas, newly arrived in Madrid from the provinces, attended the lectures of the Krausists Alfredo Adolfo Camús and Nicolás Salmerón at a time when Krausism still retained the prestige of novelty. In October 1871, three years after Sanz del Río's death, his students echoed his doctrines with almost religious veneration. Alas absorbed this reverence, and henceforward, his Catholicism would combat his Krausist intellectualism. Since Isabella II's minister had expelled Sanz del Río from his chair of Metaphysics, this expulsion served as the best propaganda in favor of Krausism. Every individual who prided himself on being politically liberal necessarily had to espouse Krausist philosophy.[3] Alas belonged to a group of four liberal-minded Krausist students who identified themselves as "the boys from Oviedo" ("los de Oviedo").

Eventually, Alas would form part of the Oviedo circle of Krausism, which María Dolores Gómez-Molleda regards as the most compact and solid of all Krausist groups in late nineteenth-century Spain. Of the older Krausists who helped found that circle in Oviedo, José Manuel Piernas y Hurtado, who occupied a chair in Political Economy, Statistics, and Public Finance from 1870 to 1876, had helped educate such distinguished thinkers as Leopoldo Alas himself and his intimate friend Adolfo Posada.[4] In Madrid, Alas earned his Ph.D. in law in 1878 with a thesis examining a typical Krausist theme, "Law and Morality."[5] He dedicated the dissertation to his thesis director, D. Francisco Giner de los Ríos, everywhere present in his thinking, as Alas there acknowledges.[6] In 1882, Alas won the chair of Roman Law at the University of Saragossa, and the following year he transferred to Oviedo, where he became a leading member of the Oviedo circle of Krausists.

In his prologue to a book of critical essays on Goethe by his own Krausist teacher Urbano González Serrano, Leopoldo Alas displays his respect for Spanish Krausism, which seems to account for his love of German literature and philosophy in general. In a letter of 12 March 1888 to Marcelino Menéndez y Pelayo, he reveals that as a youth studying in Madrid, he devoured as much German letters and philosophy as he could get his hands on, including the correspondence and works of Schiller, Goethe, Humboldt, Hegel,

Vischer, Schopenhauer, and Helmholtz. Sergio Beser believes that the majority of these authors came to Clarín's attention through the influence of his Krausist teachers: Giner, González Serrano, Canalejas, and perhaps Revilla,[7] for, like those Krausists, Alas felt that true Spanishness consisted of importing elements worthy of acclimating to Spanish soil. He recommended studying with care to assimilate everything non-Spanish deserving to be seen and learned in Spain.[8] This attitude of openness for patriotic purposes he explicitly attributed to Spanish Krausism. He regarded it as an injustice that the Spanish Krausists had been ostracized for their dogmatic exclusiveness, and he found González Serrano's book on Goethe ample evidence of the falseness of that judgment, for so complex a figure as Goethe could not have been understood and judged by a spirit of sectarianism. Alas concurred with González Serrano in finding Goethe by successive degrees superstitious, mystical, pantheistic, eclectic, perhaps skeptical, and perhaps sensualistic, but all without any true contradiction.[9] Goethe struck Alas as a poet-philosopher, the most philosophical of all poets.[10] Unquestionably, Alas measured himself against Goethe in his own literary career. Guided by Krausist openness to numerous critical currents, he prided himself on his open-mindedness as a critic, his willingness to embrace numerous movements. Yet he showed reluctance to see himself as a dilettante in the process.[11] Moreover, as a poet in the sense of a creator of prose fiction, he may well have viewed himself as deserving of writing in accordance with Krausist philosophy.

Of all the works of Spanish Krausism, according to Jiménez García,[12] none has affected several generations so deeply as Julián Sanz del Río's *Ideal of Mankind for Life*. Taking Sanz del Río at his word in his introduction, critics for thirty years had regarded this work as an adaptation of Krause's philosophical treatise *Das Urbild der Menschheit* (The Ideal of Mankind, 1811) to the spirit, needs, and characteristics of the Spanish people. However, in 1987, Enrique Menéndez Ureña systematically demonstrated that Sanz del Río had not really translated the *Urbild* at all, but instead other texts of Krause published in 1811, which centered on the same themes. The texts directly translated by Sanz del Río came from the *Tagblatt des Menschheitlebens* (Journal of Mankind's Life). They were philosophical articles titled "Alliance of Mankind," the incomplete "Development and Ideal Presentation of the Idea of the Alliance of Mankind from the Perspective of Life," and the "Commandments of Mankind." It turns out, therefore, that Sanz del Río, belonging to the European tradition of Krause's students, felt it incumbent upon himself to popularize his teacher's works in Spain. Hence, he opted for bringing to the general Spanish public not Krause's basic works, difficult and dense, but other writings in which Krause offered his social and pedagogical philosophy to the public at large.[13]

What scholars have not recognized is the heavy impact of *Ideal of Mankind for Life* on the fiction of Leopoldo Alas. Both a philosophical anthropology and a philosophy of history, the book takes as its point of departure metaphysical definitions of man before examining the mission and destiny of mankind on earth; moreover, it studies humanity in its divine origin and as the unveiling of the essence of God in time. According to Juan López-Morillas,[14] Sanz del Río's work has a tripartite division: the first part studies humankind as an archetype; the second, humankind as a historical reality; and the third, humankind as a universal aspiration. The first part provides metaphysical and anthropological definitions of man and humanity that function throughout the whole work. Man is defined as the perfect, harmonious synthesis between nature and spirit. In its progressive process of self-perfection, this synthesis is to achieve its proper destiny in a union with God and the world. For Krause and Sanz del Río, "man, living image of God, capable of progressive perfection, should live in religion united with God, subordinated to God. In his place and limited sphere, he should realize the harmony of universal life, and he should show this harmony in a beautiful outer form; he should come to know God and the world within science; in the clear cognition of his destiny, he should educate himself."[15] Herein, according to López-Morillas, lies the essence of Krausist philosophy: first, the vision of man as an idea, an archetype, insofar as he is presented to us as a living image of God; second, the view of man as history insofar as his evolution brings about the gradual materialization of that archetypal idea in time; and third, the notion of man as moral will, since all his actions should promote that destiny.[16]

In their works, Krause and Sanz del Río envision human society as a function of humankind's self-realization.[17] The fulfillment of human destiny requires the association of the individual with other human beings in complementary relationships. Such associations form the various social spheres through which human beings progress toward their destiny as a harmonious mankind.[18] Societies seem to Krause and Sanz del Río to fall into three types: personal, real, and formal. Personal societies, so called because of the persons of which they are comprised, include the family, friendship, and the people or nation. These societies demand the personal surmounting of particular interests for the greater good of the group. The second type of society, the real, is constituted by virtue of real human works: science and art.[19] Through science, the human spirit achieves the analogy with God in His infinite intelligence. Through art, complement of science, a living and progressive revelation of godhood among men is given to mankind. The third type of society, the formal, includes morality, law, the state, and religion. Morality regulates all human acts in accordance with the imperative to act in conformity with the individual's good nature in God. Law offers the necessary conditions for the materialization of human destiny. The state is the public manifestation of law. The various states form mere steppingstones to the city of God on earth. Finally, religion consists of the rational development of this cosmopolis of faith.[20]

The development of mankind, according to Krause and Sanz del Río, implies three historical stages, in a relationship of thesis, antithesis, and synthesis, or unity, opposition, and harmony.[21] The first stage is the absolute past, an age of innocence, a lost golden age in which man lived in unity with God. The second stage is the historical present, an age of evil and egoism, giving rise to conflicts and wars. In religion, polytheism prevails. The third age, or the future, is that of harmony, with absolute happiness and perfection. In religion, this final period is characterized by monotheism. Leopoldo Alas transforms this manner of reckoning history to his own Krauso-positivism by autobiographically pinpointing the premises of Krause. The age of innocence was to correspond to the period in Spanish history when that country enjoyed its greatest intellectual freedom in the nineteenth century: from 1868 to 1874, an era on which Alas looked back with nostalgia; the age of corruption would describe the restoration of the Bourbon monarchy as of 1874; and the future would remain in abeyance as an ever receding utopia of social, moral, and intellectual reform in the Spain shown in Alas's writings.

During the six years of freedom of press and opinion, initiated by the "Glorious Revolution" of 1868 and culminating in the First Spanish Republic (1873), the open-mindedness and universality of Krausist liberalism made possible the importation into Spain of new currents of thinking previously unnoticed. One of these currents was positivism. Eusebio Fernández has distinguished five different varieties of positivism introduced into Spain: (1) naturalistic positivism directly derived from the natural sciences and practiced by certain Spanish physicians; (2) a weak Comtism professed by certain Catalan conservatives; (3) a Darwinian and Spencerian evolutionism; (4) a neo-Kantian positivism; (5) finally, a Krauso-positivism defended by the philosophers of the Institución Libre de Enseñanza: Nicolás Salmerón, Francisco Giner de los Ríos, Urbano González Serrano, Adolfo Posada,[22] and, as I shall here prove, Leopoldo Alas, who even as early as in his doctoral dissertation shows his acquaintance with the various forms of positivism.[23] Krauso-positivism, as understood by A. Jiménez García,[24] consists of the logical and necessary evolution of Krausism toward positivistic philosophy: it is influenced especially by the methods of positivism and tries to harmonize them with its own idealism. What emerges is harmony between speculation (Krausism) and experience (positivism), which surmounts the rationalistic dualism of the modern world.

To summarize, Alas's Krausism is basically mediated by two instances: first, Sanz del Río's need to popularize Krause, and second, the historical introduction of positivism in Spain around the 1870s. Let us now examine the presence of this Krauso-positivism in Alas's great fiction: his two long novels, *The Regent's Wife* and *Su único hijo* (His Only Son, 1891) on the one hand, and short stories with a marked Krausist accent on the other.

The Regent's Wife allegorizes a general Krausist speculative premise, which in turn is buttressed by positivistic proofs devised by analogy with the natural sciences and espoused by Émile Zola's school of literary naturalism. Man, for Krause an archetype or a living image of God, is evolving toward his ideal of harmony between spirit and nature, between God and the world, yet encounters obstacles in his path in the guise of social institutions that, through self-seeking, impede the progress of self-realization. Sanz del Río, translating Krause, affirms the historical problem in the following terms, evidently incorporated by Alas with little changes into his novel: "Is there health for man? Everything at our side, in pure spirit and in pure nature, seems to be where it belongs, everything seems to adjust to everything else in its species, and to move with assurance toward its respective goal; only man lives as in an alien land, alternating between spirit and nature, and alternately hurled from one kingdom and from the other like a stranger in his house, like an exile without fatherland or home."[25]

The conflict of Alas's protagonist Ana Ozores—an orphan soul, alternately tossed between spirit and nature in the city of Vetusta where she resides—reflects the metaphysical dilemma of Krause's human being: "At that moment, [Ana] saw all the Vetustans happy at her side, some engaged in vice, others in any madness, but all of them satisfied. Only she abided there as in an exile. But, alas!, she was an exile who had no fatherland to which to return, nor for which to yearn."[26] Note the analogues between Krause and Clarín: both authors at once establish a contrast between the individual and the beings at its side; both counterpose the types of pursuits of these beings; both, however, resolve the antithesis by pointing out the self-sufficiency of these beings; yet both painfully perceive the radical deficiency of the human being immersed among this cosmic self-satisfaction like an exile in its very home. This is the Krausist premise of Clarín's novel, and he buttresses that premise throughout with naturalistic methods, as Zola would, minutely portraying the *race*, the *moment*, and the *milieu* that has brought about Ana's sense of existential exile and that will eventually result in her fall. In sum, *La Regenta* is unquestionably classifiable as Spanish Krauso-positivism—the greatest literary work which that philosophy has produced.

The theme of the novel amounts to Ana's gradual loss of psychophysical health, understood in the Krausist sense of harmony between spirit and nature, between intimacy and external being. Consider the forces in Restoration Spain, symbolized by Vetusta, vying for control of the heroine of the novel: on the one hand, the church, personified by its most powerful member in the city, the herculean vicar general of the diocese, Don Fermín de Pas; and, on the other hand, the state, embodied by the most potent politician, the seductive Don Álvaro Mesía. Whereas for Krause the state should constitute the lawful steppingstone to the kingdom of God on earth, he recognizes that, in fact, in the historical present, the state operates in its own interests.[27] Nothing better describes the statecraft of Álvaro Mesía: he is ostensibly the head of the Liberal Party in Vetusta, but in secret he also dominates the Marquis of Vegallana, head of the city's Conservative Party.[28] Mesía channels the considerable resources of Vegallana, together with those of the Liberal casino, into the project of conquering Ana's love while defeating his rival Fermín de Pas. Krause holds that the church should consist of the rational unfolding of the city of God on earth, but in fact, in the second stage of humanity, is self-centered and intolerant.[29] In *La Regenta*, Fermín de Pas uses the formidable power of his reason to convert Ana into a virtual slave of the church, forced to perform pious acts that show her fanaticism while displaying de Pas's secular superiority to Mesía. Buffeted between church and state, between the tyranny of the spirit and the dominion of nature, Ana continually complains of feeling her psyche being rent asunder within her.

The consequences are tragic: Ana oscillates between ever greater extremes of pseudomystic piety and pagan eroticism until she succumbs to adultery and public disgrace, which leads to the death of her husband. At every point, Krausist idealism contrasts with its positivistic corroboration by the facts. For instance, Krause once defined religion as "the intimate intercourse of man with God" ("der innere Umgang des Menschen mit Gott").[30] Ana Ozores, at the point of giving a public display of her piety, reflects that her late father, a freethinker, held that "religion is an inner homage of man to God" ("la religión es un homenaje interior del hombre a Dios").[31] Nonetheless, inner as well as outer religious piety presents extremes that, for the sake of maintaining a well-balanced personality, are to be avoided. In the worship of God, Krause has recommended the alliance of spirits and bodies.[32] Hence, during a novena of the Virgin of Sorrows, Ana Ozores realizes that in the new religiousness she is seeking, the senses have to play an important role.[33] On hearing the *Stabat Mater* of Rossini, she feels a sense of universal charity, particularly for her spiritual guide Don Fermín de Pas, who has claimed to be the victim of general calumny. Therefore, misguided by him at a point in history in which the church, according to Krause, acts out of selfish motives and unknowingly encourages idol worship, a penitent Ana decides to participate in a Holy Week procession dressed as the Virgin and walking through the streets of Vetusta with bare feet. By her side, Alas situates a masochistic schoolmaster nicknamed "Vinegar," who spends all year punishing his students except on Good Friday, when in penance he marches through Vetusta wearing a crown of thorns. Guided by the *Ideal of Mankind for Life*, Alas's admired teacher, the Krauso-positivist Giner de los Ríos, held that "the salvation of the country depended on the radical reform of teaching at all levels, especially the elementary and the secondary."[34] It follows that if Ana has let herself be prostituted to the will of Fermín de Pas to the point that she has made a spectacle of herself, allowing no one contemplating the Good Friday procession to think pious thoughts,[35] it is because she lacks the religious and secular education needed to save her person. No wonder, then, that her religious faith all but disappears, her spirit loses dominion over her body, and she succumbs to the influence of nature and an adulterous love affair. As her physician Benítez says of Ana, "yesterday she was a mystic ... now she eats well, walks outdoors ... and holds a love for the merry life, for Nature."[36]

Nevertheless, the new imbalance will eventually lead to the death of Ana's husband Víctor Quintanar. The self-seeking, jealous cleric, Fermín de Pas, arranges for him to discover his own dishonor.[37] In the duel that ensues between Quintanar and his dishonorer Don Álvaro Mesía, Quintanar, the better shot, decides not to kill his opponent. The omniscient narrator explains that "philosophy and religion were triumphing in the mind of Don Víctor." We can easily identify this religious philosophy as Krausism. Krause's twenty-second commandment of mankind in relation to individuals includes the following: "Thou shalt fight error with science ... sin with virtue ... hate with love ... provocation with firm sereneness and equanimity ... vengeance with forgiveness."[38] Hence, in the middle of the duel, Quintanar thinks to himself that he no longer abhors Don Alvaro. Face to face with his enemy, according to the narrator, Quintanar feels tears well up in his eyes. "At that instant," reports the narrator, "he would gladly have screamed, 'I forgive! I forgive!,' ... like Jesus on the cross."[39] However, Don Alvaro does not share Quintanar's philosophy. A symbol of the state, as unmindful of sacred conjugal bonds as the church, embodied by Fermín, Alvaro kills Quintanar out of fear.[40] This great novel does not exemplify pure Krausism, but Krausopositivism, criticizing the Spanish Restoration for failing to advance the Krausist ideals of humanity.

Alas's second novel, *His Only Son*, develops in positivistic fashion a Krausist idea that constitutes a secondary theme of *The Regent's Wife*: the doctrine that the family represents a sacred social sphere as the most intimate one of mankind, from which sprang all other social spheres.[41] Yet Krause and his Spanish translator Sanz del Río regret that in the present moment of history, the family does not reflect the law of mankind to realize the fullness of its archetypal idea. Woman does not receive all her human rights in the family; children are not accorded the treatment of disinterested love in accordance with their rights.[42] In *His Only Son*, Alas ironically reverses the traditional family pattern, and instead of presenting a patriarchal tyranny, he shows a husband under the sway of a domineering wife, whose whims deprive him of his conjugal rights to self-fulfillment. "Emma," writes the narrator, "was the head of the family; what is more, as has already been said, she was its tyrant."[43] She scorns her husband Bonifacio Reyes each day more, reducing him to nothing but an attractive physique.[44] Bonifacio, incapable of constant, serious work—a sine qua non of the Krausist ethic—decides to seek meaning in his life by filling it with music.[45] This sensuous cult of philharmonics will eventually train him for the self-fulfilling exercise of fatherhood, for, as Sanz del Río, translating Krause, writes, "the artistic conception and creation, however excellent it may be, is particular, is only one form of the complete human life; nor does the artistic goal fill all the heart, all the spirit, of man. For the sake of our favorite art, we easily forget the total art of life and of beautiful actions."[46] Blinded by the representation of the beautiful ideal, and concerned with the exclusive love of that goal, artists at times lose interest in the immediate beauty of virtue. Love of mankind grows cold in them. Then arises the need to "dispense with the human being in order to love the artist" ("prescindir del hombre para amar al artista").[47] This is precisely what happens to Bonifacio. An orphan like Ana Ozores, seeking motherly tenderness in all his social relationships, Bonifacio falls in love with the voice of the second-rate operatic soprano Serafina Gorgheggi for its motherliness.[48] In short, as the narrator puts it, with a phrase that gives an almost crudely empirical, positivistic sense to the idea quoted here from Krause/Sanz del Río, Bonifacio "loved art for the sake of the artist" ("amaba el arte por el artista").[49] Impervious to the generically human, biographical side of artists, he romanticizes everything to do with them. In his adulterous love with Serafina, he discovers a "lover and a mother and a muse in one piece" ("amante y madre y musa en una pieza.").[50] Bonifacio begins living the fictional life of a hero in a cheap romantic novel,[51] to which he becomes ever more attached every day. At times, when in the presence of his wife his conscience protests, he finds it the conscience belonging to a husband, a "virtual" father of the family.[52]

His opportunity arises to change virtuality into materiality. Having dreamed of being a father, with its "dignity" proper to a "priesthood,"[53] Bonifacio has a pseudomystic experience, like that of Ana Ozores in the cathedral on hearing Rossini's *Stabat Mater*. In his *Synthetics*, Sanz del Río holds that God in His providence is capable of descending to finite beings and establishing a relationship with them signified by the word "grace."[54] Something analogous seems to happen to Bonifacio Reyes upon hearing Serafina Gorgheggi sing a prayer to the Virgin in concert one evening. Serafina's maternal voice seems to announce to Bonifacio the virgin birth within himself of his own son, and this notion completely fills Bonifacio's soul as nothing else ever has.[55] Upon subsequently learning of the pregnancy of his wife Emma, Bonifacio feels like a "new man" ("hombre nuevo") in the ethical sense used by Giner to denote the individual who begins to live by religious and moral imperatives.[56] Then he comes to realize that his love of his own son has a greater depth and seriousness than his love of art,[57] as Krause would have agreed. Fatherhood is Bonifacio's vocation, and for Giner, vocation demands sacrifice.⁵⁸ Accordingly, in true Krauso-positivist fashion, Bonifacio decides to give up his mistress in the interest of raising his new son in a peaceful, legitimate home. The "grace that God was sending him in the form of vocation,... vocation as father,"⁵⁹ brings Bonifacio into a powerful confrontation with his ex-mistress Serafina on the final page of the novel. She informs him that his will to sacrifice their relationship for the happiness of his newborn son has no substance. It appears that positive prosaic reality is about to defeat Krausist premises when Serafina reveals to Bonifacio Reyes that not he but another member of the opera company has fathered the new baby. Nevertheless, idealism wins out in this novel as Bonifacio affirms his own faith in the child being his. Faithful to Sanz del Río's commandments of mankind, Bonifacio exercises forgiveness, not vengeance, toward Serafina for her painful revelation. His faith in his fatherhood, like Clarín's own religious faith, is perpetually called upon to surmount doubts.⁶⁰

The same Krauso-positivistic themes that I have just analyzed in Alas's two long novels recur in his short stories. In these tales, the idealism of Krausism cannot dispense with the solid evidence of positivistic methods, nor can the lowliness of positivism do without the universal vision of Krausism. In proof of my first thesis, I offer Alas's fable "The Talking Fly" (La mosca sabia, 1881);⁶¹ in proof of its antithesis, I point to his story "Zurita" (1884).⁶² "The Talking Fly" is a humorous critique of philosophy so closed and dogmatic (like orthodox Krausism) that it prefers to obliterate the facts to save its own theories. In examining Alas's life, we earlier noted that Krausism, as interpreted by Sanz del Río, taught Alas an attitude of openness to all veracious systems and an aversion to intellectual exclusivity, an opposition visible in his literary criticism. To symbolize censurable closed-mindedness, Alas sets his fable in the library of an over-eloquent egghead, Don Eufrasio Macrocéfalo, a library so "hermetically sealed from every gust of air ... that no one ever recalled anyone having coughed there or having shown any sign of an approaching stuffed nose."⁶³ So claustrophobic were those walls of books that the narrator's fantasy had no freedom of flight. However, the presence there of a talking fly offers relief to his fantasy. Don Eufrasio considers that fly his intellectual enemy, because its very existence demonstrates the contrary of everything he wishes to prove. Convinced with Descartes that animals are mere machines, incapable of any intelligent activity, Don Eufrasio wishes to swat the fly to death to preserve his theory. Yet, like Scheherazade's murderous monarch in

The Arabian Nights, he keeps postponing the execution, in his case until he can reason down to the first principle of his insecticidal act. Nonetheless, one day an excess of study deprives the talking fly of its will to live. Analogously, in Alas's own biography, an exposure to Krausism produced an everlasting crisis in his existence, causing his reason to battle with life. The talking fly discovers, in its readings, that its best beloved, a black Venus of a fly, belongs to a repugnant species, *Musca vomitoria*. As a result, our flying protagonist commits existential suicide, alighting on the pate of Don Eufrasio and stinging him until the sage, even before reasoning down to his first principle, swats him to death.[64]

Whereas excessive intellectualism becomes the butt of Alas's humor in "The Talking Fly," excessive attachment to positive facts inspires the hilarious story of "Zurita." Indeed, the biography of Zurita runs suspiciously parallel to that of Urbano González Serrano, Alas's one-time Krausist mentor and friend, who started out subscribing to Krausist metaphysics but ended up, like Zurita, a professor of psychology, logic, and ethics who adhered ever increasingly (though never exclusively like the mature Zurita) to positive facts.[65] The process of Zurita's disillusionment by gradual stages marks his descent from the intellectually sublime to the factually ridiculous, lacking the theoretical elevation of universality, for Zurita has an essential character flaw: he lives dazzled by everything around him, filled with admiration, without possessing enough critical irony to achieve the intellectual independence that Clarín's contact with Giner had taught him. For instance, when a Madrid philosophy professor mocks Zurita's first name, Aquiles, in front of the entire class, the antiheroic student rationalizes that perhaps such humor at his personal expense is "something good. Didn't some German aestheticians affirm that humor is the highest degree of mind? (The Germans! What a great thing it is to be German!)."[66] Aquiles's intellectual servitude attains such extremes that he becomes a Krausist in imitation of a philosopher who happens to be lodging at the same cheap inn as himself.[67] That philosopher, Don Cipriano, exhorts Zurita to love knowledge for its own sake and to have, as he does, mystic communion with God in accordance with the second part of Sanz del Río's *System of Philosophy* or *Synthetics*. However, as much as Aquiles tries, he seems unable to dispense with his finite self in order to enter into the ego in itself, and from there eventually into the being in unity which is God. The ironic narrator relates that God takes pity on Aquiles, causes Don Cipriano to move to another inn, brings new philosophical currents to Spain, and changes Aquiles's mind.

Under the pressure of the new Spanish positivists, Zurita eventually becomes a positivist, though more in a biographical than in a philosophical sense: lured by a flirtatious landlady who cooks him crabs, oysters, lobsters, and squid, he becomes a gourmet of seafood, the supreme delight of a positivist's palate.[68] Clearly Clarín is suggesting that neither Krausism nor positivism is sufficient in and of itself for the uncritical mind.

What, then, is Clarín's final philosophical solution? Evidently, a rational experience that would put him in direct contact with the absolute as Zurita desired in his youth, yet would at the same time afford him positive evidence of its efficacy, as Zurita wanted at maturity. This ultimate solution of Spanish Krauso-positivism appears in the short story "Cambio de luz" (A Change of Light, 1892) that Clarín's biographer Juan Antonio Cabezas deems autobiographical,[69] but which merits precise comparison with Krause's doctrine of synthesis and Sanz del Río's derivative notion of the real truth. Laura de los Ríos connects "A Change of Light" with a personal letter written by Alas in 1888 to Menéndez y Pelayo, in which he makes an apology of Krausism and in which he writes, "As for me, I firmly believe that if there is, as I do not doubt, God and a divine order, etc., etc., the [universal] Law is what Krause says [it is]."[70] The clearest, most concise exposition of Krausist theology appears in an 1869 lecture by Tomás Tapia, a student of Sanz del Río and a professor of systems of philosophy:

> But that God of Whom we speak,... does He exist? Is He an objective reality?... If He exists, demonstrate it.
>
> If God did not exist, He would not be the infinitely perfect God that we think. He would lack existence, which is an immense perfection; in the very fact of thinking an infinitely perfect being, He should necessarily exist. Otherwise, from where would our spirit receive that infinite thought of an infinitely perfect being, when my senses merely give knowledge of the finite, the imperfect, and my finite individuality that I perceive only gives me the finite ...? ... That sublime thought should be necessarily produced by an infinitely perfect being existing in and outside of ourselves.[71]

This describes the experience of Alas's protagonist in "A Change of Light," Jorge Arial, a middle-class intellectual and a talented, hard-working essayist and historian of art, devoted to his family. He has only one pang in life: religious doubt, for he holds that if God exists, all is well; if not, all is evil. Excessive work causes him to go blind, to lose the light of day, but also to achieve the light of faith. He attains this "change of light" through rational reflection, as Krause and Sanz del Río recommend. I quote the text of the story: "With soul, with logic, with deep intuition, he felt his brain philosophize and attack face to face the most formidable sources of atheistic science; then he saw the reality of the divine, not with mathematical evidence, which he well knew was relative and conditional and precarious, but with 'essential' evidence; he saw the truth of God."[72]

The evidence of which the narrator speaks is what logicians call a truth *per se nota*, not needing demonstration. I believe I am the first to point out that Arial arrives at what Sanz del Río has called the "real vision of being" ("vista real del Ser"), which is God.[73] The result is a new, more reliable orientation that allows Arial to cope with daily existence.

In summary, I have attempted to show that Clarín consistently adheres to a unique kind of Krauso-positivism in his most respected fictions. Whereas Laura de los Ríos finds Alas's attitude as a fiction writer "eclectic and fluctuating" when treating Krausism in its various manifestations,[74] I discover in him a clear, unswerving resolve to choose a middle course between idealist speculation and factual underpinning—with humor varying between raucous and sweetly melancholic—to correct the extremes of these two attitudes. Rigorous comparison between his fiction and his probable philosophical sources reveals no difference in this respect between the two long novels and the short stories. In *The Regent's Wife*, Alas fictionalizes with naturalistic detail the second phase of human history as interpreted by Krause and Sanz del Río, in which institutions like church and state deprive individuals like Ana and Fermín of their right to self-realization. In *His Only Son*, Krausist subthemes from *La Regenta* step to the foreground as an excessive passion for art leads the protagonist toward a sacred vocation of stable family life and fatherhood, an affirmation of idealism that overcomes self-seeking and moral squalor. Of the three short stories considered here, "The Talking Fly" deserves mention for its relationship to fictionalized satires of different aspects of Krausism. Just as in this fable Clarín mocks the hermetically sealed mind, so in short stories not analyzed here, like "Doctor Pértinax," "Doctor Angelicus," and "Doctor Sutilis," he ridicules Krausist linguistic obscurity.[75] His teacher Giner always preferred conceptual clarity. Also, Clarín does poke fun at Krausist doctrines not susceptible, at the time, of rigorous proof: Krause and Sanz del Río's conviction of life on other planets,[76] or of the persistence of the species and the disappearance of the individual after death.[77] Still, a story like "Zurita" shows that Alas advocated neither pure

Krausist idealism, nor unmitigated empirical positivism, but rather a philosophical attitude reconciling the two in a kind of rational intercourse with divinity as in "A Change of Light." The role of the various Krauso-positivisms in Spanish literary history has yet to be written in monograph form. Undoubtedly, the great novelist Leopoldo Alas would occupy a lengthy first chapter, in which it would be shown that he left an astonishingly rich doctrinal legacy for Unamuno's Generation of 1898 and Ortega y Gasset's Generation of 1914.

Notes

1. According to Noël Valis, "Clarín," *Dictionary of the Literature of the Iberian Peninsula*, ed. Germán Bleiberg, Maureen Ihrie, and Janet Pérez (Westport, Conn., and London, 1993), vol. 1, pp. 411–414. Gonzalo Sobejano and Mario Vargas Llosa, among others, view *La Regenta* (The Regent's Wife) as "the most significant novel of the last century (along with the quite different *Fortunata y Jacinta*, by Galdós)."
2. *Fondo y forma del humorismo de Leopoldo Alas, "Clarín"* (Oviedo, 1958), pp. 13–14.
3. Juan Antonio Cabezas, *"Clarín": el provinciano universal* (Madrid, 1962), pp. 63–64.
4. Dolores Gómez-Molleda, *Los reformadores de la España contemporánea* (Madrid, 1966), pp. 312–314.
5. Antonio Jiménez García, *El krausismo y la Institución Libre de Enseñanza* (Madrid, 1985), p. 111.
6. *El derecho y la moralidad: determinación concepto del derecho y sus relaciones con el de la moralidad* (Madrid, 1878), no. 1, p. 146.
7. Sergio Beser, *Leopoldo Alas, crítico literario* (Madrid, 1968), p. 38.
8. Leopoldo Alas, "Prólogo" to *Goethe: ensayos críticos*, ed. Urbano González Serrano, 3rd rev. ed. (Madrid, 1900), p. 9.
9. Ibid., p. 22.
10. Ibid., p. 14.
11. Beser, *Leopoldo Alas*, p. 73.
12. Jiménez García, *El krausismo*, p. 79.
13. Antonio Jiménez García, "Menéndez Ureña, E., Fernández Fernández, J. L. y Seidel, J.: 'El "Ideal de la Humanidad" de Sanz del Río y su original alemán.' Universidad Pontificia, Comillas, Madrid, 1993, 1 + 238 pp.," *Asociación de hispanismo filosófico*, vol. 6 (1994), pp. 15–16.
14. Juan López-Morillas, *El krausismo español: perfil de una aventura intelectual* (Madrid, 1980), p. 79.

15. "El hombre, imagen viva de Dios y capaz de progresiva perfección, debe vivir en la religión unido con Dios, y subordinado a Dios; debe realizar en su lugar y esfera limitada la armonía de la vida universal, y mostrar esta armonía en bella forma exterior; debe conocer en la ciencia a Dios y el mundo; debe en el claro conocimiento de su destino educarse a sí mismo." Carl Christian Friedrich Krause, *Ideal de la humanidad para la vida*, trans. Julián Sanz del Río (Madrid, 1960), p. 33.
16. Jiménez García, *El krausismo*, p. 15.
17. Krause, *Ideal de la humanidad*, p. 37.
18. Ibid., pp. 33–34.
19. Ibid., p. 155.
20. Jiménez García, *El krausismo*, pp. 86–88.
21. Krause, *Ideal de la humanidad*, p. 252.
22. Antonio Jiménez García, "Urbano González Serrano y la fundamentación del krauso-positivismo español," *Letras Peninsulares*, vol. 4, no. 1 (Spring 1991), p. 187.
23. In *El derecho y la moralidad*, naturalistic positivists include the psychologists Théodule Ribot (p. 9) and Wilhelm Wundt (pp. 14–15); Auguste Comte, the French founder of positivism, is mentioned several times (pp. 7, 153), as is Herbert Spencer (pp. 22, 154–157). Leopoldo Alas's thesis includes a critique of positivism that, in my judgment, stays constant through the years. It maintains that positivism, when it tries to deny to metaphysics the possibility of scientific validity, lapses into the same dogmatic skepticism that it tries to avoid (p. 23); for, according to Alas (p. 39), "in every particular object like law, the metaphysical part, the essential part, is not something stuck onto it, but the basis of the object itself" ("en todo objeto particular como el derecho lo metafísico, lo esencial no es algo pegadizo, sino el fondo del objeto mismo"). With his usual perspicacity, Gonzalo Sobejano has written, "educated in Krausism and idealistic by inclination, [Alas] took from positivism and literary naturalism only what he judged opportune for the progress of culture in Spain, without ever losing his metaphysical yearning nor his spiritual and religious restlessness" ("Educado en el krausismo e idealista por inclinación, tomó del positivismo, y del naturalismo literario, sólo aquello que para el progreso de la cultura en España juzgó oportuno, sin perder nunca apetencia metafísica ni inquietud espiritual y religiosa"), "Introducción" to *La Regenta* by Leopoldo Alas, "Clarín" (Madrid, 1981), vol. 1, p. 10.
24. Jiménez García, *El krausismo*, p. 114.
25. "¿Hay salud para el hombre? Todo á nuestro lado, en el espíritu puro y en la naturaleza pura, parece estar en su asiento, cada cosa parece ajustar con las demás de su género, y caminar con seguridad hácia su fin respectivo; sólo el hombre vive como en tierra ajena, alternativamente en el espíritu y en la naturaleza, y alternativamente arrojado del un reino, y del otro como extranjero en su casa, como desterrado sin patria ni hogar." Krause, *Ideal de la humanidad*, p. 15.
26. "En aquel momento vió a todos los vetustenses felices a su lado, entregados unos al vicio, otros a cualquier manía, pero todos satisfechos. Sólo ella estaba allí como en un destierro. Pero ¡ay!, era una desterrada que no tenía patria a donde volver, ni por la cual suspirar." Leopoldo Alas, *La Regenta*, in *Obras selectas de Leopoldo Alas "Clarín"* (Madrid, 1947), p. 150.
27. Krause, *Ideal de la humanidad*, pp. 224–225.
28. Alas, *La Regenta*, p. 113.
29. Krause, *Ideal de la humanidad*, p. 253.

30. C. Chr. Fr. Krause, *Das Urbild der Menschheit*, 2nd ed. (Göttingen, 1851), p. 3.
31. Alas, *La Regenta*, p. 439.
32. Krause, *Das Urbild*, p. 18.
33. Alas, *La Regenta*, p. 439.
34. Juan López-Morillas, *Racionalismo pragmático: el pensamiento de Francisco Giner de los Ríos* (Madrid, 1988), p. 52.
35. Alas, *La Regenta*, p. 456.
36. "Ayer era mística ... ahora come bien, se pasea al aire libre ... y tiene un amor de la vida alegre, de la Naturaleza." Ibid., p. 478.
37. Ibid., p. 513.
38. "Combatirás el error con la ciencia ... el pecado con la virtud ... el odio con el amor ... la provocación con la firme serenidad y la igualdad de ánimo." Krause, *Ideal de la humanidad*, p. 101.
39. "En aquel instante hubiera gritado de buena gana: "¡Perdono! ¡Perdono!" ..., como Jesús en la cruz." Alas, *La Regenta*, p. 543.
40. Ibid., p. 544.
41. Krause, *Ideal de la humanidad*, pp. 43–44.
42. Ibid., pp. 68–69.
43. "Emma era el jefe de la familia; era más, según ya se ha dicho, su tirano." L. Alas, *Su único hijo*, in *Obras selectas de Leopoldo Alas "Clarín,"* p. 560.
44. Ibid., p. 562.
45. Ibid., p. 559.
46. " ... la concepción y la producción artística, por excelente que sea, es particular, es sólo una forma de la vida total humana; tampoco el fin artístico llena todo el corazón, todo el espíritu, del hombre. Fácilmente olvidamos por el arte nuestro predilecto el arte total de la vida y del bello obrar." Krause, *Ideal de la humanidad*, p. 65.
47. Ibid., p. 66.
48. Alas, *Su único hijo*, p. 573.
49. Ibid., p. 574.
50. Ibid., p. 596.
51. Ibid., p. 601.
52. Ibid., p. 609.
53. Ibid., p. 621.
54. Fernando Martín Buezas, *La teología de Sanz del Río y del krausismo español* (Madrid, 1977), p. 260.
55. Alas, *Su único hijo*, p. 651.
56. Francisco Giner de los Ríos, *Ensayos*, ed. Juan López-Morillas (Madrid, 1969), p. 210.
57. Alas, *Su único hijo*, p. 665.
58. Giner de los Ríos, *Ensayos*, p. 116.
59. "Gracia que Dios le enviaba en forma de vocación,... de vocación de padre." Alas, *Su único hijo*, p. 709.
60. Ibid., p. 713.
61. For the dating of the story, I rely on Laura de los Ríos, *Los cuentos de Clarín: proyección de una vida* (Madrid, 1965), p. 300.
62. For the dating, I count on ibid., p. 161.
63. L. Alas, "La mosca sabia," in *Obras selectas de Leopoldo Alas "Clarín,"* p. 929.
64. Ibid., p. 939.
65. Jiménez García, "Urbano González Serrano," pp. 194, 203.

66. "Cosa buena. ¿No aseguraban algunos estéticos alemanes (¡los alemanes!, ¡qué gran cosa ser alemán!) que el humorismo es el grado más alto del ingenio?" L. Alas, "Zurita," in *Obras selectas de Leopoldo Alas "Clarín,"* p. 900.
67. Ibid., p. 904.
68. Ibid., p. 919.
69. Cabezas, *"Clarín,"* p. 183.
70. "En cuanto a mí, creo firmemente que si hay, como no dudo, Dios y orden divino, etc., etcétera, el Derecho es lo que dice Krause." L. de los Ríos, *Los cuentos de Clarín*, p. 162.
71. "Pero ese Dios de que hablamos ... ¿existe?, ¿es una realidad objetiva? ... Si existe, demuéstralo. Si Dios no existiera, no sería el Dios infinitamente perfecto que pensamos, le faltaría la existencia, que es una inmensa perfección; en el hecho mismo de pensar un ser infinitamente perfecto debe existir necesariamente; ¿de dónde, si no, vendría a nuestro espíritu ese infinito pensamiento de un ser infinitamente perfecto, cuando mis sentidos sólo dan a conocer lo finito, lo imperfecto? ... Ese sublime pensamiento debe de ser producido necesariamente por el ser infinitamente perfecto existiendo en, y fuera de nosotros." Martín Buezas, *La teología de Sanz del Río*, p. 117.
72. "Con alma, con lógica, con profunda intuición, sintió filosofar a su cerebro y atacar de frente los más formidables fuentes de la ciencia atea; vio entonces la realidad de lo divino, no con evidencia matemática, que bien sabía él que ésta era relativa y condicional y precaria, sino con evidencia *esencial*; vio la verdad de Dios." Cabezas, *"Clarín,"* p. 182.
73. Martín Buezas, *La teología de Sanz del Río*, pp. 116–117.
74. L. de los Ríos, *Los cuentos de Clarín*, p. 160.
75. See especially L. Alas, "El doctor Pértinax," in *Obras selectas de Leopoldo Alas "Clarín,"* p. 944.
76. On life on other planets, see Krause, *Ideal de la humanidad*, p. 317; cf. Alas, "El doctor Pértinax," pp. 945–946, and L. Alas, "Doctor Sutilis," in *Obras selectas de Leopoldo Alas "Clarín,"* p. 923.
77. Krause, *Ideal de la humanidad*, p. 217; cf. Alas, "El doctor Pértinax," p. 941.

– 12 –

CONFIGURATIONS OF GERMAN AND SPANISH INTELLECTUAL HISTORY AND AESTHETICS

Goethe, Novalis, Ortega y Gasset, and Unamuno

Francisco LaRubia-Prado

The purpose of this study is to establish an association between two German and two Spanish authors whose work was carried out at different moments of modern history. This association will yield some tentative theoretical conclusions regarding two competing cultural views of our time, modernity and postmodernity, and their connection with what I will call the classical and the romantic paradigms. I must clarify from the very outset that in this essay I am not interested in the understanding of certain authors as "sources" of other authors. Thus, I will associate texts and authors that so far have been unrelated by critics (or related for very different reasons) in order to explore how earlier writers (Goethe and Novalis) can be relevant to our time through texts and ideas produced by more contemporary writers (Ortega and Unamuno). The main issue confronted in this paper can perhaps be summarized in the shift from Matthew Arnold's question about Virgil—"'*Is he adequate*?' to represent the era in which he lived"[1]—to Ortega's question about the relevance of classic authors to the present: can we *live* today based on the legacy of our classics?[2]

Goethe and Ortega y Gasset

As is well known, Johann Wolfgang von Goethe (1749–1832), after the early Sturm und Drang days when his work was dominated by the power of emotions and rebelliousness, changed his intellectual and artistic orientation. He subsequently developed into what in general terms can be understood as a "classicist." Goethe's new classicism became more apparent as a result of a trip to Italy in 1786 and 1787. According to Atkins, "Although Goethe's aesthetic theories are thus not rigidly neoclassical, almost all his writings on art reflect ... [a] strong ... preference for the forms and values of ancient and Renaissance idealizing classicism."[3]

An archetypal example of Goethe's classical aesthetics is his *Iphigenie auf Tauris* (1787). In *Iphigenie*—whose Greek predecessor is Euripides' *Iphigenia in Tauris*—the heroine, Iphigenia, who is Diana's priestess in Tauris (now the Crimea), is eager to return to Greece and join her siblings, Electra and Orestes, to redeem the cursed "House of Tantalus." Iphigenia confesses the long-kept secret of her origin to Thoas, king of Tauris, who had been her protector and who wants to marry her. In Tauris, she has convinced the king to spare the lives of foreigners, who have been ritually sacrificed to the goddess under an ancient custom of the land. However, Iphigenia rejects Thoas's advances, and the king reinstitutes human sacrifices. In fact, Iphigenia herself is instructed to prepare for the sacrifice of two captive Greeks. After speaking with the captives, Iphigenia realizes that one of them is her own brother, Orestes, who is in Tauris following the instruction of an oracle from Apollo in Delphi to take the sacred image of Diana to Athens. By doing so, he would end the curse haunting him for having killed their mother Clytemnestra (who, along with her lover Aegisthus, had killed Iphigenia's and Orestes' father, King Agamemnon). Iphigenia, Orestes, and his friend Pylades plot to escape, but Iphigenia discloses the plot to Thoas since she feels that she cannot betray her protector by lying to him. Orestes and his men are then discovered, but Thoas lets the Greeks, including Iphigenia, return to Greece.

In *Iphigenie*, the two main characters, Iphigenia and Orestes, are haunted by memories of pain, and they suffer throughout the play. Whereas Iphigenia had been separated from her family and country in her childhood, Orestes had killed his mother and is being persecuted by the Furies. However, their belief in the disclosure of truth as a means toward the resolution of problems is intended to appeal to everyone's humanity, including that of the king in a land of "barbarians" where human sacrifices were routinely performed. Ultimately, as Dieckmann has suggested, *Iphigenie* shows a strong belief in the Enlightenment notion of the perfectibility of human beings,[4] a perfectibility achievable only through fulfillment of moral obligation and articulated through psychological motivation. In what constitutes the central theme of the play, Iphigenia makes a strong case for the notion of *individual life*. She strives toward reconciling what she understands as her own destiny—her return to her family and her land and the redemption of the cursed House of Tantalus—with her actual existence as an exile in a foreign land. Finally, her return to Greece from Tauris represents the beginning of the fulfillment of her own existential project, a project in which ethical values are indeed paramount.

In the classical world-view, it is possible to reach generalizations regarding the goodness or evil of certain ethical positions or values suggested in the work of art, or regarding the aesthetic form in which those ethical positions are put forward. Furthermore, the possibility of reaching valid generalizations through art embraces all realms of culture within the classicist's credo. This certainly was the position of Goethe, for whom the values conveyed in the unique expression of a work of art go beyond the specific historical moment in which the work was produced; they are intended to be *universal* values. Not only are they universal, but they are understood as *atemporal* and *transcultural*, as well. In the case of *Iphigenie*, values such as those mentioned above appeal to the humanity, individuality, and perfectibility of all human beings—including the barbarians in Tauris and their king Thoas. Some of these values, such as individuality and the perfectibility of all human beings, are certainly more an inheritance of the Enlightenment than of classical Greece.[5]

If the psychological motivation or impetus in Goethe's classicism is always attached to the ethics of his works, his treatment of ethical problems also requires psychological justification. In fact, psychology, ethical values, and everything relevant to the "human condition" achieve in the classicist Goethe their unique cultural embodiment through the work of art: "The work of art, existing through and for man, gives form to the familiar or unfamiliar elements (*Stoff*)—lines, colors, words, motifs, themes, objects—that it may comprise; not engendered in the neutral realm of nature, this form always exists to convey import (*Gehalt*—meaning, feeling, something uniquely relevant to the human condition); and so it cannot be confused with a natural object or phenomenon that may, but does not necessarily or always, produce this response."[6]

Part of the same cultural discourse, in which the ethical and the aesthetic join forces without becoming the same thing, is evidenced in Iphigenia's rejection of Thoas. Even though a change of heart could save the life of her brother, who is about to be sacrificed, she insists on protecting her virginity as a way of redeeming her house. Prudhoe makes sense of this behavior through the Kantian notions of "reason" and "understanding": "Iphigenia is not deaf to Reason but rather to Understanding. For it is Understanding which judges according to particular circumstances. It is Reason, however, which tells us that certain actions are *always* good or bad, *regardless* of particular circumstances. Thus, Understanding, using the voice of Pylades, might be held to urge that Iphigenia should offer up a lie in order to circumvent the grim atrocity of double murder. But Reason issues a categorical command, 'Thou shalt not lie,' which overrides it."[7]

This connection between Goethe and Immanuel Kant (1724–1804) is hardly surprising since, as Wilhelm Windelband observed, Kant's *Critique of Judgment* (1790) was "a priori the concept of Goethe's poetry." In this sense, according to Windelband, what Goethe represents in aesthetic achievement is "founded and demanded in ... [Kant] by the pure necessity of philosophical thought."[8] Windelband's observation seems to me particularly apt if we take into consideration that both Goethe and Kant, vis-à-vis Baumgarten, agreed not to "bring the critical treatment of the beautiful under rational principles, and so to raise its rules to the rank of science."[9]

Yet despite the flourishing of neoclassical aesthetics and thought in his time, Goethe critics such as Reed underline the curious paradox of Goethe's classicism: "'Classicism' always implies harmony and control and a restraining or supportive order, but these things are usually derived from outside, often from a stable society whose ethos is reflected ... in art. Goethe had no such community to give him support or make demands; there was in his time virtually no 'German society,' at all events none coherent enough for that cultural role. In its absence, he created a one man's order."[10]

This observation about Goethe can be applied, mutatis mutandis, to José Ortega y Gasset's (1883–1955) case, as well. Not only was Ortega a cultural crusader in a country that, in many respects, had been lagging behind the most advanced European countries since the seventeenth century, but his own classicism was scarcely shared in Spain, where the baroque and even the romantic traditions were more deeply rooted than classicism. Furthermore, unlike the case of Goethe, where there is more of a critical consensus with respect to his classicism, the notion that Ortega was a classicist beyond his days of philosophical apprenticeship in Marburg under Hermann Cohen is not an accepted one by most Ortega critics.[11] Yet that is precisely one of the suggestions I wish to make in this study. Furthermore, I would like to propose an important connection between Goethe's and Ortega's thinking via their shared classicism.

Despite the fact that we can find many pages on Goethe in Ortega's posthumously published *Obras completas* (Complete Works, 1983), I would like to pursue the connection between these two authors by focusing less on those pages than on Ortega's text *Ideas sobre la novela* (Notes on the Novel) of 1924.[12] There, Ortega offers some ideas to reinvigorate the novel as a genre. More specifically, Ortega is suggesting a model for modernity's novel.[13] There are three features that Ortega deems essential for the renewal of the novel as genre:

1. *Autopsy*. What constitutes characters is not supposed to be "explained" or "defined" by the narrative voice to the reader. Instead, the characters are supposed to be shown doing what makes them unique and interesting. In this *re-presentation*—the aesthetic achievement—of something human, the reader acquires a more distinctive understanding or view of the subject of representation than the one obtainable in everyday life.[14]

2. *Sluggishness*. Ortega clearly places action at the service of characters; action must be a "mere pretext," and we must be able to summarize it briefly. While the intrigue of a novel is not of primary interest, "we want the novelist to linger and to grant us good long looks at his personages, their being, and their environment."[15] For Ortega, what interests the reader is not action—what the characters do—rather, it is the characters themselves, their motivations and psychology.

3. *Imperviousness*. This creation of an insular literary space was the main principle for Ortega's idea of modernity's novel. To achieve the effect of "imperviousness," "the author must begin by luring us into the closed precinct that is his novel and then keep us there cut off from any possible retreat to the real space we left behind .... The author must build around us a wall without chinks or loopholes through which we might catch, from within the novel, a glimpse of the outside world."[16] To this, Ortega adds that "imperviousness is but the special form adopted on in the novel by the generic imperative of art: to be

without transcending consequence."[17] In other words, readers cannot be trapped in the "closed precinct" of the novel if they are thinking more about everyday affairs than about the aesthetic experience to which they are being lured.

Surprisingly enough, Ortega finds the model for his new novel in classicism: "Should we, by any chance, now be again in the process of turning from action to the person, from function to substance? Such a transition would be indicative of an *emerging classicism.*"[18] The obvious answer to Ortega's question, as we suspect and will eventually verify, is "yes." Let us see how.

Ortega begins his revisitation of classicism with a comparison between French classical theater and Spanish theater of the Golden Age, *La Comedia.* Ortega sees Spanish theater as a *popular* theater that appeals to the masses, and thus is aimed at an audience interested in "vital emotion" ("apasionamiento vital") and lacking in consciousness and reflection. For him, Spanish theater is based on adventures and the proliferation of many events rather than on a detailed presentation of the characters' feelings and psychology. Consequently, the ethical dimension that these vague and ill-defined characters project is, at best, negligible.

Diametrically opposed in Ortega's view to the *Comedia*, which he defines as an "art of adventures," is French classical theater, an "art of figures." French classical theater is not aimed at the people, but at the "aristocracy of the spirit," a definitely more select audience. It is based not on action, but on contemplation, reflection, and analysis of the characters' psychology. Thus, the ethical dimension of these plays is crucial. Instead of presenting constant action, the classical playwright emphasizes only two or three exemplary moments of the story at hand in order to pose the "inner problems" of the soul and of human existence. In this theater, as in the later Goethe, psychology is a tool that serves to underscore "the exemplary type of reaction" that art invites the audience to emulate.[19]

If in Spanish theater of the Golden Age the characters are ill defined as human beings and exemplify everyday reality, the characters of French classical theater are "heroes, exalted characters, prototypes of magnanimity,"[20] and they are presented to an audience concerned with moral conflicts. Classical theater is also the opposite of popular theater in that it channels passions and frames feelings in both a particular language and a particular behavior, in acts that overcome the state of nature through conscious reflection and a self-demanding attitude.

The characteristics that Ortega praises in French classical theater are clearly found in Goethe's *Iphigenie*. As a matter of fact, both Ortega and Goethe found a model of aesthetic achievement in Jean Baptiste Racine (1639–1699). Whereas Ortega approves of Racine's construction of characters in *Notes on the Novel*,[21] critics such as Dieckmann claim that *Iphigenie*, in an assertion that can be extended to other works by Goethe, "resembles Racine's plays much more than those of Sophocles."[22] In fact, it is Goethe—in so many ways the inheritor of the Enlightenment, and thus a much closer presence to what Ortega would call his own "circumstance"—who is the most authorized classical playwright to verify the features that Ortega considers essential for the renewal of the novel as a genre.

It is not surprising that Ortega finds in the theater a model to illustrate what he means by "autopsy," or the nondefinition of characters, since the absence of a narrator leaves the development of behavior as the only activity on display. Whereas in Sophocles, the chorus serves to comment on the action, and thus defines to some extent the development of the play (or its understanding by the spectator), in more modern classical drama, such as Goethe's *Iphigenie*, there is no chorus. Consequently, we have before us only the unfolding of the psychological and ethical motivations of the characters.

"Sluggishness," which describes a focus on the development of character, instead of an emphasis on action, is another characteristic that seems inspired by ancient or modern classical drama, since it is not only the feature that stresses technique and form, but also the foundation of the "art of figures" exemplified by classical heroes in the midst of agonizing conflicts, in which destiny and human fallibility converge to determine changes of fortunes.[23] In *Iphigenie*, the heroine's change of fortune—for the better, even if her victory is painful—is accomplished not only in the succession of scenes, but also in the density of the dialogues, as Ortega suggested.

When Ortega says that "the generic imperative of art ... [is] to be without transcending consequence,"[24] he essentially means that art must be "self-sufficient," that is, that art is first and foremost art, and not something else.[25] Despite their emphasis on the ethical aspect of art, both Goethe and Ortega—in a Kantian fashion, as we have already seen with respect to Goethe—consider that the work of art is a unique statement, different from any other realm of culture, including the ethical.

But as Ortega says, the lack of transcendence is only a general feature that is actualized in the novel in the form of imperviousness.

Goethe's *Iphigenie* certainly entraps the reader in that impervious space, in which it is very hard to identify the reader's everyday reality because the characters are, as Ortega observes with respect to classical drama, "heroes, exalted characters, prototypes of magnanimity";[26] and yet what is being treated in the play is appealing to the reader. True, Goethe develops in *Iphigenie* issues that can be seen, from the classicist's point of view, as being of universal concern, but they are not presented from an "everyday life" point of view because of both the larger-than-life characters involved and the "abstract" (universal) perspective from which the ethical point of view of the play is conceived. In this sense, the distinction between real and fictitious worlds is firmly maintained.

I suggest that classicism, then, is the deepest point of encounter between Goethe and Ortega. Both assume that "the ancient can be more or less immediately relevant and available, in a sense contemporaneous with the modern—or anyway, that its nature is such that it can, by strategies of accommodation, be made so."[27] But as Ortega says, Goethe is the "patrician" among the classics, since he has been sustained by all the classics past.[28] Classics must justify themselves vis-à-vis life, and one of the most powerful ways in which Goethe justifies his presence among the moderns is by passionately believing in the necessity of merging one's own destiny with one's own life, which is, as I have suggested, the main—and eminently modern—theme of *Iphigenie auf Tauris*.

As a critic of modernity, Ortega brings up to date the legacy of Goethe's classical aesthetics and converts them into a form that inspires nothing less than the renewal of the novel for the modern time.[29] By doing so, Ortega can be seen as making the case far earlier than T. S. Eliot for the contemporaneousness of the classic—a contemporaneousness predicated on the belief, as stated by Eliot, "that the modern is not absolutely new, but a renovation of the classic."[30]

Novalis and Unamuno

The notion of historical unity and its echoes,[31] the completed form, and closure of the work of art have traditionally been attached to classicism, and are exemplified by Iphigenia's return home, or by the conclusion of *Wilhelm Meisters Lehrjahre*. As opposed to classicism, romanticism entails fragmentation. Perhaps no other German text illustrates the romantic fragmentary imperative so well as *Heinrich von Ofterdingen* (1802), Novalis's answer to Goethe's foundational *Bildungsroman*, *Wilhelm Meisters Lehrjahre* (1795–96).

In Novalis's *Notebooks* (1802), the author contrasts the romantic character of his novel *Heinrich*—and indeed the romantic novel as subgenre—and Goethe's *Wilhelm Meister*, which he calls a "bürgerlicher Roman" (bourgeois novel). In the romantic novel, says Novalis, the pseudonym of Friedrich von Hardenberg (1772–1801), the writer works with acts and dialogues, with reflections and representations, to create poetry. In novels such as *Wilhelm Meister*, the writer reports on everyday life—illness, clothing, lifestyles, marriage, and so on.[32] In other words, Novalis sees in Goethe's classical Bildungsroman a linear narrative that constitutes a direct and unproblematic representation of life. Novalis is extremely critical of Goethe's novel. In fact, he calls it "a fatal and idiotic book," "pretentious" and "unpoetic." Novalis goes on to acknowledge the writer's effort to "calm down" the reader through an embarrassing reconciliation with bourgeois life after the highly charged and interesting events of the first two parts of the novel. He describes *Wilhelm Meisters Lehrjahre* as a "pilgrimage to the nobility diploma" and calls Goethe's text a *Candide* directed against poetry. On the other hand, Novalis refers to his own "romantic works" as fragmentary and restless. Thus, while Novalis sees in the traditional *Bildungsreise* (educational travel) a clear linearity, an appreciation of well-traveled paths and lives, and, finally, an end that formally and thematically implies a supposedly "ennobling closure," his own romantic writing is poetic because it challenges totality and is thematically and structurally open.[33]

As Azade Seyhan has shown, *Heinrich von Ofterdingen*, which she calls a "novel fragment," "is a configuration of various literary forms which narrate the story of their own historical and formal production."[34] The fragmentation of this novel is the result not only of those diverse literary forms, but also of the constant interpolation of new stories and the repeated shift of temporal and even spatial "representations of reality." In fact, the presence of these stories constitutes a major factor in the creation of romantic poetry: "The tales and fables within the novel constitute, in Schlegel's definition of romantic poetry, the endless series of mirrors that reflect the thematic concerns of the narrative."[35] The novel is divided into two parts, "Die Erwartung" (The Expectation) and "Die Erfüllung" (The Fulfillment). The second part, an oneiric and mysterious fragment, is left unfinished. Indeed, Novalis articulates the text as an unfinished fragment whose structure is prefigured in one of the interpolated stories of the novel. In that specific story—the only one to which I will refer here—Heinrich, in the company of an old and experienced miner, explores a cave. In the last chamber of the cave they find a hermit, Count von Hohenzollern, who has been living there for years. As the count and the miner explore another cave, Heinrich stays in the count's library, looking at books. Heinrich finds a book without a title, written in a language unknown to him. However, in the book there are pictures of people and scenes familiar to Heinrich, which make him feel an irresistible attraction to it. Suddenly, while looking at the pictures, he finds images of different moments and stages of his own life. He even finds himself in the cave with the count and the miner, and then he sees his parents and other figures of his past, along with unknown figures that, we eventually learn, will be part of his future. Saddened by the fact that he cannot understand the book, Heinrich is informed by the count, upon his return from exploring the cave, that it is written in Provençal, and that it narrates the life of a poet and exalts poetic art.

This fragment of *Heinrich* has striking parallels to a Spanish text, *Cómo se hace una novela* (How to Make a Novel, 1927) by Miguel de Unamuno (1864–1936). Before I begin analyzing and drawing conclusions about the implications of Heinrich's story in the cave, I would first like to introduce this extremely complex work by Unamuno. *Cómo se hace una novela*, like *Heinrich von Ofterdingen*, is composed of many fragments. An initial problem relating to its composition is that after Unamuno wrote it while exiled in France, he gave the original to a French friend (Jean Cassou), who translated and published it in French before it could be published in Spanish. The version included in Unamuno's *Obras completas* (1958) is a second translation back into Spanish, by Unamuno himself, of Cassou's translation of the original text. What seems to have lost priority in this chain of translations is the *original* text itself. Thus, *Cómo se hace una novela* exhibits a clear antiteleological nature, since by de-emphasizing the relevance of the original form and exposing itself to different translations (and, as we will see, to many later additions and comments), it valorizes change and open-endedness as the very basis of its own ontology. What we now consider the standard text of *Cómo se hace una novela* consists of the following parts or fragments: a prologue by Unamuno, a portrait of Unamuno by Cassou, a commentary by Unamuno on Cassou's portrait, the text proper of *Cómo se hace una novela*, and a so-called "Continuation" of the text, which, after a few pages, turns into a sort of diary, thus obviously increasing the structural fragmentation of the text. To this accumulation of forms and fragments, we must add the commentaries that Unamuno progressively added as he was translating Cassou's own translation. Therefore, like the German romantics, Unamuno demonstrates in his writings, and especially in *Cómo se hace una novela*, a particular affinity with the fragment.

If we focus on the section entitled "Cómo se hace una novela" alone, we observe first of all that it is divided into formal fragments. In addition, the text constantly shifts through a fragmented articulation from the writer's present-day existence to his comments on many issues, including poetry, the indivisibility of literature and life, the conflict between his public self and his private self, Spain's political situation under the dictatorship of Primo de Rivera, and the miseries of living in exile. One of the narrative lines in this text is the story of U. Jugo de la Raza: U. (Unamuno) Jugo (last name of Unamuno's maternal grandfather) de la Raza (play of words on "Larraza," the last name of Unamuno's paternal grandmother); the translation of this last name in Spanish would be "Juice of the Race."[36] U. Jugo de la Raza, then, is an alias for the writer himself, Unamuno. And yet, given the nature of the character's experience in the text, most human beings could potentially identify themselves with Jugo de la Raza.

As Jugo strolls one day by the bank of the river Seine in Paris, where even today one can see the used bookstalls, he browses through a book at a stall and begins reading it. Jugo feels from the very first moment a very powerful attraction toward this book, a novel—"a romantic autobiographical confession."[37] As he reads, he begins to realize that the novel is providing him with a sense of purpose, a sort of existential project for his own life. Suddenly, he falls upon these words: "When the reader comes to the end of this painful story he will die with me."[38] Thus, just as he begins to feel "alive" (for at the beginning we are told that before he starts reading the book, he "is beset with a sovereign ennui"),[39] Jugo de la Raza develops an awareness of death: as a result of *reading* the book, death appears on the horizon, and he is faced with his own mortality. After reading the words, Jugo experiences the existential fear that both Martin Heidegger (1889–1976) and Unamuno call "anxiety" (*Sein und Zeit* and *Cómo se hace una novela* were written the same year), and, terrified, he drops the book and runs away from the bookstall. But from that moment on, he lives his life in agony: "Poor Jugo de la Raza could not live without the book, without that book. His life, his inner existence, his reality, his true reality was now definitively and irrevocably joined to that of the central figure of the novel. If he continued reading it, living it, he ran the risk of dying when the central figure of the novel died. But if he did not read any further, if he did not live the book any longer, would he live at all?"[40]

For a while, Jugo resists the temptation of buying and reading the book, although he is convinced that he will eventually acquire it. In fact, Jugo does end up purchasing the novel, and once at home, as he continues reading, the character of the book repeats to him, "I must tell my reader again that he will die with me."[41] Jugo faints. When he wakes up, he burns the book and then falls asleep. In the morning, as he contemplates the ashes of the book, he feels tormented, since now he will never know the end of the story, and he finds himself condemned to wonder about the end of the/his story for the rest of his life.

As we are beginning to see, the tale of the cave in *Heinrich von Ofterdingen* and the story of Jugo in *Cómo se hace una novela* share many important elements. First, both *Heinrich von Ofterdingen* and *Cómo se hace una novela* consist of a book within a book; in each case, the "outer" book is made up of fragments and has no end, while the "inner book" constitutes one of those fragments and does not have an end either. Thus, the inner book prefigures the structure of the outer book in both instances, serving as its mirror. Neither of the inner books has a title, and they are both autobiographies. The Provençal book deals with Heinrich's life and his education to become a poet. As I have mentioned, the book that Jugo de la Raza reads is considered "a romantic autobiographical confession." Furthermore, according to Unamuno, living is the task of forging oneself as a poet. As Lacoue-Labarthe and Nancy state, "What makes an individual ... is the 'systasis' that produces it. What makes its individuality is its capacity to produce, and to produce itself, first of all, by means of its internal 'formative force'"; likewise, they add from the *Athenäum*, "every man should be a poet."[42] In the same way, Unamuno believes that a human being must become a reflection of God as creator in the experience of existence.[43] The Provençal book leaves Heinrich ignorant about the specifics of how to become a poet, since he cannot read Provençal, and yet, through images, he is clearly informed about the chance that life is giving him to become one. It will be his exclusive responsibility to actualize that chance as an individual. The same can be said about *Cómo se hace una novela*, since Jugo reads only the portion or portions of the book that will make him aware of his own existence as a "project," as the chance to become a poet. Burning the book is a confirmation that what defines human life (in the case of *Cómo se hace una novela*, the life of Jugo de la Raza) is the possibility of becoming who one is—that is, who one can become: a poet. In the mysterious experience of life, this process is defined as much by its open-endedness as by death.

Finally, the burning of the book of life in *Cómo se hace una novela* makes the information contained in it inaccessible to Jugo, and the fact that the book in *Heinrich* is not only unfinished but also in Provençal, and thus incomprehensible to Heinrich, points to the impossibility of representing reality, either past, present, or future. Hints of that reality are made briefly available in the lines that Jugo reads in the "book of life," or in the images that Heinrich sees—all fragments. They are also present for us, as readers of *Cómo se hace una novela* and *Heinrich von Ofterdingen*, but in a similarly fragmentary way, the only way in which the romantics thought representation was possible. This similarity between Novalis's and Unamuno's texts leads to the conclusion that in both works, representation is defined by an infinite postponement in its pursuit to capture reality, the reality of Heinrich's and Jugo's *lives*—even if the two texts are powerful enough to provoke immense excitement in both characters (in the case of the latter, it even takes him out of his "sovereign ennui").

The distance between experience and representation makes these texts, insofar as they attempt to represent life, allegories. As Seyhan suggests, "allegory signifies an approximation ... the absence of an ultimate referent in terms of concept and time and recover[s] it [the referent] only as poetic representation."[44] In my own reading of *Heinrich von Ofterdingen* and *Cómo se hace una novela*, representation is posed first and foremost at the level of *human life*: the characters are not allowed to access the representation of their lives, a denial that symbolizes the impossibility of representation itself. Their lives are an open, blank book, upon which only experience can write in an intelligible language. Now it is up to them to fulfill their destinies. From this perspective, both the story of the cave in *Heinrich von Ofterdingen* and *Como se hace una novela* are allegories not so much in a purely romantic sense, which pursues the "representation of an intercepted infinity,"[45] but in a postmodern sense, because their always postponed object of representation can exist only in the empirical world. Whereas in the romantic allegory of Schlegel, the impossibility of representation occurs vis-à-vis the absolute, in postmodern allegory, representation never refers to any absolute but only to the reality of human beings and/or nature. Thus, Novalis's and Unamuno's texts can be considered postmodern allegories, and it is here where the two authors' works converge in a connection highly relevant to contemporary critical concerns.[46]

Classic/Romantic; Modernity/Postmodernity

Underlying the idea of romanticism informing my study is Schlegel's notion that the romantic poet creates his or her own laws in order to accomplish the textual construction that we call representation. The process of creation versus discovery undertaken by the romantic poet carries within its implied world-view a sense of becoming and open-endedness (fragmentation) that is at odds with the atemporal foundation of the classical text (whose essence takes precedence over the activity of its author). That is why in my treatment of Novalis and Unamuno, I have focused on the paradigmatic figures of this open-endedness: the fragment and allegory. Romantic open-endedness is largely prefigured by Kant's distinction between determinative and reflective judgments in the *Critique of Judgment*. For Kant, whereas determinate judgments formulate objective criteria—a fundamental tenet of classicism—reflective judgments propose unregimented operations or transgressive constructions—activities closely aligned with romanticism—and constitute features of what can be termed the "romantic paradigm."[47] This paradigm—a phenomenon not fully developed here—can be understood as a precursor of postmodernism, a world-view associated with a lack of constitutive metaphysics, an abandonment of the will to find the true nature of things, and a rejection of the rational argumentation operative in Kant's determinative judgments. These are the very features embodied by allegory, as seen in Novalis and Unamuno.

In contrast, the "classical paradigm" asserts order, extratemporal truth, reason, universality, certainty, transparency, and natural order. Furthermore, classicism understands these notions as not only relevant, but also, as previously stated, eternally available. This is why for the modern classicist—that is, the modernist—modernity is not only an incomplete project, but a project that *cannot* be completed. Thus, Ortega's recovery of Goethe's classicism only prefigures the never-ending retrieval of an atemporal legacy whose linearity is believed by classicists, as well as by modernists like Ortega himself, to be endless.

Notes

1. Frank Kermode, *The Classic* (Cambridge, Mass., 1983), p. 18.
2. José Ortega y Gasset, *Obras completas* (Madrid, 1987), vol. 4, p. 398.
3. Stuart Atkins, "On Goethe's Classicism," *Goethe Proceedings: Essays Commemorating the Goethe Sesquicentennial at the University of California, Davis*, ed. Clifford Bernd and Timothy Lulofs (Columbia, S.C., 1984), p. 12. Goethe's main works in the classical tradition are *Egmont, Iphigenie auf Tauris, Torquato Tasso, Faust,* and *Wilhelm Meister Lehrjahre*. According to Jenkins, Goethe's classicism is already perceptible before his travels in Italy. See Sylvia P. Jenkins, ed., *Iphigenie auf Tauris* (London, 1958), p. xv.
4. Liselotte Dieckmann, *Johann Wolfgang Goethe* (New York, 1974), p. 98.
5. But if the validity of the tenets maintained in the classical work of art transcend time and become transcultural, their universality seems, paradoxically, aimed at a selected audience. This was Goethe's case, but, on the other hand, the immutability of general principles that constitute the classical world-view clashes with Goethe's challenges to the already established taste among his audience. See Atkins, "On Goethe's Classism," p. 8.
6. Ibid., pp. 9–10.
7. John Prudhoe, "Introduction," *Iphigenie in Tauris* (Manchester, 1966), p. xxiii. The following are Pylades' words to Iphigenia in the same edition, p. 54:

    Stern purity was yours within this temple,
    But life persuades us we must deal more gently
    Both with ourselves and others! You will learn it.
    Humanity is fashioned with such wonder,
    So subtly interwoven, so conjoined,
    That no man lives, alone or in society,
    Untainted and uncompromised. The gods
    Did not appoint us judges of ourselves.
    Our duty, first and last, is to proceed
    Along the immediate ways we can determine.
    Rarely can man evaluate the past,
    Never, perhaps, judge rightly of the present.

8. I am citing Wilhelm Windelband through Ernst Cassirer, *The Philosophy of the Enlightenment*, trans. Fritz Koelln and James Pettegrove (Princeton, 1968), p. 278.
9. Cited in W. H. Walsh, "Kant," *The Encyclopedia of Philosophy*, ed. Paul Edwards (New York, 1972), vol. 4, p. 319. This does not mean that Alexander Gottlieb Baumgarten did not exercise a great deal of influence over Goethe's aesthetics, as Ernst Cassirer affirms in his *The Philosophy of the Enlightenment*, pp. 345, 351. However, the differentiation between the realm of aesthetics and any other realm is clear in Goethe, as shown in his *Leipzig Song Book*, where he points out that under the microscope, the scientist finds out the "objective nature" of a dragonfly, but its aesthetic dimension is totally lost. Thus, we find in Cassirer, *Philosophy*, pp. 344–345:

    Fluttering the fountain nigh
    The iridescent dragonfly
    An hour mine eye has dwelt upon;
    Now dark, now light alternately
    Like the chameleon;

> Now red, now blue,
> Now blue, now green:
> How would its hues appear
> If one could but come near!
> It flits and hovers, resting not—
> Hush! on a willow bough it lights;
> I have it in my fingers caught,
> And now I seek its colors true,
> and find a melancholy blue—
> Such is thy lot, dissector of delights!

10. T. J. Reed, *Goethe* (Oxford, 1984), p. 54.
11. The relation between Ortega and Cohen, with regard to aesthetics, is treated by Ciriaco M. Arroyo, *El sistema de Ortega y Gasset* (Madrid, 1968), pp. 365–368.
12. Ortega's writings on Goethe are divided among his "Goethe desde dentro" ("Goethe from Within," 1932) and his lectures in Aspen, Colorado, and in Germany on the bicentennial of Goethe's birth in 1949. Although it would be lengthy to elaborate on the content of these writings, I will point out that they essentially deal with (1) Goethe's idea of personality (*Persönlichkeit*); (2) Goethe's notion that culture must serve the fulfillment of human life, and not the opposite; and (3) what Ortega considers "the great Goethian task" for Europe—a Europe most definitely in crisis in 1949—namely, to learn about human limitations and to build a future based on resignation (*Entsagung*). See Ortega y Gasset, *Obras completas*, vol. 4, pp. 383–428; and vol. 9, pp. 551–608.
13. Ortega is also the author of *El tema de nuestro tiempo* (The Modern Theme), a philosophical manifesto of the avant-garde, and of *La deshumanización del arte* (The Dehumanization of Art), in which, as Ortega says, he "attempts" to understand and explain the tenets of avant-garde art.
14. José Ortega y Gasset, *The Dehumanization of Art and Notes on the Novel*, trans. Helene Weil (Princeton, 1948), pp. 60–62.
15. Ibid., p. 66.
16. Ibid., pp. 91–92.
17. Ibid., p. 93.
18. Ibid., p. 67. My italics.
19. Ibid., p. 69.
20. Ibid.
21. Ibid., p. 73.
22. Dieckmann, *Johann Wolfgang Goethe*, p. 32.
23. This "art of figures" is opposed not only to Spanish theater of the Golden Age, an art of "action," but also to romance. For more about Ortega's conception of the novel vis-à-vis romance, see my "Pío Baroja y el retorno del *romance*: hacia una textualidad posmoderna," *Letras Peninsulares*, vol. 2, no. 1 (1996), pp. 93–115. Ortega praises the sluggishness of Dostoevski's novels, which is accomplished through the use of the classical unities: "The concentration of the plot in time and space, so characteristic of Dostoevski's technique, brings to mind, in an unexpected sense, the venerable *unities of classical tragedy*" (emphasis added). He also understands Dostoevski's art according to a poetics closer to the Enlightenment than to romanticism; for him, Dostoevski was not a "genius" but "a conscientious craftsman." See Ortega, *The Dehumanization of Art*, pp. 76–77.
24. Ibid., p. 93.

25. The novel has its own reality, different from the reality of the reader in the empirical world, and that reality may contain, as Ortega says, sociology, psychology, anthropology, etc., as long as they are "ultimately derealized and confined within the inner world of the novel; i.e., if it remains without actual and effective validity." Ibid., p. 103.
26. Ibid., p. 69.
27. Kermode, *The Classic*, pp. 15–16.
28. Ortega, *Obras Completas*, vol. 4, p. 398.
29. In my interpretation of Goethe's and Ortega's classicism, Ortega makes Goethe's legacy more relevant to modernity—and in a more conscious way than, for instance, Bertolt Brecht, in spite of Brecht's interest in Sophocles. See Brecht on classicism in *Brecht on Theater* (New York, 1994), pp. 181–182 and pp. 272–273.
30. Cited in Kermode, *The Classic*, p. 20.
31. Ibid.
32. Novalis, *Schriften*, ed. Richard Samuel, vol. 3 (Stuttgart, 1960), p. 649. The translation from the *Notebooks* is mine.
33. Ibid., p. 647.
34. Azade Seyhan, *Representation and Its Discontents: The Critical Legacy of German Romanticism* (Berkeley, Calif., 1992), p. 116.
35. Ibid., pp. 118–119.
36. This would be the translation provided the word "jugo" were Spanish (which in this case it is not, since it is Basque). However, it seems clear that the play on words is intended to mean "Juice of the Race."
37. Miguel de Unamuno, *How to Make a Novel*, trans. Anthony Kerrigan (Princeton, 1976), p. 421.
38. Ibid., p. 422.
39. Ibid., p. 420.
40. Ibid., p. 423.
41. Ibid., p. 427.
42. Philippe Lacoue-Labarthe and Jean-Luc Nancy, *The Literary Absolute: The Theory of Literature in German Romanticism*, trans. Philip Barnard and Cheryl Lester (Albany, N.Y., 1988), p. 49.
43. Miguel de Unamuno, *Obras completas* (Madrid, 1958), vol. 9, pp. 419–420.
44. Seyhan, *Representation and Its Discontents*, p. 67.
45. Ibid., p. 67.
46. According to Paul de Man, "it remains necessary if there is going to be allegory, that the allegorical refer to another sign that precedes it. The meaning constituted by the allegorical sign can then consist only in the *repetition* ... of a previous sign with which it can never coincide, since it is of the essence of this previous sign to be pure anteriority" (emphasis de Man). Later he adds that "allegory designates primarily a *distance in relation to its own origin, and, renouncing the nostalgia and the desire to coincide*, it establishes its language in the void of this temporal difference. In so doing, it prevents the self from an illusory identification with the nonself" (emphasis added); Paul de Man, *Blindness and Insight* (Minneapolis, 1983), p. 207.
47. For more discussion of the distinction between judgments in Kant and what I call the romantic and the classical paradigms, see Richard Rorty, "Nineteenth-Century Idealism and Twentieth-Century Textualism," *The Monist*, vol. 64 (1981), p. 158.

– 13 –

THE FAME OF MIGUEL DE UNAMUNO IN GERMANY

Its Growth and Decline, 1924–1930

Shirley King

A Story of Exile

In the Café de la Rotonde in Paris, famous as a modern international Bohemia, "are forever the same youth, full of hope, lacking all hope, the same ones who believe they will conquer the century with cubism and jazz and free love."[1] So it was explained by Ivan Goll on the last day of December 1924. "At the far end of the café," Goll wrote, "for a few weeks, many of the little round marble tables have been pulled together to form a single one, and so the Spanish table was created. The quiet old man with golden glasses, and a pointed trim little beard, who seemed to feel very comfortable in this society," was Miguel de Unamuno, surrounded every day by "a troop of black-haired, wildly effervescent, loudly laughing young people."[2]

In the above article, Goll identified Don Miguel de Unamuno (1864–1936) as "the greatest living poet and novelist of Spain, the current national martyr."[3] Unamuno was described as excitedly hitting the table with his hand, laughing like the youngest student in his entourage, and wearing a small, formless felt cap on his head. "One wonders," questioned Goll, "is that a university president, … the man whom the entire world honors as the strongest revolutionary against the sword of a general?... From Paris, Unamuno conducts his fight,"[4] wrote Goll, and he said that the Spanish dictator and general, Miguel Primo de Rivera, dubbed here "the Modern Inquisitor," was "biting his fingernails."

Originally from the northern coastal town of Bilbao in the Basque country, Unamuno had risen to the position of president of the University of Salamanca. He had earned a reputation in Spain as the boldest of critics. For years, he had made his voice heard by repeatedly publishing newspaper articles critical of education, religion, and politics. It was for being so outspoken about politics in particular that Unamuno had been exiled from Spain by the Spanish dictator and general Miguel Primo de Rivera (1870–1930), who sent him to Fuerteventura in the isolated Canary Islands off the northwest coast of Africa. From there Unamuno fled to France, where he arrived in July 1924. Unamuno was also not a silent observer in France. The newly recognized Spanish celebrity continued to criticize his government and his king—so strongly that dictator Primo was provoked into answering him in an open letter in *Le Quotidien*.

In October, Unamuno had spoken at a meeting of the Club de Faubourg de Montmartre in the Theatre de la Fourni in northern Paris. This was reported in the *Weltbühne*.[5] Ignaz Wrobel (a.k.a. Kurt Tucholsky) retold in this article the story of Unamuno's fleeing Spain and of the island, "which surely would have brought him death." Don Miguel, speaking softly, delivered his speech in French and switched to Spanish when foreign words failed him. Some well-known characters of the day were present. The majority of the audience was made up of what the writer called "Latins." Most reacted positively to Unamuno's political attitude, but Tucholsky questioned whether anyone besides the "Latins" understood his point of view. The journalist reflected upon how the "intelligentsia" (*Gelehrtenköpfe*) of Germany might compare with the crowd he saw there, in the way they think as well as in their public behavior. He asked himself rhetorically, "Who worries about Unamuno in Germany, and about foreign problems? Who knows about that?"[6]

Indeed, who worried about Unamuno in Germany? It is not difficult to see, from the concentration of articles about Unamuno beginning around March 1924, that his exile was the cause of his sudden recognition in Germany. Gerhart Hoffmeister called him a "European figure ever since his exile in Hendaye" ("figura europea desde su exilio en Hendaya"),[7] and the now famous epithet of E. R. Curtius, "*Excitator Hispaniae*," reflects Unamuno's reputation in

Germany as the Spaniard with the fiery personality.[8] An article in the Buenos Aires paper *Nosotros* said, "The list of notes or references published in Germany about Unamuno and his difficulties with the administration would be very long."[9] However, references to Unamuno's exile normally did not deal with Unamuno's own literary merit or philosophy, but rather with his political image.

All of Unamuno's works that were eventually translated into German had been written before his 1924 exile, with the exception of *La agonía del cristianismo* (The Agony of Christianity), published in Paris, and the play *El otro* (The Other), which, because of its low budget and poor management, had a very short and unsuccessful stage history. So what the German public would read of Don Miguel even after 1924 would be "old news," and only a partial representation of his personality and views. German readers did not have access to what amounted to an enormous proportion of his literary production, namely the hundreds of newspaper articles per year he sent on a daily basis to Spanish-language publications. The Unamuno that the Spanish public knew was a man physically isolated, teaching Greek in an ancient university, yet still able to make his voice boom throughout the country with intense and unrelenting criticism of institutions considered sacred, from educational to governmental to religious. Although there is much evidence to suggest that his novels and major works were read in Germany, only a handful of German reactions to his abundant newspaper essays in the Spanish language can be found. The contributions he did make to larger journals in Germany were few.[10]

The following will outline the translations of works by Miguel de Unamuno into the German language. There were five articles on socialism and Spain appearing in *Der Sozialistische Akademiker* between February 1895 and November 1897, and then there was nothing until November 1915, when a submission of Unamuno entitled "Das geistige Spanien und Deutschland" appeared in *Der Neue Merkur*. Over five years later, "Spaniens Philosophie" was printed in *Wissen und Leben* (1 February and 15 February 1921). Unamuno, an exceedingly prolific writer in Spain, was nearly sixty years old before a book-length manuscript was to appear on the German market. This occurred in October 1924, when *Ein ganzer Mann* or *Nada menos que todo un hombre* (Nothing Less Than a Complete Man) was scheduled in the first issue of a publication entitled *Uhu*. It was in that same month that the German firm Meyer & Jessen received from the Spanish author the rights to all German translations of his works and set themselves to the task of getting them published. In the week of 22 November 1924, three of

Unamuno's novels appeared in major German newspapers. A year later, three independent volumes were released (*Das tragische Lebensgefühl* [*Del sentimiento trágico de la vida* or *The Tragic Sense of Life*], *Abel Sánchez*, and *Der Spiegel des Todes* [*El espejo de la muerte* or *The Mirror of Death*, containing *Tres novelas ejemplares* or *Three Exemplary Novels*]). A few months following, between 28 May and 14 April 1926, *Das Leben Don Quijotes und Sanchos* (*La vida de don Quijote y Sancho* or *The Life of Don Quixote and Sancho*) and *Nebel* (*Niebla* or *Fog*) came out. Over the course of the next four years, two more works were printed, *Tante Tula* (*La tía Tula* or *Aunt Tula*) and *Frieden im Krieg* (*Paz en la guerra* or *Peace in War*), and by April of 1931, two of his plays were performed on German stages: *Nothing Less Than a Complete Man* in Berlin, Osnabrück, and Hamburg, and *The Other* as a radio play in Leipzig. From what the available documents can tell us, these works all became known to the German reading public during a span of seven years, between his 1924 exile and a year after his return to Spain.

On Unamuno's homecoming to Spain on 9 February 1930, there were reports of some five thousand people at the Hendaye/Irún border, and twenty thousand in Bilbao, waiting to greet the returned exile. This activity sparked a series of articles in major European papers. The *Berliner Tageblatt* ran six front-page articles in the month of February alone with Miguel de Unamuno as the central figure. This Berlin paper sent its correspondent to Salamanca for a personal interview.[11] Mr. Joel told his German readers of Don Miguel's plans for the future. Reportedly, the Spanish professor was to be offered a place at the university in Madrid, and he planned to refuse, fighting for his right to his former position in Salamanca.

Articles in other papers were near facsimiles of the information in Joel's report. Close observation was made of Unamuno for a few weeks until the storm died down, then relatively little attention was paid in Germany to the Spanish writer. There was occasional mention of the political noise he was making, but media attention quickly turned to other momentous events taking place in Europe in the l930s.

Unamuno's German Journal Publications

Unamuno was not averse to being in the limelight, but he was selective. For example, in late April 1928, Albert Theile, the editor of *Die Böttcherstraße*, sent a letter to Miguel de Unamuno at the Hotel Broca in Hendaye requesting a ten- to fifteen-page unpublished manuscript for inclusion in the new magazine. *Die Böttcherstraße* was a publication dedicated to fine literature and the arts and was associated with Worpswede, the artists' colony that still thrives outside the city of Bremen. Again in June, a similar request came along with a copy of the first issue, for which Jaime Ibarra had written a short article introducing Unamuno to the journal's readers; however, no article from Unamuno was ever included in this magazine. This was not the first time—nor the last—that he would be asked for a contribution to a German journal. Evidence of some of these requests exists in Unamuno's library, for instance, letters from the following individuals and organizations: (1) Paul Feldkeller (publisher), 30 April 1923, *Reichls Philosophischer Almanach*, Schönewalde bei Berlin; (2) Leo Stahl, 16 December 1924, *Frankfurter Zeitung*, special Christmas issue; (3) *Die Laterne*, 21 January 1926, Berlin; (4) Max Hochdorf (editor), 13 May 1927, *Europa-Magazin. Illustrierte Weltrevue für Wissen und Unterhaltung*, Berlin; (5) Dr. Ernst Leopold Stahl (theatrical scholar and dramatist), 2 July 1928, *Das Prisma*, Berlin; (6) Inés E. Manz (freelance journalist), 22 November 1929, 15 July 1930, 8 November 1930, Munich; (7) Victor Wittner, 25 April 1930, *Der Querschnitt*, Berlin; (8) Harold Braun (editor), 16 April 1931, *Eckart*, Berlin; (9) Walter Küchler (institute director), 4 November 1931, Institut für Romanische Sprachen und Kultur, Hamburg; (10) 1932 and 1934, *Brockhaus Encyclopedie*, Leipzig (there was consequently no entry for Miguel de Unamuno in the 1932 and 1934 editions of this reference work); and (11) Ria Schmidt-Koch, 28 February 1935, Pädagogisches Seminar der Universität Berlin (Sociedad Kantiana). Rarely did Unamuno comply with such requests. This is also reminiscent of the contacts attempted by different publishing houses that wanted to translate his works into German.

It is a little surprising to note to which papers Unamuno did, in fact, send articles. According to letters he received, he seemed to ignore requests from better known journals in favor of papers like *Der Sozialistische Akademiker* (1895) and *Eiserne Blätter*, both publications of "alternative politics" with limited readership.[12] It is clear where Unamuno's priorities lay, but one begins to question his judgment as far as the quality of his choices is concerned. Certainly, his expressed goal of reaching people in other countries in order to diffuse his political opinions would have been better served had he more carefully targeted publications that were apt to reach a greater number of readers.

While enduring his exile in Paris, Unamuno busily wrote articles to the French press—one outlet still available to him. When he was invited by Paul Medina of Ernst Rowohlt Publishing Company to contribute to a special issue of the journal *Die Literarische Welt* in honor of the anniversary of Goethe's birth, he decided to comply.[13] In the October 1925 issue of this weekly magazine, Unamuno shared a page with Paul Valéry, Pierre Mac Orlan, Max Jacob, and Thomas Mann.[14] The question all were invited to answer was, "For what are you indebted to the German spirit?" ("Was verdanken Sie dem deutschen Geist?"). Perhaps the fact that Unamuno was invited to participate is more significant than what he wrote. In his lengthy answer, Unamuno decided that it was in fact the German language he had most to thank. He said that he did not know exactly what the "German spirit" was, and moreover, he was as skeptical of the idea of a national spirit as he was of the notion of race.

How curious this statement might seem to a reader who has stumbled through *The Life of Don Quixote and Sancho* or *En torno al casticismo* (On Racial Purity)! Unamuno's own concept of *casticismo* implied a "pure Spanishness." His term *intrahistory*, meaning culture at its simplest or the basis of culture, indicated that he did, indeed, believe in a national spirit and race. This leaves little question that there existed for him something like a national spirit. The contradiction presented in this German article might be explained by the whimsical advantage that Unamuno often assumed: that by attempting to shorten the distance between the "German" spirit and the "Spanish," he conveniently appeared more European, which was his goal in this case. And in other instances, when he wanted to show Spain as separate and equal to, or better than, the rest of Europe, he could be just as divisional and "Spanish-spirited."

Language, he wrote in *Die Literarische Welt*, is the lifeblood of what we call the spirit, adding confidently, "could I not read German, I would not dare to say what I have to thank the German spirit for, no matter how many German works I had read in translation."[15] The play with prefixes and suffixes in the German language, he theorized, makes possible a continuity and a shifting from one idea to another, thereby enabling ideas to move into formations of thoughts. This notion is compatible with his theory of the impossibility of thought without language, as expounded, for example, in *The Tragic Sense of Life*. He was of the opinion, however, that the necessarily abstract roots in German makes it difficult to express something concrete. "But," he rambled characteristically, "what is abstract and what is concrete? Does one arrive at more concreteness through language?"[16] Finally, at the end of this piece, he noted that he was dependent upon translators because his ability in German was not sufficient to write the article!

Unamuno's Climb to Literary Fame in Germany

Don Miguel's first German book translations were about to be released in November 1925, when Ernst Robert Curtius (1886–1956) published his article "Unamuno oder die Philosophie des Tragischen" ("Unamuno or the Philosophy of the Tragic") in the *Neue Zürcher Zeitung*.[17] This was probably the first German-language newspaper article that discussed Unamuno's works in a scholarly way, not playing on his publicity but rather extolling his literary accomplishments. E. R. Curtius, the Heidelberg historian, along with Hermann Bahr (1863–1934), one of the leading literary personalities in turn-of-the-century Vienna, probably did more than anyone else to bring the young Spanish generation of writers closer to literary Germany.[18] Curtius published numerous articles on Unamuno and books about Spanish literature. In the essay at hand, he chose to write about *On Racial Purity* as the definitive work that represents Unamuno's philosophical viewpoint. The article concentrated on this work exclusively, notwithstanding the fact that *On Racial Purity*, thirty years old by that time, was not one of the translations that were shortly to go to press. This fact may either eliminate or reinforce the possibility that the article was simply propaganda to advertise Unamuno's works.

Unamuno had become a celebrity, but he was still relatively unknown to Germans as a man of letters. The Madrid correspondent for the *Berliner Tageblatt* revealed just how unknown he was. He explained in his December 1925 report that the first editions of the works of Unamuno in German were being released by Meyer & Jessen, and that this publisher had sent him copies of the works with a request for an article, "telling what there was to tell about this Spaniard."[19] In other words, the page on Unamuno in Germany was blank. It is difficult to say whether this journalist left his readers with a clearer understanding and appreciation of our writer, or just muddied the waters, for he wrote, "Thank God that Unamuno is finally being translated. I have tried three times to tackle him, and have given up each time—so atrociously irritable ("scrub-brushy") is the Spanish that he writes."[20] He concluded that one probably must be a Spaniard to find pleasure in Unamuno's harshness.

And so 1925 came to an end. Unamuno had been out of Spain for more than a year and a half, and three of his works had been translated into German and published under their own cover. According to figures provided to Unamuno by Meyer & Jessen, sales of his novellas in German by the end of the first quarter of 1926 totaled around one thousand copies each for the three works in the five months' time after their releases.[21] Aside from payment for these volumes, the records show that Unamuno had already received from Meyer & Jessen several hundred German marks for his articles published in various German newspapers.

Four months later, in April 1926, *Der Querschnitt* ran a special issue of articles by and about influential Spanish personalities. Unamuno, however, was not mentioned in the issue, which included writings of Ramón Pérez de Ayala, Luis Araquistaín, José Ortega y Gasset, José Martínez Ruiz, Federico García Lorca, and Manuel Machado, among others, and also articles about Juan Gris, Miguel Primo de Rivera, important Spanish families, and even bullfighting and Spanish dancers.[22] To leave Unamuno out of an edition so expressly devoted to contemporary Spanish writers was indicative of an ignorance of his scholarship and his importance on the stage of world literature.

By 1927, Miguel de Unamuno had already been in France for over two years. The novelty of his exile had worn off. His collected works had been translated, sales had peaked, but the book-signing trips he had promised to make to Germany had never materialized, and his publisher, Meyer & Jessen, had not been able to make arrangements adequately or timely enough in getting his plays onto German stages. The German media did not know what to do with an exiled Spanish author in France whose situation was not changing, and who apparently had said all he was about to say for a while.

The first series of articles in Germany about Unamuno had centered on the adventurous aspects of his experiences: his daring escape from the Spanish island of Fuerteventura by boat at night, his public fight for justice, and the personal hardships of his existence as an exile. Antonina Vallentin remarked that the description of his flight, the details of which one awaited anxiously, was like an episode from Karl May or an adventure film.[23] Our longing for adventure (*Abenteuersehnsucht*) wants fulfillment. "Don Quixote lives," she professed, "in spite of all the Primo de Riveras."[24] Unamuno was at first a heroic underdog figure in the public eye. Then, after his literary creations were translated, he became recognized as an author, and later special interest groups began to study his unique philosophical viewpoint. Not only did Miguel de Unamuno's banishment from Spain put him in the public eye in Germany, but his exile, to no small degree, also brought Spanish problems into world view.

Politics or Religion?

From his exile, Don Miguel published *The Agony of Christianity* (1925) in French, which was soon after translated into German as *Die Agonie des Christentums*. Years later, after his return to Spain, it would be printed in Spanish. The work's theme, of interest to a wider audience in Spain, attracted in Germany only certain journals of a religious nature, minor publications directed toward limited, specific audiences. Documented by letters now in Don Miguel's estate, several of these smaller journals solicited Unamuno's input on the topic of *Unsterblichkeit*, or immortality. This was, at the time, a subject of great concern—even a stylish one—in such magazines.

Other smaller journals, on the lookout for either a dissenting viewpoint or an ultraconservative opinion, welcomed the diversion of a popular Spanish exile preaching social and religious reform. Unamuno's submission of March 1927 to the journal *Individualität*, entitled "A Guide to Meditation for the Festival of Resurrection," along with *The Agony of Christianity*, earned him recognition in quite a number of reviews. Here was a niche created for Unamuno. He added fuel to their kindled religious fire, and his controversial and contradictory pages kept them warm for a few years to come. These journals obviously belong in a separate category from the articles in well-known publications read by the general public, for example, the *Vossische Zeitung* or *Berliner Tageblatt*.

One might expect to find Unamuno among those Spaniards whose existential leanings found some affinity in Germany. Existentialism, however, was for the most part not a term associated with Unamuno in that country in the 1920s. In fact, in a 1928 article by Dr. Otto Forst de Battaglia about Spanish literature, the subject comes up (with a group of other "-isms"), but Unamuno's name is not mentioned. Instead, the aging Salamanca University president is listed among what were then called the "new youth" of Spain (those who dealt with questions of the influence of the war experience on society), along with Blasco Ibáñez, Benito Pérez Galdós, Pío Baroja, and Ramón del Valle Inclán.[25] The recognition Unamuno earned through these publications did not always result in favorable criticism. As a rule, there were no middle-of-the-road opinions on Unamuno; one article would be wildly in favor, another highly negative, though enthusiasm seems to have been strongest in special-interest publications.

In *Der Gral*, a journal dedicated to matters of religious philosophy, critic Friedrich Mackermann expressed sharp criticism of both Miguel de Unamuno and his work *The Agony of Christianity*, typical of the reactions that appeared in this type of alternative publication.[26] Mackermann called the work an "unrefreshing mixture of mysticism and dialectic," the inspiration for which being completely unoriginal. Mackermann stood up against the powerful *Vossische Zeitung* in a recent issue of which Unamuno was dubbed "the greatest European writer of world renown." "Or," Mackermann questioned, "are non-science, lack of logic, unoriginality, thoroughly confusing mysticisms really the characteristics which assure world renown today?"[27]

Another journalist, Rudolf Pick-Seewart, wrote an article praising Unamuno almost to the point of idolatry.[28] The critic simplified and probably misunderstood Unamuno's main and all-consuming question to be, why is the individual not happy? Pick-Seewart's answer: because he does not believe in personal salvation. He deduced that Unamuno's great discovery was that Western Europeans needed "religion" desperately. This article is reminiscent of a certain percentage of the fan mail Don Miguel received from Germans who were in awe of his studies and had become very inspired by his "philosophy."[29] They had fallen in love with what they thought to be an exclusively religious message. Unamuno's *Tragic Sense of Life*, to which Pick-Seewart referred specifically, had to do with the author's difficulty in believing in immortality. The religious agony of Unamuno arose from his struggle between logic and desire: a logic he believed dictated that life is an end in itself, and a desire for an eternal continuation of the human spirit. But it was also about his struggle to maintain his deep faith in Spain, the homeland he could not abandon, but which in his view seemed to have abandoned itself.

Philosophie und Leben dedicated an entire issue in 1926 to the problem of immortality. The journal's editor, August Messer, discussed Unamuno's theories, striking them down here and there, with points of contradiction. Messer emphasized that Unamuno "engaged himself in feeling," which is rooted in desire and is not logical. According to Messer, Unamuno made a caricature out of reason in his fight against so-called rationalism and intellectualism, but, he said, this was really only a "fight against windmills."

Don Miguel should not have told Messer, "I just don't want to die. No, I don't want it, and neither do I want to want it. I want to live forever, and ever, and ever. And I want to live as the same poor 'I,' as the 'I' that I feel here and now."[30] Messer found this naive confession "deserving of thanks" and "psychologically interesting," but thought reality would pay no attention to the desire for everlasting life of "an Unamuno." He labeled Don Miguel an irrational philosopher with his whining, his feelings, his intuiting, his fighting for his conviction with rhetoric, and his unwillingness to concede that his ideas could be disproved or to search for truth together with his opponent. The journalist had the feeling that Unamuno's fight was becoming a kind of sport, one which he played in all seriousness.

Further on the subject of immortality, reference was made to Unamuno as arrogant and godforsaken. Kurt Krippendorf implied that Unamuno's work was not "real" philosophy.[31] He said that his judgments, colored by sentiment, were based on fantasy, as Unamuno himself, of course, would have been the first to admit. Unamuno's work is useful, suggested Krippendorf, in allowing us to see the Spanish mentality, the "Catholic consciousness," expressing not only Unamuno's own soul, but the soul of Spain as well.

This was, to a large extent, the central problem: Germans of the time could not know or understand firsthand the style of life that had shaped Unamuno's philosophy. Each of these two exceedingly dissimilar cultures had its own social and administrative problems; therefore, it is not surprising that the reactions to Unamuno in Germany would be so wildly divergent.

The Constant Reintroduction of Miguel de Unamuno

Unamuno seems to have been known to the general public as a "personality," and to specialized groups more extensively, either as a writer, as a political figure, or as an advocate of philosophical and religious viewpoints. But he was nevertheless, even as late as 1928, still being constantly "reintroduced" in many articles. His life story became an oft-told tale of his Basque heritage, his history as the president of a large Spanish university, and his political exile by dictator Primo de Rivera. There were just as many German articles about Unamuno as a personality as there were about his writings. The theme mattered little; most reports began with an introduction of who Miguel de Unamuno was. The reason for this cannot be purely that his circumstances were an icebreaker into the topic, or because, as Leo Hirsch noted in the *Berliner Tageblatt*, "We love biography!"[32]

Biographical material about Unamuno can be found in a variety of unexpected places, not only in religious journals, as was already mentioned, but also, for example, in the publication *Die*

Freude, subtitled "Monthly Magazine for Free Life Fashioning," which was, by all indications, a journal for literary nudists. Although Ivan Goll had previously said that Unamuno was the greatest living poet and novelist of Spain—the "current national martyr"—perhaps Hans Harbeck in *Die Freude* was closer to the truth regarding Unamuno's reception in Germany when he wrote, "the masses hardly know about him."[33]

E. V. Zenker, in the magazine *Freie Welt*, defended Spain against its reputation as an unproductive, passive nation.[34] "History classifies people," he wrote, and he cited the damage done by the Inquisition and clericalism as the foremost reasons for the unfortunate nonrecognition of what he called remarkable literary and artistic accomplishments. He distinguished Unamuno from the popular line of philosophers (James, Bergson) as too independent, and he linked Unamuno to the German world of thought, as many others have done since.

The Critics

E. R. Curtius's piece, entitled "Unamuno," which appeared in the February 1926 issue of *Die Literararische Welt*, was not intended to be the same type of critical essay in which he had previously mentioned Unamuno.[35] Instead, its purpose was to awaken the public's desire to read Unamuno's works. Curtius began by mentioning that Unamuno was a poet in exile, "which is typical for Latins,"[36] though in just a few years Curtius would see the same trend among German writers and artists, who, by virtue of their critical stance against the government as well as their race, would become a politically endangered species.

Cervantes' *Don Quixote* (part one) was published in 1605, and Unamuno's *The Life of Don Quixote and Sancho* exactly three hundred years later, in 1905. Curtius believed the dates were merely coincidental, and that Unamuno's work was not intended as a festschrift. Curtius felt, moreover, that Unamuno's work was a great violation of the original *Don Quixote*. He said that the abundant humor of Cervantes' work and divinely calm solutions were born out of tears and laughter. But Unamuno, Curtius wrote, was a man without humor. He quoted Unamuno, who himself said that the atmosphere of modern Spain was filled with weighty earnestness, and that "no people are as incapable these days of understanding and feeling humor as the Spanish."[37] Curtius wrote that Unamuno "wants to breathe only tragic air. He can live only in tension."[38]

It is a vicious circle of criticism from which Unamuno never seemed to escape. One must understand, wrote Curtius, that Unamuno altered Cervantes' figure of Don Quixote due to the overwhelming pressure of his own heart. One would have to be "dead in the soul" not to sense the pathos in Unamuno's plight, "not to feel the drama of our human existence, in these scruples, weaknesses, uncertainties, and human frailties."[39]

Otto Freiherr von Taube, the German poet and translator of Pedro Calderón de la Barca and Félix Lope de Vega, wrote some remarks about Unamuno that were to a great extent stereotypical, expounding commonly held conceptions about Spain and Spaniards. Von Taube noted the many contradictions in the personality and works of Don Miguel, observable in the translations published in German. He explained away these contradictions by the fact that Unamuno was from Spain, "land of contradictions."[40]

Detectable in an essay by Eberhard Vogel is a constant subsurface comparison of Spain to Germany.[41] The critic had analyzed Spain and had found it lacking. As one example, his essay elaborates on what the Spanish landscape does *not* have; what it does have, though breathtakingly beautiful, is somehow made to sound like a disadvantage. Vogel speaks of the plain of Castile, "which takes in three-fourths of the whole peninsula [sic]," its monotony, its shabby-colored dress, the fleeting beauty of the falling sun, the splendor of death, and the sharp contrasts among them: lack of gradualness between day and night, shade and light, heat and cold, summer and winter, and so on. There are no forests, no meadows to waltz through, "no green valleys in which to build one's nest," and no *Bauernhof* (farm)—the mainstay of German country life. What could life possibly hold in a country with no farms? Of course, we know there were farms in Spain, even in Castile, though not the kind that Vogel was doubtless used to. One infers that, according to Vogel, the predictable demise of Spanish society could be due in part to its presumed lack of farm life.[42]

"What Unamuno has to say about Spanish people," wrote Vogel, "is so scattered throughout his writings that it is laborious to gather it all into homogeneous viewpoints. I will try to bring his thoughts into some kind of order anyhow."[43] One has to admire him for trying. But, at the same time, one wonders how much Vogel knew about the life of our author before reading and producing such a monumental report on his works. Certain statements he made contradicted what was at the time common knowledge about Unamuno in Spain, as well as in other circles of Spanish study. For example, if there was anyone at the time who could be considered an authority on the development of the Iberian Peninsula with regard to race and language, it was likely to be Unamuno. Yet Vogel stated without hesitation, "Unamuno is not enough of a scholar to research the historical roots of the Spanish people."[44] He then went on to explain those "roots" in half a page.

Some German intellectuals were at a loss to decipher Unamuno's particular brand of philosophy. It is certainly comprehensible that the German reader might not readily understand what Unamuno wanted to express through his creative literature. He was arguably the most controversial and self-contradictory writer of Spain. He approached philosophical or political questions from an ultra-individual and singularly religious viewpoint, with his writings often combining biblical references with personal paranoia. The sometimes overt, sometimes subliminal message of his writings was linked with the fate of Spain, and, in his view, its inevitable path toward self-destruction. The agony Unamuno felt in his religious consciousness was intimately connected to his obsession with Spain. Serious analysts of his texts, even those who greatly admired his works, were at a loss to offer approbation or even clear explanations of his statements, which sometimes seemed to be extraordinary to them. Otto Hachtmann said that our author misjudged both Schopenhauer and Nietzsche.[45] But, as Hermann Bahr noted, Unamuno ingested so much of German Protestant philosophy that it "spoiled his digestive system."[46] He expressed strong anti-German sentiments, so much so that it was the cause of his losing his rectorship of the University of Salamanca in 1914. Yet he professed great admiration for the German philosophers, and his library was stocked with major German works.

We come back at this point to E. R. Curtius, who addressed the subject of the Spanish condition and the relationship of Unamuno's ideas to Germany and the rest of Europe: "[Miguel de Unamuno's] is the work of a thinker who has studied all literatures and philosophies." Curtius depicted a writer who was "cosmopolitan in the world of ideas but fast rooted in the tradition of his fatherland," deep down a Spaniard, but for all that, a European, "even when he objects to the 'Europeanization' of Spain."[47] The difficulty of Unamuno's writings, Curtius implied, was his insistence on continually returning to the notion of *Unsterblichkeit*, or immortality. Curtius thought this approach lent Unamuno his originality, but he said, "We are not used to that anymore. It will fill many with mistrust. Intellectual Europe does not speak of death and eternity—it's not good manners."[48] Not only was it impolite, but it also remained uninteresting. Richard Gabel would say after six years of Unamuno's exile that his constant refrain, "think about death," attracted no modern mind.[49]

Wilhelm Muster, prologuist for the 1987 edition of *Nebel* (*Fog* or *Niebla*), was of a similar opinion. In a letter to this writer, he states,

> Unamuno's central question—What about my existence? What happens to me after death? Is there a *personal* immortality?—spoke to the readers less and less, as their living conditions improved ... The situation is surely the worst among us [Germans]. With us, death [i.e., the funeral home] comes in through the back door; one does not acknowledge it. One shoves everything away which could be bothersome in life, including the thought of death. It is interesting that questions such as "I cannot believe, but I want to believe!" or "I do not want to die, but I will die" continue to attract a few people, among them also publishers. However, most people are uncomfortable when Unamuno is so importunate, when he becomes so psychologically oppressive. What the reader would like to have is certainty. But Unamuno makes the reader uncertain. It is therefore a psychological problem, and thus a problem of sales figures. Unamuno can have the most wonderful reviews, but with us it is common for publishers to calculate not the total sales of all books, but instead book by book.[50]

Muster's point about cultural differences is an important one. The question is cultural, because it deals with religious beliefs. As a result, the Spanish author's ideas were often tucked away in ultra-religious journals in Germany. Spain being a Catholic country, Unsterblichkeit is in this sense an especially Spanish question. One German critic said that Unamuno's brain was "tied up with religious cord."[51]

One comes back to the theme of distrust in Unamuno's sincerity about his convictions. Hubert Becher would say in 1931 that Unamuno was receiving too much "frankincense" upon his homecoming, and that the politics which his name had come to symbolize were receiving the homage.[52] This writer categorically struck down the plight of Unamuno, saying it was a storm in a teacup, a publicity-getter that wouldn't last. Becher thought that the emperor was wearing no clothes: "... he flashes and glitters, but doesn't enlighten.... Followers always cling to a great man, but with Unamuno, this following lies in the system."[53] Becher was partly correct. In Spain, the circle of admirers and those influenced by Unamuno was large, but few people, if any, tried to copy his example. Followers in the sense of imitators he did not have.

In Don Miguel's library, one finds a copy of Heinrich Mann's contribution to the *Berliner Tageblatt* newspaper of 1 October 1927, containing Mann's comments on the release of *Aunt Tula*, as well as an anecdotal experience of the German author. Mann must have attended a meeting in Paris in 1925, when Unamuno unofficially represented Spain at a banquet of the PEN Club.[54] Mann described Unamuno as a "volcano"; speaking first in French, then in Spanish, Unamuno could be understood by the tone, if not the words. "We all applauded, which was unfitting. Why applaud when a great, purifying storm is over?"[55] Mann was obviously impressed with the work, and with Unamuno: "In a manner, fully unknown farther north, emerges the old spinster, no, the fanatic saint, no, a criminal, no, a phenomenon. A wonder of life comes out of this enemy of life, filled with hot life."[56]

Heinrich Mann recognized that such a character as Tula would be foreign to German eyes and might be interpreted as a ludicrous figure. Mann demonstrated the distance, more psychological than physical, between his country and that of Miguel de Unamuno: "This comes from a country which remains dark to us, out of strange traditions of the soul. She looks at us coolly, if not daydreamy, even speaks to us with a somewhat stern, unconcerned voice. But suddenly fire flashes from her eyes, and she tears apart her breast."[57]

In the final analysis, from the German critical point of view, Unamuno already may have had three strikes against him. First, he was a Spaniard, from a country allegedly full of unproductive and dreamy people. Second, Unamuno's philosophy mixed religious beliefs with logic. And third, the political events that he discussed had only a faint echo in the German society of the 1920s. There was no critical consensus on whether Miguel de Unamuno was a religious, a literary, or a political figure. In spite of the translation and distribution of a major component of his literary work, his fame was short-lived and primarily sensational in nature, from his exile in 1924 to his return to Spain in 1930.

Notes

1. "Es ist ewig dieselbe hoffnungsvolle, hoffnungslose Jugend, die mit Kubismus, Jazz und freier Liebe das Jahrhundert zu erobern glaubt." Ivan Goll, "Don Miguel de Unamuno" (also: "Miguel de Unamuno in Paris"), *Königsberger Hartungsche Handelszeitung*, 31 December 1924, reprinted in *Neue Zürcher Zeitung*, 5 January 1925, and in *Dresdner Neueste Nachrichten*, 18 January 1925.—All translations are by the author unless otherwise indicated.

2. "Seit einigen Wochen wurden am äußersten Ende des Saales mehrere der kleinen runden Marmortische zu einem einzigen zusammengerückt, und es entstand der spanische Tisch. Eine Schar schwarzhaariger, wild aufbrausender, grellauflachender Jünglinge umringt dort alltäglich ... einen stillen alten Mann mit goldener Brille, mit einem spitz zugestutzten kleinen Bärtchen, der sich in dieser jungfreudigen Gesellschaft sehr wohl zu finden scheint." Ibid. Copies of these articles were sent to Unamuno by Ivan Goll, "avec l'expression de son profonde admiration, Paris XVIe 27, Rue Jasmin." See newspaper article files in Casa-Museo Unamuno, Salamanca, Spain.
3. "... der größte Dichter und Romancier Spaniens, der heutige Nationalmärtyrer." Ibid.
4. "Man wundert sich ... ist das ein Universitätsrektor? Ist das der Mann, der heute in der ganzen Welt als der heftigste Revolutionär gegen die Säbelmacht eines Generals verehrt wird? ... Von Paris aus führt Unamuno den Kampf." Ibid.
5. Ignaz Wrobel, "Unamuno spricht," *Die Weltbühne*, 30 October 1924.
6. "Wie hat ein siegreiches Land auf das Militär reagiert? Wie reagiert ein besiegtes? Wo sind unsre Vereinigten Sozialdemokraten, diese schlimmsten Feinde eines radikalen Fortschritts, wenn Diskussionen der Geistigen anheben? Wer kümmert sich bei uns um Unamuno und um ausländische Probleme? Wer weiß davon?" Ibid.
7. Gerhart Hoffmeister, *Spanien und Deutschland: Geschichte und Dokumentation der literarischen Beziehungen* (Berlin, 1976), p. 27.
8. E. R. Curtius, "Ortega y Gasset," in *Kritische Essays zur europäischen Literatur* (Berne, 1950), p. 221. Curtius's article originally appeared in 1924.
9. Anonymous, "Las Revistas: Unamuno en Alemania: Un estudio de Curtius," *Nosotros*, vol. 54, 1926.
10. Miguel de Unamuno, "Spaniens Philosophie," *Wissen und Leben*, vol. 14, no. 8. (l and 15 February 1921), pp. 341–356. See also idem, "Das sogenannte 'Neue Regime' in Spanien," *Die Weltbühne*, 27 March 1924, also in *Frankfurter Zeitung*, 4 May 1924; idem, "Was verdanken Sie dem deutschen Geist?" *Die Literarische Welt*, 16 October 1925; idem, "Gruß an Romain Rolland," *Die Literarische Welt*, 29 January 1926; and idem, "Stimme des spanischen Dichters," *Berliner Tageblatt*, 1 January 1927.
11. H. Th. Joel, "Gespräch mit Unamuno," *Berliner Tageblatt*, 15 February 1930.
12. Unamuno's article in the latter publication was entitled "Autorität und Macht oder Christus und der Pharisäer" ("Authority and Power or Christ and the Pharisee") and was (appropriately) published on 25 December 1931. *Eiserne Blätter: Wochenschrift für deutsche Politik und Kultur* (a socialist weekly), vol. l3, no. 43, pp. 697–698. This was translated into German by Inés Manz, according to her letters to Unamuno; see reference to letters of 1929 and 1930 in preceding paragraph in text.
13. See unpublished letters from Berlin to Paris, 9 and 17 July 1925, Casa-Museo Unamuno, Salamanca. Founded in 1925 by Rowohlt, and edited by Willy Haas until 1933, *Die Literarische Welt* was a unique Berlin literary publication with writings by and about the most important intellectuals of the day. Peter de Mendelssohn, in his work *Zeitungsstadt Berlin* (Frankfurt, 1982), says of *Die Literarische Welt* that it was a periodical "das es bis dahin in Deutschland nicht gegeben hatte: keine gewichtige Literaturzeitschrift herkömmlichen Typs, sondern nach dem Vorbild der Pariser Nouvelles Littéraires eine literarische Wochenzeitung. Sie brachte natürlich regelmäßig lange und gewichtige Essays,

auch Novellen und Gedichte, aber ihr Hauptnachdruck lag, wie es sich bei einer Zeitung gehört, auf Nachrichten, und der größte Teil jeder Nummer war mit aktuellen Neuigkeiten aus der Literatur-, Theater- und Kunstwelt gefüllt, und zwar nicht nur aus Deutschland, sondern aus der ganzen Welt. In dieser schrankenlosen ... Aufnahmefreudigkeit war auch sie ein sehr berlinisches Produkt. Es ist heute fast unvorstellbar, was mir damals zur Verfügung stand, schrieb ihr Herausgeber ein Vierteljahrhundert später in seinen Lebenserinnerungen. *Die Literarische Welt* ... kann heute nicht wiederholt werden ... Es fehlt die ganze, ungemein breite Basis, das unermeßlich reiche Material ... Man mußte gleichsam eine redaktionelle Idee nur träumen, und sie war schon halb ausgeführt. Ich habe nie das Gefühl gehabt, daß es da irgendwelche Grenzen gab," p. 324. ("[It was a kind of publication] that had not existed in Germany until that time: not a weighty literature magazine of the traditional type, instead it was, modeled after the example of the Parisian *nouvelles littéraires*, a literary weekly. It regularly published long and weighty essays, also novellas and poetry, but its main focus was, as is proper with a 'newspaper,' the news, and the biggest part of each issue was filled with current events from the literary, theatrical, and artistic world, and indeed not only from Germany, but from all over the world. It was also a very Berlin-like product. 'It is almost unimaginable what was at that time at my disposal,' wrote its editor a quarter century later in his memoirs. '*Die Literarische Welt* ... cannot be repeated today ... The whole uncommonly broad basis is lacking, the immeasurably rich material ... One only had to dream about a publishing idea, and it was already half realized. I never had the feeling that there existed any kind of limits.'")
14. The other contributors to this three-part series were: André Germain, Henri Barbusse, Jean Cocteau, Ilya Ehrenburg, Jules Sauerwein, Maurice Barrès, and Joséphin Péladan.
15. "Und könnte ich nicht deutsch lesen, so würde ich es nicht wagen zu sagen, was ich dem deutschen Geiste zu verdanken glaube, so viele deutsche Werke ich auch in Übersetzungen gelesen hätte." Miguel de Unamuno, "Was verdanken Sie dem deutschen Geist?" *Die Literarische Welt*, 1925, no. 2 (16 October 1925), p. 2.
16. "Aber was ist das Abstrakte, und was ist das Konkrete? Erreicht man in einer Sprache ... eine schärfere Konkretheit?" Ibid.
17. E. R. Curtius, "Unamuno oder die Philosophie des Tragischen," *Neue Zürcher Zeitung*, 8 October 1925.
18. Hermann Bahr, whose comments figure later in this discussion, contributed to the well-known *Notizen zur neueren spanischen Literatur* (Berlin, 1926), no. 20 in the series *Preußische Jahrbücher*. Bahr, essentially a journalist, worked as theater critic for over twenty years for the *Deutsche Zeitung*, and was known as the "seismograph of his age." Highly politically active, his writings produced theatrical scandals in Berlin and elsewhere. See David G. Daviau, *The Letters of Arthur Schnitzler to Hermann Bahr* (Chapel Hill, N.C., 1978).
19. "Die Redaktion sandte mir diese Bände hierher und fordert mich auf ... zu sagen, was über diesen Spanier zu sagen ist." Victor Auburtin, "Unamuno," *Berliner Tageblatt*, 20 December 1925.
20. "Gott sei Dank, daß Unamuno endlich übersetzt wird. Ich habe mich schon dreimal an ihn herangemacht und es jedesmal wieder aufgegeben; so entsetzlich kratzbürstig ist das Spanisch, das er schreibt." Ibid.
21. Sales of November 1925–30 March 1926, Casa-Museo Unamuno, Salamanca.

22. *Der Querschnitt*, April 1926, vol. 1, no. 4. The founder of this Berlin magazine was Alfred Flechtheim, who sold it to Ullstein in 1924. At its highest moment of circulation, this exclusive journal sold about 25,000 copies and was read by at most around 125,000 people. However, the newspaper exercised an influence that stretched far beyond its immediate readers. Peter de Mendelssohn said of *Der Querschnitt*, "Wer heute an dieses Jahrzehnt [des Berlins der Zwanziger Jahre] zurückdenkt ... faßt es in seiner Vorstellung unwillkürlich in dem Begriff Querschnitt zusammen. Dieser Name ist heute, ein halbes Jahrhundert später, geradezu zum Wahrzeichen einer ganzen Zeit geworden ... 'Querschnitt' war das Gegenteil von umfassend. Er war ausgesprochen 'exklusiv'. Er war das Gegenteil von populär. Er war ... keineswegs frei von snobistischem Hochmut. Er war alles andere als gemeinverständlich; er sprach geradezu eine Geheimsprache. Er war nicht einfach; er war 'getüftelt', überspitzt ... Er war keineswegs weit verbreitet; aber jedermann wußte von ihm." Peter de Mendelssohn, *Zeitungsstadt Berlin* (Berlin, 1982), pp. 321–323. ("Anyone who thinks back to this decade [of Berlin of the twenties] ... automatically conceives it in his imagination together with the concept of *Querschnitt*. This name has today, a half century later, become a landmark of an entire age ... *Querschnitt* was the opposite of comprehensive. It was downright 'exclusive.' It was the opposite of popular. It was in no way free from snobbish arrogance. It was anything but understandable by the masses; it almost spoke a secret language. It was not easy; it was 'subtle,' in fact too subtle ... It was not at all widely distributed, but everyone knew about it.")
23. Antonina Vallentin, "Unamuno's Don Quijote," *Vossische Zeitung*, 14 August 1924. Karl May (1842–1912) began publishing short stories and novels serially in periodicals after 1874. His popularity soared in the 1890s with his adventure stories. May is perhaps most famous in Germany for his series based on the fictional Native American "Winnetou." He is one of the world's all-time fiction bestsellers, though he is virtually unknown in the United States.
24. Ibid.
25. Otto Forst de Battaglia, "Querschnitt durch die europäische Literatur der Gegenwart, VI. Die spanische Literatur," *Rhein/Main Volkszeitung*, 1 June 1928.
26. Friedrich Mackermann, "Dichtung und Leben," *Der Gral: Monatsschrift für schöne Literatur*, vol. 6, no. 22 (1927–28), pp. 759–763.
27. "Oder sind Unwissenschaftlichkeit, Mangel an Logik, Unselbständigkeit, durch und durch konfuser Mystizismus wirklich die Eigenschaften, die heute Weltruf sichern?" Mackermann, *Der Gral*, p. 759.
28. Rudolf Pick-Seewart, "Miguel de Unamuno: Tragisches Lebensgefühl," *Zeitschrift für individualpsychologische Pädagogik und Psychohygiene*, vol. 1, nos. 5–6 (July–August 1928).
29. For example, see in the archive of Casa-Museo Unamuno, Salamanca: 30 May 1927 from Elfriede Clement, Berlin; 28 June 1927 from Dr. Fr. Munker, Nuremberg; September and October 1927, from Max Victor Depta, Silesia; 10 August 1927 from Ernst Fritz Katz, Frankfurt; 12 February 1928 from Madonin Astrow, Munich; etc.
30. "Ich will eben nicht sterben. Nein, ich will es nicht, und ich will es auch nicht wollen. Ich will immer, immer, immer leben! Und ich will leben, als das gleiche armselige Ich, als das ich mich heute und hier fühle." August Messer, "Unamuno über die Unsterblichkeit," *Philosophie und Leben*, vol. 1 (1926), pp. 277–278.

31. Review of *Das tragische Lebensgefühl* by Kurt Krippendorf in *Kantstudium*, vol. 23 (1928).
32. "Man liebt jetzt bei uns Biographie," in Leo Hirsch, "Jakob Wassermann: Christoph Colombus," *Berliner Tageblatt*, 4 December 1929 (article in Casa-Museo Unamuno library, Salamanca).
33. "Die große Masse der Leser hat noch kaum Notiz von ihm genommen." Hans Harbeck, "Unamuno," *Die Freude: Monatshefte für freie Lebensgestaltung*, vol. 2, no. 5 (February 1928), p. 91.
34. E. V. Zenker, "Don Miguel de Unamuno," *Freie Welt*, no. 145 (1926), pp. 7–16.
35. See, for example, Curtius, "Ortega y Gasset," p. 221.
36. "Der Dichter in der Verbannung—das ist eine der Situationen, die wir als typisch für den lateinischen Stil der Geschichte empfinden. Elegisch bei Ovid, heroisch bei Dante, theatralisch bei Victor Hugo, wiederholt sie sich aktuell bei Miguel de Unamuno." Ibid. ("The poet in exile—that is one of the situations which we perceive as typical for the Latin style of history. Elegic with Ovid, heroic with Dante, theatrical with Victor Hugo, it repeats itself currently with Miguel de Unamuno.")
37. "... daß kein Volk heute so unfähig sei, Humor zu verstehen und zu fühlen, wie das spanische." Ibid.
38. "Er will nur tragische Luft atmen. Er kann nur in Spannung leben." Ibid.
39. "Aber man müßte seelisch fühllos sein, um nicht auch in diesen Skrupeln, Schwächen, Unsicherheiten, Menschlichkeiten das Pathos zu empfinden, das dem Drama unseres Menschentums innewohnt." Ibid.
40. Otto von Taube, "Randbemerkungen," *Zeitwende*, no. 2 (January 1926).
41. Eberhard Vogel, "Miguel de Unamuno: Ein spanischer Publizist und Philosoph," *Hochland*, no. 23, pt. 2 (February 1926), pp. 214–231.
42. An intriguing concept that Vogel introduced into his discussion of the Spanish character, to go along with this lack of farm life theory, is the purportedly Spanish attitude toward animals: "Die Freude am Tier ist in Spanien selten, was für die Kinder den empfindlichen Ausfall eines Erziehungselementes bedeutet." Ibid. ("The pleasure in animals is rare in Spain, which for children means the absence of a significant component in their education.")
43. "Was Unamuno vom spanischen Menschen und von seiner Kultur zu sagen hat, ist so durch seine Schriften zerstreut, daß es mühselig ist, es unter einigende Gesichtspunkte zu fassen ... Ich werde gleichwohl versuchen, seine Gedanken in einiger Ordnung vorzutragen." Ibid.
44. "Unamuno ist zu wenig Gelehrter, um nach den geschichtlichen Wurzeln des spanischen Menschen zu forschen." Ibid.
45. Otto Hachtmann, "Das tragische Lebensgefühl," *Literarische Wochenschrift*, 12 June 1926, pp. 696–697.
46. "Er hat sich ... an deutscher (protestantischer) Philosophie den Magen verdorben." Bahr, *Notizen zur neueren spanischen Literatur*.
47. "Es ist das Werk eines Denkers, der alle Literaturen und Philosophien durchstreift hat. Fest in seiner vaterländischen Tradition verwurzelt, ist Unamuno zugleich ein Kosmopolit der Ideenwelt; Europäer, selbst wenn er sich gegen die 'Europäisierung' Spaniens wendet." E. R. Curtius, "Unamuno oder die Philosophie des Tragischen," *Neue Zürcher Zeitung*, 8 October 1925.
48. "Wir sind das nicht mehr gewöhnt ... es wird viele mit Mißtrauen erfüllen ... Es gehört zum guten Ton des intellektuellen Europa, von Tod und Ewigkeit nicht zu sprechen." Ibid.

49. Richard Gabel, "Don Quichotte im Exil: Über den fünfundsechzigjährigen Unamuno," *Die Neue Bücherschau*, vol. 7, no. 8 (August 1929).
50. "Unamunos zentrale Frage: wie steht es mit meiner Existenz? Was geschieht nach meinem Tod? Gibt es eine *persönliche* Unsterblichkeit? haben die Leser umso weniger angesprochen, je besser sie lebten ... Am schlimmsten ist es ... sicher bei uns. Bei uns kommt der Tod (die Bestattungsanstalt) zur Hintertüre herein, man nimmt ihn nicht zur Kenntnis, man schiebt alles, was einen im Leben stören könnte, weg, so eben auch den Gedanken an den Tod. Interessant ist, daß Fragen wie: 'Ich kann nicht glauben, aber ich will glauben!' oder: 'Ich will nicht sterben—aber ich werde sterben', zwar ein paar Menschen immer wieder anziehen, darunter auch Verleger, daß es den meisten Leuten aber unheimlich ist, wenn ihnen Unamuno so auf den Pelz rückt, so drängend wird: was der Leser gern hätte, ist Sicherheit, Unamuno aber macht unsicher. Es ist also ein psychologisches Problem, und damit ein Problem der Verkaufszahlen. U. kann die schönsten Kritiken haben—bei uns ist es üblich, daß der Verleger nicht die Summe seiner Bücher berechnet, sondern Buch für Buch." Wilhelm Muster, 17 February 1989, personal communication to author.
51. "... sein religiös verschnürtes Gehirn." Gabel, "Don Quichotte im Exil."
52. "Miguel de Unamuno," *Der Gral*, no. 2 (1930–31), pp. 1016–1018.
53. "Er ist ein Mensch, der sich wie nur einer nach dem Unendlichen ausstreckt, der es aber—wir wollen einfach sprechen—nicht fertig bringt, seine Seele zu verlieren, um sie zu gewinnen ... Wir sprechen nicht so sehr von seinem Stil und seiner literarischen Form—er ist nie weich und zart, fast nie harmonisch; er ... blitzt und funkelt, aber erleuchtet nicht. Wir sprechen auch nicht von seiner Politik ... Wir sprechen von seiner menschlichen Wirksamkeit, die er auf sein Volk und seine Zeit hat ... Epigonen heften sich immer an den großen Menschen, bei Unamuno liegt das Epigonen-weckende im System. Und so reißt Unamunos Geist die Gegensätze Spaniens noch mehr auseinander, ohne zu heilen, und das geistige Leben vieler bleibt fruchtlos." Ibid., p. 1018.
54. Miguel de Unamuno's presence at that meeting was as symbolic as that of Heinrich Mann. The International PEN Club, since its London founding just a few years prior in 1920 by John Galsworthy and others, was quickly developing its reputation as a strong proponent of authors' rights.
55. "... denn wozu Beifall, wenn ein großes, reines Gewitter vorüber ist?" Heinrich Mann, *Berliner Tageblatt*, 1 October 1927.
56. "Hieraus wird, in einem weiter nordwärts völlig unbekannten Format, die alte Jungfer, nein, die fanatische Heilige, nein, eine Verbrecherin, nein, ein Phänomen. Es wird ein Lebenswunder aus dieser von heißem Leben erfüllten Feindin des Lebens." Ibid.
57. "Diese hier tritt hervor aus einem Land, das uns dunkel bleibt, aus fremden Überlieferungen der Seele. Sie sieht uns kühl, wenn nicht versonnen, an, spricht auch mit etwas harter, unbekümmerter Stimme zu uns. Plötzlich bricht aus ihrem Auge Feuer, und sie zerfleischt sich die Brust." Ibid.

Part III

From the Spanish Civil War to the Present

– 14 –

HITLER AND THE SPANISH CIVIL WAR

A Shifting Balance of Power

Robert H. Whealey

The Spanish Civil War lasted from July 1936 to the last day of March 1939, a time of major changes in both Spain and Europe. Looking back sixty years, it appears that Adolf Hitler (1889–1945) won the Civil War for the Third Reich and for General Francisco Franco (1892–1975). To understand why, one must focus on two different arenas: the first is Spain itself, and the second considers the European balance of power. In mid-February 1936, a very close election involving a dozen or so Spanish parties was won by a left-wing coalition known as the Popular Front. The 4.7 million to 4.5 million vote tally set the stage for the Civil War that erupted six months later because the people did not settle down after the February elections. Civil unrest escalated, including political assassinations and the burning of churches. The losing voters on the right—parts of the Catholic hierarchy and Catholic journalists, monarchists, fascists, landlords, capitalists, and military officers—began to consider overthrowing the elected government.

Military plotters launched a coup d'état on 17 July 1936, the insurgent generals and colonels assuming they would win quickly. However, the liberal government countered by passing out weapons to socialist and anarchist labor unions interested in social revolution, which formed independent leftist militia units. These militias defeated the garrisons in major cities, including Madrid,

Barcelona, Bilbao, Valencia, and Málaga. General Franco flew to Spanish Morocco and assumed command of the mercenary army he had led in the 1920s. He saw that with Italian and German airplanes, he could transport troops across the Strait of Gibraltar—a novel plan at the time.

Late on 25 July 1936, General Franco's emissary, Johannes Bernhardt, a Nazi merchant living in Spanish Morocco, arrived in Bayreuth with an urgent request to Hitler for transport planes and bombers for the rebel Spanish army. Simultaneously, Franco sent another emissary to Rome to secure aid from Benito Mussolini (1883–1945). Indeed, Nazi and Fascist military aid helped Franco to become Nationalist Spain's chief of state on 1 October 1936 over rival generals.

The first consideration of the Nazis was to prevent the "Reds," the Popular Front, from winning the Civil War in Spain. A second concern of Hitler and his propaganda minister Joseph Goebbels (1897–1945) in the fall of 1936 was that the Spanish traditionalist, monarchist Carlists leaned toward the British.[1] The Nazis saw Franco to the left of the Carlists and as a potential ally, not as a puppet of either Berlin or Rome. Franco answered the Carlist problem by creating a united totalitarian party of the Carlists and the Falange, of which in April 1937 he became Caudillo.

Meanwhile, European leftists and Soviet Russia began aiding the Republic. Franco's military drive on Madrid failed to take the capital by November 1936, in part because of resistance mounted by the International Brigades. In June 1937, Bilbao and the Basque region fell to the Nationalists. After hard fighting in Aragon, Franco split the Republican territory in two when he reached the Mediterranean in the spring of 1938. But he still had to fight on the Ebro River and drive into Catalonia; General Franco had to win his war in Spain by military conquest.

In late January 1939, as Franco's armies were marching into Barcelona, Hitler told Goebbels that the Spanish war would soon be over and that he would be happy if Spain were benevolently neutral in the next war. Yet he hoped that Franco's new Spain would not look inward but would instead challenge France and Great Britain in the Mediterranean. In Hitler's mind, Spain was from the beginning a burden primarily for Mussolini, who was loudly trumpeting his Mediterranean ambitions.

The Spanish Civil War was a prime factor creating the Rome-Berlin Axis Pact of October 1936. Hitler cultivated Mussolini's Spanish policy for the sake of Axis solidarity. However, the Nazis also directly pushed Franco into a bilateral relationship to gain economic concessions, at the same time encouraging "Il duce" to send more military supplies and men to Franco. Hitler's and Mussolini's ideology seemed to be the wave of the future in 1939. After learning that Franco had signed Joachim von Ribbentrop's (1893–1946) Anti-Comintern Pact on 27 March 1939, seemingly bringing Nationalist Spain firmly onto the side of the Rome-Berlin alliance, Goebbels commented that the democracies—not the Soviet Union—had lost another battle.

Yet Franco could not be considered a mere tool of Hitler, who dealt with the Caudillo through Hermann Göring (1893–1946), Ribbentrop, and Goebbels.[2] The propaganda minister had his eye mainly on the person most favorable toward fascist thinking among Nationalist ministers, Franco's brother-in-law, Minister of Interior Ramón Serrano Suñer. Educated in Fascist Italy, Serrano was in charge of police and propaganda.[3] Although Serrano preferred the Italian brand of fascism, the Nazis trusted that the new Spain would continue its anticommunist, anti-Jewish, and anti-Masonic solidarity with Berlin and Rome in 1939.[4]

In the imperialistic 1930s, the European balance of power dominated the world. During the Spanish Civil War, Hitler cleverly applied classic balance of power pressures to volatile Spain. In 1936, the balance of power in Europe was shifting: Britain, largely because of economic reasons, was in danger of losing its dominance. The carnage of World War I made France somewhat hesitant about continuing as a major actor. Germany and Italy, both nationalist, expansionist, and popular dictatorships, were pressing forward. For Spain in 1936, this meant that the Republic had to face indifference or even hostility from the four capitalist European great powers, finding only Mexico and Soviet Russia friendly. The British and U.S. governments were basically neutral. The French were badly divided between a pro-British foreign office and a recently elected Popular Front government, which sought the aid of the Soviet Union to check growing German power in eastern Europe.

The balance of power system is complex. While balance of power politics are influenced first of all by geography, historians, political theorists, and politicians use the term "balance of power" to cover at least three different political and economic situations. First is the assumption that a neutral state can balance rival sovereign states, as Britain did in Europe from the Peace of Paris in 1856 to the outbreak of World War I in 1914. Second, diplomats might refer to a coalition of weak states balancing a single large state—like the alliances that coalesced during the wars of Louis XIV. Third, a coalition can balance another coalition or bloc of states.

Different diplomats at different times in history see their national situations differently. Some heads of state and politicians seek the predominant place for their own state or their own national interests, while others prefer a defensive approach as part of an alliance system or coalition. Some politicians are confused about the exact status of their own country as a member of one side of the balance or the other. Sometimes they choose the "wrong side" because of misunderstanding the relative importance of the multiple factors affecting power. These include, among others, size and location, readiness of armed forces, technological skills of the labor force, natural resources, ideological coherence, and political and economic talent. When a big state chooses to move from the neutral camp or from one side to the other, it can decisively tip the balance of power toward either peace or war.

On the eve of World War I, the European states that could tilt the balance of power suddenly created a new alignment of coalitions. The Entente Powers, consisting initially of the empires of Britain, France, and Russia, on the one side, militarily balanced themselves against the imperial Central Powers of Germany, Austria-Hungary, and Turkey on the other. The horrific result was four years of bloody, stalemated trench warfare on the western and eastern fronts. Although imperial Russia collapsed into revolution in 1917, U.S. entry into the war tipped the military balance on the western front, enabling the Allies to win. In 1919, the victorious powers imposed the treaties of Paris and Versailles, dismembering the vanquished Central Powers, but the United States then lapsed back into isolationism.

On the ideological level, World War I spawned international communism and nationalistic-imperialistic fascism. The new Soviet Russia emerged as a fifth great European power, but one that was weak economically, politically, and militarily. Ideologically, however, Moscow went on the offensive, so that in 1936 Stalin was seen in London and Paris as more powerful than he was in reality. During the Spanish Civil War from 1936 to 1939, wartime conditions made the power system more dynamic and unstable. Each of the five powers intervened for different reasons, hoping to tilt the European balance in its favor.

Britain and France lost the Spanish campaign essentially because they did not balance their own internal military, political, ideological, and economic assets and liabilities or factors of power. Politicians in London and Paris initiated the Non-Intervention

Committee without clear foresight into the potentialities of Mussolini, Hitler, or Stalin. The British and French governments had already launched their appeasement policies before July 1936, and the Spanish Civil War increased that tendency, occasionally to the point of paralyzing inaction. Internal dissension and short-lived French cabinets weakened France, while politicians in London exaggerated the threat of a largely imaginary Bolshevik-style revolution in Spain. The ruling Tory Party discounted how its strategic or economic position might be affected if the Axis powers took over Spain or reduced it to satellite status.

Hitler had played his cards very well since coming to power in January 1933. To begin with, he quickly consolidated Nazi control in Germany. Paradoxically, the Führer, the man with insane ambitions to take over the USSR and rid Europe of Jews, played the diplomatic game quite skillfully before his 1939 invasion of Poland. From 1933 to 1939, Hitler would win some dozen diplomatic moves, including the complex Spanish operation, before Anglo-German war broke out in September 1939. He scored points by resigning from the London Disarmament Conference in October 1933, by signing up Poland to an anticommunist nonaggression pact in January 1934, by unilaterally announcing a draft and rearmament program in March 1935, by concluding an Anglo-German naval agreement in June 1935, and by marching into the demilitarized Rhineland in March 1936, all of which further weakened France.

In the first part of July 1936, Hitler came to an agreement with Italy over Austria, thereby removing a bone of contention with Mussolini. The Spanish war that erupted on 17 July prompted the Führer to appoint in August 1936 his Nazi Party foreign policy expert Ribbentrop as ambassador to London. There Ribbentrop, having recently secured the Japanese signature on his Anti-Comintern Pact, continued to preach anticommunism.

The outbreak of the Spanish Civil War explosively expanded the specter of international communism. Exploiting the ideological side of the war, Hitler and Goebbels were propagandizing National Socialist ideas and Hitler's mission as the savior of European civilization from the "menace of Bolshevism" in France, England, Poland, and Spain. For Hitler and Goebbels, Bolshevism did not represent a territorial threat by Moscow so much as an international subversive movement bent on undermining German and European social and economic structures. This fascist stand aroused the sympathy of conservatives around the world.

Despite political differences between the diverse groups on the Spanish radical right and the Nazis, Hitler supported Franco and his military efforts and used the Civil War to his political advantage. By cleverly alluding to communism, socialism, Bolshevism, and Marxism, Hitler exploited ideas to influence Franco and Mussolini, to create the Axis, and to expand fascism among the Catholics and conservatives of Eastern Europe and Latin America. Berlin thus isolated and weakened French Premier León Blum (1872–1950) and the delicate balance of French-Soviet relations.

Foreign Minister Konstantin von Neurath (1873–1956), whom Hitler inherited from the conservative National People's Party (DNVP) of the Weimar Republic, busied himself with messages to and from the Non-Intervention Committee (NIC) in London. This committee of ambassadors met ostensibly to implement an Anglo-French plan to keep weapons and foreign troops out of Spain. German merchant vessels flying Panamanian flags violated the committee's ineffective patrols, and Italy also flouted the NIC's strictures. Non-intervention failed because Hitler, Mussolini, and Stalin had no interest in carrying it out. The Anglo-French democratic diplomats did not care that much who won the Spanish war, while two of the dictators worked for Franco to win, and only Stalin hoped he would lose.

The Führer saw Spain in economic terms as a source of raw materials, and in September 1936 he delegated to Göring the task of preparing the Third Reich's economy for world war within four years. The merchant who carried Franco's request to Hitler for airplanes became a millionaire by setting up two joint Spanish-German corporations called HISMA and ROWAK, which would continue operations until 1945. Borrowing money from the German finance ministry, Bernhardt served as an agent of Göring and was making a commission on every tank, gun, and spark plug imported by Franco, as well as a second commission on every shipment of copper ore, lead ore, wolfram, pyrites, and hides imported from Spain into Germany.[5] Hitler sold the services of Condor Legion military specialists for cash and credit, obtaining Spanish raw materials and investments in mines. The Third Reich provided just enough military aid to ensure Franco's victory, while encouraging Mussolini to contribute even more.

In July 1937, the Germans achieved important economic concessions from Spain by three treaties. On 31 July, when he reviewed for Goebbels the past year's Spanish activities, Hitler felt quite satisfied with his decision of 25–26 July 1936 to aid Franco. The Führer boasted that the Nazis had made many gains since then.[6]

Militarily, the Nazis used the Spanish Civil War for training and experimentation by their army, navy, and air force. The smokescreen provided by Spain assisted the German military to pass through the "danger zone" of rearmament against France during the 1936–37 period. From September 1936 to the end of the war, Göring, who held the two vital posts of Luftwaffe chief and commissioner for the Four Year Plan, played major military and economic roles in Spain, overseeing both Condor Legion operations and German-Spanish trade.

In addition to Ribbentrop, Göring, and Goebbels, Hitler also took advice from Admiral Canaris. Wilhelm Canaris (1887–1945), chief of military intelligence, a Spanish expert and informal liaison between Hitler and Franco, spoke with a fourth voice. His position often wavered between supporting Ribbentrop and supporting Göring. A conservative spymaster but never a Nazi, sometime in 1938 Canaris began secretly but ineffectively to oppose Hitler's Eastern European ambitions when they risked war with Britain. Hitler got much of his Spanish information from Canaris, a career naval officer who first operated in Spain in 1916. During the regime of dictator Miguel Primo de Rivera (1870–1930), which had lasted from 1923 to 1930, Canaris had worked to circumvent the Treaty of Versailles by building submarines for Germany in Spain. Canaris also had visited the Canary Islands in 1927 to help establish a Lufthansa base.[7] A secret supply service, the Etappendienst (ETO), was reorganized in September 1933 as a subbranch of the Abwehr, or German military intelligence; by March 1934, operations in the Canary Islands began.[8]

Canaris personally served as Hitler's emissary to Franco during the Spanish Civil War at least four or five times, including a crucial first documented mission in September 1936 to assess Nationalist military needs. Canaris and Italian military intelligence chief Colonel Mario Roatta had met in the first week of August 1936 to consider Franco's military problems, as German transport planes were ferrying Franco's Moroccan legion across the Strait of Gibraltar. Hitler discussed the Spanish situation with German army leaders from 7 to 12 August. The first German pilots had left in July. Other pilots and tank and radio experts were reinforced in Spain in late September, and in early November, the 4,500-man Condor Legion, Hitler's third operation, was dispatched. In December, Hitler decided to maintain the legion at 4,500 to 5,000 technical experts, an elite regiment that continued operations until the end of the war in 1939. Hitler's December 1936 decision to limit German military activities in Spain allowed Mussolini to take the military lead, and Il duce sent much larger numbers of ground troops and even fighter aircraft and provided more naval support to the Spanish Nationalists for the rest of the war.

The Condor Legion bombing of Guernica in late April 1937 became the most notorious atrocity of the Spanish Civil War, thanks partly to Pablo Picasso's surreal rendering of the scene. On 26 April 1937, the Condor Legion and the Italian Aviation Legion firebombed the ancient Basque town of Guernica, killing from 200 to 1,600 civilians.[9] According to another interpretation by a U.S. Air Force historian, the bombing of Guernica killed about 500 people, mostly civilians.[10] On the other hand, this source thinks that there has been too much focus on Guernica and not enough on the Condor Legion as a whole. Earlier in the war, from 14 to 23 November 1936, several German air raids on Madrid had killed 244 civilians. The Guernica bombing experiment, approved by the chief of the Nationalist air force, proved ineffective, even counterproductive. The motives of General Emilio Mola and his German advisors in bombing Guernica were tactical and not strategic. After the incident, although Franco's propaganda denied that the Nationalists, Italians, and Germans had ever bombed the Basque town, Franco and the Condor Legion mostly abandoned the tactic of bombing civilians in Spanish towns.

Generally, the Luftwaffe was more effective than the Italian Royal Air Force in Spain, although the Italians sent their most modern aircraft models, which up to 1938 had greater performance characteristics than their German counterparts. The Italian problem was not technological but rather stemmed from faulty doctrine. Italian pilots in the 1930s were dominated by the strategic bombing theories of General Giulio Douhet (1869–1930), who invented the terror bombing theory in 1919. The theory postulated that the terror bombing of masses of civilians would force a government to surrender. In May 1938, Mussolini and General Giuseppe Valle from Rome decided to bomb the city of Barcelona as such an act of terror.

From the beginning, Hitler and Mussolini cooperated in Spain, and their relations soon warmed into the Axis protocols. Both men were masters of propaganda, with Mussolini having first made his name as a socialist journalist. In the first week of August 1936, Goebbels talked with his Italian counterpart, Minister of Popular Culture Dino Alfieri, about a joint propaganda agreement, and on 23 October, Italian foreign minister Count Galeazzo Ciano (1903–1944), until June 1936 propaganda minister, visited Munich and Berlin to sign the Axis pact.

In Hitler's mind, the Axis accord was aimed at weakening France and checking British influence on the Continent. Hitler and

Goebbels were initially more enthusiastic for this bilateral entente, which over the years became an alliance, than the somewhat independent Mussolini. On 18 November, the Germans and Italians jointly recognized the Franco government. Their two navies cooperated well in supplying the Nationalists and sinking merchant marine provisioning the Republicans.[11]

For over a year, Hitler encouraged a visit by Mussolini to the Third Reich, where the two dictators celebrated the first anniversary of the Axis pact in glorious festivities at the end of September 1937. Goebbels accurately predicted that Mussolini, on ideological grounds, would go with Berlin to the end. Amidst anti-Bolshevik speechmaking that touched on events in Spain, Italian Fascist leaders toured German military installations and attended the Nuremberg Nazi Party rally. Il duce assured the Führer that, as Germany's partner, Italy would do nothing on the Spanish question without prior German agreement. In October 1937, Mussolini joined Ribbentrop's Anti-Comintern Pact, which turned the Axis into a triangle with Japan, ostensibly aimed at isolating the USSR.

The victories of Mussolini, Hitler, and Franco weakened France's international position in the balance of power between 1936 and 1938. French-Italian naval rivalry in the Mediterranean was heightened by Italy's partial occupation of the Balearic Islands and claims to Nice, Corsica, and Tunis. The French were technically allied with many countries against their increasingly dangerous neighbors, Fascist Italy and Nazi Germany. However, friendships with Britain, Republican Spain, the USSR, Poland, Czechoslovakia, Yugoslavia, and Romania presented France with more burdens than reliable allies. France's seven friends were too hostile to each other for Paris to forge a seven-power multilateral military agreement against the menacing Rome-Berlin Axis. The anticommunist preachers in five of those seven countries, plus in half of France itself, nullified the impossible dreams of the Quai d'Orsay for an anti-German alliance system. French conservatives, faced with a choice between Great Britain and the USSR, thought that aid to the Spanish Republic would only strengthen Soviet Communism. The generally forgotten Bonnet-Ribbentrop Non-Aggression Pact, signed in Paris in December 1938, signaled that France was no longer a great power and willing to try Poland's ploy of 1934. Georges Bonnet, French foreign minister, turned out to be an even bigger appeaser than either Chamberlain or Stalin.

The outbreak of the Sino-Japanese War in July 1937 weakened both the USSR and Britain by diverting some of their energies and attention from the European-Spanish crisis to defend China, also divided by civil war. In March 1938, Hitler annexed Austria with Mussolini's blessing and without firing a shot. Then, in September 1938, London and Paris put pressure on Prague to cede the Sudetenland to Hitler, in the most famous of Prime Minister Neville Chamberlain's (1869–1940) sellouts. In retrospect, the Munich Agreement would be Britain's last major stand for isolationist appeasement. France had signed a 1925 military treaty to protect a democratic Czechoslovakia, so that the four-power Munich Agreement between Great Britain, France, Italy, and Germany was a clear violation of international law. To Hitler, the Sudetenland and Czechoslovakia were merely stepping-stones in his imperial expansion program against Eastern Europe and the Soviet Union. But the French and the British failed to foresee Hitler's next moves on Prague, Danzig (Gdánsk), and Poland in 1939. Meanwhile, during this period, the United States was, by choice, a neutral isolationist nation, largely withdrawn from the European power struggle.

One of the major lessons of the Munich Agreement was that leading French and British politicians failed in playing the balance of power game, a struggle to determine who would dominate the future of Europe. Hitler, by appealing to anticommunism and Anglo-French guilt for the harsh terms of the Versailles treaty, secured British and French cooperation for partitioning a democratic Czechoslovakia and keeping Stalin isolated. Excessive fear of Leninism and social revolution betrayed democracy at home and in Czechoslovakia and Spain. For Stalin, it meant giving up on the dying French-Soviet Pact of 1935, resulting in a gradual Soviet shift away from the Popular Front, pro-French line.

After the Munich Agreement, Franco's victory was assured, as new German and Italian aid flowed to the Nationalists, and the International Brigades evacuated the leftist zone of Spain late in 1938. While Franco was mopping up the last resistance in Spain in the spring of 1939, Hitler's forces seized Prague on 16 March. Slovakia and Hungary became satellite allies by joining the side of the Axis through the burgeoning Anti-Comintern Pact. Hitler next turned his full attention to Danzig and Poland. A major concern in London and Paris up to May 1939 was whether Mussolini and Hitler would withdraw their troops and dismantle their naval bases in Spain, as they had promised many times since 1936. Only a minority in Britain felt threatened by Franco's vague ambition to retake Gibraltar. Stalin repaid the Western appeasers in kind by signing the famous Non-Aggression Pact on 23 August. By this Nazi-Soviet pact, the USSR protected itself, at least temporarily, from the coming European war, and Stalin joined the ranks of those who had appeased Hitler. After Britain and France went to war with Hitler in September 1939, Nationalist Spain remained basically, albeit malevolently, neutral toward Britain until June 1941. Then, when Hitler attacked the USSR, Franco partly repaid the Condor Legion war debt by sending the Spanish Blue Division to the Soviet front.

Hitler and Mussolini first fought together in Spain and thereby gained ground for the Axis in the European balance of power from 1936 to 1939. The collaboration of Hitler's and Mussolini's troops supports a historical interpretation, espoused by American Ambassador Claude Bowers at the time, that views the Spanish Civil War as the opening round of World War II.

Notes

1. See *Die Tagebücher von Joseph Goebbels: Sämtliche Fragmente,* ed. Elke Fröhlich (Munich, 1987). Vol. 2 covers to 31 December 1936; vol. 3 covers 1 January 1937 to 31 December 1939. On Carlism, cf. diary entry 5–6 November 1936. See also Robert H. Whealey, "Goebbels and the Spanish Civil War," in *The Historian,* vol. 61 (Winter 1999), pp. 341–360.
2. Actually, this exaggerates the significance of Ribbentrop on Spanish affairs, as opposed to the general ideological relationship of communism, Britain, and the USSR as seen in Berlin. See G. T. Waddington, "Ribbentrop and the Soviet Union, 1937–1941," in *Barbarossa: The Axis and the Allies,* ed. John Erickson and D. N. Dilks (Edinburgh, 1995), pp. 7–33. Waddington says that then Ambassador to Britain Ribbentrop turned against Britain in December 1937. Robert H. Whealey, *Hitler and Spain: The Nazi Role in the Spanish Civil War, 1936–1939* (Lexington, Ky., 1989), believes the decisive turning point of Anglo-German relations was in May of 1937; see pp. 110–111.
3. Serrano attempted to unify Franco's new totalitarian party, the FET y JONS, with the traditional local administrative caciques. See Antonio Cazorla-Sánchez, University of Granada, "What Should We Do with Caciques? Old Politics in the Francoist New State, 1938–1941," paper at the Society of Spanish and Portuguese Historians, University of Minnesota, Minneapolis, April 1997.
4. J. A. Ferrer Benimeli, *El Contubernio Judeo-Masónico-Comunista: del Satanismo al escándalo de la P-2* (Madrid, 1982), sheds light on the many reactionaries in Spain who held to the absurd theory that a single Masonic-Jewish-communist conspiracy was causing social revolution in Spain. Although the main thrust of Spanish reactionary thinking was anti-Masonic, many Spanish journalists made naive comments on the forged *Protocols of the Elders of Zion* (1899), as did one of the founders of the Falange y JONS, Onésimo Redondo, in 1932.
5. Christian Leitz, *Economic Relations between Nazi Germany and Franco's Spain, 1936–1945* (New York, 1996), pp. 36–37.
6. *Die Tagebücher von Joseph Goebbels,* 1 August 1937. On the treaties see Whealey, *Hitler and Spain,* p. 89.

7. Whealey, *Hitler and Spain*, p. 202, n. 7; Angel Viñas, *La Alemania nazi y el 18 de Julio: antecedentes de la intervención alemana en la guerra civil española* (Madrid, 1974), pp. 29–80; R. H. Whealey, "Anglo-American Oil Confronts Spanish Nationalism, 1927–31: A Study of Economic Imperialism," *Diplomatic History*, vol. 12 (1988), pp. 111–126, here p. 115, n. 11. More details about Lufthansa in the Atlantic islands in Marion Einhorn, *Die ökonomischen Hintergründe der faschistischen deutschen Intervention in Spanien, 1936–1939* (Berlin, 1962), pp. 36–42.
8. Memorandum, Abwehr Lt. Vehrmehren to Lt. Cmd. G. Krüger, Abw. Sect. V, Conversation with Kapt. Lt. John T. Essberger (German Naval Reserve and captain and owner of a commercial shipping line), OKM Docs., PG 49087, pp. 7a, 16–17. The Abwehr sent agent Christopher Jansen to negotiate with CEPSA in Tenerife. Jansen had worked in the islands and in Madeira in World War I as a coal merchant.
9. Ferdinando Pedriali, *Guerra di spagna e aviazione italiana* (Pinerlo, 1983), documents the Italian participation in the raid. For Goebbels's comments, see his *Tagebücher*, 30 April 1937, 4 and 5 May 1937. On the propaganda surrounding the incident, see H. R. Southworth, *Guernica! Guernica! A Study of Journalism, Diplomacy, and History* (Berkeley, Calif., 1977). Statistics on Guernica casualties vary greatly. Southworth claims the maximum of 1,600 deaths. However, a later book by Jesús Salas Larrazabal, *Guernica: el bombadero* (Madrid, 1981), claims that the bombing caused only 200 deaths; this estimate is accepted by Pedriali. K. A. Maier, in his article "Guernica: Fakten und Mythen," *German Studies Review*, vol. 18 (1995), pp. 465–470, cites Salas but does not add any new information on the number of casualties.
10. J. S. Corum, "The Luftwaffe and the Coalition Air War in Spain, 1936–1939," in *Airpower: Theory and Practice*, ed. John Gooch (London, 1995), pp. 68–90.
11. Contrary to an interpretation of the conflict that is suggested in my book *Hitler and Spain*, Italian research shows that the Axis agreement worked well on the naval level. Italian warships used the Enigma Code and assisted the German Condor Legion in bombing Republican vessels in the Mediterranean. They also cooperated in the Battle of Málaga. On 10 December 1936, Captain Giovanni Ferretti met with Franco's naval minister, Admiral Juan Cervera, and German Rear Admiral Hermann Boehm on the cruiser *Nürnberg* off the coast of Ceuta to map out a naval strategy for the entire war. This was followed up by a second three-way naval conference near Cádiz on 30 December between Admiral Cervera, Admiral Moreno, Commander Hermann von Fischel, and Italian Rear Admiral Angelo Iaccino on the battleship *Graf Spree*. See Franco Bargoni, *L'Impegno navale italiano durante la guerra civile spagnola, 1936–1939* (Rome, 1992), pp. 153–161, 444–457. Bargoni's book, subsequent to the publication of *Hitler and Spain*, supplements the German naval story. According to the contemporary German Navy's Pistorius Report (see Whealey, *Hitler and Spain*, p. 203, n. 23), the Germans sent 154 vessels with men and supplies, the first one leaving Hamburg on 31 July for Cádiz. Later, most of the German vessels resupplying the Condor Legion arrived in Vigo.

– 15 –

WHAT THE CONDOR SAW

Nazi Propaganda Images of the
Spanish Civil War

Conrad Kent

When the Condor Legion returned to Germany after the Spanish Civil War, many "legionnaires" narrated their stories to an eager German public. Within months of their return in 1939, tales of heroism and the epic grandeur of German warplanes thrilled the country. The anonymous *Deutsche kämpfen in Spanien*, Karl Georg von Stackelberg's *Legion Condor*, and Wulf Bley's collection of twenty-seven aviators' stories in *Das Buch der Spanienflieger* recounted in poetry, anecdote, and nostalgic reveries the exploits of German soldiers and pilots. Max Graf Hoyos, liaison officer between the Spanish and German forces, was still looking back on his chivalric adventures as an aviator from the first days of the war through the conquest of Bilbao in the summer of 1937. A year later, Werner Beumelburg, an established writer of Great War tales, attempted to formalize the history of the Condor Legion in *Kampf um Spanien: Die Geschichte der Legion Condor* by providing a semblance of objectivity to what George L. Mosse has described as the myth of the war experience. Widely disseminated, these memoirs extolled the gallantry of German officers who fought in primitive conditions and energized a nation prepared for the next war. Relying on all the heroic conventions of war, especially the medievalizing conventions of World War I, the returning legionnaires told of a conflict to which the German presence had given a mythic order and meaning.[1]

Yet these legionnaire tales do not tell another story, that of the remarkable process by which the German military experimented in modern warfare. Improvement in supply procedures, the concentration of armor in spearheads, the coordination of armor and bombing to create panic, the rapid adjustment of airplanes to new combat conditions, and new forms of protecting aircraft were among what Robert H. Whealey has called the nine lessons of modern warfare that the Germans learned in Spain.[2] By the time they had left Spain in the late spring of 1939, the German military was mobilized and expeditious, eminently capable of rapid deployment of arms in a kind of war very different from World War I. While much of the world dwelled in an older conception of combat—the French buttressing their immobile defenses even further against attack along the Maginot line—the Germans unrelentingly explored ways to avoid stationary battle lines and the concentration of forces in inert defensive blocks. That the lessons in military efficiency and flexibility the Condor Legion had learned in the field and in the air in Spain would quickly revolutionize the practice of warfare in Europe was to be expected. What is surprising is that the experience produced no corresponding revision of perspectives in the representation of war and political conflict. Entrenched in an anachronistic world-view, the German military continued to frame the war in monumentalist images founded on mythic assumptions little affected by the fluidity and complexity of their own experience in combat or the technical advances in photography, which were already highly developed at the time. Moreover, it is not clear that the heroic vision was self-consciously controlled as a mask for the brutality of war as it had been in the first war. In photography more than in any other medium, the dual nature of the German experience in Spain reveals itself to be deeply rooted and shared by many different individuals.

Technical Advances: The Miniature Camera

By the time the Spanish Civil War had begun, photography was clearly an obsession in Germany. Many of the nineteen thousand Germans who served in Spain carried with them the miniature cameras with which German industry had revolutionized photography in the 1920s. Soldiers and commercial photographers alike carried the continuously updated small Leica cameras first introduced in 1925 by Leitz of Wetzlar. Not much larger than today's point-and-shoot cameras, the cameras with which they captured their images were the Leica II and IIIa screwmounts, the optical counterpoint to the mobility and flexibility of the modern war machine. Cameras from the other German manufacturer of miniature cameras, Zeiss Ikon of Jena, whose Contax model had been introduced in 1926, were there when the Leica was not.

Leicas and Contaxes simplified the photographic operation and made possible a spontaneity of image for a culture of picture-taking hobbyists as well as a corps of European street photographers, like Cartier-Bresson and André Kertész, whose work fundamentally altered modern photography during the decade from the mid-1920s to the mid-1930s. Even General Erwin Rommel had become a "shutterbug," weighing the relative merits of Contax construction and the Leica viewfinder in informal photographic discussion groups. Equipping amateur and professional alike with dependable, lightweight cameras with interchangeable, astonishingly fast lenses and the capability for both rapidity and accuracy in focusing even in low-light situations, Leitz and Zeiss Ikon provided the technology for a new, candid photography, capable not just of sequential images, but also of multiple angles of vision of the same event. Capturing the unplanned moment, the masters of that period left a legacy of lessons so deep and so widespread that they could not have escaped the attention of the German photographers who went to Spain during the Civil War. By the summer of 1936, the first German soldiers and civilian advisers were beginning to record the warfare with this new photographic technology. With Leica and Contax cameras, they could quickly focus subjects both stationary and in motion at speeds of up to 1/500th of a second, shooting frame after frame of roll film, another innovation, as easily as they typed reports on recently improved typewriters.[3]

Occasionally, the extant photographs of this era show the unvarnished images we might expect of candid photography. In figure 1, we see a photograph that appears to be unstaged, taken as a photographer encountered Francisco Franco's (1892–1975) Moroccan troops on a country road. Intrigued by the soldiers trudging in the opposite direction, the photographer leaned forward from the back seat and spontaneously lifted the camera to his eye, perhaps to capture the sight of African exotics. Improvising, he framed his image of the soldiers in a foreground we would have seen if we had been looking over the photographer's shoulder. We see the Moroccans, the steering wheel, the driver's right hand,

FIGURE 1: Franco's Moroccan troops in February 1937.

Photo credit: Zentralbild. Bundesarchiv der Bundesrepublik Deutschland (hereafter "Bundesarchiv"), no. H27143.

and the rear-view mirror reflecting the back of a cap of a soldier already past the viewfinder in a layered composition of unplanned complexity. Yet as we shall see, even the apparent spontaneity of the image coincides with a reductive attitude toward the Moroccan soldiers as exotic curios on the margins of the war that the Condor Legion and the Spanish Nationalists were waging. Capable of capturing the multiplicity of the war experience, the new Leicas were made to serve very much as the heavy cameras that they had supplanted throughout Europe and America for nearly a decade. The camera could not refocus the eye beyond its viewfinder.

The Photographers

The photographers who took the images of this German adventure in Spain carried with them the paradoxes that would extend to so many aspects of this war and the larger one that was looming.

When Germany agreed early in the Nationalist uprising against the Republic to side with the rebels, some eighty-five "volunteers" arrived in August of 1936, and by September, they had already seen action in Irún. Bearing ideals of courage, patriotism, and camaraderie, as they had been shaped in World War I, these soldiers were nevertheless the scouts of a new school of military tactics. They assisted Franco's troops with a cold efficiency while still maintaining the altruistic semblance of helping a sacred cause.

At first, the Germans were minimally engaged in the war as a visual experience. English news agencies supplied various archival photographs of these early troops and of the first members of the Condor Legion, who arrived during the first week of November 1936. Even with the choreographed Olympic Games of 1936, the Nazis were slow in developing an appropriate ministry for the collection of the visual record of their exploits in Spain. Spain was too remote from the Reich to be easily integrated into Germany's propaganda strategies. It was not until General Wilhelm Keitel (1882–1946) suggested the creation of a Wehrmacht propaganda ministry in February 1937 that the German armed forces began to develop a program for taking and filing their own photographs. And yet even then, images followed received patterns of visualizing war, perhaps because the Reichsministerium was not yet in a position to demand photographs for immediate publication and distribution. Adolf Hitler (1889–1945) kept the deployment of the German troops in Spain an open secret until the very end of the war. Not until 30 January 1939 did Hitler make their presence public.

With the accessibility of the new cameras and the dawning awareness of the value of the Spanish Civil War for propaganda purposes, an archival collection with German photographs did develop over the course of the war. The photographer Stempka provided the Reichsministerium with images through the Scherl Bilderdienst of Berlin during the first half of the war. Mensing photographed images of the German war schools in Ávila and Salamanca during the spring of 1938, and a Dr. Franz provided images of the last year of the war to the Reichsministerium, again through the Scherl agency. Many photographs were provided by Zentralbild of Berlin and by the Fulgur agency of Paris toward the end of the war. Some anonymous German photographs represent military intelligence photography. Members of the Condor Legion also made souvenir photographs of the war, publishing images in a half dozen conventionalized memoirs published in Germany in 1939 and 1940.

The Legacy

In the midst of reshaping warfare to maximize technological capabilities, the Germans in Spain subordinated technological innovation in photographing war to a received world-view. Instead of producing spontaneous compositions commensurate with Germany's many military innovations, the photographers compiled a record of staged performances of only a few of those innovations. Of the thousands of photographs the Germans took of the Spanish Civil War, most pretended to memorialize war heroism of a kind ponderously waged on World War I battlefields and paraded along bannered avenues. Perhaps not coincidentally, these images seem to evoke the élan and victory celebrations denied to the Germans after suffering in the trenches of Verdun and Château-Thierry. Here they were making Spain the surrogate venue for the 1918 victory parades that had been celebrated on Fifth Avenue, Trafalgar Square, and the Champs Elysées.

Stuck in an archaic vision despite new technology, the photographers assembled for the Reichsministerium a collection of conventions. They could not escape the formulaic patterns of mind that led to discrepancies between pragmatism and pseudoheroic fancy. The first category of images from Spain illustrates how the Germans adapted to their own needs the binary oppositions constructed by ultraconservative Spanish propaganda between the pious, heroic Spaniard and the dangerously monstrous Spanish left. The images show simple distinctions between good and bad Spaniards, including militarized Bolshevik women in juxtaposition with saintly iconic women of tradition. Second, the Germans concerned themselves with monuments and ruins as emblems through which Francoist action and German intervention were justified. Third, images pertaining to the Condor Legion itself do exist, even though Hitler did not officially admit its presence in Spain until early 1939. Included in this section are the aerial photographs taken by Germans for intelligence purposes. A fourth category of images pertains to a sustained fixation on Franco's Moroccan soldiers, both as soldiers in the field and as exotic knights of the desert who became Franco's flamboyant ceremonial guard in victory parades and related celebrations. A fifth important category of images collected by the propagandists pertains to Catalonia and the pictorial evidence of the crucial campaign to conquer Barcelona during late 1938 and the first months of 1939. A final collection of images celebrates the Condor Legion, both in Spain and in Germany in 1939. Through these last images we see the

Germans of the Condor Legion in high profile—festooned and bemedaled—as they preened in victory marches in the early summer before the German invasion of Poland of September 1939.

The Opposition between Good and Evil

Since the early months of the war, the Reichsministerium had gathered images of Spain from other sources. The war had begun before the creation of the Reichsministerium in early 1937, and the photographs were borrowed largely from Spanish propagandists. Images of Republican social chaos, Bolshevik sacrilege, and militarized women were the conventional visual language of the Spanish ultraconservatives, including the Spanish church. Like the poster propaganda from both camps that demonized the enemy, the photographs flattened perspectives and juxtaposed exaggerated images in caricature.

German propagandists made indirect use of the sacred images that the Spanish church used in its own defense. Although the Reich had signed a condordat with the Vatican in 1933, the Spanish Nationalist forces were, of course, much closer to the church. Spanish church-sponsored periodicals had railed against the "godless Republic" throughout the prewar period; Pope Pius XI rejoiced at the fall of Málaga; and, by July 1937, the bishops of Spain proclaimed their support for Franco. The German agency merely appropriated the received images for their own crusade against the Bolsheviks. For the Germans, the religious program inherent in many of the Spanish photographs was secondary to the impression of communist chaos and disintegration that the Nazis were seeking to communicate to the German public. The Spanish images therefore served to repudiate Bolsheviks for their disorganization, Republican crowds for their violence and lack of discipline, the leftist body politic for its decay, and the socialist imagination for its lack of spirit.

The photomontage of figure 2 dramatizes the effect of Spanish leftist ravages. Assembled in such a way as to emphasize Republican destructiveness, the montage evokes the various aspects of Spanish tradition against which the Bolsheviks warred. It therefore more closely resembles a devotional image of popular piety than an avant-garde photomontage of the same period.

As a documentary corollary to the photomontage, photographs of Republican Madrid were compiled to document the living chaos of the city under Republican auspices. In one image taken without

FIGURE 2: A Spanish photograph appropriated for an anticommunist Nazi propaganda exhibition at the Reichstag: "Bolschewismus ohne Maske" (Bolshevism unmasked).

Anonymous photograph, with elements recalling the work of the Spanish photographer Brangulí. Bundesarchiv, no. R95/4/27a.

FIGURE 3: Refugees in Madrid.

Anonymous photograph. Bundesarchiv, no. 95/67/17.

attribution in 1936 (fig. 3), hopelessly displaced people suggest the fragmentation and disorder of life under the Republic—evidence of Republican instability, rather than rebel aggression.

Another visual formula shared by both the Spanish and the German photographers was their fixation on the role of women in public life. For both German and Spanish Nationalist propagandists, the leftist female was an angry demon who showed no respect for order or discipline. The militarized woman in particular became a monster governed by dark passions, the most visible demonstration of the Republic's violation of the laws of nature (fig. 4). By contrast, the iconic madonna nurturing ultraconservative Spanish Catholic values was a pliant, all-suffering saint placed on a domestic pedestal. Nationalist females were nurses, dispensers of charity, mothers, homemakers, and orderly participants in the Sección Feminina of the Falange (fig. 5). Conventionally composed without ambiguous margins or exaggerated individual details, these photographs extol the pious joy of the people whom the Francoists pretended to liberate from the prison of the Republic.

The Heroic Building: Monuments and Ruins

German and Spanish Nationalist propagandists alike made frequent use of imposing structures in the built landscape. For both the Nazis and the Francoists, colossal historic piles were symbolic of a mythic past, threatened by the new Bolsheviks. Painters from Germany and Spain produced huge canvases on which spectacular relics of historical culture formed the backdrop for current gestures of heroism. Replicating the same model, photographers for the Condor Legion and the Spanish Nationalists also sought out massive structures to dominate their own images of defense of the deepest traditions of the land. With miniature cameras at their disposal, and a residual romantic taste for the cult of the exotic in remote places like Spain, the German photographers conflated various visual conventions into a bizarre collection of monumental images. They both yearned for the heroic stability of ancient times and amused themselves with condescending folkloric depictions.[4]

Throughout the 1920s, "most of the German professors longed for the return of the glory days of Bismarck's empire."[5] Both scholars and amateur archaists promoted austere monuments as popular excursion destinations for an expanding industrial population. Hoary ruins in the romantic lithograph were transferred to the steel engraving and finally to the photograph, where they exploded onto

FIGURE 4: Communist on her way to the front to fight with the volunteers.

Anonymous photograph. Bundesarchiv, no. R68/50/8.

hundreds of thousands of postcards and stereopticon images. A quaint decrepitude befitting romantic idylls of the past became a patina of legitimacy, authenticating ancient grandeur.

Salamanca, the seat of Franco's military government from late September 1936, and the seat of his political government beginning in 1937, offered a heroic stage on which the Nazi photographers constructed some of their early monumentalist images. The city was an ensemble of venerable buildings with an imperial past, propitious for evoking atmospheric images for the German audience. German images of Salamanca made the medieval and Golden Age architecture the backdrop for depicting the traditional

FIGURE 5: The "Margaritas" who aided the Falange by sewing woolens for the battle of San Sebastián.

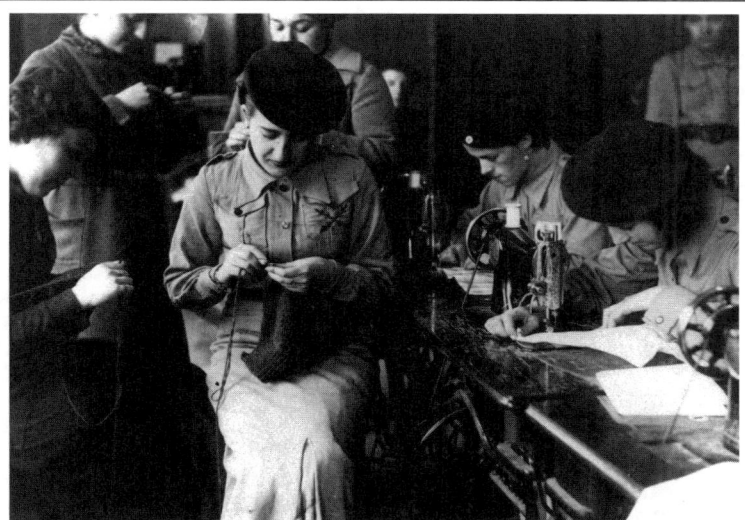

Photo credit: Stempka. Bundesarchiv, no. 95/67/27.

life Franco claimed to be protecting. Photographs of Salamanca predictably include traditional archetypes: peasants with their donkeys on the Roman bridge over the River Tormes; the urban poor sitting with their children in the shadow of a great tower, quaintly inhabiting a place of ancient romance; locals promenading in the Plaza Mayor; and crude dwellings huddled below the towers of the old and new cathedrals (fig. 6). Such photographs recall the albums of itinerant romantic artists indulging in nostalgic reveries. In the 1930s, however, the compositions of the German photographers were not far removed from Hollywood set designs in which monuments were props for actions only marginally related to them.

In the wonderland of Francoist and Nazi propaganda, solid monuments became instant ruins, and war-ravaged ruins became shining monuments to recent victories. For the Francoists, the demolished Alcazar of Toledo became a primary symbol of their martyrdom. For the German photographers, scenes of urban devastation were depicted frontally and with a grandeur modeled on the same visual tactics with which the photographers had portrayed the venerable towers of Salamanca. Ironically, the ruins the German photographers selected were the bombed buildings and

FIGURE 6: The Renaissance tower, the "Torre del Clavero," as part of the architectural and military heritage of Salamanca.

Photo credit: Kautschoumoff. Bundesarchiv, no. 95/68/35.

shattered cities that the Nationalists and the Condor Legion had destroyed in their methodical aggression against the Republic. In one image, smiling officers survey the ruins. With their relaxed pose, the soldiers recall the nineteenth-century travelers who were often photographed inspecting architectural curiosities in faraway places (fig. 7).

Guernica is the paragon of all Civil War ruins, both for the Republic and for the Germans. The bombing of Guernica occurred on 26 April 1937. The Sygma Agency photograph in the German archives (fig. 8) was probably taken when General Mola's troops entered Guernica at noon on 29 April, two and one-half days after

FIGURE 7: Francoist forces examining the destruction of buildings in Madrid.

Anonymous photograph. Bundesarchiv, no. 95/67/28.

the bombing. The photograph shows the fires still burning, but the presence of a dazed dog would suggest a scene following the bombing itself. Another photograph assembled from four later photographs of Guernica taken by Zentralbild is a devastating record of Guernica, seen in pseudomonumental grandeur on a grotesque scale.

Herbert Southworth had documented the Spanish Nationalists' attempts to attribute the destruction of Guernica to Republican elements.[6] Pro-Nationalists perpetuated this claim for thirty years; then, in the last years of the Franco era, Francoists changed the official position to blame the Germans in order to exculpate the

Figure 8: Guernica after the bombing of 26 April 1937.

Photo credit: Sygma Agency through Zentralbild. Bundesarchiv, no. S30063.

Spanish Nationalists. Francoist forces appear to have requested the bombing of Guernica, during which both Italian and German planes dropped Thermit bombs, burning the wooden structures of the city with temperatures rising to 3,000 degrees centigrade. Southworth also presents evidence to suggest that Spaniards ordered the bombing, and that Italian and German planes may have dropped the bombs without the knowledge of the German High Command in Berlin. Perhaps one or the other of the German leaders in Spain during the spring of 1937 had encouraged Franco, or were persuaded by him, to bomb Guernica. In any case, the gung-ho Nazi-affiliated German ambassador Wilhelm von Faupel was replaced by the career diplomat Eberhard von Stohrer

FIGURE 9: Guernica several days after the bombing.

Photo credit: Europa Press through Zentralbild. Bundesarchiv, no. T1128/312.

in the late summer of 1937, and the head of the Condor Legion, Hugo Sperrle, with whom Faupel had been in continuous conflict, was himself replaced by Helmuth Volkmann on 31 October 1937.

Southworth also points out that the pro-Nationalist French news service Havas was slow to provide information on the Guernica event, even though English and other news services had featured the story on 27 April. Pablo Picasso (1881–1973), who was living in Paris, would have picked up bits and pieces of information, but no photographs, in the few days following the event. By 29 April, all Paris would have known of the bombing, and by 1 May, Picasso had started work on his painting devoted to the subject. He could conceivably have had access to the kind of photograph taken by the French agency, Europa Press (fig. 9).

Monumentalizing the New Technology

The mechanized warfare with which the Germans were experimenting in the Spanish Civil War represented a curious challenge to the photographer. On the one hand, the war was being depicted in epic terms; photographers made visual euphemisms of even bombed-out buildings. On the other hand, fascination with the instruments of war and the existence of new, prototype planes and tanks created the necessity to integrate images of the new technology into archaic visual formulas. Often photographs pertaining to technology were therefore framed in traditional contexts or assembled in images dissociated from contemporary invention.

Some documentary images associated with war technology and training appear to be the result of military assignments. At the end of March 1938, the German photographer Mensing documented the German military schools in Ávila and Salamanca (fig. 10). German officers typically appear in the center of the image, leading Spanish "volunteers" through training sessions. Several images are of German officers formally inspecting the Spanish trainees on parade grounds. On one occasion, an image of German officers inspecting modern artillery highlights the contrast between German machines and picturesque Spanish resources (fig. 11). With these photographs, Berlin wanted to see—or rather the Condor Legion wanted Berlin to see—evidence of an efficient military operation in Spain. In fact, due in part to the strain of the unfinished war, 1938 became a difficult year for the Condor Legion, and by October, Wolfram von Richthofen, former chief of staff, had to assume charge of rebuilding the German forces in Spain.

Images taken at the "Gasschule" on 30 March 1938 in Salamanca are documentary photographs of Spanish "volunteers" in a Condor Legion training center (fig. 12). The Spanish soldiers, participating in what was called the Servicio de Guerra Química, were photographed against a distant background of Salamanca. Additional photographs in this series demonstrate other aspects of chemical warfare and flamethrowing exercises. Such images stand in contrast with the folklorish, pseudoheroic German images of historic Salamanca.

The Condor Legion's role in the air war is documented by the photographic record. Although many of the photographs were standard air shots of bombings, harbor scenes, and cityscapes, the photographs from the air resemble all aerial photography of the period. Here photographic technology took precedence over monumentalizing aspirations. From on high, and with virtually no heroic precedents to follow, image-makers allowed technology and intelligence requirements to supersede propaganda.

Such was not the case in the photography of the German planes themselves. These new machines were assimilated into the conventional categories with which the Condor Legion conceptualized their Spanish expedition. If aerial photography was largely

FIGURE 10: German instructors in the Ávila training grounds.

Photo credit: Mensing. Bundesarchiv, no. R68/48/79.

FIGURE 11: Moving artillery with beasts of burden at the Ávila training grounds.

Anonymous photograph. Bundesarchiv, no. R74/127/13.

FIGURE 12: Chemical warfare exercises at the Salamanca "Gasschule."

Anonymous photograph. Bundesarchiv, no. 68/49/75a.

FIGURE 13: A photomontage of Ju 52 planes over Burgos.

Anonymous image. Bundesarchiv, no. R73/36/25.

What the Condor Saw | 343

FIGURE 14: Moroccan soldiers leaving the city of Leganés.

Photo credit: H.G.v. Studnitz. Bundesarchiv, no. 95/70/17a.

FIGURE 15: Captured Republican soldiers guarded by the Moroccan soldiers.

Anonymous photograph. Bundesarchiv, no. PO 220/511.

FIGURE 16: Moroccan soldiers rendered as leisurely cosmopolites in Barcelona, March 1939.

Photo credit: Zentralbild. Bundesarchiv, no. E20106/25.

FIGURE 17: Italian propaganda photograph of Franco's Moroccan color guard, 22 February 1939.

Photo credit: "Vedo" (Rome). Bundesarchiv, no. 95/71/25.

FIGURE 18: A Moroccan guardsman preparing for a ceremonial march in Barcelona, March 1939.

Anonymous photograph. Bundesarchiv, no. R99360.

FIGURE 19: Republican refugees moving toward the French border at Perthus, January 1939.

Photo credit: Zentralbild. Bundesarchiv, no. P0305/508.

functional, photography of German planes was either monumentalist or campy. Figure 13 is a propaganda photomontage of Ju 52 aircraft and the city of Burgos. These planes were known as the Condor Lufthansa and were the inspiration for the name of the Legion. Burgos was the first political capital of the Franco government and one of the symbolic centers of conservative Spanish culture. A virtual fascist devotional image, the photomontage shows German "Condors" protectively flocking over the hieratic Spanish city.

Franco's Moroccan Troops

If the Condor Legion kept a low profile, the opposite was true of the troops who fought with Franco from the earliest days of the rebellion against the Republic. German photographers were fascinated by Franco's Moroccan troops in both their rough appearance in battle and their exotic parade regalia in victory celebrations. In keeping with the formulaic character of the Nazi vision, the strangeness of

FIGURE 20: Republican refugees on entering France at Perthus, January 1939.

Photo credit: Fulgur Agency (Paris). Bundesarchiv, no. 95/70/30a.

the Moroccans, seen alternately as grotesque monsters or as brave desert warriors, captivated the German photographer throughout the war. Through reductive conventions, moreover, the Nazis were able to sublimate their own racist attitudes toward the Arabs as their allies. In any guise, the Arabic figures were visual symbols of the colonial aura in which the German military wrapped the Spanish experience. In their photographs and in their narrative memoirs, the Moroccans were central to the pseudomedieval fantasy of the Germans in Spain.

For Franco, the Moroccan troops, or *Moros*, were the legacy of the Africanist military campaigns that had divided the Spanish nation in its last efforts to retain vestiges of a once legendary colonial power. As soldiers, the Moroccans were an effective military force, flamboyant extras in Franco's formal military reviews, and devices of psychological warfare against the Republic. For the German photographers, they were either menacing savages or exotic color guards. Especially during the first years of the war, the German photographers depicted them as rustic curiosities, dark savages fighting on the same side through an accident of history. Nazi photographers captured them on film as a glum and ragtag outfit; spontaneous compositions of the Moroccans seem to be appropriate for the ragged and unvarnished troops. The depiction of these soldiers on the run has the grab-shot quality made possible by the miniature Leica and Contax cameras. The Nazi photographers apparently did not regard the subject, or the captured Republicans, as worthy of heroic framing. The gritty immediacy of war was not erased from the composition when the Nazis aggressively pointed their small cameras at these subjects. In a strategy similar to the medieval artist depicting peasants, rogues, and sinners in their crude vernacular traits, the photographer's rough-and-tumble images of aliens and enemies provided confirmation of the natural law of the world's hierarchy and an extension of the Third Reich's neomedieval fantasy and racist arrogance (figs. 14 and 15).

At the conclusion of the war, a different kind of photography shows the Moroccans graciously at ease in the cafés of Barcelona and in magnificent regalia in the victory parade on the Gran Via. As figures of leisure after the war, they were depicted as patronizing and compassionate—welcomed by the population as protectors (fig. 16). As flamboyant warriors of the desert, they added a movie-set cachet to the victory parade in Barcelona, followed by the culminating celebration in Madrid. Ceremoniously exploited throughout the war in such centers as Burgos and Salamanca, they were now dressed up to add pomp to Franco's victory parades. Accompanying goose-stepping Condor Legionnaires, Franco's turbaned warriors of the desert appear to fulfill the Spanish Arabic colonial fantasy (figs. 17 and 18).

Catalonia

In early 1939, the Nazis and their German photo agencies were mesmerized by the collapse of Catalonia. German photographers hovered over the flight of hundreds of thousands of Catalan people and Republican sympathizers from other parts of Spain. From late 1938 through the first months of 1939, the photographers recorded thousands of people lurching to borders already closed

FIGURE 21: Spanish Nationalist officers at leisure in a captured Barcelona.

Anonymous photograph. Bundesarchiv, no. 95/67/10.

FIGURE 22: Spanish Nationalist soldiers in a café.

Photo credit: Zentralbild. Bundesarchiv, no. E20120/26.

FIGURE 23: A Gypsy offering to tell the fortune of a soldier in Barcelona after the fall of the city.

Photo credit: Dr. Franz. Bundesarchiv, no. 95/68/28.

to many by the French. On 30 January 1939, Hitler proclaimed to the world that the Germans had been helping to make the Nationalist victory possible. The world was now free to see the evidence of German military prowess and the last desperate scramble of the "red peril" in Spain. The photographs from this period through the fall of Catalonia in March emphasize the disorder in the streets and on the roads, much like the first images of Madrid in 1936. In the mountains and at the French border, the fleeing throngs again conjured the dreaded specter of the disintegration of social order (figs. 19 and 20).

FIGURE 24: A market in Barcelona during the last weeks of the war.

Photo credit: Dr. Franz, Scherl Bilderdienst. Bundesarchiv, no. 95/68/29.

Catalonia's state of collapse gave the German photographers license to evoke a leisurely expansiveness in the cafés and boulevards of Barcelona. Suddenly, the work of sophisticated photographers began to appear. In addition to recording the trappings of victory, these photographers noticed the casual encounters in the afterglow of Barcelona's nightlife. Dimly lit interiors and figures out of focus in both the foreground and the background capture a fleeting world of café pleasures. As in the demimonde explored by Brassaï (1899–1984) in his book of this period, *Paris by Night*,[7] a photographer has represented a Nationalist officer in elegant nonchalance against the backdrop of an out-of-focus waiter and nested among blurred comrades in arms and the civilian upper crust in suits (fig. 21). The man's pose suggests urbanity made possible through victory in the war, just as the photographer has refocused his heroic lens to capture the pleasures of leisure after victory. In another scene from this period, probably the same photographer captured Spanish military men of lesser rank and a woman drinking from coarse bar glasses. Yet here, too, the German photographer

FIGURE 25: Franco's victory parade in Madrid, 19 May 1939.

Anonymous photograph. Bundesarchiv, no. 95/67/19.

has appropriated surface aspects of the avant-garde street photographer for a tribute to military prowess—a world apart from the café scenes of Brassaï and his contemporaries (fig. 22).

One photographer of the later group of confident German travelers to Spain, Dr. Franz, could not resist temptations similar to those experienced by the nineteenth-century traveler indulging in Orientalist fantasies in the legendary sites of the Iberian Peninsula. Confirming the colorful strangeness of Barcelona were images of Gypsy fortunetellers and singers (fig. 23). Distracted by exotic types, including Gypsies in various traditional poses, Dr. Franz also contrived strategies by which destitute Barcelona city

FIGURE 26: Maidens adorning the legionnaires with flowers in Hamburg.

Anonymous photograph. Bundesarchiv, no. 95/68/37.

dwellers, forced to survive as street peddlers, appeared as if they were the denizens of an ancient village (fig. 24).

The Final Victory Marches

After Barcelona fell, Toledo and Madrid were brought under Francoist control. With all of Spain now dominated by Francoist forces, the victory celebrations rehearsed in Barcelona were brought to Madrid. On 17 May 1939, at Barajas airport in Madrid, Franco awarded Condor Legion aviators with medals of commendation; on 19 May, he staged his victory parade in Madrid with Moroccans standing guard at the base of a wooden arch of triumph.

Figure 27: Hitler and his staff honoring the Condor Legion, 6 June 1939.

Photo credit: Zentralbild. Bundesarchiv, no. E7195.

Figure 28: Generals Wilhelm Keitel, Wolfram von Richthofen, Walther von Brauchitsch, and Erhard Milch, Admiral Erich Raeder, Field Marshall Hermann Göring, and Adolf Hitler celebrate the returning German legionnaires.

Anonymous photograph. Bundesarchiv, no. E 7214.

FIGURE 29: Condor legionnaires at the Brandenburg gate, 6 June 1939.

Anonymous photograph. Bundesarchiv, no. R79.89.25.

Reviewing his assembled forces, Franco celebrated the first event of the long postwar era (fig. 25).

For the German Condor Legion, the Spanish adventure would quickly recede into anecdotal memoirs and conventional photographic images. When they first returned to Germany in the spring of 1939, however, the Condor legionnaires enjoyed festivities as a rehearsal for other promised victory parades. Maidens adorned the exalted heroes with garlands in Hamburg on 31 May (fig. 26). On 6 June, Hitler and the High Command gave the Condor legionnaires an extravagant reception (figs. 27 to 29). By early September of that same year, the German army would invade

Poland with all the military intelligence techniques and mechanized warfare that had been refined in Spain, but also with the same aura of chivalric invincibility with which they had carried out their mission in Spain for two and a half years. As the German military readied their now more effective modern war machines for battle, they continued to reinforce the Wehrmacht with images of epic heroism. Spain had accommodated the German military's need for both a field for military experimentation and a faux-medieval environment in which they could rehearse their archaist self-perception.

Hitler and Franco sparred over the role of Spain in the dawning world war in which the Nazis were now engaged. On 23 October 1940, Hitler and Franco met in Hendaye, in France but near the Spanish border. Spain gave little to Germany, although in a symbolic gesture, Franco volunteered men for Hitler's invasion of the Soviet Union, as the Bolsheviks were a mutual enemy. The División Azul arrived in France in June 1941 (fig. 30). In Paris, they were depicted as playful, wholesome, and nonchalant. The German photographer captured them in a mock bullfight, a game played by virtually every Spanish boy of the 1920s and 1930s (fig. 31). By December, the Spanish volunteers faced the ferocious weather of Leningrad and the beginning of the deconstruction of the mythologies by which the Nazi vision exalted itself in Spain and justified the initiation of World War II.

Conclusion

From the memoirs of Spaniards, we know that most of Spain hoped for German victory during World War II. The publisher Carlos Barral, for example, describes teachers and priests who affected German accents.[8] Part hoax and part murderous reality, the Condor Legion abided in the Spanish mind and political institutions long after the Axis powers had been defeated in 1945. For individual members of the Condor Legion, the Spanish adventure had inspired cavalier memoirs, virtually all published in 1939 and 1940, before the full dimension of World War II was recognized. For Germany, however, the pseudomedievalism of the Condor Legion that had encouraged the whole country to pursue its fantasy of imperial expansion was soon brutally submerged in the realities of World War II. Yet for a brief period, the Condor's visual record, like the origins of the fascist imagination itself, hovered in European archaism and neocolonial posturing.

FIGURE 30: The División Azul arriving by train in France in June 1941.

Anonymous photograph. Bundesarchiv, no. 67/2450/7.

FIGURE 31: Members of the Spanish División Azul in Paris before transfer to the Russian front.

Anonymous photograph. Bundesarchiv, no. 68/2461/28a.

Above all, the photographic record reveals the deep wound of frustrated colonial pretensions behind Germany's ostensibly modern military campaign in Spain. Denied access to far-flung possessions shared by even lesser European powers both before and after the Great War, the Germans had allowed themselves to believe that their advanced technologies could help them realize an ancient dream. Spain in the 1930s was fated to become the theater for the German effort to compensate for past failures, a place where the Reich might rehearse for what proved to be a short-lived equilibrium between the old fantasies and the new technologies. While civil war burned through the peninsula for two and a half years, German photographers mounted their own expedition to a land viewed as primitive and remote. Deriving inspiration from romantic conventions and reducing Spain to a venerable and vulnerable kingdom, the photographers labored to accumulate visual evidence to justify the war itself. At once heroic, monumental, quaint, and condescending, these photographs of the 1930s evoke not the origins of modern combat photography, but stiff and posturing images that had been used to justify European expansionism in an earlier era.

Notes

1. See *Deutsche kämpfen in Spanien* (Berlin, 1939); Karl Georg von Stackelberg, *Legion Condor: Deutsche Freiwillige in Spanien* (Berlin, 1939); Wulf Bley, *Das Buch der Spanienflieger: Die Feuertaufe der neuen deutschen Luftwaffe* (Leipzig, 1939); Max Graf Hoyos, *Pedros y Pablos: Fliegen, Erleben, Kämpfen in Spanien* (Munich, 1939); and Werner Beumelburg, *Kampf um Spanien: Die Geschichte der Legion Condor* (Oldenburg and Berlin, 1940). For a critical perspective on the mythologies of war in the twentieth century, see George L. Mosse, *Fallen Soldiers: Reshaping the Memory of the World Wars* (New York, 1990). For a general review of the work of Werner Beumelburg and other German propagandists who wrote on the Spanish Civil War, see Peter Monteath, "The Nazi Literature of the Spanish Civil War," in *German and International Perspectives on the Spanish Civil War: The Aesthetics of Partisanship*, ed. Luis Costa et al. (Columbia, S.C., 1992), pp. 129–148. According to Monteath, in the Nazi literature of the war, "Discipline, an unquestioning obedience to the Führer und a sense of solidarity and duty in the face of a common enemy were the key qualities which were to ensure the required functionality and uniformity of society" (p. 144). See also Joachim Schmitt-Sasse, "'… Madrid has fallen!' The Spanish Civil War in the *Völkischer Beobachter* and Other Third Reich Media," in ibid., pp. 149–165; and Christoph Eykman, "The Spanish Civil War in German Publications during the Nazi Years," in ibid., pp. 166–178.

2. Robert H. Whealey, *Hitler and Spain: The Nazi Role in the Spanish Civil War, 1936–1939* (Lexington, Ky., 1989), pp. 104–108.
3. Sigrid Schneider, "Manipulating Images: Photojournalism from the Spanish Civil War," in *German and International Perspectives on the Spanish Civil War*, pp. 179–198, also notes the impact of the small cameras on war photography in Spain, and argues that between fascist and antifascist photographs "Principal differences in the visual language are not detectable" (p. 192).
4. Among the most widely circulated nineteenth-century German photographic volumes of Spanish monuments was Max Junghändel, *Die Baukunst Spaniens* (Dresden, 1891–98). The photographs of this collection, dating from the 1880s, replicate the widely circulated 1850s images of the Englishman Charles Clifford and the 1860s and 1870s images of the Frenchman Jean Laurent. For a commentary on German travel literature and tourism in Spain, see Peter Antonio, *Das Spanienbild in den Massenmedien des Dritten Reiches, 1933–1945* (Frankfurt, 1992), pp. 41–83.
5. Norman F. Cantor, *Inventing the Middle Ages: The Lives, Works, and Ideas of the Great Medievalists of the Twentieth Century* (New York, 1991), p. 87.
6. Herbert Southworth, *Guernica! Guernica! A Study of Journalism, Diplomacy, Propaganda and History* (Berkeley, Calif., 1977), pp. 32–43.
7. Brassaï, *Paris de nuit* [Paris by Night] (Paris, 1933).
8. Carlos Barral, *Años de penitencia* (Barcelona, 1990).

– 16 –

WRITING WAR

German Women and the Spanish Civil War

Friederike B. Emonds

When Ruth Berlau (1906–1974) returned to Denmark from the 1937 Second International Writers Congress for the Defense of Culture held in Spain, Bertolt Brecht (1898–1956) was impatiently awaiting her description of her experiences and impressions surrounding the conference. In her memoirs, *Living for Brecht* (1987), she recalls, "I returned to Brecht with stories of this nature, and he was not satisfied. He was hoping for an account of the political background to the Civil War, and all I could talk about was fantastic experiences. I was, of course, much too emotional."[1] She elaborates on Brecht's reaction to her report: "In a political sense I was still far too immature for Spain. Though I had seen a lot, Brecht was cross with me for not being able to tell him everything he wanted to know. For the first time he shouted at me."[2] What in Berlau's report (or lacking in it) provoked such irritation on Brecht's part? Why did she, even in retrospect, judge herself and her account in such harsh terms as "too emotional" and "far too immature"?

Both Brecht and Berlau, among some two hundred writers and intellectuals from thirty countries, had participated at the opening ceremony of the Second International Writers Congress for the Defense of Culture held in Paris in the summer of 1937. However, the conference was then moved to various cities in war-torn Spain to support the Republican efforts to defend the democratically elected government against the Nationalist attacks led by General Francisco Franco (1892–1975). While Berlau traveled from Paris to Spain with most of the other conference participants, Brecht returned to Denmark because, as Berlau laconically commented, "he had no great liking for bombs."[3] In Madrid, Berlau met with soldiers of the International Brigades, actively supported the Spanish Republic, and, together with some other writers, even visited the front. Upon her return to Denmark, her account to Brecht about the Civil War in Spain included the following experiences:

> I also visited the fighters at the front. The Red Army soldiers slept beneath their tanks. Among them was a woman whose name I shall not reveal here. She was about to return to Moscow. Before leaving, she went among the soldiers, offering to take letters or verbal greetings home with her. She knew intuitively that very few of them would ever return. During the night she came to me with a request to prepare a hot bath for her. She had not wanted the soldiers to contract syphilis or any other disease from the Spanish whores. To my regret I was unable to provide her with a bath. This was the finest example of understanding for the soldiers that I came across from any woman out there.[4]

This report to Brecht was apparently so utterly inadequate that he not only scolded her but also later, as Berlau recalls, "collected a large group of returned fighters around him for discussions" to find out about the "real" war events.[5]

Even though Berlau based her report on her own firsthand war experiences, her depictions clearly did not fulfill Brecht's demands of a war report. The above example shows that she did not focus on risky combat action, dangerous political controversies, or strategic war maneuvers, but instead drew attention to a specific case of human action in wartime in her representation of the Spanish Civil War. Berlau added a distinct human dimension to her war representations with the remarkable example of the single woman among the Red Army soldiers at the front. Brecht's reaction suggests that those kinds of incidents, examples, and experiences were typically deemed unworthy and too unimportant to be included in the writing or making of traditional war histories. In her subsequent writings, Berlau avoided any descriptions of her Spanish Civil War adventures, perhaps discouraged by Brecht's harsh reaction. Her many impressions and experiences from war-torn Spain remained unwritten, apparently silenced by more powerful voices such as Brecht's, so that her female perspective was not recorded and included in the canon of war narratives.

Was Brecht's dismissive reaction unique, or does it signify a remnant of the past? With a few exceptions in German scholarship today, women's voices from the Spanish Civil War are still suppressed, silenced, and/or simply discarded as politically irrelevant and historically inconsequential. In contrast to these conventional treatments, I contend that it is, in fact, women's political conviction and ideological stance that predominantly shaped their war narratives. Why, then, are women's texts still excluded from so many academic discourses on war? Why is their political agenda so blatantly ignored or downplayed? This study centers on the striking contrast between the exclusion of and disregard for women's war texts in German literary history and war historiography, and the inherent political character of their writings. In my opinion, two factors are responsible for this paradox: the genre of these experiential war narratives and the gender of their authors. I argue that the point of contention is located in the intersection of authorial credibility and restrictively constituted genre specifications.

To illustrate my claim, in the first part of this study I will present an overview of the current reception of women's participation in the Spanish Civil War. I will then examine stylistic, structural, and topical characteristics that seem to be more common in women's writings than in men's texts about the Spanish Civil War. Analyzing the impact of these narrative differences, I will explore the discrepancy between the political and historical significance of women's writings and the lack of attention they received in the postwar era. Furthermore, I maintain that the political agenda inherent in women's war writings was and still is often undermined by the explicit reference to the gender of the author. Since by law German women were not allowed to engage in combat action at the front, their literary capability to represent war in their writings was automatically discredited. The underlying premise that emerges in such a conflation of author, gender, and war experience is, of course, that realistic and politically relevant literary representations of war events have to be based on personal combat and front experiences. Lacking this seminal experience, women authors, however, were and still are denied authenticity and political agency in their writings about the Spanish Civil War.

In the second part of this essay, I will examine selected war texts by German women according to the specific political agenda that motivated their writings. Naturally, the list of names and works referred to in this study is not at all exhaustive and comprises only the better known authors whose works appeared between 1936 and 1939. Much research still needs to be done in this area in order to uncover the many still unknown accounts by women whose voices and experiences have been denied, avoided, or forgotten. Once brought to light, the wealth of the different representations of the Spanish Civil War from distinct women's perspectives will inevitably broaden the prevailing discourse on war to include more diverse aspects. This development will hopefully also lead to significant changes, especially in German historiographies of this war.

In 1991, Shirley Mangini lamented the still obvious neglect of Spanish women's voices in the histories about the Spanish Civil War. In her article entitled "Memories of Resistance: Women Activists from the Spanish Civil War," she asserts, "Of the thousands of articles and books about the Spanish civil war [sic], few contain information about women's role in the war and its aftermath, except for brief descriptions or scant references in footnotes."[6] In the meantime, however, several publications in English helped fill that void, such as her own work and those of Mary Nash and Martha Ackelsberg—just to mention a few of the major studies on the Spanish Civil War in English with a distinct focus on gender.[7] Similarly, the involvement of women from countries other than Spain in the Civil War has also been slowly reappraised. Recently published anthologies and articles about women in the Spanish Civil War—such as Petra Lataster-Czisch's collection of interviews *Eigentlich rede ich nicht gern über mich: Lebenserinnerungen von Frauen aus dem Spanischen Bürgerkrieg, 1936–1939* (1990), as well as *Women's Voices from the Spanish Civil War* (1991), edited by Jim Fyrth and Sally Alexander, among many other publications—confirm the wealth of perspectives, insights, and experiences of women in the Spanish Civil War. In the introduction of the latter work, Jim Fyrth writes, "Our women come from English-speaking nations. We have not included the French—probably the largest contingent—nor the Czechs, Scandinavians, Poles, Dutch, Belgians, Latin Americans, or others, or the refugees from fascist countries."[8] It is striking that Fyrth did not mention any of the German-speaking countries. Clearly, Germany, Austria, and Switzerland cannot all be subsumed under "fascist countries," nor does it suffice to include them under the category of "others." In contrast, I argue that Spanish Civil War experiences of women from German-speaking countries add unique perspectives and informative insights not only to the representations of the Spanish Civil War, but also to the politics and dominating ideologies of their own countries that played key roles in the political arena of Europe on the eve of World War II.

A significant number of women from German-speaking countries experienced the Spanish Civil War firsthand. At a time when women's emancipation was nearly reversed by the restorative ideologies of reactionary politics, particularly in Germany, it was fairly unusual for women to travel abroad alone, especially to a war-torn country such as Spain. Clearly, the reasons and motives for German women to participate in the Spanish Civil War varied drastically according to their ideological beliefs and political orientations. Hence, it is not surprising that women supported both sides of the fight: the fascist and the antifascist, including various political splinter groups that divided up both sides, respectively.

Political activists and writers such as Klara Blum, Ilsa Kulcsar, Erika Mann, Maria Osten, Anna Seghers, Anna Siemsen, Clara Thalmann, and Ilse Wolff represent the antifascist perspective. On the Nationalist side are accounts by women writers such as Therese Bauer, Rima Lascoiti, Maria de Smeth, Maria Stona, and perhaps Juanita von Waldingau; these accounts draw a sharp contrast to the previous testimonies. With the exception of von Waldingau, all of the writers mentioned above based their accounts on their own wartime experiences in Spain. While some of them already lived in Spain at the time the war broke out, others traveled to Spain with the express intention to participate in the war in some capacity. Though it is difficult to categorize their accounts according to conventional genre specification—a claim I will substantiate further in this study—one might argue that autobiographical writings as well as travel reports prevail among these women's war narratives. Another striking number of texts shows characteristics of the then rather new genre of reportage, because many female journalists traveled to Spain as war correspondents.[9] In contrast to the three categories mentioned above, there appears to be only a small number of women writers at the time who reworked their war experiences into more traditional forms of fiction such as novel, drama, or poem. Notable exceptions are Klara Blum's poems "Bäuerin in der Sierra" (1937) and "Letzte Fahrt"(1938), as well as her poetry collection *Die Antwort* (1939), and Juanita von Waldingau's novel *Der unsterbliche Gott: Roman aus dem heutigen Spanien* (1938).[10]

Though only a few of the women writers actually depict fighting at the front and general combat action in their writings, several present more than a mere civilian perspective. Apart from detailed descriptions of women's various tasks in this war and nationalistic statements of professed goals interspersed with the respective political propaganda (from either side), the writers also included bombardments and air raids as well as sudden assaults, violent attacks, and particular deployments of troops. However, characteristic of most of these experiential war narratives is that they appear to be de-centered, that is, without a continuous thread or story line. Rather, their portrayals of the war remind the reader of a mosaic of numerous smaller, seemingly unrelated historical incidents and political occurrences as well as cultural events and social circumstances. Combined, the various pieces of information form the background on which the writers analyze and/or portray the complex wartime situation in Spain. Ruth Berlau's silenced attempt to relate the war events to Bertolt Brecht can be regarded as an example of such a technique. In what way does this kind of de-centered writing style clash with conventional notions of this experiential genre and its practice of ascribing political agency to its authors?

In her article "Behind the Lines: The Spanish Civil War and Women Writers," Janet Pérez claims that Spanish women writers "adher[e] closely to empirically observed bases and personal experience for their war narratives ... Nearly all present some varia": "tion upon the theme that war is hell, and most prefer the reconstruction of small, seemingly insignificant moments overlooked or forgotten in the larger scheme of things, ignored or scorned by historians and chroniclers of war's 'major' events. Their sphere is largely war's 'intra-history,' as Unamuno would have termed it, the effects upon the daily and the future lives of unsung and largely unknown, concrete individuals whose collective human history is more 'typical' and authentic than the abstract dates and solidarity heroes found in historians' texts."[11]

However, while Pérez claims a similar narrative technique to be typical for women's writings about the Spanish Civil War, she also asserts that "possibly many Spaniards, including some women writers, indeed did not understand the complex and tangled ideologies in conflict in the war," and that "[m]ost are ignorant of political issues."[12] She concludes that this apolitical way of writing is characterized by a "reluctance ... generally to view the conflicts from a fixed ideological stance."[13]

Pérez's hypothesis may be based on well-founded claims and convincing textual evidence within Spanish literature, yet in the context of German literary history, these assertions that label women's war writings as apolitical and ahistorical evoke the kind of gender stereotypes that have excluded and/or marginalized women's writing for too long. I concede that on a surface level, the often stylistic and compositional mixtures of women's writings vacillating between travel report, autobiography, war reportage, and social observations may be compared to a miscellaneous assortment of impressions thrown together by an accidental tourist surprised by the precipitating political events of a war. However, this misreading of women's war narratives results from an already biased evaluation based on the literary-historical definition and narrative standard of war narratives as a literary subgenre in which certain constituent aspects are deemed politically and historically relevant.

Indeed, analyzing the makeup of conventional war narratives of the same time period, one finds that the discussed texts by women draw a stark contrast to the former. Very often, conventional war texts are also based on the writer's own experience in the war.[14] Typically, these authors sequence their narratives chronologically, portraying a convincing and plausible image of the war events with the focus on thrilling combat action, clever militaristic maneuvers, and persuasive examples of the immediate danger created by the enemy's capabilities. Another important characteristic of these narratives is the way the authors build up suspense, namely by weaving a logical yet increasingly tighter plot line interspersed with occasional moments of dramatic relief, only to emphasize the magnified tension induced by the next incident. Clearly, in such war texts, style and composition are aimed at constructing the kind of "realistic" war atmosphere that the reader expects and is able to identify with. The text appears as an immediate reflection of the war events. Reading, then, becomes an act of vicarious participation in the war. For the reader, the author's own war experience guarantees the authenticity and flawlessness of his war descriptions. The authority of his experience as a soldier is transferred to the text and confers on the narrator political agency and historical credibility. By essentializing the writer's experience, the reader is led to take the story at face value and not as a representation constructed from a wide variety of war discourses. The author's story becomes history, hence politically meaningful and historically relevant.

The texts under discussion in this study, however, fail to achieve the genre-determined characteristics of atmospheric immediacy and close identification between reader and protagonist. Their lack of a clearly defined genre, of narrative continuities, and of climactic narrative structure still evoke doubt as to the authenticity and significance of these works, as well as the historical and political competency of their authors. All of these unusual and deviating narrative characteristics cause literary critics and historians to dispute the political claim inherent in women's war works. At the same time that women's experiences during war have been challenged and/or denied, their accounts have been characterized as hysterical, melodramatic, and most of all unpolitical, hence historically irrelevant and inconsequential.[15]

Contrary to such conventional readings of women's war narratives, I contend—as I have claimed earlier—that most women incorporated their political convictions and specific ideological stances into their writings.[16] In fact, their narratives often served the decided purpose of conveying their political convictions to a broader audience. While methods and means, weapons and capabilities also vary among the many women who were actively engaged in the various goals of the war, the women were united in their firm belief that their political intervention would make a difference. For this reason, the Spanish Civil War comprises an important moment in the history of women's political activism. With the possible exception of the impact of the 1917 Russian Revolution, the Spanish Civil War denotes one of the earliest and at the same time most striking examples in which political conviction and responsibility led women to travel abroad and fight in a war not for national reasons, that is, to defend their homeland against foreign threats and potential invasion, but to fight for their own, supranational, ideological beliefs. In the second part of this study, I examine selected textual examples that particularly illustrate the kind of political fervor and ideological intensity that inspired these women writers.

Former East German writer Anna Seghers (1900–1983) is perhaps the most prominent representative of the antifascist perspective. Seghers had experienced the dangerous power and political threat of National Socialism in Germany firsthand: as a member of the Communist Party (KPD), Seghers had been arrested in 1933, yet managed to escape to France. In Paris, she joined the Schutzverband deutscher Schriftsteller (SDS: Protective Association of German Writers), which at that time was particularly devoted to the support and aid of the Republican side in the Spanish Civil War. Seghers organized and participated in numerous discussion groups, talks, meetings, readings, and benefit functions in support of the Spanish freedom fighters and, in particular, the International Brigades.[17] She also played a key role in the organization of solidarity groups, relief efforts, and other political activities.

Like many exiled writers at that time, Seghers admired the spontaneity, political consciousness, and self-determination of the Spanish people in their struggle against a fascist takeover led by General Franco. Underlying her respect for the Spanish Republicans was her hope for a similar popular uprising against Hitler's National Socialist regime in Germany. As an antifascist intellectual, Seghers was clearly aware of the political correlation between Germany and Spain and the historical relevance of the Spanish Civil War on a wider global scale. Having already usurped Germany and Italy and now threatening to take over Spain, too, fascism for Seghers represented an immediate global danger that had to be fought against with worldwide efforts.

Seghers's tireless support of the Spanish Republicans and her outspoken political convictions led to her participation at the Second International Writers Congress as one of the few female official representatives. In her powerful speech "Gruß an den II. Internationalen Schriftstellerkongreß 1937," at the conference in Madrid, she emphasized the solidarity between German and Spanish antifascists.[18] Moreover, she appealed specifically to the moral duties of all writers by emphasizing the importance of the word as a powerful tool not only to raise political consciousness in the populace, but also to translate that awareness into political action. Echoing the imperative demand of writer and soldier Ludwig Renn to "exchange the pen for the rifle," Seghers strongly accentuated the activist role of the intellectual.[19] She mobilized her fellow writers to participate in the war because, as she declared, "it is written and expressed in all languages in the world that the battles at Madrid are not only fought for the freedom of Spain but for the freedom of the entire world."[20] In a longer essay written at the same time, "Zum Schriftstellerkongreß in Madrid" (1937), she was even more outspoken in her appeal to the writers' responsibilities to defend Spain, drawing a direct parallel between the defense of Spain and the defense of culture in general: "Our congress was conceived from the beginning as a demonstrative congress. Whereas at the first congress it was a matter of working out, of formulating our terms, in this congress it was a matter of bearing witness, namely, to the defense of culture, which today is identical with the defense of Spain."[21]

As is illustrated in these two texts, Seghers's agitative use of language and her persuasive rhetoric emphasized her passion as well as her ideological vigor and political conviction towards the Spanish Civil War. Surprisingly, these two texts, referring directly to the Civil War, have been treated negligently in the academic discourses on Anna Seghers as well as on the Spanish Civil War. Already at the time of the war, Seghers was an important political writer within the German exile community in France and the Soviet Union, yet the speech she delivered at the conference was not published along with many other speeches in the dedicated volume of the exile journal *Das Wort* (1937).[22] In fact, her speech only survived in the Spanish translation of its original German version and had to be translated back into German for inclusion into her collected essayistic works, *Über Kunst und Wirklichkeit* (1971).[23]

To counter any doubts and suspicion about Seghers's serious commitment to and preoccupation with the Spanish Civil War, it should be stated that her subsequent writings prove that these two texts did not remain isolated incidents in her support of the Republican forces against Franco. In fact, the Spanish Civil War and its political impact left a long-lasting impression on Seghers, even though, as Gertraud Gutzmann pointed out, her firsthand experience of the Spanish Civil War was based only on her participation in the International Writers Congress and therefore was rather limited in its scope. Though Seghers never directly depicted the actual war, she nevertheless incorporated the theme of the Civil War in two of her later novels, *Die Entscheidung* (The Decision, 1959) and *Das Vertrauen* (The Trust, 1968), as well as in several other stories, long after the battles were decided.[24] In both novels, though in different ways, the Spanish Civil War symbolizes the kind of unwavering political belief in and commitment to antifascism that she considered particularly crucial in her own country, especially in the years following the political upheavals in the German Democratic Republic (GDR) in June 1953. Seghers emphasizes a parallel between the fight against fascism in Spain in the mid-1930s and the fight for socialism in the GDR in the early 1950s, thereby placing the new socialist government of the GDR as the legitimate heir to antifascist causes. Similarly, she defined the tasks of the writers in the GDR to educate the masses—this time, however, about the concepts of socialism in order "to show the magnificent, only possible future."[25] Clearly, for Seghers the Spanish Civil War did not constitute an isolated historical incident but an important political moment in history, which shaped her political expectations and beliefs up to her death in 1983.

Perhaps less known, though just as tireless and passionate in her antifascist efforts in Spain, was German political activist and writer Maria Osten (1908–1942). As did Seghers, Osten understood writing to be a political act. In this respect, much of the strength of her writing resides in the fact that she often examined life, reality, and sociopolitical structures in a sharp-minded yet sensitive way to expose power relations and challenge decrepit foundations of authority. Her ideological convictions and political commitment eventually led her to exile from Germany when Hitler came to power in 1933.[26]

Osten emigrated to Moscow, where she joined the German section of the Soviet Writers Union and took part in the literary life established by the numerous other German writers already in Soviet exile. Apart from her own literary success in Moscow, Osten assisted in the realization of the international anthology *Den Mira*— a work commissioned by novelist Maxim Gorky (1868–1936) at the Soviet Writers Congress in 1934.[27] In addition, she played a key role in the founding and organization of the German exile journal *Das Wort* in 1936.[28] During its three years of existence, this periodical proved to be an important venue for many exiled writers to report on the antifascist efforts against Hitler all over the world—but especially in Spain during its Civil War.

Later that same year, Osten traveled to Spain to cover the Spanish Civil War for the *Deutsche Zentral-Zeitung*. In contrast to Seghers, she intended to stay in Spain for a longer period of time and experience the war firsthand. As war correspondent, she reported from the front with detailed descriptions of war events, including the bombing of Madrid in 1936. However, in her reports, she also attended to current political issues and social concerns, portrayed Spanish women, and gave voice to the many young men and women fighting in this war. Sylvia Schlenstedt asserts that Maria Osten belonged to a special kind of war correspondent covering the Spanish Civil War:

> To report about the terror and the enormous difficulties of this war in such a way that sympathy and understanding was raised in the readership; to report about the resistance and commitment of the antifascists in such a way that on the one hand, nobody could jump to reassuring conclusions, while on the other hand, smooth and polished heroic images could not be constructed; to acknowledge individual successes and deeds in such a way that rash generalizations about the invincible force of the freedom fighters could not be drawn—this contradictory task was not easy to solve, especially in newspaper reporting. There were always contradictions of impressions and experiences that had to be overcome—and all of that our author was able to make evident in her best reports.[29]

Osten's journalistic talents were founded on her refined and sensitive ability to observe social sentiments while at the same time analyzing military circumstances in Spain. Endowed with these gifts and an extreme sense of justice, Osten was able to make sense out of the chaos and disruption of the Civil War without indulging in heroic glorification of the antifascist troops at one extreme, or getting lost in the horror and panic of the war at the other. For her inspired accounts of the Spanish Civil War, Osten found a rather successful venue in the genre of war reportage. Despite the chaos of the war and her own doubly outside position as a woman and a non-Spaniard, Osten succeeded in conveying informed and yet compelling impressions of the war events. Though her reports appear to be very detailed and specific as to certain incidents, in order to give her readers a better understanding of the war situation in Spain, she did not lose sight of the war's international effects, particularly in Europe on the eve of World War II. Clearly, her accounts reflect her strong political awareness in a wider, global context.

In addition, her motivation to write was guided by her political conviction and a sense of personal responsibility to recount the injustice of this war to the whole world and to convey the desperation and urgency of this fight against fascism as illustrated by her article "Spring in Madrid" ("Frühling in Madrid"), dated 28 August 1937:

> This is not an accusation. This is not an appeal. Both of these, the quill could endure. What is difficult is to get the truth, the reality closer to the people through writing, so that they take up arms. When we tell about Madrid, the quill should be filming the events at the same time, it should be painting in colors, taking pictures, and talking to each individually, so that they feel everything in their hearts, so that they experience it with us, so that they cannot sleep until they communicate it to someone else and together they are ready to help. In the same hour in which reports of artillery bombardments of Madrid are related, the writer hears new explosions. And what the writer speaks of right now is not old but has just happened; it has repeated itself in a new, perhaps even more horrible variation.[30]

This excerpt exemplifies, according to Schlenstedt, Osten's inner tension and committed awareness that made her unique as a war correspondent. However, more than that, her impassioned rhetoric and compelling diction in this brief metadiscourse on the genre of war reportage draw attention to the improbability of recording the true facts and the horrible reality of this war. She compares her work to more "objective" visual media such as film and photography in terms of achieving greater reliability and verisimilitude for her readers. For the same reasons, she injects herself into the narrative as an eyewitness close to the war action. On the other hand, however, her report transcends the realm of political abstraction and offers a frank account of her own subjective experiences in this war. This necessarily limited point of view does not at all compromise her mission nor her qualities as a war correspondent, but quite the opposite: it makes her reportage deeply personal. Political critique does not contradict personal experience in her writings. As a consequence, the Spanish Civil War becomes more comprehensible and compelling for her many readers, dispersed all over the world. Though she identified and characterized the war as an international political affair, she also convincingly reinscribed the war on a personal level, postulating that its goals and impact should subjectively affect and mobilize everybody. Osten thereby emerges as a passionate and partisan observer of the war—an observer who is also a participant in it. With the irony already evident in the title of her reportage, "Frühling in Madrid" exemplifies the kind of "mixing of subjectivity and objectivity, the blurring of distinctions between fact and fiction" that Peter Monteath considers characteristic for the reportage of the Spanish Civil War.[31]

Already in 1937, as one of the earliest books on the Spanish Civil War to appear, Osten's collection of reports from the front was published in Russian as *Spanish Reportages*.[32] In addition to her writings about the Spanish Civil War, she composed several short stories and narrative sketches, and she started writing a novel that remained a fragment. She was also involved in various other political activities, such as publishing, editing, and other organizational work. For example, at the Second International Writers Congress for the Defense of Culture, where Osten also delivered a passionate speech,[33] she was appointed to write and compile a history of the Thälmann Brigade—a work that she never completed. In 1938, she worked as coeditor of a German book series that was to appear in the newly founded publishing house *Verlag 10. Mai*.[34] Though Osten remained actively involved in the antifascist causes of the Spanish Civil War until her return to Moscow in 1939 (followed by her death in Stalinist purges in 1942),[35] her works have almost entirely been forgotten. Her reportages from the Civil War, though so insightful in their war representations, are rarely included in academic discourses on the Civil War in German literature.

While both Seghers and Osten firmly believed in their mission to fight against fascism in Europe by recording the injustice of the Spanish Civil War and reporting it to the entire world, there were numerous other forgotten women who actually fought fascism on a more immediate front—not with words and language, but with their own hands. Already alerted by the political situation in

Germany and the increasing sense of powerlessness experienced in their own country, these women regarded it as their responsibility to fight fascism where there was still a chance to succeed. This sentiment can best be illustrated by the vivid oral testimony of Spanish Civil War volunteer Lenchen Jans (born 1898), who was stationed in Barcelona as an international brigader (Spanish war volunteer) from April 1937 to October 1938. In a 1990 interview with Petra Lataster-Czisch in Germany, she explained, "The First World War was a bourgeois war, let's just say. And the Spanish war was *our* war, wasn't it? For *our* freedom. And that was something entirely different."[36]

Consequently, in the winter of 1936–37, Jans took her two sons, left her comfortable middle-class life in Germany behind, and started the adventurous journey to Barcelona in order to help fight against the fascists. There she worked as a nurse in a hospital while her two sons and her husband, who had arrived in Spain a few months earlier, fought at the front. Jans endured tremendous hardship not only because of the often life-threatening situations she experienced—the incessant misery, death, and war atrocities she encountered every day in the hospital—but also because of the constant worries and sorrows for her husband and sons, who were wounded and captured by the enemies several times. Even when her youngest son was severely injured, deported to Germany, and later killed in the concentration camp in Dachau, she maintained, "I am proud that I was in Spain. I am proud of that, I say that to everybody."[37] And about her son, who had the chance to save his life if he had only agreed to join the SS, she says, "As a mother, to lose one's child is very terrible, the pain is tremendous. But I do say to anybody who will listen: my joy is larger, because my son Willi said: SS member? No way! I'm proud of that! Thank God my son did not become a member of the SS."[38] Jans sums up her experience, "it had to be, we had to fight against the fascists. It was our duty."[39]

The sense of duty so forceful and compelling in Jans's account, imbued with the strong identification of the common goal of combating fascism in Spain, characterizes the reports of most women writers supporting the Republican side. Because of their clear ideological stance and political convictions, the women strongly identified with "the cause" and unconditionally fought for its realization, even in times of personal loss, hardship, and misery. Courage and conviction in the face of violence, devastation, and war marked the lives of women like Seghers, Osten, and Jans, who got involved in a war that had already been lost in their own country, Germany.

Maria de Smeth's (1903–1976) involvement in the Spanish Civil War diverges from that of the previous women due to her opposing political convictions and ideological stance, namely her strong support of Franco's fascist forces in Spain and her deep abhorrence of communism. Her account also contrasts with the previous women's testimonies in that de Smeth did not volunteer to travel to Spain but was summoned by the German propaganda ministry to undertake a secret war mission in Spain. Her task was to collect evidence of Soviet intervention in the Spanish Civil War while at the same time reporting about the latest front activities. In her autobiography *Roter Kaviar—Hauptmann Maria* (1965), she reconstructs the conversation she had with Dr. Taubert, an official working for the ministry of propaganda, who explained her task: "Russia supports Spain, which means the Popular Front government (*Volksfront-Regierung*) intervenes in internal Spanish affairs. We urgently need valid proof for this intervention. Party member Schulze told me that you are an expert on questions of active communism. You will understand what is important. Moreover, you are a Dutch citizen, which for us is especially valuable. This fact could also make your task easier. Would you go to Spain, if we sent you there?"[40]

De Smeth emphasizes that she initially refused to accept this assignment, arguing, "To a country in which the Soviets have their hands? No thanks ... I have had all I can take from my experiences in Russia."[41] However, after initial hesitation, she finally did agree to her task, rationalizing her acceptance in retrospect: "As a very visual person, I could literally see in this conversation about the danger of communism the gigantic green space that the Soviet Union occupied on the global map. If Spain turned communist, too, then Moscow would have all of Europe in its pinchers. Suddenly, it became clear to me that the fight about Spain was part of the danger I still feared, and that one had to do something against it."[42]

The argument de Smeth uses to legitimize her acceptance even almost thirty years later needs to be situated in the context of Hitler's profound anticommunist propaganda efforts. As historian Robert H. Whealey affirms, already in the late 1920s Hitler used "fear of communism as political formula for diplomatic maneuvering."[43] He "exploited the slogan 'anticommunism' to facilitate his relations not only with other governments but also with corporate, ecclesiastical, and press leaders."[44] In his fascist rhetoric, Hitler conflated fear of social revolution, atheism, and loss of nation with the goals of communism set forth by the Soviet Bolsheviks, who were "only the front for an (imaginary) anti-German Jewish International."[45] In this context, the impact of this powerful visual image of the Soviet Union on the Nazi world map intertwined with Hitler's anticommunist propaganda and use of scare tactics turned de Smeth's rigid ideological stance into political action.

In her autobiography, however, de Smeth rejects the mere passive influence of Nazi propaganda by referring to the memory of her own experience with communism when she was imprisoned in Moscow for five months. Specifying her abhorrence for communism lends to her political judgment the kind of credibility that is supposed to make her decision not only understandable for the reader thirty years later, but also in retrospect plausible and even compelling in her particular situation. In addition, Taubert's earlier reference to her as an "expert on questions of active communism" seems to confirm the assumption that de Smeth did not simply fall for the Nazis' anticommunist propaganda but also consciously contributed to the Nazi-shaped conceptual image of the communist enemy. Indeed, as de Smeth asserts in her memoirs, after her release from Moscow she went on numerous lecture tours throughout Germany to report about her experience in the infamous Soviet prison "Lubjanka."

In mid-November 1936, the same month in which Hitler officially recognized the new Nationalist regime at Burgos and covertly deployed the Condor Legion to Spain in support of Franco's troops, Maria de Smeth left Germany on her secret mission to Spain.[46] Upon her arrival in Salamanca, the *Generalstab* provided her with a car and a chauffeur to facilitate her search for communist propaganda material. Equipped with a special pass that allowed her to drive all the way up to the front lines, she traveled 38,000 kilometers throughout the national territory of Spain, mostly along the front. On her travels she collected all sorts of material that she considered to be tools of communist propaganda, or "red material" as she called it, such as Soviet emblems, red neckties with hammer and sickle symbols, magazines, newspapers, notebooks, and scrap paper with messages in Russian.[47] She was particularly intrigued by the many findings of pornographic magazines, about which she commented, "In their choice of means, the Reds are really not particularly choosy."[48]

While on the one hand she collected "red material," on the other hand she distributed German National Socialist propaganda material, especially books and magazines. By far the most popular item out of her German treasures, however, was a portrait of Hitler. Overall, she resumed, "Everything German is very highly regarded in Spain; I enjoy being German for them. According to my bloodline, I am after all German [though Dutch by citizenship]. However, Mussolini is more famous. There are portraits of him everywhere."[49]

Upon her return to Germany, in late April 1937, de Smeth prepared an official account of her trip for the Anti-Comintern. This report, *Das Rotbuch über Spanien*, was edited by Alfred Gielen, a member of the Reichsministerium für Volksaufklärung und Propaganda, and published in 1937 by the Gesamtverband deutscher antikommunistischer Vereinigungen. Moreover, according to de Smeth's autobiography, her report served as the main source for Nazi propaganda minister Joseph Goebbels's (1897–1945) anticommunist speech "The Truth about Spain" ("Die Wahrheit über Spanien") at the *Reichsparteitag* in 1937. Almost thirty years after her trip, de Smeth commented in her autobiography: "I was more than a little proud when I listened to the radio broadcasting of his speech and noticed that he had based two-thirds of his elaboration about the communist influence on the Spanish Civil War on my own report, and that he even adopted my own formulations."[50] In his study *Die deutsche Politik im spanischen Bürgerkrieg* (1969), German historian Manfred Merkes confirmed de Smeth's influence on Goebbels's speech as well as on the press release that was issued at a press conference on 13 October 1937. Merkes explained that de Smeth was a member of the Sonderstab of the ministry of propaganda. According to Whealey, this special Anti-Comintern section, founded by Hitler in 1935, specifically turned their attention to Spain in the spring of 1936 in order "to direct a war of words toward 'fighting bolshevism.' Its indirect approach was to induce the world press to accept National Socialist and anti-bolshevik publicity."[51]

In 1937, de Smeth published her impressions and experiences of the five months she visited Spain—this time, however, under her own name. This text, entitled *Viva España, Arriba España*, was geared toward a broader audience and, according to the author, was so well received that de Smeth went on several lecture tours throughout Germany to report on her experiences in Spain.

De Smeth's work is carefully disguised as a travel account of war-torn Spain, though she does mention that she visited the country in her function as a press officer. However, de Smeth does not elaborate on her special assignment, nor does she reveal her close connection to the German propaganda ministry or disclose the military intervention of German troops and fighter planes of the Condor Legion.[52] As literary scholar Günther Schmigalle stated, "de Smeth had to solve the delicate task to represent not only travel impressions in her 1937 published book but also to present a political analysis without mentioning the German-Italian intervention in the Civil War."[53] I agree with Schmigalle's further elaboration that the author succeeded in her goal to conceal and distort political facts and de-emphasize the use of ideological propaganda. Hence, at the time of its publication, the work did not appear to be a "pure" tool of Nazi propaganda, but a rather harmlessly subjective account by a politically minded civilian, and a woman at that. To achieve this goal, de Smeth employed a simple yet effective writing technique. She interposed her personal experience with the Spanish people (particularly soldiers, clergymen, women, and children) with comments and opinions (including her own) on Spanish politics, language, society, as well as Spain's old customs, rich traditions, and cultural wealth, along with its beautiful landscape. In the context of these impressions and descriptions, she charged the "Reds" for the lack of organization and discipline and supply problems in their occupied areas, as well as blaming them for the plundering and destruction of churches, museums, and other religious and cultural institutions. Hence, instead of explicitly constructing yet another account focusing on the alleged violence and unscrupulousness, in short the "red terror" of the Republican forces—a topic that basically constitutes the center of the official Anti-Comintern report *Das Rotbuch über Spanien*—she systematically undermined the authority and credibility of the enemy. By repeatedly ascribing social chaos and political instability to their regime, induced by the supposed deterioration of conservative morals and values, she insinuated that the events in war-torn Spain were similar to the political upheavals of the Weimar Republic and prerevolutionary Russia. Subtly expanding on the already present fear of revolutionary ideas of social, economic, and political change that many conservative Germans found embodied in the Soviet regime, de Smeth's work at the time emerged as a rather clever and effective means of Nazi propaganda to divert attention away from Germany's own war preparations and to cast the Soviet Union as the principal enemy of the Western capitalist world. In other words, de Smeth's account of Spain functioned on two levels simultaneously: while it clearly manipulated people's general opinion about the Spanish Civil War in favor of Franco and against the Spanish Popular Front government, it also ostensibly contributed to the conceptual construction of the communist enemy.

The testimonies of Anna Seghers, Maria Osten, Lenchen Jans, and Maria de Smeth differ drastically in their representations of the Spanish Civil War in terms of topics, style, diction, and atmosphere as well as in their descriptions of their own roles in the war. Yet despite the many differences, all four women emphasize their strong political identity in this fight that for them transcended national borders. On both sides of the ideological divide, the authors fear an expansion and violent takeover of most of Europe by the enemy nation and its totalitarian regime. While both Seghers's and Osten's writings are informed by the collective experience of political activists exiled from Germany, Jans's testimony is driven by the collective experience of German communists who remained in Germany after Hitler came to power in the hope of undermining his authority and power from within. All three women recognized Hitler's victory as a tremendous defeat for their own political agenda and a great threat to democracy and political rights. Hence, their political conviction was guided by their belief that one had to fight fascism where it was still possible. In contrast, de Smeth arrived at her political awareness via her strong national identity. Her testimony was motivated by her belief in and active support of the National Socialist regime. Due to her own encounter with communism, she not only found her personal experiences confirmed in Hitler's anticommunist indoctrination, but also contributed to the scare tactics of the National Socialist propaganda machinery.

Interestingly, nowhere in the texts did the four women explicitly refer to their gendered identity, nor did they emphasize their collective experience as women in war, yet their testimonies are very often dismissed as subjective, thus historically unreliable and typically feminine. In order to change this distorted image of women's testimonies from the Spanish Civil War, much research still needs to be done. Apart from thorough stylistic analyses of individual war texts, future research in this area may explore the following questions: What were the various different roles of women (including Spanish women) in the Civil War, and how did women writers characterize them in their own texts? What role does gender play in the representation of the Spanish Civil War? Are gender-specific goals and issues represented in these texts or are they completely blurred by the generalized struggle against fascism or communism respectively? To what extent did the political agenda of the authors result in a loss of specific female identity and the subordination of women's issues to the overall cause of the war (on each respective side)?

The goal of this study was to show women's representations of the war events in Spain as legitimate, thematically important, and structurally innovative articulations that significantly affect the representations and understanding of the Spanish Civil War in German literature and history. Within the scope of this essay, I had to necessarily limit my topic to present a contextualized overview of some of the war texts published between 1936 and 1939 by German women. Nevertheless, I hope that this essay may serve as an impetus to inspire further investigations into the neglected field of German women's involvement in the Spanish Civil War.

Acknowledgment

I would like to thank Rick Francis for his encouragement and valuable suggestions on earlier drafts of this essay.

Notes

1. Ruth Berlau, *Living for Brecht*, ed. Hans Bunge, trans. Geoffrey Skelton (New York, 1987), p. 49.
2. Ibid., p. 50.
3. Ibid., p. 47.
4. Ibid., p. 49.
5. Ibid.
6. Shirley Mangini, "Memories of Resistance: Women Activists from the Spanish Civil War," *Signs*, vol. 17, no. 1 (1991), p. 171.
7. Shirley Mangini, *Memories of Resistance: Women's Voices from the Spanish Civil War* (New Haven, Conn., 1995); Mary Nash, *Defying Male Civilization: Women in the Spanish Civil War* (Denver, Colo., 1995); and Martha Ackelsberg, *Free Women of Spain* (Bloomington, Ind., 1991). Apart from these sources in English, quite a number of studies have been published in Spanish. For a detailed and updated bibliography on works in Spanish, see Mary Nash's book.
8. Jim Fyrth and Sally Alexander, eds., *Women Voices from the Spanish Civil War* (London, 1991), p. 24.
9. For a further discussion on the importance of the reportage genre in the depiction of the Spanish Civil War, see Peter Monteath, "The Spanish Civil War and the Aesthetics of Reportage," in *Literature and War* (Amsterdam, 1990), pp. 69–86.
10. Zhidong Yang mentions in his recent study that Blum had evidently requested to be deployed to the front in Spain but for some reason never actually went there. Unfortunately, Yang's biography of Blum is rather inconclusive at this point, for he does not follow up on this particular event in her life. See Zhidong Yang, *Klara Blum—Zhu Bailan, 1904–1971* (Frankfurt, 1996), p. 22.
11. Janet Pérez, "Behind the Lines: The Spanish Civil War and Women Writers," *The Spanish Civil War in Literature*, ed. Janet Pérez and Wendell Aycock (Lubbock, Tex., 1990), p. 172.
12. Ibid., p. 164.
13. Ibid., p. 165.
14. See, for example, Gustav Regler, *Das große Beispiel: Roman einer internationalen Brigade* (Cologne, 1976); Willi Bredel, *Begegnung am Ebro* (Paris, 1939); Ludwig

Renn, *Der spanische Krieg* (Berlin, 1955); and Bodo Uhse, *Die erste Schlacht: Vom Werden und von den ersten Kämpfen des Bataillons Edgar André* (Strasbourg, 1938). See also the many short stories and reportages on the Spanish Civil War published in the exile journal *Das Wort* between 1937 and 1939.
15. See for example Günther Schmigalle's otherwise excellent study "Deutsche schreiben für Hitler und Franco: Vierzig biobibliographische Porträts," in *Der spanische Bürgerkrieg: Literatur und Geschichte*, ed. Günther Schmigalle (Frankfurt, 1986), pp. 197–244.
16. Waldingau's novel is an exception. Her almost entirely allegorical treatment of the Spanish Civil War provides merely a background for her otherwise mostly religious novel. While the political as well as the sociohistorical context of the war remains a mere sketch in her novel, the author focuses instead on the kind of religious quest and search for the existence of God that the protagonist Raimund Brückner has to go through before he finds salvation in his death. Supposedly, it is not political conviction that led the protagonist to join the Francoist foreign legion, but rather necessity, since he is forced to leave Austria after a dueling incident. However, the possibility that he could also have fought in the International Brigades instead is never even considered in the narrative. For a more detailed discussion on Waldingau's novel, see Georg Pichler, *Der spanische Bürgerkrieg (1936–1939) im deutschsprachigen Roman* (Frankfurt, 1991), pp. 330–418.
17. For example, the SDS helped arrange the premiere of Bertolt Brecht's Spanish Civil War play *Die Gewehre der Frau Carrar* in Paris in October 1937.
18. Anna Seghers, "Gruß an den II. Internationalen Schriftstellerkongreß 1937," in *Über Kunst und Wirklichkeit* (Berlin, 1970), vol. 1, pp. 66–67. Seghers was one of the official representatives of Germany to the congress, and the only woman writer, as far as I could determine.
19. Seghers, "II. Kongreß der Internationalen Schriftstellervereinigung zur Verteidigung der Kultur," *Das Wort*, vol. 10 (October 1937), p. 78. During 1936 and 1937, political writer Ludwig Renn served as a general in the International Brigades in Spain. He wrote several famous accounts on the Spanish war such as *Die Schlacht bei Guadalajara* (1955) and *Der Spanische Krieg* (1955; 1959 as *Im Spanischen Krieg*), based on his personal experiences as an officer in the International Brigades.
20. "In allen Sprachen der Welt wird geschrieben und ausgesprochen, daß vor Madrid nicht nur für die Freiheit Spaniens, sondern für die Freiheit der ganzen Welt gekämpft wird." Seghers, "Gruß an den II. Internationalen Schriftstellerkongreß 1937," p. 67.
21. Anna Seghers, *Gesammelte Werke in Einzelausgaben*, vol. 13 (Berlin, 1984), p. 40. Here cited after the translation by Peter Monteath in Peter Monteath, *Writing the Good Fight: Political Commitment in the International Literature of the Spanish Civil War* (Westport, Conn., 1994), pp. 68–69.
22. See *Das Wort*, vol. 10 (1937).
23. The Spanish translation appeared in the newspaper *Hora de España* in 1937. See Anna Seghers, *Über Kunst und Wirklichkeit*, vol. 1 (Berlin, 1970), pp. 279–280. Seghers's 1937 essay on the Spanish Civil War first appeared in *Die Internationale*, vols. 5/6, no. 2 (1937).
24. See also her texts *Transit* (Boston, 1944, in English; Konstanz, 1948, in German) and *Steinzeit; Wiederbegegnung: Zwei Erzählungen* (Berlin and Weimar, 1977). Strikingly, Seghers even referred to the Spanish Civil War in several of her interviews and book reviews published in the three volumes of *Über Kunst*

und Wirklichkeit. For a detailed discussion on Seghers's use of the Spanish Civil War theme in her texts, see Gertraud Gutzmann, "Representations of the Spanish Civil War in the Works of Anna Seghers," *German and International Perspectives on the Spanish Civil War: The Aesthetics of Partisanship,* ed. Luis Costa et al. (Columbia, S.C., 1992), pp. 450–461.
25. Anna Seghers, "Rede auf dem II. Deutschen Schriftstellerkongreß 1950," in *Über Kunst und Wirklichkeit,* vol. 1, p. 81.
26. In the late 1920s and up until her emigration to Moscow, Osten worked as secretary at the Malik publishing house in Berlin.
27. According to Silvia Schlenstedt, the German translation of this title is *Ein Tag der Welt.* See Silvia Schlenstedt's valuable study on Spain in Klaus Hermsdorf, Hugo Fetting, and Silvia Schlenstedt, *Exil in den Niederlanden und in Spanien* (Frankfurt, 1981), p. 303. In English, the title could be roughly translated as "A Day in (of) the World." I am indebted to my Russian colleague Charles L. Byrd for clarification on the multiple meanings of "mir" in Russian. For more information on Maria Osten's career as a novelist, see the same study, pp. 302–305.
28. In fact, in January 1938, Osten was appointed to head the newly established editorial office of *Das Wort* in Paris. She later shared the responsibilities of this position with Willi Bredel. For more detailed information, see Hermsdorf, Fetting, Schlenstedt, *Exil in den Niederlanden und in Spanien,* pp. 303–304.
29. This passage is taken from Hermsdorf, Fetting, Schlenstedt, *Exil in den Niederlanden und in Spanien,* pp. 303–304.
30. Maria Osten, "Frühling in Madrid" (1937), in *Geschichten aus der Geschichte des Spanischen Bürgerkriegs,* ed. Erich Hackl and Cristina Timón Solinís (Darmstadt, 1986), pp. 104–105.
31. See Peter Monteath, "The Spanish Civil War and the Aesthetics of Reportage," p. 81.
32. Silvia Schlenstedt mentions only the German title of this particular work by Maria Osten: *Spanische Reportagen.* See Hermsdorf, Fetting, Schlenstedt, *Exil in den Niederlanden und in Spanien,* p. 301.
33. See Gunnar Müller-Waldeck, "Maria Osten zum Gedenken," *Notate,* vol. 2 (1990), p. 14.
34. While Schlenstedt presents Osten as a coeditor of this series together with Willi Bredel, David Pike in his study states that Osten merely "assisted in technical matters" (p. 197). Pike claims that originally Bredel received permission and financial support from Mikhail Koltsov, at that time head of the foreign bureau of the Soviet Writers' Union, to establish a small publishing press to print the works of German communists and Popular Front writers. Heinrich Mann's *Mut* and Bredel's *Begegnung am Ebro* were two out of eight works approved to appear in this series. Quoting Bredel, Pike implies that Osten was brought into this project only through her connection with Koltsov, her common-law husband (pp. 196–197). Contrasting the merely tangential association Osten supposedly held with the new publishing press, Schlenstedt asserts that one of Osten's own narratives was slated to be published in this series, too. See David Pike, *German Writers in Soviet Exile* (Chapel Hill, N.C., 1982), pp. 196–197, and Hermsdorf, Fetting, Schlenstedt, *Exil in den Niederlanden und in Spanien,* pp. 304–305.
35. According to John Fuegi and Gunnar Müller-Waldeck, Maria Osten was shot for "espionage" on 8 August 1942. Clearly a victim of the tremendous purges of Stalinism during that time, her charges of spying for France seem to be a pretext in order to cover up the real reason, namely her association with the

arrested Mikhail Koltsov. See Gunnar Müller-Waldeck, "Maria Osten zum Gedenken," p. 14, and John Fuegi, *Brecht & Co.: Sex, Politics, and the Making of Modern Drama* (New York, 1994), p. 405.
36. Petra Lataster-Czisch, ed., *Eigentlich rede ich nicht gern über mich: Lebenserinnerungen von Frauen aus dem Spanischen Bürgerkrieg, 1936–1939* (Leipzig, 1990), p. 192.
37. Ibid., p. 205.
38. Ibid., p. 224.
39. Ibid., p. 226.
40. Maria de Smeth, *Roter Kaviar—Hauptmann Maria* (Berlin, 1965), p. 199. Taubert particularly emphasized two qualities that rendered de Smeth a perfect candidate for the job in Spain: her expertise in "questions of active communism" and her Dutch citizenship. De Smeth was born in Bavaria around the turn of the century. In 1923, she married a wealthy Dutch businessman, thereby acquiring Dutch citizenship. After his early death, she returned to Germany to support herself. She held various jobs as a photographer and a journalist, which provided her with the rare opportunity to travel extensively throughout Europe. In 1932, on one of her trips, she was captured by Soviet troops and sent to Moscow. According to her own testimony, she spent five months (from September 1932 until January 1933) in the infamous "Lubjanka" prison in Moscow. For reasons that remain utterly unclear in her autobiography, she was released and sent back to Germany.
41. Ibid., p. 199.
42. Ibid., p. 200.
43. Robert H. Whealey, *Hitler and Spain: The Nazi Role in the Spanish Civil War, 1936–1939* (Lexington, Ky., 1989), p. 29.
44. Ibid., p. 26.
45. Ibid., p. 30.
46. Hitler postponed publicly admitting German intervention in the Spanish Civil War until near the end of the war (see ibid., p. 28). De Smeth claims that she even had to swear an oath that she would not talk to anybody about her mission in Spain, not even to her mother (see de Smeth, *Roter Kaviar*, p. 201).
47. Maria de Smeth, *Viva España! Arriba España!* (Berlin, 1937), p. 28.
48. Ibid., p. 58.
49. Ibid., p. 86.
50. De Smeth, *Roter Kaviar*, pp. 314–315.
51. Whealey, *Hitler and Spain*, p. 32. Experts on propaganda as well as journalists, photographers, writers, artists, and film and radio experts constituted this group of undercover agents spying in Spain for Hitler's National Socialist regime. Their main contact person was German ambassador Wilhelm von Faupel; in fact, in June 1937, the organization was renamed Presseabteilung der deutschen Botschaft (Press Department of the German Embassy).
52. In her autobiography, de Smeth regrets that she was not allowed to mention the German and Italian troops deployed in Spain in her monograph *Viva España! Arriba España!* She was convinced that the inclusion of especially the German intervention would have greatly contributed to the larger success of her earlier book on Spain, though she still claims that her book on Spain superseded Karl Silex's and Edwin Erich Dwinger's works in popularity at that time. See de Smeth, *Roter Kaviar*, p. 315.
53. Günther Schmigalle, "Deutsche schreiben für Hitler und Franco," p. 204.

– 17 –

THE RELUCTANT BELLIGERENT

Franco's Spain and Hitler's War

Norman J. W. Goda

Shortly after World War II, Francisco Franco's government argued before the world that Spain never wished to enter the conflict on the side of Adolf Hitler's Germany. True, Spain had supplied the Germans with vital war materials, a Spanish division had fought against the Soviets, and the Spanish press had openly favored the Axis.[1] But Spain, so the official story went, had to comply with Adolf Hitler (1889–1945) to a certain degree, lest the Germans, who stood at the Pyrenees by June 1940, overrun the country. Franco (1892–1975) had thus shielded his nation from invasion by providing Germany with minimal help and friendly rhetoric.[2] These arguments influenced the historiography of the war until the 1970s,[3] when Franco's death, key memoirs by subordinates, and the opening of some Spanish records began to change it.[4] At the very least, Franco seriously entertained the idea of belligerence; at most, he was completely enthralled with Hitler's victories.[5] The truth may lie somewhere in between, and this essay will argue as follows: the Franco government held imperialist aims that could have been won only through a French defeat; Spain nearly entered the war of its own accord thanks to France's defeat in 1940; and Madrid abstained from war only when it became clear that Germany itself had become the greatest threat to Spanish imperial aims.

As early as the 1920s, Franco shared with the Spanish right the belief that national renewal was attainable in large part through the reconquest of empire abroad. For Franco, the empire centered on Morocco. Franco and other *Africanistas* in the army had built their military careers there in the 1920s fighting the Rif rebellion under Abd-el-Krim.[6] In 1924, when the Spanish dictator Miguel Primo de Rivera (1870–1930) argued for a withdrawal from Morocco, Lieutenant Colonel Franco countered that "Morocco is Spanish earth because it has been acquired at the highest price ... Spanish blood."[7] On the eve of his victory in Spain, General Franco commented that the possibility of restoring Spain's greatness lay ultimately in Africa.[8] Franco, wrote his brother-in-law and onetime minister Ramón Serrano Suñer, "was a man of Africa. In Morocco he had brilliantly made his entire career, and in Morocco his destiny seemed to lie."[9]

The delineation of the Moroccan protectorate zones had long angered Spanish nationalists. Despite the promise of a large zone in 1902, Spain's zone was shrunk, mainly by the French. The division of Morocco in 1912 left France with most of Morocco and Spain with what the Italian king Victor Emmanuel III (1869–1947) called the bone of the Moroccan cutlet—a mountainous coastal strip of 20,000 square kilometers, nearly impossible to conquer and barely worth improving.[10] The zone was shrunk even more after World War I. In 1923, Tangier was placed under French-dominated international administration,[11] and in 1925 France occupied three tribal areas in the Spanish zone as part of its military contribution against Abd-el-Krim.[12]

On assuming power, then, the Franco government worked to build Spain's position in Morocco at France's expense. The most active figure was Colonel Juan Beigbeder, an expert on Morocco who served as high commissioner in Tetuán from April 1937 to August 1939.[13] During the Spanish Civil War, Beigbeder kept the tribal leaders loyal to Franco—sixty thousand Moroccan troops fought on his side—by granting a degree of autonomy yet unseen in either zone. Beigbeder also built an Institute for Moroccan Studies, while allowing the Moroccan press in the Spanish zone to blast the neighboring French administration. None of this sat well with Paris, which had enough problems without the addition of nationalist agitation in Morocco.[14]

The German government was pleased to augment French headaches, and thus relations between the High Commissariat and Herbert Georg Richter, the German consul in Tetuán, were quite friendly. Beigbeder set up German contacts with Moroccan nationalists in the French zone, and, beginning in 1939, Richter funneled cash to nationalists in French Morocco while promoting German propaganda in both zones.[15] Beigbeder naturally expected Spain to be the beneficiary of this sort of activity. While praising Beigbeder to the German Foreign Ministry upon the colonel's promotion to the office of foreign minister in August 1939, Richter commented that "Beigbeder's personal wish is to incorporate Tangier into the Spanish zone and also to advance the frontiers against French Morocco; nonetheless, he openly admits that this [would only be] possible in the event of a general conflict."[16]

Franco did not plan to enter Hitler's war when it erupted in September 1939. Spain, he said privately, would need five years to recover from its civil war, and on 4 September, Madrid proclaimed strict neutrality.[17] Yet the French disasters of May and June 1940 opened doors which seemingly offered inexpensive passage. "We believed then certainly in a German victory," wrote Ramón Serrano Suñer, "and we had to ... foresee the accommodation of Spain in the European order."[18] Air Minister Juan Yagüe was hardly joking when he commented to the Germans in May that "the Spanish Air Force rejoices in this victory as if it were our own."[19] Beigbeder meanwhile informed the German ambassador that Spain's national claims included French Morocco and said that he would regret an Italian occupation of Morocco.[20] The Spanish press, meanwhile, spoke openly about demands in Africa, and during a speech commemorating the rebellion on 18 July, Franco himself announced that it was necessary "to make a nation, to forge an empire. To do that, our first task must be to strengthen the unity of Spain. There remains a duty and mission, the command of Gibraltar, African expansion, and the permanence of a policy of unity."[21]

Action indeed accompanied polemic, and it is interesting that at first Madrid preferred not to consult Berlin. On 12 June, the Franco government announced that it was no longer neutral, but a "non-belligerent."[22] A united Morocco under Spanish protection now became the overriding aim. Tangier was the first objective. Despite the international administration, the chief of the Tangier Control Commission had always been French, which had piqued the Spaniards in general and Beigbeder in particular.[23] Yet a beleaguered French Foreign Ministry agreed on 13 June to allow Spain to occupy Tangier temporarily to maintain the city's neutrality. The next morning, before French officers in Morocco were even informed, Spain acted. Beigbeder was visibly pleased with himself for days, and though Madrid characterized the occupation as temporary in its explanatory notes to most capitals, its notes to

Berlin and Rome deliberately omitted this proviso.[24] Spain's subsequent measures to replace international control with that of Tetuán revealed further that Tangier was to become part of Spanish Morocco.[25]

Yet would Madrid be as daring with French Morocco? Here Spanish intentions are murkier, but from available evidence it appears that Madrid seriously considered an invasion in the days preceding the French surrender.[26] On 15 June, the day following the Tangier occupation, Eberhard von Stohrer, the German ambassador to Madrid, visited Beigbeder, found him fully preoccupied with maps of French Morocco, and cabled Berlin that Spain would take action in the French zone soon.[27] The same day in Tetuán, General Carlos Asensio, the new Spanish high commissioner, told Richter that Spanish action was forthcoming.[28] The next day, Franco's chief of staff, Jorge Vigón, visited Hitler in France. While promising nothing, Vigón announced Spain's expectation of a united Morocco. Hitler's answer, however, could not have pleased Madrid. Though the Germans were willing to allow Spain to have Gibraltar, Hitler warned that Germany and possibly Italy also had interests in Morocco.[29] Indeed, Germany was developing an intense interest in Morocco, for reasons which will be seen below.

Madrid concluded for the moment that it would have to win Morocco itself, but the question of how remained open. Richter reported considerable Spanish troop movements at the French zonal frontier during the next week; he reported that the marching order was to have come from Madrid on 16 or 17 June 1940, but that it had been delayed. Asensio, meanwhile, predicted a large-scale Spanish advance while nervously awaiting orders.[30] Why did Spanish troops not march? One explanation lies in the shrewd French request in the small hours of 17 June that Spain mediate a Franco-German cease-fire.[31] The request stunned Madrid, which had expected the Swiss to perform this favor; yet as Spain's ambassador in France noted, the request was an appeal to the moral stature of Spain and of Franco himself.[32] Honor aside, there were also military factors for the delay. Richter learned on 19 June that the Spaniards believed French ground forces to remain formidable, and the movement of French aircraft to North Africa further dissuaded the Spaniards. Richter himself was relieved by Franco's restraint, commenting, "One cannot describe the Spanish military organization here in bad enough terms."[33]

A disappointed Beigbeder attempted on 17 June to negotiate with France an extension of the zonal frontier. But despite the foreign minister's argument that France should prefer to lose part of its empire to Spain than to Germany, the French did not yield. There was no intention, especially on the part of the French resident general in Rabat, General Charles-August Noguès, of allowing another Tangier to occur.[34] The road to Morocco would thus have to wind through Berlin. Too late to take advantage of Hitler's victory over France, Madrid hoped that there was still time to capitalize on the impending victory over Great Britain. On 19 June, Beigbeder informed the Germans that Spain would enter the war against Britain in return for territorial prizes, which featured a united Moroccan protectorate, the Oran district of Algeria, an extension of the Spanish Sahara, an enlargement of Spanish Guinea, and Gibraltar. Madrid also wanted material aid for the attack on Gibraltar, German help in defending the Canary Islands, and food.[35] Why did Madrid make this offer now? It was Madrid's last hope for an empire in French Northwest Africa. With the exception of Gibraltar, all Spanish claims were on French territory. Spain had made no suggestion up to this time that it wanted a war with Great Britain. Aside from the occasional Madrid street demonstration, the Spanish government had not pressed the British on Gibraltar and, in fact, lacked any prepared plans for an attack there.[36] French Morocco was another matter, but to have it, Spain would have to join Germany's war and thus make the claim recognized in Berlin.

Berlin, as matters turned out, was interested in Northwest Africa as well. Morocco offered strategic base sites that the Germans could develop and use in a future struggle, most likely with the United States. German naval and aircraft firms had already received official contracts for the construction of a fleet of 56,000-ton battleships (*Bismarck* and *Tirpitz* were a mere 48,000 tons) and for the Messerschmitt 264—a four-engine, long-distance bomber that would be able to traverse the Atlantic.[37] With this in mind, Hitler demanded from the French eight air bases near Casablanca in July 1940. When the French rejected the demand, Berlin began to view Spain and the Gibraltar strait as a route by which it could place troops in Northwest Africa and perhaps take coastal bases on its own. Hitler and the German navy also coveted a base in Spain's own Canary Islands. The Germans began serious talks with the Spaniards in August 1940, and on 16 September, Franco's interior minister, Ramón Serrano Suñer, arrived in Berlin for talks with Hitler and Foreign Minister Joachim von Ribbentrop (1893–1946). The Germans had yet to reveal to the Spaniards the true nature of their aims, and even as the Germans spoke to Serrano Suñer in

Berlin, a secret German Luftwaffe mission was in Casablanca reconnoitering base sites.[38] Though unaware of the German agents in Casablanca, Serrano Suñer knew of Berlin's earlier demand for air bases there thanks to a deliberate French Foreign Ministry leak.[39] He thus launched into a lengthy treatise on Spain's claim to a united Morocco, insisting that it was the "natural and historical objective of Spanish expansion."[40] The Germans accepted the idea of a united Morocco under Spanish rule, but then requested that Spain cede to Germany two bases there (Agadir and Mogador), as well as one of the Canary Islands, for base development. Serrano was visibly upset, and an indignant Franco would comment privately that "the world is big enough so that Spain need not suffer any mortgage on its territories."[41] Serrano Suñer's subsequent comments to Benito Mussolini (1883–1945) were damning enough that they had to be deleted from the discussion record handed to the Germans.[42] Still, Franco remained hopeful that he could find an arrangement with Berlin over Morocco. His letters from Madrid to Hitler and Serrano Suñer reveal that he even accepted the possibility of a long war and that he banked on a long-term alliance.[43] Later in September 1940, Madrid even rejected a French offer to adjust Morocco's zonal borders, thus signifying Franco's continued belief that he could still get a better deal from the Germans.[44]

It is within this context that the famous meetings at Hendaye on 23 October 1940 between Franco and Serrano Suñer (now Franco's foreign minister) on the one hand, and Hitler and Ribbentrop on the other, must be seen. Yet the Hendaye meetings were a disappointment as well.[45] Hitler, thanks to the Anglo-Gaullist raid on Dakar on 23 September, now feared handing too much of the French empire to Spain, lest the French not defend their imperial holdings against future attacks. Spain, he said, would have to accept smaller—and unspecified—rewards. The so-called Hendaye Protocol, which the Germans presented during the meeting as a regulative document for Spain's entry into the war, thus had no clear provisions concerning Spain's future in Africa.[46] Franco and Serrano Suñer, who had thought Hitler was bringing good news to Hendaye, were stunned. Franco was fully alive to the Gaullist threat, but assumed that Spain would fight it rather than sacrifice its territorial future to it. He argued that his troops in Spanish Morocco—now seven divisions—could neutralize a Gaullist movement in North Africa; he then spoke at terrific length on Spain's historic claim to Morocco, while insisting on a formal agreement concerning Morocco before Spain's entry into the war.[47]

Hitler, visibly irritated, noted privately that "nothing can be done with these people."[48] Five days later he made his famous comment to Mussolini that he would prefer to have three or four teeth removed rather than suffer another discussion with Franco.[49]

The Spaniards were irritated as well. Franco privately noted to Serrano Suñer that "this sacrifice of ours would only be justified with the counterbalance of that which is to be the basis of our imperium. After the victory, they would give us nothing if it is not agreed to now, despite what they are saying."[50] Still, the Germans rejected a proposed supplementary protocol that would have promised French Morocco to Spain, which prompted the following comment from Serrano Suñer: "I would not like to pass up this opportunity to express the bitter feeling produced in both the Caudillo and myself by the fact that, in spite of our friendship, the trivial changes which we had suggested—and which, without encroaching at all on the core of the problem or on the Führer's possibilities for negotiation, gave us a somewhat greater measure of security—were rejected."[51] Yet Franco did not give up. In his letter to Hitler of 30 October, he argued that the French lands in question were in fact not French at all, but natural *Spanish* territory that France had stolen at the time of the *Entente Cordiale*. "It is not French territory that we want," claimed Franco, "nor do we claim to profit from French blood. We want only that which a clever liberal diplomacy ... wrested from us in complete injustice ... I thus repeat the Spanish aspiration ... to the part of Morocco which is in French hands."[52]

Franco's intriguing attempt to prove that French Morocco was not French failed. In fact, Hitler believed, thanks to the letter's opening statement of solidarity with the Axis, that the document simply confirmed Franco's intention to enter the war.[53] On 4 November, Hitler told his military staff that Spain would join the conflict; Germany would soon conclude political negotiations with Spain and capture Gibraltar.[54] He also insisted that a substantial German force would then travel to Spanish Morocco.[55] Ribbentrop's invitation to Serrano Suñer to come to Berchtesgaden in mid-November to tie up loose ends was eagerly accepted by the latter, probably because Madrid saw it as a response to Franco's letter.[56] Yet it was at this meeting at Hitler's mountain retreat on 18 November that Spain's ardor for war finally cooled. Irritated at Serrano Suñer's continued insistence for a written guarantee for French Morocco, Hitler made what were for Madrid startling new revelations. Were Germany to make such public promises, he said, "Morocco would immediately break away, and the conquest of

Gibraltar would make *no sense anymore*. [A specific written agreement] would lead to the loss of the object of the agreement ... He [Hitler] would then prefer that Gibraltar remain in English hands and Africa with [the French]."[57] After the operation, he revealed, Germany would place troops in Morocco to prevent such a defection, and after the war it would claim a base on the coast. These statements were pivotal. Hitler gave no encouragement to Franco's recent letter, and worse, he revealed to a Spanish official for the first time that he would use Spanish belligerence as a reason to place German troops in Morocco—the prime objective of Spanish belligerence.

On 7 December, Franco refused the official German request that Spain enter the war by 10 January, and, when asked, he refused to say when Spain would be ready.[58] Subsequent German attempts to bully the Spaniards into the war also failed.[59] Franco blamed his country's economic difficulties, and these were certainly a factor. But Spain's economy had been wretched throughout the autumn of 1940, and the Spaniards remained willing to enter the war—even a long war—throughout that time. Madrid's reticence stemmed from German aims in Africa that Spain could not have prevented should it have entered the war and permitted German passage through the Iberian Peninsula. Much of the available evidence supports this contention. In the first place, Franco and Serrano Suñer continued to complain loudly and often even after 7 December that the Germans had not been forthcoming enough concerning territorial rewards.[60] Meanwhile, in Spain's overseas territories, German agents suddenly confronted roadblocks to their activities. In the second half of November 1940, distrustful Spanish authorities refused to cooperate with the German naval officials in augmenting the defenses in the Canaries, even though German help in defending the islands had been part of Franco's original price for belligerence in June, and the weak defenses there were among his stated reasons for remaining at peace in December. In late November, Spain's ambassador to Berlin addressed a blistering note to Ribbentrop that condemned German propaganda and other illicit activities in Morocco.[61] In Morocco itself, German agents confronted difficulties entering Tangier, and, at year's end, Richter, who had recently praised the friendliness of the Spanish High Commissariat in Tetuán, complained as follows:

> The Spanish effort to exclude us systematically from Morocco has been evident ... on unimportant occasions as well as in matters of principle. In the French zone, too, which certainly does not belong to the Spaniards,

they do not want any German influence. A shipment from the Madrid embassy to the consulate containing Arabic propaganda material, which by reason of its text and sense could only be used in the French zone, was confiscated by the High Commissariat in a way that I consider to be contrary to international law [!] ... Spanish policy here ... is a bad sign for the future, if Spain should really succeed in gaining possession of the French zone entirely or even in part. Spain would have only one aim. It would never rest until the last German had left the country.[62]

The contrast with Richter's earlier comments on Spanish-German cooperation in Morocco is particularly striking.

We should indeed lay to rest the notion that the Franco government never wished to make an ultimate commitment to Hitler's war. In the summer of 1940, the Spaniards nearly invaded French Morocco without even consulting the Germans; they then offered, with no German prodding, to enter the war against Great Britain. Yet it is also true that the Franco government considered war for Francoist aims. France's defeat presented an opportunity to realize long-standing goals in Africa, which appealed to the Spanish right, to the Spanish army, and to Franco personally. The sacrifice of Spanish interests on the altar of National Socialism as such was never considered. Once it became clear in Madrid that Germany was the new threat to Spanish territorial aims in Africa, war became a far less appealing option.

Notes

1. For consideration of these issues, see David Wingeate Pike, "Franco and the Axis Stigma," *Journal of Contemporary History*, vol. 17 (January 1982), pp. 369–480, and more recently Paul Preston, "Franco and Hitler: The Myth of Hendaye 1940," *Contemporary European History*, vol. 1 (March 1992), pp. 1–16.
2. Ramón Serrano Suñer, *Entre Hendaye y Gibraltar: noticia y reflexión, frente a una legenda, sobre nuestra politica en dos guerras* (Madrid, 1947); José María Doussinague, *España tenía razón, 1939– 1945*, 2nd ed. (Madrid, 1950).
3. Charles B. Burdick, *Germany's Military Strategy and Spain in World War II* (Syracuse, N.Y., 1968); Donald S. Detwiler, *Hitler, Franco und Gibraltar: Die Frage des spanischen Eintritts in den Zweiten Weltkrieg* (Wiesbaden, 1962).
4. Ramón Serrano Suñer, *Memorias: entre el silencio y la propaganda, la historia como fue* (Barcelona, 1977); Heleno Saña, *El franquismo sin mitos: conversaciones con Serrano Suñer* (Barcelona, 1982).
5. Various good interpretations can be found in Stanley G. Payne, *The Franco Regime, 1936–1975* (Madison, Wis., 1987); Paul Preston, *Franco: A Biography*

(New York, 1994); and Xavier Tusell and Genoveva García Queipo de Llano, *Franco y Mussolini: la politica española durante la Segunda Guerra Mundial* (Barcelona, 1985).

6. David S. Woolman, *Rebels in the Rif: Abd el Krim and the Rif Rebellion* (Stanford, Calif., 1968); J. W. D. Trythall, *El Caudillo: A Political Biography of Franco* (New York, 1970), pp. 29–51; Preston, *Franco: A Biography*, pp. 31–68.
7. Quoted in Woolman, *Rebels in the Rif*, p. 132.
8. Denis Smyth, *Diplomacy and Strategy of Survival: British Policy and Franco's Spain, 1940–41* (Cambridge, 1986), p. 45.
9. Serrano Suñer, *Memorias*, p. 285.
10. Christopher M. Andrew, *Théophile Delcassé and the Making of the Entente Cordiale: A Reappraisal of French Foreign Policy, 1898–1905* (London, 1968), pp. 191–193, 216–217; William A. Hoisington, Jr., *The Casablanca Connection: French Colonial Policy, 1936–1943* (Chapel Hill, N.C., 1984), pp. 136–137. The best treatment of Spanish claims in Morocco is in the contemporary Spanish official account, José María de Areilza and Fernando María Castiella, *Reivindicaciones de España*, 2nd ed. (Madrid, 1941), pp. 267–501. The account is polemical but complete and with excellent maps. For Spain's problems in its zone, see Victor Morales Lezcano, *España y el Norte de Africa: el Protectorado en Marruecos (1912–1956)*, 2nd ed. (Madrid, 1986), pp. 163–217.
11. Charles R. Halstead and Carolyn J. Halstead, "Aborted Imperialism: Spain's Occupation of Tangier 1940–1945," *Iberian Studies*, vol. 7 (Autumn 1978), pp. 53–55; Hoisington, *The Casablanca Connection*, p. 150.
12. Ibid., p. 153; Woolman, *Rebels in the Rif*, pp. 165–66, 208–209. De Areilza and Castiella, *Reivindicaciones de España*, pp. 420–432, contains the documentation on the 1925 border agreement.
13. Charles R. Halstead, "A 'Somewhat Machiavellian' Face: Colonel Juan Beigbeder as High Commissioner in Spanish Morocco, 1937–1939," *The Historian*, vol. 37 (November 1974), pp. 46–66; idem, "Un africain méconnu: le colonel Juan Beigbeder," *Revue d'histoire de la deuxième guerre mondiale*, vol. 21 (July 1971), pp. 31–60.
14. Hoisington, *The Casablanca Connection*, p. 149. See also Foreign Ministry (Berlin), to Deutsche Botschaft [DB] Madrid, Pol III 359g, 18 February 1939, Politisches Archiv des Auswärtigen Amtes (Bonn) [AA], DB Madrid, "Frankreich und Beziehungen zu Spanien"; Estado Español, SIPM, no. 10/8–390, 6 May 1939, Archivo General del Ministerio de Asuntos Exteriores (Madrid) [AMAE], Legajo 1065, Expediente 5.
15. Richter to Stohrer, Unnumbered, 24 June 1940, AA, DB Madrid, Marokko-Allgemein, vol. 5; Richter to Foreign Ministry, no. 469/40, 15 April 1940, ibid; Richter to Foreign Ministry, no. 915/Sekr., 26 June 1939, ibid.
16. Richter to Foreign Ministry no. 1192/39, 11 August 1939, enclosed in Foreign Ministry to DB Paris, Pol III 3318, 18 August 1939, AA, DB Paris, Spanien: Politische Akten, Bndl 1363. The new Spanish administration in Tetuán was also headed by staunch Africanistas friendly to the German Consulate. The high commissioner was General Carlos Asensio, a divisional commander during the Civil War, and the new general secretary of the administration, Tomás García Figueras, was an expert on Morocco who had long polemicized on the Spanish protectorate. See Richter to Foreign Ministry, no. 1231/ Pol III, 18 August 1939, enclosed in Foreign Ministry to DB Paris, Pol. III 3380, ibid; Richter to Foreign Ministry, no. 626/41, 10 May 1941, AA, DB

Madrid, Marokko-Allgemein, vol. 5. On García Figueras's views, see his *Marruecos: la acción de España en el Norte de África* (Madrid, 1939).
17. Victor Morales Lezcano, *Historia de la no-beligerancia española durante la Segunda Guerra Mundial (VI, 1940–X, 1943)* (Las Palmas, 1980), pp. 25–26.
18. Serrano Suñer, *Memorias*, p. 288.
19. Stohrer to Foreign Ministry, no. 1496/20, 20 May 1940, AA, DB Madrid, Entwicklung der allgemeinen Lage, vol. 1.
20. Stohrer to Foreign Ministry, 3 June 1940, Germany, Auswärtiges Amt, *Akten zur deutschen auswärtigen Politik, 1918–1945* (Baden-Baden, 1950ff.). Hereafter cited as *ADAP* with series, volume, and document number: series D, vol. 9, no. 380.
21. Quoted in Samuel Hoare (Viscount Templewood), *Ambassador on Special Mission* (London, 1946), p. 48. See also Smyth, *Diplomacy and Strategy of Survival*, pp. 41–42. On Spanish press comments, see *ADAP*, D, IX, no. 380; Stohrer to Foreign Ministry, 7 June 1940, no. 1769, AA, Büro des Staatssekretärs [StS], Marokko, vol. 1.
22. Victor Morales Lezcano, "Las causas de la no-beligerancia española, reconsideradas," *Revista de Estudios Internacionales*, vol. 5 (July–September 1984), pp. 609–631.
23. On Tangier, see Halstead and Halstead, "Aborted Imperialism," pp. 54–55; Hoisington, *The Casablanca Connection*, pp. 150–151. For Spanish irritation, see the newspaper articles by Beigbeder's press chief, Enrique Arquéz," ¿Ha sido Tánger neutral alguna vez?," *España*, 8 June 1939, and the "prize-winning" "Cómo perdimos Tánger," ibid., 8 January 1940. *España*, a Tangier newspaper under Arquéz's editorship, was generally recognized as Beigbeder's voice. Richter still called it "Das Blatt Beigbeders" even after Beigbeder had become foreign minister. Beigbeder commented to Richter in June 1939 that he aimed to keep polemic over Tangier at a steady flow so that the question would remain open. See Richter to Foreign Ministry, no. 839/Pol. III, 12 June 1939, AA, DB Madrid, Tanger Zone, vol. 3; Richter to Foreign Ministry, no. 30/Pol. VII, 10 January 1940, ibid. Arquéz later wrote a polemic on Morocco entitled *El momento de España en Marruecos* (Madrid, 1942).
24. On the background, negotiations for, and execution of the Tangier occupation see AMAE, L 1217, Ex 69. See also Stohrer to Foreign Ministry, no. 2621/40, 17 June 1940, AA, DB Madrid, Tanger Zone, vol. 3.
25. Ibid., passim; Hoisington, *The Casablanca Connection*, pp. 150–152; Halstead and Halstead, "Aborted Imperialism," pp. 55–57; Smyth, *Diplomacy and Strategy of Survival*, vol. 46, pp. 133–172.
26. The lack of clarity is due in part to the Servicio Historico Militar, which presently claims that no records from the Army of Africa exist from the period of World War II.
27. Stohrer to Foreign Ministry, no. 1906, 15 June 1940, AA, StS, Marokko, vol. 1; Payne, *The Franco Regime*, p. 270, states that there had been military plans for an advance in northwest Africa since June 1940.
28. Richter to Foreign Ministry, no. 8, 15 June 1940, AA, StS, Marokko, vol. 1.
29. For the protocol, see *ADAP*, D, IX, no. 465. For Franco's letter to Hitler, delivered by Vigón but dated 3 June, see ibid., p. 378. Asensio had told Richter on 15 June that the imminent Spanish advance into Morocco hinged on the outcome of the negotiations in Berlin with Franco's representative. Asensio no doubt meant the negotiations with Vigón. See Richter to Foreign Ministry, no. 8, 15 June 1940, AA, St.S., Marokko, vol. 1.

30. Richter to Foreign Ministry, no. 725/40, 20 June 1940, enclosed in Foreign Ministry to DB Rome, Pol III 1734, 4 July 1940, AA, DB Rom, Lage an der französisch-spanischen Zonengrenze. For Italian perspectives see Italy, Ministro degli Affari Esteri, *I Documenti Diplomatici Italiani*, series 9, vol. 5 (Rome, 1962)(hereafter cited as *DDI*), no. 42.
31. *ADAP*, D, IX, no. 459 and no. 1.
32. Lequerica to Beigbeder, no. 824, 18 June 1940, AMAE, L 2295, Ex 4; Lequerica to Beigbeder, unnumbered, 16 June 1940, ibid., L 1217, Ex 69.
33. See Richter to Foreign Ministry, no. 725/40, 20 June 1940, enclosed in Foreign Ministry to DB Rome, Pol III 1734g, 4 July 1940, AA, DB Rom, Lage an der französisch-spanischen Zonengrenze; Richter to Foreign Ministry, no. 732/40, 25 June 1940, enclosed in Foreign Ministry to DB Rome, Pol III 1765g, 4 July 1940, ibid.; Richter to Stohrer, unnumbered, 24 June 1940, AA, DB Madrid, Marokko-Allgemein, vol. 5. On the deployment of French troops, see Hoisington, *The Casablanca Connection*, p. 152, no. 53. On Spanish concerns on French air power estimates, see Stohrer to Foreign Ministry, 23 June 1940, *ADAP*, D, X, no. 3; see also Zoppi to Ciano, 22 June 1940, *DDI*, 9, V, no. 86.
34. Hoisington, *The Casablanca Connection*, pp. 150–155; François Charles-Roux, *Cinq mois tragiques aux affaires étrangères (21 mai–1er novembre 1940)* (Paris, 1949), pp. 224–248.
35. Stohrer to Foreign Ministry, no. 1971, 19 June 1940, AA, StS, Marokko, vol. 1; *ADAP*, D, IX, no. 488. The Spaniards gave an analogous message in Rome, omitting the requests for weapons and foodstuffs. See *DDI*, 9, V, no. 54.
36. Smyth, *Diplomacy and Strategy of Survival*, pp. 32–33, 42–44, 47–49; Burdick, *Germany's Military Strategy*, p. 25.
37. On the naval contracts, see Jost Dülffer, *Weimar, Hitler und die Marine: Reichspolitik und Flottenbau, 1920–1939* (Düsseldorf, 1973). On the Messerschmitt 264, see Jochen Thies, *Architekt der Weltherrschaft: Die "Endziele" Hitlers* (Düsseldorf, 1980).
38. For these issues, see my "The Riddle of the Rock: A Reassessment of German Motives for the Capture of Gibraltar in the Second World War," *Journal of Contemporary History*, vol. 28 (April 1993), pp. 297–314; and my "Hitler's Demand for Casablanca in 1940: Incident or Policy?" *International History Review*, vol. 16 (August 1994), pp. 491–510.
39. Lequerica to Beigbeder, unnumbered, 18 July 1940, AMAE, L 1190, Ex 97; Lequerica to Beigbeder, nos. 526–529, 20 July 1940, ibid. Beigbeder had in fact hinted to Stohrer in late July that a demand for German installations in Morocco could push the French colonies into the arms of Charles de Gaulle. See *ADAP*, D, X, no. 231.
40. ' For Serrano Suñer's five September meetings in Madrid, see ibid., XI, nos. 63, 66, 67, 97, 117; Espinosa de los Monteros to Beigbeder, 3 October 1940, AMAE, L 1188, Ex 3.
41. Franco to Serrano Suñer, 21 September 1940, Serrano Suñer, *Memorias*, pp. 331–340.
42. Malcolm Muggeridge, ed., *Ciano's Diary, 1939–1943* (London, 1947), 1, 5 October 1940; idem, ed., *Ciano's Diplomatic Papers* (London, 1948), pp. 393–394; Tusell and Queipo de Llano, *Franco y Mussolini*, pp. 107–108.
43. Franco to Serrano Suñer, 21 September 1940, Serrano Suñer, *Memorias*, pp. 331–340. Franco to Hitler, 22 September 1940, *ADAP*, D, XI, no. 88. See also ibid., no. 172. Regarding the possibility of German bases in Morocco, Franco would go no further than a ninety-nine year lease on Mogador.

44. On Spanish-French talks concerning the Moroccan border, see Lequerica to Beigbeder, no. 1137, 30 September 1940, AMAE, L 2295, Ex 5; Charles-Roux, *Cinq mois tragiques*, pp. 243–248. French Chief of State Marshal Henri Philippe Pétain was aptly concerned that Hitler was using Franco to push into North Africa. See Matthieu Séguéla, *Pétain-Franco: les secrets d'une alliance* (Paris, 1992), pp. 119–156.
45. For a full consideration of this meeting, its sources, and its controversies, see Preston, "Franco and Hitler," and my own *Tomorrow the World: Hitler, Northwest Africa, and the Path toward America* (College Station, Tex., 1998), pp. 103–106. For the protocols of the Hendaye meetings between Hitler and Franco and Serrano Suñer and Ribbentrop, respectively, see *ADAP*, D, XI, nos. 220, 221. See also Serrano Suñer, *Memorias*, pp. 289–301.
46. See *ADAP*, D, XI, pp. 466–467, for the only surviving version of the protocol, which had been revised from the original presented at Hendaye. The controversial article five, which dealt with compensation to Spain, reads as follows:

> 5. Apart from the reunion of Gibraltar with Spain, the Axis powers state that in principle they are ready to provide, in the course of a new general settlement in Africa, such as is to be carried out in the peace treaties after the defeat of England, that Spain be ceded certain areas in Africa in precisely the same extent to which France can be compensated by other cessions of territorial possessions in Africa of equal value. The claims to be made on France by Germany shall not be affected thereby.

47. Franco's explanation on what Spain could do militarily to minimize the Gaullist threat in North Africa is not contained in the incomplete protocol of the Franco-Hitler discussion, but he must have gone into considerable detail. Both Ribbentrop and Hitler would tell the Italians after the Hendaye meeting that the Spaniards grossly overestimated their capabilities in North Africa, and that it had been difficult to convince them that they could not handle the Gaullist threat alone. See *ADAP*, D, XI, nos. 228, 246.
48. For Hitler's comments, see Pike, "Franco and the Axis Stigma," pp. 376–378, and Payne, *The Franco Regime*, p. 273. The German memoir literature cited in Detwiler, *Hitler, Franco and Gibraltar*, p. 59, n. 25, says that Hitler lost his patience and threatened to leave on one or two occasions. Serrano Suñer, *Memorias*, pp. 298–299, states that Hitler never made this threat, but that he was reduced to yawns during Franco's monologue.
49. Muggeridge, *Ciano's Diplomatic Papers*, p. 402. Hitler's comment that his meeting with Franco lasted nine hours is an exaggeration. It is likely that subsequent dinner discussion was included in the figure. Serrano Suñer, *Memorias*, p. 299, states that the meeting lasted three hours.
50. Quoted in ibid., p. 299.
51. Stohrer to Ribbentrop, 26 October 1940, *ADAP*, D, XI, no. 235. For the draft of the Spanish supplementary protocol see ibid., no. 222. For German comment, see AA, StS, Spanien, vol. 2, frame 74442-3.
52. Printed in Serrano Suñer, *Memorias*, pp. 301–305. Serrano Suñer's claim that the letter was written to buy time does not ring true. On 2 November, he told Stohrer that the intent of the letter lay in clarification of the issues discussed at Hendaye. Stohrer to Foreign Ministry, no. 3718, 2 November 1940, AA, StS, Spanien, vol. 2.
53. Hitler received Franco's letter of 30 October on 3 November by a special courier from Serrano Suñer's secretariat, who waited in Berlin to take back a

reply from Hitler. Yet Hitler made no reply. See Stohrer to Foreign Ministry, 1 November 1940, *ADAP*, D, XI, no. 273; Memorandum by Weizsäcker, AA, StS, Spanien, vol. 2, frame 74440.
54. Percy Ernst Schramm, gen. ed., *Kriegstagebuch des Oberkommandos der Wehrmacht (Wehrmachtführungsstab)*, 4 vols. (Frankfurt, 1961–65), vol. 1: *1 August 1940–31 Dezember 1941*, ed. Hans-Adolf Jacobsen (hereafter cited as *KTB/ OKW*), 4 November 1940; Hans-Adolf Jacobsen, ed., *Generaloberst Halder: Kriegstagebuch*, vol. 2: *Von der geplanten Landung in England bis zum Beginn des Ostfeldzuges* (Stuttgart, 1963), 4 November 1940.
55. Halder and Brauchitsch decided later in the day that the Third Armored Division, which had until that day been earmarked for service in the Italian North African campaign, would be one of the units sent to Morocco. The SS Division Adolf Hitler was also contemplated for service in Morocco. Subsequent planning revealed that the troops would cross the Strait of Gibraltar on German ships, then located in Italy. See *Halder Kriegstagebuch*, vol. 2, 7 November 1940.
56. Serrano Suñer was given ample opportunity to reject the invitation had he wished to do so. See my *Tomorrow the World*, p. 124.
57. *ADAP*, D, XI, no. 352. My italics.
58. *KTB/OKW*, I, entry of 8 December 1940; *ADAP*, D, XI, no. 500.
59. See my *Tomorrow the World*, pp. 159–162.
60. Stohrer to Ribbentrop, 25 November 1940, *ADAP*, D, XI, no. 398; Stohrer to Foreign Ministry, 28 November 1940, ibid., no. 414; Stohrer to Ribbentrop, 29 November 1940, ibid., no. 420; see also Franco's statements to Mussolini at their February 1941 meeting in Bordighera in Memorandum by Weizsäcker, 14 February 1941, ibid., XII, no. 49; Muggeridge, *Ciano's Diplomatic Papers*, pp. 422–426.
61. For the German navy's problems with the Canary Islands in late November and early December 1940, see my *Tomorrow the World*, pp. 132–134. For Spanish complaints on German activity in Morocco, see Eugenio Espinosa de los Monteros to Ribbentrop, no. 620, 30 November 1940, AA, StS, Marokko, vol. 1.
62. Herbert Georg Richter to Foreign Ministry, 26 December 1940, *ADAP*, D, XI, no. 273. On the problems of German activity in Morocco see my *Tomorrow the World*, pp. 129–131.

– 18 –

THE LAST DEFENDERS OF THE NEW ORDER

Spaniards and Nazi Germany,
August 1944–May 1945

Wayne Bowen

During the last nine months of World War II, the split between Francisco Franco's (1892–1975) Spain and Adolf Hitler's (1889–1945) Germany became a deep chasm. The physical separation after the Allied conquest of France was echoed in political, economic, and diplomatic conflicts between the two governments. Despite the imminent collapse of Nazism, several thousand Spaniards remained loyal to the New Order and the Third Reich. They continued to offer their labor and lives in defense of their dream: a new European order, led by Germany but not only for Germany. Throughout this period, German leaders used these collaborators cynically—as spies, soldiers, and workers—never intending to grant Spaniards equal status in a Nazi-dominated Europe. To the end of the war, prominent Nazis hoped to use their Spanish allies to replace Franco, whom they viewed as disloyal and ungrateful. When the last forces of the Thousand Year Reich surrendered in 1945, their failure also signaled the political demise of the Falange (the official state political party in Spain from 1936 on), forever stained by its identification with National Socialism. The last months of World War II were a dismal period for Spanish supporters of the New

Order. Whatever hopes had stayed alive after the Axis defeats of 1943 and early 1944 were now buried under the rubble of a bombed and burned-out Germany. In August 1944, it was still possible to believe that Germany could, if not win, at least fight the war to a draw. With Nazi *Wunderwaffen* coming into action and conflicts brewing within the Allied coalition, it was still possible to hope for an alternative to unconditional surrender. After German expulsion from France and most of Eastern Europe in late 1944, the war was effectively over. Only Hitler's defiance of reality kept the battles raging into 1945.

While Franco's government, which had maintained an official position of wartime neutrality, made haste to repair its relationship with the Allies during this period, thousands of Spaniards continued to support the New Order.[1] Even after D-Day (6 June 1944) and Soviet victories in the east, Spanish workers, soldiers, and political activists continued to work for closer official Hispano-German coordination and, when this proved impossible, defied the restrictions of their own government in this regard. Allied pressure and Franco's recognition of the changed realities made 1944–45 a difficult time for German agents and their collaborators in Spain. Surprisingly, however, even when the fortunes of the Third Reich seemed in inevitable decline, new Spanish recruits for Nazi military forces continued to enlist, risking their lives and citizenship in the process. With Allied armies advancing toward the Rhine and Vistula, hundreds of Spanish workers in Germany voluntarily renewed their work contracts. Germany's willingness to accept these soldiers and workers was understandable, given its acute labor and military necessities, but Spanish motivations are not so immediately evident.[2] Why would citizens of a neutral nation risk their lives in service to the Third Reich, by 1944 suffering under daily bombardment and constant military defeats? A few reasons stand out most dramatically. The most universal motivation was a search for adventure. The hard work of reconstruction, the pervasiveness of corruption, and the empty rituals of Spanish public life and politics compared unfavorably with the excitement and passions of the war in Europe. Serving in the Wehrmacht or laboring in German factories, even in the final months of the war, a young Spaniard could feel part of a great cause, rather than just another worker in Spain. Another important factor driving Spaniards into the arms of the Nazis was admiration for the Third Reich. Many had been impressed by the efficiency of the Condor Legion and the speed with which Hitler had rebuilt German strength and the power of the Wehrmacht. Even under the burden of war,

Germany seemed a tower of discipline and order in a chaotic world. With its rallies, parades of storm troopers, and commitment to social justice, the Nazi Party, too, awed many Spaniards, while the work of Nazi social and labor organizations inspired imitation in Spain.

A third motivation was financial need or ambition. After the destruction of a civil war, many parts of Spain were in severe depression and famine. Desperate to save themselves and their families, thousands of men from the poorest regions of Spain volunteered to work in Germany. Others, less poverty-stricken, used their trips to and from Germany for black market profits. By selling smuggled cognac, cigarettes, and coffee in Germany, a Spaniard could become wealthy in a short time. Through the system of wire and bank transfers set up by the Spanish and German governments, these black marketeers could then transfer this wealth back to Madrid. The final and most important reason was purely ideological: belief in the New Order and in Germany as its wellspring. By aligning with the Third Reich in uniform or as workers, these men hoped to bolster the new Europe and win places in its future. They saw Spain's natural role as an ally of Germany; service to Hitler was a direct outgrowth of this identification. The history of the Spaniards who aligned themselves with the Third Reich is part of the greater tragedy of World War II. Caught up in the revolutionary fervor of the New Order, they worked for this vision even after there was no possibility of success. In their misdirected idealism, they defended to the last the Nazi empire, sacrificing themselves for a lie.

With the withdrawal of German forces from France, Nazi intelligence agencies operating in Spain underwent dramatic changes. With nearly all German forces evicted from France by August 1944, the Allies began to pressure Spain to expel the Nazi spy network, presenting lists of German officials and private citizens considered agents of Berlin. Under Allied economic pressure, the Spanish Foreign Office reluctantly and incompletely complied with these requests, dealing successive blows to Axis intelligence gathering.[3] Recognizing this threat to their activities, the SS department in Madrid, a branch of the Reichssicherheitshauptamt (RSHA—Reich Central Security Office), proposed to Berlin the creation of a second, stand-alone espionage network to continue activity if Spain broke relations with Germany, hoping to secure Spanish citizenship for as many of its agents as possible "to forestall possible expulsion."[4] After receiving a rejection of this proposal, the Madrid RSHA warned that "90% of the network's [Spanish] personnel would probably drop out" if Franco severed relations with Germany. Even with bribes and ideological solidarity working in their favor, Nazi spymasters recognized the limits to which they could push their Spanish operatives.[5]

Nonetheless, the Nazis continued to find recruits among Falangist activists and veterans of the División Azul (Blue Division), which had fought aslongside German troops in Russia. With the return in early 1944 of the Blue Legion (the final elements of the Blue Division), the pool of potentially radical Naziphiles grew dramatically. Allied planners worried that these men, numbering over eight thousand, could prove dangerous advocates of Nazi interests in the peninsula.[6] Even with the blows to their organizations, the Nazis had many agents and sympathizers in Spain, controlled by the German embassy in Madrid and other consular offices. In early 1945, the Nazis could still count on reliable agents in the Spanish police forces, army, Falange, railroad, and other party and state organizations for these purposes.[7] In any case, Spanish border restrictions had limited the utility of the Nazi spy network. Germans were routinely granted exit visas throughout the summer and fall of 1944, but without the corresponding visas allowing the right of return.[8] As the war turned increasingly in favor of the Allies, these frontier controls impinged even more on Nazi activities. Although the Spanish border was hardly watertight, Franco's government did prevent a flood of Nazis from escaping the Allies.[9]

The breaking of the land link between Spain and Germany had greater significance. While the link had been shaky since the Allied assault on Normandy in June, it was the Allied landings in southern France in August that finally closed the land routes between Berlin and Madrid. Normal mail service was interrupted during July and August, resuming only sporadically thereafter with the continuation of air connections.[10] The Hispano-German trade relationship, and the agreements that codified it, effectively ended after the middle of August 1944.[11] Telephone service, even routed through Switzerland, was unreliable and plagued by bad connections, thereby limiting communication to telegraph cables.[12] Rail transportation between Spain and Germany ended completely after 8 July, so that only limited economic relations continued, such as German advertising in Spanish newspapers.[13] Direct trade plummeted, with Spanish companies canceling over RM 70,000 in orders from German firms in less than two weeks, from 30 August to 11 September.[14] The removal of Germany as a factor in the military balance of southwest Europe, ending the latent Nazi threat to

Spain, was the most visible result of this change, however. Just ahead of General Dwight D. Eisenhower's (1890–1969) armies, the once proud troops of the Thousand Year Reich scrambled to evacuate themselves from France, leaving behind a rear guard of resistance around Atlantic submarine bases and major communication centers, in the faint hope that the swastika would soon return to flutter over French soil.[15]

The German Labor Ministry's offices in Madrid continued to find hundreds of volunteers to work in Germany, however, even after D-Day, with radical Falangists and veterans of the División Azul as their main recruiting sources.[16] Given the difficulties of transport across France, some of these workers never made it beyond Irún; others traveled on blockade runners in the Mediterranean.[17] Recognizing the danger facing these volunteers, and under Allied pressure, the Spanish government placed obstacles to these departures, denying the validity of contracts, restricting passports, and conscripting military-age males.[18] Those who did make it to Nazi-occupied regions did not remain far from the minds of their compatriots, however. Parents, friends, and relatives desperate to get their sons back from France and Germany wrote frantic letters to the Spanish Foreign Ministry and other government agencies. Young men also ran away from home to enlist in the German army and Waffen-SS, much to the consternation of the Franco regime.[19] The Spanish government's attempts to lobby the German government for the return of these men and boys were unsuccessful. Franco's ambassador in Berlin tried his best to rescue these Spaniards, but informed the Spanish Foreign Ministry that Berlin was unlikely to surrender precious volunteer laborers and soldiers to an increasingly unfriendly Madrid.[20]

The Allies protested strongly to the Spanish Foreign Ministry about the enlistments of Spanish nationals in German military and intelligence services.[21] Of particular concern to the United States and the Free French representative in Madrid was the service in the Gestapo of dozens of Spaniards in France, and rumors that hundreds more were preparing to join them.[22] The Spanish Foreign Ministry vehemently, and deceptively, denied knowledge of any enlistments or service in the German military, indicating that perhaps these soldiers and agents might be Spanish expatriate Republicans who, for "the spirit of adventure and economic necessity," may have enlisted. In any case, the Spanish government asserted that their numbers could not compare with those of Spaniards enlisting in the ranks of the Allies.[23] According to the Spanish foreign minister, the Spanish government had not and would not authorize the enlistment of Spaniards, whether División Azul veterans or not, in German military, security, or police forces, nor allow them to aid German forces in France. The foreign minister did, however, admit knowledge of the many Spaniards who had joined the Maquis (French Resistance) or were fighting for the Allies in northern Italy. Despite these enlistments on both sides, he declared that Spain would not deviate from its "strict neutrality."[24] At the same time, however, the Spanish Foreign Ministry sent a letter to Falangist Secretary-General Arrese, asking if he knew anything about a group of four hundred Falangists allegedly preparing to leave Spain for France to join German occupation forces there.[25] The Foreign Ministry, despite its statements to the Allies, had extensive knowledge about Spaniards serving in the Waffen-SS and Wehrmacht.

As early as the spring of 1944, the Spanish Foreign Ministry had confirmed reports from its European embassies that Spaniards were enlisting in German military and intelligence services.[26] This information came, in its most direct form, from Spanish veterans of German service, who began to show up at Spanish diplomatic offices throughout Europe in early 1944. These often destitute Spaniards told stories of service in the Balkans, France, and the eastern front.[27] While many claimed to have served in the German army, most had worn the uniform of the Waffen-SS.[28] The Foreign Ministry was also well aware that recruitment of Spaniards occurred in Spain as well as in Nazi-occupied Europe.[29] The Spanish government likewise knew that German offices in Madrid, formerly used to recruit workers, were responsible for much of this activity, providing papers, funds, and directions to Spaniards wishing to enlist in the Nazi cause. The Germans even established a special unit, Sonderstab F (Special Staff, or Office, F), to supervise the movement of these Spaniards from Madrid to Nazi-occupied territory.[30] The main recruiting pools were veterans of the División Azul and Spaniards who were or had already been in Germany. Once these Spaniards made it across the frontier into France, the Sonderstab F provided them with transportation to Germany, work contracts, and identity documents.[31] Spanish workers already in Germany, displaced by air raids or other dislocations, had the option of joining the Todt Organization (OT), the Waffen-SS, or a Spanish Legion within the Wehrmacht.[32]

Even after the dissolution of the División Azul in late 1943 and the Blue Legion in the spring of 1944, Spaniards served in the German armed forces. Most served in two companies of a unit in the Waffen-SS, the Spanische Freiwilligen Einheit, recruited from

Spanish workers in Germany, veterans of the División Azul, and a few adventurers who had crossed illegally from Spain into German-held France.[33] Others served with Léon Degrelle's SS-Freiwilligen-Grenadierdivision-Wallonie after the summer of 1944, incorporated into the organization as the Third Spanish Company of the First Battalion.[34]

Throughout the rest of the shrinking Nazi empire, other small units of Spaniards were organized in late 1944 to fight against the Allies in northern Italy, near Potsdam, on the Franco-German border, and elsewhere.[35] The unit in Italy, under the command of a Lieutenant Ortiz, fought against partisans in northern Italy and Yugoslavia. Unlike other Spanish units, however, it gained a mixed reputation, with accusations of looting, rape, and plunder.[36] Another unit, the 101st Company of Spanish Volunteers, fought a desperate rear guard action near Vatra-Dornei, Romania, defending the Carpathian mountain passes against the Red Army. Led by a German officer, this unit contained some two hundred men, mostly veterans of the División Azul and the Spanish labor force in Germany. During the last half of August 1944, these Spaniards fought doggedly until the defection of Romania on 27 August. Turning their backs to the advancing Soviets on 31 August, what was left of the 101st began a slow retreat northwest. Fighting against attacks from both Soviet forces and Romanian guerrillas, and deserted by the Wehrmacht and Waffen-SS, the unit was caught between Soviet armies in Hungary and Romania. At the end of October, the few dozen survivors of the unit finally reached Austria.[37] Another company, the 102nd, had fought Tito's Yugoslav partisans in Slovenia and Croatia during the summer of 1944 and had been as mangled as the 101st. These units also suffered desertions, as soldiers fled to seek what they hoped would be safety in the hands of the Allies or in the interior of Germany.[38]

Miguel Ezquerra, a veteran of the División Azul and then a *Hauptsturmführer* in the Waffen-SS, led another small unit into the Battle of the Bulge.[39] He and his men had previously served the Abwehr in France, fighting against Spanish exiles in the Resistance. Later called the Einheit Ezquerra, this unit was closely linked to General Wilhelm von Faupel and the Ibero-American Institute.[40] In January 1945, Ezquerra was commissioned to enlist all the Spaniards he could find into one unit, which he would command as a Waffen-SS *Sturmbannführer*.[41] All of these enlistments greatly troubled the Spanish government, which viewed with alarm news of Spaniards serving in the SS and other Nazi organizations. Apart from the dangers confronting these men, the Franco regime was concerned that they were still wearing the emblem of the División Azul on their uniforms, an obvious and visible compromise of Spanish neutrality.[42]

After the loss of France came Germany's Black September, with the Finno-Soviet peace treaty, the Romanian and Bulgarian defections, and the entry of Soviet troops into East Prussia.[43] Berlin could find small comfort in Madrid, where Spanish relations with the Allies continued to improve. These changes led U.S. Ambassador Carlton Hayes to declare at a press conference that Spain was "making great efforts to collaborate with the Allies."[44] Germany continued to fret over its deteriorating relations with Spain, fearing that Allied pressure and self-interest might nudge Franco into breaking diplomatic ties with Berlin.[45] While Spain was not Germany's highest priority at this late date, it did want to preserve its intelligence networks, political connections, and limited trade with the remaining neutral states.

After the end of rail, road, and sea traffic between Spain and Germany, the only remaining transport link was by air, through a sporadically operating Lufthansa service from Barcelona to Stuttgart. Seats on these flights were tightly controlled: even the Servicio Exterior had to use political pressure from the highest ranks of the Falange to get seats for its officers and functionaries to return to Berlin.[46] Germans were also in the same predicament, a condition which often left businessmen and engineers stranded in Madrid long past their expected stays. Leaders of such important firms as Skoda and Siemens could extract their employees from Spain only by exerting pressure on "high German authorities" in Berlin.[47] Cargo to Germany included animal waste (for explosives), lemon juice (for nutritional supplements), and diplomatic mail. On return flights to Spain, the Germans sent newspapers, films, and more diplomatic mail. Using, among other aircraft, an American-made DC-3, Lufthansa continued to fly between Spain and Germany until just before the end of the war.[48] Falangist journalists, expected by German authorities to write sympathetic articles for the Spanish press, were among those given priority on these flights.[49] This Lufthansa air bridge continued to operate despite Allied pressure to end it. Franco was understandably unwilling to sever this last connection to Spanish nationals in Central Europe, at least until air routes opened between Switzerland and Spain.[50]

Germanophiles continued to lose ground in the Spanish press apparatus. The National Press Delegation, for example, dismissed Laurentino Moreno Munguia from his position as editor of the newspaper *El Alcázar* for his stories about German Wunderwaffen and for his refusal to emphasize Allied successes on the battlefield. At the same time, some of the most prominent German journalists were recalled to Berlin, presumably for their inability to prevent the reversal in Spanish press behavior.[51] One of Germany's strongest friends in Spain, Manuel Mora Figueroa, vice secretary general of the Falange, had been earlier dismissed for similar intransigent Naziphilism. Mora, a veteran of the División Azul, had allowed the distribution of Falangist "propaganda leaflets threatening violence if any attempt were made ... to destroy the Movement."[52] Franco replaced Mora with Rodrigo Vivar Téllez, a government lawyer and jurist, expected to be more reasonable and adaptable to the changing circumstances. As a consolation, Mora was awarded the *Gran Cruz de Cisneros* and thanked for his efforts on behalf of the Falange, thereafter fading into the political background.[53]

Franco continued to distance himself from the Axis throughout 1944, at times testing the credulity of the world with his brazenness. On 6 November 1944, this movement reached its highest point. In an interview with United Press, Franco declared that Spain was "already a true democracy." By "democracy," Franco meant "an organic democracy ... of the sum of individual wills." As the Caudillo, the general embodied something like the general will of all Spaniards. Even with this qualification, Franco's declaration seemed a bit incredible. Franco went on to express his opinion that "no obstacles existed in the interior regime of Spain (which would prevent) its collaboration with the principal Allied powers." Even the dispatch of the División Azul should not pose difficulties, according to Franco, as this effort was an expression of anticommunism, not hatred of Russia.[54] Although the reaction by the Allies to the statements was very unfavorable, at least London and Washington could see that the Spanish government was still committed publicly to moving away from the Axis.[55] Faupel's newspaper *Enlace* responded vehemently against Franco's change of stripe. After a front-page editorial extolling the importance of truth and honesty, the paper used parallel columns on the following page to compare Franco's words in 1944 to his speeches in previous years. The Caudillo's friendly words for Germany and Italy, his disdain for democracy, and his enthusiasm for the División Azul contrasted embarrassingly with his new perspectives.[56]

In other areas, Spain demonstrated its opposition to Nazi racial policies. Throughout the fall of 1944, Spain's diplomats used what little influence they had left in the Third Reich to continue rescuing Jews. With the strong efforts of Jordana and then Lequerica in

Madrid, Spain's ambassadors in Berlin, Bucharest, Budapest, and other capitals managed to save thousands of Jews by the end of the war.[57] While the Spanish government could have acted more energetically in this regard, even "England and the United States did not regard the rescue of Jews as an important issue of the war" until too late to accomplish much.[58] Understanding the Spanish position on this issue and the general deterioration of relations, Germany did not invite Spanish representatives to the "International Anti-Jewish Congress" of 1944, held at Cracow in July. Unlike at previous Nazi-run meetings, no Falangist shared the stage with Nazi and Fascist leaders.[59]

As the Allies closed in on Germany, the Spanish government did what it could to move its citizens away from the front lines. Antonio de la Fuente, delegado especial for the supervision of Spanish workers in Germany, received in late November promises from the Deutsche Arbeitsfront (German Labor Front, DAF) and German Labor Ministry that all Spanish workers in Austria and Alsace-Lorraine would be evacuated to Berlin. The Nazis also promised that Spaniards would not be used in building fortifications.[60] Instead of trying to bring more workers to Germany, as they had from 1941 to 1943, de la Fuente and his staff spent their time digging out from under air raids, helping to find shelter for destitute Spaniards, searching for missing laborers, tracking down workers who were joining the Waffen-SS, and planning for the evacuation of the colony.[61] De la Fuente's struggle was made even more difficult by delays of up to three months in payments by the Spanish government to his office and by Madrid's demands for audits of all accounts. After months of intense air raids, fires, and personnel losses, de la Fuente was only just able to evaluate his current expenses, much less account for money spent by the his office over the past year.[62]

Air raids exacted a heavy toll on the Spanish colony. Along with direct hits on Spanish diplomatic offices, British and American bombers found Falangist offices as well. The previous August alone, Allied strikes had destroyed Falangist regional offices in Stuttgart, Königsberg, Hamburg, and Wiesbaden.[63] Workers were not spared, either, suffering along with the general population, with dozens dying in air raids during the last months of the war, sometimes because they refused to go into air raid shelters. On 16 January, for example, seven Spanish workers employed at an IG Farben factory in Bitterfeld lost their lives in the barracks for this reason, while forty-nine others lost all of their possessions in the destruction.[64]

In November 1944, Ambassador Vidal indicated to the German Foreign Office that he wanted to move his diplomatic offices out of Berlin, away from constant air raids, shortages, and the approaching Red Army.[65] Ribbentrop's ministry refused to grant facilities outside Berlin, claiming that diplomacy could not be conducted in such a dispersed manner. By this time, however, Nazi diplomacy was almost a nonissue. Apart from representatives of Japan and Axis satellites, only the neutrals Ireland, Spain, Portugal, Switzerland, Sweden, and the Vatican maintained diplomats in Germany.[66] Ribbentrop, who continued to make life difficult for the representatives of legitimate governments, was by now obsessed with exile movements, including Serbians, Romanians, Vlasov's Russian forces, and the squabbling Vichy collaborators. Hoping to mimic British success with similar movements, the Nazi minister tried to bolster these remnants of the New Order with pep talks, diplomatic recognition, and other forms of support.[67]

No thanks to Ribbentrop and Nazi authorities, the treatment of Spaniards in Germany worsened with the general conditions. In Vienna, the Spanish consul complained that his countrymen were being treated as prisoners of war, convicts, or members of an inferior race, in direct opposition to the solemn promises of the German government.[68] In response to this, Lequerica sent a stern note to the German embassy in Madrid and to Ribbentrop through the Spanish embassy in Berlin, demanding better treatment for Spaniards in Germany.[69] With the support of the Spanish Foreign Ministry, Spanish diplomats at the same time intervened on behalf of Spanish exiles in France and Germany, issuing identification papers and visas to these supporters of the defeated Spanish Republic.[70] To enable their representatives to better protect Spanish workers in the deteriorating situation, the Spanish government secured diplomatic immunity for Antonio de la Fuente by appointing him as a consular official to the Spanish Legation in Switzerland. De la Fuente needed all the support he could get, as the German government, especially the DAF, proved increasingly hostile to his advocacy of Spanish workers and citizens.[71] Other Spanish officials also received diplomatic portfolios to aid in the repatriation of the approximately one thousand Spanish workers remaining in Germany by the end of 1944.[72] While placing obstacles in the way of the Spanish government, the Germans continued to recognize the contributions of these workers, awarding German Bronze Service Medals (*Deutsche Bronzene Verdienstmedaillen*) to distinguished laborers.[73]

While the conditions of Spanish workers continued to deteriorate, those of the Falangist leadership in Germany were not much better. Sergio Cifuentes, national secretary of the Falange Exterior, directed Pablo de Pedraza in Berlin to conduct a general purge of the organization, removing from the membership Spaniards whose "attitude or comportment" did not fit the standards of the party. Cifuentes also directed Pedraza to appoint a new head of the Sección Femenina, conduct a complete inventory of all property of the Falange, and begin an investigation of improprieties in the organization. Pedraza, sent to Berlin in early 1944, had previously concluded that, according to the rolls, the German Falange had exactly three hundred members in the Third Reich, but he admitted that he could not locate addresses of the majority of these Falangists.[74] Of greater concern to Falangist leaders in Madrid was the behavior of Rafael Gascón, leader of the Frente de Juventudes (FJ) in Germany, who was accused of gross negligence and dereliction of duty.[75] These charges arose from a series of incidents during the summer and fall of 1944. During July 1944, while on an inspection visit to a regional FJ office in Germany, Gascón was robbed of his identity documents, as well as of all the official documents of the Frente de Juventudes. To explain this last event, and to replace his personal documents, Gascón returned to Spain on 20 September without informing Falangist authorities. Unable to convince his superiors of his veracity, and severely ill with chronic bronchitis, Gascón withdrew to the safety of a Madrid hospital.

In Berlin, the Spanish community continued with life as normally as possible, commemorating Catholic and Falangist festivals as if nothing was changing. The Falange in Berlin also continued to operate, advertising in late December Spanish lessons to "beginners and advanced students."[76] Celia Giménez, the former godmother (*madrina*) of the División Azul, continued to work for Radio Nacional de España and Deutschlandsender, transmitting news and entertainment nightly back to Spain until the early fall of 1944. The Spanish press community in Berlin, led by Ismael Herraiz, correspondent for *Arriba*, still enjoyed favored treatment, being feted by the German Ministries of Foreign Affairs and Propaganda with real coffee, private clubs, and meetings with Nazi leaders.[77] This semblance of normality was, however, belied by the ongoing air war above Germany, strict rationing, and strained communications between Berlin and Madrid: even official correspondence took over one month to travel from Germany to Spain.[78]

By November, the Berlin Falange was again in organizational shambles. The party headquarters, on the third floor of an office building at Motzstraße 5, had suffered the cumulative effects of numerous air raids. While the structure was intact, the roof had numerous holes in it, and windows had been shattered. Another house, leased by the Falange, was in better condition, but was inhabited by several shady characters. The Berlin Falange had only one typewriter, another having been lost by Gascón. From what had once been an extensive teaching library, only a few volumes remained, effectively ending proposals to teach Spanish language courses. Despite his initial efforts, Pedraza's career as a foreign correspondent for Spanish newspapers kept him away from Falangist work, leaving the organization in a sorry state. The leadership of the Berlin Falange was in full retreat: Pedraza kept away from Berlin on journalistic assignments, Gascón was in Madrid, and Celia Giménez had disappeared. Only the Sindicato Español Universitario (Spanish University Syndicate, SEU), working for the evacuation of Spanish students from Germany, continued to function with any success. Other problems also beset the organization: corruption, misuse of documents, and black market involvement.[79]

Even the Ibero-American Institute, long a stalwart ally of the Falange, had turned against the Spanish party. Still under the direction of General Faupel, the institute had taken over the publication of *Enlace*, formerly printed by de la Fuente's office. Edited by Martin Arrizubieta, a defrocked Basque priest and former Loyalist captain in the Spanish Civil War, the newspaper took on a decidedly anti-Francoist bent in the fall of 1944. Promoting a strange mixture of Nazism and Basque separatism, the paper, continuing under its old title, produced a great deal of confusion among the remaining members of the Spanish colony in Germany.[80] Claiming to be both Falangist and National Socialist, the paper insisted that "the salvation of humanity … is … in us, the defenders of the New Order."[81] Along with complete identification with Nazism, Arrizubieta promoted anti-Francoist sentiments among Spanish workers, declaring that "if Germany wins the war, it should not respect the Spanish frontier."[82] Faupel, still bitter at Franco for asking Hitler to replace him as ambassador to Spain in 1937, fought to assert control over the dwindling Spanish colony of 1944–45. Together with his wife Edith, the old general won over the most ardent Falangists left in Berlin. Along with elements of the Abwehr and SS, the Faupels hoped to use these collaborators someday to overthrow the Franco regime.[83] By December, however, even the most stalwart Naziphiles could see that the end was near for the Hitlerian experiment. Nazi radio broadcasts, always a staple of German propaganda, were losing listeners in Spain at an alarming rate.[84] Nazi film studios continued to send newsreels and full-length features to Spain, using up critical cargo space on

Lufthansa flights, but even the best films and newsreels could not reverse the genuine decline of Nazi power and prestige in Spain.[85] While the Germans struggled to maintain connections with Spain, the Allies in December 1944 established international air routes between Spain and the U.S. and reopened rail traffic between Madrid and Paris: disheartening signs to Germany of the increasing ties between Spain and the Allies.[86]

Even the División Azul, long the darling of the Spanish government, became unwieldy baggage in this time of Allied ascendancy. After years of praise and financial support to veterans and their families, in late 1944, all such assistance ended. The support offices of the unit in Madrid and the provinces were closed, and the Spanish War Ministry indefinitely postponed questions about veterans' pensions, promotions, and decorations.[87] A few Falangist stalwarts in Spain did what they could to prop up the collapsing Nazi war effort—smuggling supplies to German redoubts in France, spying on the Allies, and protecting German citizens from Allied expulsion demands—but these efforts were irrelevant to the general picture of deteriorating Spanish relations with the Third Reich.[88]

Elements of the Falange also tried to comfort Germany in print. Despite a dramatic shift away from pro-Axis reporting, the Falangist press still had words of praise for the courage of the German military and the Hitler Youth: "[S]trong, healthy in body and soul, patriotic, (and) full of a fanatic will to victory ... How beautiful the scene of those children-soldiers, those twelve-year-old heroes!"[89] Even as the Third Reich was crumbling about them, Hitler's satraps were grateful for this sympathy, pronouncing their praises of the Falange and the Spanish press, while getting in a few last insults targeting Franco.[90] In their time of desperation, the Germans continued to support veterans of the División Azul, sending 10,000 to 15,000 pesetas per month for "pensions and the organization of reunion evenings," struggling to maintain a base of support in Spain for whatever contingencies might arise.[91]

Even as some Spanish leaders praised the Third Reich and the New Order, others did their best to abandon it. As early as February, Ambassador Vidal and the embassy staff in Berlin began to consider evacuation plans.[92] In mid-February, the Spanish government formally requested permission from the Nazis to evacuate the seven hundred remaining Spanish workers from Berlin.[93] At this point, the Nazis still controlled most of Germany, the northern Netherlands, Austria, western Hungary, most of Czechoslovakia, northern Italy, Denmark, Norway, and northwest Yugoslavia, but were retreating on all fronts.[94] The end was in sight, and the Spanish government saw no need to allow its representatives to die along with Hitler's empire. On 15 February, Lequerica ordered the closing of the Spanish Legation in Bucharest, leaving the remaining Spanish nationals under the care of the Swedish Legation. Eight days later, he instructed the Spanish diplomatic representation in Salzburg to secure exit visas for the twenty-five members of the Spanish colony in Prague.[95] At the same time, in February, Ribbentrop tried to maintain a front of normalcy in Berlin, deciding "to inaugurate a weekly tea-party for such foreign diplomats and journalists as remained in the capital."[96] To preserve Hitler's illusions, Ribbentrop ordered all foreign missions to stay in Berlin, rescinding previous exit permission.[97] The Spanish ambassador continued with his plans.

While more practical Spaniards prepared to leave Germany, the intransigence of radical Falangists and other elements of the New Order continued, even in the face of certain defeat. Jesús Suevos, *camisa vieja* and member of the Consejo Nacional, remained in Paris to serve as a liaison between the Falange and Doriot's collaborationist Parti Populaire Français (PPF).[98] The PPF, which hoped to form a "White Resistance" movement against de Gaulle and the communist-led French Resistance, was to receive clandestine aid from Spain. This action, reasoned Suevos, would provide a buffer against the anti-Franco plans of Spaniards in the Maquis. The rapid collapse of German occupation, the unpopularity of the collaborationist movements, and the strength of the Free French, however, made this plan unrealistic at best.[99] After the withdrawal of German troops, Suevos remained in Paris until December 1945 as Spanish press attaché, watching the triumphant entry of General de Gaulle and his forces into the capital. At victory parades, Suevos ruefully noted the presence of a column of Iberian troops: Spanish Republican exiles who had fought on the side of the Allies.[100]

This refusal to abandon the New Order was also strong among Spaniards in Germany. Even as the Battle of Berlin was underway in late March 1945, two leaders of the Berlin Falange, who had returned briefly to Madrid on political business, tried to gain official permission, passports, and Lufthansa reservations to return to Germany. These men, José Luis de la Rosa, chief of the Frente de Juventudes and Sindicato Español Universitario in Germany, and José Luis Yriarte Betancourt, territorial secretary of the Berlin Falange, returned to supervise the evacuation of the Spanish colony.[101] Gonzalo Rodríguez del Castillo, journalist for *El Español*, refused to evacuate Berlin even in the face of Soviet tanks, preferring to bear witness to the fall of the Reich.[102]

The Spanish foreign minister, however, continued to order evacuations. On 16 March, Lequerica ordered the closing of the Prague Consulate, the evacuation of the Spanish colony from Bohemia-Moravia, and the removal of the diplomatic archive to Vienna or Munich. He also ordered the Spanish consul in Bad Wiessee, Bavaria, to help evacuate thirty Spanish students from Munich.[103] The challenge of evacuation was no small task, as the size of the Spanish colony in Germany in March 1945 continued to be substantial. From the Andalusian province of Huelva alone, 330 draft-age Spanish men were still registered as workers in Germany. These were among the 1,200 workers and 200 men, women, and children of the permanent colony evacuated by Antonio de la Fuente and Rodríguez de Castillo during the last two months of the war.[104]

The Red Army launched its final offensive against Berlin on 16 April. Rejecting the pleas of his military and political advisers to fly out of the Berlin pocket, Hitler decided to remain and personally lead the defense of the city, entrusting Goebbels to embolden the last defenders of Nazism.[105] The Battle of Berlin was an international struggle, pitting Stalin's multiethnic Soviet Army against the ragtag remnants of Hitler's New Order. The vast majority of Berlin's defenders were Germans; however, Frenchmen, Norwegians, Danes, Italians, Dutch, Romanians, Belgians, Hungarians, and other nationals, mostly in the Waffen-SS, also defended the dying capital of the Third Reich. In the "apocalyptic atmosphere" of this brutal battle, Spanish accents could be heard from the band of Iberians remaining in Germany.[106]

Those non-Germans who kept fighting had abandoned their homes and families to fight for the disappearing dream of the New Order. By 1945, this continental vision was confined to a shrunken remnant of Central Europe, stretching from the Alps to the Norwegian Arctic Circle. The strategic situation was so desperate in the final months that only the most deluded could have expectations of victory.[107] Fantasy was all that remained, with the surviving Spanish soldiers perhaps dreaming of a last desperate battle, where, by the force of will, Germany and its remaining supporters would expel the invaders from the home of the New Order. What else could they do? They had made their choices: 1945 was not a time for second thoughts. Surrender meant imprisonment or death at the hands of the Allies, while desertion was a capital crime in Germany. In uniform, these exiles could at least hope to die among comrades.

From January to April, the Einheit Ezquerra fought on what remained of the eastern front, suffering tremendous casualties without much result. After additional recruiting and transfers from other units, by mid-April, Ezquerra cobbled together just over one hundred Spaniards for the final defense of Berlin.[108] This recruitment was stymied by the actions of Antonio de la Fuente and the journalist and press attaché Rodríguez del Castillo, who used their contacts in the Nazi government to secure exit permission, work releases, and safe-conduct passes for several hundred Spanish workers. Most of these fleeing Spaniards traveled south to Switzerland, but others, including Rodríguez, sought refuge in Denmark.[109]

For all of their efforts, Spain's representatives in Germany had to leave behind their once luxurious embassy, its basements full of precious goods, valuable scientific instruments, and the personal possessions of dozens of diplomats, workers, and other members of the colony. With Stalin's tanks fast approaching, Rodríguez could do little more than inventory the embassy and try, unsuccessfully, to affix posters to the exterior, declaring its extraterritoriality and diplomatic immunity from expected ransacking at the hands of the Soviet Army. The Swedish Legation, which had promised at the end of March to safeguard the Spanish embassy, had fled by 7 April. By this time, all neutral diplomats had evacuated Berlin except for the Portuguese minister.[110] Finally, on 22 April, Rodríguez and his small band of refugees left for Denmark, carrying with them from the embassy only the flags of Spain and the Falange, a few important documents, and the movie ¡Presente!, about the life of Spanish dictator Miguel Primo de Rivera (1870–1930).[111] Another casualty of the evacuation was the archive of the Berlin Falange, carried south in the final exodus. Four suitcases of documents and one typewriter had to be abandoned in Bad Wiessee am Tegernsee and Blumgarten, towns near Munich.[112]

As their compatriots evacuated, Spaniards fought as they had in the frozen lands of Russia: tenacious in the defense, foolhardy in the attack. Alongside the final shattered units of the Charlemagne Division, these men threw down their lives for a vanished dream.[113] Convinced that they had fought for a New Order in Spain and Europe, they had sacrificed everything for the racist and evil vision of Hitler. The number of Spaniards in this final battle is uncertain. Whether dozens or hundreds, their presence signaled their misguided loyalties in this moment of death and desperation. Spaniards died in the defense of Berlin and Hitler's *Führerbunker*, even after the Nazi dictator's suicide. To the southeast, the 101st and 102nd companies also fought in Slovakia to the end of the war, until the final survivors escaped west or were captured by the Soviet army. The mastermind behind Nazi-Falangist collaboration, Wilhelm von Faupel, could not bear to see the destruction of his life's work. As Soviet troops entered the capital, the old general and his wife committed suicide in Berlin.[114]

In Bavaria, Antonio de la Fuente continued to supervise the exodus of Spanish workers from Germany.[115] Back in Spain, the government prepared to receive thousands of destitute repatriates, readying stockpiles of food, medical care, rail tickets, clothing, short-term loans, even tobacco. In a reversal of previous years, the regime authorized the distribution of clothing and supplies previously reserved for workers going to Germany. Some of these items had been sold by the Spanish government, but enough probably remained to provide for the emergency needs of refugees.[116] In just two years, the export of Spanish laborers and warriors had become the import of Spanish refugees.

Falangist ideology did not in its beginnings depend upon Nazi inspiration and power, but the vision of a New Order did. Without the military and industrial engine of the Third Reich, the collaborationist movements of Europe had no future. The end of World War II also ended the political viability of Nazism, Fascism, Rexism, Falangism, and all other movements and regimes of the New Order. Even in Spain, where the regime survived, the Falange quickly became just the *Movimiento* (Movement), not much more than a Francoist admiration society and bureaucratic behemoth. With the Anglo-Saxon Allies promoting democratic capitalism in the west and the Soviet Union installing Stalinism in the east, there was no longer room for a Third Path or a New Order. Nazi ideology and the ideas of the New Order, which had risen in tandem with the victories of the swastika, faded away with the "definitive defeat" of the Third Reich.[117] The failure of Hitler and his allies to create a new world system was also the failure of Naziphiles in the Falange. Spain in the 1930s and 1940s was too weak to make its own way in the world, but was not without choices. Franco could have aligned himself with Hitler, attempting to break away from Western capitalism and world markets. In the summer and fall of 1940, the Spanish dictator could have altered the course of World War II in favor of the Axis. That he did not do so is a tribute to Hitler's mishandling of the Iberian Peninsula.

Had Spanish Naziphiles been in charge of the peninsula in 1940, this decision could have gone in another direction. Spain could have permitted the Wehrmacht to attack Gibraltar, launch submarines against Britain, and seize French territories in North Africa. The Falange could have ridden to power on the backs of *Panzer*, launching their promised social revolution. This did not happen, but that does not mean it was not a possibility. Instead of rising to power in Spain, however, most of the pro-Nazi elements of the Falange were destroyed by their collaboration with Germany. Led to destruction by Hitler's hubris, the Spanish vision of the New Order died, swept away by Franco like an embarrassing mistake.

For Germany, the New Order was never more than a cover for ruthless exploitation of the continent. Hitler and other Nazi leaders saw Europe as theirs to remake racially, politically, and economically. German interests were their sole preoccupation; there was no room for the ambitions of Spaniards, Belgians, Italians, Hungarians, Frenchmen, or any of the other nationalities who produced willing collaborators in the Nazis' continental project. If it is possible to understand the early attractiveness of the Nazi regime, it is less easy to comprehend collaboration with the Third Reich after the days of victory were gone. For Spaniards, the vision of the New Order was far different. Falangists dreamed that Spain would return to a position of world leadership, with a cultural empire in the Americas and a territorial empire in Africa. They hoped that Spain would become a partner to the Axis, taking its place alongside Germany and Italy as one of the arbiters of Europe. This vision, never fulfilled, was a costly one at the end of the story, but it did not seem so in 1940–41. Spanish commitment to the New Order, partial and hesitant though it was, was made in the flush of three victories: Franco's over the Spanish Republic, Hitler's over France, and the expected victory of Germany over Stalin's Russia. Of these triumphs, only Franco's was not reversed by 1945.

The destruction of the Third Reich signaled more than just the end to Hitler's racial and geopolitical ambitions. Across Europe, the former supporters of the New Order went on trial, escaped to South America, or hid as best they could among the millions of displaced persons. A few Nazis and European collaborators found refuge in Spain, but Franco was smart enough to conform to Allied demands and handed over nearly all Germans residing in Spain. Allied suspicions that many high-ranking Nazis, including Wilhelm von Faupel, had taken refuge in Spain proved unfounded.[118] To prevent the escape of Nazis and the survival of their ideology, the Allies launched Operation Safehaven to deny them sanctuary.[119] No such pressures were applied to the thousands of Spaniards who had pledged themselves to Hitler and a new Europe, however. While thousands of Spanish workers and soldiers died in defense of the New Order, thousands more returned to Spain during and after the war. Many veterans of the Blue Division, Legion, and Squadron rose to prominence in Franco's Spain, especially after the cold war improved the acceptability in the West of Spain's anticommunist legacy.

Just after the Nazi surrender, *Pueblo* published a column by Antonio Tovar, one of Nazi Germany's closest collaborators in the Falange. In this bittersweet column, "My Berlin," Tovar recounted his earlier years in Berlin, just after the Nazi seizure of power. He did not want to dwell on politics—a wise decision given world events—but wrote a mournful piece about the fallen glories of Berlin:

> I was a student in Berlin. Those were the initial years of the National Socialist regime, when here (in Spain) and in France, the Popular Front was incubating. A great sensation of purity, novelty, revolution, and the disappearance of filth was felt in the Berlin of those times! I had taken casual notice in Paris of the lives of some Marxist and Radical deputies and personalities, and consoled myself that I was far from this putrefaction of drugs, gluttony, and filth in the new Berlin: athletic, militarized, full of martial music and marching and singing youth groups. I remember that I was enthusiastic about it all ... and from the first moment understood that it was something new.[120]

These words recounted all of what Falangists in the 1930s and 1940s had found attractive in Nazi Germany: "purity, novelty, revolution, and the disappearance of filth." Tovar and his fellow Naziphiles did not realize it at the time, but the bright and wonderful promises of the New Order delivered a terrible result: Continental war and genocide.

The pivotal difference between Franco and radical Falangists was their commitment to the New Order. To Franco, the New Order meant substituting one set of great powers with another set. He was primarily interested in defending Spain's interests and ambitions in a traditional balance of power. Of course, Franco hoped for an expansion of the Spanish empire, but he did not want to turn the world upside down. Radical Falangists expected the New Order to be a revolution, replacing the world system with an international regime of social justice and authoritarian states. Their intent was to lead Spain into a new golden age, as partners with Nazi Germany and Fascist Italy at the head of a new Europe. Even as they gave their lives in the final defense of the Third Reich, they believed they were defending

Spain and Europe. Franco, who had boldly declared in 1942 that one million Spaniards would defend Berlin if need be, retreated from these declarations as soon as the course of the war changed. The Spaniards who wore Nazi uniforms after D-Day made no such retreat. Franco survived the war intact; they and their ideology did not.

Notes

1. On changes in Spanish policy, see a report from late 1944, purportedly written by Falangist leader Manuel Valdés Larrañaga: United States National Archives (USNA), Office of Strategic Services (OSS) Report, 24 October 1944, Record Group (RG) 226, OSS E21, Box 418.
2. The leadership of the SS even allowed Spaniards to enlist without receiving the standard tattoo of blood type. Archivo del Ministerio de Asuntos Exteriores (AMAE), LegR2192/32. Report, 23 September 1945, police attaché, Spanish embassy in Rome.
3. USNA, *Magic*, 13 August 1944.
4. Ibid., 26 December 1944.
5. Ibid., 6 August 1944.
6. USNA, OSS Report, 1 March 1944, RG226, OSS E97, Box 29, Folder 508.
7. AMAE, LegR2299/3. Report, 8 January 1945, Spanish police attaché, Berlin, to MAE.
8. USNA, OSS Report from Polish intelligence, 7 September 1944. RG 226, OSS E 21, Box 395.
9. After the war, the Spanish government confiscated war booty, interned thousands of Germans, and cooperated with the Allies in bringing Nazis to justice. Carlton Hayes, *Wartime Mission in Spain* (New York, 1976), pp. 263–264.
10. USNA, OSS Report, 7 August 1944, RG226, OSS E21, Box 369.
11. Rafael García Pérez, *Franquismo y Tercer Reich* (Madrid, 1994), pp. 499–502.
12. USNA, OSS Report, 12 February 1945, RG226, OSS E21, Box 428.
13. Ibid., 11 July 1944, RG226, OSS E21, Box 348. For example, see Bayer pharmaceutical ads in *Arriba,* 5 August and 5, 15, 26 September 1944, and Telefunken radio ad, 24 September 1944.
14. Ibid., 12 September 1944, RG226, OSS E21, Box 392.
15. *Pueblo,* 22 August 1944.
16. Rafael García Pérez, "Trabajadores españoles a Alemania durante la II Guerra Mundial," *Hispania,* no. 170 (1988), p. 1055.
17. USNA, OSS Report, 14 June 1944, RG226, OSS E127, Box 31, Folder 217.
18. AGA, Trabajo (T), 16256. Various reports, August 1944 and other months. For example, from late June to early November 1944, the Interministerial Commission for the Sending of Workers to Germany (Comisión interministerial para el envío de trabajadores a Alemania), a Spanish agency formed in 1941, requested passports for only four medical doctors to go to Germany, compared to thirty-two for the first six months of 1944. AGA, T 16255. Various reports and document registers, 1944.

19. AMAE, LegR 2192/31–32. Various letters, 1943–1945, from parents and relatives to MAE.
20. AMAE, LegR2192/31. Letter, 27 September 1944, from Ambassador Vidal to Foreign Minister Lequerica; and LegR2225/1, 6. Various documents, 1944–1945.
21. AMAE, LegR2192/32. Diplomatic Notes, 7 and 11 August 1944, from the British and U.S. embassies in Madrid, to the Spanish foreign minister, respectively.
22. Ibid. Diplomatic Note, 8 August 1944, from Jacques Truelle, minister plenipotentiary of the Provisional French Republic to subsecretary, Foreign Ministry Pan de Soraluce.
23. Ibid. Diplomatic Note, 2 August 1944, from foreign minister to U.S. ambassador.
24. AMAE, LegR2192/31. Diplomatic Note, 31 August 1944, from MAE to British ambassador.
25. AMAE, LegR2192/32. Letter, 8 August 1944, from Subsecretary Pan de Soraluce to Arrese.
26. See also Raymond Proctor, *Agony of a Neutral: Spanish-German Relations and the División Azul* (Moscow, Idaho, 1974), pp. 263–271.
27. AMAE, R 2192/ 32. Letter, 21 April 1945, from Luis de Torres-Quevedo, chargé d'affaires, Spanish Legation, Bratislava, Slovakia, to the foreign minister.
28. AMAE, LegR 2192/31. Letter, 5 June 1944, from Urbano Feyjóo de Sotomayor, Spanish consul in Berlin, to the foreign minister. G. R. Kleinfeld and L. A. Tambs, *Hitler's Spanish Legion: The Blue Division in Russia* (Carbondale, Ill., 1979), p. 345.
29. AMAE, R2192/31. Letter, 6 July 1944, from ambassador in Berlin to foreign minister, warning him that "many" Spaniards, mostly veterans of the Blue Division and Legion, were crossing the Pyrenees to enlist in the SS. In combat, many wore Spanish national emblems on their SS uniforms.
30. Ibid. Letter, 19 June 44, from Dirección General de Seguridad, Servicio Interior, to Subsecretary Doussinague, Foreign Ministry; and letter, 19 May 1944, from Ambassador Vidal in Berlin to Foreign Minister Jordana. USNA, T77, Roll 885, Frames 5634559–5634594.
31. AMAE, LegR 2192/31. Letter, 19 May 1944, from ambassador in Berlin to foreign minister, regarding the clandestine entry of Spaniards into German-occupied France, based on reports from the Delegado Especial para la Inspección y Tutela de Trabajadores Españoles en Alemania.
32. USNA, letter, 28 July 1944, from Third Secretary Robert Brandin, U.S. embassy, Madrid, to W. Walton Butterworth, U.S. chargé d'affaires, Madrid, based on the report of a Spanish informant, recently returned from Germany. RG226, OSS E127, Box 33, Folder 229.
33. AMAE, LegR2192/32. Report, 23 September 1945, police attaché, Spanish embassy, Rome. Felix Steiner, *Die Freiwilligen der Waffen-SS: Idee und Opfergang* (Oldendorf, 1973), p. 135. Estimates of the number of Spaniards who served in the Waffen-SS during the war vary upward from eight hundred (Hans Werner Neulen, *Eurofaschismus und der Zweite Weltkrieg* [Munich, 1980], p. 170). Fernando Vadillo, *Los irreductibles* (Granada, 1993), p. 275, for example, argues that hundreds fought in the Battle of Berlin alone.
34. Vadillo, *Los irreductibles*, pp. 91–96, 100–101.
35. Ibid., pp. 106–107, 218–223.
36. AMAE, LegR2192/32. Report, 23 September 1945, from police attaché, Spanish embassy in Rome.
37. Vadillo, *Los irreductibles*, pp. 53–65, 67–68.
38. AMAE, LegR2192/32. Report, 23 September 1945, from police attaché, Spanish Embassy in Rome. Vadillo, *Los irreductibles*, pp. 68–74.

39. Equivalent to a captain in the U.S. Army. Vadillo, *Los irreductibles*, pp. 108–110. Ezquerra later wrote an exaggerated account of his own adventures, in which he claimed to have had tea with Goebbels and an interview with Hitler in the *Führerbunker,* where the dictator awarded him the Knight's Cross and offered him German citizenship. His promotion to the rank of lieutenant colonel (*Obersturmbannführer*) in the Waffen-SS and claims of secret missions in France are also dubious. Miguel Ezquerra, *Berlin, a vida o muerte* (Barcelona, 1975).
40. Faupel, ambassador to Spain, 1936–37, used the Ibero-American Institute to promote the status of Naziphiles within the Falange. Vadillo, *Los irreductibles*, pp. 119, 127–129.
41. Equivalent to a major in the U.S. Army. Vadillo, *Los irreductibles*, pp. 128–130. Ezquerra, *Berlin, a vida o muerte*, pp. 89–96.
42. AMAE, LegR2299/3. Report, 8 January 1945, from Spanish police attaché in Berlin embassy to MAE.
43. *Arriba,* 5, 7, 9, 14 September 1944. *Pueblo*, 9, 19 September 1944.
44. *Arriba*, 2 September 1944.
45. USNA, *Magic*, 25 September 1944.
46. AGA, P, SGM 64. Letter, 1 September 1944, from Sergio Cifuentes, national secretary, Delegación Nacional del Servicio Exterior (DNSE), to Sigismund Freiherr von Bibra, chargé d'affaires, Madrid.
47. USNA, OSS Reports, 20 September 1944, RG226, OSS E21, Box 396 and 25 September 1944, RG226, OSS E16, Box 1113.
48. Ibid., 26 February 1945, RG226, OSS E16, Box 1354; 8 February 1945, RG226, OSS E127, Box 31; and 30 August 1944, RG226, OSS E134, Box 183, Folder 1159.
49. Two such correspondents were Gonzalo Rodríguez del Castillo, of the Spanish EFE wire service, and José Luis Navarro, of the newspaper *El Español*. Despite the hopes of Nazi officials, most Spanish journalists could find little in the Third Reich about which to be optimistic. Even the most pro-German writers could not deny that Hitler's capital was in ruins and the Wehrmacht in full retreat. Vadillo, *Los irreductibles*, pp. 115–116.
50. USNA, *Magic*, 17 February 1945. The last Nazi flight out of Spain left Barcelona on 17 April 1945. Its cargo consisted of 1,150 kgs of diplomatic mail, 79 kgs of animal wastes and 380 kgs of regular mail. The six passengers—a diplomatic courier, a businessman, two German sailors, and two unnamed Spaniards—narrowly avoided being caught in Spain, for on 21 April, Franco's government ordered the internment of all remaining German aircraft. USNA, OSS Report, 23 April 1945, RG226, OSS E127, Box 31, Folder 212. The Spanish government interned two German aircraft, a Ju-290 and a DC-3, both of which were experiencing mechanical difficulties preventing them from leaving Spain under their own power. In the months previous, Franco had authorized the use of Spanish airfields by U.S. Army Air Corps planes, a privilege never extended to the Luftwaffe, even in the days of Nazi triumph. Hayes, *Wartime Mission in Spain*, p. 292.
51. USNA, OSS Report, 10 October 1944, RG226, OSS E16, Box 1190.
52. Ibid., 20 September 1944, RG226, OSS E19, Box 22.
53. *Pueblo*, 18 September 1944.
54. Ibid., 6 November 1944.
55. Paul Preston, *Franco* (London, 1993), pp. 519–520.
56. *Enlace*, 23 November 1944.
57. Luis Suárez Fernández, *Francisco Franco y su tiempo*, vol. 3 (Madrid, 1984), pp. 535–541. AMAE, LegR 2303/10. Letter, 22 March 1944, from Manuel G. de

Barzanallana, Spanish minister in Romania, to Jordana. Estimates of the number of Jews saved by the Franco regime vary, from 11,535 (plus 30,000 allowed transit through to Portugal; Haim Avni, *Spain, the Jews and Franco* [Philadelphia, 1982], p. 186) to approximately 50,000 (Chaim Lipschitz, *Franco, Spain, the Jews and the Holocaust* [New York, 1984], p. 178). Antonio Marquina and Gloria Inés Ospina, *España y los judíos en el siglo XX* (Madrid, 1984), pp. 145–232.
58. Avni, *Spain, the Jews and Franco*, p. 199.
59. USNA, *Magic*, 2 May and 30 June 1944.
60. AMAE, LegR2225/1. Letter, 23 November 1944, from Ambassador Vidal to Spanish foreign minister.
61. AGA, T 16259. Various CIPETA documents, October–December 1944. Despite the dramatic changes in the European situation, as late as October 1944, some Spanish workers still begged to be allowed to travel to Germany. AGA, T 16258, letter, 17 October 1944, from Bernardo Acosta and Manuel López to CIPETA.
62. AGA, T 16258. Various documents, October–December 1944, between Catalá and de la Fuente.
63. AGA, P, SGM 54. Letter, 31 August 1944, from Pablo de Pedraza, Berlin Falange, to DNSE.
64. AMAE, LegR2225/6. Letter, 25 January 1945, from Ambassador Vidal to Lequerica.
65. The shortage of gasoline was particularly acute after further reductions in monthly allotments during the spring and summer of 1944. In early September, these already strict rations were reduced by an additional forty percent. USNA, *Magic*, 14 October 1944.
66. USNA, *Magic*, 6 November 1944.
67. Michael Bloch, *Ribbentrop: A Biography* (New York, 1992), pp. 414–416, 418.
68. AMAE, LegR2225/1. Letter, 17 December 1944, from the Spanish consul in Vienna to MAE.
69. Ibid. Note, 26 January 1945, from Lequerica.
70. Ibid. Letter, 17 January 1945, from Spanish consul in Munich to Spanish foreign ministry. Letter, 16 February 1945, from Doussinague to the consul in Munich. USNA, OSS Report, 11 August 1944, RG226, OSS E21, Box 371.
71. Ibid. Letter, 26 March 1945, from the consul in Munich to MAE; letter, 28 December 1944, from Girón to MAE.
72. AMAE, R2225/3. Letters, April 1945, from Doussinague to the Spanish legations in Switzerland and Denmark. García Pérez, "Trabajadores españoles a Alemania," p. 1057.
73. USNA, German Foreign Ministry report, 26 October 1944, in OSS documents, E19, Box 222. In the province of Thuringia alone, these Spaniards worked in the metal, glass, textile, and office machinery industries in Jena, Weimar, Gera, Erfurt, and Halle. Various documents, June–December 1944. USNA, T175, R472, 2993500–2993590. At least fifty were employed by IG Farben at its Bitterfeld works. AMAE, LegR2225/6. Various documents, 1944–1945.
74. AGA, P, SGM 54. Letter, 1 December 1944, from Cifuentes to Pedraza. Of these, 204 were men and 96 were women. Ibid. Letter, 25 August 1944, from Pedraza to DNSE. This list was incomplete, as Pablo de Pedraza, a leader of the Berlin Falange, was not included. There was also no indication of members joining after December 1942, despite the added presence in Germany of hundreds of Spaniards after that date, including Spanish workers who arrived during 1943 and members of the Blue Division and Blue Legion who refused to be repatriated with their demobilizing units. This list also does not

include those applications being processed at the time, which in February 1944 included fifty-seven Spaniards and eight "foreign sympathizers." Ibid. Letter, 18 February 1944, from Sergio Cifuentes to the Berlin Falange.
75. Ibid. Letter, 1 December 1944, from Antonio Riestra, delegado nacional, Servicio Exterior, to José Antonio Elola-Olaso, delegado nacional, Frente de Juventudes.
76. *Deutsche Allgemeine Zeitung*, 24 December 1944, quoted in USNA, OSS Report, 9 January 1945, RG226, OSS E16, Box 1272.
77. Vadillo, *Los irreductibles*, pp. 117, 120.
78. AGA, P, SGM 54. Letter, 31 October 1944, from Yriarte Betancourt, Berlin territorial secretary, to DNSE.
79. Ibid. Report, 11 November 1944, from Yriarte Betancourt, Berlin territorial secretary, to DNSE.
80. Ibid.
81. *Enlace*, 23 November 1944.
82. AMAE, LegR2299/3. Report, 26 December 1944, from Spanish police attaché in Berlin to MAE.
83. Vadillo, *Los irreductibles*, pp. 123–125. Ezquerra, *Berlin, a vida o muerte*, pp. 92–105.
84. USNA, OSS Report, 15 December 1944, RG226, OSS E21, Box 418.
85. Ibid., 11 September 1944, RG226, OSS E21, Box 390.
86. Hayes, *Wartime Mission in Spain*, p. 272. *Pueblo*, 2 December 1944.
87. USNA, OSS Report, 4 December 1944, RG226, OSS E21, Box 420.
88. USNA, *Magic*, 3 November 1944, 31 January and 23 April 1945.
89. *Mayo*, 4 January 1945. Even after Hitler's death, Naziphiles in the Spanish press could not restrain their admiration for the Führer, remarking that "men of good will must incline themselves … toward the example of his life." *Pueblo*, 2 May 1945.
90. Joseph Goebbels, *Final Entries 1945*, ed. Hugh Trevor-Roper (New York, 1978) 1 March 1945, p. 17.
91. USNA, *Magic*, 19 March 1945 and 10 March 1945.
92. Ramón Garriga, *La España de Franco* (Madrid, 1976), pp. 272–273. At the same time, Vidal requested, and received, Swiss visas for his diplomatic staff. Vadillo, *Los irreductibles*, p. 158.
93. AMAE, R2225/3. Letter, 17 February 1945, from Catalá to Alfred Mehne, German Labor Ministry representative in Madrid; LegR2225/6. Letter, 17 February 1945, from Catalá to Doussinague; LegR2299/3. Letter, 16 February 1945, from José de Carcer, ministro consejero, Berlin (then in Berne, Switzerland) to MAE. At the same time, the FJ evacuated seventy-five Spanish children from Germany.
94. *Pueblo*, 21 February 1945.
95. USNA, OSS Reports, 23 February 1945, RG226, OSS E16, Box 1342 and 16 February 1945, RG226, OSS E21, Box 430.
96. Bloch, *Ribbentrop: A Biography*, p. 423.
97. USNA, *Magic*, 11 April 1945. On 7 February, the German Foreign Office had "advised … (all diplomatic missions) … to leave Berlin with all possible speed." USNA, *Magic*, 16 February 1945.
98. USNA, OSS Report, 26 September 1944, RG226, OSS E127, Box 31, Folder 215. The OSS knew Suevos, former chief of the Falange in Portugal, was in Paris, but not the purpose of his mission.
99. AGA, P, SGM 67. Report, 10 April 1945, from Mario Peña to DNSE.
100. Vadillo, *Los irreductibles*, pp. 46–47.

101. AGA, P, SGM 70. Letters, 26 March 1945, from national secretary, DNSE, to subsecretary, MAE; letter, 18 October 1945, from Carlos María R. de Valcárcel, Falange secretariat general, to Alberto Martín Artajo, foreign minister. Vadillo, *Los irreductibles*, p. 121.
102. Vadillo, *Los irreductibles*, pp. 163–164.
103. USNA, OSS Reports, 14 March 1945, RG226, OSS E16, Box 1374 and 31 March 1945, RG226, OSS E21, Box 434. It is inaccurate to say that the Spanish government did not give every possible aid to its nationals trying to evacuate from Germany. García Pérez, *Franquismo y Tercer Reich*, pp. 503–504.
104. AGA, T 16255. Letter and name list, 7 March 1945, from Catalá to Jefe, Provincial Service of Statistics and Employment, Huelva. AMAE, LegR2229/3, Letter, 15 May 1945, from Gonzalo Rodríguez Castillo, in Copenhagen, to subsecretary, MAE.
105. Werner Haupt, *Berlin 1945*, trans. Angel Sabrido (Barcelona, 1964), pp. 7–8, 13, 57, 61, 77.
106. Jean Mabire, *Morir en Berlin: los SS franceses* (Madrid, 1976), pp. 11, 91, 151–153, 254, 276, 310. Haupt, *Berlin 1945*, p. 71. Steiner, *Die Freiwilligen der Waffen-SS*, p. 329.
107. Mabire, *Morir in Berlin*, p. 74–76. Haupt, *Berlin 1945*, p. 91.
108. Vadillo, *Los irreductibles*, pp. 181–184. Ezquerra, *Berlin, a vida o muerte*, p. 105.
109. Rodríguez del Castillo was also instrumental in the evacuation of the families of these laborers. AMAE, LegR2229/3, letter, 15 May 1945, from Gonzalo Rodríguez Castillo, in Copenhagen, to subsecretary, MAE; AMAE, LegR2229/3, report, 7 April 1945, from Col. Marín de Bernardo, Spanish military attaché in Berlin (then in Bregenz); and letter, 14 April 1945, from Carlos Sánchez Alterhoff, in Konstanz, Germany, to Cristobal del Castillo, subsecretary, MAE, Madrid. Vadillo, *Los irreductibles*, pp. 256–259.
110. USNA, *Magic*, 10 April 1945.
111. AMAE, LegR2229/3, letter, 15 May 1945, from Gonzalo Rodríguez Castillo, in Copenhagen, to subsecretary, MAE.
112. AGA, P, SGM 70. Letter, 16 August 1945, from Spanish Minister in Denmark to MAE.
113. Ricardo de la Cierva, *Historia del franquismo* (Barcelona, 1975), p. 300. Haupt, *Berlin 1945*, pp. 192–193, 253. Vadillo, *Los irreductibles*, pp. 231–239.
114. Vadillo, *Los irreductibles*, pp. 150–156, 165–167, 193–210, 241–263, 289–291. Ezquerra, *Berlin, a vida o muerte*, pp. 105–132, 169.
115. AGA, T 16259. Letter, 21 April 1945, Antonio de la Fuente, Munich, to Carlos Sanchez Alterhoff, Berlin.
116. Ibid. Memo, 25 April 1945, from Marcelo Catalá, CIPETA technical secretary, and other documents, 1945–46. AMAE, LegR2225/7. CIPETA inventory of goods, 26 June 1945. Few returned from Germany in 1945, however. Most had to wait months for transport home by sea or rail.
117. García Pérez, "La idea de la 'Nueva Europa' en el pensamiento nacionalista español de la inmediata posguerra, 1939–1944," *Revista del Centro de Estudios Constitucionales* (January–March 1990), pp. 238–239.
118. The most prominent to find refuge was the Rexist leader Léon Degrelle, who landed in Spain on 8 May 1945. USNA, *Magic*, 9 July 1945. USNA, OSS Report, 17 May 1945, RG226, OSS E134, Box 183, Folder 1156.
119. USNA, OSS Report, 6 April 1945, RG226, OSS E134, Box 183, Folder 1156.
120. *Pueblo*, 2 May 1945.

–19–

Pablo Neruda and the German Literary Exile Community

Vera Stegmann

Der Paß ist der edelste Teil von einem Menschen. Er kommt auch nicht auf so einfache Weise zustand wie ein Mensch. Ein Mensch kann überall zustandkommen, auf die leichtsinnigste Art und ohne gescheiten Grund, aber ein Paß niemals. Dafür wird er auch anerkannt, wenn er gut ist, während ein Mensch noch so gut sein kann und doch nicht anerkannt wird.

The passport is the noblest part of a person. It also doesn't come about as easily as a person. A person can come about anywhere, in the most careless fashion and without a particular reason, but a passport never. Therefore, it is recognized if it is good, whereas even a good person often won't be recognized.

Bertolt Brecht, *Flüchtlingsgespräche*
(Conversations among Refugees)

Exile literature usually occurs on the margins of any national literature or culture, but given the tragic developments in German history earlier in this century, one can easily argue that the margin moved to the center, since Germany's greatest writers and artists were driven out of their country. Between 1933 and 1945, German literature took place largely in exile. Most German writers, like Bertolt Brecht, Thomas Mann, and Lion Feuchtwanger, eventually opted for the United States and spent the Hitler years either in New York or in California, but a sizable group of artists, such as Anna Seghers, Egon Erwin Kisch, Bodo Uhse, Gustav Regler, and Ludwig Renn, went to Mexico instead. In Mexico City, they came into contact with another displaced writer, the Chilean poet who had wandered the world and who was working as consul general in Mexico at the time: Pablo Neruda (1904–1973). Ever since the publication of his *Veinte poemas de amor y una canción desesperada* (Twenty Love Poems and a Song of Despair, 1924) had brought him worldwide success, Neruda was able to combine the career of a diplomat with the vocation of a poet. In his dual role as poet and politician, he followed a tradition quite characteristic of Latin American countries, or even of European nations where Romance languages are spoken—Octavio Paz and Carlos Fuentes of Mexico, Paul Claudel of France, and Saint-John Perse of Guadeloupe come to mind. The German poet Hans Magnus Enzensberger suggested in an essay on Neruda that Germany might learn some lessons from these Latin countries, where poetry enjoys a more public status and diplomats, or the people representing a nation, are often creative masters of their language, rather than primarily bureaucrats.[1]

Besides being a poet and a politician, Neruda also knew the experience of exile, although not until later in his life. In 1946, Neruda became national campaign manager for the candidate González Videla, who turned against Neruda upon his election as president and outlawed the Communist Party, which Neruda had joined the previous year. When Neruda, who had been elected to the Senate in 1945, retaliated by publishing his "Intimate Letter to Millions of Men" and by delivering a Senate speech under the Zola-inspired title "I accuse," the order for his arrest was issued. From 1948 until 1949, Neruda went into a year-long period of hiding, staying at a different home each night to escape his persecutors and writing large sections of his groundbreaking epic *Canto General* (1950). Like the German artists whom he met during the Spanish Civil War and later in Mexico, Neruda thus understood the interaction between alienation through exile and intense poetic creativity.

In this essay, I will explore the friendships, the political collaborations, the cultural exchanges, and the literary influences between Neruda and the German artists who spent their exile in Mexico or Latin America in the 1940s. From childhood on, Neruda had read German authors; in his *Confieso que he vivido* (translated as *Memoirs*), he refers particularly to Brecht, Heine, Hölderlin, and Rilke. He also understood the dangers of German fascism and fought against it both in Chile and in Mexico. Some of Neruda's poems that incorporate these German themes will be discussed later in the essay, along with the enormous influence that Neruda has exerted on modern German literature.

Although Neruda has come to be regarded as a poet who represented Latin American Indian cultures and origins and who defended the *indígena* cause, he had from his earliest years on received a European, or rather Eurocentric, education, and in his later years as a diplomat, he not only grew to understand, but even participated in the antifascist struggles that were at the center of the German émigrés' cause. A brief historical and biographical introduction to Neruda's European and specifically German contacts therefore seems inevitable.

Already in high school, Neruda once commented, his classmates had mostly European-sounding names. Besides a few Araucanian and many Spanish names, Neruda recalled names of English, French, German, Irish, Norwegian, Polish, and Sephardic origin. The local indigenous population of Neruda's hometown Temuco, the Mapuche, lived in an entirely separate area a few miles away.[2] This absence of any contacts with the local Mapuche in his youth may have later sparked Neruda's intense interest in the forgotten or "forsaken" people—as he also referred to Latin Americans[3]—but his childhood education was dominated by a Eurocentric focus. As a boy, Neruda had already acquired an understanding of European politics, when, during World War I, for example, two groups were forming in his high school, the "Allies" and the "Germans." Several boys even returned to Europe to participate in the war on the side of the countries of their foreign-born parents.[4]

Due to Latin America's colonial history, therefore, Neruda witnessed European affairs from an early age. Later, Neruda suggested that Latin America has been colonized twice, first by the Spaniards, and then in the twentieth century by the United States.[5] But besides these two major players, other European countries also tried to extend their spheres of influence. The British and the French were there; indeed, French was, until the early twentieth century, the principal foreign language in Latin America and carried the prestige of being the language of culture.[6] Neruda, who majored in French at the university and at one point considered making a living as a French teacher, read much of the German literature that he knew in French translation. In 1926, he published his translation of fragments from Rainer-Maria Rilke's *Notebooks of Malte Laurids Brigge* in the journal *Claridad*. However, he did not translate this work from German into Spanish, but from a French translation into his native Spanish. European colonization had brought German workers and artisans to Latin America as well.[7] By the early 1930s, more than a million Germans lived in Latin America, the large majority in Brazil and Argentina, but many also settled in Chile, Mexico, Paraguay, and Uruguay.[8] Compared to the German immigrants in North America, who made an effort to blend into U.S. culture, the Latin American Germans did not integrate themselves into their new societies nearly as quickly, often remaining in isolated colonies. For this reason, Germans in Latin America have in the past tended to preserve a conservative or nationalistic attitude, and especially right before and during World War II, many became vulnerable to fascist propaganda by German Nazis, who worked on manipulating them into loyalties to Hitler's Germany rather than to their new country of residence.[9] The success of this Nazi propaganda, combined with the friendly support or tolerance by certain Latin American rulers, explains why German fascism could make its influence felt in regions as remote from Europe as Latin America.

Neruda witnessed some of these developments in Chile. Volodia Teitelboim, one of Neruda's major biographers and a politician and writer himself, describes frequent street confrontations between the Popular Front—comprised of Democrats, Socialists, Communists, and the Chilean Workers' Confederation—and the Chilean version of Nazism, headed by González von Marées.[10] Neruda was at the time deeply involved in helping the Republicans in the Spanish Civil War, and during World War II, he continued to participate in the antifascist struggle. In his *Memoirs*, he devotes a small section to the subject "Nazis in Chile."[11] While he claims that Latin America did not produce eminent writers such as Louis-Ferdinand Céline, Pierre Drieu la Rochelle, and Ezra Pound who were seduced by the false persuasions of fascism, parafascist groups did spring up throughout Chile. Neruda relates that on several occasions he had to walk through the streets under forests of swastikas, and once he was even forced to salute the Führer involuntarily, when picking up the receiver in order to place a phone call, because the telephone was installed high on the wall under a portrait of Hitler. Even the Nazis' book burnings had their moderate counterparts in Chile, when the Chilean National Library tried to replace German books with fascist propaganda literature. In a memorable passage, Neruda recounts his courageous efforts to block those attempts and to bring good German literature back into the library:

I was editor of the magazine *Aurora de Chile*. All its literary weapons (we had no other) were aimed at the Nazis, who were swallowing country after country. Hitler's ambassador to Chile donated books, by authors of the so-called neo-German culture, to the National Library. We countered by asking our readers to send us German books that were faithful to the real Germany, the Germany banned by Hitler. It was a momentous experience. I received death threats. And many neatly wrapped packages arrived with books smeared with filth. We also received whole collections of *Der Stürmer*, a pornographic periodical that was sadistic and anti-Semitic, edited by Julius Streicher, deservedly hanged in Nuremberg years later. German-language editions of Heinrich Heine, Thomas Mann, Anna Seghers, Einstein, Arnold Zweig also trickled in. And when we had nearly five hundred volumes, we took them to the National Library.

We were in for a surprise. The National Library had padlocked its doors to us.

Then we organized a march and entered the university's hall of honor carrying pictures of the Reverend Niemöller and Carl von Ossietzky. Some kind of ceremonial act was taking place, presided over by Don Miguel Cruchaga Tocornal, the foreign minister. We set the books and portraits down carefully on the speaker's dais. The battle was won. The books were accepted.[12]

Fascism confronted Neruda as well in Mexico, when he lived and worked in Mexico City from 1940 until 1943 as consul general. After the Nazi invasion of the Soviet Union, Neruda wrote the poem "Song to Stalingrad," which was posted all over the walls in Mexico City. Since his political call to help the Soviet Union went unheeded, he published a second poem, "A New Love Song to Stalingrad,"[13] which he read at a banquet for intellectuals in support of the Soviet Union, at which Anna Seghers (1900–1983) also spoke. Her novel *Das siebte Kreuz* (The Seventh Cross, 1942), about seven prisoners who escape from a Nazi concentration camp, was turned into a 1944 Hollywood film. During this politically charged period, on an afternoon in December 1941, Neruda was beaten and injured in a fistfight started by a group of Nazis in a restaurant in Cuernavaca, forty miles south of Mexico City. As a result, hundreds of intellectuals throughout the Americas raised their voices in support of Neruda. After his recovery, Neruda responded to his attackers by writing the prologue to Ilya Ehrenburg's book *Death to the Invader*. Hannes Meyer, the Swiss architect and former Bauhaus director living in Mexico at the time, created the artistic design of this book, rich in illustrations by Mexican and Soviet painters.

Neruda's Mexican years also comprise the period of his closest collaborations with German antifascists. The vast majority of

German exiles chose the United States, but since Mexico, in contrast to the U.S., did not set any political restrictions to emigration, Mexico became the most important country in the Western Hemisphere offering refuge to left-wing intellectuals and Communists. Among the most prominent German-speaking literary and cultural figures who received asylum in Mexico were Anna Seghers, Bodo Uhse, Gustav Regler, Ludwig Renn, Otto Katz (alias André Simone), the composer Hanns Eisler, the Czech writer Egon Erwin Kisch, and the Swiss architect Hannes Meyer. Even Bertolt Brecht had a visa for Mexico, which Gustav Regler had helped him obtain, but he ultimately chose the United States.

Several of Neruda's friendships with German exiles date back to the Spanish Civil War. As a diplomat in Spain, where Neruda helped some four thousand Spaniards emigrate to Chile on the ship *Winnipeg*, he was also in contact with Germans who served in the International Brigades, especially Anna Seghers and "el comandante" Ludwig Renn. He even published an ode to them in the Mexican exile journal *Freies Deutschland*.[14] In Mexico, he developed deep friendships with Anna Seghers, Egon Erwin Kisch, Ludwig Renn, and Bodo Uhse, who were frequent guests at Neruda's Mexico City apartment on Revillagigedo Street and at his later residence, Villa Rosa María.

The friendship between Neruda and Seghers lasted for several decades. When Neruda was awarded the Nobel Prize for literature in 1971, Seghers sent him a long and personal letter from the German Democratic Republic (GDR), in which she expresses what Neruda has meant to her and to the world, and in which she remembers their encounters, from their work in the International Brigades in Spain, to the exile years in Mexico, and to their common engagement in the postwar world peace movement.[15]

Egon Erwin Kisch, the journalist and self-styled "racing reporter" whose many travel accounts on Prague, America, China, and Mexico raised the skill of journalistic writing to the level of literary art, had also known Neruda since Spain. Neruda shares several memories of this "Czech humorist" in his *Memoirs*.[16] One anecdote refers to Kisch's curiosity about Neruda's motivations for his choice of a Czech pseudonym, after the writer Jan Neruda, since Neruda had been born as Neftalí Ricardo Reyes Basoalto. He asked Neruda at the various places they met—Spain, Mexico, Prague—but throughout his life, Neruda did not disclose his secret to his Czech friend.[17]

Ludwig Renn, who had gained fame as editor of the journals *Aufbau* and *Linkskurve* and as author of the novels *Krieg* (1928) and

Nachkrieg (1930), participated in the Spanish Civil War as leader of the Thälmann battalion. During his Mexican years (1939–47), he was president of the organizations Bewegung Freies Deutschland in Mexico and Lateinamerikanisches Komitee der Freien Deutschen, as well as professor for modern European history and languages at the University of Morelia between 1940 and 1941. The writer Bodo Uhse, who had also fought in Spain, spent the years 1940 to 1948 in Mexico, where he collaborated with the major exile organizations and published his most important novel, *Lieutenant Bertram*, in 1944.

Mexico, the only country besides the Soviet Union not to recognize Hitler's annexation of Austria, became, in Neruda's words, "the salt of the earth,"[18] the major Latin American nation from which German exiles directed cultural and political activities against the fascists. The first such organization that formed in Mexico, the Liga Pro Cultura Alemana en Mexico (LPC), was founded following a suggestion by the expressionist and revolutionary writer Ernst Toller, who traveled to Mexico City in 1937 from his New York exile to give a talk in the Palacio de Bellas Artes. The society constituted itself in March 1938 and was officially neutral, although a communist branch developed later. Its leading minds were Heinrich (Enrique) Gutmann, Paul Elle, Erwin Friedeberg, Alfred Miller, Mauricio Luft, and Joseph Zaunboss. Hannes Meyer, Bodo Uhse, Ludwig Renn, and Franz Feuchtwanger joined later. The LPC organized lectures, publications, and performances promoting nonfascist German culture and tried to inform the Mexican public on the dangers of Nazism. The LPC existed until 1943, when political and internal conflicts dissolved the group. Neruda followed their activities closely and even became mildly involved in some of their inner affairs when he participated in the discussions about the writer Gustav Regler, a former communist who withdrew into political silence in Mexico and was accused by some of becoming a renegade.[19]

Emerging from the left-wing circles within the LPC, one of the most important exile journals, *Freies Deutschland*, developed in Mexico. Apart from *Alemania Libre* and the newspapers *Deutsch-Mexikaner* and *Demokratische Post*, *Freies Deutschland* became the major publication for German exiles in Mexico. The first issue, published in November 1941, already contained poetry and prose by some of the most important writers of the time: Pablo Neruda, Thomas Mann, Lion Feuchtwanger, and Friedrich Wolf. Both Anna Seghers and Egon Erwin Kisch participated in producing the journal, and Heinrich Mann sent frequent contributions. Brecht's contributions to *Freies Deutschland* usually dated from earlier years and had been previously published.[20] But he read the journal regularly in his California exile and commented, "I like the journal very much; it is a small miracle that you were able to produce something like that."[21] *Freies Deutschland* became an essential outlet for antifascist literary voices in exile. Closely associated with the journal was the Bewegung Freies Deutschland (BFD) that formed on 30 January 1942, a coalition of left-wing antifascists that strove to create a democratic Germany and to support their host country, Mexico, in breaking the impact of Nazi ideology abroad. Ludwig Renn became president of the organization. An association with similar goals was the Mexico chapter of the LAK, the Lateinamerikanisches Komitee der Freien Deutschen.[22] Neruda sent a greeting to the BFD in the Mexico City exile paper *Demokratische Post*: "I am greeting the Freies Deutschland that so courageously stands for the victory of freedom, in spite of its open and hidden enemies. I am with you because you already fought against Hitler when some of those who attack you today were still worshiping the future Hitlers of their own countries."[23]

Another cultural organization, which formed in November 1941, was the Heinrich Heine Club, or the Club Enrique Heine, Asociación de Intelectuales Antinazi de Habla Alemana. Anna Seghers was elected as president, and Ernst Römer and Leo Deutsch (later succeeded by Egon Erwin Kisch) became vice presidents. The idea was to found a cultural association similar to the ones organized by exile Germans in European capitals like Paris, where their activities drew large groups of visitors. The name of Heine, who shared the experiences of expulsion from his native country, censorship, and homesickness with the modern émigré artists, seemed the perfect emblem to unite this group. Between 1941 and 1946, the Heinrich Heine Club offered literary and musical evenings, political and scientific lectures, film screenings, and seven theater performances. Among the most notable of these was the first Mexican performance of *The Threepenny Opera*. The actors were chosen from the émigré community (Steffie Spira, Günter Ruschin, Ernst Robicek, Viktor Blum); Ernst Römer and Egon Neumann were responsible for the music. The Mexican muralist Xavier Guerrero, a friend of Anna Seghers and a onetime companion of Tina Modotti, created the stage design. The performance was a success and received favorable reviews from the Mexican newspaper *El Nacional*. Given the public attention, it is likely that Neruda attended this or other events presented by the Heine Club.

A major literary event in the history of the German exiles in Mexico, the foundation of the publishing house El Libro Libre, was celebrated in Mexico City's Palacio de Bellas Artes, which incidentally had been built on the site of a former *quemadero*, a place where the Spanish Inquisition burnt heretics. Ironically, this same beautiful building became host to a ceremony commemorating the infamous Nazi book burnings in Berlin on 10 May 1933: on 9 May 1942, El Libro Libre was founded in memory of the destruction of books in Germany. Neruda attended this inauguration, and, in addition to Ludwig Renn, Anna Seghers, Bruno Frei, and the president of the Mexican PEN section Enrique González Martínez, Neruda was one of the scheduled speakers. On the following day, the evening of 10 May 1942, a radio program of the Bewegung Freies Deutschland informed the Mexican public about the anniversary of the book burnings and presented, among other contributions, a reading of poetry and prose by Brecht and Seghers in Spanish translation. In the years to come, Neruda continued to collaborate with the publishing collective of El Libro Libre by speaking at several of their cultural or fundraising events.[24] Among the books published by El Libro Libre were Kisch's *Marktplatz der Sensationen* and his *Entdeckungen in Mexiko*, Seghers' *Das siebte Kreuz*, Lion Feuchtwanger's *Unholdes Frankreich*, Uhse's *Leutnant Bertram*, and Renn's *Adel im Untergang*. A gesture by the Mexican president Ávila Camacho, who invited Kisch, Renn, Seghers, and Uhse to his residence in Los Pinos on 24 July 1942, shows the extent to which the Mexican government officially supported El Libro Libre. Camacho even provided financial assistance for a publication, *El Libro Negro*, a *Schwarzbuch* about Hitler's terror in Europe, that commemorated the ten-year anniversary of the Reichstag burning. Many internationally established authors sent contributions to this volume, although Brecht, Neruda, and Ilya Ehrenburg, who were originally included as authors, ultimately did not write for *El Libro Negro*.[25]

Neruda's sensibilities to the wide spectrum of German issues, from high literature to the political threat of fascism, were thus intensely acute from early on. He had felt the dangers of Nazism personally, and in Mexico he worked together with the German émigré community in the struggle against Hitler. So deeply had these events shaped Neruda's thinking that he mentioned them in Chile in his maiden speech in the Senate on 30 May 1945. He ended his inaugural speech as senator for the provinces Tarapacá and Antofagasta with a reference to the "madman ... who, under the banner of anticommunism, massacred and destroyed, defiled and blasphemed, invaded and murdered human beings, cities, fields and villages, peoples and cultures."[26] The Red Army had entered Berlin a few weeks earlier, and, hoping for the Soviet Union's role in restoring world peace and human dignity, Neruda joined the Chilean Communist Party on 8 July 1945. He had also befriended the Russian Communist writer Ilya Ehrenburg, who had gained fame for his novels and journalistic writings exposing crimes of German fascists.

Ehrenburg was close to Brecht and to many German exile writers. His novel *Padenie Pariža* (The Fall of Paris, 1941) had been distributed by the Mexican publishing house El Libro Libre. The Russian author thus became a further cultural intermediary between Neruda and the scene of German writers. When Brecht was awarded the International Stalin Peace Prize in 1954 in Moscow, Neruda was on the committee for this prize that he himself had received in 1950. Neruda made special efforts to support Brecht: "There was a secret alliance between Aragon, Ehrenburg, and me which had enabled us to see that the prize was given, in other years, to Picasso, Bertolt Brecht, and Rafael Alberti. It had not been easy, of course."[27]

After the war, Neruda visited Berlin on a number of occasions. From 5–19 August 1951 he attended the World Youth Festival in East Berlin, where he met Brecht in the company of Erich Arendt, an East Berlin poet who later became Neruda's most prolific translator into German. In 1951, Neruda also became a member of the East German Academy of the Arts in Berlin. In 1952, he spent July and August in Berlin and Denmark, and in 1965 he participated in the International Writer's Meeting in Berlin and Weimar. In 1968–69, Neruda was awarded an honorary doctorate from Karl-Marx-Universität in Leipzig. Neruda also lobbied for East Germany's admittance to the United Nations.[28] On at least one of his Berlin visits, Neruda attended a performance of the Berliner Ensemble. He recounts this episode in a 1969 letter to Mexican President Gustavo Díaz Ordaz, in which he describes his contacts with the Revueltas family and demands the release of the imprisoned writer José Revueltas:

> [O]nce in Berlin I was invited by Helene Weigel, the widow of Bertolt Brecht, to a performance of the Berliner Ensemble. They were performing some nineteenth-century Russian play—in German, of course—with a large cast of ladies and gentlemen dressed for the hunt. The leading lady was beautiful, feted, fatally attractive, and very natural. I looked at the program. The actress was the sister of Silvestre and José, the dark-skinned Mexican Rosaura Revueltas. There she was, black

eyes glittering and sparkling, speaking German in a European capital, the center of the most famous theater troupe in the world.

After the performance, I asked her, "How did you manage to look so fair among all those blonds? I thought you'd look like a fly in a bowl of milk. Did they use light makeup on you?"

"No," she replied. "You'll never guess what they did. They used dark makeup on all the others."[29]

Quite possibly, Neruda paid several visits to the Berliner Ensemble or had the opportunity to see Brecht's plays performed during his stays in France, where the ensemble toured frequently. Neruda's 1967 play *Fulgor y muerte de Joaquin Murieta* (Splendor and Death of Joaquin Murieta) shows many elements of Brecht/Weill's *Threepenny Opera* and *Rise and Fall of the City of Mahagonny*.

The above pages may help elucidate Neruda's contacts with German literary émigrés, starting in Spain and Mexico and continuing with postwar meetings in Moscow and Berlin. Furthermore, some of Neruda's works incorporate German subjects. Compared to Neruda's vast lyrical output, these poems are few in number, and they mostly belong to the period of the 1940s and 1950s, during which Neruda's poetic focus was strongly politicized. But a closer look at his poems with references to Germany also reveals *in nuce* some aspects of Neruda's poetic development. The poems are contained in four of his collections: *Tercera residencia* (Third Residence), *Canto General*, *Las uvas y el viento* (The Grapes and the Wind), and *Extravagaria*.

The third volume of *Residence on Earth* departs sharply from the dark and surrealist images or the hermetic, inward looking, ivory tower approach to poetry in the prior two *Residences*. Published as a cycle in 1947 and written between the years 1935 and 1945, it reflects a period in which Neruda was deeply affected by the Spanish Civil War and in particular by the death of his close poet friend, Federico García Lorca, who was murdered by the Falangists. In his poem "I Explain a Few Things,"[30] as well as in his "Manifesto for an Impure Poetry,"[31] he justifies his shift from his earlier *l'art pour l'art* style to a more socially engaged poetry. Part IV of the *Third Residence*, "Spain in Our Hearts," Neruda's poetic reaction to his experience in the Spanish Civil War, is the first example of his political and "impure" poetry. The poem "Song to the Rivers of Germany," a response to World War II included in part V of the *Third Residence*, may equally be seen in this light.

"Song to the Rivers of Germany" is divided into ten stanzas. The first five stanzas evoke the main German rivers, national symbols and images of German romantic poetry. Neruda distorts these traditional symbols, since the Rhine, Elbe, and Oder do not carry water, a sign of creativity, but rather tears and even blood. The last five stanzas address the resistance fighters and Alemania Libre, which refers both to the general hope for a future free Germany, as well as specifically to the group of exile Germans in Mexico, whose organization, Alemania Libre, set itself the goal to help prepare the downfall of fascism. The poem's message is quite straightforward and ultimately optimistic, yet its form introduces several complexities. The poem is based on the *ronda*, a didactic children's song that employs the principles of repetition and variation.[32] The first stanza exemplifies this literary form:

> Sobre el Rhin, en la noche, lleva el agua una boca
> y la boca una voz y la voz una lágrima
> y una lágrima corre por todo el Rhin dorado
> donde la dulzura de Lorelei no vive,
> una lágrima empapa las cepas cenicientas
> para que el vino tenga también sabor de lágrimas.
> Sobre el Rhin, en la noche, lleva el agua una lágrima,
> una voz, una boca que lo llena de sal.[33]

> Upon the Rhine, in the night, the water bears a mouth
> and the mouth a voice and the voice a tear
> and a tear flows all along the golden Rhine
> where Lorelei's sweetness no longer lives,
> a tear soaks the ashen roots
> so that the wine too may have a taste of tears.
> Upon the Rhine, in the night, the water bears a tear,
> a voice, a mouth, that fills it with salt.

The contrast between the seemingly innocent, playful children's form of the ronda and the tragic subject of war intensifies the sense of suffering that the poem evokes. Besides its ironic use of the ronda form, the poem also alludes to nature images of German romantic poetry and alienates them. The poetry of Heine or Eichendorff, or the songs of Schubert, repeatedly speak of rivers, especially the Rhine, as the symbol of Germany, or more abstractly as representations of creativity or life. But here the Lorelei, the Rhine's best-known myth, is dead, and the river, rather than opening up into a huge ocean, dries up as salt. In the first five stanzas, Neruda perverts traditional images that the romantics associated with water and rivers: the rivers here cover the earth with "salty roots," the Elbe and its "icy tongue" need to stay silent, the Oder does not carry songs or water, but gathers the blood of its people, and all the rivers have become "old blue veins."[34] Neruda himself had started out as a romantic, and besides the political reference, his distortions of nature imagery may also reflect on his own earlier poetry.

Beginning in stanza six, Neruda greets "Alemania Libre," and he picks up on this hope for renewal in the last and tenth stanza by addressing in reversed word order "Libre Alemania," which could still be the group of exile artists or the freed Germany that they have created. Stanza seven speaks to "brigades of German brothers," since many members of Alemania Libre—like Seghers, Kisch, and Renn—had joined the International Brigades in Spain and had met Neruda there. Stanza eight mentions the true "rivers," whose waters have remained fresh and not polluted with salt or blood: the voices of Einstein, Heine, Mendelssohn, or Thälmann, the Communist Party leader who was murdered in Buchenwald. The association of rivers and voices here emphasizes once more the close symbolic link between water and creativity. The poem closes with a confident hope in the "secret voice" of the "sunken man" ("hombre sumergido") who will rise up and walk.[35] Later, in *Canto General*, Neruda applies a similar metaphor to the Latin American continent, which he describes as "sunken bride" ("novia sumergida").[36] "Song to the Rivers of Germany" thus represents a poem that blends surrealist images of Neruda's earlier periods with new political themes.

Canto General, Neruda's epic masterpiece on Latin America, is more overtly political. German subjects enter only marginally here in a few poems: in "Prestes del Brasil (1949)" of section IV, entitled "The Liberators," and in poems 2 and 3 of section IX, entitled "Let the Woodcutter Awaken." When it was published in 1950, *Canto General* created a sensation because the work presented a new and at the time revolutionary poetic history of Latin America, seen not from the perspective of the colonialists or the industrial nations, but from an indigenous viewpoint. "The Liberators" contains a series of poems that honor a wholly new group of heroes, among them Luis Carlos Prestes, a Brazilian Communist leader who spent nine years in prison for political reasons. "Prestes del Brasil (1949)" also relates the tragic story of Prestes's wife, a German-Jewish communist who was deported to Nazi Germany and died in prison after giving birth to a girl. In the midst of his narration, Neruda interrupts himself by emphasizing his new aesthetics in a parenthetical note in the poem:

> Poeta, buscas en tu libro
> los antiguos dolores griegos ...

> y no ves en tu propia puenta
> los océanos que golpean
> el oscuro pecho del pueblo.³⁷
>
> Poet, in your book you seek
> ancient Greek sorrows ...
> and you don't see at your own doorstep
> the oceans that pound
> the people's dark breast.

Like a theatrical aside, much in the manner of Brecht, who frequently inserted political or aesthetic comments in his works, Neruda here argues within his poem against aesthetic escapism and for a socially committed poetry.

Section IX of *Canto General,* "Let the Woodcutter Awaken," mostly deals with Latin America's complex and at times problematic relationship to its northern neighbor, the United States. The woodcutter—"leñador"—stands for Lincoln and his ideals of democracy and social justice, and this group of poems may be read as Latin America's appeal to the United States to implement Lincoln's principles. Some of the language in this section uses classic cold war rhetoric. The few references to Germany, in poems 2 and 3, occur in this cold war context. Poem 2 polemically describes the American press in fascist metaphors—"the press distills ancient poison, cultivated in Berlin"—and points to "Hearst, who sang the Nazis a love song."³⁸ Indeed, William Randolph Hearst, the American newspaper tycoon eternalized in Orson Welles's *Citizen Kane,* had visited Hitler on one occasion and shared at least a nationalist agenda with him. Poem 3 of this section refers to the liberation of Berlin by the Soviet Army and proceeds to a poetic praise of Stalin.

Las uvas y el viento, published in 1954, is possibly Neruda's most heavily political book, following a Stalinist line and written in the style of socialist realism. For this reason it may today be among Neruda's least read collections, and an American translation of the volume has not yet been published. It contains Neruda's impressions of his extended travels throughout postwar Eastern Europe, and among this vast geographic range of topics, several poems also address Germany. The poem "Las ruinas en el Báltico" ("Ruins in the Baltic") in section III makes a fleeting reference to the war damages and sufferings in Madrid, Berlin, and Warsaw; and the entire section X, entitled "La sangre dividida" ("Blood Divided"), with its three poems "En Berlín la mañana" ("Berlin in the Morning"), "Jóvenes alemanes" ("Young Germans"), and "La ciudad herida" ("The Wounded City"), concentrates on Berlin. Broken up into a three-part, cyclical structure, the first poem, "En Berlín la mañana," shows the poet waking up in the train and arriving in Berlin, where he witnesses the immense destruction, anguish, and ashes that the war has produced. The second poem, "Jóvenes alemanes," talks about the new life that is slowly arising in Berlin, because the "hombre común," the "nuevo hombre"—or the socialist human being—has begun to create a new society.[39] While this poem already follows the official GDR view of its own state and may be regarded as a textbook example of socialist realist worker's literature, the third and final poem, "La ciudad herida," continues the cold war rhetoric in more aggressively propagandist terms. West Berlin personifies evil, which the poem describes in horrid metaphors: "La pústula del rostro antiguo de Europa," the city overflows with "alcohólico carmín," "viejos zorros nazis," "Coca-Cola y antisemitismo," "pederastas," and "lesbianas."[40] Neruda also follows socialist realist aesthetics by including a critique of Western abstract art and its soul-searching emphasis on "el conflicto del 'alma'" in the poem.[41] East Berlin, in contrast, embodies the new humanist society, and the poem concludes on a hopeful note, associating rejuvenating images with the East: "huele a agua fresca, / huele a panadería,/ huele a verdad y a viento" ("It smells of fresh water / It smells of a bakery / It smells of truth and wind").[42]

The revelations about Stalin at the twentieth congress of the Communist Party in 1956 in Moscow prompted a period of introspection in Neruda; his 1958 collection of poems, *Extravagaria*, presents a departure from the political passions that governed his prior poetry. The original Spanish title, *Estravagario*, a term invented by Neruda, refers to a collection of little extravaganzas. In this volume, Neruda utilizes some of Nicanor Parra's techniques of the antipoet: he questions the seriousness of poetry, he employs humorous visual illustrations, and he develops a poetic style that is playful, individualistic, and almost colloquial. One of the poems in *Extravagaria*, "Horses," striking in its simplicity, takes place in Berlin. Once again, as in the Berlin poems of *Las uvas y el viento*, the poet looks out of the window. But he doesn't see a black-and-white image of two Berlins—one decadent and corrupt, one pure. Rather, he sees a gray city: "The light was without light, the sky skyless."[43] In this colorless environment, the poet witnesses a circus and a man leading ten horses to the arena. This scene incites the poet's imagination; soon, the foggy air is filled with colors, with fiery flames, with odors of honey and oranges, and the circus horses become ten gods, dancing a golden dance. The poem closes with the lines, "I have obliterated that gloomy Berlin winter. / I shall not forget the light from these horses."[44] Reality lies in its creation, the poem suggests, and the images here are more personal and deeply felt than the political propaganda of *Las uvas y el viento*. In some instances, as in the dream world he creates around the circus horses, Neruda picks up on the surrealist style of his very early poetry.

These few references to Germany may thus also serve to illuminate the changes in Neruda's aesthetics, from his origins in romanticism, still evident in the *Residence* cycle, to the historical and political content in *Canto General*, which takes on stronger and more polemical tones in *Las uvas y el viento*, to a return to a more individualistic and introspective poetry in *Extravagaria*. Not only are German subjects present in Neruda's oeuvre, but his stylistic and formal approaches also reveal an awareness of German literature. He himself has mentioned his admiration of Heine and Hölderlin, and Neruda's biographer, Teitelboim, shows several parallels between Neruda and Goethe.[45] Furthermore, Neruda applied concepts of twentieth-century German literature: *Canto General*, his epic poem about the Latin American continent, employs many devices of Brecht's alienation effect by including multiple narrators, changes in perspective, and episodic and almost cinematographic treatments of history, and by interrupting his narration with an authorial interlude.[46]

Conversely, and even more so, Neruda was extremely influential in twentieth-century German literature. In 1949, Anna Seghers and Stephan Hermlin edited a volume of Neruda's poetry, entitled *Beleidigtes Land*, translated by Hermlin, with a foreword by Seghers. Neruda, in turn, translated some poems by Hermlin. Neruda's major translator into German was Erich Arendt, himself a poet who had fought in the Spanish Civil War, where he became acquainted with the Spanish language. Arendt then emigrated via Marseilles to Bogotá, Colombia, where he spent eight exile years and collaborated with antifascist movements such as the ANFB (Antinazi-Freiheitsbewegung). Upon his return to East Berlin in 1949, Arendt became one of the main transmitters of Latin American literature to Germany. Besides translating works by Neruda, Rafael Alberti, and Nicolás Guillén, a personal friend of his, Arendt wrote his own poetry. Some of his poetry volumes—such as *Gesang der sieben Inseln* (1957), *Flug-Oden* (1959), and *Unter den Hufen des Winds* (1966)—reflect a close reading of Latin American literature and the incorporation of Latin American images and themes, as well as a much more emotional and baroque style than was prevalent in Germany at the time. Before finishing his translation of Neruda's *Canto General* in 1953, Arendt had selected several poems from this opus—among them the entire section "Let the Woodcutter Awaken" and an almost complete text from "The Heights of Macchu Picchu"—to be printed in German in the East Berlin journal *Sinn und Form* between the years 1950 and 1952. Of these selections, Brecht adapted "Peace for the Coming Twilights"—the last and climactic poem in "Let the Woodcutter Awaken" and Neruda's hymn to peace—into his "Peace Song," which was subsequently set to music by both Paul Dessau and Hanns Eisler. For a while, Eisler's version became a well-known folk song in the German Democratic Republic.

Christa Wolf included Neruda quotes in her novel *Kindheitsmuster* (Patterns of Childhood, 1989). She preceded the novel with a poem from Neruda's *Libro de las preguntas* (Book of Questions), and chapter 8 refers to the 1973 military coup in Chile, to Allende's murder and Neruda's death, and to the importance of Neruda's last irreplaceable manuscript.[47] In Wolf's novel, Neruda's life and work become a vehicle for the author's reflections on Germany's past.

Anna Seghers, Neruda's long-time friend, not only wrote prose in Mexico, but also some works on Mexican or Latin American subjects. While living in Mexico, she felt she understood too little about the country in order to write about it and rather published novels and stories with German and antifascist content, such as *Das siebte Kreuz* (The Seventh Cross) or "Der Ausflug der toten Mädchen" (The Excursion of the Dead Girls). In the latter work, an autobiographical short story, Mexico serves merely as a frame for the narration or a scenic backdrop, a mountainous landscape resembling a vague "Mondgebirge."[48] Later, in the GDR, Seghers reflected in greater depth on Mexico, where she had befriended several artists besides Neruda, such as the painters Xavier Guerrero, Clara Porset, and Diego Rivera. Her Mexican experiences play a more prominent role in some of her works published in the GDR, in the short stories "Crisanta," "Agathe Schweigert," "Die Heimkehr des verlorenen Volkes," and "Das wirkliche Blau: Eine Geschichte aus Mexiko." A closer study of these Latin American or Neruda-inspired writings would open up a new subject of literary investigation.

Notes

1. Hans Magnus Enzensberger, *Einzelheiten* (Frankfurt, 1962), p. 324.
2. Volodia Teitelboim, *Neruda: An Intimate Biography*, trans. Beverly J. DeLong-Tonelly (Austin, Tex., 1991), p. 16.
3. Pablo Neruda, *Canto General*, trans. Jack Schmitt (Berkeley, Calif., 1991), p. 40.
4. Teitelboim, *Neruda*, p. 32.
5. Neruda, *Canto General*, pp. 149–201.
6. Teitelboim, *Neruda*, p. 50.
7. Ibid., p. 15.
8. Wolfgang Kießling, *Exil in Lateinamerika* (Leipzig, 1980), p. 55.
9. Ibid., p. 56.
10. Teitelboim, *Neruda*, p. 219.
11. Pablo Neruda, *Memoirs*, trans. Hardie St. Martin (New York, 1977), pp. 138–139.
12. Ibid.
13. Pablo Neruda, *Residence on Earth*, trans. Donald D. Walsh (New York, 1973), pp. 308–323.
14. Kießling, *Exil in Lateinamerika*, p. 295.
15. Thomas Billhardt et al., eds., *Chile: Gesang und Bericht* (Halle, 1975), pp. 219–220.
16. Neruda, *Memoirs*, pp. 157–158.
17. Teitelboim, *Neruda*, pp. 49–50.
18. Neruda, *Memoirs*, p. 157.
19. Kießling, *Exil in Lateinamerika*, pp. 198–199. See also Fritz Pohle, *Das mexikanische Exil: Ein Beitrag zur Geschichte der politisch-kulturellen Emigration aus Deutschland,1937–46* (Stuttgart, 1986), pp. 145 and 157.
20. Pohle, *Das mexikanische Exil*, p. 219.
21. "Die Zeitschrift gefällt mir sehr gut, es ist ein kleines Wunder, daß Ihr so was zustande gebracht habt." In Kießling, *Exil in Lateinamerika*, p. 311.
22. Pohle, *Das mexikanische Exil*, p. 201.
23. "Ich grüße das *Freie Deutschland*, das all seinen offenen und verkappten Feinden zum Trotz so mutig für den Sieg der Freiheit eintritt. Ich bin mit Euch, denn Ihr kämpftet schon gegen Hitler, als manche von denen, die Euch heute angreifen, noch die zukünftigen Hitlers ihrer Länder anbeteten." In Bonnie Beckett, *The Reception of Pablo Neruda's Works in the German Democratic Republic* (Berne, 1981), p. 61.
24. Kießling, *Exil in Lateinamerika*, p. 395.
25. Ibid., p. 448.
26. Teitelboim, *Neruda*, p. 273.
27. Neruda, *Memoirs*, p. 204.
28. Beckett, *The Reception of Pablo Neruda's Works*, p. 121.
29. Pablo Neruda, *Passions and Impressions*, ed. Matilde Neruda and Miguel Otero Silva, trans. Margaret Sayers Peden (New York, 1983), pp. 115–116.
30. Neruda, *Residence on Earth*, pp. 254–260.
31. Pablo Neruda, *Obras Completas* (Buenos Aires, 1957), vol. 2, pp. 1040–1041.
32. René de Costa, *The Poetry of Pablo Neruda* (Cambridge, Mass., 1979), p. 101.
33. Neruda, *Residence on Earth*, pp. 338–339.
34. Ibid., pp. 339–341.
35. Ibid., p. 343.
36. Neruda, *Canto General*, p. 39.
37. Ibid., p. 142.

38. Ibid., p. 259.
39. Neruda, *Obras Completas*, vol. 1, p. 836.
40. Ibid., p. 840.
41. Ibid., p. 841.
42. Ibid., p. 842.
43. Pablo Neruda, *Extravagaria*, trans. Alastair Reid (New York, 1974), p. 87.
44. Ibid., p. 89.
45. Teitelboim, *Neruda*, pp. 331–332.
46. Costa, *The Poetry of Pablo Neruda*, p. 126.
47. Christa Wolf, *Kindheitsmuster* (Frankfurt, 1989), pp. 222, 232.
48. Anna Seghers, *Werke* (Darmstadt and Neuwied, 1977), vol. 9, p. 135.

LA INSURRECCIÓN/DER AUFSTAND

Cultural Synergy, Film, and Revolution

Rachel J. Halverson and Ana María Rodríguez-Vivaldi

In the twentieth century, the growth of relations between Germany and certain Latin American countries has increased due to the rapid economic recovery of the postwar period and the active role Germany has taken in the democratization of, for example, Chile and Nicaragua.[1] For the West Germans, who began to acquire a stronger presence and expertise in the region since the 1960s, cultural relationships became a "channel for the transmission of ideas, support, and resources"[2] that would advance social and political agendas. Related to this, many Latin Americans have considered that "at least some of the political and social currents in Europe would understand and sympathize with Latin American dilemmas."[3] Thus, from a macrocosmic perspective, certain synergistic interactions were established and developed in view of common geopolitical, social, and financial goals.

Appropriately, one of the areas in which common interaction has found an outlet for creative endeavors between Germany and Latin America has been the media. Within this field, film has become an important forum for cultural diplomacy and a clear point of contact. It is, after all, a collective art by definition and a medium that has emerged in this century as a significant intersection of the narrative and the audiovisual. In a way, then, film embodies a synergistic relationship in its act of communication and, as such, becomes an appropriate medium for human collaboration as well. Latin American cinema has been a precarious industry, and its development has depended consistently on imported technology and foreign resources.[4] Coproductions abound and have been a significant factor in the international success of many Latin American cinematic works.

The cross-cultural communication inherent in these coproductions is enhanced when its collaborators have a particularly deep knowledge of each others' countries, cultures, and social situations. Such is the case of Peter Lilienthal (born in Berlin, Germany, in 1929) and Antonio Skármeta (born in Antofagasta, Chile, in 1940). Due to particular aspects of their formative years—Skármeta became an exile in West Berlin from 1973 to 1990, while Lilienthal lived from 1939 to 1956 in Uruguay—it can be argued that they reached a unique understanding of each others' backgrounds, a knowledge that is reflected in their joint productions as filmmakers.[5] In their collaborative work, Lilienthal and Skármeta share the credit for scripts that touch upon such diverse and contrasting topics as political struggle on a large scale and the struggle of the individual in sports. They demonstrate how the fusion of individual interests and production can become a joint project and a shared vision across cultures.

In this study of Lilienthal's and Skármeta's œuvre, we will focus on the film *La insurrección/Der Aufstand* (*The Uprising*, 1980), a film which showcases the unique strengths of their cross-cultural partnership. It is based on the true story of the Sandinista revolution in Nicaragua in the 1970s.[6] The two filmmakers had previously dealt with the failure of a communist regime in Chile in their film *Calm Prevails over the Country* (1975); the Nicaraguan crisis offered the opportunity to portray a successful contemporary revolution. Culminating in 1979, the Nicaraguan revolution was directed against a dictatorship and temporarily implemented a communist-oriented government and economy. Each film contains the theme of struggle: people fighting for what they perceive to be just, for the defense of their beliefs, and for their own destiny. The support for this leftist movement implied in Lilienthal and Skármeta's selection of topic and their portrayal of the triumphant revolutionaries reveals the filmmakers' personal politics, particularly in response to the United States' interventionist policy in Latin America. In order to expose the significance of Lilienthal's and Skármeta's collaboration in *La insurrección/Der Aufstand*, we will examine their respective careers, the four main themes in the film, and the film's structure. Our analysis will demonstrate that these artists met at a precise moment when a strong message of solidarity arose that would bind Europe and Latin America, as "a substantial groundswell of popular and political opinion in Europe was strongly critical of the U.S. policy in Latin America."[7] After the chaos of the 1960s, Lilienthal and Skármeta provided Europe and Latin America with a paradigm for successful revolution and hope for the future. This is not to say that their work was able to change this dynamic, but rather that they were responding to the mood of the times.

The recognition Peter Lilienthal's films have garnered speaks for his status as one of the major German filmmakers of the 1960s and 1970s. Although not as well known as his compatriots Rainer Werner Fassbinder, Werner Herzog, and Volker Schlöndorff, several of Lilienthal's films have earned critical acclaim and received highly competitive awards.[8] *Malastesta* (1969) won the *Bundesfilmpreis* and was entered by the Federal Republic of Germany at the Cannes Film Festival in 1970. His film *La Victoria* (1973) won the Special Prize of the Prague Television Festival and the Television Prize of the German Academy of Performing Arts in Frankfurt. *Schoolmaster Hofer* (1974) was awarded second prize in the 1978 Human Rights Film Festival in Strasbourg. In 1975, his film *Calm Prevails over the Country* (1975) was recognized with the West German Film Critics Prize. Lilienthal reached the pinnacle of his career with his film *David* (1979), which captured first prize at the Berlin International Film Festival.[9]

Lilienthal's work with Skármeta brings together many strands of his life: his interest in Latin America, his leftist politics, his exile experience, his life as an immigrant, and revolution.[10] These have much to do with Lilienthal's own experiences as a young German Jew in exile in Uruguay. In an interview with Annette Insdorf in *Cineaste* just before the U.S. release of *David* (1979) and *La insurrección/Der Aufstand* (1980), Lilienthal described his feelings toward Latin America and its peoples: "To get into Uruguay in this period, you needed money, so many rich Jewish people came. They always felt superior, unconcerned with Latin America, their new country. Whatever these cultivated Europeans said to me, I didn't understand. I really loved Latin Americans. I learned that it makes sense to have a social behavior, and that it's too easy to talk about socialist conviction. Whoever can really embrace someone, I'll give him a hand and look him in the eyes. I was always bored with rich people. I haven't changed."[11]

Clearly, Lilienthal perceives himself as different from the majority of European Jewish exiles in Latin America, who were wealthy and quite aware of class boundaries. He did not consider himself separate from Latin Americans while living there, but rather has come to consider it important to embody political convictions in both word and deed due to his experience of growing up in a foreign culture. In fact, one may go so far as to say that Lilienthal feels more Latin American than German. As he stated in an interview, "I grew up with Spanish and not with German. I understand the gestures, the eye contact, the behavior of the people there better than that of the people here [in Germany], who are always so reserved, sometimes even cold."[12] This attitude finds resonance in his films, which for the most part take place in various Latin American countries and deal with political and social issues on the grassroots level.

As we have seen, Lilienthal's connection to Latin America is unique. Born into a Jewish family in Berlin, the growing threat of Hitler, National Socialism, and increasing antisemitic hostilities forced his family to emigrate to Uruguay in 1939. He was only ten years old at the time, and he did not visit Germany again until 1954, spending his formative years in exile. His mother ran a second-class hotel, and it was there that Lilienthal, as he put it, "[had] the chance to understand basic political realities."[13] Uruguay from the late 1940s to the 1960s was going through a particularly positive economic and sociopolitical period, thanks to the protectionism of national products and the gradual industrial development after World War II.[14] Long known as the "Switzerland of the Americas" for its strong democratic tradition as well as its strong social programs that produced a highly urbanized population with literacy percentages mirroring or even exceeding those of some industrialized nations,[15] the country was a safe haven for a youth, such as Lilienthal, escaping from the horrors of Nazi Germany.

Lilienthal's counterpart in our study is Antonio Skármeta, a descendant of Polish immigrants and, as such, an insider with access to the outsider's view of his culture. As a writer, he is linked to the latest generation of narrators, the "Postboom" that succeeds well-known "Boom" era literary works such as Julio Cortázar's *Hopscotch* (1963) or Gabriel García Márquez' *One Hundred Years of Solitude* (1967). This "Postboom" designation is more than simply a generational link; it denotes certain convictions that cross over to Lilienthal's film work, as demonstrated by the consistent presence in his novels and films of the social and political situation in Latin America. Among other theories, he has proposed the idea that Latin American artistic expression should go back to a direct observation of its reality,[16] even if that reality will be transformed by its emotional impact upon the author.[17] Skármeta's generation proposes that Latin American literature should avoid the excesses in technical experimentation with form and the constant use of the fantastic in the interest of communicating the story. This is because contemporary Latin America has experienced such a wide variety of problems that literature must reflect its needs without providing a magical gloss that would detract from the stark reality of life on many parts of its continent.

As a professor of literature at the University of Chile from 1967 to 1973, Skármeta had exposure to the latest literary trends, but he was also living through one of the most active political times in the history of his country. He had always demonstrated a moderate support of leftist politics and criticism of bourgeois life in Chile and the United States, but his views became radicalized after the coup of 1973 that deposed the communist government of Salvador Allende. The impact of this change can be felt very clearly in *La insurrección/Der Aufstand*: Skármeta became convinced that literature should place more emphasis on "man as positioned in history." Apart from this radical effect on his ideology, the military coup caused his departure and exile in Berlin. After 1981, he also lived for short periods of time in other European countries and in the United States, working as a writer, as a film and theater director, and as a visiting professor at various universities.[18] In 1990, he left Germany and returned to Santiago de Chile, where he worked for the Goethe Institute. Currently, he produces and presents the award-winning series *El show de los libros* (The Book Show) for Chilean national television.

The year 1973 became a crossroads for Skármeta and Lilienthal in more ways than one since Lilienthal facilitated Skármeta's eventual exile to Germany after the fall of the Allende government. In 1972, Lilienthal had visited Chile because he was interested in the political process that was developing there—the first democratically elected communist government in Latin America. As the German filmmaker searched for someone who could write a screenplay based on this series of events, he was directed to Skármeta, who had published various collections of short stories. Interestingly enough, when the two met, they did not hit it off immediately, their temperaments being too dissimilar. Skármeta hesitated to collaborate on the project, but Lilienthal thought that their differences would ensure a positive working relationship, as he liked to be challenged. As Lilienthal pointed out in an interview, "I was a bit too European, and Skármeta gave me support to be a little bit [more Latin American] ... He knows my weaknesses and has beautiful intuitions about what I'm doing."[19] Eventually, they worked together in what would be their first film: *La Victoria*.

After the coup, Lilienthal felt that their collaboration was more important than ever, since the German public—indeed the European public—needed to be kept abreast of the reality and the problems in Chile. In fact, following the opening of *La insurrección/Der Aufstand*, Lilienthal received numerous letters from "Chile Committees" in Germany, which demonstrated that Germans had an increased awareness of the political situation in Latin America and contributed to keeping the Chilean situation in the public eye.[20] A month after the coup, Lilienthal obtained a contract for Skármeta from a German television station to write a second script, one which became *Calm Prevails over the Country*. Later, Skármeta was awarded a scholarship from the Arts Program of Berlin and lived there with his family until 1989.[21]

Skármeta readily admits the impact of German culture on his own style of writing: "I had as a calling an unreal, experimental language, with a lot of images sometimes bordering on the chaotic, and a way of thinking not in rational terms, but rather metaphorically and visually. Lately, in contact with this [German] culture and with another kind of language and literature, I have considered it expedient to discipline my expressive modes a bit.... My own stylistic preferences ... have been modified."[22] The sociopolitical experience that preceded his exile in a foreign country, as well as the exile experience itself, taught him two basic things: on the one hand, he found a need within himself to avoid "an individualistic and egocentric kind of literature," to dwell within a realistic appreciation of the political situation of his country; on the other, more personal note, he felt an impulse toward "the other" ("lo otro"), not only to learn to love it, but to be able to embrace it as a "social corpus."[23] The culmination of socialism in Chile and the subsequent trauma caused by the coup and exile brought the author to a closer identification with proletarian struggles. This radicalization in his ideology carried with it a realization that collaborative work can have a supreme aesthetic value, since "the true identity of the writer cannot be separated from the liberty of his country."[24] The new attraction of collaborative work as a true expression of the solidarity of this artist with the social struggles of his people became clear immediately as Skármeta started working with Lilienthal in Germany and found success in many of their projects together. In light of both artists' views of their collaborative work, it becomes clear that their synergy has had a positive effect on their productivity and has resulted in a complementary vision perhaps far exceeding their potential as single creators.

It is also significant that the time Skármeta spent in Germany took place in Berlin. His perception of Germany comes through this exposure to the Berlin way of life, and the city has essentially become the bridge for Skármeta to German culture as a whole, coloring his understanding of his hosts' approach to life. The West Berlin of the 1970s and the 1980s was marked by cold war and détente, and life in that divided city produced individuals with special or different needs and qualities. It was, and still is, considered to be the center of alternative culture, avant-garde art, theater and film, and political radicalism in Germany. It is to this implicit Berlin audience that Skármeta directed his images, and with which as an exile from another culture he identified. It was a city with its feet in both camps: half socialist, half democratic. It had to deal with the sociopolitical problems of both worlds and, as a result, reached a perhaps unique comparative view that is still functional.

The selection of the Nicaraguan revolution as the topic for the film also speaks to a need that Skármeta perceived in Germans, particularly in the youth in Berlin. According to him, the insularity of the city has created a thirst for knowledge about the outside world, about other cultures, that sometimes becomes a passion and at other times a profession. In a society as structured as Germany, many of the essential problems have been solved, and each nascent generation in its quest for change and renovation faces a very limited scope for action. In a way, Skármeta feels that because the system works, it has become stagnant.[25] On the other hand, he feels that Berlin's society "did not integrate its different segments ... [As a city,] it had a difficult identity, a broken identity ... and as such did not impose upon you a cliché.... You could create your own city." This mindset is reflected in its citizens, and, while undeniably liberating, it also presents another challenge, even a need, to search for the meaning of unity in other parts of the world. In Skármeta's opinion, this is the reason why the West Berlin youth looked toward Latin America; there they perceived the movement of history, the urgency and solidarity that arises from the common struggles of societies in formation.[26] *La insurrección/Der Aufstand* speaks to this idea: it presents clearly what the human spirit can achieve through hard work, planning, and, above all, solidarity. These realities will become more and more important as we study Lilienthal and Skármeta's decision to organize the film *La insurrección/Der Aufstand* around the universal themes of family, class, and religion within the framework of political struggle.

As is often the case in civil or internal wars, the family in *La insurrección/Der Aufstand* becomes the arena for conflict, a microcosm of political dissension—just as León, the city in which it takes place, is a microcosm of the entire country. Father and son are pitted against each other, but the film subverts the more typical dynamic of conservative father versus radical son. Here it is the father, Antonio Menor, who supports the Sandinistas, and the son, Agustín Menor, who is a part of the repressive National Guard. The conflict is extended to encompass a third character, Captain Flores, Agustín's superior officer, who becomes a kind of pseudo-father figure and protector for Agustín with promises of lucrative study in the United States. This triangular relationship forces Agustín to choose between "fathers," just as his nation must choose between governments.

The women in the family add another dimension to the already complex father-son triangle. Both Agustín's mother and his sister identify with the Sandinistas; in fact, the sister leaves her university studies to join the guerrillas. This action becomes particularly poignant due to the close relationship between Agustín and his sister, contrasted with the fact that she is actively involved in the killing of soldiers like him, whereas he has been excluded from killing actions by his status as a technician. Eventually, this dynamic imbalances the familial harmony, pitting the son against not only the father, but against the entire family. A further complication arises from the fact that Agustín joined the National Guard to help support the family after his father lost his job, probably due to his political convictions, and thus feels a responsibility to remain in the military even in the face of familial opposition. The mounting pressures from his family to desert place Agustín between obeying his parents and adhering to his oath to military service. Leaving the military under such conditions would not only make him a criminal and jeopardize his life and the lives of his family, who would be killed as a result, but would also force him to give up his dream of studying engineering in the United States. Agustín's internal struggle convinces the audience of the depth of his convictions and the seriousness of this change in political stance. Just as many Nicaraguans grappled with the decision to support the Sandinistas, Agustín must go through a process of enlightenment. His eventual act of desertion parallels the actions of people who have become fed up with the abuses of a corrupt dictatorship.

The film provides a problematical model for resistance that speaks both to the conflict in Skármeta's homeland—as well as to those of other nations where similar processes take place—and to a German audience familiar with the criticism of their own limited popular resistance to the abuses of the National Socialists in Nazi Germany. Given that Lilienthal is Jewish, this criticism is implicitly present in the film. At the end of *La insurrección/Der Aufstand*, Agustín makes his personal choice to rally with the revolutionary forces and to provide critical technical support to the uprising. In the bloody confrontation between the Sandinistas and the National Guard, which marks the triumph of the former, Agustín dies when he confronts Captain Flores, who had been using Antonio Menor as a human shield to protect himself from the rebels' gunfire. When confronted by his traitorous protégé, Captain Flores abandons caution in his desire for revenge. He is killed just as the military he represents is defeated. Agustín must also die: as with tragically flawed characters in classical drama, his previous military allegiances tainted him, and to pay for his doubts, he must sacrifice himself.

The theme of class reinforces the father dichotomy established by Captain Flores and Antonio Menor. Captain Flores is a scion of an upper-class family, replete with all of the trappings of the privileged class: artwork, servants, and leisure. In keeping with the tradition of his class, he followed a military career. Essentially, Captain Flores, with his promises to Agustín of study in the U.S., represents a way up the social ladder for Agustín, a temptation, in effect, for Agustín to forget his working-class origins. Antonio Menor, on the other hand, is at this point unable to even provide for his family. As is common in many Latin American countries, he also has to support his extended family, a task which has been complicated by the loss of his job. Unlike Captain Flores, who was born into his wealth and yet cannot instill respect in his own daughters, Antonio Menor gains the respect and commitment of his family by eking out an existence from menial jobs and begging from his neighbors. Agustín's decision to side with his father signifies more than just family loyalty; it embodies his acceptance of his heritage and a realization that the Sandinista movement has more to do with dignity and identity than with wealth and personal gains.

La insurrección/Der Aufstand also explores the racial dimension of the revolution in Nicaragua. Captain Flores, with his more European features and tall stature, has an added advantage, a perceived superiority over Agustín, who has Indian features, darker coloring, and shorter stature. The Sandinista movement brought together disparate racial backgrounds under the umbrella of the common goal of justice for the majority. In the ideal society that was to be born out of this movement, racial differences would cease to be significant. This is particularly appealing to Agustín, who is acutely aware of the racial differences at play in Captain Flores's home as he sees his face mirrored by those of the servants. In a significant act of defiance, he purposely breaks a priceless vase he has been packing for the Flores family's move to the U.S., symbolically avenging the humiliations inflicted on the servants and himself.

Ultimately, the real issue behind differences in class and race is power. This is symbolized most graphically in the film by Captain Flores and his Mercedes-Benz. As the camera lingers on the universally distinctive Mercedes logo (which is, of course, frighteningly similar to the peace symbol), the audience is made aware of the power Captain Flores wields in his milieu: this man has power over life and death. With a single arbitrary command, he can send a soldier into a home to kill its residents, or rescind the order on a whim—a power which is starkly depicted in the film.

The influence of the Catholic Church and its contradictory role—performing at times as a conservative bastion, and at others as a supporter of liberal views—is also considered in *La insurrección/Der Aufstand*. As has been stated, the church's power "is still substantial, though commonly exaggerated ... [and] the region has a long history of Church-state conflict in republican times."[27] The film chooses to depict the church's more grassroots role in supporting and providing sanctuary for opponents of the existing regime. The faction of the church that has been identified as the "theology of liberation" has close ties to the actual revolutionary movement, as seen clearly in the figure of the priest who hides one of the fleeing revolutionaries and allows his church to be used in promoting the uprising. The National Guards call this priest "Cura Satanás" (Father Devil) in an effort to vilify his actions, yet the film portrays him as a true believer in the justice that the movement promises its adherents, and, as such, he is aligned with what the film supports as "good," as opposed to the implied "evilness" of the government's thugs. Though it would seem simplistic, the film clearly establishes a return to the Manichaean world-view, which had been lost in the twentieth century.[28]

The theme of political struggle frames the narrative of Agustín's journey to enlightenment as well as all other themes at play in the film. Even for an audience not well versed in Latin American politics, the political clash is obvious enough to have meaning because it is expressed in the polarities of good and evil. Given Germany's National Socialist past, a German audience would condemn the excesses of a dictatorial regime and would resonate with the insurgents' political awareness. In contrast, Latin American audiences would either support or reject the scenario along a clear liberal/conservative polarity.

The quasi-documentary style of the film aims to establish a sort of cinema verité that will have a *Verfremdungseffekt* (distancing effect) on the viewer, objectifying the political struggle portrayed, since the filmmakers want to prevent the romanticization of Third World political strife. This was a particular danger for a young leftist Western European audience that had dealt with Marxist theory only in the abstract and not in practice, an audience which perhaps had never even experienced firsthand a Third World country. At the same time that the film presents a veneer of objectivity for the audience, it also separates the filmmaker from any blatant expression of approval, though by the selection of topic and point of view, that approval is implied. Key to this documentary style are the understated development of the characters and their limited emotional responses. The film's commitment to realism is also reflected in the exclusive use of nonprofessional actors, except for Oscar Castillo, who plays Captain Flores.

The structure of *La insurrección/Der Aufstand* is, in turn, both circular and linear. Visually, the film opens with a shot of a mural proclaiming the triumph of the Sandinistas, thus emphasizing popular art as a medium for protest. This is accompanied by an off-camera voice shouting "¡Patria libre!"—the cry that announces the beginning of every battle in the film and the enunciation of the insurgents' goal. Here the idea of the voice functions clearly as the carrier of messages in the absence of access to other media. The dictator controlled radio, television, film, and the presses; the voice thus highlights the importance of oral traditions to movements with limited access to the printed word, as well as the popular roots of those movements, which rely to some degree on word of mouth to propagate their ideals. This concept of oral tradition comes full circle with the closing scene of the film, when, during the victory celebration, the children crowd around one of the rebels to listen to his story. He tells of shooting his gun at a military plane just as a foreign correspondent photographed his challenge to the mighty powers. The film thus depicts the birth of a legend that will imprint the identities of generations to come, just as epic poems have guided the beginning of nations and the seeding of national identity since recorded history. In its linearity, the film follows the chronology of the Sandinista uprising in the city of León. In order to underscore the enormity of the struggle, the film begins with characters who function more as types than as individuals with distinct identities. In the course of the film, however, we learn more and more about these players in the movement, including their names and relationships, their virtues and vices. Little by little, each individual voice gains identity and joins the orchestration of the revolution. This joining of voices is metaphorically supported in certain scenes, such as the contrast between the empty streets of the opening frames and the festive crowds populating the streets at the conclusion of the film.

In the process of collaborating on a film of this epic scope, Lilienthal and Skármeta have imprinted Nicaragua's historical process with their own perspectives and desires. Their film is a creation that depicts the destruction of an old order and the substitution of the prevalent social contract with that of a new popular vision and reach. In the pre-Reagan era, before the fall of communism and the reunification of Germany, *La insurrección/Der Aufstand* could be interpreted as a celebration of human strife, perhaps naive in view of what was to come, but nevertheless sincere. Through their management of the universal themes of family, class, and religion, they point toward the creation of a system that, ideally, will bring about the happiness that has eluded the Nicaraguans. The political struggle of these people becomes, in truth, a search for dignity. It is a search for a place in history, for respect as human beings. The impact of the family on the political process, as represented in this film, is toward nonconformity, rather than toward compliance with society's mores that have marginalized a large part of its members. Class and race are reviewed and discounted as the Sandinista movement is identified as one that forgoes elitist distinctions in order to pursue the benefit of the whole. Religion is also represented as having a supporting role in the emergence of this system, particularly as Marxism is downplayed to highlight the human struggle, which transcends ideological boundaries. Through the filmmakers' eyes, then, the audience is allowed a directed view of a beginning, of a utopian society in which virtue will be rewarded and corruption will find its proper, fiery end.

Thus, the film represents a fusion of outlooks: that of the European who has found a voice and a way to express his desires in a culture not his own, but in the process of formation; and that of the Latin American who celebrates his people's capacity for survival, even in the midst of apparent destruction, and showcases it so that others in his adopted country can understand and keep their own vitality alive. With Lilienthal's and Skármeta's collaboration in *La insurrección/Der Aufstand*, the Old and the New Worlds meet and cooperate. The personal synergy which is generated between these two creative individuals is part of a larger geopolitical trend. *La insurrección/Der Aufstand* is a microcosm of their interaction and functions as a statement of goals that extend beyond the particular scenario portrayed in the film. Ultimately, the film represents a macrocosmic view of the larger dynamics between Germany and Latin America.

Notes

1. *Latin America in Perspective: Oxford Analytica* (Boston, 1991), p. 272.
2. Ibid.
3. Ibid., pp. 272–273.
4. Ibid., p. 71ff.
5. Lilienthal and Skármeta collaborated on the following films: *La Victoria* (1973), *Calm Prevails over the Country* (1975), *The Uprising* (1979), and *The Bicyclist of San Cristobal* (1988).
6. The political history of Nicaragua in the twentieth century has been marked by war and civil strife. Between 1912 and 1932, the country was occupied by the United States Marine Corps. In the struggle against them, general Augusto César Sandino was one of the main leaders. He was assassinated in 1934 by the leader of the National Guard Corps, created during the American occupation. The assassin was Anastasio Somoza, who, in 1936, staged a coup against the constitutional government and began a dictatorship that lasted until his own assassination in 1956. His son Luis Somoza succeeded him. After an interruption, power returned to the family when Anastasio Somoza, Jr. was elected president in 1967. As was the case with his father and brother, his government was marked by authoritarianism and corruption. It is said that he became rich due to all of the international funds sent to Nicaragua for aid after the 1972 earthquake that devastated Managua. The opposition groups—the Sandinista guerrillas, the factory workers, farmworkers, students, even industrialists—united against his government and denounced the corruption and abuses of his administration. The United States eventually canceled all financial and military aid, and in 1979, the Organization of American States (OAS) asked for Somoza's dismissal. The popular revolution and its eventual triumph that year led to his exile. See Juan Kattán-Ibarra, *Perspectivas culturales de Hispanoamérica* (Lincolnwood, Ill., 1995), pp. 127–129.
7. *Latin America in Perspective*, p. 272.
8. In terms of sheer numbers of pages, Fassbinder, Herzog, and Schlöndorff receive greater attention in German film scholarship. See Timothy Corrigan, *New German Film: The Displaced Image* (Austin, Tex., 1983); Thomas Elsaesser, *New German Cinema: A History* (New Brunswick, N.J., 1989); and Anton Kaes, *From Hitler to Heimat: The Return of History as Film* (Cambridge, Mass., 1989), for representative treatments of Lilienthal's work within the body of literature on German cinema.

9. Lynne Layton, "Peter Lilienthal: Decisions before Twelve," in *New German Filmmakers: From Oberhausen through the 1970s*, ed. Klaus Phillips (New York, 1984), pp. 233–241.
10. Ibid., p. 232.
11. Annette Insdorf, "A Passion for Social Justice: An Interview with Peter Lilienthal," *Cineaste*, vol. 11, no. 4 (1982), p. 38.
12. "Ich bin mit Spanisch und nicht mit Deutsch aufgewachsen. Ich verstehe die Gesten, die Blicke, die Verhaltensweisen der Menschen dort besser als die Menschen hier, die immer so zurückhaltend, manchmal auch eisig sind." In Gregor Dotzauer, "Politik der Gesten: Peter Lilienthal wurde sechzig," *Kulturchronik*, vol. 2 (1990), p. 44.
13. Insdorf, "A Passion for Social Justice," p. 38.
14. Kattán-Ibarra, *Perspectivas culturales de Hispanoamérica*, p. 110.
15. The 1987 percentage of gross enrollment ratios for higher education in Uruguay was 41.61 percent, as compared to 30.0 percent for Spain and 24.3 percent for Italy, both of which are industrialized countries with market economies that have had strong links to Uruguay through migration or economic exchange (*Latin America in Perspective*, p. 61).
16. Donald Shaw, "Skármeta: contexto e ideas literarias," *Revista Iberoamericana*, nos. 168–169 (July–December 1994), p. 1054.
17. Ibid., p. 1058.
18. Skármeta wrote the novel on which *Il postino* (1994) was based and also received credit for the script. He had adapted the same novel for the 1983 film *Ardiente paciencia*, which he directed. For more information on Latin American film, see Zuzana M. Pick, *The New Latin American Cinema: A Continental Project* (Austin, Tex., 1993); John King, *Magical Reels: A History of Cinema in Latin America* (London, 1990); and Julianne Burton, *Cinema and Social Change in Latin America: Conversations with Filmmakers* (Austin, Tex., 1986).
19. Insdorf, "A Passion for Social Justice," p. 38.
20. Ibid.
21. These anecdotes were summarized from an interview between Skármeta and Andrea Pagni, "Entrevista con Antonio Skármeta, *Discurso Literario*, vol. 1 (1987), pp. 59–73.
22. "Yo tenía por vocación un lenguaje irrealista, experimental, de muchas imágenes a veces caóticas, y un modo de pensar no racional, sino metafórico y visual … En este último tiempo, en contacto con esa cultura, y con otro tipo de lenguaje y de literatura, estimé conveniente disciplinar mis medios expresivos … mis propias preferencias estilísticas … se han ido modificando." Andrea Pagni, "Entrevista con Antonio Skármeta," pp. 66–67.
23. "Antes … en Chile, mi literatura era individualista y egocéntrica. El auge del socialismo, por el contrario, conllevó la necesidad de hacer una apreciacíon realista de la situación política del país, y en el terreno personal me impulsó hacia lo 'otro', no sólo para amarlo, sino para abarcarlo en tanto que cuerpo social." Quoted in Menene Gras Balaguer, "Entrevista con Antonio Skármeta," *Ínsula*, vol. 478 (1986), p. 14. Cited in Shaw, "Skármeta," p. 1057.
24. Cristián Cortés, "Leer la realidad desde la distancia," *Encuentro Latinoamericano*, vol. 19 (1980), p. 55.
25. Of course, we should note that Skármeta is speaking before the fall of the Berlin Wall in 1989 and the reunification of Germany in 1990. The incorporation of a population that has lived in a different world has placed Germans in a position of movement and change that becomes equivalent to the social

process in Latin America with its trend toward the integration of minorities, and so forth.

26. Pagni, "Entrevista con Antonio Skármeta," p. 63.
27. *Latin America in Perspective*, p. 129.
28. This is not new, of course, as that is the classical paradigm also used in many Hollywood movies: "This narrative model is based on a conflict between a protagonist, who initiates the action, and an antagonist who resists it." Louis D. Giannetti, *Understanding Movies* (Englewood Cliffs, N.J., 1990), p. 304.

– 21 –

THE RECEPTION OF SPANISH-AMERICAN FICTION IN GERMANY

The Tide of Bestsellers, 1980–1995—
Rising and Ebbing?

Meg H. Brown

The history of Spanish-American fiction in Germany has been uneven, to say the least. To be sure, it has been a drought ... and then a flood. Before 1980, no Latin American works had been on the *Spiegel/Buchreport* bestseller list. Yet in the subsequent years, from 1981 to 1995, sixteen books from Central and South America made the list. By 1985, there was a clear trend of Latin American literature in Germany. What caused such a turnaround in reception and then a surge of Spanish-American fiction so suddenly and so dramatically? Now that the Germans have discovered Latin American writing, what is the status of the rising tide of South American fiction in Germany today?

Here, I will present the background of the process of reception of Spanish-American bestsellers in Germany. Then I will examine the reception of more recent works from Latin America since 1992, using bestseller lists and the earlier set of literary expectations from the 1980s that the Germans had to compare with features found in the works of the 1990s, in order to determine the standing of Spanish-American prose in Germany today.

The trend started slowly but then accelerated quickly. The first Latin American author to have a work become a bestseller in

Germany was, as one might expect, Nobel Prize winner Gabriel García Márquez (born 1928); the first book by García Márquez to secure bestseller standing was *Crónica de una muerte anunciada* (Chronicle of a Death Foretold) for three weeks in 1981. It was only after García Márquez's 1982 Nobel Prize that his *Cien años de soledad* (One Hundred Years of Solitude), translated into German in 1971, became a bestseller for four months. But, on the other hand, beginning in 1984, Isabel Allende's (born 1942) *La casa de los espíritus* (The House of the Spirits) was on the list for four and a half years, and her *De amor y de sombra* (Of Love and Shadows, 1986),[1] *Eva Luna* (1988), and *Cuentos de Eva Luna* (The Stories of Eva Luna, 1990) were each on the list for approximately fifteen months. Allende's style of basic storytelling appealed to popular German taste. García Márquez's subsequent works, *El amor en los tiempos del cólera* (Love in the Time of Cholera, 1987) and *El general en su laberinto* (The General in His Labyrinth, 1989), were then also tremendously successful, again due to accessible storytelling. Indeed, García Márquez's and Allende's success in Germany prepared the reading public for prose written by other Latin Americans, paving the way for Ángeles Mastretta's (born 1949) novel *Arráncame la vida* (Mexican Bolero, 1988) and Mario Vargas Llosa's (born 1936) *Elogio de la madrastra* (In Praise of the Stepmother, 1989) and *El hablador* (The Storyteller, 1990) to become bestsellers by changing and crystallizing, or "concretizing," the German reading public's horizon or set of expectations. Mastretta's and Vargas Llosa's novels were surprisingly more popular in Germany than in many other countries.

Clearly, the Germans were searching for and finding in the Hispano-American prose certain literary qualities that they were not finding collectively in the belles-lettres from other cultures, nor from their own. In an interview, the *Kempinski Journal* asked translator Curt Meyer-Clason what distinguishes Latin American literature and makes it so interesting for the Germans. He answered, "it has everything that the German literature lacks. The wonderful world of the South American has not yet been spoiled by logic. It begins with the five senses and comes from ... daily social life and from a direct contact with nature. While we Europeans put logic and intelligence above all, for Latin Americans, feelings and the miracle of our existence are more important."[2]

An analysis of the reviews of Spanish-American bestsellers in Germany shows a definite pattern in the reception and thus also in the horizon of expectations of the German readers with respect to Latin American literature. The characteristics of this set of expectations were the return to storytelling; Latin American history, culture, and politics; and the exotic, the magic, the color, and the vitality of everyday life that Germans associate with Latin America. These themes are found repeatedly in the reviews of bestselling Spanish-American fiction in Germany from 1981 to 1991. By examining the reviews and reception history of the later works in relation to the established pattern and set of expectations, a determination of the status of Latin American literary reception in Germany today can be reached.

The horizon of expectations was in place when later novels from South America were published in Germany. Laura Esquivel's (born 1950) *Como agua para chocolate* (Like Water for Chocolate, 1992) weaves together a love affair and the magic of cooking, so that those who eat the foods prepared by the Mexican main character take on the emotion she was feeling when she cooked the dish. Isabel Allende's *El plan infinito* (The Infinite Plan, 1992), a family history focusing on a white boy who grows up with Chicanos in the ghettos of Los Angeles, deals with prejudice, failed marriages, Vietnam, drug-dependent children, and the Chicano experience. In *Paula* (1995), written as a letter to her daughter, who was in a coma for about a year before she died, Allende relates her family history. García Márquez's *Doce cuentos peregrinos* (Strange Pilgrims, 1993) is a collection of twelve stories about Latin Americans living or visiting in Europe. He published the book in Spanish in 1992, the "Columbus year." His *Del amor y otros demonios* (Of Love and Other Demons, 1994) takes place in colonial Colombia and begins with a young girl being bitten by a rabid dog. She is sent to a cloister to be cared for by nuns. Ultimately, a young priest overseeing her falls in love with her, but the authorities, including the Catholic Church, obstruct any chance of their love, and the girl dies. Three of these five latest well-received South American works of fiction differ greatly in content from the earlier group. By examining reviews, we will find whether the literary expectations were being met in these works.

The opinion of literary critics is multifaceted: it represents the views and the expectations of a body of readers; at the same time, the critics influence public opinion by disseminating their own views. They thus belong to that process of "concretization" of the set of public literary expectations. They may be viewed as opinion reflectors, makers, and disseminators.

As with the former bestsellers, critics often refer back to an earlier and therefore better known work or author in order to give the reader a point of reference—or sometimes just to make a wordplay.

A number of reviews of García Márquez's *Strange Pilgrims* have references to Franz Kafka, such as the following: "... without the help of [García Márquez's] familiarity with Kafka's *Metamorphosis*, the poet in the journalist would not have been born—the poet who elevates the unlikely and fantastic to be the central event of his poetics of matter-of-factness."³ Others use the review title or a phrase to connect the piece to an earlier work by the same author or by another bestselling Latin American writer. For example, reviews of *Of Love and Other Demons* refer back to García Márquez's own *Love in the Time of Cholera* with such phrases as "Love in the Time of the Inquisition,"⁴ "Love in the Times of the Baroque and Enlightenment,"⁵ and "Love in the Time of Rabies."⁶ Other reviews connect two later works to García Márquez's *Chronicle of a Death Foretold*. One review title of García Márquez's *Of Love and Other Demons* is "Chronicle of a Tragedy Foretold,"⁷ while another calls Allende's *Paula* "[t]his chronicle 'of a death foretold.'"⁸ By making these connections, the critics can suggest the parameters of the public's set of expectations upon encountering a new Spanish-American text.

We can now survey the individual characteristics that the German readers had come to expect from Spanish-American fiction. Here, I refer to results of my investigation *The Reception of Spanish American Fiction in West Germany, 1981–1991: A Study of Best Sellers*.⁹ Naturally, it is to be expected that the Germans perceived "the exotic" as belonging to Latin American literature. However, it was only in the 1980s, after Hispanic-American literature had become more accessible and more easily understood and the exotic elements more concrete and less threatening, that the common German reader became more interested in South American fiction. Prior to the 1980s, literature from Latin America was too distant, too different, and too incomprehensible for most Germans, and critics of Latin American fiction used more frequently the vague expression "exotic." In contrast, the reviews of Latin American works from 1981 to 1991 were more likely to name specific exotic characteristics, though often trite, stereotypical, and false—for example, "Caribbean Village," "Music in the Blood," "Ballroom Dance on the Volcano of the Mexican Revolution," "In the Jungle of Politics," "Jungle Scenes," and "Indian Fantasy." In the reviews of the popular Latin American fiction after 1991, there was a break in this tendency, partly as a result of a difference in the novels themselves: *The Infinite Plan* takes place in the United States, and in *Strange Pilgrims*, Latin Americans are in Europe. *Paula* is Allende's life story in letter form and narrates events in

Chile, Venezuela, and the United States; but any mention of exoticism, connotatively or denotatively, is decidedly missing from the reviews of the work.

Reviews of the other two works do include "exoticism." A critic of Esquivel's *Like Water for Chocolate* makes a direct reference to exoticism: "Or turkey in *mole* ... with almonds and sesame seeds. Purely exotic things."[10] In some reviews of García Márquez's *Of Love and Other Demons*, one finds more indirect suggestions of the exotic: "If the reader pauses confused, that may be caused by the intensity and density of the novel, which unfolds like an equatorial jungle on the pages";[11] "Cloisters, young priests, slaves, orgies, the sun of the Caribbean";[12] and "Maybe the momentary weariness of South America, the weariness of Cuba, the weariness of Haiti, and especially the weariness of Colombia have made it the minor work that it is."[13] Critics of Esquivel's novel offer fewer exotic images and, with a few exceptions, mention the word "exotic" less often, even though the book is filled with such elements. The same holds true for García Márquez's *Of Love and Other Demons*. While such references can be found, they are less frequent. One has the sense that the Germans have had enough of the exotic—they feel a "Müdigkeit der Exotik," a weariness of the exotic.

Another quality that belongs to Latin American literature is "magic realism," a term first used by Cuban writer Alejo Carpentier. As with exoticism, for the German readers there should not be too much—"a little seasoned, but not too strong."[14] Magic realism is a difficult concept for the average German reader, who often views it as an obstacle to understanding Latin American literature. Reviews of the Spanish-American novels that have been popular in Germany since 1991 mention magic realism even less frequently than those before, and the more concrete expression "magic" ("Magie" and "Zauber") is found more often. The title of one review of *Like Water for Chocolate* is "Kitchen Magic and Love."[15] In a review of *Strange Pilgrims*, this question is raised: "Does the magical world of the Latin Americans not remain foreign to us?"[16] Some reviews combine magic with other concepts, such as in the following critique of *Of Love and Other Demons*: "a grand script for a colorful, historical film";[17] and "great literature, bittersweet, in the vividly colorful tradition of magic realism."[18] Similar combinations are found in reviews of Allende's *The Infinite Plan*, "The colorful and also magical world of the Latin Americans,"[19] while a critic of *Paula* believes that "Magic realism has lost its magic."[20]

As several of these reviews suggest, there is a lack of enthusiasm for either the magic realism that is currently found in the works from Latin America or for magic realism itself as a genre. While the reviews show disappointment in the current magic realism, they continue to demonstrate that Germans find the colorfulness that they perceive in Latin American literature very enticing. Other phrases found frequently in reviews are "colorful images" ("farbige Bilder"), "colorful life" ("buntes Leben"), and "richly colored prose" ("farbenreiche Prosa"). One review calls the work *Of Love and Other Demons* "a fresco-like painting, glittering in all its colorfulness" ("ein freskoartiges Gemälde, das in seiner Buntheit schillert").[21]

Hand in hand with this celebration of color is the German perception of "Vitalität" ("vitality"), a term found in a tremendous number of reviews of earlier Latin American bestsellers. One example was the pleasure taken in the recognition of Latin American life and vitality in this 1988 review of Mastretta's *Mexican Bolero*: "Mexico! There one expects thundering life in a colorfulness that one does not know here at all."[22]

However, with the later set of popular Spanish-American fiction since 1992, such expressions of "Lebendigkeit" ("vividness") and "Vitalität" are far fewer. This, once again, may have to do with the nature of the works written during this time. One reviewer of *Of Love and Other Demons* even seems to suggest that the existence of a special Latin American vitality is merely a myth: "It would be a misunderstanding to believe that such an absolute love is the sign of the unbroken vitality of a younger world, far away from Europe's whitewashed politeness."[23] An exception is found in a review of *Like Water for Chocolate*: "Interested readers can now get a taste of the vitality of Mexican literature."[24]

It does seem surprising that some of the characteristics that the Germans had initially found most appealing in Spanish-American fiction would be so lacking in the later reviews. Nevertheless, there is the continued sense that Latin American literature has something to offer that European, and more specifically German, works do not have, as we saw above and again in a critic's review of *Strange Pilgrims*: "The [book] reads at times like a parable of the confrontation of the highly technologized, rationalistic Europe with Latin America and its mentality that appears to be archaic."[25] Of *Of Love and Other Demons*, another critic notes: "[García Márquez] has made us all addicted to the tropics, infected us with incurable passions, and spoiled for us the anemic prose of many German authors."[26] One must note, however, that such stirring remarks are almost exclusively found in reviews of García Márquez's works and rarely in reviews of works by the other authors.

The differentiation between Europe and South America extends to the interest in accessible Latin American history and politics, particularly in Esquivel's *Like Water for Chocolate*, Allende's *Paula*, and García Márquez's *Of Love and Other Demons*. Notes one critic of *Like Water for Chocolate*, "Sparing references to historical and technical developments suggest a diffuse 'Once upon a time' at the time of the revolution in Mexico."[27]

Furthermore, in a review of García Márquez's *Of Love and Other Demons*, the critic makes the point that the story is a metaphor for Latin American history: "It will certainly become an endless age of bloody revolutions and dictatorships, of eternal inquisitions, persecutions, and tortures, fear of death and terror; until the present day, the demons of darkness flutter through the reality of Latin America."[28]

In looking back at the recent works and the set of German expectations for fiction from Latin America, we can determine that there was indeed a disruption in the trend. First of all, two of the publications did not follow the expectation of the Latin American setting—Allende's *The Infinite Plan*, set in the United States, and García Márquez's *Strange Pilgrims*, set in Europe. García Márquez's *Of Love and Other Demons* and Esquivel's *Like Water for Chocolate* have the most characteristics of what Germans expect from Spanish-American fiction. Nevertheless, of the five works, it was *Like Water for Chocolate* that failed to make the published *Spiegel/Buchreport* bestseller list. This is true in spite of the fact that it was published by the "sister publishing house" of the one that publishes Allende's works, and that Allende and Esquivel share the same editor, Jürgen Dormagen. Theoretically, Allende and Mastretta had prepared the German reader for popular Spanish-American prose written by a woman. *Like Water for Chocolate* was presented at the 1992 Frankfurt Book Fair, the theme of which was "Mexican Literature." Laura Esquivel herself made appearances and gave talks and interviews there. Moreover, the film based on her book came out in 1993; still, *Like Water for Chocolate* did not appear on the German bestseller list. Allende and García Márquez have been the only Latin American authors to attain bestseller status, and their works no longer remain on the list for years as they had earlier. In fact, none of their bestsellers since 1991 has stayed on the list for even a year. Furthermore, not one of their publications since 1991 has secured the number one position on the list, whereas four had done so before 1992. It may very well be that the authors themselves have not produced any "super bestsellers."[29] In any case, we must come to the conclusion that the trend of

Spanish-American bestsellers in Germany has reached its peak and is on the decline. Allende and García Márquez remain bestselling authors in their own right, just as Siegfried Lenz had been years earlier when it was written that Lenz had "established himself in the mind of certain buyers, which results in permanently high sales of his books."[30] It is plausible that, had the trend still been alive, Esquivel's novel would have become a bestseller as had the works by Mastretta and Vargas Llosa. But since this was not the case, we are left with the determination that the Spanish-American tide in Germany is indeed ebbing.

Notes

1. The dates shown indicate the year the work was published in German.
2. Interview with Curt Meyer-Clason, "Vermittler einer wunderbaren Welt," *Kempinski Journal*, September 1993.
3. The translations of the reviews are mine. The original text reads, "ohne die Hebammendienste durch seine Bekanntschaft mit Kafkas *Verwandlung* wäre in dem Journalisten der Dichter ... nicht zur Welt gekommen, der das Unwahrscheinlich-Phantastische zum Zentral-Ereignis seiner Poetik des Selbstverständlichen machte." "Die Einsamkeit der Latinos in Europa," *Frankfurter Rundschau*, 27 March 1993.
4. Wolf Scheller, "Liebe in der Zeit der Inquisition," *Main-Echo*, 23 January 1995.
5. Jörg Sobiella, "Frühstücksjournal," Mitteldeutsches Radio, 9 September 1994.
6. Klaus Laabs, "Liebe in den Zeiten der Tollwut," *Freitag*, 4 November 1994.
7. Ernst Bockrandt, "Chronik einer angekündigten Tragödie," *Muritz-Nordkurier*, 1 October 1994.
8. *Elle*, April 1995.
9. Meg H. Brown, *The Reception of Spanish American Fiction in West Germany, 1981–1991: A Study of Best Sellers* (Tübingen, 1994).
10. "Oder Puter in Mole ... mit Mandeln und Sesamsamen. Lauter exotische Sachen." Benjamin Jakob, "Gertrudis schwitzt Rosenduft: Roman um Kochrezepte von Laura Esquivel," *Neues Deutschland*, 9 July 1993.
11. "Wenn der Leser trotzdem verwirrt innehält, mag das an der Intensität und Dichte des Romans liegen, der sich wie ein äquatorialer Dschungel auf den Seiten ausbreitet." Christian Lorenz, "Prächtig-faulig schillernde Welt der Tropen," *Hamburger Abendblatt*, date unknown. All reviews come from the archives of the publishers Suhrkamp, Insel, and Kiepenheuer & Witsch. On occasion, bibliographic information on the original articles in the archives is missing or unclear.
12. "Nonnenkloster, junge Priester, Sklaven, Orgien, die Sonne der Karibik," *Bild-Zeitung*, 19 September 1994.
13. "Vielleicht hat die augenblickliche Müdigkeit Südamerikas, die Müdigkeit Kubas, die Müdigkeit Haitis und ganz besonders die Müdigkeit Kolumbiens

das Buch zu dem Nebenwerk gemacht, das es ist." Andreas Kilb, "Tollwut und andere Kleinigkeiten," *Die Zeit*, 7 October 1994.
14. Dr. Vittoria Borsò, personal interview.
15. "Küchenzauber und Liebe: Noch einmal Mexiko," *Wiesbadener Tagblatt*, 12 November 1992.
16. "Bleibt diese magische Welt der Lateinamerikaner uns nicht fremd?" "Vermittler einer wunderbaren Welt," *Kempinski Journal*, September 1993. In *Kempinski Journal*'s interview with Curt Meyer-Clason, his answer was, "Nein, ich denke nicht. Denn das Wunderbare ist nicht aufgesetzt, ist keine Schminke, sondern kommt aus den Menschen selbst. Sie leben mit dem Zauber der Natur, mit dem Glauben an Offenbarungen und Enthüllungen, die es immer wieder gibt." While all this may be true, he not only does not answer the question, but I maintain that Meyer-Clason, as a specialist in the field, is not a representative of the average German reader as is, more likely, the interviewer who asked the question.
17. "... ein grandioses Filmszenario für einen farbenprächtigen historischen Film." Wolfram Schütte, "Maria von allen karibischen Engeln und Teufeln," *Frankfurter Rundschau*, 3 September 1994.
18. "'Von der Liebe und anderen Dämonen'—das ist große Literatur Marke zartbitter, in den bunten Farben des realismo magico [sic], des 'magischen Realismus.'" Matthias Grau, "Buchtip 6: Gabriel García Márquez, 'Von der Liebe und anderen Dämonen,'" Bayerisches Radio—Bayern 3, date unknown.
19. "Die farbenprächtige, auch magische Welt der Lateinamerikaner." "Erzählteppich mit vielen Farben," *Darmstädter Echo*, 2 September 1992.
20. "Der magische Realismus hatte seinen Zauber verloren." Lilo Solcher, "Brief an die Bewußtlose," *Allgäuer Zeitung*, 13 April 1995.
21. Hans-Jürgen Schmitt, "Meinungen über Bücher," Westdeutscher Rundfunk, 23 August 1994.
22. "Mexiko! Da erwartet man donnerndes Leben, in einer Farbigkeit, wie man sie bei uns gar nicht kennt!" Bernhard Lassahn, "Tango in der mörderischen Macho-Welt: Der preisgekrönte Roman von Angeles Mastretta," *Szene*, August 1988.
23. "Doch es wäre ein Mißverständnis zu glauben, solche Unbedingtheit der Liebe sei das Zeichen der ungebrochenen Vitalität einer jüngeren Welt fern von Europas übertünchter Höflichkeit." Gustav Seibt, "Von der Liebe und anderen Dämonen," *Frankfurter Allgemeine Zeitung*, 12 July 1994.
24. "Literarisch interessierte Leser [können] nun einen Eindruck von der Vitalität der mexikanischen Literatur gewinnen." Susanne Kleinert, "Was ist mexikanisch an Mexikos Literatur?" *Saarbrücker Zeitung*, 22 October 1992.
25. "Die 'Zwölf Geschichten aus der Fremde' lesen sich zuweilen wie eine Parabel der Konfrontation des hochtechnisierten, rationalistischen Europas mit Lateinamerika und seiner archaisch anmutenden Vorstellungswelt." Katharina Posada, "Sonderbare Pilgerreisen," *Rhein-Neckar-Zeitung*, 5 May 1993.
26. "[García Márquez] hat uns alle tropensüchtig gemacht, uns mit unheilbaren Leidenschaften infiziert und für die blutarme Prosa vieler deutscher Autoren verdorben." Hartmut Wilmes, "Tollwut, Teufel und Liebesqual," *Kölnische Rundschau*, 27 August 1994.
27. "Sparsame Hinweise auf historische und technische Entwicklungen suggerieren ein diffuses 'Es war einmal' zur Zeit der Revolution in Mexiko." Renate Miehe, "Bittere Kekse in der Küche," *Frankfurter Allgemeine Zeitung*, 24 November 1992.

28. "Doch es wird ein endloses Zeitalter der blutigen Revolutionen und Diktaturen werden, der ewigen Inquisitionen, Verfolgungen und Folterungen, der Todesfurcht und des Schreckens, und bis zum heutigen Tag flattern die Dämonen der Finsternis durch die Wirklichkeit Lateinamerikas." Gunar Ortlepp, "Satansbrut der Karibik," *Der Spiegel*, 22 August 1994.
29. Bärbel Flad, personal interview.
30. "[Lenz] hat sich im Bewußtsein bestimmter Käufer festgesetzt, was sich ... in permanenten Absatzerfolgen der betreffenden Bücher äußert." Burkhart R. Lauterbach, *Bestseller: Produktions- und Verkaufsstrategien* (Tübingen, 1979), p. 170.

NOTES ON CONTRIBUTORS

Berit Balzer is Associate Professor at the Universidad Complutense de Madrid from where she has received her Ph.D. She has written numerous articles on German and Spanish literature of the nineteenth and twentieth centuries, including essays on Günter Grass, Heinrich Heine, Otto Ludwig, Ingeborg Bachmann, and Christa Wolf. She authored *"Zwischen Himmel und Erde" de Otto Ludwig: la problemática del realismo literario alemán* (Madrid: Editorial Complutense, 1991) and edited *Heinrich Heine: Gedichte-Auswahl— Antología poética* (Madrid: Ediciones de la Torre, 1995).

Wayne Bowen is Assistant Professor of History at Ouachita Baptist University. He received his M.A. and Ph.D. in European History from Northwestern University. His articles and reviews have appeared in various journals, including *H-Net*, *German Studies Review*, *The Bulletin of Spanish and Portuguese Historical Studies*, and *Resisting the Holocaust* (Oxford and New York: Berg Publishers, 1998). He is currently revising his dissertation, *Spaniards and Nazi Germany: Visions of a New Order*, for publication.

Meg H. Brown is Associate Professor of German and Spanish at Murray State University. She received her Ph.D. from the University of Texas at Austin. Her research in Germany as a Fulbright Fellow led to the publication of *The Reception of Spanish American Fiction in West Germany 1981–1991: A Study of Best Sellers* (Tübingen: Niemeyer, 1994). She has delivered numerous conference presentations and has written various essays on Isabel Allende, Gabriel García Márquez, Ángeles Mastretta, Laura Esquivel, and Alfred Döblin.

Albrecht Classen is Professor of German at the University of Arizona. He received his Ph.D. from the University of Virginia. He is assistant editor of *Mediaevistik*, book review editor of the *Journal of the Rocky Mountain Medieval and Renaissance Association*, and the editor of *Tristania*. His has written numerous articles and edited several volumes. His many books include *Oswald von Wolkenstein* (Göttingen: Kümmerle, 1987), *Wolfram von Eschenbach* (Heidelberg: Winter-Universitätsverlag, 1990), *Tristan als Mönch* (Greifswald: Reineke, 1995), and *The German Volksbuch* (Lewiston, N.Y.: Edwin Mellen Press, 1995).

Friederike B. Emonds is Assistant Professor of German and a member of the Women's Studies Program at the University of Toledo. She received her Ph.D. from the University of California at Davis with a dissertation on nineteenth- and twentieth-century women dramatists. She has published articles on women's reactions to and representations of World War I and the Spanish Civil War in theater, dance, and literature. She is currently working on a book concerning women's representations of war and exile in the twentieth century.

Norman J. W. Goda is Associate Professor of History at Ohio University. He received his Ph.D. at the University of North Carolina, Chapel Hill. He has held a Fulbright Graduate Fellowship at the Universität Bonn and Universität Freiburg (1989). He has written essays on international relations during World War II for the *International History Review* and the *Journal of Contemporary History*. His book *Tomorrow the World: Hitler, Northwest Africa, and the Struggle for Global Supremacy* appeared in 1998 (College Station: Texas A&M University Press).

Rachel J. Halverson is Associate Professor of German at Washington State University. She received her Ph.D. from the University of Texas at Austin. She has published articles on Jurek Becker, Günter de Bruyn, Siegfried Lenz, and the *Historikerstreit*.

Cameron M. K. Hewitt is a 1998 Phi Beta Kappa graduate of Ohio Wesleyan University and a student of both Spanish and German literature.

Conrad Kent is Professor of Modern Foreign Languages and Humanities/Classics at Ohio Wesleyan University. He earned his M.A. and Ph.D. at Harvard University, and he has taught at Harvard, Amherst, and Ohio Wesleyan. He authored *La Plaza Mayor de Salamanca: historia fotográfica de un espacio público* (Salamanca: Ayuntamiento de Salamanca and Junta de Castilla y León, 1998) and, with Dennis Prindle, *Park Güell* (New York:

Princeton Architectural Press, 1993). He has edited *Salamanca en la edad de oro* (Salamanca: Librería Cervantes, 1995), *Salamanca en el siglo XX* (Salamanca: Librería Cervantes, 1998), and, with María Dolores de la Calle, *Visiones salmantinas,1898/1998* (Salamanca: Universidad de Salamanca and Ohio Wesleyan University, 1998).

Shirley King received her Ph.D. from the University of Washington in Seattle and has studied at universities in Madrid, Mexico City, Frankfurt, and Berlin. Formerly an Associate Professor of Spanish, she is currently owner of South of the Border, an interpreting and cultural consulting agency. Her publications include the article "*San Manuel Bueno* and Unamuno's Reading of Hauptmann" in *Revista de Estudios Hispánicos*.

John W. Kronik is Professor of Romance Studies at Cornell University and has held visiting appointments at the University of California, Berkeley and Irvine; Brigham Young; Columbia; Colorado; Purdue; Syracuse; and the Colby and Middlebury Summer Schools of Spanish. He served as editor of *PMLA* from 1985 to 1992 and of *Anales Galdosianos* from 1985 to 1990. His various authored books include *La Farsa (1927–1936) y el teatro español de preguerra* (Chapel Hill: University of North Carolina, 1971). With Jeanne P. Brownlow, he has edited *Intertextual Pursuits: Literary Mediations in Modern Spanish Narrative* (Lewisburg, Penn.: Bucknell University Press; London: Associated University Presses, 1998). See also Susan L. Fischer, *Self-Conscious Art: A Tribute to John W. Kronik* (Lewisburg, Penn.: Bucknell University Press; London: Associated University Presses, 1998).

Francisco LaRubia-Prado is Professor of Spanish at Georgetown University. He has written two books on Miguel de Unamuno—*Alegorías de la voluntad* (Madrid: Libertarias/Prodhufi, 1996) and *Unamuno y la vida como ficción* (Madrid: Gredos, 1999). He is also the editor of several scholarly works and the author of many articles.

Donald E. Lenfest is Professor of Modern Foreign Languages at Ohio Wesleyan University. He earned his Ph.D. at the University of Illinois. He has been a Fulbright Lecturer in linguistics at the Universidad Católica in Santiago de Chile and at the Escuela Politécnica in Quito, Ecuador. He has contributed several essays on linguistics to *Hispania* and other journals.

Nelson R. Orringer is Professor of Spanish and Comparative Literature and Chair of the Spanish Ph.D. Program at the University of Connecticut. Brown University awarded him his Ph.D. and, years later, the 1999 Distinguished Graduate Alumnus Award. He has held two Fulbright Postdoctoral Research Fellowships. His books include *Ortega y sus fuentes germánicas* (Madrid: Gredos, 1979), its sequel *Nuevas fuentes germánicas de ¿Qué es filosofía? de Ortega* (Madrid: Consejo Superior de Investigaciones Científicas, 1984), *Unamuno y los protestantes liberales* (Madrid: Gredos, 1985), *La aventura de curar: la antropología médica de Pedro Laín Entralgo* (Barcelona: Galaxia Gutenberg—Circulo de Lectores, 1997), and *Ángel Ganivet (1865–1898): la inteligencia escindida* (Madrid: Ediciones del Orto, 1998). He has authored 110 articles comparing contemporary Spanish thought with that of Kant, Goethe, Nietzsche, Simmel, and Scheler.

Joseph F. Patrouch is Associate Professor of Early Modern European History at Florida International University. He received his Ph.D. from the University of California, Berkeley, and he has been a Fulbright Student at the Johannes Kepler Universität, Linz, Austria. He has also been a Fulbright Research Scholar affiliated with the Viennese Institut für die Erforschung der frühen Neuzeit. He has written various essays in German, Czech, Austrian, and U.S. publications.

Ana María Rodríguez-Vivaldi is Associate Professor of Spanish and Graduate Studies Advisor at Washington State University. She received her Ph.D. at the University of Massachusetts at Amherst. Her publications include essays on contemporary Latin American narrative, theater, and film.

Magdalena S. Sánchez is Associate Professor of History at Gettysburg College. She received her Ph.D. from the Johns Hopkins University. She is the author of *The Empress, the Queen, and the Nun: Women and Power at the Court of Philip III of Spain* (Baltimore: Johns Hopkins University Press, 1998). With Alain Saint-Saëns, she edited *Spanish Women in the Golden Age: Images and Realities* (Westport, Conn.: Greenwood Press, 1996).

Rachel Schmidt is Associate Professor of Spanish at the University of Calgary. Her recent publications include the book *Critical Images: The Canonization of Don Quixote through Illustrated Editions of the Eighteenth Century* (Montreal and Kingston: McGill-Queen's University Press, 1999).

Contributors | 471

Vera Stegmann is Associate Professor of German at Lehigh University in Bethlehem, Pennsylvania. She received an M.A. in Spanish at the University of Missouri and a Ph.D. in German at Indiana University. She specializes in twentieth-century German literature, German theater, comparative arts, and German-Romance cultural and literary relations. She edited *Communications from the International Brecht Society* from 1991 to 1995, and authored the book *Das epische Musiktheater bei Strawinsky und Brecht* (New York: P. Lang, 1991), as well as articles on Bertolt Brecht, Ferruccio Busoni, Thomas Bernhard, and Kurt Weill.

Christopher D. Storrs is Lecturer in History at the University of Dundee, Scotland. He received his M.A. from the London School of Economics and his D.Phil. from the University of London. He is the author of essays on English and continental diplomatic history and the European nobility from the sixteenth through the seventeenth centuries.

Henry W. Sullivan is Professor of Spanish and Portuguese in Golden Age Literature at Tulane University. A graduate of Queen's College, Oxford, he received his Ph.D. from Harvard University and has held fellowships from the National Endowment for the Humanities, the Alexander von Humboldt Foundation, and the Guggenheim Foundation. He has also been a Visiting Fellow at Clare Hall College, Cambridge University. His various authored books include *Juan del Encina* (Boston: Twayne, 1976), *Tirso de Molina and the Drama of the Counter Reformation* (Amsterdam: Rodopi, 1976), *Calderón in the German Lands* (Cambridge and New York: Cambridge University Press, 1983), *The Beatles with Lacan: Rock 'n' Roll as Requiem for the Modern Age* (New York: P. Lang, 1995), and *Grotesque Purgatory: A Study of Cervantes's Don Quixote, Part II* (University Park: Pennsylvania State University Press, 1996).

Robert H. Whealey is Associate Professor of History at Ohio University. He received his Ph.D. from the University of Michigan. He has published *Hitler and Spain: The Nazi Role in the Spanish Civil War* (Lexington, Ky: University Press of Kentucky, 1989). He has written numerous articles on the Spanish Civil War for scholarly journals and encyclopedias.

Thomas K. Wolber is Assistant Professor of Modern Foreign Languages at Ohio Wesleyan University. He received his M.A. and Ph.D. from the University of Wisconsin, Madison. He has written articles and reviewed books on Germanic culture and literature in the *GDR Bulletin, German Studies Review, Germanic Notes and Review, The Journal of the Gypsy Lore Society, Habsburg-L, The Historian, Lessing Yearbook, Modern Austrian Literature, Monatshefte für den deutschen Unterricht, Society for German-American Studies Newsletter, Trans-Lit, Die Unterrichtspraxis,* and the *Women in German Newsletter.*

Patricia D. Zecevic, who received her Ph.D. from the University of Glasgow, is Lecturer in Hispanic Studies at the University of Glasgow and Assistant Editor of the *Bulletin of Hispanic Studies*. She has written articles on German and Hispanic studies, and on the cultural relations between the two. She has also written on Portuguese language and culture, Spanish Golden Age literature, and Women's Studies. Her forthcoming book is a study of the reception of the Spanish Kabbalah in sixteenth-century Spain and eighteenth-century Germany.

BIBLIOGRAPHY

This interdisciplinary bibliography draws from the essays of the volume and other reliable sources. Although no such list can be definitive, the selection has been intended to encourage and facilitate further research into the cross-fertilization of culture and social life in the Germanic and Hispanic worlds. The most exhaustive bibliography of earlier references remains Gerhart Hoffmeister, *Spanien und Deutschland: Geschichte und Dokumentation der literarischen Beziehungen* (Berlin: E. Schmidt, 1976).

Abendroth, Hans Henning. *Hitler in der spanischen Arena: Die deutsch-spanischen Beziehungen im Spannungsfeld der europäischen Interessenpolitik vom Ausbruch des Bürgerkrieges bis zum Ausbruch des Weltkrieges, 1936–1939.* Paderborn: Schöningh, 1973.
———. *Mittelsmann zwischen Franco und Hitler: Johannes Bernhardt erinnert 1936.* Marktheidenfeld: Schleunung, 1978.
Actas de las primeras jornadas de hispanistas en Austria: Viena, 19–20 de mayo de 1995. Vienna: Edition Praesens, 1996.
Actas del simposio sobre "La imagen de España en la ilustración alemana," Madrid, 22 a 24 de mayo de 1991. Madrid: Görres-Gesellschaft, 1991.
Adalbert of Bavaria. *Mariana de Neoburgo, reina de España.* Madrid, 1938.
Aktuelle Kunst aus Kuba. Stuttgart: Institut für Auslandsbeziehungen, 1990.
Alas, Leopoldo. *El derecho y la moralidad: determinación del concepto del derecho y sus relaciones con el de la moralidad.* Madrid: Casa Editorial de Medina, 1878.
———. *Obras selectas de Leopoldo Alas "Clarín."* Madrid: Biblioteca Nueva, 1947.
———. "Prólogo." In *Goethe: ensayos críticos*, 3rd rev. ed. Ed. Urbano González Serrano, pp. 5–26. Madrid: Librería Internacional de Fernández Villegas y Cía., 1900.
———. *La Regenta.* Trans. John Rutherford. Athens, Ga.: University of Georgia Press, 1984.
Alba Vega, Carlos, comp. *México y Alemania: dos países en transición.* Mexico City: El Colegio de México, 1996.
Alpert, Michael. *A New International History of the Spanish Civil War.* New York: St. Martin's Press, 1994.
Die Alte und die Neue Welt: Mittel- und Südamerika in alten Büchern. Ausstellung zur 500. Wiederkehr der Landung von Christoph Columbus in Amerika. Ed. Christina Hofmann-Randall, Hans-Joachim König, and Peer Schmidt. Eichstätt: Universitätsbibliothek Eichstätt, 1992.

Altermatt, Urs, Adrian Holderegger, and Pedro Ramírez, eds. *Zur Wieder-Entdekkung der gemeinsamen Geschichte: 500 Jahre Lateinamerika und Europa.* Freiburg [Switzerland]: Universitätsverlag, 1992.

Alvarez Guerrero, Osvaldo. *El radicalismo y la ética social: Irigoyen y el krausismo. Orígenes ideológicos de la UCR.* Fuerte General Roca, Argentinia: Editorial de la Patagonia, 1983.

———. *El radicalismo y la ética social: Irigoyen y el krausismo.* Buenos Aires: Editorial Leviatán, 1986.

Amadis. Frankfurt: Hieronymus Feyrabend, 1569–72. Reprint Berne and New York: Peter Lang, 1988ff.

Anderson, Vernon Lockwood. *Hugo von Hofmannsthal and Pedro Calderón de la Barca: A Comparative Study.* Ph.D. Diss. Stanford University, 1954.

Andics, Hellmut. *Die Frauen der Habsburger.* Vienna: Jugend und Volk, 1991.

Andres, Stefan. *Wir sind Utopia: Novelle.* Berlin: Riemerschmidt, 1943.

Angulo y Heredia, Antonio. *Goethe y Schiller: su vida, sus obras y su influencia en Alemania.* Madrid: M. Galiano, 1863.

Archila, Ricardo. *Alemania y Venezuela: vínculos médicos.* Caracas, 1978.

Aregger, Agnes J. *Heine und Larra: Wirkungsgeschichte eines deutschen Schriftstellers in Spanien.* Zurich: Verlag Reihe W, 1981.

Areilza, José María de, and Fernando María Castiella. *Reivindicaciones de España.* 2nd ed. Madrid: Instituto de Estudios Politicos, 1941.

Arens, Arnold. *Zur Tradition und Gestaltung des Cid-Stoffes.* Frankfurt: Akademische Verlagsgesellschaft, 1975.

Armamento de los ejércitos de Carlos V en la guerra de Alemania, 1546–1547. Ed. Servicio Histórico Militar, Estado Major Central del Ejército. Madrid: Imprenta de Servicio Geográfico del Ejército, 1947.

Armbruster, Claudius, and Karin Hopfe, eds. *Horizontverschiebungen: Interkulturelles Verstehen und Heterogenität in der Romania. Festschrift für Karsten Garscha zum 60. Geburtstag.* Tübingen: Narr, 1998.

Arráez Cerdá, Juan. *Los cazadores de la Legión Condor.* Valladolid: Quirón Ediciones, 1993.

Arroyo, Ciriaco M. *El sistema de Ortega y Gasset.* Madrid: Alcalá, 1968.

Asch, Ronald G., and Adolf M. Birke, eds. *Princes, Patronage, and the Nobility: The Court at the Beginning of the Modern Age, c. 1450–1650.* London: Oxford University Press, 1991.

Ashoff, Guido. *Argentina: Economic Cooperation with the Federal Republic of Germany and the European Community. Problems and Prospects.* Berlin: German Development Institute, 1985.

Atkins, Stuart. "Goethe, Calderón and Faust: Der Tragödie zweiter Teil." *Germanic Review,* vol. 28 (1953), pp. 83–98.

Aub, Max. *Manual de historia de la literatura española.* Madrid: Akal, 1974.

———. "Notas acerca de Heine." In *Pruebas,* pp. 9–68. Madrid: Ciencia Nueva, 1967.

Baasner, Frank, ed. *Spanische Literatur—Literatur Europas: Wido Hempel zum 65. Geburtstag.* Tübingen: Niemeyer, 1995.

Balzer, Berit. "*Die Blechtrommel* von Günter Grass: Ein moderner Schelmenroman?" In *Der deutsche und spanische Schelmenroman.* Ed. Margit Raders and Luisa Schelling. Madrid: Ediciones del Orto, 1995.

———. "Menschenhaß aus Kunstliebe: E. T. A. Hoffmanns Hund Berganza vor dem Hintergrund des Cervantinischen Textes," *Revista de Filología Alemana,* vol. 3 (1996).

Barber, Sigmund J. *"Amadis de Gaule" and the German Enlightenment*. New York: Peter Lang, 1984.
Barton, E. R. *Die spanische Literatur in Deutschland im Zeitalter des Barock: Ein Forschungsbericht*. Ph.D. Diss. University of Nebraska, 1972.
Bastian, Gert, and Petra Kelly, eds. *Guernica und die Deutschen: Dokumentation einer gescheiterten Wiedergutmachung*. Darmstadt: Luchterhand, 1992.
Bauer, Matthias. *Der Schelmenroman*. Stuttgart: Metzler, 1994.
Bauer, Therese. *Spaniens Himmel und Hölle: Erlebnisse einer Deutschen in Spanien in den Jahren 1915–1936*. Heilbronn: Eugen Salzer, 1938.
Bauschinger, Sigrid, and Susan L. Cocalis. *"Neue Welt" / "Dritte Welt": Interkulturelle Beziehungen Deutschlands zu Lateinamerika und der Karibik*. Tübingen and Basel: Francke, 1994.
Becker, Félix, comp. *América Latina en las letras y ciencias sociales alemanas*. Caracas: Monte Avila Editores, 1988.
Becker, Heribert, et al. *Lateinamerika und der Surrealismus: Museum Bochum, 22. Mai–18. Juli 1993*. 2 vols. Bochum: Kordt, 1993.
Becker-Cantarino, Barbara. "The Rediscovery of Spain in Enlightened and Romantic Germany." In *Monatshefte*, vol. 72 (1980), pp. 121–134.
Beckett, Bonnie A. *The Reception of Pablo Neruda's Works in the German Democratic Republic*. Berne: Peter Lang, 1981.
Behler, Ernst. "The Reception of Calderón among the German Romantics." In *Studies in Romanticism*, vol. 20 (1981), pp. 437–460.
Benecke, Dieter W., et al. *Die Beziehungen der Bundesrepublik Deutschland zu Lateinamerika: Bestandsaufnahme und Empfehlungen*. Bonn: Friedrich-Ebert-Stiftung, 1983.
———. *The Relations between the Federal Republic of Germany and Latin America*. Bonn: Friedrich-Ebert-Stiftung, 1984.
Beneyto, José Maria. *Politische Theologie als politische Theorie: Eine Untersuchung zur Rechts- und Staatstheorie Carl Schmitts und zu ihrer Wirklungsgeschichte in Spanien*. Berlin: Duncker & Humblot, 1983.
Beng, Dieter. *Die sozialen Bewegungen in Lateinamerika*. Hamburg: VSA-Verlag, 1998.
Benito-Vessels, Carmen, and Michael Zappala, eds. *The Picaresque: A Symposium on the Rogue's Tale*. Cranbury, N.J.: University of Delaware Press, 1994.
Bensch, K., and R. Tießler. *Der Jakobsweg nach Santiago de Compostela: Spurensuche auf einer großen Pilgerstraße*. Darmstadt: Wissenschaftliche Buchgesellschaft, 1991.
Benson, Frederick R. *Writers in Arms: The Literary Impact of the Spanish Civil War. Hemingway, Koestler, Malraux, Bernanos, Orwell, Regler*. New York: New York University Press, 1967.
Berchem, Theodor, and Siegfried Sudhof, eds. *Pedro Calderón de la Barca: Vorträge anläßlich der Jahrestagung der Görres-Gesellschaft 1978*. Berlin: E. Schmidt, 1983.
Berenger, Jean. *Histoire de l'Empire des Habsbourg, 1273–1918*. Paris: Fayard, 1990.
———. *A History of the Habsburg Empire, 1700–1918*. Trans. C. A. Simpson. White Plains: Longman, 1997.
Bergel, Lienhard. "Cervantes in Germany." In *Cervantes across the Centuries*. Ed. Angel Flores and Maír José Benardete. New York: Gordion Press, 1969.
Berlau, Ruth. *Living for Brecht*. Ed. Hans Bunge, trans. Geoffrey Skelton. New York: Fromm, 1987.
Berman, Antoine. *L'épreuve de l'étranger: culture et traduction dans l'Allemagne romantique. Herder, Goethe, Schlegel, Novalis, Humboldt, Schleiermacher, Hölderlin*. Paris: Gallimard, 1984.

———. *The Experience of the Foreign: Culture and Translation in Romantic Germany.* Trans. S. Heyvaert. Albany: State University of New York Press, 1992.
Bernecker, Walther L. *Krieg in Spanien, 1936–1939.* Darmstadt: Wissenschaftliche Buchgesellschaft, 1991.
———. "Neutralität wider Willen: Spaniens verhinderter Kriegseintritt." In *Kriegsausbruch 1939: Beteiligte, Betroffene, Neutrale,* pp. 153–177. Ed. Helmut Altrichter and Josef Becker. Munich: Beck, 1989.
———. *Die Schweiz und Lateinamerika im 20. Jahrhundert: Aspekte ihrer Wirtschafts- und Finanzbeziehungen.* Frankfurt and New York: Peter Lang, 1997.
———. *Spaniens Geschichte seit dem Bürgerkrieg.* 3rd ed. Munich: Beck, 1997.
Bernecker, Walther L., ed. *España y Alemania en la edad contemporánea.* Frankfurt: Vervuert, 1992.
———. *Handbuch der Geschichte Lateinamerikas.* Stuttgart: Klett-Cotta, 1992ff.
Bernecker, Walther L., and Klaus Dirscherl, eds. *Spanien heute.* 3rd ed. Darmstadt: Wissenschaftliche Buchgesellschaft, 1998.
Bernecker, Walther L., and Thomas Fischer, eds. *Unheimliche Geschäfte: Schweizer Rüstungsexporte nach Lateinamerika im 20. Jahrhundert.* Zurich: Chronos, 1991.
Bernecker, Walther L., and Gertrut Krömer, eds. *Die Wiederentdeckung Lateinamerikas: Die Erfahrung des Subkontinents in Reiseberichten des 19. Jahrhunderts.* Frankfurt: Vervuert, 1997.
Bernecker, Walther L., and José Manuel López de Abiada, eds. *Die Lateinamerikanistik in der Schweiz.* Frankfurt: Vervuert, 1993.
Bernecker, Walther L., and Horst Pietschmann. *Geschichte Spaniens: Von der frühen Neuzeit bis zur Gegenwart.* 1st ed.: Stuttgart: Kohlhammer, 1993. 2nd ed.: Stuttgart: Kohlhammer, 1996.
Bernhofer, Martin. *Valle-Inclán und die spanische Kultur im Silbernen Zeitalter.* Darmstadt: Wissenschaftliche Buchgesellschaft, 1992.
Berschin, Walter, and Arnold Rothe, eds. *Ernst Robert Curtius: Werk, Wirkung, Zukunftsperspektiven. Heidelberger Symposion zum hundertsten Geburtstag 1986.* Heidelberg: C. Winter, 1989.
Bertrand, Jean-Jacques Achille. *Cervantes en el país de Fausto.* Trans. José Perdomo García. Madrid: Ediciones Cultura Hispánica, 1950.
———. *Cervantes et le romantisme allemand.* Paris: F. Alcan, 1914.
———. "Encuentros de F. Schiller con España." *Clavileño,* vol. 6, no. 35 (1955), pp. 38–42.
———. *Ludwig Tieck et le théâtre espagnol.* Paris: R. Rieder & Cie, 1914.
Bertuch, F. J. *Magazin der spanischen und portugiesischen Literatur,* vols. 1–3. Karlsruhe: Schmieder, 1778–1785.
Beser, Sergio. *Leopoldo Alas: crítico literario.* Madrid: Gredos, 1968.
Beumelberg, Werner. *Kampf um Spanien: Die Geschichte der Legion Condor.* Berlin: Stalling, 1940.
Beutler, Gisela, ed. *"Sieh den Fluß der Sterne strömen": Hispanoamerikanische Lyrik der Gegenwart.* Darmstadt: Wissenschaftliche Buchgesellschaft, 1990.
Beyer, Paul. *Der junge Heine.* Berlin: Grote, 1911.
Die Beziehungen zwischen Lateinamerika und der Bundesrepublik Deutschland = Las Relaciones América Latina—República Federal de Alemania. 2nd ed. Hamburg: Institut für Iberoamerika-Kunde, 1980.
Bieber, León Enrique. *Las relaciones económicas de Bolivia con Alemania, 1880–1920.* Berlin: Colloquium, 1984.
Biha, Otto. *Spanien zwischen Tod und Geburt.* [Germany]: 1937.

Billhardt, Thomas, et al., eds. *Chile: Gesang und Bericht*. Halle: Mitteldeutscher Verlag, 1975.
Bitterli, Urs. *Die Entdeckung Amerikas: Von Kolumbus bis Alexander von Humboldt*. 4th ed. Munich: C. H. Beck, 1992.
Bjornson, Richard. *The Picaresque Hero in European Fiction*. Madison: University of Wisconsin Press, 1977.
Blei, Franz. "Miguel de Unamuno." In *Schriften in Auswahl*, pp. 230–234. Munich: Biederstein, 1960.
Bley, Wulf. *Das Buch der Spanienflieger: Die Feuertaufe der neuen deutschen Luftwaffe*. Leipzig: Hafe & Koehler, 1939.
Blum, Klara. "Bäuerin in der Sierra." *Das Wort: Literarische Monatsschrift*, vol. 9 (1937), p. 87.
———. "Letzte Fahrt." *Das Wort: Literarische Monatsschrift*, vol. 10 (1938), p. 17.
———. *Die Antwort*. Moscow: Iskra Revoluzii, 1939.
Bodo Uhse, Eduard Claudius: Abriß der Spanienliteratur. Ed. Kollektiv für Literaturgeschichte im Volkseigenen Verlag Volk und Wissen. Berlin: Volk und Wissen, 1961.
Bofill y Ferro, Jaime, ed. *La poesía alemana de los primitivos al romanticismo*. Trans. Jaime Bofill y Ferro and Fernando Gutiérrez. Barcelona: J. Janés, 1947.
Bollinger, Armin. *Drei Körner von gelbem Mais: Neue Erzählungen aus Lateinamerika*. Zurich: NZZ-Buchverlag; Graz, etc.: Styria, 1976.
———. *El Curandero: Der Wunderheiler und andere Erzählungen aus Südamerika*. Wald: Im Waldgut, 1980.
Bolzern, Rudolf. *Spanien, Mailand und die katholische Eidgenossenschaft: Militärische, wirtschaftliche und politische Beziehungen zur Zeit des Gesandten Alfonso Casati, 1594–1621*. Lucerne: Rex, 1982.
Bonilla y San Martín, Adolfo. *Las leyendas de Wagner en la literatura española: con un apéndice sobre el Santo Grial en el "Lanzarote del Lago" castellano*. Madrid: Asociación Wagneriana de Madrid, 1913.
Boris, Dieter. *Arbeiterbewegung in Lateinamerika*. Marburg: Verlag Arbeiterbewegung und Gesellschaftswissenschaft, 1990.
———. *Die sozialen Bewegungen in Lateinamerika*. Hamburg: VSA-Verlag, 1998.
Borkenau, Franz. *Kampfplatz Spanien: Politische und soziale Konflikte im Spanischen Bürgerkrieg. Ein Augenzeugenbericht*. Stuttgart: Klett/Cotta, 1986.
Born, Sigrid, and Birgit Reuter. *Deutsche Zusammenarbeit mit Lateinamerika: Studium in Deutschland, Wissenschaftleraustausch und Hochschulkooperation für künftige Führungskräfte*. Bonn: Inter Nationes, n.d.
Bosse, Monika, and André Stoll, eds. *Theatrum mundi: Figuren der Barockästhetik in Spanien und Hispano-Amerika. Literatur, Kunst, Bildmedien*. Bielefeld: Aisthesis, 1997.
Branceforte, Charlotte L. *Fridericus Berghius' Partial Latin Translation of Lazarillo de Tormes and Its Relationship to the Early Lazarillo Translations in Germany: Study and Edition*. Madison, Wis.: Hispanic Seminary of Medieval Studies, 1983.
Brandáriz, Gustavo A., et al. *Alemania en la Argentina*. Buenos Aires: Manrique Zago Ediciones, 1997.
Brans, J. V. L. *Hieronymus Bosch (El Bosco) en el Prado y en el Escorial*. Barcelona: Omega, 1948.
Bräutigam, Thomas. *Hispanistik im Dritten Reich: Eine wissenschaftsgeschichtliche Studie*. Frankfurt: Vervuert, 1997.
Brecht, Bertolt. *Werke: Große kommentierte Berliner und Frankfurter Ausgabe*. Frankfurt: Suhrkamp, 1993.

Bredel, Willi. *Spanienkrieg*. 2 vols. Ed. Manfred Hahn. Berlin and Weimar: Aufbau, 1977.
Brinkmann Scheihing, Beatriz. *Spanische Romanzen in der Übersetzung von Diez, Geibel und von Schack: Analyse und Vergleich*. Marburg: N.G. Elwert, 1975.
Brockstedt, Jürgen. *Die Schiffahrts- und Handelsbeziehungen Schleswig-Holsteins nach Lateinamerika, 1815–1848*. Cologne: Böhlau, 1975.
Brown, Cedric, and Therese Fischer-Seidel, eds. *Cultural Negotiations: Sichtweisen des Anderen*. Tübingen and Basel: Francke, 1998.
Brown, Meg H. *The Reception of Spanish American Fiction in West Germany 1981–1991: A Study of Best Sellers*. Tübingen: Niemeyer, 1994.
———. "Die Rezeption von Laura Esquivels *Como agua para chocolate* in Deutschland: Schäumend oder bittersüß?" In *Actas del VIII Congreso Latinoamericano de Estudios Germanísticos*, pp. 248–255. Ed. Dietrich and Marlene Rall. Mexico: Diseño Editorial, Universidad Nacional Autónoma de México, 1996.
Broyles, Yolanda J. *The German Response to Latin American Literature and the Reception of Jorge Luis Borges and Pablo Neruda*. Heidelberg: C. Winter, 1981.
Brücker, Christian Ludwig. *Donauschwaben in Nordamerika, in Südamerika und in Australien*. Munich: Donauschwäbische Kulturstiftung, 1990.
Brüggemann, Werner. *Cervantes und die Figur des Don Quijote in Kunstanschauung und Dichtung der deutschen Romantik*. Münster, Westfalen: Aschendorff, 1958.
———. *Spanisches Theater und deutsche Romantik*. Münster, Westfalen: Aschendorff, 1964ff.
Bumke, Joachim. *Die romanisch-deutschen Literaturbeziehungen im Mittelalter: Ein Überblick*. Heidelberg: C. Winter, 1967.
Die Bundesrepublik Deutschland und Lateinamerika: Dokumentation. Bonn: Auswärtiges Amt, 1987.
Burdick, Charles B. *Germany's Military Strategy and Spain in World War II*. Syracuse, N.Y.: Syracuse University Press, 1968.
———. "'Moro': The Resupply of German Submarines in Spain, 1939–1942." *Contemporary European History*, vol. 3 (1970), pp. 256–284.
Burton, Julianne, ed. *Cinema and Social Change in Latin America: Conversations with Filmmakers*. Austin, Tex.: University of Texas Press, 1986.
Busch, Fritz Otto. *Kampf vor Spaniens Küsten: Deutsche Marine im spanischen Bürgerkriege*. Berlin and Leipzig, 1939.
Busta Vargas, Jorge del. *La filosofía de Oswald Spengler*. Lima, Peru, 1944.
Bynum, Caroline Walker. *Holy Feast and Holy Fast: The Religious Significance of Food to Medieval Women*. Berkeley: University of California Press, 1987.
Cabezas, Juan Antonio. "*Clarín*": *el provinciano universal*. Madrid: Espasa-Calpe, 1962.
Caller Iberico, Clorinda. *María Reiche y los dioses de Nazca = Maria Reiche and Nazda's Gods*. Lima, Peru: Editorial Horizonte, 1984.
Cámara de Comercio Alemana para España, 1917–1967: 50 años al servicio del comercio hispana-aleman = Deutsche Handelskammer für Spanien, 1917–1967: 50 Jahre im Dienste der deutsch-spanischen Wirtschaft. Madrid: Gráficas Hispano, 1967.
Campe, Elisabeth. *Aus dem Leben von Johann Diederich Gries*. Leipzig: Brockhaus, 1855.
Canedo, Lino Gómez. *Don Juan de Carvajal, un español al servicio de la Santa Sede: Cardenal de Sant'Angelo legado en Alemania y Hungría, 1399?-1469*. Madrid: Consejo Superior de Investigaciones Científicas, Instituto Jerónimo Zurita, 1947.
Canicio, Víctor. *Vida de un emigrante español: el testimonio auténtico de un obrero que emigró a Alemania*. Barcelona: GEDISA, 1979.

Cantarutti, Giulia, and Hans Schumacher, eds. *Germania, Romania: Studien zur Begegnung der deutschen und romanischen Kultur*. Frankfurt: Lang, 1990.
Carande, Ramón. *Carlos V y sus banqueros*. 3 vols. Madrid: Socieded de Estudios y Publicaciones, 1949.
Carandell, José María. *Hermann Hesse*. Barcelona: Dopesa, 1975.
―――. *Peter Weiss: Poesía y verdad*. Barcelona: Taurus, 1969.
Cassirer, Ernst. *The Philosophy of the Enlightenment*. Trans. Fritz Koelln and James Pettegrove. Princeton: Princeton University Press, 1968.
Castillejo Gorráiz, Miguel. *El fundador del krausismo, etapa andaluza*. Córdoba: Banco Occidental, 1980.
Charles-Roux, François. *Cinq mois tragiques aux affaires étrangères (21 mai–1er novembre 1940)*. Paris: Plon, 1949.
Christmann, Hans Helmut. *Ernst Robert Curtius und die deutschen Romanisten*. Mainz: Akademie der Wissenschaften und der Literatur; Stuttgart: F. Steiner Verlag Wiesbaden, 1987.
Chuboda, Bohdan. *Spain and the Empire, 1519–1643*. New York: Octagon, 1977.
Cichon, Peter, ed. *Das sprachliche Erbe des Kolonialismus in Afrika und Lateinamerika: Bestandaufnahme und Perspektiven aus romanistischer Sicht*. Vienna: Edition Praesens, 1996.
Cierva, Ricardo de la. *Hendaya: Punto Final*. Barcelona: Planeta, 1981.
Claudius, Eduard. *Grüne Oliven und nackte Berge*. Zurich: Steinberg, 1945.
Coello, Francisco. *La conferencia de Berlin y la cuestión de las Carolinas: discursos pronunciados en la Sociedad Geográfica de Madrid*. Madrid: Fortanet, 1885.
El Comercio entre México y Alemania y sus corredores de transporte. Sanfandila, Qro: Instituto Mexicano del Transporte, Secretaría de Comunicaciones y Transportes, 1995.
Conde, José Antonio. *Geschichte der Herrschaft der Mauren in Spanien*. Trans. K. Rutschmann. Karlsruhe, 1824.
Constante, Mariano. *Los años rojos: españoles en los campos nazis*. Barcelona: Ediciones Martínez Roca, 1974.
―――. *Yo fui ordenanza de los SS*. Barcelona: Editiones Martínez Roca, 1976.
Conta, Manfred von. *Reportagen aus Lateinamerika*. Zurich: Diogenes, 1982.
Coreth, Anna. *Pietas Austriaca: Österreichische Frömmigkeit im Barock*. 2nd ed. Vienna: Verlag für Geschichte und Politik Wien, 1982.
Corral Salvador, Carlos Manuel, and Mariano Baena del Alcázar, eds. *Constitución y acuerdos iglesia-estado: actas del II Simposio Hispano-Alemán*. Madrid: UPCM, 1988.
Corral Salvador, Carlos Manuel, and Franco Díaz de Cerio. *El conflicto sobre las Islas Carolinas entre España y Alemania (1885): la mediación internacional de León XIII*. Madrid: Complutense, Universidad Pontificia Comillas, 1995.
Corum, J. S. "The Luftwaffe and the Coalition Air War in Spain, 1936–1939." In *Airpower: Theory and Practice*. Ed. John Gooch, pp. 68–90. London: Frank Cass, 1995.
Cossío, José María de. *Cincuenta años de poesía española, 1850–1950*. 2 vols. Madrid: Espasa-Calpe, 1960.
Costa, René de. *The Poetry of Pablo Neruda*. Cambridge: Harvard University Press, 1979.
Costa, Luis, et al., eds. *German and International Perspectives on the Spanish Civil War: The Aesthetics of Partisanship*. Columbia, S.C.: Camden House, 1992.
Crantford, Carey S. "German Lyric Poetry in Spanish Translation through 1915." *Dissertation Abstracts*, vol. 22 (1962), pp. 3658–3659.

Curtius, Ernst Robert. *Essays on European Literature*. Trans. Michael Kowal. Princeton: Princeton University Press, 1973.

———. *Europäische Literatur und lateinisches Mittelalter*. Berne: Francke, 1948.

———. *Kritische Essays zur europäischen Literaturgeschichte*. Berne: Francke, 1950.

———. "Unamuno oder die Philosophie des Tragischen." *Neue Zürcher Zeitung*. 8 October 1925.

DeBruck, Edelgard E., and William C. McDonald, eds. *The Current State of Research in Fifteenth-Century Literature: Germania-Romania*. Lewiston, N.Y.: Mellen, 1996.

Demokratische Post: Organo de los Antinazis Alemandes de Mexico y Centro-America. Mexico: Carmen Otero y Gama. [Succeeds *Alemania libre* and its supplement *El Germano-Mexico*.]

Deterning, Susanne. *Kolumbus, Cortes, Montezuma: Die Entdeckung und Eroberung Lateinamerikas als literarische Sujets in der Aufklärung und im 20. Jahrhundert*. Weimar: VDG Verlag, 1996.

Detwiler, Donald S. *Hitler, Franco und Gibraltar: Die Frage des spanischen Eintritts in den Zweiten Weltkrieg*. Wiesbaden: Steiner, 1962.

Deutsche kämpfen in Spanien. Ed. Legion Condor. Berlin: Wilhelm, 1939.

Deutschland und Mexiko: Perspektiven für das Jahr 2000. Bericht der Kommission Mexiko-Deutschland 2000. Hamburg: Ibero-Amerika Verein, Institut für Iberoamerika-Kunde, 1994.

Díaz, Elías. *La filosofía social del krausismo español*. Valencia: Torres, 1983.

Dickens, Arthur G., *The Counter Reformation*. New York: Harcourt, Brace & World, 1969.

Dickens, Arthur G., ed. *The Courts of Europe: Politics, Patronage and Royalty, 1400–1800*. New York: McGraw-Hill, 1977.

Dieterich, Anton. *Zentral-Spanien: Kunst und Kultur in Madrid, El Escorial, Toledo und Aranjeuz, Avila, Segovia, Alcalá de Henares*. Cologne: DuMont Schauberg, 1975. 2nd ed.: Cologne: DuMont Schauberg, 1978.

Dietrich, Donald J. *Goethezeit and the Metamorphosis of Catholic Theology in the Age of Idealism*. Bonn: Bouvier, 1981.

Díez Taboada, Juan María. "El germanismo y la renovación de la lírica española en el siglo XIX, 1840–1870." *Filología Moderna*, vol. 2, no. 5 (1961), pp. 21–55.

Documentos secretos sobre España: documentos secretos del Ministerio de Asuntos Exteriores de Alemania sobre la guerra civil española. Trans. Eduardo Méndez Riestra. Madrid: Júcar, 1978.

Domínguez, Javier. *El hombre mercancia: españoles en Alemania*. Bilbao: Desclée de Brouwer, 1976.

Douer, Alisa, and Ursula Seeber, eds. *Wie weit ist Wien: Lateinamerika als Exil für österreichische Schriftsteller und Künstler*. Vienna: Picus, 1995.

Doussinague, José María. *España tenía razón, 1939–1945*. 2nd ed. Madrid: Espasa Calpe, 1950.

Driesch, Wilhelm von den. *Die ausländischen Kaufleute während des 18. Jahrhunderts in Spanien und ihre Beteiligung am Kolonialhandel*. Cologne and Vienna: Böhlau, 1972.

Driesch, Wilhelm von den, ed. *Die Fuggersche Spanienkorrespondenz, 1560–1594*. 4 vols. Frankfurt: P. Lang, 1998–2001.

Duchardt, H., and C. Strosetzki, eds. *Siglo de Oro—Decadencia: Spaniens Kultur und Politik in der ersten Hälfte des 17. Jahrhunderts*. Cologne: Böhlau, 1996.

Dülffer, Jost. *Weimar, Hitler und die Marine: Reichspolitik und Flottenbau, 1920–1939*. Düsseldorf: Droste, 1973.

Durzak, Manfred, ed. *Die deutsche Exilliteratur, 1933–1945*. Stuttgart: Reclam, 1973.
Dwinger, Edwin Erich. *Spanische Silhouetten: Tagebuch einer Frontreise*. Jena: Diederichs, 1937.
Ebert, A. "Litterarische Wechselwirkungen Spaniens und Deutschlands." *Deutsche Vierteljahrsschrift für Literaturwissenschaft und Geistesgeschichte*, 1857, pp. 86–121.
Edelmayer, Friedrich, and Alfred Kohler, eds. *Kaiser Maximilian II: Kultur und Politik im 16. Jahrhundert*. Vienna: Verlag für Geschichte und Politik, 1992.
Ehrenburg, Ilya. *Memoirs: 1921–1941*. Trans. Tatiana Shebunina. Cleveland: World Publishing Co., 1964.
Einhorn, Marion. *Die ökonomischen Hintergründe der faschistischen deutschen Intervention in Spanien, 1936–1939*. Berlin: Akademie-Verlag, 1962.
Eisenberger, Gert, ed. *Lebenswege: 15 Biographien zwischen Europa und Lateinamerika*. Hamburg: Verlag Libertäre Assoziation, 1995.
Elliott, John H. *Imperial Spain, 1469–1716*. New York: Saint Martin's, 1964.
Elstob, Peter. *Condor Legion*. New York: Ballantine Books, 1973.
———. *La Legión Condor: España, 1936–39*. Trans. Diorki. Madrid: San Martín, 1973.
Englekirk, John E. "*El Museo Universal* (1857–69): Mirror of Transition Years." *PMLA*, vol. 70 (1955), pp. 350–374.
Enzensberger, Hans Magnus. *Einzelheiten*. 2 vols. Frankfurt: Suhrkamp, 1962–70.
———. *Fray Bartolomé de las Casas: una retrospectiva al futuro*. Trans. Christian von Randow. Mexico: Coordinación de Difusión Cultural, Dirección de Literatura, UNAM, 1987.
———. *El interrogatorio de La Habana: autorretrato de la contrarrevolución y otros ensayos políticos*. Trans. Michael Faber-Kaiser. Barcelona: Anagrama, 1973.
———. *Der kurze Sommer der Anarchie: Buenaventura Durrutis Leben und Tod*. Frankfurt: Suhrkamp, 1972.
———. *Das Verhör von Habana*. Frankfurt: Suhrkamp, 1970.
Enzensberger, Hans Magnus, ed. *Bartholomé de Las Casas, Kurzgefaßter Bericht von der Verwüstung der westindischen Länder*. Frankfurt: Insel, 1966.
Erfen, Irene, and Karl-Heinz Spiess. *Fremdheit und Reisen im Mittelalter*. Stuttgart: Steiner, 1997.
Erichsen, Hans-Uwe, ed. *Lateinamerika und Europa im Dialog: Menschenrechte, wirtschaftliche Verflechtung, Menschenbild, Minderheiten, Medien, politische Beziehungen. Öffentliche Vorträge und Berichte aus den wissenschaftlichen Werkstätten des Lateinamerika-Kongresses 1987 der Westfälischen Wilhelms-Universität Münster*. Berlin: Duncker & Humblot, 1989.
Ernst, Hildegard. *Madrid und Wien, 1632–1637: Politik und Finanzen in den Beziehungen zwischen Philipp IV. und Ferdinand II.* Münster: Aschendorff, 1991.
Esebeck, Hans Gert Freiherr von. *Spanien: Land der Entscheidung*. Bayreuth: Gauverlag Bayrische Ostmark, 1939.
Esteban Infantes, Emilio. *"Blaue Division": Spaniens Freiwillige an der Ostfront*. Trans. Werner Haupt. Leoni am Starnberger See: Druffel, 1977.
Evans, Robert J. W. *The Making of the Habsburg Monarchy, 1550–1700*. New York: Oxford University Press, 1979.
Everard, C. *Luftkampf über Spanien*. Berlin: Scherl, 1937.
Expresionismo en Alemania: exposición conmemorativa del décimo aniversario de la Fundación de la Asociación Cultural Humboldt. Caracas: La Asociación, 1959.
Farinelli, Arturo. *Die Beziehungen zwischen Spanien und Deutschland in der Litteratur der beiden Länder*. Berlin: A. Haack, 1892.

———. *Guillaume de Humboldt et l'Espagne.* Paris: Revue Hispanique, 1898.
———. "Spanien und die spanische Literatur im Lichte der deutschen Kritik und Poesie." *Zeitschrift für vergleichende Literaturgeschichte,* new series, vol. 5 (1892), pp. 135–276, and vol. 8 (1895), pp. 318–407.
Feis, Herbert. *The Spanish Story: Franco and the Nations at War.* New York: Knopf, 1948; reprint ed., New York: Norton, 1966.
Fernández Matheu, José. "Estudios de literatura alemana." *El Museo Universal,* vol. 11 (1867), pp. 19, 131, 162, 323, 330, 347, 354.
Fernández Guerra, A., et al. *Historia de España desde la invasión de los pueblos germánicos hasta la ruina de la monarquía visigoda.* 2 vols. Madrid, 1890.
Fernández Martín, Luis. "La Marquesa del Valle: una vida dramática en la corte de los Austrias." *Hispania,* vol. 39, no. 143 (1979), pp. 559–638.
Ferno, Renate, and Wolfgang Grenz, eds. *Handbuch der deutschen Lateinamerika-Forschung: Institute, Wissenschaftler und Experten in der Bundesrepublik Deutschland und Berlin (West). Neuere Veröffentlichungen.* Hamburg: Dokumentations-Leitstelle Lateinamerika; Bonn: Deutscher Akademischer Austauschdienst, n.d.
Feßler, Ignaz Aurelius. *Versuch einer Geschichte der spanischen Nation (Die alten und die neuen Spanier: Ein Völkerspiegel).* 2 vols. Berlin: Maurer, 1810.
Fichtner, Paula Sutter. *Ferdinand I of Austria: The Politics of Dynasticism in the Age of the Reformation.* New York: Eastern European Monographs, 1982.
Fiebig-von Hase, Ragnhild. *Lateinamerika als Konfliktherd der deutsch-amerikanischen Beziehungen, 1890–1903: Vom Beginn der Panamerikapolitik bis zur Venezuelakrise von 1902/03.* Göttingen: Vandenhoeck & Ruprecht, 1986ff.
Fischer, Martin Bodo. "Frühling in Spanien ... einer neuen, großen Zukunft entgegen: Zwei deutsche Reiseberichte aus den dreißiger Jahren (Klara Rumbacher und Maria Stona)." *Tranvía: Revue der Iberischen Halbinsel,* no. 37 (June, 1995).
Flasche, Hans. "Calderón, the German Idealist Philosophers, and the Question of Christian Tragedy." In *Calderón de la Barca at the Tercentenary: Comparative Views,* pp. 51–69. Ed. Wendell M. Aycock. Lubbock: Texas Tech Press, 1981.
———. *Geschichte der spanischen Literatur.* Berne: Francke, 1977ff.
Flemming, Willi, ed. *Jeronimo, Marschalck in Hispanien: Das deutsche Wandertruppen-Manuskript der "Spanish Tragedy" von Thomas Kyd.* Hildesheim and New York: Olms, 1973.
Floeck, Wilfried. *Spanisches Gegenwartstheater.* Vol. 1: *Eine Einführung,* vol. 2: *Eine Anthologie.* Tübingen and Basel: Francke, 1997.
Fornet-Betancourt, Raúl. *Ein anderer Marxismus? Die philosophische Rezeption des Marxismus in Lateinamerika.* Mainz: Matthias-Grünewald-Verlag, 1994.
———. *Lateinamerika-Forschung an deutschen Hochschulen: Eine bibliographische Annäherung.* Aachen: Verlag der Augustinus-Buchhandlung, 1990.
Fornet-Betancourt, Raúl, and Celina A. Lértora Mendoza, eds. *Ethik in Deutschland und Lateinamerika heute: Akten der 1. Germano-Iberoamerikanischen Ethik-Tage.* Frankfurt, etc.: Lang, 1987.
Forssmann, Knut. *Baltasar Gracián und die deutsche Literatur zwischen Barock und Frühaufklärung.* Ph.D. Diss. Universität Mainz, 1976.
Francis, D. "Prince George of Hesse-Darmstadt and the Plans for the Expedition to Spain of 1702." *Bulletin of the Institute of Historical Research,* vol. 42 (1969), p. 58ff.
Franz, Marie. *Die Darstellung von Faschismus und Antifaschismus in den Romanen von Anna Seghers, 1933–1949.* Frankfurt and New York: Peter Lang, 1987.

Franzbach, Martin. *La traducción de Huarte por Lessing (1752): recepción e historia de la influencia del "Examen de ingenios para las ciencias" (1575) en Alemania*. Trans. Luis Ruiz Hernández. Pamplona: Ditutación Foral de Navarra, Institución Príncipe de Viana; Madrid: Consejo Superior de Investigaciones Científicas, 1978.
Franzl, Johann. *Ferdinand II.: Kaiser im Zwiespalt der Zeit*. Graz: Verlag Styria, 1978.
Freigang, Christian, ed. *Gotische Architektur in Spanien: Akten des Kolloquiums der Carl-Justi-Vereinigung und des Kunstgeschichtlichen Seminars der Universität Göttingen, 4.-6. Februar 1994*. Frankfurt: Vervuert; Madrid: Iberoamericana, 1999.
Frey, Marsha. "A Question of Empire: Leopold I and the War of Spanish Succession, 1701–1705." *The Austrian History Yearbook*, vol. 14 (1978).
Friedrich, Hugo. *Der fremde Calderón*. Freiburg i.Br.: Schultz, 1955.
Fries, Fritz Rudolf, ed. *Amadís von Gallien: Nach alten Chroniken überarbeitet, erweitert und verbessert durch Garcí Ordoñez de Montalvo im Jahre 1508*. Trans. Fritz Rudolf Fries and Eberhard Wesemann. Leipzig: Insel, 1973.
Frisch, Max. *Stiller*. Frankfurt: Suhrkamp, 1954.
Froembgen, Johann. *Franco: Ein Leben für Spanien*. Leipzig: Goten-Verlag Eisentraut, 1939.
Fröschle, Hartmut, ed. *Americana Germanica: Bibliographie zur deutschen Sprache und deutschsprachigen Literatur in Nord- und Lateinamerika*. Hildesheim and New York: Olms, 1991.
———. *Die Deutschen in Lateinamerika: Schicksal und Leistung*. Tübingen and Basel: Erdmann, 1979.
Fuegi, John. *Brecht & Co.: Sex, Politics, and the Making of Modern Drama*. New York: Grove, 1994.
Führing, Hellmut H. *Wir funken für Franco: Einer von der Legion Condor erzählt*. Gütersloh: Bertelsmann, 1939.
Fyrth, Jim, and Sally Alexander, eds. *Women's Voices from the Spanish Civil War*. London: Lawrence and Wishart, 1991.
Ganz-Blättler, Ursula. *Andacht und Abenteuer: Berichte europäischer Jerusalem- und Santiago-Pilger, 1320–1520*. Tübingen: Narr, 1990.
García Casanova, Juan Francisco. *Hegel y el republicanismo en la España del XIX*. Granada: Universidad de Granada, 1982.
García Cue, Juan Ramón. *Aproximación al estudio del krausismo andaluz*. Madrid: Tecnos, Fundación Cultural E. Luño Peña, 1985.
García Pérez, Rafael. "Trabajadores españoles a Alemania durante II Guerra Mundial." *Hispania*, no. 170 (1988).
———. *Franquismo y Tercer Reich: Las relaciones económicas hispano-alemanas durante la Segunda Guerra Mundial*. Madrid: Centro de Estudios Constitucionales, 1994.
Garmendia, José Antonio. *Alemania: exilio del emigrante*. Barcelona: Plaza & Janés, 1970.
Garriga, Ramón. *Berlín: años cuarenta*. Barcelona: Editorial Planeta, 1983.
———. *La España de Franco*. Vol. 1: *Las relaciones con Hitler*. Madrid: Gregorio del Toro, 1976.
———. *La Legión Condor*. Madrid: G. del Toro, 1975.
———. *La Legión Condor*. Esplugas de Llobregat: Plaza Janés, 1978.
———. *Las relaciones secretas entre Franco y Hitler*. Buenos Aires: J. Alvarez, 1965.
Gautier, Théophile. *Premières poésies, 1830–1845*. Paris, 1870.
Geißler, Rolf. "Der Spanische Bürgerkrieg im Spiegel der deutschen Literatur: Report und Reflexion." *Literatur für Leser: Zeitschrift für Interpretationspraxis und geschichtliche Texterkenntnis*, 1979, pp. 184–200.

Geldrich, Hanna. *Heine und der spanisch-amerikanische Modernismo.* Berne: H. Lang, 1971.
George, Uta, and Mark Arenhövel, eds. *Lateinamerika, Kontinent vor dem Morgengrauen: Nachdenken über ein schwieriges Verhältnis—Lateinamerika und Deutschland.* Münster: Unrast, 1992.
Gil Novales, Albert, ed. *La revolución burguesa en España: actas del Coloquio Hispano-Alemán, celebrado en Leipzig los días 17 y 18 de noviembre de 1983.* Madrid: Universidad Complutense, 1985.
Gimber, Arno. "Von Perlen, Mond und Wasserfrauen: Die Heine-Rezeption in der spanischen Literatur der Jahrhundertwende." In *Aufklärung und Skepsis: Internationaler Heine-Kongreß zum 200. Geburtstag...*, pp. 210–721. Ed. Joseph A. Kruse, Bernd Witte, and Karin Füllner. Stuttgart: Metzler, 1999.
Giner de los Ríos, Francisco. *Ensayos.* Ed. Juan López-Morillas. Madrid: Alianza, 1969.
Gleich, Albrecht von, et al. *Wirtschaftspartner Lateinamerika: Stand der Beziehungen und Erfahrungen. Aus der Praxis der deutschen Außenwirtschaftsförderung. Regionalkonferenz des Auswärtigen Amtes, Caracas, 24.-26. November 1987.* Hamburg: Institut für Iberoamerika-Kunde, 1988.
Gleich, Albrecht von, Gerd Kohlhepp, and Manfred Mols, eds. *Neue Konzepte in der Entwicklungszusammenarbeit mit Lateinamerika? Ein Dialog zwischen Entwicklungspolitik und Wissenschaft.* Hamburg: Institut für Iberoamerika-Kunde, 1991.
Gleich, Albrecht von, and Germán Kratochwil, eds. *Denkanstöße aus Lateinamerika: Theologen, Soziologen, Politik- und Wirtschaftswissenschaftler berichten.* Hamburg: Institut für Iberoamerika-Kunde, 1976.
Gleim, Johann Wilhelm Ludwig. *Romanzen.* Berlin, 1756.
Goda, Norman J. W., "The Riddle of the Rock: A Reassessment of German Motives for the Capture of Gibraltar in the Second World War." *Journal of Contemporary History,* vol. 28 (April 1993), pp. 297–314.
———. *Tomorrow the World: Hitler, Northwest Africa, and the Path toward America.* College Station, Tex.: Texas A&M University Press, 1998.
Goede, Wolfgang C. *Lateinamerika im Griff der deutschen Wirtschaft: Eine entwicklungspolitische Bilanz der 70er Jahre.* Munich: Holler, 1984.
Goethe, Johann Wolfgang. *Goethes Werke in 14 Bänden: Hamburger Ausgabe.* Ed. Erich Trunz. Hamburg, 1949ff.
Göller, Josef-Thomas. *Auf der Suche nach El Dorado: Südamerika—die Geschichte eines deutschen Traums.* Bergisch Gladbach: Lübbe, 1992.
Gómez Molleda, María Dolores. *Los reformadores de la España contemporánea.* Madrid: CSIC, 1966.
Gómez Tello, J. L. *Canción de invierno en el este: Crónicas de la División Azul.* Barcelona: Luis de Caralt, 1945.
Gonda, Imre, and Emil Niederhauser. *Die Habsburger: Ein europäisches Phänomen.* Vienna: Kremayr & Scheriau, 1983.
Görlach, Manfred, ed. *Max und Moritz in romanischen Sprachen.* Essen: Die Blaue Eule, 1994.
Görrisch, Walter. *Fünf Patronenhülsen.* Berlin: Aufbau, 1960.
Gramberg, Eduard Johannes. *Fondo y forma del humorismo de Leopoldo Alas, "Clarín."* Oviedo: Diputación de Asturias, 1958.
Gray, Rockwell. *The Imperative of Modernity: An Intellectual Biography of José Ortega y Gasset.* Berkeley: University of California Press, 1989.
Grenz, Wolfgang, ed. *Deutschsprachige Lateinamerika-Forschung = Investigación sobre América Latina en los países de habla alemana: Institutionen, Wissenschaftler*

und Experten in Deutschland, Österreich und der Schweiz. Neuere Veröffentlichungen. Ed. Institut für Iberoamerika-Kunde. Frankfurt: Vervuert, 1993.

Gross, Stefan. *Ernst Robert Curtius und die deutsche Romanistik der zwanziger Jahre: Zum Problem nationaler Images in der Literaturwissenschaft*. Bonn: Bouvier, 1980.

Groth, Hendrik. *Das Argentinische Tageblatt: Sprachrohr der demokratischen Deutschen und der deutsch-jüdischen Emigration*. Münster: Lit, 1996.

Gubar, Susan. "'This Is My Rifle, This Is My Gun': World War II and the Blitz on Women." In *Behind the Lines: Gender and the Two World Wars*. Ed. Margaret Randolph Higonnet et al., pp. 227–259. New Haven: Yale University Press, 1987.

Günther, Dieter. *Die lateinamerikanische Literatur von ihren Anfängen bis heute*. Frankfurt: R. G. Fischer, 1995.

Guthke, Karl S. *B. Traven: Biographie eines Rätsels*. Frankfurt: Büchergilde Gutenberg, 1987.

Gutierrez, Ellen Turner. *The Reception of the Picaresque in the French, English, and German Traditions*. New York: P. Lang, 1995.

Guzmán, Diego de. *Reina Católica: vida y muerte de Doña Margarita de Austria, Reina de España*. Madrid, 1617.

Haab, Barbara. *Weg und Wandlung: Zur Spiritualität heutiger Jakobspilger und -pilgerinnen*. Freiburg [Switzerland]: Universitätsverlag, 1998.

Haas, Helmuth de. *Hofmannsthals Weg zu Calderón*. Ph.D. Diss. University of Munich, 1955.

Hamann, Brigitte, ed. *Die Habsburger: Ein biographisches Lexikon*. Munich: Piper, 1988.

Handke, Peter. *Versuch über die Jukebox*. Frankfurt: Suhrkamp, 1990.

———. *Ensayos sobre el Jukebox*. Trans. Eustaquio Barjau. Madrid: Alianza, 1992.

Hanffstengel, Renate von. *Mexiko im Werk von Bodo Uhse: Das nie verlassene Exil*. New York: P. Lang, 1995.

Hanffstengel, Renata von, Cecilia Tercera, and Silke Wehner Franco, eds. *Mexiko, das wohltemperierte Exil*. Mexico: Instituto de Investigaciones Interculturales Germano-Mexicanas, 1995.

Hanssen, Friedrich. *Spanische Grammatik auf historischer Grundlage*. Halle: Max Niemeyer, 1910.

Harms, Wolfgang, and C. Stephen Jaeger, eds. *Fremdes wahrnehmen—fremdes Wahrnehmen: Studien zur Geschichte der Wahrnehmung und zur Begegnung von Kulturen in Mittelalter und früher Neuzeit*. Stuttgart: Hirzel, 1997.

Harper, Glenn T. *German Economic Policy in Spain during the Spanish Civil War, 1936–1939*. The Hague and Paris: Mouton, 1967.

Hauschild-Thiessen, Renate, and Elfriede Bachmann. *Führer durch die Quellen zur Geschichte Lateinamerikas in der Bundesrepublik Deutschland*. Bremen: Schünemann, 1972.

Havemann, Nils. *Spanien im Kalkül der deutschen Außenpolitik: Von den letzten Jahren der Ära Bismarck bis zum Beginn der Wilhelmischen Weltpolitik, 1883–1899*. Berlin: Duncker & Humblot, 1997.

Havemann, Wilhelm. *Darstellungen aus der inneren Geschichte Spaniens während des 15., 16. und 17. Jahrhunderts*. Göttingen: Dieterich, 1850.

Heidenreich, Helmut, ed. *Pikarische Welt: Schriften zum europäischen Schelmenroman*. Darmstadt: Wissenschaftliche Buchgesellschaft, 1969.

Heine, Heinrich. "Einleitung zu 'Der sinnreiche Junker Don Quixote von La Mancha, von Miguel Cervantes de Saavedra.'" In *Heine Säkulärausgabe*, vol. 9, pp. 137–152.

———. *Joyas prusianas: intermedio, regreso y nueva primavera*. With a biographical study by Manuel María Fernández y Gonzalez. Madrid: J. Velada, 1873.

Hell, Vera, and Hellmut Hell. *Die große Wallfahrt des Mittelalters: Kunst an den romanischen Pilgerstraßen durch Frankreich und Spanien nach Santiago de Compostela*. Vienna: Buchgemeinschaft Donauland, 1965. 3rd ed. Tübingen: Wasmuth, 1979.

Helmes, Günter, and Petra Hennecke, eds. *Don Juan: Fünfzig deutschsprachige Variationen eines europäischen Mythos*. Paderborn: Igel, 1994.

Hempel, Wido, and Dietrich Briesemeister, eds. *Actas del Coloquio Hispano-Alemán Ramón Menéndez Pidal: Madrid, 31 de marzo a 2 de abril de 1978*. Tübingen: Niemeyer, 1982.

Herbers, Klaus, ed. *Deutsche Jakobspilger und ihre Berichte*. Tübingen: Narr, 1988.

———. *Der Jakobusweg: Mit einem mittelalterlichen Pilgerführer unterwegs nach Santiago de Compostela*. Tübingen: Narr, 1997.

Herbers, Klaus, and Robert Plötz, eds. *Der Jakobuskult in Kunst und Literatur: Zeugnisse in Bild, Monument, Schrift und Ton*. Tübingen: Narr, 1998.

Hermsdorf, Klaus, Hugo Fetting, and Silvia Schlenstedt. *Exil in den Niederlanden und in Spanien*. Frankfurt: Röderberg, 1981.

Herrero, Javier. *Ángel Ganivet: un iluminado*. Madrid: Gredos, 1966.

Herrmann, Helene. *Studien zu Heines Romanzero*. Berlin: Weidmann, 1906.

Hess, Steven. *Ramón Menéndez Pidal*. Boston: Twayne, 1982.

Heydenreich, Titus, ed. *Der Umgang mit dem Fremden: Beiträge zur Literatur aus und über Lateinamerika*. Munich: Fink, 1986.

Hielscher, Martin, ed. *Fluchtort Mexiko: Ein Asylland für die Literatur*. Hamburg: Luchterhand, 1992.

Hillen, Ursula. *Wegbereiter der romanischen Philologie: Ph. A. Becker im Gespräch mit G. Gröber, J. Bédier und E. R. Curtius*. Frankfurt and New York: Lang, 1993.

Hödl, Günther. *Habsburg und Österreich, 1273–1493: Gestalten und Gestalt des österreichischen Spätmittelalters*. Vienna and Cologne: Böhlau, 1988.

Hoffmann, Rosemary. "Spanish Painting, Spanish Landscape and the German Imagination." In *Spain, Espagne, Spanien: Foreign Artists Discover Spain, 1800–1900*. Ed. Suzanne L. Stratton. New York: The Equitable Gallery in Association with the Spanish Institute, 1993.

Hoffmeister, Gerhart. *Deutsche und europäische Barockliteratur*. Stuttgart: Metzler, 1987.

———. *Deutsche und europäische Romantik*. Stuttgart: Metzler, 1978.

———. *Der deutsche Schelmenroman im europäischen Kontext: Rezeption, Interpretation, Bibliographie*. Amsterdam: Rodopi, 1987.

———. *Der deutsche Schelmenroman in europäischer Barockliteratur*. Stuttgart: Metzler, 1990.

———. *España y Alemania: historia y documentación de sus relaciones literarias*. Trans. Isidro Gómez Romero. Madrid: Gredos, 1980.

———. *Spanien und Deutschland: Geschichte und Dokumentation der literarischen Beziehungen*. Berlin: E. Schmidt, 1976.

———. *Die spanische Diana in Deutschland: Vergleichende Untersuchungen zu Stilwandel und Weltbild des Schäferromans im 17. Jahrhundert*. Berlin: E. Schmidt, 1972.

Höfs-Kahl, Marion. *Zur Rezeption der lateinamerikanischen Literatur in der Bundesrepublik Deutschland: Das Beispiel Octavio Paz*. Frankfurt: Haag + Herchen, 1990.

Hölz, Karl. *Das Fremde, das Eigene, das Andere: Die Inszenierung kultureller und geschlechtlicher Identität in Lateinamerika*. Berlin: E. Schmidt, 1998.

Homeyer, Gerda, ed. *Beiträge zur Geschichte der deutschen Romanistik: Unveröffentlichte Korrepondenz zwischen Alfred Bassermann, Adolf Gaspary, Adolf Tobler,*

Gustav Körting, Hugo Schuchardt u.a. mit Bonaventura Zumbini. Frankfurt: Haag + Herchen, 1989.
Hörr, Beate. *Tragödie und Ideologie: Tragödienkonzepte in Spanien und Deutschland in der ersten Hälfte des 20. Jahrhunderts.* Würzburg: Königshausen und Neumann, 1997.
Horton, Albert Cary. *Germany and the Spanish Civil War.* Ph.D. Diss. Columbia University, 1966.
Hoyos, Max Graf. *Pedros y Pablos: Fliegen, Erleben, Kämpfen in Spanien.* Munich: Bruckmann, 1939.
Hüffer, Hermann H. *Las relaciones germano-españolas durante el reinado de Carlos V: ponencia.* Madrid: Ciudad Universitaria, 1958.
Humboldt, Alexander von. *Die Forschungsreise in den Tropen Amerikas.* Ed. Hanno Beck. 3 vols. Darmstadt: Wissenschaftliche Buchgesellschaft, 1997.
Hurter, Friedrich von. *Bild einer christlichen Fürstin: Maria, Erzherzogin zu Österreich, Herzogin von Bayern.* Schaffhausen, Fr. Hurter'sche Buchhandlung, 1860.
Hüttl, Ludwig. *Max Emanuel, der Blaue Kurfürst, 1679–1726: Eine politische Biographie.* Munich: Süddeutscher Verlag, 1976.
Ibáñez Hernandez, Rafael. "De Madrid a Grafenwöhr: el nacimiento de la División." *Defensa,* special issue, No. 16 (June 1991).
Ilg, Karl. *Heimat Südamerika: Brasilien und Peru. Leistung und Schicksal deutschsprachiger Siedler.* 2nd ed. Innsbruck: Tyrolia-Verlag, 1982.
Illi, Manfred. *Die deutsche Auswanderung nach Lateinamerika: Eine Literaturübersicht.* Munich: Fink, 1977.
Informativo REAAL: noticias sobre las relaciones políticas, económicas y culturales entre Alemania y América Latina. Hamburg: Instituto de Estudios Iberoamericanos. (Description based on no. 4 [October–December 1992]).
Ingrao, Charles W. *The Habsburg Monarchy, 1618–1815.* Cambridge and New York: Cambridge University Press, 1994.
Inter Nationes e.V. *Spanisch-deutscher Kulturdialog: Ein Handbuch deutscher Aktivitäten.* Ed. Bertelsmann Stiftung. Gütersloh: Verlag Bertelsmann Stiftung, 1990.
Interbrigadisten: Der Kampf deutscher Kommunisten und anderer Antifaschisten im national-revolutionären Krieg des spanischen Volkes, 1936–1939. Ed. Lehrstuhl Geschichte der deutschen Arbeiterbewegung an der Fakultät für Gesellschaftswissenschaften der Militärakademie Friedrich Engels. Berlin: Deutscher Militärverlag, 1966.
Jacob-Wendler, Gerhart. *Deutsche Elektroindustrie in Lateinamerika: Siemens und AEG, 1890–1914.* Stuttgart: In Kommission bei Klett-Cotta, 1982.
Jacobs, Jürgen. *Der deutsche Schelmenroman: Eine Einführung.* Munich: Artemis, 1983.
———. "Der späte Heine und die Utopie." *Études germaniques,* vol. 22 (1967), pp. 511–516.
Jacquemard de Gemeaux, Christine. *Ernst Robert Curtius (1886–1956): Origines et cheminements d'un esprit européen.* Berne, etc.: P. Lang, 1998.
Jané Carbó, Jordi. "Deutsche Schriftsteller im Exil 1933–1945 und ihr Wirken in Spanien." *Universitas Tarraconensis,* vol. 13 (1990/91), pp. 143–182.
Jehle, Peter. *Werner Krauss und die Romanistik im NS-Staat.* Hamburg: Argument, 1996.
Jerofke, Hans-Christoph. *Der Wiederaufbau der deutschen Wirtschaftsbeziehungen mit Südamerika nach dem Zweiten Weltkrieg: Die Genesis der vertraglichen Rahmenbedingungen 1949 bis 1958.* Frankfurt and New York: P. Lang, 1993.
Jiménez García, Antonio. *El krausismo y la Institución Libre de Enseñanza.* Madrid: Cincel, 1985.

———. "Menéndez Ureña, E., Fernández Fernández, J. L. y Seidel, J.: El 'Ideal de la Humanidad' de Sanz del Río y su original alemán. Universidad Pontificia, Comillas, Madrid, 1993, L + 238 pp." *Asociación de hispanismo filosófico*, vol. 6 (1994), pp. 15–16.

———. "Urbano González Serrano y la fundamentación del krauso-positivismo español." *Letras Peninsulares*, vol. 4, no. 1 (Spring 1991), pp. 185–206.

Jongh-Rossel, Elena M. de. *El krausismo y la generación de 1898*. Valencia: Albatros Hispanófila, 1985.

Jordan, Lothar, and Bernd Kortländer, eds. *Nationale Grenzen und internationaler Austausch: Studien zum Kultur- und Wissenschaftstransfer in Europa*. Tübingen: Niemeyer, 1995.

Jornadas sobre nuevas universidades en Alemania y en España: Castellón de la Plana, noviembre de 1992. [Castellón de la Plana:] Publicacions de la Universidad Jaume I, 1993.

Juhl, Paulgeorg. *Deutsche Direktinvestitionen in Lateinamerika*. Tübingen: Mohr, 1979.

Junghändel, Max. *Die Baukunst Spaniens*. Dresden: J. Bleyl, 1891–98.

Juretschke, Hans, ed. *Zum Spanienbild der Deutschen in der Zeit der Aufklärung: Eine historische Übersicht*. Münster: Aschendorff, 1997.

Juretschke, Hans, Alexander Hollerbach, and Jesús Iturrioz. *Aspectos del humanismo alemán: conferencias pronunciadas en la Fundación Universitaria Española y en la Sociedad Görres los días 23, 25 y 30 de octubre de 1979*. Madrid: Fundación Universitaria Española, 1981.

———. "La recepción de la cultura y ciencia alemana en España durante la época romántica." In *Estudios románticos*, pp. 63–120. Valladolid: Casa-Museo de Zorrilla, 1975.

Kahle, Günter. *Lateinamerika in der Politik der europäischen Mächte, 1492–1810*. Cologne: Böhlau, 1993.

Kamen, Henry. *Philip of Spain*. New Haven and London: Yale University Press, 1997.

———. *Spain, 1469–1714: A Society in Conflict*. 2nd ed. London: Longman, 1991.

———. *Spain in the Later Seventeenth Century, 1665–1700*. London: Longman, 1980.

Kann, Robert A. *A History of the Habsburg Empire, 1526–1918*. Berkeley: University of California Press, 1974.

Kantorowicz, Alfred. *Spanisches Kriegstagebuch*. Frankfurt: Fischer Taschenbuch Verlag, 1982.

Kaufmann, Brigitte. *Die comedia Calderóns: Studien zur Interdependenz von Autor, Publikum und Bühne*. Berne, Frankfurt, and Munich: Lang, 1976.

Kaufmann, Thomas DaCosta. *The School of Prague: Painting at the Court of Rudolf II*. Chicago: University of Chicago Press, 1988.

Kayser, W. *Die iberische Welt im Denken J. G. Herders*. Hamburg, 1945.

Keding, Karl. *Feldgeistlicher bei Legion Condor: Spanisches Kriegstagebuch eines evangelischen Legionspfarrers*. Berlin: Ostwerk, 1939.

Kehrer, Hugo. *Deutschland in Spanien: Beziehung, Einfluß und Abhängigkeit*. Munich: Callwey, 1953.

———. *Alemania en España: influjos y contactos a través de los siglos*. Madrid: Aguilar, 1966.

Kent, Conrad, and Dennis Prindle. *Park Güell*. New York: Princeton Architectural Press, 1993.

Kesten, Hermann. *Die Kinder von Gernika: Roman*. Wiesbaden: Limes, 1948; Leipzig: Reclam, 1985.

Kiehl, Heinz. *Kampfgeschwader "Legion Condor" 53: Berichte, Erlebnisse, Dokumente, 1936–1945. Eine Chronik*. Stuttgart: Motorbuch, 1983.
Kießling, Wolfgang. *Alemania Libre in Mexico*. 2 vols. Berlin: Akademie, 1974.
———. *Exil in Lateinamerika*. Leipzig: Philipp Reclam, 1980.
Kircher, Hartmut. *Heinrich Heine und das Judentum*. Bonn: Bouvier, 1973.
Kirsch, Hans-Christian, ed. *Der Spanische Bürgerkrieg in Augenzeugenberichten*. Düsseldorf: Rauch, 1967.
Klein, Wolfgang, and Brigitte Sändig, eds. *Zur Rezeption der Aufklärung in der Romania im 19./20. Jahrhundert: Beiträge zum Romanistentag in Potsdam 1993*. Rheinfelden: Schäuble, 1994.
Kleinfeld, Gerald R., and Lewis A. Tambs. *Hitler's Spanish Legion: The Blue Division in Russia*. Carbondale: Southern Illinois University Press, 1979.
Klengel, Susanne, ed. *Contextos, historias y transferencias en los estudios latinoamericanistas europeos: los casos de Alemania, España y Francia*. Frankfurt: Vervuert, 1997.
Knabe, Peter-Eckhard, and Johannes Thiele, eds. *Über Texte: Festschrift für Karl-Ludwig Selig*. Tübingen: Stauffenburg, 1997.
Knefelkamp, Ulrich, and Hans-Joachim König, eds. *Die neuen Welten in alten Büchern: Entdeckung und Eroberung in frühen deutschen Schrift- und Bildzeugnissen*. Bamberg: Staatsbibliothek, 1988.
Kneipp, Sebastian. *Meine Wasser-Kur, durch mehr als 30 Jahre erprobt und geschrieben zur Heilung der Krankheiten und Erhaltung der Gesundheit*. 11th ed. Kempten: J. Kösel, 1889.
———. *Mi testamento*. 4th ed. Barcelona: Asociación Médico-Kneippista, 1904.
Koch, Herbert, and Gabriele Staubwasser de Mohorn. *Schiller y España*. Madrid: Ediciones Cultura Hispánica del Centro Iberoamericano de Cooperación, 1978.
Kodalle, Klaus-M., ed. *Karl Christian Friedrich Krause, 1781–1832: Studien zu seiner Philosophie und zum Krausismo*. Hamburg: Meiner, 1985.
Koestler, Arthur. *Ein spanisches Testament: Aufzeichnungen aus dem Bürgerkrieg*. Frankfurt: S. Fischer, 1980.
Kohl, Hermann. *Deutsche Flieger über Spanien*. Reutlingen, 1939.
Kohler, Alfred, and Friedrich Edelmayer, eds. *Hispania-Austria: Die Katholischen Könige, Maximilian I. und die Anfänge der Casa de Austria in Spanien. Akten des Historischen Gespräches, Innsbruck, Juli 1992*. Vienna: Verlag für Geschichte und Politik; Munich: Oldenbourg, 1993.
Köhler, Klaus. *Kriegsfreiwilliger 1937: Tagebuch eines Kriegsfreiwilligen der Legion Condor*. Leipzig: Der Nationale Aufbau, 1939.
Kohut, Karl, ed. *Deutsche in Lateinamerika—Lateinamerika in Deutschland*. Frankfurt: Vervuert, 1996.
———. *Der eroberte Kontinent: Historische Realität, Rechtfertigung und literarische Darstellung der Kolonisation Amerikas*. Frankfurt: Vervuert, 1991.
———. *La recepción de la cultura alemana en América Latina: cinco visiones*. Eichstätt: Zentralinstitut für Lateinamerika-Studien, 1998.
———. *Von der Weltkarte zum Kuriositätenkabinett: Amerika im deutschen Humanismus und Barock*. Frankfurt: Vervuert, 1995.
Kohut, Karl, Dietrich Briesemeister, and Gustav Siebenmann, eds. *Deutsche in Lateinamerika—Lateinamerika in Deutschland*. Frankfurt: Vervuert, 1996.
Kohut, Karl, and Patrik von zur Mühlen, eds. *Alternative Lateinamerika: Das deutsche Exil in der Zeit des Nationalsozialismus*. Frankfurt: Vervuert, 1994.
Koller, Erwin, and Hugo Laitenberger, eds. *Suevos—Schwaben: Das Königreich der Sueben auf der Iberarischen Halbinsel, 411–585. Interdisziplinäres Kolloquium Braga 1996*. Tübingen: Narr, 1998.

Koniecki, Dieter, and Juan Manuel Almarza-Meññica, eds. *Martín Lutero, 1483–1983: jornadas hispano-alemanas sobre la personalidad y la obra de Martín Lutero en el V centenario de su nacimiento, Salamanca, 9–12 de noviembre 1983.* Madrid: Fundación Friedrich Ebert, 1984.

König, Andreas. *Zur spanischen Kultur und Identität. Ein Literaturbericht zum Thema "kulturanthropologische Länderkunde": Spanien.* Frankfurt: IKO-Verlag, 1996.

König, Hans-Joachim, and Stefan Rinke, eds. *Transatlantische Perzeptionen: Lateinamerika—USA—Europa in Geschichte und Gegenwart.* Stuttgart: Hans-Dieter Heinz Akademischer Verlag, 1998.

Körting, Gustav. *Handbuch der romanischen Philologie.* Leipzig: O. R. Reisland, 1896.

Kossok, Manfred. *Im Schatten der Heiligen Allianz: Deutschland und Lateinamerika 1815–1830. Zur Politik der deutschen Staaten gegenüber der Unabhängigkeitsbewegung Mittel- und Südamerikas.* Berlin: Akademie, 1964.

Krause, Carl Christian Friedrich. *Ideal de la humanidad para la vida.* Trans. D. Julian Sanz del Río. Madrid: Manuel Galiano, 1860.

———. *Das Urbild der Menschheit.* 2nd ed. Göttingen: Dietrich, 1851.

Krauss, Werner. *Die Aufklärung in Spanien, Portugal und Lateinamerika.* Munich: Fink, 1973.

———. *Das wissenschaftliche Werk.* Ed. Werner Bahner, Manfred Naumann, and Heinrich Scheel. 2nd ed. Berlin: Akademie and Aufbau, 1987ff.

Kremer, Harry Andreas, ed. *Die Bundesrepublik Deutschland und das Königreich Spanien 1992: Die Rolle der Länder und der "comunidades autónomas" im europäischen Integrationsprozeß.* Munich: Bayerischer Landtag, 1990.

Kreuzer, Helmut. "Zum Spanienkrieg: Prosa deutscher Exilautoren." *Lili: Zeitschrift für Literaturwissenschaft und Linguistik,* no. 60 (1985), pp. 10–45.

Krieger, Karl Friedrich. *Die Habsburger im Mittelalter: Von Rudolf I. bis Friedrich III.* Stuttgart: Kohlhammer, 1994.

Kroch, Ernesto. *Exil in der Heimat, heim ins Exil: Erinnerungen aus Europa und Lateinamerika.* Frankfurt: Dipa-Verlag, 1990.

Kroetz, Franz Xaver. *Brasilien-Peru-Aufzeichnungen.* Frankfurt: Suhrkamp, 1991.

———. *Nicaragua-Tagebuch: Roman.* Hamburg: Konkret, 1985.

Krömer, Wolfram, ed. *1492–1992: Spanien, Österreich und Iberoamerika: Akten des siebten Spanisch-Österreichischen Symposions (16.-21. März 1992 in Innsbruck).* Innsbruck: Institut für Sprachwissenschaft der Universität Innsbruck, 1993.

———. *Spanien und Österreich, 1800–1850: Akten des Symposions vom 21.-26. September 1980 in Innsbruck-Igls.* Innsbruck: Institut für Sprachwissenschaft der Universität Innsbruck, 1982.

———. *Spanien und Österreich im Barockzeitalter: Akten des dritten Spanisch-Österreichischen Symposions (Kremsmünster, 25.-30. September 1983).* Innsbruck: Institut für Sprachwissenschaft der Universität Innsbruck, 1985.

———. *Spanien und Österreich in der Renaissance: Akten des fünften Spanisch-Österreichischen Symposions 21.-25. September 1987.* Innsbruck: Institut für Sprachwissenschaft der Universität Innsbruck, 1989.

Kruse, Felicitas, et al. *Schieß gut, aber freu dich nicht: Österreicherinnen und Österreicher im Spanischen Bürgerkrieg 1936–1939. Photographien und Interviews.* Innsbruck: Haymon, 1998.

Kuehne, Alyce de. "Influencias de Pirandello y de Brecht en Mario Benedetti." *Hispania,* vol. 51 (1968), pp. 408–415.

Kühnhardt, Ludger, and Dario Valcárcel, eds. *Spanien und Deutschland als EU-Partner.* Baden-Baden: Nomos, 1999.

Kulístikov, Vladímir. "América Latina en los planes estratégicos del Tercer Reich." *América Latina*, no. 10 (1984).

Der Kulturdialog zwischen Spanien und Deutschland im Rahmen Europas: Ein Symposium am 27. und 28. Mai 1988 in Santillana del Mar. Gütersloh: Bertelsmann-Stiftung, 1989.

Kunst aus Kuba: Eine Ausstellung im Forum für Kulturaustausch, Stuttgart, und in der IfA Galerie, Bonn. Stuttgart: Institut für Auslandsbeziehungen, 1984.

LaBahn, Kathleen J. *Anna Seghers' Exile Literature: The Mexican Years, 1941–1947.* New York: Lang, 1986.

Lacasta Zabalza, José Ignacio. *Hegel en España: un estudio sobre la mentalidad social del hegelismo hispánico.* Madrid: Centro de Estudios Constitucionales, 1984.

Laferl, Christopher F. *Die Kultur der Spanier in Österreich unter Ferdinand I., 1522–1564.* Vienna: Böhlau, 1997.

Lahne, Werner. *Spaniens Freiwillige an der Ostfront.* [Germany:] Propaganda-Kompanie der Armee Busch, 1942.

Lanz, Johann. *Die 32 Ahnen der Habsburger: Von Rudolf I. bis Maria Theresia.* Vienna: Heraldisch-Genealogische Gesellschaft "Adler," 1993.

Lascoiti, Rima. *In der Hölle von Madrid: Erlebnisse einer Frau.* Berlin: Deutscher Verlag für Politik und Wirtschaft, 1939.

Lataster-Czisch, Petra, ed. *Eigentlich rede ich nicht gern über mich: Lebenserinnerungen von Frauen aus dem Spanischen Bürgerkrieg, 1936–1939.* Leipzig: Kiepenheuer, 1990.

Latin America in Perspective: Oxford Analytica. Boston: Houghton Mifflin, 1991.

Lehmann, Hartmut. *Alte Welt und Neue Welt in wechselseitiger Sicht: Studien zu den transatlantischen Beziehungen im 19. und 20. Jahrhundert.* Göttingen: Vandenhoeck & Ruprecht, 1995.

Leitz, Christian. *Economic Relations between Nazi Germany and Franco's Spain, 1936–1945.* New York: Oxford University Press, 1996.

Lemm, Robert. *Die spanische Inquisition: Geschichte und Legende.* Munich: Deutscher Taschenbuch Verlag, 1996.

Lent, Alfred. *Wir kämpften für Spanien: Erlebnisse eines deutschen Freiwilligen im spanischen Bürgerkrieg.* Oldenburg and Berlin: Stalling, 1939.

Lentzen, Manfred. *Der Spanische Bürgerkrieg und die Dichter: Beispiele des politischen Engagements in der Literatur.* Heidelberg: Carl Winter, 1985.

Lewalter, Ernst. *Spanisch-jesuitische und deutsch-lutherarische Metaphysik des 17. Jahrhunderts: Ein Beitrag zur Geschichte der iberisch-deutschen Kulturbeziehungen und zur Vorgeschichte des deutschen Idealismus.* Darmstadt: Wissenschaftliche Buchgesellschaft, 1967.

Lewis, Ward B. "Literature in Exile: Paul Zech." *German Quarterly*, vol. 43 (1970), pp. 535–538.

———. *Poetry and Exile: An Annotated Bibliography of the Works and Criticism of Paul Zech.* Berne and New York: Lang, 1975.

Linke, Reinhard, ed. *Die Frauen der Habsburger: Glanz und Schicksal der Frauen des Hauses Habsburg.* Vienna: Marchfelder Schlösserverein, 1995.

Lipschitz, Chaim U. *Franco's Spain, the Jews, and the Holocaust.* New York: Ktav, 1984.

Literature and the Delinquent: The Picaresque Novel in Spain and Europe, 1599–1753. Edinburgh: Edinburgh University Press, 1967.

Lope, Hans-Joachim. "Das kritische Bild Spaniens in Zedlers Universal-Lexikon (1730–1754). In *Aufsätze zur Literaturgeschichte in Frankreich, Belgien und Spanien.* Ed. H.-J. Lope. Frankfurt and New York: Lang, 1985.

Lope, Hans-Joachim, ed. *Antonio Ponz, 1725–1792: coloquio hispano-alemán organizado a la Biblioteca Ducal de Wolfenbüttel (3 y 4 de diciembre de 1992) con motivo del segundo centenario de su muerte.* Frankfurt and New York: P. Lang, 1995.
López Alvarez, Juan. *El krausismo en los escritos de A. Machado y Álvarez, "Demófilo."* Cádiz: Universidad de Cádiz, Servicio de Publicaciones, 1996.
López de Abiada, José Manuel, and Gustav Siebenmann. *Lateinamerika im deutschen Sprachraum—América Latina en el ámbito cultural alemán: Eine Auswahlbibliographie—Selección bibliográfica.* Tübingen: Niemeyer, 1998.
López Molina, Luis, ed. *Miscelánea de estudios hispánicos: homenaje de los hispanistas de Suiza, a Ramon Sugranyes de Franch.* Montserrat: Publicaciones de L'Abadia de Montserrat, 1982.
López-Morillas, Juan. *Krausismo: estética y literatura.* 2nd ed. Barcelona: Editorial Lumen, 1990.
———. *El krausismo español: perfil de una aventura intelectual.* 2nd ed. Madrid: Fondo de Cultura Económica, 1980.
———. *The Krausist Movement and Ideological Change in Spain, 1854–1874.* Trans. Frances M. López-Morillas. 2nd ed. Cambridge and New York: Cambridge University Press, 1981.
———. *Racionalismo pragmático: el pensamiento de Francisco Giner de los Ríos.* Madrid: Alianza, 1988.
Lorenz, Gunter W., ed. *Literatur in Lateinamerika.* St. Gallen: Edition Galerie Press, 1967.
Lorenzo, Emilio. "Goethe, visto por los españoles." *Boletín Informativo* (Fundación Juan March), no. 122 (January 1983), pp. 38–40.
———. "Goethe, visto por los españoles del siglo XIX." *Cuadernos Hispanoamericanos,* no. 88 (1957), pp. 53–72.
———. "Schiller y los españoles." *Arbor,* vol. 45 (1960), pp. 339–356.
Lovett, A. W. *Early Habsburg Spain, 1517–1598.* Oxford: Oxford University Press, 1986.
Ludwig, Jörg. *Der Handel Sachsens nach Spanien und Lateinamerika, 1760–1830: Warenexport, Unternehmerinteressen und staatliche Politik.* Leipzig: Nouvelle Alliance, 1994.
Lux, Werner. *Doña Manuela: Erzählungen aus Südamerika.* Zurich: Orell Füssli, 1979.
Lynch, John. *Spain under the Hapsburgs.* Oxford: Basil Blackwell, 1965.
Lyte, Herbert O. *Spanish Literature and Spain in Some of the Leading German Magazines of the Second Half of the Eighteenth Century.* Madison: University of Wisconsin, 1932.
———. *A Tentative Bibliography of Spanish-German Literary and Cultural Relations.* Minneapolis, 1936.
Madersbacher, Lukas, ed. *Hispania-Austria: Die Katholischen Könige, Maxmilian I. und die Anfänge der Casa de Austria in Spanien: Kunst um 1492.* Milan: Electa, 1992.
Mai, Kim Thuan. *Das Bild der "Dritten Welt" in Werken der deutschen Gegenwartsliteratur vom Ausgang der vierziger bis in die achtziger Jahre.* Frankfurt: P. Lang, 1995.
Maier, Klaus A. *Guernica 26.4.1937: Die deutsche Intervention in Spanien und der "Fall Guernica."* Freiburg i.Br.: Rombach, 1975.
Maier, Linda S. *Borges and the European Avant-garde.* New York: Peter Lang, 1996.
Mangini, Shirley. "Memories of Resistance: Women Activists from the Spanish Civil War." *Signs,* vol. 23 (1991), pp. 171–186.

———. *Memories of Resistance: Women's Voices from the Spanish Civil War.* New Haven: Yale University Press, 1995.
Mann, Heinrich. "Unamuno." *Berliner Tageblatt,* 1 October 1927.
Maravall, José Antonio. *Utopía y reformismo en la España de los Austrias.* Madrid: Siglo Ventiuno de España, 1982.
Marín-Medine, José, comp. *Spanische Plastik der Gegenwart: Neue Berliner Galerie im Alten Museum, Februar–März 1987.* Ed. Ministerium für Kultur der DDR, trans. Elisabeth Peter. Berlin: Das Zentrum, 1987.
Márquez Carrillo, Jesús. *Las aguas profundas: política y krausismo en Puebla, 1880–1910.* Puebla, Mexico: H. Ayuntamiento del Municipio de Pueblo, 1995.
Marquina, Antonio. "La iglesia española y los planes culturales alemanes para España." *Razón y Fe,* no. 975 (1979).
Martín Buezas, Fernando. *El krausismo español desde dentro: Sanz del Río, autobiografía de intimidad.* Madrid: Tecnos, D.L., 1978.
———. *La teología de Sanz del Río y del krausismo español.* Madrid: Gredos, 1977.
Martínez Esparza, José. *Con la División Azul en Rusia.* Madrid: Ediciones Ejército, 1943.
Martz, Linda. *Poverty and Welfare in Habsburg Spain: The Example of Toledo.* Cambridge: Cambridge University Press, 1983.
Mate, Reye, and Friedrich Niewöhner, eds. *La ilustración en España y Alemania.* Barcelona: Anthropos, 1989.
Matulka, Barbara. *The Novels of Juan de Flores and Their European Diffusion: A Study in Comparative Literature.* New York: Institute of French Studies, 1931.
Maura y Gamazo, Don Gabriel. *Vida y reinado de Carlos II.* 3 vol.s in 1, ed. P. Gimferrer. Madrid, 1990.
Maura y Gamazo, Don Gabriel, and Adalbert of Bavaria, eds. *Documentos inéditos referentes a las postrimérias de la Casa de Austria.* 5 vols. Madrid, 1927–35.
Mayobre Rodríguez, Purificación. *O krausismo en Galicia e Portugal.* Sada, a Coruña: Ediciós do Castro, 1994.
McDonald, William C., ed. *The Current State of Research in Fifteenth-Century Literature: Germania-Romania.* Göttingen: Kümmerle, 1986.
McDonald, William C., and Edelgard E. DuBruck, eds. *The Current State of Research in Fifteenth-Century Literature: Germania-Romania. Vol. II: 1985–1995.* Lewiston, N.Y.: Mellen, 1996.
Medicus, Thomas. *Städte der Habsburger.* Frankfurt: Hain, 1991.
Meding, Holger M. *Flucht vor Nürnberg? Deutsche und österreichische Einwanderung in Argentinien, 1945–1955.* Cologne: Böhlau, 1992.
Meding, Holger M., ed. *Nationalsozialismus und Argentinien: Beziehungen, Einflüsse und Nachwirkungen.* Frankfurt and New York: P. Lang, 1995.
Mende, Fritz. *Heine-Chronik.* Berlin: Akademie, 1970.
Menéndez Pidal, Ramón. *Manual de gramática histórica española.* 15th ed. Madrid: Espasa-Calpe, 1977.
———. *Orígenes del español.* 5th ed. Madrid: Espasa-Calpe, 1977.
Menéndez Ureña, Enrique. *Cincuenta cartas inéditas entre Sanz del Río y krausistas alemanes, 1844–1969: con introducción y notas.* Madrid: UPCO, 1993.
Menéndez y Pelayo, Marcelino. *Historia de las ideas estéticas en España.* Madrid: A. Pérez Dubrull, 1883.
Merkes, Manfred. *Die deutsche Politik gegenüber dem Spanischen Bürgerkrieg, 1936–1939.* Bonn: Röhrscheid, 1969.
Messner, Dieter. *Ibero-romanisch: Einführung in Sprache und Literatur.* Darmstadt: Wissenschaftliche Buchgesellschaft, 1983.

Mews, Siegfried, ed. *A Bertolt Brecht Reference Companion*. Westport, Conn.: Greenwood, 1997.

Meyer-Clason, Curt. *Erstens die Freiheit: Tagebuch einer Reise durch Argentinien und Brasilien*. Wuppertal: Hammer, 1978.

Meyer-Lübke, Wilhelm. *Grammaire des langues romanes*. Trans. Auguste and Georges Doutrepont. Paris: H. Welkter, 1890–1906.

———. *Grammatik der romanischen Sprachen*. 4 vols. Darmstadt: Wissenschaftliche Buchgesellschaft, 1972.

Mikusch, Dagobert von. *Franco befreit Spanien*. Leipzig: List, 1939.

Millet, Victor. *Waltharius—Gaiferos: Über den Ursprung der Walthersage und ihre Beziehung zur Romanze von Gaiferos und zur Ballade von Escriveta*. Frankfurt and New York: P. Lang, 1992.

Mir, Santiago, ed. *La reforma del derecho penal II: jornadas hispano-alemanas sobre la reforma del derecho penal, Universidad Autónoma de Barcelona, Marzo, 1980*. Bellaterra: Universidad Autónoma de Barcelona, 1981.

Moeller, Hans-Bernhard, ed. *Latin America and the Literature of Exile: A Comparative View of the 20th-Century European Refugee Writers in the New World*. Heidelberg: Carl Winter, 1983.

Mols, Manfred, and Christoph Wagner, eds. *Deutschland—Lateinamerika: Geschichte, Gegenwart und Perspektiven*. Frankfurt: Vervuert, 1994.

Monreal, Susana. *Krausismo en el Uruguay: algunos fundamentos del estado tutor*. Montevideo: Universidad Católica del Uruguay Dámaso A. Larrañaga, 1993.

Monteath, Peter. "Die Legion Condor im Spiegel der Literatur." *Lili: Zeitschrift für Literaturwissenschaft und Linguistik*, no. 60 (1985), pp. 94–111.

———. "The Spanish Civil War and the Aesthetics of Reportage." In *Literature and War*. Ed. David Bevan, pp. 69–86. Amsterdam: Rodopi, 1990.

———. *Writing the Good Fight: Political Commitment in the International Literature of the Spanish Civil War*. Westport, Conn.: Greenwood, 1994.

Monteath, Peter, and Elke Nicolai. *Zur Spanienkriegsliteratur: Die Literatur des Dritten Reiches zum Spanischen Bürgerkrieg. Mit einer Bibliographie zur internationalen Spanienkriegsliteratur*. Frankfurt, Berne, and New York: P. Lang, 1986.

Morales Lezcano, Victor. *España y el norte de Africa: el protectorado en Marruecos, 1912–1956*. 2nd ed. Madrid: Universidad Nacional de Educación a la Distancia, 1986.

———. *Historia de la no-beligerancia española durante la segunda guerra mundial (VI, 1940–X, 1943)*. Valencia: Excma; Las Palmas: Plan Cultural, 1980.

Morgan, B. Q. "Rüedegêr." *Beiträge zur Geschichte der deutschen Sprache und Literatur*, vol. 37 (1911), no. 2, pp. 325–336.

Mühlen, Patrik von zur. "'Das Atavistische in diesem Krieg.' Spanien in der *Ästhetik des Widerstands* von Peter Weiss." *Lili: Zeitschrift für Literaturwissenschaft und Linguistik*, no. 60 (1986), pp. 112–123.

———. *Fluchtziel Lateinamerika: Die deutsche Emigration, 1933–1945. Politische Aktivitäten und soziokulturelle Integration*. Bonn: Neue Gesellschaft, 1988.

———. "Säuberungen unter deutschen Spanienkämpfern." *Exilforschung*, vol. 1 (1983), pp. 165–176.

———. *Spanien war ihre Hoffnung: Die deutsche Linke im Spanischen Bürgerkrieg 1936 bis 1939*. Bonn: Verlag Neue Gesellschaft, 1983.

———. "Der spanische Bürgerkrieg: Eine Bilanz von fünfzig Jahren." *Exilforschung*, vol. 4 (1986), pp. 186–195.

Mulhall, Michael G. *Rio Grande do Sul and Its German Colonies*. London: Longmans, Green & Co., 1873.

Müller, Bodo. "La agogida de la literatura alemana en España." *Humboldt*, vol. 11, no. 43 (1970), pp. 58–68.
———. "Die Rezeption der deutschen Literatur in Spanien." *Arcadia*, vol. 2 (1967), pp. 257–276.
Müller, Jürgen. *Nationalsozialismus in Lateinamerika: Die Auslandsorganisation der NSDAP in Argentinien, Brasilien, Chile und Mexiko, 1931–1945*. Stuttgart: Heinz, 1997.
Müller, Ralf. *Die Wirtschaftsbeziehungen Hamburgs mit Lateinamerika: Trends und Perspektiven*. Hamburg: HWWA-Institut für Wirtschaftsforschung, 1993.
Müller-Kampel, Beatrix. *Dämon—Schwärmer—Biedermann: Don Juan in der deutschen Literatur bis 1918*. Berlin: E. Schmidt, 1993.
Müller-Waldeck, Gunnar. "Maria Osten zum Gedenken." *Notate*, vol. 2 (1990), pp. 14–15.
Münnig, Elisabeth. *Calderón und die ältere deutsche Romantik*. Berlin, 1912.
Nader, Helen. *Liberty in Absolutist Spain: The Habsburg Sale of Towns, 1516–1700*. Baltimore: Johns Hopkins University Press, 1990.
Namuth, Hans, and Georg Reisner. *Spanisches Tagebuch 1936: Fotografien und Texte aus den ersten Monaten des Bürgerkriegs*. Ed. Diethart Kerbs. Berlin: Nishen, 1986.
Nash, Mary. *Defying Male Civilization: Women in the Spanish Civil War*. Denver: Arden, 1995.
Nelles, Dieter. "Deutsche Anarchosyndikalisten und Freiwillige in anarchistischen Milizen im Spanischen Bürgerkrieg." *Internationale Wissenschaftliche Korrespondenz zur Geschichte der deutschen Arbeiterbewegung*, vol. 33 (1997), pp. 500–518.
Nelson, R. J. "Hieronymous Bosch y el Otoño de la Edad Media." *Hispania*, vol. 70 (1987), no. 3, pp. 422–430.
Neruda, Pablo. "Gruß an die DDR." *Weltbühne*, vol. 69, no. 39 (1974), pp. 1217–1219.
———. *Memoirs*. Trans. Hardie St. Martin. New York: Farrar, Straus and Giroux, 1977.
———. *Obras Completas*. 2 vols. Buenos Aires: Editorial Losada, 1957.
———. *Poésie Impure*. Ed. and trans. Hans Magnus Enzensberger. Hamburg: Hoffmann und Campe, 1968.
———. *Residence on Earth*. Trans. Donald D. Walsh. New York: New Directions, 1973.
Neuschäfer, Hans-Jörg. *Macht und Ohnmacht der Zensur: Literatur, Theater und Film in Spanien, 1933–1976*. Stuttgart: Metzler, 1991.
Ngouebeng, Ebol. *Die Entwicklungsproblematik der mexikanischen Gesellschaft und die Indianerfrage in den Romanen von B. Traven*. Pfaffenweiler: Centaurus, 1996.
Niederehe, Hans-Josef, ed. *Schwerpunkt Siglo de oro: Akten des Deutschen Hispanistentages, Wolfenbüttel, 28.2.-1.3.1985*. Hamburg: Buske, 1986.
Niederehe, Hans-Josef, and Harald Haarmann. *In memoriam Friedrich Diez: Akten des Kolloquiums zur Wissenschaftsgeschichte der Romanistik, Trier, 2.-4. Oktober 1975*. Amsterdam: John Benjamins, 1976.
Noeske, Jürgen. *Freies/neues Deutschland = Alemania Libre: Zur Inszenierung von Wirklichkeit in einer Exilzeitschrift*. Bamberg: Schadel, 1980.
Novalis [Friedrich von Hardenberg]. *Henry of Ofterdingen*. Trans. Palmer Hilty. New York: Ungar, 1964.
Núñez de Arce, Gaspar. *Gritos del combate*. Madrid: F. Fé, 1930.
O'Callaghan, Joseph F. *A History of Medieval Spain*. Ithaca: Cornell University Press, 1975.

Ohler, Norbert. *Pilgerleben im Mittelalter: Zwischen Andacht und Abenteuer*. Freiburg i.Br.: Herder, 1994.
Ojeda-Ebert, Gerardo Jorge. *Deutsche Einwanderung und Herausbildung der chilenischen Nation, 1846–1920*. Munich: Fink, 1984.
Olives Canals, Santiago. *Bergnes de las Casas, helenista y editor*. Barcelona: Escuela de Filología, 1947.
Olmedo Moreno, Miguel. *El pensamiento de Ganivet*. Madrid: Revista de Occidente, 1965.
Opll, Ferdinand, and Karl Rudolf. *Spanien und Österreich*. Vienna: Jugend und Volk, 1991.
Orden Jiménez, Rafael V. *Las habilitaciones filosóficas de Krause: con estudio preliminar y notas*. Madrid: UPCO, 1996.
Oria, Tomás G. *Martí y el krausismo*. Boulder, Colo.: Society of Spanish and Spanish-American Studies, 1987.
Orringer, Nelson R. *Ortega y sus fuentes germánicas*. Madrid: Gredos, 1979.
———. *Nuevas fuentes germánicas de "Qué es filosofía?" de Ortega*. Madrid: Consejo Superior de Investigaciones Científicas, Instituto de Filosofía "Luis Vives," 1984.
———. *Unamuno y los protestantes liberales (1912): sobre las fuentes de "Del sentimiento trágico de la vida."* Madrid: Gredos, 1985.
Ortega y Gasset, José. *Obras completas*. 12 vols. Madrid: Alianza, 1987.
Ortiz, Héctor V., coord. *La filosofía hoy en Alemania y América Latina: jornados realizadas en Córdoba entre el 21 y el 24 de septiembre de 1983*. Córdoba: Círculos de Amigos del Instituto Goethe, 1984.
Osten, Maria. "Frühling in Madrid (1937)." In *Geschichten aus der Geschichte des Spanischen Bürgerkriegs*. Ed. Erich Hackl and Cristina Timón Solinís, pp. 104–107. Darmstadt: Luchterhand, 1986.
Otto, Wolfgang. *Conquista, Kultur und Ketzerwahn: Spanien im Jahrhundert seiner Weltherrschaft*. Göttingen: Vandenhoeck & Ruprecht, 1992.
Oven, Wilfried von. *Hitler und der Spanische Bürgerkrieg: Mission und Schicksal der Legion Condor*. Tübingen: Grabert, 1978.
Overy, R. J. *War and Economy in the Third Reich*. New York: Oxford University Press, 1994.
Owen, Claude. *Heine im spanischen Sprachgebiet*. Münster: Aschendorff, 1968.
———. "Ramiro de Maeztu über Heinrich Heine." *Heine-Jahrbuch* (1967), pp. 91–98.
Pade, Werner. *Deutschland und Argentinien 1917/18–1933: Studien zur Expansion des deutschen Kapitals nach Lateinamerika in der Weimarer Republik*. Ph.D. Diss. University of Rostock, 1971.
Pageard, Robert. *Goethe en España*. Trans. Francisco de A. Caballero. Madrid: CSIC, 1958.
Pageard, Robert, and G. W. Ribbans. "'Heine and Byron' in the *Semanario Popular* (1862–1865)." *Bulletin of Hispanic Studies*, vol. 33 (1956), pp. 78–86.
Pailler, Claire, ed. *Les Amériques et l'Europe: voyage, émigration, exil. Actes de la 3ème semaine latino-américaine, Université de Toulouse-Le Mirail, 12–15 mars 1984*. Toulouse: Université de Toulouse-Le Mirail, 1985.
Pardo Bazán, Emilia. "Fortuna española de Heine." *Revista de España*, no. 110 (1886), pp. 481–496.
Parker, Geoffrey. *The Army of Flanders and the Spanish Road, 1567–1659*. Cambridge, Mass., 1972.
———. *Philip II*. Boston: Little, Brown, 1978.

———. *Spain and the Netherlands, 1559–1659: Ten Studies*. London: Fontana Press, 1990.
Parrilla, Justo P. *Conflicto hispano-alemán: descripción geográfico-histórica de las islas Marianas y Carolinas, acompañada de una carta marítima del océano Pacífico*. Havanna: La Propaganda literaria, 1885.
Pass, Walter. *Musik und Musiker am Hof Maximilians II*. Tutzing: Schneider, 1980.
Paulin, Roger. *Ludwig Tieck: A Literary Biography*. Oxford: Clarendon Press, 1986.
Payne, Stanley G. *The Franco Regime, 1936–1975*. Madison: University of Wisconsin Press, 1987.
———. *Franco's Spain*. New York: Crowell, 1967.
———. *Politics and the Military in Modern Spain*. Stanford, Calif.: Stanford University Press, 1967.
Payne, Stanley G., and Javier Tusell, eds. *La Guerra Civil: una nueva visión del conflicto que dividió España*. Madrid: Temas de Hoy, 1996.
Pecellín Lancharro, Manuel. *El krausismo en Badajoz: Tomás Romero de Castilla*. Extremedura: Universidad de Extremadura, Servicio de Publicaciones, 1987.
Pellicer, Alexandre Cirici, et al. *Spanische Kunst heute: 11.II.–3.III.1968*. Bochum: Städtische Kunstgallerie, 1968.
Peñalver Castillo, Manuel. *La escuela de Menéndez Pidal y la historiografía lingüística hispánica, aproxomación a su estudio*. Almería: Universidad de Almería, 1995.
Peréz Lopez, Ana. "In den Augen der anderen: Spanische Germanisten zu ihrer Begegnung mit der DDR-Literatur," *Weimarer Beiträge*, vol. 9 (1987).
Peter, Antonio. *Das Spanienbild in den Massenmedien des Dritten Reiches, 1933–1945*. Frankfurt: P. Lang, 1992.
Pettegree, Andrew, ed. *The Early Reformation in Europe*. Cambridge: Cambridge University Press, 1992.
Pérez, Janet, and Wendell Aycock, eds. *The Spanish Civil War in Literature*. Lubbock: Texas Technical University Press, 1990.
Pérez Bustamante, Ciriaco. *La España de Felipe III*, 3rd ed. Madrid: Espasa-Calpe, 1983.
Pérez Martín, María Jesús. *Margarita de Austria, reina de España*. Madrid: Espasa-Calpe, 1961.
Pérez Sánchez, Alfonso E. "The Madrid-Prague Axis." In *The Arcimboldo Effect: Transformations of the Face of the Sixteenth to the Twentieth Century*. Ed. Ponus Hulten. New York: Abbeville, 1987.
Pérez Villanueva, Joaquín. *Ramón Menéndez Pidal: su vida y su tiempo*. Madrid: Espasa-Calpe, 1991.
Petriconi, Hellmuth. *Die spanische Literatur der Gegenwart*. Wiesbaden, 1926.
Pfandl, Ludwig. *Carlos II*. Madrid, 1947.
———. *Cultura y costumbres del pueblo español de los siglos XVI y XVII*. Barcelona: Araluce, 1929.
———. *Geschichte der spanischen Nationalliteratur in ihrer Blütezeit*. Freiburg i.Br.: Herder, 1929.
———. *Historia de la literatura nacional española en la edad de oro*. Barcelona: Gili, 1933.
———. *Spanische Kultur und Sitte des 16. und 17. Jahrhunderts*. Kempten: Kösel and Pustet, 1924.
Pfanner, Helmut F., ed. *Kulturelle Wechselbeziehungen im Exil*. Bonn: Bouvier, 1986.
Pfeifer, Martin, ed. *Hermann Hesses weltweite Wirkung: Internationale Rezeptionsgeschichte*. 3 vols. Frankfurt: Suhrkamp, 1977–91.
Pfeiffer, Erna, and Hugo Kubarth, eds. *Canticum Ibericum: Neuere spanische, portugiesische und lateinamerikanische Literatur im Spiegel von Interpretation und Übersetzung. Georg Rudolf Lind zum Gedenken*. Frankfurt: Vervuert, 1991.

Phillips, Carla Rahn, and William D. Phillips, Jr. *Spain's Golden Fleece: Wool Production and the Wool Trade from the Middle Ages to the Nineteenth Century*. Baltimore, Md.: Johns Hopkins University Press, 1997.
Pichler, Georg. *Der spanische Bürgerkrieg (1936–1939) im deutschsprachigen Roman*. Frankfurt: Lang, 1991.
Pike, David Wingeate. "Franco and the Axis Stigma." *Journal of Contemporary History*, vol. 17 (January 1982), pp. 369–407.
Plitt, Gustav Leopold, ed. *Aus Schellings Leben in Briefen*. 3 vols. Leipzig: Hirzel, 1869.
Po-chia Hsia, R. *The World of Catholic Renewal, 1540–1770*. New York: Cambridge University Press, 1998.
Pohl, Walter, and Karl Vocelka. *Die Habsburger: Eine europäische Familiengeschichte*. Ed. Brigitte Vacha. Graz: Styria, 1992.
Pohle, Fritz. *Emigrationstheater in Südamerika abseits der "Freien Deutschen Bühne" Buenos Aires*. Hamburg: Hamburger Arbeitsstelle für Deutsche Exilliteratur, 1989.
———. *Das mexikanische Exil: Ein Beitrag zur Geschichte der kulturellen Emigration aus Deutschland, 1937–1946*. Stuttgart: Metzler, 1986.
Polleross, Friedrich B., et al., eds. *Federschmuck und Kaiserkrone: Das barocke Amerikabild in den habsburgischen Ländern. 10. Mai–13. September 1992, Schloßhof im Marchfeld*. Vienna: Bundesministerium für Wissenschaft und Forschung, 1992.
Pollmann, Leo. *Geschichte des lateinamerikanischen Romans*. 2 vols. Berlin: E. Schmidt, 1982–84.
Pommerin, Reiner. *Das Dritte Reich und Lateinamerika: Die deutsche Politik gegenüber Süd- und Mittelamerika, 1939–1942*. Düsseldorf: Droste, 1977.
Posada, Adolfo. *Breve historia del krausismo español*. Oviedo: Universidad, Servicio de Publicaciones, D.L., 1981.
Prawer, Siegbert. "Heine's Return." *German Life and Letters*, vol. 9 (1955/56), pp. 171–180.
Preston, Paul. *Franco: A Biography*. New York: Basic Books, 1994.
———. "Franco and Hitler: The Myth of Hendaye 1940," *Contemporary European History*, vol. 1 (March 1992), pp. 1–16.
Preston, Paul, ed. *Revolution and War in Spain, 1931–1939*. London and New York: Methuen, 1984.
Preston, Paul, and Ann L. Mackenzie, eds. *The Republic Besieged: Civil War in Spain, 1936–1939*. Edinburgh: Edinburgh University Press, 1996.
Prien, Hans-Jürgen, ed. *Verzeichnis der Veröffentlichungen zur Iberischen Halbinsel und Lateinamerika*. Münster: Lit, 1990.
Proctor, Raymond L. *Agony of a Neutral: Spanish-German Wartime Relations and the "Blue Division."* Moscow, Idaho: Idaho Research Foundation, 1974.
———. *Hitler's Luftwaffe in the Spanish Civil War*. Westport, Conn.: Greenwood Press, 1983.
———. "The Spanish Army and the Nationalists' Moroccan Allies." *Bulletin of the Society for Spanish and Portuguese Historical Studies*, vol. 9 (October 1984), pp. 18–19.
Prüfer-Leske, Irene. "Übersetzungen deutscher Kinderliteratur in Spanien," *Lengua y literatura de los países de habla alemana y didáctica del Alemán*, 1997–98.
Raders, Margit. "Zur spanischen Rezeption des Werks der Schriftstellerfamilie Mann anhand der Übersetzungen." *Actas de los IV Encuentros Complutenses en torno a la Traducción*, pp. 569–583. Ed. Margit Raders and Rafael Martín-Gaitero. Madrid: Editorial Complutense, 1994.

———. "Zur spanischen Rezeption des Werks der Schriftstellerfamilie Mann anhand der Übersetzungen: Golo Mann." *Actas de los V Encuentros Complutenses en torno a la Traducción*, pp. 417–429. Ed. Margit Raders and Rafael Martín-Gaitero. Madrid: Editorial Complutense, 1995.
Raders, Margit, and Luisa Schelling, eds. *Der deutsche und der spanische Schelmenroman*. Madrid: Ediciones del Orto, 1995.
———. *Deutsch-spanische Literatur- und Kulturbeziehungen: Rezeptionsgeschichte = Relaciones hispano-alemanas en la literatura y la cultura: historia de la recepción*. Madrid: Ediciones del Orto, 1995.
Rausse, Hubert. *Zur Geschichte des spanischen Schelmenromans in Deutschland*. Münster, Westfalen: H. Schöningh, 1908.
Reboredo Olivenza, José Daniel. *Krausismo y contrarrevolución en el País Vasco: La Universidad Literaria de Vitoria, 1869–1873*. Vitoria-Gasteiz: J. D. Reboredo Olivenza, 1996.
Reck, Hanne Gabriele. *Die spanische Romanze im Werke Heinrich Heines*. Frankfurt: P. Lang, 1987.
Regler, Gustav. *The Great Crusade*. New York and Toronto: Longmans, Green and Co., 1940.
———. *Das große Beispiel*: Roman einer internationalen Brigade. Cologne: Kiepenheuer & Witsch, 1976.
Rehm, Walther. *Götterstille und Göttertrauer: Aufsätze zur deutsch-antiken Begegnung*. Berne: Francke, 1951.
Reichardt, Dieter. *Autorenlexikon Lateinamerika*. Frankfurt: Suhrkamp, 1992.
———. *Lateinamerikanische Autoren: Literaturlexikon und Bibliographie der deutschen Übersetzungen*. Ed. Institut für Iberoamerika-Kunde. Tübingen: Erdmann, 1972.
Reiche, Maria. *Contribuciones a la geometría y astronomía en el antiguo Perú*. Lima, Peru: Asociación María Reiche para las Líneas de Nasca, 1993.
———. *Conversaciones con María Reiche*. Ed. Clorinda Caller Iberico. Lima, Peru: Editorial Horizonte, 1992.
———. *Peruanische Erdzeichen = Peruvian Ground Drawings*. Ed. Hermann Kern. Munich: Kunstraum München, 1974.
Reifenscheid, Richard. *Die Habsburger in Lebensbildern: Von Rudolf I. bis Karl I.* Graz: Styria, 1982.
Reinhart, Karla. *Jene Lilien von Valois: Eine spanische Königin in der Geschichte des 16. Jahrhunderts, in Schillers "Don Karlos" und in Verdis "Don Carlos."* Frankfurt: Lang, 1997.
Reiss, H. S. "The Criticism of Heine since the War: An Assessment." *German Life and Letters*, vol. 9 (1955/56), pp. 210–219.
Renn, Ludwig. *In Mexiko*. Berlin and Weimar: Aufbau, 1979.
———. *Im spanischen Krieg*. Berlin and Weimar: Aufbau, 1977.
Retornado: algunas apreciaciones sobre el retorno de los exilados chilenos residentes en Alemania a su patria. Rostock: Universität Rostock, 1995.
Reuter, Wolfgang. *The Lippizaners and the Spanish Riding School*. Trans. J. M. Abbot. Innsbruck: Pinguin, 1969.
Revista de Filología Alemana. Madrid: Universidad Complutense, vol. 1 (1993) ff.
Ribas, Pedro, ed. *Verbreitung und Rezeption der Werke von Marx und Engels in Spanien*. Trier: Karl-Marx-Haus, 1994.
Richards, Earl Jeffrey. *Modernism, Medievalism, and Humanism: A Research Bibliography on the Reception of the Works of Ernst Robert Curtius*. Tübingen: Niemeyer, 1983.

Riedel, Volker. *Freies Deutschland, México, 1941–1946: Bibliographie einer Zeitschrift.* Berlin and Weimar: Aufbau, 1975.
Ries, Karl, and Hans Ring. *Legion Condor, 1936–1939: Eine illustrierte Dokumentation.* Mainz: Dieter Hoffmann, 1980.
———. *The Condor Legion: A History of the Luftwaffe in the Spanish Civil War, 1936–1939.* Trans. David Johnston. West Chester, Penn.: Schiffer Military History, 1992.
Rincón, Carlos, and Gerda Schattenberg-Rincón, eds. *Moderne Lyrik aus Nikaragua: Spanisch und deutsch.* Leipzig: Reclam, 1981.
Ríos, Laura de los. *Los cuentos de Clarín: proyección de una vida.* Madrid: Revista de Occidente, 1965.
Rodiek, Christoph. *Sujet—Kontext—Gattung: Die internationale Cid-Rezeption.* Berlin and New York, 1990.
Rodríguez-Arana Muñoz, Xaime, ed. *Reforma administrativa: seminario bilateral hispano-alemán sobre reforma administrativa, Santiago de Compostela, 20 e 21 de setembro de 1993.* Santiago de Compostela: Escola Galega de Administración Pública, 1993.
Roggausch, Werner. *Das Exilwerk von Anna Seghers, 1933–1939: Volksfront und antifaschistische Literatur.* Munich: Minerva, 1979.
Rohde, Erich, ed. *Ludwig Renn zum 70. Geburtstag.* Berlin: Aufbau, 1959.
Roloff, Volker, and Harald Wentzlaff-Eggebert, eds. *Der spanische Roman vom Mittelalter bis zur Gegenwart.* Düsseldorf: Schwann Bagel, 1986.
Romero, Christiane Zehl. *Anna Seghers.* Hamburg: Rowohlt, 1993.
Rosenthal, Ludwig. *Heinrich Heine als Jude.* Frankfurt: Ullstein, 1973.
Rössig, Wolfgang. *Literaturen der Welt in deutscher Übersetzung: Eine chronologische Bibliographie.* Stuttgart: Metzler, 1997.
Rössner, Michael. *Auf der Suche nach dem verlorenen Paradies: Zum mythischen Bewußtsein in der Literatur des 20. Jahrhunderts.* Frankfurt: Athenäum, 1988.
Das Rotbuch über Spanien: Bilder, Dokumente, Zeugenaussagen. Ed. Anti-Komintern. Berlin and Leipzig: Nibelungen, 1937.
Rothe, Hans, ed. *Deutsche in der Habsburger Monarchie.* Cologne: Böhlau, 1989.
Rötzer, Hans Gerd. *Picaro—Landstörtzer—Simplicius: Studien zum niederen Roman in Spanien und Deutschland.* Darmstadt: Wissenschaftliche Buchgesellschaft, 1972.
Rüchardt, Benedikt. *Deutsch-spanische Beziehungen.* Freising: Graphischer Betrieb Kratzl & Goerge, 1988.
Ruhl, Klaus-Jörg. *Franco, Falange y "Tercer Reich": España en la Segunda Guerra Mundial.* Madrid: Ediciones Akal, 1986.
———. *Spanien im Zweiten Weltkrieg: Franco, die Falange und das "Dritte Reich."* Hamburg: Hoffman und Campe, 1975.
Rukser, Udo. *Goethe in der hispanischen Welt.* Stuttgart: Metzler, 1958.
———. *Goethe en el mundo hispánico.* Trans. Carlos Gerhard. Mexico City: Fondo de Cultura Económica, 1977.
———. "Heine in der hispanischen Welt." *Deutsche Vierteljahrsschrift für Literaturwissenschaft und Geistesgeschichte,* vol. 30 (1956), pp. 474–510.
Rumold, Inca. "Lorca and Neruda in Erich Arendt's Poetry." *Monatshefte,* vol. 77, no. 2 (Summer 1985), pp. 143–150.
Rusin, Beatrix Maria. *Mensch und Urwald im hispano-amerikanischen Roman.* Vienna: Böhlau, 1981.
Sachs, Michael. *Die religiöse Poesie der Juden in Spanien.* Berlin, 1845.
Salas Larrazabal, Jesús. *Air War over Spain.* Trans. M. A. Kelley. London: Allan, 1974.

Salisbury, Joyce E. *Iberian Popular Religion 600 B.C. to 700 A.D.: Celts, Visigoths, Romans*. Lewiston, N.Y.: Mellen, 1985.

Sánchez, Magdalena S. *The Empress, the Queen, and the Nun: Women and Power at the Court of Philip III of Spain*. Baltimore: Johns Hopkins University Press, 1998.

Sánchez Fernández, Beatriz. *Proteccionismo y liberalismo: las relaciones comerciales entre Suiza y España, 1869–1935*. Frankfurt: Vervuert; Madrid: Iberoamericana, 1996.

San Miguel, Ángel, ed. *Calderón: Fremdheit und Nähe eines spanischen Barockdramatikers. Akten des internationalen Kongresses anläßlich der Bamberger Calderón-Tage 1987*. Frankfurt: Vervuert, 1988.

Santí, Enrico Mario. "Introducción." In Pablo Neruda, *Canto General*, pp. 11–99. Madrid: Cátedra, 1995.

Sanz del Río, Julián. *Cincuenta cartas inéditas entre Sanz del Río y krausistas alemanes, 1844–1969: con introducción y notas*. Ed. Enrique M. Ureña. Madrid: UPCO, 1993.

Sapper, Christian. "Casa de Austria: The Austro-Spanish Family Chronicle." *Austria Today*, 1992, no. 3, pp. 29–35.

Sauder, Gerhard. "Blasphemisch-religiöse Körperwelt. Heinrich Heines 'Hebräische Melodien.'" In *Heinrich Heine: Artistik und Engagement*. Ed. Wolfgang Kuttenkeuler, pp. 118–143. Stuttgart: Metzler, 1977.

Schack, Adolf Friedrich von. *Geschichte der dramatischen Literatur und Kunst in Spanien*. Berlin 1845–54. Reprint Hildesheim and New York: Olms, 1975.

Schaefer, Camillo. *Gewaltig viele Noten: Die Musik der Habsburger*. Vienna: Überreuter, 1996.

Schaeffer, Adolf. *Geschichte des spanischen Nationaldramas*. 2 vols. Leipzig: Brockhaus, 1890.

Scharlau, Birgit, ed. *Bild, Wort, Schrift: Beiträge zur Lateinamerika-Sektion des Freiburger Romanistentages*. Tübingen: Narr, 1989.

Schempp, Otto. *Das autoritäre Spanien*. Leipzig: Goldmann, 1939.

Scherfenberg, Ulrich. *Die auswärtige Kulturpolitik der Bundesrepublik Deutschland in der peripheren Region Lateinamerika: Rahmenbedingungen, Formen, Inhalte, Ziele und Auswirkungen*. Munich: Fink, 1984.

Schiller, Johann Christoph Friedrich von. *Die Braut von Messina, oder die feindlichen Brüder. Ein Trauerspiel mit Chören*. In *Werke*, vol. 2: *Dramen II*. Ed. Herbert Kraft. Frankfurt: Insel, 1966.

———. *Über naive und sentimentalische Dichtung*. Oxford: Basil Blackwell, 1951.

Schlegel, August Wilhelm. *Kritische Schriften und Briefe*. Ed. Edgar Lohner. Stuttgart: Kohlhammer, 1962.

———. *Schauspiele von Don Pedro Calderón de la Barca*. 2 vols. Berlin: Hitzig, 1803–09.

———. *Das spanische Theater*. 2 vols. Berlin: Reimer, 1803–09.

———. *Das spanische Theater*. 2 vols. Ed. Eduard Böcking. Leipzig: Wiedmann, 1945.

Schlegel, Friedrich von. *Geschichte der europäischen Literatur*. In *Kritische Friedrich-Schlegel-Ausgabe*. Ed. Ernst Behler. Vol. 11. Paderborn and Munich: F. Schöningh, 1958.

Schlenstedt, Dieter. *Egon Erwin Kisch: Leben und Werk*. Berlin: das europäische buch, 1985.

Schlenstedt, Silvia. "Neues Nachdenken über Spanien und deutsche Antifaschisten." *Weimarer Beiträge*, vol. 7 (1986), pp. 1125–1143.

Schlenstedt, Silvia, ed. *Spanien-Akte Arendt: Aufgefundene Texte Erich Arendts aus dem Spanienkrieg*. Rostock: Hinstorff, 1986.

Schmidt-Brabant, Manfred. *Sternenwege: Von den alten zu den neuen Mysterien. Die Hintergründe des Camino nach Santiago de Compostela*. Dornach: Verlag am Goetheanum, 1996.

Schmieder, Ulrike. *Lateinamerika in Periodika deutscher Regionen: Die Widerspiegelung der gesellschaftlichen Transformation Lateinamerikas in publizistischen Quellen, 1760–1850*. Hamburg: Kovac, 1998.

Schmigalle, Günther, ed. *Der spanische Bürgerkrieg: Literatur und Geschichte*. Frankfurt: Vervuert, 1986.

Schneider, Adam. *Spaniens Anteil an der deutschen Literatur des 16. und 17. Jahrhunderts*. Strasbourg: Schlesier & Schweikhardt, 1898.

Schneider, F. G. A. *Béquer: Leben und Schaffen*. Bonn and Leipzig, 1914.

Schneider, Reinhold. *Gesammelte Werke*. Ed. Edwin Maria Landau. 10 vols. Frankfurt: Insel, 1977–81.

Schoepp, Sebastian. *Das "Argentinische Tageblatt" 1933 bis 1945: Ein Forum der antinationalsozialistischen Emigration*. Berlin: Wissenschaftlicher Verlag, 1996.

Schönwald, Matthias. *Deutschland und Argentinien nach dem Zweiten Weltkrieg: Politische und wirtschaftliche Beziehungen und deutsche Auswanderung 1945–1955*. Paderborn: Schöningh, 1998.

Schoonover, Thomas. *Germany in Central America: Competitive Imperialism, 1821–1929*. Tuscaloosa: University of Alabama Press, 1998.

Schrader, Achim, ed. *Deutsche Beziehungen zu Lateinamerika*. Münster: Lit, 1991.

Schrader, Achim, and Karl Heinrich Rengstorf, eds. *Europäische Juden in Lateinamerika*. St. Ingbert: Röhrig, 1989.

Schrader, Ludwig, ed. *Von Góngora bis Nicolás Guillén: Spanische und lateinamerikanische Literatur in deutscher Übersetzung—Erfahrungen und Perspektiven. Akten des internationalen Kolloquiums Düsseldorf vom 21.-22.5.1992*. Tübingen: Narr, 1993.

Schramm, E. "Einwirkung der spanischen Literatur auf die deutsche." *Deutsche Philologie im Aufriß*, vol. 3 (1957), pp. 261–306.

Schreiber, Georg. *Habsburger auf Reisen*. Vienna: Überreuter, 1994.

Schuler, Friedrich E. *Mexico between Hitler and Roosevelt: Mexican Foreign Relations in the Age of Lázaro Cárdenas, 1934–1940*. Albuquerque: University of New Mexico Press, 1998.

Schumacher, Ernst, and Renate Schumacher. *Leben Brechts in Wort und Bild*. Berlin: Henschel, 1978.

Schütz, Günther. *Epistolario de Rufino José Cuervo con filólogos de Alemania, Austria y Suiza y noticias de las demás relaciones de Cuervo con estos países y sus representantes*. 2 vols. Bogota: Instituto Caro y Cuervo, 1976.

Schwarz, Egon. "Exilliteratur." In *Deutsche Literatur: Eine Sozialgeschichte*, vol. 9, pp. 302–317. Ed. Horst Albert Glaser. Reinbek: Rowohlt, 1980ff.

———. "Joan Maragall, Catalan Mediator of German Literature." *Modern Language Notes*, vol. 76 (1961), pp. 800–807.

———. *Hofmannsthal und Calderon*. Cambridge, Mass.: Harvard University Press, 1962.

———. *Keine Zeit für Eichendorff: Chronik unfreiwilliger Wanderjahre*. Frankfurt: Gutenberg, 1992.

———. "The Reception of German Culture in Spain." *Yearbook of Comparative and General Literature*, vol. 14 (1965), pp. 16–39.

Schwartz, Wilhelm. *August Wilhelm Schlegels Verhältnis zur spanischen und portugiesischen Literatur*. Halle a.d.S.: E. Karras, 1913.

Schwarz, Reingard. *Die Dichtergruppe Cántico und ihre Zeitschrift, 1947–1957: Ein Beispiel andalusischer Lyrik der Nachkriegszeit.* Vienna: Böhlau, 1989.
Schweitzer, Christoph E. *Spanien in der deutschen Literatur des 17. Jahrhunderts.* Ph.D. Diss. Yale University, 1954.
Schwering, Julius. *Litterarische Beziehungen zwischen Spanien und Deutschland: Eine Streitschrift gegen Dr. A. Farinelli.* Münster: Heinrich Schöningh, 1902.
Seghers, Anna: *Gesammelte Werke in Einzelbänden.* 14 vols. Berlin: Aufbau-Verlag, 1984.
———. "Gruß an den II. Internationalen Schriftstellerkongreß 1937." In *Über Kunstwerk und Wirklichkeit.* Ed. Sigrid Bock. Vol. 1, pp. 66–67. Berlin: Akademie Verlag, 1970.
———. "Rede auf dem II. Deutschen Schriftstellerkongreß 1950." In *Über Kunstwerk und Wirklichkeit.* Ed. Sigrid Bock. Vol. 1, pp. 76–84. Berlin: Akademie Verlag, 1970.
———. *Werke in zehn Bänden.* Darmstadt and Neuwied: Luchterhand, 1977.
Seghers, Anna, and Wieland Herzfelde. *Gewöhnliches und gefährliches Leben: Ein Briefwechsel aus der Zeit des Exils, 1939–1946.* Darmstadt: Luchterhand, 1986.
Selig, Karl-Ludwig. "Another Inventory of a German Collection of Spanish Books." In *Bibliothèque de Manisme et Renaissance,* vol. 21 (1959), pp. 613–615.
———. "Garcilaso in 17th-Century Germany: Two Citations and an Excursus Bibliographicus." In *Revista hispánica moderna,* vol. 40 (1978/79), pp. 72–75.
———. "A German Library of Spanish Books (Cat. Bavaricus 110)." In *Bibliothèque de Manisme et Renaissance,* vol. 19 (1957), pp. 51–79.
———. *The Library of Vincencio Juan de Lastanosa, Patron of Gracián.* Geneva: E. Droz, 1960.
———. "Los proverbios españoles de Daniel Georg Morhof." In *Estudios sobre el Siglo de Oro: En homenaje a Raymond R. MacCurdy,* pp. 327–332. Ed. Ángel González et al. Albuquerque, N.M., and Madrid: Cátedra, 1983.
———. "The Spanish Proverbs in Hieronymus Megiserus." *Proverbium* [Helsinki], vol. 16 (1972), p. 576.
Sell, Hans Joachim. *Das Drama Unamuno: Ein Vortrag zur 100. Wiederkehr des Geburtstages des spanischen Dichters und Philosophen Miguel de Unamuno.* Munich: Ellermann, 1965.
———. *Der rote Priester: Eine spanische Erfahrung.* Düsseldorf: Claassen, 1976.
Sepasgosarian, Ramin Alexander. *Eine ungetrübte Freundschaft? Deutschland und Spanien, 1918–1933.* Saarbrücken and Fort Lauterdale: Breitenbach, 1993.
Serrano Suñer, Ramón. *Entre Hendaye y Gibraltar: noticia y reflexión, frente a una legenda, sobre nuestra politica en dos guerras.* Madrid: Ediciones y Publicaciones Españolas, S.A., 1947.
———. *Memorias: entre el silencio y la propaganda, la historia como fue.* Barcelona: Planeta, 1977.
Seyhan, Azade. *Representation and Its Discontents: The Critical Legacy of German Romanticism.* Berkeley: University of California Press, 1992.
Siebenmann, Gustav. *Die lateinamerikanische Lyrik, 1892–1992.* Berlin: E. Schmidt, 1993.
Siebenmann, Gustav, and Hans-Joachim König, eds. *Das Bild Lateinamerikas im deutschen Sprachraum: Ein Arbeitsgespräch an der Herzog August-Bibliothek Wolfenbüttel, 15.-17. März 1989.* Tübingen, 1992.
Siebenmann, Gustav, and José Manuel Lopez, eds. *Spanische Lyrik des 20. Jahrhunderts.* Stuttgart: Philipp Reclam, 1985.

Siefer, Elisabeth. *Epische Stilelemente im Canto General von Pablo Neruda*. Munich: Fink, 1970.

Siefer, Elisabeth, ed. *Neuere deutsche Lateinamerika-Forschung: Institute und Bibliotheken in der Bundesrepublik Deutschland und in Berlin (West)*. Hamburg: Arbeitsgemeinschaft Deutsche Lateinamerikaforschung, 1971.

Siemsen, Anna. *Spanisches Bilderbuch*. Düsseldorf: Komet, 1947.

Siera, Ana. *El mundo como volundad y representación: Borges y Schopenhauer*. Potomac, Md.: Scripta Humanistica, 1997.

Siguan Bohemer, María Luísa. "La recepción de las literaruras hispánicas en Alemania: Una imagen de España." In *Homenaje al profesor Antonio Vilanova*. Coord. Adolfo Sotelo Vásquez, ed. Marta Cristina Carbonell. Barcelona: Universidad de Barcelona, 1989.

Siguan Bohemer, María Luísa, and Jordi Jané Carbó. "El Fausto de Goethe en España." *Revista Libros*, no. 21 (1983), pp. 12–17.

Simmer, Götz. *Die deutsche Auswanderung nach Mittel- und Südamerika im 16. und frühen 17. Jahrhundert*. Bamberg: Förderverein Forschungsstiftung für vergleichende europäische Überseegeschichte, 1993.

Simposio Internacional Influencias Científicas Alemanas en la Argentina: actas del simposio, 18 al 20 de agosto de 1992. Ed. Embajada de la República Federal de Alemania en Buenos Aires [and the] Institución Cultural Argentino-Germana, 1993.

Smeth, Maria de. *Viva España! Arriba España! Eine Frau erlebt den spanischen Krieg*. Berlin: Nibelungen, 1937.

———. *Roter Kaviar—Hauptmann Maria: Odyssee einer Frau im 20. Jahrhundert*. Wels: Welsermühl, 1965.

Smitten, Theo in der. *Don Quixote (der "richtige" und der "falsche") und sieben deutsche Leser: Rezeptionsästhetische leseaktorientierte vergleichende Analysen an spanischen Ur-Quixote-Ausgaben von 1604/5 bis 1615 und sechs deutschen Übersetzungen von 1648 bis 1883*. 2 vols. Berne and New York: Peter Lang, 1986.

Sobejano, Gonzalo. "Introducción." In *Leopoldo Alas, "Clarín": La Regenta*, vol. 1, pp. 7–67. Madrid: Castalia, 1981.

Sofer, Johann. *Die Welttheater Hugo von Hofmannsthals und ihre Voraussetzungen bei Heraklit und Calderón*. Vienna: Mayer, 1934.

De Soto de Clonard. *Historia orgánica de las armas de infantería y caballería española desde la creación del ejercito permanente hasta el dia*. 16 vols. Madrid, 1851–62.

Southworth, Herbert. *Guernica! Guernica! A Study of Journalism, Diplomacy, Propaganda and History*. Berkeley: University of California Press, 1977.

Spaniens Freiwillige an der Ostfront = Los voluntarios españoles en el frente: Ein Bildbuch von der Blauen Division. Ed. Propaganda-Kompanie der Armee Busch. Kauen [Lithuania], 1942.

Spielmann, Peter, ed. *Für Spanien: Internationale Kunst und Kultur zum spanischen Bürgerkrieg. Zum Gedenken an den 50. Jahrestag des Anfanges des spanischen Bürgerkrieges, 28.9.-23.11.1986*. Bochum: Museum Bochum, 1986.

Spitta, Arnold. *Paul Zech im südamerikanischen Exil, 1933–1946: Ein Beitrag zur Geschichte der deutschen Emigration in Argentinien*. Berlin: Colloquium, 1978.

Spitzer, Leo (1887–1960). *Romanische Literaturstudien, 1936–1965*. Tübingen: Niemeyer, 1959.

———. *Syntaktische Studien zum Catalanischen*. Göthen: O. Schulze, 1915.

———. "Zur Kunst Quevedos in seinem 'Buscón.'" *Archivum Romanicum*, no. 11 (October–December 1927), pp. 511–580.

Spitzer, Leo (1939–). *Hotel Bolivia: The Culture of Memory in a Refuge from Nazism*. New York: Hill and Wang, 1998.

Sprunck, A. "Die Trierer Kurfürsten Karl Kaspar von der Leyen und Johann Hugo von Oberseck und die Statthalter der Spanischen Niederlande von 1675–1700." *Rheinische Vierteljahrsblätter*, vol. 32 (1968), p. 318ff.

Stache, Rudolf. *Armee mit geheimem Auftrag: Die deutsche Legion Condor in Spanien*. Berlin, 1939.

Stackelberg, Karl Georg von. *Legion Condor: Deutsche Freiwillige in Spanien*. Berlin: Heimbücherei, 1939.

Stark, Michael, ed. *Der "Kondor-Krieg": Ein deutscher Literaturstreit*. Bamberg: Otto-Friedrich-Universität, 1996.

Staub, M. *Die spanische Romanze in der Dichtung der deutschen Romantik, mit besonderer Berücksichtigung des Romanzenwerkes von Tieck, Brentano und Heine*. Ph.D. Dissertation University of Hamburg, 1970.

Stauf, Renate. *Der problematische Europäer: Heinrich Heine im Konflikt zwischen Nationenkritik und gesellschaftlicher Utopie*. Heidelberg: C. Winter, 1997.

Steger, Hanns-Albert, Achim Schrader, and Jürgen Gräbener. *Lateinamerika-Forschung in der Bundesrepublik Deutschland und in Berlin (West)*. Dortmund: Universität Münster, 1966.

Stephan, Alexander, ed. *Anna Seghers im Exil: Essays, Texte, Dokumente*. Bonn: Bouvier, 1993.

Stoll, André, ed. *Sepharden, Morisken, IndianerInnen und ihresgleichen: Die andere Seite der hispanischen Kulturen*. Bielefeld: Aisthesis, 1995.

Stona, Maria. *Das schöne Spanien: Eine Reise*. Berlin: AGV, 1940.

Storrs, Christopher. "The Army of Lombardy and the Resilience of Spanish Power in Italy in the Reign of Carlos II, 1665–1700 (Part One)." *War in History*, vol. 4, no. 4 (1997), p. 371ff.

———. *Diplomatic Relations between Victor Amadeus II of Savoy and William III, 1690–96*. Ph.D. Diss. University of London, 1990.

Storz, Gerhard. *Heinrich Heines lyrische Dichtung*. Stuttgart: Klett, 1971.

Stötzel, Monika. *Lateinamerika—Bundesrepublik Deutschland: Institutionen zur Pflege der gegenseitigen Beziehungen in der Bundesrepublik Deutschland und Berlin (West)*. Bonn: Inter Nationes, 1986.

Strack, Thomas. "Alexander von Humboldts amerikanisches Reisewerk: Ethnographie und Kulturkritik um 1800." *The German Quarterly*, vol. 69 (1996), pp. 233–246.

———. *Exotische Erfahrung und Intersubjektivität: Reiseberichte im 17. und 18. Jahrhundert. Genregeschichtliche Untersuchung zu Adam Olearius, Hans Egede, Georg Forster*. Paderborn: Igel Verlag Wissenschaft, 1994.

Stradling, R. A. *Europe and the Decline of Spain, 1580–1720*. London and Boston: Allen & Unwin, 1981.

———. *Spain's Struggle for Europe, 1598–1668*. London and Rio Grande, Ohio: Hambledon Press, 1994.

Straub, Eberhard. *Pax et Imperium: Spaniens Kampf um seine Friedensordnung in Europa zwischen 1617 und 1635*. Paderborn: Schöningh, 1980.

Strausfeld, Michi. *Spanische Literatur des 20. Jahrhunderts in deutschen Übersetzungen. Mit einer Ergänzung: Lateinamerikanische Literatur der Gegenwart in deutschen Übersetzungen. Ein Auswahlverzeichnis*. Dortmund: Stadtbücherei Dortmund, 1984.

Strosetzki, Christoph, ed. *Juan Luis Vives: Sein Werk und seine Bedeutung für Spanien und Deutschland. Akten der internationalen Tagung vom 14.-15. Dezember 1992 in Münster*. Frankfurt: Vervuert, 1995.

Strosetzki, Christoph, and André Stoll, eds. *Spanische Bilderwelten: Literatur, Kunst und Film im intermedialen Dialog*. Akten der Sektion Bild und Text des Deutschen Hispanistentages, Göttingen 1991. Frankfurt: Vervuert, 1993.

Strosetzki, Christoph, and Manfred Tietz, eds. *Einheit und Vielfalt der Iberoromania: Geschichte und Gegenwart*. Akten des Deutschen Hispanistentages, Passau, 26.2.-1.3.1987. Hamburg: Buske, 1989.

Studemund-Halévy, Michael, ed. *Die Sefarden in Hamburg*. Hamburg: Buske, 1994ff.

Sullivan, Henry W. *El Calderón alemán: recepción e influencia de un genio hispano, 1654–1980*. Trans. Milena Grass. Frankfurt: Vervuert; Madrid: Iberoamericana, 1998.

———. *Calderón in the German Lands and the Low Countries: His Reception and Influence, 1654–1980*. Cambridge and New York: Cambridge University Press, 1983.

———. "Calderón, the German Idealist Philosophers, and the Question of Christian Tragedy." In *Calderón de la Barca at the Tercentenary: Comparative Views*, pp. 51–69. Ed. Wendell M. Aycock. Lubbock: Texas Tech Press, 1981.

———. "Un manuscrito desconocido de la refundición por Goethe del *Standhafter Prinz* (Calderón/A. G. Schlegel)." In *Hacia Calderón: V Coloquio Anglogermano (Oxford 1978)*, pp. 74–82. Ed. Hans Flasche. Wiesbaden: Steiner, 1981.

———. *Tirso de Molina and the Drama of the Counter Reformation*. Amsterdam: Rodopi, 1976.

———. "Ein unbekanntes Manuskript von Goethes Bearbeitung des *Standhaften Prinzen* (Calderón/August Wilhelm Schlegel)." In *Pedro Calderón de la Barca: Vorträge anläßlich der Jahrestagung der Görres-Gesellschaft (1978)*, pp. 58–68. Ed. Theodor Berchem and Siegfried Sudhof. Berlin: E. Schmidt, 1983.

Szirmai, László. *América Latina: Lateinamerika in der bildenden Kunst der DDR*. Berlin: Verband der Bildenden Künstler der DDR, 1988.

Tanner, S. *German Naval Intervention in the Spanish Civil War as Reflected in the German Records*. Ph.D. Diss. The American University, 1976.

Tausendjähriges Wien = Viena milenaria. Trans. Klaus Lohrmann. Madrid: Joyas Bibliográficas, 1982.

Teitelboim, Volodia. *Neruda: An Intimate Biography*. Trans. Beverly J. DeLong-Tonelly. Austin: University of Texas Press, 1991.

———. *Pablo Neruda: Ein Lebensweg*. Trans. Wilhelm Plackmeyer. Berlin: Aufbau, 1987.

Teraoka, Arlene Akiko. *East, West, and Others: The Third World in Postwar German Literature*. Lincoln: University of Nebraska Press, 1996.

Tgahrt, Reinhard, comp. *Weltliteratur: Die Lust am Übersetzen im Jahrhundert Goethes. Eine Ausstellung des Deutschen Literaturarchivs im Schiller-Nationalmuseum Marbach am Neckar*. Marbach: Deutsche Schillergesellschaft, 1982.

Thalmann, Clara, and Paul Thalmann. *Revolution für die Freiheit: Stationen eines politischen Kampfes. Moskau/Madrid/Paris*. Hamburg: Association, 1977.

Thelen, Albert Vigoleis. *Die Insel des zweiten Gesichts: Aus den angewandten Erinnerungen des Vigoleis*. Düsseldorf: Diederichs, n.d.

Thies, Jochen. *Architekt der Weltherrschaft: Die "Endziele" Hitlers*. Düsseldorf: Droste, 1980.

Thomas, Hugh. *The Spanish Civil War*. 3rd ed. New York: Harper, 1986.

Thompson, I. A. A. *War and Government in Habsburg Spain, 1560–1620*. London: Athlone Press, 1976.

———. *War and Society in Habsburg Spain*. Aldershot, Great Britain: Variorum, 1992.

Thürmer-Rohr, Christina. *Mittäterschaft und Entdeckungslust*. Berlin: Orlanda, 1989.
Tiemann, Hermann. *Das spanische Schrifttum in Deutschland von der Renaissance bis zur Romantik: Eine Vortragsreihe*. Hamburg: Ibero-Amerikanisches Institut, 1936. Reprint Hildesheim, 1971.
Timm, Uwe. *Der Schlangenbaum*. Cologne: Kiepenheuer & Witsch, 1986.
———. *The Snake Tree*. Trans. Peter Tegel. New York: New Directions, 1989.
Timmermanns, Rudolf. *General Franco*. Olten: Otto Walter, 1937.
Tötschinger, Gerhard. *Auf den Spuren der Habsburger*. Vienna: Amalthea, 1992.
Traine, Martin. *Die Sehnsucht nach dem ganz Anderen: Die Frankfurter Schule und Lateinamerika*. Aachen: Verlag der Augustinus-Buchhandlung, 1994.
Trautloft, Hannes. *Als Jagdflieger in Spanien: Aus dem Tagebuch eines deutschen Legionärs*. Berlin: Nauck, 1940.
Troncoso, José M. "Con la División Española de Voluntarios en un campamento aleman." *Ejercito*, no. 25 (February 1942).
Tusell, Xavier, and Genoveva García Queipo de Llano. *Franco y Mussolini: la politica española durante la Segunda Guerra Mundial*. Barcelona: Planeta, 1985.
Uerlings, Herbert. *Poetiken der Interkulturalität: Haiti bei Kleist, Seghers, Müller, Buch und Fichte*. Tübingen: Niemeyer, 1997.
Uhse, Bodo. *Die erste Schlacht: Vom Werden und von den ersten Kämpfen des Bataillons Edgar André*. Strasbourg: Editions Prométhée, 1938.
Unamuno, Miguel de. *Abel Sánchez: Die Geschichte einer Leidenschaft*. Trans. W. v. Wartburg. Munich: Meyer & Jessen, 1925.
———. *Die Agonie des Christentums*. Munich: Meyer & Jessen, 1928.
———. *Frieden im Krieg: Ein Roman aus dem Carlistenaufstand*. Trans. Otto Buek. Berlin: Wegweiser Verlag, 1929.
———. *Die Höhle des Schweigens*. Trans. Otto Buek and Oswald Jahns. Leipzig: Reclam, 1930.
———. *How to Make a Novel*. Trans. Anthony Kerrigan, Bollinger Series. Princeton: Princeton University Press, 1976.
———. *Das Leben Don Quijotes und Sanchos*. Trans. Otto Buek. Munich: Meyer & Jessen, 1926.
———. *Lesebuch der spanischen Literatur des XIX. und XX. Jahrhunderts*. [Germany:] Niedermayer, 1928.
———. *Nebel*. Trans. Otto Buek. Munich: Meyer & Jessen, 1926.
———. *Obras completas*. 18 vols. Madrid: Afrodisio Aguado 1958.
———. *Der Spiegel des Todes*. Munich: Meyer & Jessen, 1925.
———. *Tante Tula*. Trans. Otto Buek. Munich: Meyer & Jessen, 1927.
———. *Das tragische Lebensgefühl*. Trans. Robert Friesé (a.k.a. Paul Adler). Munich: Meyer & Jessen, 1925.
———. "Was verdanken Sie dem deutschen Geist?" *Literarische Welt*, 16 October 1925.
Ureña, Enrique M., José Luis Fernández, and Johannes Seidel. *El "Ideal de la Humanidad" de Sanz del Río y su original aleman: textos comparados con una introducción*. Madrid: UPCO, 1992.
Vadillo, Fernando. *Los irreducibles*. Alicante: García Hispan, 1993.
Valis, Noël. "Clarín." In *Dictionary of the Literature of the Iberian Peninsula*. Ed. Germán Bleiberg, Maureen Ihrie, and Janet Pérez, vol. 1, pp. 411–414. Westport, Conn.: Greenwood, 1993.
Varela Martínez, María Jesús. "Der junge Eichendorff und die spanische Welt." In *Oberschlesisches Jahrbuch*, vol. 2 (1986), pp. 184–198.
Vesper, Will. *Im Flug durch Spanien: Erzählungen von einer Reise*. Gütersloh, 1943.

Vey, Horst, and Xavier de Salas, eds. *German and Spanish Art to 1900*. New York: F. Watts, 1965.
Vicente Álvarez, Saturnino. "El Lazarillo de Tormes en las traducciones alemanas." *Yelmo*, nos. 21–32 (1981–84).
Vinas, Angel. *La Alemania nazi y el 18 de julio: antecedentes de la intervención alemana en la guerra civil española*. Madrid: Alianza, 1974.
Vocelka, Karl, and Lynne Heller. *Die Lebenswelt der Habsburger: Kultur- und Mentalitätsgeschichte einer Familie*. Graz: Styria, 1997.
———. *Die private Welt der Habsburger: Leben und Alltag einer Familie*. Graz: Styria, 1998.
Volberg, Heinrich. *Deutsche Kolonialbestrebungen in Südamerika nach dem Dreißigjährigen Kriege, insbesondere die Bemühungen von Johann Joachim Becher*. Cologne and Vienna: Böhlau, 1977.
Vordtriede, Werner. "Wilhelm Heinse's Share in the German Interest in Spanish Literature." *The Journal of English and Germanic Philology*, vol. 48 (1949), pp. 88–96.
Voßler, Karl. *Algunos caracteres de la cultura española*. Buenos Aires: Espasa-Calpe, 1942.
———. *Einführung in die spanische Dichtung des goldenen Zeitalters*. Hamburg: Behre, 1939.
———. *Introducción a la literatura española del Siglo de Oro*. Buenos Aires: Espasa-Calpe, 1945.
———. *Lope de Vega und sein Zeitalter*. Munich: Beck, 1932.
———. *Lope de Vega y su tiempo*. Madrid: Revista de Occidente, 1933.
———. *Realismus in der spanischen Dichtung der Blütezeit*. Munich: Bayerische Akademie der Wissenschaften, 1926.
———. *Die romanische Welt: Gesammelte Aufsätze*. Munich: Piper, 1965.
———. *Die romanischen Kulturen und der deutsche Geist*. Stuttgart: Klett, 1948.
———. *Spanien und Europa*. Munich: Kösel, 1952.
Wagner, B. A. *Zu Lessings spanischen Studien*. Berlin: R. Gaentner, H. Heyfelder, 1883.
Waldingau, Juanita von. *Der unsterbliche Gott: Roman aus dem heutigen Spanien*. Basel: Geering, 1938.
Walter, Hans-Albert. *Deutsche Exilliteratur, 1933–1950*. 7 vols. Stuttgart: Metzler, 1978ff.
———. "No pasarán! Deutsche Exilschriftsteller im Spanischen Bürgerkrieg." *Kürbiskern*, vol. 1 (1967), pp. 5–27.
Walter, Rolf. *Der Traum vom Eldorado: Die deutsche Conquista in Venezuela im 16. Jahrhundert*. Munich: Eberhard, 1992.
Walter, Rolf, et al. *Preußen und Venezuela: Edition der preußischen Konsularberichte über Venezuela, 1842–1850*. Frankfurt: Vervuert, 1991.
Walther, Klaus. *Bodo Uhse: Leben und Werk*. Dresden: Volk und Wissen, 1984.
Wegner, Sonja. "German-speaking Emigrants in Uruguay, 1933–1945." *Leo Baeck Institute Yearbook* 1997.
Weinberg, Gerhard L. *World in the Balance: Behind the Scenes of World War II*. Hanover, N.H.: University Press of New England, 1981.
———. *A World at Arms: A Global History of World War II*. Cambridge: Cambridge University Press, 1994.
Weinert, Erich, ed. *Die Fahne der Solidarität: Deutsche Schriftsteller in der Spanischen Freiheitsarmee, 1936–1939*. Berlin: Aufbau, 1953.

Weinrich, Marie Mathilda. *Goethe's Interest in Spanish Literature: Its Influence on His Own Works, and His General Relation to Spain.* Ph.D. Diss. Washington University, 1937.
Weinstein, Donald, and Rudolph M. Bell. *Saints and Society: The Two Worlds of Western Christendom, 1000–1700.* Chicago: University of Chicago Press, 1982.
Weiß, Peter. *Die Ästhetik des Widerstands.* 3 vols. Frankfurt: Suhrkamp, 1975–81.
Werz, Nikolaus, ed. *Handbuch der deutschsprachigen Lateinamerikakunde.* Freiburg i.Br.: Arnold-Bergsträsser-Instiutut, 1992.
Whealey, Robert H. *Hitler and Spain: The Nazi Role in the Spanish Civil War, 1936–1939.* Lexington: University Press of Kentucky, 1989.
Wheatcroft, Andrew. *The Habsburgs: Embodying Empire.* London and New York: Viking, 1995.
Wilke, Jürgen, and Siegfried Quandt, eds. *Deutschland und Lateinamerika: Imagebildung und Informationslage.* Frankfurt: Vervuert, 1987.
Willett, John. *Brecht in Context: Comparative Approaches.* London: Methuen, 1984.
Williams, Raymond L. *The Postmodern Novel in Latin America.* New York: St. Martin's, 1995; London: Macmillan, 1997.
Willkomm, B. "Deutsch-spanische Beziehungen im Mittelalter." *Zeitschrift für Auslandskunde,* vol. 3 (1921), pp. 141–192.
Winkler, Markus. *Mythisches Denken zwischen Romantik und Realismus: Zur Erfahrung kultureller Fremdheit im Werk Heinrich Heines.* Tübingen: Niemeyer, 1995.
Wir kämpften in Spanien: Männer der deutschen Legion Condor berichten von ihren Erlebnissen auf dem spanischen Kriegsschauplatz. Berlin: Verlag Die Wehrmacht, 1939.
Wisser, Burkhard. *Der rote Atem der Sonne: Erfahrungen in Spanien und Lateinamerika. Erzählungen und Gedichte.* Karlsruhe: von Loeper, 1987.
Wittschier, Heinz Willi. *Geschichte der spanischen Literatur vom Kubakrieg bis zu Francos Tod, 1898–1975.* Rheinfelden: Schäuble, 1982.
Wöhlcke, Manfred. *Lateinamerika in der Presse: Inhaltsanalytische Untersuchung der Lateinamerika-Berichterstattung.* Stuttgart: Klett, 1973.
Wölfel, Dominik Josef. *So ist Spanien: Geheimgeschichte eines Bürgerkrieges.* Mauer bei Wien and Leipzig: Kühne, 1937.
Wolffsohn, Michael. *Spanien, Deutschland und die "Jüdische Weltmacht": Über Moral, Realpolitik und Vergangenheitsbewältigung.* Munich: Bertelsmann, 1991.
Wolffsohn, Michael, and Reinhard Niederfeld. *Politik als Investitionsmotor? Deutsche "Multis" in Lateinamerika.* Frankfurt and New York: P. Lang, 1985.
Wolfram, Herwig, ed. *Österreichische Geschichte in zehn Bänden.* Vienna: Überreuter, 1995ff.
Wulschner, Hans Joachim ed. *Vom Rio Grande zum La Plata: Deutsche Reiseberichte des 19. Jahrhunderts aus dem südlichen Amerika.* Tübingen: Erdmann, 1975.
Yang, Zhidong. *Klara Blum—Zhu Bailan (1904–1971): Leben und Werk einer österreichisch-chinesischen Schriftstellerin.* Frankfurt and New York: Peter Lang, 1996.
Zantop, Susanne. *Colonial Fantasies: Conquest, Family, and Nation in Precolonial Germany, 1770–1870.* Durham, N.C.: Duke University Press, 1997.
———. "Zwischen Aneignung und Enteignung: Heine in Südeuropa." In *Nationale Grenzen und internationaler Austausch,* pp. 94–108. Ed. Lothar Jordan. Tübingen: Niemeyer, 1995.
Zeuske, Michael, and Bernd Schröter, eds. *Alexander von Humboldt und das neue Geschichtsbild von Lateinamerika.* Leipzig: Leipziger Universitätsverlag, 1992.

Zeuske, Michael, Bernd Schröter, and Jörg Ludwig, eds. *Sachsen und Lateinamerika: Begegnungen in vier Jahrhunderten*. Frankfurt: Vervuert, 1995.
Zimmels, Hirsch Jakob. *Ashkenazim and Sephardim*. Farnborough, England: Gregg International Publishers, 1969.
Zimmermann, Christian von. *Reiseberichte und Romanzen: Kulturgeschichtliche Studien zur Perzeption und Rezeption Spaniens im deutschen Sprachraum des 18. Jahrhunderts*. Tübingen: Niemeyer, 1997.
Zybura, Marek. *Ludwig Tieck als Übersetzer und Herausgeber: Zur frühromantischen Idee einer "deutschen Weltliteratur."* Heidelberg: C. Winter, 1994.

INDEX OF NAMES

Abd-el-Krim, 384
Abulafia, Abraham, 175n. 11
Abusch, Alexander, 32
Ackelsberg, Martha, 363
Adalbert of Bavaria, 124n. 1
Adam von Dietrichstein, 81
Adenauer, Konrad, 32
Agrippa, Cornelius Henricus, 157, 170
Alas, Leopoldo ("Clarín"), 19–20, 248, 255–272
Alba, Duke of, 14
Albéniz, Isaac, 22
Albert, Archduke of Austria and Flanders, 97–98
Albert V, Duke of Wittelsbach, 91
Albert, Georgia, 196
Alberti, Rafael, 432, 438
Albertus Magnus, St., 62
Alemán, Mateo, 11
Alexander, Sally, 363
Alfieri, Dino, 320
Alfonso I, King of Aragon, 61
Alfonso II, King of Castile, 5
Alfonso V, King of Aragon, 65
Alfonso VII, King of Spain, 61
Alford, Steven E., 209n. 25
Allende, Isabel, 34, 35, 457–466 *passim*
Allende, Salvador, 33, 439, 446
Alonso, Amado, 181
Álvarez Oller, Maite, xii, 6
Andrade, Mário de, 36
Andritsch, Johann, 104n. 14
Angulo y Heredia, Antonio, 248
Anna (mother of Maria of Bavaria), 91
Anna, Archduchess of Austria and Queen of Spain, 9, 78, 82
Anna, Queen of Bohemia and Hungary and Empress (wife of Ferdinand I), 78

Anna Dorothea, Marquise de Austria, 80, 95
Aquinas, St. Thomas, 142
Aragon, Louis, 432
Araquistaín, Luis, 297
Aregger, Agnes, 222, 226
Areilza, José María de, 392n. 10
Arendt, Erich, 33, 432, 438–439
Ariosto, Lodovico, 191
Aristophanes, 226
Aristotle, 182
Arndt, Ernst Moritz, 245
Arnim, Achim von, 16, 253n. 26
Arnold, Gottfried, 171
Arnold, Matthew, 273
Arp, Hans, 23
Arquéz, Enrique, 393n. 23
Arreola, Juan José, 31
Arrese (Falangist Secretary-General), 402
Arrizubieta, Martín, 409
Asensio, Carlos, 386, 392n. 16, 393n. 29
Astrow, Madonin, 308n. 29
Asturias, Miguel Ángel, 36
Atkins, Stuart, 274
Aub, Max, 32–33, 44n. 56, 227, 229n. 7, 234n. 64
Auburtin, Victor, 307n. 19
Auerbach, Erich, 25
d'Aulnoy, Marie-Catherine, 230n. 16
Avellaneda, Alonso. *See* Fernández de Avellaneda, Alonso
Averroës, 62
Azorín (José Martínez Ruiz), 297

Baader, Franz, 16
Bahr, Hermann, 22, 296, 303, 307n. 18
Baist, Gottfried, 181, 182, 183
Bakhtin, Mikhail, 207

512 | Index of Names

Bakunin, Mikhail, 18
Baldung, Hans (Grien), 6
Balzer, Berit, xiii, 2, 18
Barbusse, Henri, 307n. 14
Bargoni, Franco, 324n. 11
Baroja, Pío, 20, 225, 233n. 54, 235, 298
Barral, Carlos, 30, 356
Barrès, Maurice, 307n. 14
Bataillon, Marcel, 39n. 9
Baudelaire, Charles, 223
Bauer, Therese, 364
Baumgarten, Alexander Gottlieb, 276, 287n. 9
Bayle, Pierre, 12
Beatrice of Swabia, 5
Becher, Hubert, 304
Bécquer, Gustavo Adolfo, 18, 178, 223, 224, 225, 227, 232n. 45, 234n. 64, 249, 253n. 22
Behler, Ernst, 191, 196, 208n. 11, 209n. 21
Beigbeder, Juan, 384–387, 393n. 23, 394n. 39
Bello, Andrés, 181, 183
Benavente, Countess of, 122
Benedict, St., 85
Berengaria, Queen of León, 5
Berghahn, Marion, xii
Bergnes de las Casas, Antonio, 239–254 *passim*
Bergson, Henri, 301
Berlau, Ruth, 360–361, 365
Berlepsch, Countess of (Gertrudis Maria Josefa Bohl von Gutenberg), 121–122, 128n. 61
Bernhardt, Johannes, 314, 318
Bertrand, Jean Jacques Achille, 133
Bertuch, Friedrich Justin, 13, 206, 218
Beser, Sergio, 257
Beumelburg, Werner, 325, 358n. 1
Beyer, Paul, 230n. 16
Bismarck, Otto von, 225, 333
Bizet, George, 20
Blackall, Eric A., 169
Blessin, Stefan, 176n. 31
Bley, Wulf, 325
Blum, Klara (Zhu Bailan), 364, 379n. 10
Blum, León, 318
Blum, Viktor, 430
Boabdil, King of the Moors, 220, 232n. 31

Boccaccio, Giovanni, 191, 208n. 12, 209n. 18
Bodmer, Johann Jacob, 247, 252n. 12
Boehm, Hermann, 324n. 11
Böhl de Faber, Cecilia ("Fernán Caballero"), 20, 42n. 32
Böhl von Faber, Johann Nikolas, 20, 233n. 49, 251n. 3
Bohl von Gutenberg, Gertrudis Maria Josefa (Countess of Berlepsch), 121–122, 128n. 61
Böhme, Jakob, 156, 171
Boileau, Nicolas, 12
Bolívar, Simón, 34
Bonnet, Georges, 321
Bopp, Franz, 177, 184
Borges, Jorge Luis, 34, 35, 36
Bosch, Hieronymus, 6
Botrel, Jean-François, 251n. 1
Bourciez, Édouard, 181
Bowen, Wayne, xii, 2, 28–29
Bowers, Claude, 323
Brangulí (Spanish photographer), 332f. 2
Brantôme, Seigneur de, 88n. 12
Brassaï (Gyula Halasz), 351–352
Brauchitsch, Walther von, 354f. 28, 396n. 55
Braun, Harold, 294
Braun, Volker, 34
Brecht, Bertolt, 30, 33, 289n. 29, 360–362, 365, 380n. 17, 423, 424, 428, 429–430, 431, 432–433, 436, 438, 439
Bredel, Willi, 381nn. 28, 34
Brentano, Clemens, 218, 230n. 16, 253n. 26
Brown, Kenneth, xii, 12
Brown, Meg H., xii, 2, 34
Brueghel family, 6
Brüggemann, Werner, 207n. 1
Brugmann, Karl, 177, 185, 186
Bruyn, Günter de, 35
Buch, Hans Christoph, 36
Büchner, Georg, 19, 30, 253n. 26
Buñuel, Luis, 42n. 37
Bürger, Gottfried, 246
Burgos, Mateo de, 98
Bynum, Caroline Walker, 104n. 10
Byrd, Charles L., 381n. 27
Byron, Lord, 18, 218, 224

Cabezas, Juan Antonio, 267
Calderón de la Barca, Pedro, 14, 16–17, 20, 25, 35, 40n. 20, 41n. 24, 49, 133–151 *passim*, 188, 302
Camacho, Ávila, 431
Campoamor, Ramón de, 223, 225
Camús, Alfredo Adolfo, 256
Canalejas, Francisco de Paula, 257
Canaris, Wilhelm, 319
Carande, Ramón, 40n. 10
Carandell, José María, 30
Cardinal, Marie, 169
Cardona, Antonio de, 81
Cardona, Margarita de, 81
Carpentier, Alejo, 36, 461
Cartier-Bresson, Henri, 327
Cassirer, Ernst, 287n. 9
Cassou, Jean, 282–283
Castel Rodrigo, Marquis of, 111
Castellet, José María, 18
Castiella, Fernando María, 392n. 10
Castillejo, Cristóbal de, 49, 81
Castillo, Oscar, 452
Castro, Américo, 180
Castro, Fidel, 35
Castro, Rosalía de, 18, 223, 232n. 45
Casulana da Mazari, Maddelena, 82
Catherina de Medici, Queen of France, 79
Céline, Louis-Ferdinand, 426
Cervantes, Miguel de, 11, 13, 16, 17, 24, 25, 41n. 24, 49, 181, 188–213 *passim*, 220, 301–02
Cervera, Juan, 324n. 11
Chamberlain, Neville, 321–322
Chambers, David, 85
Charlemagne, Emperor, 4, 54–58
Charles I/V, King of Spain and Holy Roman Emperor, 6–8, 40n. 10, 53, 78, 95, 96, 108
Charles II, King of Spain, 9–10, 12, 108–129 *passim*
Charles III, King of Spain, 13
Charles VI, Holy Roman Emperor, 117
Charles IX, King of France, 9, 79, 84, 85
Charles Philip (brother of Mariana of Neuburg), 119
Chateaubriand, François René, 224, 232n. 31
Chénier, Louis de, 218
Chindaswinth, King of the Visigoths, 3

Chrétien de Troyes, 59
Ciano, Galeazzo, 320
Cifuentes, Sergio, 408
Clarín (Leopoldo Alas), 19–20, 248, 255–272 *passim*
Clark, Jaime, 222
Classen, Albrecht, xii, 2, 4–5
Claudel, Paul, 424
Clement, Elfriede, 308n. 29
Clifford, Charles, 20, 359n. 4
Close, Anthony, 189, 208n. 4
Cocteau, Jean, 307n. 14
Cohen, Hermann, 277, 288n. 11
Comte, Auguste, 259, 270n. 23
Corradi, Fernando, 226
Cortázar, Julio, 34, 445
Corzana, Count of, 120
Cossío, José María de, 238, 244
Costa, Luis, 28
Cramer, H. M. A., 218
Croy, Guillaume de, 129n. 65
Cruchaga Tocornal, Miguel, 427
Cuervo, Rufino José, 181, 183, 184, 185
Curtius, Ernst Robert, 22–23, 25, 291, 296, 301–302, 303

Dalí, Salvador, 23, 42n. 37
Dante Alighieri, 188, 190–191, 192, 193, 203, 243, 247, 309n. 36
Darío, Rubén, 222, 223
Darwin, Charles, 260
Degrelle, Léon, 403, 422n. 118
Delbrück, Berthold, 185
Demosthenes, 204
Depta, Max Victor, 308n. 29
Descartes, René, 12, 265
Dessau, Paul, 439
Deutsch, Leo, 430
Díaz Ordaz, Gustavo, 432
Dieckmann, Liselotte, 275, 279
Diez, Friedrich, 16, 179, 180, 181, 183, 184, 185
Díez Taboada, Juan María, 249
Disney, Walt, 29
Dombay, Franz von, 218
Dominic, St., 85
Donatus, Aelius, 183
Doriot, Jacques, 411
Dormagen, Jürgen, 463
Dostoevski, Fedor M., 288n. 23
Douhet, Giulio, 320

Doutrepont brothers (Auguste and
  Georges Doutrepont), 179
Dozy, Reinhart, 184
Drieu la Rochelle, Pierre, 426
Dürer, Albrecht, 6
Dwinger, Edwin Erich, 382n. 52

Eckermann, Johann Peter, 148, 246, 248
Eckhart, Johannes ("Meister Eckhart"),
  30
Ehrenburg, Ilya, 307n. 14, 427, 431, 432
Eichendorff, Joseph von, 17, 19, 42n.
  33, 253n. 26, 434
Eichner, Hans, 191, 208n. 11
Einstein, Albert, 427, 435
Eisenhower, Dwight D., 401
Eisler, Hanns, 439, 428
Eleanora (daughter of Maria of
  Bavaria), 95
Eliot, T. S., 280
Elizabeth, Archduchess of Austria and
  Queen of France, 9, 77–90 passim
Elizabeth I, Queen of England, 91,
  104nn. 13, 23
Elizabeth of Thuringia, St., 79
Elizabeth Amalia of Hesse, 118
Elle, Paul, 429
Emonds, Friederike B., xii, 2, 27
Engelmann, Willem Herman, 184
Enzensberger, Hans Magnus, 30,
  35, 424
Erasmus of Rotterdam, 6–7
Ernst, Archduke of Austria, 9, 78–79,
  80, 81, 84, 85
Ernst, Max, 30
Ernst Ludwig, Landgrave of Hesse-
  Darmstadt, 119
Escobar, José, 251n. 1
Espronceda, José de, 18
Esquivel, Laura, 459, 461, 463, 464
Essberger, John T., 324n. 8
Euripides, 274
Eyck, Jan van, 5
Ezekiel, 156
Ezquerra, Miguel, 403, 413, 419n. 39

Fàbregas, Francesc, 24
Falla, Manuel de, 22
Farinelli, Arturo, 252n. 14
Fassbinder, Rainer Werner, 444, 454n. 8
Faupel, Edith von, 409, 414

Faupel, Wilhelm von, 338–339, 382n.
  51, 403, 405, 409, 414, 415, 419n. 40
Feise, Ernst, 222
Feldkeller, Paul, 294
Feliu de la Penya, Narciso, 121,
  128n. 60
Fendri, Mounir, 231n. 30, 232n. 31
Ferdinand the Catholic, King of Castile
  and Aragon, 6, 51, 125n. 5, 164, 218
Ferdinand I, King of Aragon, 65
Ferdinand I, King of Bohemia and
  Hungary and Holy Roman
  Emperor, 78, 79, 81, 83
Ferdinand II, Holy Roman Emperor,
  9–10, 92, 93, 95–102 passim
Ferdinand II of Tyrol, Archduke of
  Austria, 89–90n. 41
Ferdinand III, King of Castile, 5
Ferdinand VII, King of Spain, 225, 226
Fernández, Eusebio, 259
Fernández, M. M., 234n. 66
Fernández de Avellaneda, Alonso, 205
Fernández Matheu, José, 237, 246, 247,
  253nn. 25, 27
Ferrán, Augusto, 223, 232n. 44
Ferrer Benimeli, José Antonio, 323n. 4
Ferretti, Giovanni, 324n. 11
Feßler, Ignaz, 215
Feuchtwanger, Franz, 429
Feuchtwanger, Lion, 423, 429, 431
Feuerbach, Ludwig, 18, 41n. 26, 245
Fichte, Hubert, 35–36
Fichte, Johann Gottlieb, 192, 209n. 21
Finke, Heinrich, 69
Fischel, Hermann von, 324n. 11
Flecha, Matteo, 82–83
Flechtheim, Alfred, 308n. 22
Font y Guitart, Juan, 239, 244, 245, 249
Fontcuberta, José Andrés, 222, 226
Forst de Battaglia, Otto, 298
Förster, Paul, 183
Fouqué, Friedrich de la Motte, 218,
  219, 230n. 16, 231n. 19
Francis, St., 63
Francis, Rick, 379
Franco, Francisco, 18, 25, 26–29, 30,
  124n. 1, 235, 313–324 passim,
  325–359 passim, 361, 367, 369, 374,
  375, 383–396 passim, 397–421 passim
Franz (German photographer), 329,
  350f. 23, 351f. 24, 352–353

Frederick III, Holy Roman Emperor, 68
Frederick William, Great Elector of
    Brandenburg, 113–114
Frei, Bruno, 431
Freiligrath, Ferdinand, 245
Freud, Sigmund, 23, 42n. 37
Freundlich, Otto, 23
Friedeberg, Erwin, 429
Fries, Fritz Rudolf, 35
Friesé, Robert, 26
Fritsche, Willy, 29
Fuegi, John 381–382n. 35
Fuensalida, Count, 114, 126n. 34
Fuente, Antonio de la, 406, 407, 409,
    412, 413, 414
Fuentes, Carlos, 35, 424
Fugger, House of, 8, 40n. 10
Fusch, Richard D., xiv
Fyrth, Jim, 363

Gabel, Richard, 303–304
Galsworthy, John, 310n. 54
Ganivet, Ángel, xii, 20, 42n. 33, 183,
    225, 228, 233n. 53
García Figueras, Tomás, 392–393n. 16
García Lorca, Federico, 297, 433
García Márquez, Gabriel, x, 34, 35, 445,
    457–466 *passim*
Garcilaso de la Vega, 49, 81
Garnier, Charles, 21
Gascón, Rafael, 408, 409
Gastañaga, Marquis of, 115
Gaudí, Antoni, 21, 22
Gaulle, Charles de, 394n. 39, 411
Gautier, Théophile, 232n. 31
Geldrich, Hanna, 222
Georg von Ehingen, 67, 69
George, St., 63
George, Prince of Hesse-Darmstadt,
    119–121, 122, 123, 128nn. 56–60
George, Stefan, 23
Germain, André, 307n. 14
Gerstenberg, Heinrich von, 246, 247
Geßner, E., 181, 183
Geßner, Salomon, 247
Gielen, Alfred, 376
Gil de Biedma, Jaime, 18
Gil Polo, Gaspar, 40n. 11
Giménez, Celia, 408, 409
Giner de los Ríos, Francisco, 20, 256,
    257, 260, 262, 264, 266, 268

Gleim, Johann Wilhelm Ludwig, 13,
    215, 216, 229–230n. 9
Goda, Norman J. W., xii, 2, 28
Goebbels, Joseph, 314, 315, 317, 318,
    319, 320, 321, 323n. 1, 376, 412,
    419n. 39
Goethe, Johann Wolfgang von, xiii, 13,
    14–15, 17, 19, 22, 23, 24, 40n. 19,
    41n. 29, 133, 135, 136, 148–149,
    152–176 *passim*, 178, 181, 182, 212n.
    67, 222, 223, 224, 227, 232n. 36, 235,
    237, 243–254 *passim*, 256, 257,
    273–280 *passim*, 281, 286, 287nn. 3,
    5, 9, 288n. 12, 289n. 29, 295, 438
Goldsmith, Oliver, 169, 251n. 5
Goll, Ivan, 290–291, 301, 306n. 2
Gómez-Molleda, María Dolores, 256
González, Felipe, 36
González Agejas, Lorenzo, 233n. 62
González Martínez, Enrique, 431
González Serrano, Urbano, 256, 257,
    260, 266
González Videla, Gabriel, 424
González von Marées, Jorge, 426
Göring, Hermann, 28, 315, 318, 319,
    354f. 28
Gorky, Maxim, 370
Görres, Joseph, 16
Gotfrid von Pullen, 53
Gottfried von Straßburg, 63, 64
Goya, Francisco de, 13, 25
Goyri, María, 178
Goytisolo, José Agustín, 30
Goytisolo, Juan, 18
Gracián, Baltasar, 17
Gramberg, Eduard, 255
Granada, Luis de, 86
Granados, Enrique, 22
Grappin, Pierre, 230n. 16
Gravenitz, Gerhart von, 195
Gries, Christian, 89–90n. 41
Gries, Johann Diederich, 17, 137, 138
Grillparzer, Franz, 17, 141, 235
Grimm, Jacob, 177, 178, 184
Grimm, Wilhelm, 246
Grimm brothers, 16, 135, 178, 247,
    253n. 23
Grimmelshausen, Hans Jakob
    Christoffel von, 11, 169
Gris, Juan, 297
Gröber, Gustav, 16, 180–181, 182, 185

Gropius, Walter, 24
Gross, Arthur, 62
Guarini, Battista, 191
Guberman, Karen, 175n. 15
Gudannes, Marchioness of, 129n. 65
Guerrero, Xavier, 430, 439
Guevara, Che, 34
Guillén, Nicolás, 438
Guimerà, Ángel, 20
Guitart y Buch, Miguel, 239
Günther, Johann Christian, 245
Gutenberg, Johann, 52
Gutiérrez Nájera, Manuel, 222
Gutmann, Heinrich/Enrique, 429
Gutzmann, Gertraud, 369
Guzmán, Abimael, 35
Guzmán, Magdalena de. *See* Valle, Marquesa del
Guzmán, Martín de, 81

Haas, Willy, 306–307n. 13
Hachtmann, Otto, 303
Hacks, Peter, 34
Halder, Franz, 396n. 55
Haller, Richard, 95, 98–99, 100
Halverson, Rachel, J., xiii, 2, 33–34
Hammel, Claus, 34
Hampson, Norman, 12
Handke, Peter, 38
Hans von Köln, 5
Hanssen, Friedrich/Federico, 181, 183, 184
Harbeck, Hans, 301
Hartmann, Paul, 29
Hartmann, Sieglinde, 76n. 88
Hartzenbusch, Juan Eugenio, 20
Hauptmann, Gerhart, 20
Havemann, Wilhelm, 216, 229n. 6
Hayes, Carlton, 404
Head, Randolph C., 89n. 40
Hearst, William Randolph, 436
Hebbel, Friedrich, 19, 253n. 26
Hebel, Johann Peter, 244, 245
Hegel, Georg Wilhelm Friedrich, 18, 35, 41n. 29, 226, 227, 236, 245, 256
Heidegger, Martin, 35, 283
Heine, Heinrich, xiii, 18, 19, 33, 178, 182, 214–234 *passim*, 237, 244–254 *passim*, 424, 427, 430, 438
Heine, Maxmilian, 231n. 30
Heinse, Wilhelm, 13

Helmholtz, Hermann von, 257
Henry IV, King of Castile and León, 5
Henry the Lion, Duke of Saxony and Bavaria, 54, 55
Herder, Johann Gottfried, 13, 16, 19, 171, 190, 212n. 58, 215, 216, 217, 230nn. 10, 13, 16, 231n. 22, 232n. 31, 244, 245
Hermannus Teutonicus, 62
Hermlin, Stephan, 438
Hernández, A., 232nn. 35, 45
Herraiz, Ismael, 408
Herrero, José J., 222, 225, 233n. 47
Herrerra, Alonso de, 92, 93, 94, 104nn. 19, 25
Herrig, R., 182
Herzog, Werner, 31, 444, 454n. 8
Hesse, Hermann, 23, 30
Hewitt, Cameron M. K., xiv
Hirsch, Leo, 300
Hirschfelder, Gunther, 52
Hitler, Adolf, 26–29, 124n. 1, 313–324 *passim*, 325–359 *passim*, 368, 374–375, 376, 378, 382n. 46, 383–396 *passim*, 397–422 *passim*, 423, 426, 427, 430, 431, 445
Hochdorf, Max, 294
Hoffmann, Ernst Theodor Amadeus, 245
Hoffmeister, Gerhart, x, xiii-xiv, 8, 40n. 11, 291
Hofmannsthal, Hugo von, 25–26, 42n. 40
Holbein the Younger, Hans, 6
Hölderlin, Friedrich, 19, 33, 253n. 26, 424, 438
Hölty, Ludwig, 247
Honecker, Erich, 34
Hoyos, Max Graf, 325
Hrotsvita von Gandersheim, 62
Hüffer, Hermann J., 62
Hugo, Victor, 224, 309n. 36
Humboldt, Alexander von, 15, 34, 40–41n. 21, 240, 252n. 14
Humboldt, Wilhelm von, 15, 181, 185, 256
Humboldt brothers, 135
Hume, David, 12
Humperdinck, Engelbert, 21
Hurtado de Mendoza, Francisco, 105n. 45
Hutten, Ulrich von, 49

Index of Names | 517

Iaccino, Angelo, 324n. 11
Ibáñez, Blasco, 298
Ibarra, Jaime, 294
Ignatius of Loyola, St., 171
Immerman, Karl, 246
Insdorf, Annette, 444
Irigaray, Luce, 15, 152–158 *passim*, 161, 174n. 5, 175nn. 16, 22
Irving, Washington, 232n. 31, 243
Isabella, Empress, 78
Isabella, Infanta (daughter of Philip II), 127n. 44
Isabella I, the Catholic, 6, 51, 125n. 5, 164
Isabella II, Queen of Spain, 256
Isocrates, 239
Israel, J. I., 125n. 11

Jacob, Max, 295
Jacobi, Johann Georg, 13
James, St., 5
James, William, 301
Jans, Lenchen, 373, 377–378
Jansen, Christopher, 324n. 8
Jaspers, Karl, 35
Jean Paul (Johann Paul Friedrich Richter), 19, 41n. 29, 242, 244, 245, 247, 254n. 32
Jeanroy, Alfred, 182
Jehuda ben Halevi, 215, 221, 229n. 7
Jenkins, Sylvia P., 287n. 3
Jesus Christ, 85, 122, 263
Jiménez, Juan Ramón, 223
Jiménez García, Antonio, 255, 257, 260
Joannot (illustrator), 231n. 28
Joel, H. Th., 293
Johann von Gorze, 62
Johann von Würzburg, 63, 64, 69
Johann Wilhelm, Elector Palatine, 118–119
Johannes von Jandun, 62
John of Austria, the Younger (Don Juan), 121
John of Spain (husband of Margaret of Austria), 80
John of the Cross, St., 171
John II, King of Castile, 5
Jordana (Spanish ambassador), 405–406
Joseph II, Holy Roman Emperor, 80
Joseph Ferdinand (son of Max Emmanuel), 116–117

Juana, Queen of Portugal (daughter of Charles V), 80, 95, 105n. 41
Juana of Spain, 80
Jung, Carl Gustav, 23
Junghändel, Max, 21, 359n. 4

Kabel, P., 232n. 31
Kafka, Franz, 31, 460
Kamen, Henry, 124n. 1, 125n. 5
Kant, Immanuel, 35, 41n. 29, 192, 236, 260, 276, 286, 289n. 47
Karl II, Archduke of Styria, 9, 91, 92, 93, 104n. 14
Katz, Ernst Fritz, 308n. 29
Katz, Otto, 428
Kautschoumoff (photographer), 336f. 6
Kayser, Wolfgang, 25
Keitel, Wilhelm, 329, 354f. 28
Kendrick, Shawn, xiv
Kent, Conrad, xi, 2, 27
Kertész, André, 327
Kessler, Harry, 38
Khevenhüller, Johann/Hans, 96, 97, 100
King, Shirley, xii, 2, 22–23
Kirchhoff, Bodo, 36
Kirsch, Sarah, 35
Kisch, Egon Erwin, 32, 424, 428, 429, 430–431, 435
Klee, Paul, 2, 30
Kleist, Heinrich von, 19, 30, 253n. 26
Klettenberg, Susanna Katharina von, 171
Kleutgen, Joseph, 22, 42n. 36
Klinger, Friedrich Maximilian von, 13
Klopstock, Friedrich, 19, 245, 246, 247, 248
Kneipp, Sebastian, 22, 42n. 36
Knorr von Rosenroth, Christian, 170
Kohl, Helmut, 36
Koltsov, Mikhail, 381n. 34, 381–382n. 35
Königsdorf, Helga, 35
Konrad ("Pfaffe Konrad"), 4, 54–58
Körting, Gustav, 179, 181, 182, 183, 186
Körner, Christian Georg, 137
Krahl, Hilde, 29
Krause, Carl Christian Friedrich, 1, 19–20, 21, 41–42n. 29, 236, 255–272 *passim*
Kremling, Helmut J., xii, 31
Krippendorf, Kurt, 300
Kroetz, Franz Xaver, 36

Index of Names

Kronik, John W., xiii, 2, 18–19
Krummacher, Friedrich, 244, 245, 247
Küchler, Walter, 294
Kulcsar, Ilsa, 364
Kunert, Günter, 35

Lacoue-Labarthe, Philippe, 284
Lamartine, Alphonse-Marie-Louis Prat de, 224
Lamport, F. J., 133
Lamprecht von Regensburg, 63
Landsberg, Paul Ludwig, 23
Larra, Mariano José de, 18, 222, 225, 226, 227
LaRubia-Prado, Francisco, xiii, 2, 22
Las Casas, Bartolomé, 26
Lascoiti, Rima, 364
Lataster-Czisch, Petra, 363, 373
Laurent, Jean, 20, 359n. 4
Le Corbusier (Charles Édouard Jeanneret), 24
Leighton, Hera T., xii, 34
Leite de Vasconcelos, José, 180
Lenau, Nikolaus, 19, 253n. 26
Lenfest, Donald, xiii, 2, 16
Lenz, Rodolfo, 181
Lenz, Siegfried, 464
Leo XIII, Pope, 22
Leo von Rožmital, 76n. 87
Leonora, Empress (wife of Frederick III), 68–69
Leonara, Empress (wife of Leopold I), 118
Leopardi, Giacomo, 224
Leopartius, Madalena, 82
Leophart, Hanns, 82
Leopold, Archduke of Styria, 97, 99
Leopold, St., Margrave of Austria, 85
Leopold I, Holy Roman Emperor, 117, 118
Lequerica, José Félix, 405–406, 407, 411, 412
Lerma, Duke of (Francisco Gómez de Sandoval y Rojas), 97, 98, 99, 100, 101, 102, 107n. 72
Leskien, August, 186
Lessing, Gotthold Ephraim, 19, 20, 41n. 29, 138, 221, 246
Lilienthal, Peter, xiii, 33–34, 442–456 *passim*
Lincoln, Abraham, 436

Lindell, Robert, 82
Liszt, Franz, 22
Litvak, Lily, 42n 35
Liutprand of Cremona, 62
Llorente, Teodoro, 222, 246, 247, 253n. 25
Lobkowitz, Zdenek Adalbert Popel von, 80
Locke, John, 12
Lodge, Adam, 145, 147
Lope de Vega, Félix, 17, 20, 35, 49, 181, 188, 302
López de Úbeda, Francisco, xiii, 15, 152–176 *passim*
López-Morillas, Juan, 19, 255, 258
Lorenzo, Emilio, 248, 253n. 25
Louis XIV, King of France, 10, 108–112, 114–115, 123, 125n. 13, 316
Louthan, William C., xiv
Lovejoy, Arthur O., 191–192, 208n. 11
Luft, Mauricio, 429
Lukács, Georg, 207
Luther, Martin, 1, 83, 142, 170

Machado, Antonio, 38, 223
Machado, Manuel, 297
Machado da Rosa, A., 232n. 45
McKay, Derek, 124n. 1
Mackermann, Friedrich, 298–299
Mac Orlan, Pierre, 295
Macpherson, James ("Ossian"), 243
Maeterlinck, Maurice, 21, 42n. 35
Maeztu, Ramiro de, 20, 223
Magdalena de Guzmán. *See* Valle, Marquesa del
Maier, K. A., 324n. 9
Maimonides, 62
Man, Paul de, 289n. 46
Mandach, André de, 61
Mangini, Shirley, 363
Mann, Erika, 364
Mann, Heinrich, 23, 304–305, 310n. 54, 381n. 34, 429
Mann, Thomas, xi, 24–25, 30, 295, 423, 427
Manríquez de Lara, María, 80
Manz, Inés E., 294, 306n. 12
Maragall, Joan, 21, 238, 248
Marden, Charles Carroll, 180
Margaret, Queen of Aragon, 65–66
Margaret of Austria, Queen of Spain, 10, 80, 91–107 *passim*

Margaret of the Cross, Archduchess of Austria, 79, 95, 96, 99
Maria of Bavaria, Archduchess of Styria, 9–10, 91–107 passim
María of Austria, Empress, 9, 78, 79, 80, 81, 82, 95, 96, 97, 99, 105n. 45
Maria Antonia, Archduchess, 115–116
Maria Christina (daughter of Maria of Bavaria), 95
Maria Sofia, Queen of Portugal, 118
Mariana de Austria, Queen of Spain, 118
Mariana of Neuburg, Queen of Spain, 117–124 passim, 128n. 54
Marie Louise of Orleans, Queen of Spain, 118
Marie Louise of Savoy, Queen of Spain, 129n. 75
Marsé, Juan, 30
Martí, José, 222
Martín Santos, Luis, 30
Martínez Ruiz, José ("Azorín"), 297
Martínez Siliceo, Juan, 78
Marut, Ret ("B. Traven"), 31
Marx, Karl, 18, 35
Mary of Hungary, Queen of Hungary, 79
Mastretta, Ángeles, 458, 462, 463, 464
Mathesius, Vilém, 186
Matilda (wife of Henry the Lion), 54
Matute, Ana María, 30
Maura, Antonio, 124n. 1
Maura y Gamazo, Gabriel, 29, 124n. 1
Mauricio (Spanish bishop), 5
Max Emmanuel, Elector of Bavaria, 115–117, 119, 124, 127n. 45
Maximilian I, Holy Roman Emperor, 8
Maximilian II, Holy Roman Emperor, 9, 78, 82, 87n. 5, 95, 96, 104n. 14, 105n. 45
Maxwell III, John C., xiv
May, Karl, 297, 308n. 23
Mayans y Siscar, Gregorio, 206
Mayer, Hans, 30
Mayer, Paola, 212n. 61
Mazarin (cardinal), 111
Medici, Catherina de, 79
Medina, Paul, 294
Medinaceli, Duke of, 113
Mendelssohn, Peter de, 306–307n. 13, 308n. 22
Mendelssohn-Bartholdy, Felix, 435
Mendoza de Vives, María, 245

Menéndez Pidal, Juan, 177–178
Menéndez Pidal, Ramón, xiii, 16, 177–187 passim
Menéndez Ureña, Enrique, 257
Menéndez y Pelayo, Marcelino, 19, 41–42n. 29, 178–179, 223, 225, 233n. 47, 256, 267
Mennemeier, Franz Norbert, 202–203, 209n. 22
Mensing (German photographer), 329, 340, 341f. 10
Menzel, Wolfgang, 227, 231n. 18, 233n. 61, 246
Mérimée, Ernest, 180, 182
Mérimée, Prosper, 20
Merkes, Manfred, 376
Messer, August, 299–300
Meyer, Hannes, 427, 428, 429
Meyer-Clason, Curt, 458, 465n. 16
Meyer-Lübke, Wilhelm, 16, 177–187 passim
Michaëlis, C. (Carolina Michaëlis de Vasconcellos), 183
Mies van der Rohe, Ludwig, 23, 24
Milà y Fontanals, Manuel, 41n. 29, 178, 179, 183
Milch, Erhard, 354f. 28
Millardet, Georges, 181, 184
Miller, Alfred, 429
Milton, John, 243
Miró, Joan, 23, 24
Modotti, Tina, 430
Mola, Emilio, 320, 336
Molina, Luis de, 142–143
Molina, Tirso de, 20
Moncrif, François, 229n. 9
Montalto, Duke of, 128n. 65
Monteath, Peter, 358n. 1, 372
Montemayor, Jorge de, 40n. 11
Monterrey, Count of, 122
Montesquieu, Charles-Louis de, 12
Mor de Fuentes, José, 252n. 12
Mora Figueroa, Manuel, 405
Morales, Luis de, 5
Moreno (admiral), 324n. 11
Moreno Munguia, Laurentino, 404
Morf, Heinrich, 180
Morgner, Irmtraud, 35
Mörike, Eduard, 19, 253n. 26
Moritz, Karl Philipp, 19
Moscherosch, Johann Michael, 11

520 | *Index of Names*

Mosé ben Ezra, 221, 229n. 7
Moser, Moses, 219
Moses, 156
Moses de León, 169
Mosse, George L., 325
Motteux, Peter A., 206
Mozart, Wolfgang Amadeus, 37
Mueller, Dennis Melvin, 149
Müller (German gymnast), 22, 42n. 36
Müller, Adam, 1, 16
Müller, Bodo, 228
Müller, Friedrich (Max), 182, 183–84
Müller-Waldeck, Gunnar, 381–382n. 35
Müllner, Adolf, 141
Munker, Fr., 308n. 29
Munthe, Axel M., 183
Münzer, Hieronymus, 5–6
Mussolini, Benito, 313–324 *passim* 376, 388, 389, 396n. 60
Muster, Wilhelm, 304

Nancy, Jean-Luc, 284
Napoleon Bonaparte, 16
Nash, Mary, 363
Navarro, José Luis, 419n. 49
Nebrija, Antonio de, 181, 183
Nelson Jr., Lowry, 199, 209n. 21, 211n. 48, 212n. 67
Neruda, Jan, 428
Neruda, Pablo (Neftalí Ricardo Reyes Basoalto), 33, 423–441 *passim*
Nerval, Gérard de, 222
Nervo, Amado, 222
Neumann, Egon, 430
Neurath, Konstantin von, 318
Newton, Sir Isaac, 170, 176n. 47
Nezami of Ganjeh, 218
Niemöller, Martin, 427
Nietzsche, Friedrich, 20, 21, 22, 24, 42n. 33, 223, 303
Nithard, Johannes Eberhard, 121, 128n. 62
Noguès, Charles-August, 387
Nostradamus (Michel de Notredame), 85
Novalis (Friedrich von Hardenberg), 1, 16, 19, 22, 42n. 33, 203, 212n. 61, 246, 273, 280–286 *passim*
Núñez de Arce, Gaspar, 224, 225

Oedipus, 146
Oetinger, Friedrich Christoph, 171

Oliveres, Juan, 239, 242
Olives Canals, Santiago, 251n. 5, 252n. 12
Onetti, Juan Carlos, 35
Orringer, Nelson R., xi–xii, xiii, 2, 19–20, 42n. 30
d'Ors, Eugenio, 248
Ortega y Gasset, José, xii, xiii, 22, 42n. 30, 236, 248, 269, 276–280, 286, 288nn. 11–13, 23, 289n. 29, 297
Ortiz (Spanish lieutenant), 403
Ossian (James Macpherson), 243
Ossietzky, Carl von, 427
Osten, Maria, 27, 364, 369–372, 373, 377, 378, 381nn. 26–28, 32–34
Oswald von Wolkenstein, 4, 64–67, 68, 69
Otto I, Holy Roman Emperor, 62
Ovid, 309n. 36

Pageard, Robert, 248, 249, 252n. 12, 253n. 27
Paracelsus, 170
Parades, Martín de, 81
Pardo Bazán, Emilia, 224, 227, 232n. 36, 254n. 34
Paris, Gaston, 178, 179, 182, 184
Parma, Duke of, 122
Parra, Nicanor, 437
Patrouch, Joseph F., xii, xiii, 2, 8–9
Paul, Hermann, 185
Paulin, Roger, 133
Paz, Octavio, 35, 424
Pedraza, Pablo de, 408, 409, 420n. 74
Pedriali, Ferdinando, 324n. 9
Péladan, Joséphin, 307n. 14
Peñalver, Manuel, 186
Pérez, Alonso, 40n. 11
Pérez, Janet, 365
Pérez Bonalde, Juan Antonio, 222
Pérez Bustamante, Ciriaco, 107n. 72
Pérez de Ayala, Ramón, 297
Pérez de Hita, Ginés, 216, 230n. 10, 231n. 31
Pérez Galdós, Benito, 269n. 1, 298
Pérez Martín, María Jesús, 101
Pérez-Reverte, Arturo, 228
Pérez Villanueva, Joaquín, 182
Pernstein, Vratislav von, 79
Pétain, Henri Philippe, 395n. 44
Peter I, King of Castile, 221

Peter II, King of Portugal, 118
Peter III, King of Aragon, 139
Peterson, Julius, 133
Petrarch, Francesco, 188, 190–191, 192, 203, 204–205, 209n. 18
Pfandl, Ludwig, 26, 124n. 1
Pfeffel, Gottlieb, 245
Philip of Austria, 80
Philip of Swabia, Holy Roman Emperor, 5
Philip II, King of Spain, 8–9, 13, 26, 78, 79, 80, 82, 96, 97, 105n. 41, 108, 127n. 44
Philip III, King of Spain, 9–10, 78, 91–107 passim
Philip IV, King of Spain, 115
Philip V, King of Spain, 109, 120, 124, 128n. 54, 129n. 75
Philip William of Neuburg, Duke of Jülich-Berg, 118
Picasso, Pablo, 1, 23, 320, 339, 432
Pi y Margall, Francisco, 237
Pico della Mirandola, Giovanni, 156, 170, 171
Pick-Seewart, Rudolf, 299
Piernas y Hurtado, José Manuel, 256
Pike, David, 381n. 34
Pistorius (German naval commander), 324n. 11
Pius IV, Pope, 8
Pius XI, Pope, 331
Plato, 182, 204
Plotinus, 171
Poe, Edgar Allan, 223
Polheim, Karl Konrad, 195, 197, 210n. 29
Polyxena (daughter of Empress María), 80
Ponce de León, Luis, 86
Pope, Alexander, 12
Porset, Clara, 439
Portocarrero (cardinal), 116, 120, 122
Posada, Adolfo, 256–257, 260
Pound, Ezra, 426
Prawer, Siegbert S., 176n. 50, 232n. 32
Prestes, Luis Carlos, 435
Primo de Rivera, Miguel, 283, 291, 297, 300, 319, 384, 413
Prindle, Dennis, xiv–xv
Priscian, 183
Procop, St., 80, 83
Prudhoe, John, 276

Quevedo, Francisco de, 11, 218, 227
Quiroga, Antonio, 218

Racine, Jean Baptiste, 279
Raders, Margit, 37
Raeder, Erich, 354f. 28
Ramon Berenguer IV, Count of Barcelona ("Kyot"), 61
Raphael, Alice, 176n. 37
Rask, Rasmus, 177, 184
Rave, Antonio, 239
Raymond (Spanish archbishop), 62
Reagan, Ronald, 453
Recceswinth, King of the Visigoths, 3
Recesmund (Spanish bishop), 62
Reck, Hanne Gabriele, 216, 230n. 16, 232n. 31
Redondo, Onésimo, 323n. 4
Reed, T. J., 276
Regler, Gustav, 32, 424, 428, 429
Rehm, Walther, 133
Reina y Montilla, Manuel, 232n. 42
Reinbot von Durne, 63
Rembrandt van Rijn, 6
Renn, Ludwig, 32, 368, 380n. 19, 424, 428–429, 430, 431, 434
Resina, Joan Ramon, 251n. 1
Reuchlin, Johann, 170, 171
Reventós, Joan, 30
Revilla, Manuel de la, 257
Revueltas, José, 432
Revueltas, Rosaura, 432–433
Rey Hazas, Antonio, 175n. 24
Ribbans, Geoffrey W., 249
Ribbentrop, Joachim von, 315, 317, 319, 321, 323n. 2, 387, 388, 389, 390, 395nn. 45, 47, 407, 411
Ribot, Théodule, 270n. 23
Richter, Herbert Georg, 384–386, 390–391, 393n. 29
Richthofen, Wolfram von, 340, 354f. 28
Riego, Rafael de, 218
Rilke, Rainer Maria, 23, 33, 424, 425
Ríos, Laura de los, 267, 268
Ríos, Vicente de los, 206
Rivera, Diego, 439
Roatta, Mario, 319
Robicek, Ernst, 430
Roderic (Rüdiger/Rodrigo), 4, 63
Rodríguez de Castillo, Gonzalo, 411–412, 413, 419n. 49, 422n. 109

Index of Names | 521

522 | Index of Names

Rodríguez-Vivaldi, Ana María, xiii, 2, 33–34
Roh, Franz, 36
Römer, Ernst, 430
Rommel, Erwin, 327
Rosa, João Guimarães, 36
Rosa, José Luis de la, 411
Rose, William, 232n. 43
Rossini, Gioacchino, 262, 263
Rössner, Michael, 36
Rotrou II de Perche, 61
Rousseau, Jean Jacques, 12
Rubens, Peter Paul, 6
Ruck, Melchior, 113
Rückert, Friedrich, 246
Rüdiger (Rodrigo/Roderic), 4, 63
Rudolf II, Holy Roman Emperor, 9, 78, 80, 81, 84, 95, 96, 100
Rukser, Udo, 222, 249
Rumpolt, Marx, 53
Ruschin, Günter, 430
Rushdie, Salman, 232n. 31

Sábato, Ernesto, 35
Sachs, Michael, 221
Sacristán, Manuel, 30
Sagasta, Práxedes Mateo, 19
Saint-Amand, Arthur Léon Imbert de, 79
Saint-John Perse, 424
Salamanca, Gabriel de, 81
Salas Larrazabal, Jesús, 324n. 9
Salazar de Mendoza, Pedro, 92, 93, 94, 103n. 5, 104n. 19
Salmerón, Nicolás, 256, 260
Salomo ben Gabirol, 81
Salvioni, Carlo, 180
San Clemente, Guillén de, 97–98
Sánchez, Magdalena S., xiii, 2, 9–10
Sánchez Comendador, Antonio, 239
Sánchez Moguel, Antonio, 179, 180
Sandino, Augusto César, 454n. 6
Sanz, Eulogio Florentino, 222, 223, 232n. 45
Sanz del Río, Julián, 19, 41n. 29, 223, 224–225, 227, 236, 244, 255–272 passim
Sauerwein, Jules, 307n. 14
Saussure, Ferdinand de, 183, 186
Schelling, Friedrich Wilhelm Joseph von, 134, 135–136, 137, 148, 176n. 47, 226

Scherer, Georg, 85, 86
Schiller, Charlotte, 149
Schiller, Friedrich, 13–14, 15, 19, 20, 40n. 18, 133–151 passim, 181, 182, 227, 235, 243–254 passim, 256
Schilling, Luisa, 37
Schlegel, August Wilhelm, 14, 135, 136, 137, 141, 149, 215, 230n. 10, 235
Schlegel, Dorothea, 207n. 1
Schlegel, Friedrich, 14, 16, 17, 41n. 29, 147–148, 188–213 passim, 215, 227, 230nn. 11, 13, 230–231n. 18, 233n. 49, 235, 281, 285, 286
Schlegel brothers, 14, 17, 134, 135, 216, 224
Schleiermacher, Friedrich, 245
Schlenstedt, Silvia, 370–371, 381nn. 27, 32, 34
Schlesinger, Klaus, 35
Schlöndorff, Volker, 444, 454n. 8
Schmidt, Rachel, xii, 2, 17
Schmidt-Koch, Ria, 294
Schmigalle, Günther, 376–377, 380n. 15
Schneider, Reinhold, 23, 25–26
Schneider, Rolf, 35
Schneider, Sigrid, 359n. 3
Schnitzler, Arthur, 30
Scholem, Gershom Gerhard, 175nn. 11, 14
Schopenhauer, Arthur, 17, 41n. 29, 223, 226, 257, 303
Schramm, Edmund, 48–50
Schubart, Christian Friedrich, 245
Schubert, Franz, 434
Schubert, Helga, 35
Schulze (Nazi party member), 374
Schwarz, Egon, 238
Scott, Sir Walter, 178, 243
Seghers, Anna, 27, 32, 364, 367–369, 372, 373, 377–378, 380n. 18, 380–381n. 24, 424, 427–428, 429, 430, 431, 434, 438, 439
Selig, Karl-Ludwig, xiv
Sell, Hans-Joachim, 38
Sellén, Francisco, 222, 230n. 14
Serrano Suñer, Ramón, 315, 323n. 3, 383–396 passim
Sert, José Luis, 24
Sewell, Elizabeth, 174n. 4
Seyhan, Azade, 281, 285
Shaftesbury, Earl of, 171

Shakespeare, William, 17, 135, 136, 138, 188, 190–191, 192, 193, 195, 199, 201, 203, 209n. 24
Siemsen, Anna, 364
Sigismund, Holy Roman Emperor, 65
Silex, Karl, 382n. 52
Silva, José Asunción, 222
Skármeta, Antonio, xiii, 33–34, 442–456
Smeth, Maria de, 27, 364, 374–378, 382nn. 40, 46, 52
Sobejano, Gonzalo, 269n. 1, 270n. 23
Solger, Karl Wilhelm Ferdinand, 227
Solomon, King of Israel, 55
Solomon Luria, Isaac ben, 156
Somoza, Anastasio, 454n. 6
Somoza Jr., Anastasio, 34, 454n. 6
Somoza, Luis, 454n. 6
Sophocles, 85, 139, 289n. 29
Southworth, Herbert, 337–339, 324n. 9
Spencer, Herbert, 260, 270n. 23
Sperrle, Hugo, 339
Spinola, Hieronymous, 83
Spinoza, Baruch, 11, 226
Spira, Steffie, 430
Spitzer, Leo, 25
Stackelberg, Karl Georg von, 325
Staël, Germaine de, 224, 226
Staff, Erik, 181
Stahl, Ernst Leopold, 294
Stahl, Leo, 294
Stalin, Joseph, 316, 317, 318, 321, 322, 412, 413, 415, 437
Staub, M., 231n. 31
Stegmann, Vera, xiii, 2, 33
Stempka (German photographer), 329, 335f. 5
Sterne, Laurence, 169
Stohrer, Eberhard von, 338, 386, 394n. 39, 395n. 52
Stolberg, Friedrich von, 246
Stona, Maria, 364
Storrs, Christopher D. xiii, 2, 9, 10
Strakosch, Marianne, 87nn. 3–4
Streicher, Julius, 427
"Der Stricker," 54
Studnitz, H. G. von, 343f. 14
Sudermann, Hermann, 20
Sue, Eugène, 243
Suevos, Jesús, 411, 421n. 98
Sullivan, Henry W., xi-xii, 2, 14, 40n. 20

Tacitus, Cornelius, 204
Tafur, Pero, 53
Tapia, Tomás, 267
Tàpies, Antoni, 2, 30
Tasso, Torquato, 191
Taube, Otto von, 302
Taubert (Nazi official), 374, 375, 382n. 40
Teitelboim, Volodia, 426, 438
Teresa of Ávila, St., 86, 171
Thalmann, Clara, 364
Thälmann, Ernst, 435
Theile, Albert, 293
Thelen, Albert Vigoleis, 38
Thomas of Celano, 63
Thüring von Ringoltingen, 69
Thurn and Taxis, House of, 53
Tieck, Ludwig, 16, 17, 19, 41n. 24, 134, 135, 137, 188, 189, 198, 202, 203, 235, 246
Tiemann, Hermann, 133
Tierno Galván, Enrique, 18
Timm, Uwe, 36
Tito (Josip Broz), 403
Tobler, Adolf, 181
Toller, Ernst, 429
Torres Bodet, Jaime, 23
Torres Clavé, Josep, 24
Tovar, Antonio, 416
Toynbee, Arnold J., 230–231n. 18
Traven, B. (Ret Marut), 31, 43n. 47
Treves, Janine, xiv
Trubetzkoi, Nikolai Sergeevich, 186
Tucholsky, Kurt ("Ignaz Wrobel"), 291
Tuscany, Grand Duke of, 125n. 3
Twain, Mark (Samuel Langhorne Clemens), 240

Uhland, Ludwig, 230n. 16, 244, 247, 253n. 22, 254n. 34
Uhse, Bodo, 32, 424, 428, 429, 431
Unamuno, Miguel de, xi, xii, xiii, 22–23, 26, 180, 183, 223, 269, 273, 282–286, 290–310 *passim*, 365
Urquijo, Marquis of, 15

Vadillo, Fernando, 418n. 33
Valera, Juan, 224–225, 248
Valéry, Paul, 295
Valis, Noël, 269n. 1
Valle, Giuseppe, 320

Valle, Marquesa del (Magdalena de Guzmán), 101–102
Valle Inclán, Ramón del, 298
Vallentin, Antonina, 297
Van Dyck, Anthony, 6
Vargas Llosa, Mario, 35, 269n. 1, 458, 464
Varkonyi, Istvan, xii, 32
Varro, Marcus Terentius, 183
Vasconsellos, Carolina Michaëlis de (C. Michaëlis), 183
Verdi, Giuseppe, 13
Verlaine, Paul, 223
Verner, Karl, 184
Vesalius (Andreas Vesal), 7
Viardot, Louis, 231n. 28
Victor Amadeus II, Duke of Savoy, 114, 125n. 3
Victor Emmanuel III, King of Italy, 384
Vidal (Spanish ambassador), 401, 407, 410
Vigón, Jorge, 386, 393n. 29
Virgil, 273
Vischer, Friedrich Theodor, 257
Vivar Téllez, Rodrigo, 405
Vlasov, Andreaei Andreevich, 407
Vogel, Eberhard, 302–303, 309n. 42
Volkmann, Helmuth, 339
Voltaire, François, 12
Voorwinden, Norbert, 63, 75n. 71
Voragine, Jacques de, 85
Voßler, Karl, 25, 29, 42–43n. 40, 181, 185

Waddington, G. T., 323n. 2
Wagner, Richard, 1, 21, 41n. 29
Waldingau, Juanita von, 364, 380n. 16
Wallensköld, Axel Gabriel, 180
Weber, Otto, 23
Weigel, Helene, 432
Weill, Kurt, 430, 433
Weiss, Peter, 28, 30
Welles, Orson, 436
Werner, Ilse, 29
Werner, Zacharias, 141

Wezel, Johann Karl, 19
Whealey, Robert H., xii, 2, 26–27, 326, 374, 376
Wheatcroft, Andrew, 87n. 1
Whitford, Margaret, 175n. 22
Wieland, Christoph Martin, 13, 19, 253n. 26
Wiese, Benno von, 133
William III, King of England, 110, 116, 117
William V, Duke of Bavaria, 53
Wilson, Peter, 125n. 13
Winckelmann, Johann Joachim, 13, 41n. 29, 253n. 26
Windelband, Wilhelm, 276
Wirsung, Christoph, 49
Wis, Marjatta, 50, 53
Wiser, Henry, 121, 122, 128n. 61
Witiza, 63
Wittner, Victor, 294
Wolber, Thomas K., xi, xii, 25–26
Wolf, Christa, 35, 439
Wolf, Friedrich, 429
Wolff, Ilse, 364
Wolfram von Eschenbach, 4, 54, 58–62, 64, 69
Wundt, Wilhelm, 185, 270n. 23

Yagüe, Juan, 385
Yang, Zhidong, 379n. 10
Yriarte Betancourt, José Luis, 411
Yusuf III, King of the Almoravids, 66

Zantop, Susanne, 220
Zaunboss, Joseph, 429
Zauner, Adolf, 181, 183, 185
Zecevic, Patricia D., xiii, 2, 14–15
Zech, Paul, 32, 43n. 54
Zenker, Ernst Victor, 301
Zinzendorf, Nikolaus Ludwig von, 171
Zola, Émile, 255, 260, 26, 424
Zorrilla, José, 225
Zweig, Arnold, 427

INDEX OF SUBJECTS

Airplanes: 326; DC-3, 404, 419n. 50; Ju 52, 342f. 13, 346; Ju-290, 419n. 50; Messerschmitt 264, 387, 394n. 37
Anti-German sentiment in Spain, 109, 121–123, 383–396 *passim*, 397–422 *passim*
Antinazi-Freiheitsbewegung (ANFB), 438
Antisemitism, 219, 225, 315, 323n. 4
Art collecting, 6, 80, 88n. 21
Associació de Germanistes de Catalunya, 37
Avant-garde: x, 23–24, 33, 36

Balance of power, 313–324 *passim*
Barcelona: xiii, 2, 37, 52, 120, 314, 320; Cologne colony, 52; Colònia Güell, 42n. 36; Dalmau Galleries, 23; La Fundació Caixa de Catalunya, 44n. 61; G.A.T.C.P.C., 24; as gateway to Spain, 37, 236; Park Güell, 21, 42n. 36; Teatro del Liceo, 21
Baroque, 11, 49, 84
Battles: Barcelona (1697), Berlin, 411–412; Bulge, 403; D-Day (1944), 398, 401, 417, Gibraltar (1704), 121; Milan (1696), 114; Mohacs, 79; Rocroi (1643), 108; Ronceval, 54–59. *See also* Guernica
Bauhaus, 2, 23–24
Berlin: Battle of Berlin, 411–412; Berliner Ensemble, 432–433; Falange in Berlin, 408–413; Olympic Games (1936), 329; Sociedad Kantiana, 294; Verein für Kultur und Wissenschaft der Juden, 219
Bestsellers, 34, 457–466 *passim*
Bewegung Freies Deutschland (BFD), 429–430, 431
Bi- and Multilingualism, 75n. 80, 79, 89n. 40
Black legend (*leyenda negra*), 8, 12, 14, 16, 233n. 53
Black markets, 399, 409
Blue Division (División Azul), 28–29, 323, 356–357, 397–422 *passim*
Blue Legion, 400, 402, 416, 418n. 29, 420n. 74
Blue Squadron, 416
Book burnings (autos-da-fé), 218–219, 431
Book collecting, 78, 84–86, 89–90n. 41, 94
Bourbon dynasty, 10, 12, 259
Burgundian Circle, 110–112, 125n. 16

Calvinism, 93
Canary Islands, 291, 297, 319, 387–390, 396n. 61
Carlism, 314
Carolingian dynasty, 4, 54–58
Censorship, 251n. 2, 430
Charity, 84, 93–94
Chile: National Library, 427
Chile Committees, 447
El Cid, 18, 39n. 4, 66–67, 230
Cologne: trade, 51–52
Companies: Bayer, 417n. 13; IG-Farben, 406, 420n. 73; Lufthansa, 319, 324n. 7, 404, 410; Mercedes-Benz, 451; Siemens, 404; Skoda, 404; Telefunken, 417n. 13; Zeiss-Ikon, 327
Condor Legion, 26, 318–320, 323, 324n. 11, 325–359 *passim*, 375–376, 398
Concordat with the Vatican, 331
Conservative revolution (Germany), 25–26
Council of Trent, 7, 79, 84, 86, 88n. 13, 91, 92, 93, 142
Counter Reformation, 8, 9, 24, 77–107 *passim*, 142; Tridentine Catholicism, 78, 91–93
Cuisine, 53

Delegado Especial para la Inspección y Tutela de Trabajadores Españoles en Alemania, 418n. 31
Deutsche Arbeitsfront (DAF), 406
Deutscher Akademischer Austauschdienst (DAAD), 37
devotio moderna, 6–7
Dictionaries, 16, 180. *See also* Translations
Don Quixote, 13, 16–18, 25, 49, 188–213 *passim*, 220, 301–302

Enlightenment, 12–13, 206, 217–218, 221, 275
Entente Cordiale, 316, 389
Erasmian thought, 7, 39n. 9
Etappendienst (ETO), 319
European Union (EU), 36–39, 87n. 2
Evolutionism, 260
Exile literature (German), 31–34, 38, 309n. 36, 370, 360–382 *passim*, 423– 441 *passim*;

Exile literature (German) *(cont.)*
Unamuno, 290–310 *passim*
Existentialism, 30, 298
Exoticism, 30–31, 34, 36, 247, 327–328, 346–348; 435–466 *passim*
Expositions: Barcelona Universal Exposition (1929), 23; Frankfurt Book Fair, 463; International Exposition of Paris (1937), 24
Expressionism, 36–37

Falange (FET-JONS), 26–29, 313–422 *passim*
Faust, 14, 23, 246, 248
Federación de Asociaciones de Germanistas en España (FAGE), 37
Festivals: Berlin International Film Festival, 444; Cannes Film Festival, 444; Human Rights Film Festival, 444; Prague Television Festival, 444; World Youth Festival (1951), 432
Film, 29, 33–34, 442–456, 463
Folklore and folktales, 23, 340
Freemasons, 323n. 4
French culture, 16, 38–39
French mediation between Germany and Spain, 38–39, 241, 238, 425–426
French resistance movement (Maquis), 402
Frente de Juventudes (FJ), 408, 411
Fuero Juzgo, 3
Fugger Banking House, 9, 40n. 10

German Democratic Republic (GDR), 32, 34–35, 369; Academy of the Arts, 432
German postal system (Thurn and Taxis), 53
German-language periodicals: *Archiv für das Studium der neueren Sprachen und Literaturen*, 180, 182; *Aufbau*, 428; *Berliner Tageblatt*, 293, 296, 298, 300, 304–305; *Die Böttcherstraße*, 293–294; *Cineaste*, 444; *Demokratische Post*, 429, 430; *Deutsch-Mexikaner*, 429; *Deutsche Zentral-Zeitung*, 370; *Deutsche Zeitung*, 307n. 18; *Eckart*, 294; *Eiserne Blätter*, 294; *Europa-Magazin*, 294; *Frankfurter Zeitung*, 294; *Freie Welt*, 301; *Freies Deutschland/Alemania Libre*, 32, 428, 429–430, 434–435; *Die Freude*, 301; *Der Gral*, 298; *Illustrierte Weltrevue für Wissen und Unterhaltung*, 294; *Individualität*, 298; *Kempinski Journal*, 458; *Die Laterne*, 294; *Linkskurve*, 428; *Die Literarische Welt*, 295, 301, 306–307n. 13; *Der Neue Merkur*, 292; *Neue Zürcher Zeitung*, 24, 296; *Neuphilologische Mitteilungen*, 180; *Philosophie und Leben*, 299; *Preußische Jahrbücher*, 307n. 18; *Das Prisma*, 294; *Der Querschnitt*, 294, 297, 308n. 22; *Reichls Philosophischer Almanach*, 294; *Romanische Forschungen*, 182; *Sinn und Form*, 439; *Der Sozialistische Akademiker*, 292, 294; *Der Spiegel*, 457, 463; *Der Stürmer*, 427; *Uhu*, 292; *Vossische Zeitung*, 298, 299;

Die Weltbühne, 291; *Wissen und Leben*, 292; *Das Wort*, 369, 370, 380n. 14, 381n. 28; *Zeitschrift für romanische Philologie*, 180, 182, 186
Germanic tribes: Alans, 3; Suevi, 3–4; Vandals, 3; Visigoths, 3–4, 39n. 3
Gibraltar, 28, 314, 319, 322, 385, 386, 387, 364n. 55, 390, 394n. 38, 396n. 55, 414
Goethe Institute, 37, 446
Golden Age (Spain), xii, 9, 164, 278
Grail, 58–62
Guernica bombing, 320, 324n. 9, 336–339
Gypsies, 350f. 23, 352–353

Habsburg dynasty, xiii, 6–10, 77–124 *passim*
Heinrich Heine Club (Club Enrique Heine), 430
Horses, 12, 63, 74n. 68, 79
Humanism, 7, 8, 39n. 9
Hussites, 83

Ibero-American Institute, 403, 409, 419n. 40
Index librorum prohibitorum, 8
Innere Emigration (Germany), 26
Inquisition, 8, 11, 12, 13, 218, 301, 463
Institución Libre de Enseñanza, 21
International Anti-Jewish Congress (1944), 406
International Brigades, 26, 314, 322, 361, 367, 380n. 16, 428, 435
Interministerial Commission for the Sending of Workers to Germany (Comisión interministerial para el envío de trabajadores a Alemania), 417n. 18
Isabeline style, 6

Jews, 11–12, 32–33, 157, 215, 214–234 *passim*, 405–406, 420n. 57, 444–445. *See also* Antisemitism, Sacred books
Junges Deutschland (Germany), 18, 227

Knighthood: 53, 68; knight errantry, 189, 193; tournaments, 58–59, 64
Krausism, xii, 19–20, 21, 41n. 29, 223, 255–272 *passim*

Lateinamerikanisches Komitee der Freien Deutschen (LAK), 429, 430
Latin American literature, 34–35, 457–466 *passim*
League of Augsburg, 109, 112
Lex Visigothorum, 3
Liberation theology, 35, 451
El Libro Negro, 431
Liga Pro Cultura Alemana en México (LPC), 429
Literary genres: Autobiographies, 360–382 *passim*; Bildungsroman, 152–176 *passim*, 280–282; chivalric literature, 17, 47–76 *passim*, 188–213 *passim*, Golden Age

drama, 133–151 *passim*, 196, 278; magic realism, 34–35, 36, 461–462; Middle High German literature, 47–76 *passim*; Minnesang, 47, 50; novel, 17, 20, 152–176 *passim*, 188–213 *passim*, 277–278, 457–466; the picaresque, 8, 11, 15, 24, 38, 40n. 11, 49, 152–176 *passim*; *romancero*, 13, 18, 214–234 *passim*; *Schicksalsdrama*, 14, 133–151 *passim*; socialist realism, 436–437; troubadour poetry, 47, 50; *Volksbuch*, 69; Women's war narratives, 360–382 *passim*. *See also* Exile literature
Literary motifs: alienation, 31; fratricide, 133–151 *passim*; incest, 133–151 *passim*; obsession, 31

Madrid: Ateneo of Madrid, 248; Barajas airport, 353; Colegio Imperial, 143; Descalzas, 79, 95–97, 99, 105n. 41; El Escorial, 80, 105n. 41; German embassy, 407; Prado Museum, 6; SS department, 399
Marriage, 76n. 89, 78–81
Marxism, 18, 30, 41n. 28
Mexico City: Palacio de Bellas Artes, 429, 431
Missionizing, 85
Moroccan troops, 319, 327–328, 330, 343–345fs. 14–18, 346–348, 353
Morocco, 28, 314, 383–396 *passim*
Music: Court music, 81, 82, 84; *el cuplé*, 21; flamenco, 23; German, 21; Spanish, 22
Muslims (Moors, Moriscos, Saracens), 4, 13, 53, 54–58, 67–68, 73n. 46, 122, 128n. 65, 214–234 *passim*; Abencerrages, 218; Zegries, 218. *See also* Moroccan troops
Mysticism and gnosticism, 15, 69, 170

National Socialism, 26, 313–441 *passim*, 445
National Press Delegation, 404
Native Americans, 26, 85, 308n. 23, 425, 435
Naturalismus (Germany), 20
Neogrammarians (*Junggrammatiker*), 16, 177–187 *passim*
"New Order" (Spain), 397–422 *passim*
Nibelungenlied, 63
Non-Intervention Committee (NIC), 316, 318

Olympic Games (1936), 329
Oviedo circle, 256

Paris: Café de la Rotonde, 290; Champs Elysées, 330, Club de Faubourg de Montmartre, 291; International Exposition (1937), 24; Opera house, 21; Theatre de la Fourni, 291
Patronage, 8–10, 77–107 *passim*
Percival, 21, 58–62
Photography, 20–21, 27, 325–359 *passim*
Photographic agencies: Europa Press, 339, 339f. 9; Fulgur, 329, 347f. 20; Havas, 339; Scherl Bilderdienst, 329, 351f. 24; H. Sygma, 336, 338f. 8; Vedo, 344f. 14; Zentralbild, 328f. 1, 329, 337, 338f. 8, 339f. 9, 344f. 16, 346f. 19, 349f. 22, 354f. 27
Pilgrimages, 5, 39n. 5, 51–52, 95
Political parties: Communist Party (Chile), 432; Kommunistische Partei Deutschlands (KPD), 367; Deutschnationale Volkspartei (DNVP), 318; Parti Populaire François (PPF), 411; Tory Party, 317. *See also* Falange
Popular Front: Spain, 81n. 34, 313–314, 374, 377, 416; Chile, 426
Positivism, 31, 255, 259–260, 270n. 23
Printing press, 52
Prizes and awards: *Bundesfilmpreis*, 444; Deutsche Bronzene Verdienstmedaillen, 407; *Gran Cruz de Cisneros*, 405; International Stalin Peace Prize, 432; Nobel Prize, 428, 458; Order of the Golden Fleece, 119, 120; *Ritterkreuz*, 419n. 39; Television Prize of the German Academy of Performing Arts in Frankfurt, 444; West German Film Critics Prize, 444
Propaganda, 313–359 *passim*
Protocols of the Elders of Zion, 323n. 4
Protestant Reformation/Protestantism, 7–8, 49, 89n. 37, 93
Psychoanalysis, 23, 42n. 37
Publishing houses: Aufbau, 35; A. Bergnes, 252n. 12; S. Fischer, 35; Hanser, 35; Insel, 464n. 11; Kiepenheuer & Witsch, 464n. 11; El Libro Libre, 431, 432; Malik, 380n. 26; Meyer & Jessen, 292, 296–297; Juan Oliveres, 239; E. Rowohlt, 35, 294, 306n. 13; Suhrkamp, 464n. 11; Ullstein, 308n. 22; Verlag 10. Mai, 372; Vervuert, 37

Radio stations: Deutschlandsender, 408; Radio Nacional de España, 408
Reconquest (Spain), 215, 218
Reichsministerium für Volksaufklärung und Propaganda, 27, 329–331, 376
Reichssicherheitshauptamt (Reich Central Security Office, RSHA), 399
Relics, 80, 83
Religious orders: Benedictines, 83, 85; Dominicans, 85, 86, 142; Franciscans, 85, 98; Jesuits, 7, 9, 24, 53, 79, 83, 85, 86, 94, 95, 98, 142–145
Renaissance, 8–9, 39n. 9, 49, 170–171, 194
Revolutions: Bohemian revolt (1918), 102; Cuban revolution, 35; "Glorious Revolution" (1868), 259; Russian Revolution, 367; Sandinista revolution, 442–456 *passim*
Rohstoffe und Waren Einkaufsgesellschaft (ROWAK), 318
Rolandslied, 54–58
Romance languages (philology), 16, 25, 41n. 22, 177–187, 182–185
Romans, 2–3, 13

Romanticism, 16–17, 177, 188–213 passim, 224, 280–286; Jena School, 133, 207n. 1, 224

Sacred books: Bible, 157; Kabbalah, 15, 152–176 passim; Koran, 156–157; Torah, 156; Zohar, 156, 169–170, 176n. 37
Salamanca: German Military School, 340; Gasschule, 340, 342f. 12; Jesuit College, 95; Plaza Mayor, 335; Torre del Clavero, 336f. 6; University, 7–8, 291, 293, 298
Sandinistas, 33–35, 442–456 passim
Santiago de Compostela: Cathedral, 52; tomb of St. James, 51–52
Schutzstaffel (SS), 373, 399; SS-Freiwilligen-Grenadierdivision-Wallonie, 403
Shining Path (Sendero Luminoso), 35
Ships and boats: Bismarck, 387; Graf Spree, 324n. 11; Nürnberg, 321, 324n. 11; Tirpitz, 387; Winnipeg, 428; Carlos Segundo, 114; submarines, 319
Sindicato Español Universitario (SEU), 409, 411
Sociedad Hispano-Marroquí de Transportes (HISMA), 318
Sonderstab F (Special Staff, or Office, F), 402
Spanish Civil War, 26–27, 31, 33, 313–382 passim, 428–429, 433
Spanish-language periodicals: La Abeja, xiii, 18–19, 235–254 passim; La Abeja Literaria, Científica e Industrial, 253n. 23; El Alcázar, 404; La América, 237; Arriba, 408; Aurora de Chile, 427; Claridad, 33, 425; El Eco de Euterpe, 237; Enlace, 403, 405, 409; España (Tangier), 393n. 23; El Español, 411, 419n. 49; Hora de España, 380n. 23; Ilustración Española y Americana, 237; El Museo de Familias, 226; El Museo Universal, 223, 237; El Nacional, 430; El Nene, 237; Nosotros, 292; El Observador, 30; Pueblo, 416; Revista de Filología Española, 186; El Semanario Popular, 237, 249; La Vanguardia, 30
Sturm und Drang, 13–14, 138, 274
Surrealism, 23, 34–36

Teutonic Knights, 118–119
Thälmann Brigade/Battalion, 372, 429
Todt Organization (OT), 402
Trade: 5–7, 51–52, 123, 318–319, 400; Soldatenhandel, 10, 113–115; wool trade, 123
Translations, 12, 13, 16, 19, 35, 48, 49, 102, 235–254 passim, 290–310 passim, 369, 425–426, 457–466 passim. See also Dictionaries
Treaties: Anglo-German naval agreement, 317; Anti-Comintern (1939), 315, 317, 321–322, 376–377; Axis pact (1936), 314, 321; Finno-Soviet peace treaty, 404; French-German non-aggression pact (1938), 321; French-Soviet pact, 322; Munich agreement (1938), 322; Nazi-Soviet (Hitler-Stalin) pact, 322–323; Peace of Rijswijk, 120; Peace of Paris (1856), 315; Treaty of Vigevano, 114; Treaty of Versailles, 316, 319, 322
Turks (Ottomans), 67, 77–81, 93, 100

Universities: Ayacucho, 35; Barcelona, 239; Berlin, 294; Bonn, 184; Chile, 446; Fribourg, 179; Granada, 183; Heidelberg, 30; Jena, 133, 207n. 1, 224; Leipzig, 432; Madrid, 37, 178, 256, 293; Morelia, 429; Oviedo, 256; Salamanca, 7, 8, 78, 291, 293, 298; Saragossa, 256; Toulouse, 180

Vienna: Burgtheater, 25; Haus-, Hof- und Staatsarchiv, 78; Hofburg, 80; Königinkloster, 80, 83; Lippizaners, 12; Poor Clares, 83; St. Stephen's cathedral, 80; Spanish Riding School, 12, 79; Stallburg, 78–80

Wars: Dutch War, 113; Nine Years' War, 109, 110, 116, 120; Sino-Japanese War, 321; Thirty Years' War, 102, 108, 111; Wars of Louis XIV, 111, 316; War of the League of Augsburg 1688–97); War of the Spanish Succession, 10, 109, 111, 115, 124; "Wars of Truth," 7; World War I, 315–316, 317, 325, 330. See also Muslims, Spanish Civil War, Turks, World War II
Way of St. James (Jakobsweg). See Pilgrimages
Wehrmacht, 313–422 passim; Einheit Ezquerra, 403, 413; Charlemagne Division, 413; 101st Company of Spanish Volunteers, 403; Spanish legion within Wehrmacht, 402
Weimar Classicism, 13–15, 133–176 passim, 274–280
Weimar Republic, 318, 377
Wittelsbach dynasty, 9, 91, 115, 123
Women: Influence of, 9, 27, 68–69, 76n. 89, 77–90, 91–107, 118, 360–382 passim, 463; feminist discourse, 15, 152–176 passim
Women writers, 62, 360–382 passim, 427–441 passim
World War II, 27–29, 313–324 passim, 356, 363, 371, 383–422 passim, 433, 445
Writers associations: PEN Club, 305, 310n. 54, 431; Schutzverband deutscher Schriftsteller (SDS), 367; Soviet Writers Union, 370, 381n. 34
Writers congresses: International Writers Congress for the Defense of Culture, 360, 368–369, 372; International Writers Meeting in Berlin and Weimar, 432; Soviet Writers Conference, 370

Zapatistas, 31, 35